HUMAN MEMORY

HUMAN MEMORY
Theory and Practice

Alan Baddeley
MRC Applied Psychology Unit
Cambridge, UK

Allyn and Bacon

Boston ■ *London* ■ *Sydney* ■ *Toronto*

Dedication
To Hilary

 Copyright © 1990 in Canada and the U.S.A. by Allyn and Bacon
A Division of Simon & Schuster, Inc.
160 Gould Street
Needham Heights, Massachusetts 02194

Series Editor: Diane McOscar
Production Administrator: Annette Joseph
Production Coordinator: Susan Freese
Cover Administrator: Linda K. Dickinson
Manufacturing Buyer: Bill Alberti

Library of Congress Cataloging-in-Publication Data

Baddeley, Alan D.
  Human memory: theory and practice/Alan Baddeley.
    p.   cm.
  Includes bibliographical references.
  ISBN 0-205-12312-0
  1. Memory   I. Title.
BF371.B225 1990
153.1′2–dc20   89-48432
                                                    CIP

Printed in the United States of America

10   9   8   7   6   5   4   95   94   93   92   91

CONTENTS

PREFACE

In 1970 I began to write a brief elementary memory text. It eventually emerged some six years later as a rather more ambitious enterprise, which attempted to serve as both an advanced undergraduate text and as a survey of the state of memory at the time that would be useful to my colleagues. It seems to have served both these functions reasonably well – I even received notification last year that it had finally achieved the status of a "citation classic", which entitles the author to bore the readers of *Current Contents* with his hoary recollections of how and why he came to write the book. It is, of course, now long out of date, so much so that rather than attempt to revise it, I have decided to write a completely new book.

The study of the psychology of memory has been enormously active in the last ten to fifteen years, with the result that the present book differs in a number of important respects from my earlier effort. First of all, the sheer volume and breadth of research means that I can no longer even attempt the depth of coverage that characterized at least some chapters of the earlier book. I suspect that this is not entirely a bad thing, particularly for the student reader whose commitment to the more arcane reaches of iconic memory or proactive inhibition may be less than total.

However, while the coverage of memory is far from encyclopaedic, I believe that it is important to give a reasonably detailed account of major experiments and paradigms and to provide enough examples of closely argued theorectical discussion to give a genuine feel of the psychology of memory as a living and developing area of science. The reader will perhaps not be too surprised to discover that the areas chosen for more detailed treatment tend to be those in which I am most closely involved; these are obviously topics about which I can write with particular knowledge and enthusiasm. I assume that teachers using the book as a text will supplement it with their own areas of expertise, hence redressing the balance. While I anticipate that the typical reader will be either a student taking a lecture course on memory or a colleague updating his knowledge of the field, I have tried to write in a way that would make the study of memory accessible to the interested general reader. Anyone with no prior familiarity with the study of memory, however, might find it useful to begin with my brief overview entitled *Your memory: A user's guide* (Penguin Books, 1982).

The study of memory has changed and developed over the last decade, and a number of these developments are reflected in the nature of the present book. One of the most striking changes has been the increase in the number of studies of ecological or everyday memory. During the 1970s, the psychology of memory was predominantly the psychology of the verbal learning laboratory. I attempted in my previous book to speculate as to the real-world significance of these findings observed, but for the most part, this was speculation and nothing more. It is this lack of a clear link between the laboratory and the world that prompted Neisser (1978) to comment so negatively about the sterility of memory research.

Since that time there has been a burgeoning of interest in naturalistic studies of cognition, and I must confess that I began this book intending the rather ambitious, perhaps even gradiose task of providing an ecologically based account of the psychology of memory. The aim was to begin with the problems that memory has to tackle, to work from these to the theoretical questions that must be asked, and, via a combination of laboratory and real-world studies, to their answers. Perhaps unsurprisingly, this proved overambitious; although the links between theory and practice are much more extensive than ever before, there are still far too many gaps to allow a coherent text to be written.

The question of the importance of everyday memory is currently rather controversial, with protagonists such as Neisser (1978) denigrating the standard laboratory approach, while Banaji and Crowder (1989) complain of the "bankruptcy of everyday memory". I trust that what follows will make a powerful case for the view that neither of these extreme views is readily defensible. We need the control and simplicity of the laboratory to develop and test out theories, but at the same time we need to explore their adequacy and generality outside the laboratory by carrying out studies which at this stage may often be little more than natural history. At some point we shall have accumulated sufficient good observations to make such comparatively atheoretical study no longer necessary, but we are as yet far from reaching that point. For that reason, I make no apology for including data collected under natural or semi-structured conditions from barmen and divers, mothers in labour and first-aiders, and indeed anyone who has to make use of his or her memory in the rich and complex conditions of the real world. I similarly make no apology for describing many well-controlled, theorectically driven laboratory studies. We need both.

Another feature that I have tried to incorporate is an awareness of the historical continuity of work on the study of memory. Psychology has perhaps tended to be excessively driven by fashions and enthusiasms, with the danger that we are perpetually rediscovering what was known and then forgetting it again. Consequently, I have tried to emphasize the continuity of work by referring to its historical origins and make no apology for including memory phenomena that are perhaps slightly less fashionable than they were a few years ago.

A related concern has been to emphasize the continuity across fields of psychology that perhaps typically tend to be taught as separate courses. The link between memory and other aspects of cognition is, of course, particularly clear within the area of working memory; the storage capacity of any cognitive system is an integral part of its capacity to perceive, attend and reason. Similarly, the study of memory without learning is clearly a nonsense. And yet for practically a quarter of a century, theories of learning appear to have been overtly developed only in the animal laboratory. I suspect that this stemmed largely from the fact that the information-processing models of the 1960s and '70s were based on a computer model that provided a particularly implausible analogy for the process of human learning, while providing much more fruitful metaphors for other aspects of cognition. Whatever their ultimate success, I believe that the new developments in parallel distributed processing or connectionist models of learning will bring the study of theories of learning back to the centre of the scientific stage.

One final feature that differentiates the present book from its predecessor is its concern for clinical evidence. Studies of the memory performance of amnesic patients, once regarded as largely irrelevant to normal memory, now play an increasingly important role in memory theorising. There is little doubt that the unfortunate patients with memory problems have helped us understand human memory; the final chapter considers the question of whether the psychology of memory can in turn help these patients.

ACKNOWLEDGEMENTS

I have been fortunate in writing this book to be able to draw on the advice of a very wide range of friends and colleagues; I am particularly grateful to those who have helped me to approach intriguing but unfamiliar topics. My venture into behavioral approaches to learning was greatly helped by advice from Archie Levey, David Shanks and John Teasdale, while my treatment of connectionism would have been even more limited without the help of discussions with Dennis Norris, George Houghton and my son, Roland. The chapter on cognition and emotion benefited greatly from talks with Mark Williams and Fraser Watts, while my views on the application of behavioral methods and single case designs to the treatment of memory deficits were clearly much influenced by discussions with Barbara Wilson.

I am particularly grateful to a number of colleagues who were prepared to read and comment on a draft version of this book, often under unreasonably constrained time pressures. They include Robert Bjork, University of California (Los Angeles); Deborah Burke, Pomona College (Claremont, CA); Gillian Cohen, The Open University (Milton Keynes, England); John Gardiner, City University (London, England); Richard Hanley, University of Liverpool (Liverpool, England); Janet Jackson, Groningen University (The Netherlands); John Mueller, University of Missouri (Columbia) and Alan Parkin, Sussex University (Brighton, England). I am sure that the final version has benefited immeasurably, despite the fact that it has not invariably been possible to follow all their excellent suggestions.

I find that the most successful way of writing is by walking and talking into a portable taperecorder; I therefore owe a particular debt to my secretary, Julia Darling, who has regularly performed miracles of turning my garbled mumblings into beautifully typed prose. Without her help, this book certainly would not have been written. It was, in fact, principally written over a period of three summers, a process that was made much more enjoyable by the north Norfolk countryside in which it was written, and by the unfailing support of my wife, Hilary, to whom it is dedicated.

Chapter One

WHY DO WE NEED MEMORY?

UNDERSTANDING LEARNING AND MEMORY

The Scientific Approach

Philosophers have speculated about memory for at least 2,000 years, but its scientific investigation only began about 100 years ago. A German scholar, Hermann Ebbinghaus decided to apply the experimental methods that had recently been developed for the study of perception to the more ambitious investigation of "higher mental processes" and more specifically to human memory. He chose to avoid the richness and complexity of memory in everyday life, by studying the learning and forgetting of artificial materials by a single subject, himself, under rigidly controlled conditions of learning and recall. By means of this ruthless simplification, he was able to demonstrate important characteristics of human memory that were not known to earlier investigators.

The true importance of his work, however, lay less in his new discoveries than in his demonstration that the experimental method could be used to investigate something as complicated as human learning and memory. This theme, that even complicated mental functions could be studied given sufficiently simplified and controlled conditions, has dominated the scientific study of human memory ever since.

There was, however, a price to be paid for adopting this approach. Many of the richer and more intriguing aspects of human memory are difficult if not impossible to capture within the laboratory, while theories developed on the basis of simplified and artificial laboratory-based material often proved difficult to apply in the outside world. This has led to the criticism that much research on the psychology of memory is concerned with trivial and unimportant questions, being excessively concerned with exploring and developing new laboratory tasks, and paying little attention to the applicability of results to remembering in the outside world. One of the most trenchant critics of traditional memory research is Ulrich Neisser who has suggested the following "law", that "If X is an important or interesting feature of human behavior, then X has rarely been studied by psychologists" (Neisser, 1978, p.2).

I have a good deal of sympathy with this view. I believe that experimental psychologists have often been excessively timid, being obsessed with the need for experimental control, and because of this quite unwilling to step out of the laboratory to see if such theories as they have created are indeed applicable to the world outside. Far too much psychological research consists of experiments merely investigating other experiments which in turn were based on yet other experiments. It is of course necessary to examine the experimental and methodological tools that we use, but it is at least as important to concern ourselves with the validity of such tools. Elegant methods are not enough if they limit us to studying trivial questions.

The reason for these shortcomings is not difficult to see. Human memory is extremely complicated, and attempting to investigate it under uncontrolled real-world conditions is often frustratingly hard. Even merely collecting reliable results can be time-consuming and costly, while carrying out the sort of experimental test necessary for deciding between competing theories is often quite impossible.

Nonetheless, there is a tradition of memory research within the real world that extends back at least to Sir Frances Galton who was carrying out important, though largely observational work on memory at the same time as Ebbinghaus was earnestly mastering his lists of nonsense syllables. An interest in memory in the real world continued to flourish in the earlier years of this century, notably in the work of Bartlett in Britain, and of the Gestalt psychologists in Germany. In North America, where the influence of behaviorism was much stronger, the Ebbinghaus approach with its emphasis on simplification and experimental control, dominated the study of human memory up to the 1960s when the cognitive approach rapidly came to dominate the study of memory.

Cognitive Psychology and Ecological Validity

The term "cognitive psychology" is a rather loose label applied to a more flexible approach to psychology. In the case of memory, this approach was often associated with theories based on, or influenced by, the development and use of the electronic computer, which influenced psychological theory by offering new concepts and a new language, that of information processing. Computer-based terms such as "buffer store", "feedback", "encoding" and "retrieval" rapidly became absorbed into the field of memory research.

There is no doubt that this influx of new ideas substantially enriched the study of memory, and within a remarkably short period of time the older experimental techniques and concepts began to disappear from the journals. It could, however, be argued that the Ebbinghaus tradition has continued to dominate North American psychology, with a continued preoccupation with experimental control and an unwillingness to risk exposing the results of the experimental laboratory to the rigors of the world outside. This critical view of the field is cogently argued by Neisser (1976) whose earlier book entitled *Cognitive Psychology* published 10 years before had named and launched the North American cognitive psychology boom.

In his later book, Neisser (1976) makes an eloquent plea for a concern for "ecological validity". This term, associated with the work in perception of Brunswik (1957) and of Gibson (1979) emphasizes the importance of studying perception in the world rather than the laboratory.

Strongly influenced by Gibson, Neisser argues for a move away from the excessive preoccupation with laboratory control and towards an understanding and analysis of the world outside. This approach has had some success in the area of perception despite the rather Messianic fervor of some of its advocates, but has so far been much less influential in the area of human memory. Neisser's initial contribution to this area, was the publication of a book of readings entitled *Memory Observed* (Neisser, 1982) in which research on everyday memory from a wide variety of sources is collected together. It is a delightful book that is very well worth browsing through, but it does, I am afraid, tell us more about Neisser's enthusiasm and tastes than about how human memory should be studied. It offers many fascinating observations and a few intriguing experiments, but is as far from a coherent approach to the study of memory as the Victorian collections of natural history exhibits were from a modern biology laboratory. Perhaps we are still waiting for our Darwin?

While sympathizing with many of Neisser's criticisms, I myself am more of an optimist. I believe that we have made and are making very substantial progress in understanding human memory, and that much of the work carried out in the laboratory does have direct applications in the world outside. I am not of course by any means unique in this view. The comments by Neisser quoted earlier were from an address to a meeting in Wales in 1978 on "practical aspects of memory" (Neisser, 1978). It was a very large meeting in which the numerous participants discovered, with some surprise I suspect, that they were not alone in their preoccupation with memory outside the laboratory.

The proceedings of that meeting formed a landmark in research in this area, and it is now the case that far from being regarded as eccentric, or even reprehensible, work on memory outside the laboratory runs the risk of appearing too concerned with the fashion of the moment. In his closing address to the second conference on practical aspects of memory, some nine years later, Neisser acknowledges that "Time present is very different from time past. Then we were barely at the margin of respectability; now we are somewhere between a necessary evil and a wave of the future" (Neisser, 1988, p.545).

However, despite the increasing flow of ecologically relevant research, it is still far from easy to present an overall view that is not based on the laboratory. It is so much easier to carry out theoretically cogent studies under controlled conditions, that this is likely to remain the major source of theoretical development, although not necessarily of initial theoretical insights into human memory. There will, however, remain a constant need to check laboratory findings against everyday life, and of course to check our theoretical interpretations of everyday phenomena within the more tightly controlled arena of the laboratory.

There is also, of course, a need to bear both the laboratory and the world in mind in teaching the psychology of memory. Since most theoretically cogent work has been done in the laboratory, the temptation is to present a traditional laboratory-based approach, with occasional illustrations and nods in the direction of real-world application. The present book makes a conscious attempt to break away from this. Instead of listing the areas that have been explored, and then attempting to justify such research, I shall try to begin with some basic questions about memory. Questions that an intelligent Martian landing on earth might ask, based particularly on the question of what function or functions memory serves. I shall try to illustrate the importance of these various functions by describing patients who, usually as a result of brain damage have had a given function destroyed or impaired.

WHAT IS MEMORY?

The use of a single term might seem to suggest that memory is a unitary system, albeit a complicated one such as the heart or the liver. As will become obvious, it is not one system but many. The systems range in storage duration from fractions of a second up to a lifetime, and in storage capacity from tiny buffer stores to the long-term memory system that appears to far exceed in capacity and flexibility the largest available computer.

One way of gaining some appreciation of the importance of memory is to study the plight of patients whose memory has been impaired as a result of brain damage. Consider for example the case of Clive Wearing, a very intelligent and highly talented professional musician and broadcaster who in his 40s was afflicted by encephalitis, a virus that caused inflammation, and subsequently damage to his brain. He was unconscious for many weeks from an attack that would, up to recently, have been sufficient to kill him. However, drugs for treating encephalitis have improved, and his health recovered, leaving him with substantial brain damage and a very dense amnesia.

Amnesia is not an all-or-none condition, and most amnesics can appear to be relatively normal on initial meeting. Not so in the case of Clive, since his amnesia was so dense that he could remember nothing from more than a few minutes before, a state that he attributed to having just recovered consciousness. Left to his own devices, he would often be found writing down a time, for example

3.10, and the note "I have just recovered consciousness", only to cross out the 3.10 and add 3.15, followed by 3.20, etc. If his wife left the room for a few minutes, when she returned he would greet her with great joy declaring that he had not seen her for months and asking how long he had been unconscious. Experienced once, such an event could be intriguing and touching, but when it happens repeatedly day in, day out, it rapidly loses its charm.

Clive was not capable of showing new learning of people or events, rapidly becoming frustrated in a learning situation and fulminating against anyone so stupid as to waste his time on silly tests when he had only recovered consciousness a few moments before. In some patients, new learning may be impaired, while their recollection of earlier learning is normal. Not so, alas, in the case of Clive, whose capacity to recall his earlier life was patchy in the extreme. He could still remember general features, such as where he had been to school and what college he had attended at Cambridge, together with highlights such as singing for the Pope on his visit to London, and some particularly dramatic musical events he had organized. In all cases, however, his capacity to recall detail was extremely poor.

What of his semantic memory, his general knowledge of the world? Here again considerable impairment had occurred. He had written a book on Lassus, an early composer, and could still recall just a few salient features of the composer's life, but with no richness or detail. When shown pictures of Cambridge, a city in which he had spent four years of his life and subsequently visited frequently, the only scene he recognized was King's College Chapel, the best known and most distinctive Cambridge building; he did not recognize a photograph of his own college. More general knowledge was also markedly impaired for someone of his level of culture and intelligence. He could not for example remember who had written *Romeo and Juliet*, and when shown a picture of the Queen and Duke of Edinburgh identified them as singers he had known from a Catholic church.

One aspect of Clive's skills did however, appear to be remarkably well-preserved, namely his musical ability. His wife describes returning on one occasion to find that the choir that Clive had directed was visiting him, and to observe him conducting them through a complex piece of music showing all his skills and capacity to spot when someone was making a mistake. Similarly, he could play the piano or harpsichord extremely well, although initially he did encounter one particular problem. Many pieces have a point at which a return sign means that that section has to be played once again before continuing. Initially Clive ran into difficulties at this point, becoming stuck in an apparently eternal loop. Subsequently, however, he appears to have solved the problem of how to cope with this, although it is far from clear how.

The effect of Clive's memory loss on his life is, of course, devastating. If he goes out alone, he is lost and has no idea how to find his way back. He can not tell anyone who finds him where he has come from or where he is going. He has only the haziest access to his own past, and no apparent capacity to learn anything new. In his own words, his life is "Hell on earth—It's like being dead—all the bloody time".

The desperate plight of Clive and densely amnesic patients like him clearly demonstrates that memory is important, but does not tell us how we should go about investigating it. What are the important questions? Let us suppose that by some miracle of science, alas still far beyond our capabilities, that we could give Clive a new memory, working well in hot and cold weather, immersible under water and capable of withstanding the sorts of forces encountered by American football players in collision—in short, something that has most of the characteristics of a normal human memory system. What questions should we ask of such a system in order to decide whether it really was as good as Clive's old memory?

Component Processes

I might perhaps begin by asking my brand new memory box one question that is of great importance to me, if not the rest of the world, namely "Who am I?" In order to answer this, the memory box would need to have some form of *autobiographical memory*, a record of the experiences of a lifetime that go together to create myself as a person. In the case of psychologists studying normal memory, this was a topic initially raised by Galton in 1883, but largely neglected since, until a resurgence of interest in the last few years. We shall be discussing this in Chapter 12.

A second question that would interest me about my box concerns the issue of "What do I know?" Clive would find it very necessary to have a system that contained a great deal of information, not only facts about composers and choirs, but also general information about the world, how to order food, to travel on buses and carry out the wide range of skills that are essential to functioning as a normal participant in any complex society such as our own. The study of this topic, *semantic memory* was also somewhat neglected until attempts to provide a knowledge-base for computer systems stimulated an interest in the way in which this enormously important but complex facility operates in people. We shall be exploring this in Chapter 13.

A third crucial question I might want to ask my new system is "How will it learn?" Evolution has come up with two broad strategies for solving the problem of allowing complex behavior. One is to pre-program the organism so that everything that is necessary for efficient functioning is built into the genes of the organism, with a minimum of modification necessary. This occurs in the case of many insects and so-called "lower organisms". While such a solution is very rigid, organisms adopting it have been successful for far longer than man has been on the planet, and may well outlive him by a similar margin. The other strategy is to produce an organism which can learn, that is one that can modify its behavior to suit the demands of the environment. The human race is clearly the organism that is most dependent on learning and most flexible in its programing. Consequently, I would expect my new memory to be good at learning, but it would be reasonable to assume that like any other piece of equipment, I would need to know something about its learning capacities if I am to take fullest advantage of this. Chapters 7, 8 and 9 are concerned with the much studied question of how people learn.

Learning is concerned with registering and storing information. Given that information is stored, however, its efficient use must depend on access in the right form at the right time. There is nothing more frustrating than having a name or a word on the tip of one's tongue, something that you know, but simply can not produce at the crucial moment. Having good, flexible, efficient retrieval is as important as having good information storage. Indeed, storage and retrieval should not be regarded as totally separate functions; they go hand-in-hand, with the best method of retrieval depending on how material is stored. Chapters 11 and 12 describe research into the retrieval capacities of human memory.

One characteristic of human memory that makes it very different from most computer memories is that humans forget. We tend to regard this as a great nuisance, with a remarkably large number of people claiming to have "a terrible memory". There is, however, reason to believe that forgetting is actually a very useful attribute of the human memory system. It is at least plausible to assume that if we retained a record of every sensation, thought and event we had experienced, and attempted to have all of these accessible, we would need massive storage resources, and a truly incredible retrieval system. Furthermore, it would be almost entirely devoted to storing vast quantities of trivial details which are likely to be of little if any subsequent use. The process of forgetting is one whereby the important features are filtered out and preserved, while irrelevant or predictable detail is either destroyed, or stored in such a way that is not readily accessible in its original form. On balance, I would want my new device to forget, preferably showing broadly the same elegant characteristics as human forgetting. These characteristics are described in Chapter 9.

One obvious benefit of forgetting is the way in which it softens emotional pain and grief: according to popular lore "Time heals all wounds". Perhaps it would be nice to have a system that was better at remembering pleasant than unpleasant things? In fact, there is some evidence that human memory does behave in this way, but any such tendency is of course likely to have its drawbacks since it does represent a distortion of our recollection of the past. I would therefore want to know how my system was influenced, if at all, by emotional factors. Chapter 14 discusses the way in which human memory responds to the pressures of emotion.

However, while it may be useful for some purposes to think of memory as like a mysterious box, in other ways such a view is positively misleading. First of all, as mentioned earlier, memory does not comprise a single entity, but rather consists of a range of different systems which happen to have in common the capacity for storing information. Hence Clive's capacity for immediately repeating back material was comparatively normal. Working memory, however, is the term used to describe the alliance of temporary memory systems that play a crucial role in many cognitive tasks such as reasoning, learning and understanding. In general, working memory relies on different systems from those involved in long-term memory, and densely amnesic patients may have intact working memory, while patients with defective working memory may show normal long-term memory. Short-term and working memory will be discussed in Chapters 2 to 6.

A second reason why the idea of memory as a box is potentially misleading is in fostering the idea that memory storage is rather like placing items into a cupboard, or books in a library. Such analogies can be useful, but it is important to appreciate that they are analogies, ways of thinking about problems which are helpful, but which can be misleading if interpreted too literally.

LAWS, PRINCIPLES, THEORIES AND MODELS

Before concluding this introductory chapter it might perhaps be useful if I were to say a little about my own assumptions concerning the application of scientific method to psychology in general, and memory in particular. Views on the matter vary, and since mine will inevitably influence what follows, it is perhaps wise to say something about them in advance.

I begin by assuming that science is attempting to understand and represent nature, in my own case to understand human memory, and to express that understanding in some coherent way: a theory, a law or a model. Secondly, and crucially, I believe that science operates by attempting to expose such conceptualizations or models to empirical test, that is to see if they actually work when applied to a situation that is novel. The experimental method is the principal way of testing theories, typically under conditions where as many extraneous factors as possible are controlled or ruled out by the experimenter.

Experiments are not, of course, the only way of testing theories. In some subjects such as astronomy, it may be virtually impossible to manipulate or control the variables under study, but it is nevertheless possible using observational techniques to develop and test highly sophisticated theories. It is important to bear this in mind, particularly in studying memory under everyday conditions, where too strict an adherence to the Ebbinghaus laboratory tradition may suggest that studies carried out under conditions where experimental control is less complete are in some sense "unscientific". Whether they are scientific depends on the care with which the observations are made, and the conclusions drawn from them.

It is sometimes lamented that psychology, unlike physics and chemistry, apparently does not have any laws. This is not strictly true, consider for example Weber's Law in perception describing the relationship between magnitude and discriminability, Hick's Law relating reaction time to number of available choices (see Gleitman, 1986, pp.141–2), and Fitt's Law relating distance and accuracy to speed of movement (see Wickens, 1984). It is certainly true that in memory, however, there are relatively few recent laws, although some of the more ancient laws such as Ribot's Law or Jost's Law (see Woodworth, 1938) are occasionally taken out of the museum case, dusted down and cited.

Laws are essentially descriptions of regularities that occur across a wide range of observations. They summarize data, rather than explaining it. Such an atheoretical approach to the field has become rather unfashionable since the demise of the stimulus-response associationist approach that flourished in the U.S.A. between the 1930s and the 1960s, and was sometimes known as "dustbowl empiricism", because of its theoretical sterility. I believe however, that it *is* important to explore empirical findings systematically and express them clearly and succinctly, but that this needs to be combined with an attempt at understanding and explanation if the field is to flourish and grow.

Perhaps the nearest to this traditional empirical approach are the attempts to come up with broad general principles of learning and memory. An example of this is Tulving's *encoding specificity principle* (Tulving, 1983), which attempts to relate the conditions of learning to the conditions of optimal retrieval (see Chapter 11). Another example is the concept of *levels of processing* (Craik & Lockhart, 1972). This states that the more deeply and elaborately an item is processed, the greater the probability of subsequent recall.

How can something be a good principle but a poor theory? In order to answer this, we need to think about the purpose of a theory, or a model. Both theories and models are attempts to represent the processes underlying a particular area or phenomenon. Typically the term *theory* is taken to imply a rather broader and grander aim than a model, which may be something applied to a relatively limited subcomponent of a system. Hence one might talk of a theory of the whole of long-term memory, but talk about a model of a particular memory phenomenon. I regard theories and models as like maps, offering a useful way of summarizing what is known. In this respect they are similar to laws or principles. In addition to their descriptive function however, theories and models attempt to go beyond what is known, and offer a possible explanation of existing findings and suggest ways in which phenomena can be further explored. In short, laws and principles describe what we know, whereas models and theories provide tools for learning more.

Like maps in general, models and theories should not be regarded as exact copies of the processes they are attempting to explain. Theories, like maps, are tools that are devised for a particular purpose. Hence a map of the London Underground system is very well adapted to helping you travel by underground train across London, but incorporates distortions of scale and direction that would make it quite misleading as a guide to driving by car across London.

Just as different kinds of maps of London occur and are used for different purposes, so different kinds of theory of memory occur, concentrating on different aspects of the memory system. A theory giving a successful account of the neurochemical basis of long-term memory, though scientifically extremely valuable, would be unlikely to offer an equally elegant and economical account of the psychological characteristics of memory. While it may in principle one day be possible to map one theory onto the other, it will still be useful to have *both* a psychological and a physiological theory.

To use an analogy from physics, I suspect that the builders of bridges continue to use Newtonian principles in their design, despite the subsequent development of the principles of subatomic particle physics. I am sure they would not deny that subatomic physics applies to bridges, just as to other aspects of matter, but would not use it simply because the level of analysis is inappropriate for the problem they are tackling. Hence, in what follows I shall be talking about *psychological* models and *psychological* theories, and although I shall be considering the *effects* of brain damage on memory, I shall say relatively little about the associated brain structures, and even less about the underlying neurochemistry. Neurophysiology and neurochemistry are interesting and important areas, but at present they place relatively few constraints on psychological theories and models of human memory.

In conclusion, I would regard my views on science as somewhat eclectic. I regard theories and models as tools for helping us to organize what we already know, and as a means of helping us ask further questions that will extend the boundaries of what is known. In the process of doing this, the models and theories themselves will become stretched and modified so that they either grow into slightly different but more comprehensive models, or are abandoned when someone produces a better model. Models that do not give novel and testable predictions are likely to become sterile and be rejected in favor of more dynamic models.

I do not any longer, accept Karl Popper's view that the essence of a good scientific theory is that it should be readily falsifiable (Popper, 1959). Occasionally it will be possible to decide between two opposing positions by means of a crucial experiment, but this is very much the exception rather than the rule. As mentioned earlier, theories are rather like maps; occasionally a map can be shown to be fundamentally wrong, as for example in conceptualizing the world as a plane surface rather than a sphere, but much more commonly what happens is that further exploration leads to further refinement rather than simple disproof of previous beliefs. I would suggest that many of the apparently fundamental changes in memory theory are of this kind, with new information suggesting a somewhat new way of representing and conceptualizing what has gone before, rather than its complete rejection.

Models are essentially analogies, and tend to change and develop as technology develops. In the case of memory, some of the classical analogies came from natural observation such as likening the clustering of similar memories to the flocking of birds of the same species. Others came from simple technology such as that of writing, where the memory trace was likened to a mark made on a soft wax tablet. With the development of clockwork automata in the seventeenth and eighteenth centuries, mechanical analogies became more common. In the early years of this century the development of the telephone switchboard seemed to fit neatly into a view of learning involving the setting up of stimulus-response connections (see Marshall & Fryer, 1978 for an overview of the history of the use of models in memory).

Since the 1950s, cognitive psychology has been very heavily influenced by the analogy of the digital computer, tending to favor the development of models based on the serial processing of symbolic information. As we shall see in Chapter 13, this technological influence is still extremely powerful, with the development of computer systems that process in parallel rather than serially, causing a major change in the dominant models in cognitive psychology.

If models are like maps, providing a broad overview, is it possible to produce an overall model or theory of memory? I believe that it is, provided one is content to accept that what is produced is an approximation, with a great deal of disagreement, particularly about conceptualization and labeling of the components. To use our world-map analogy, there would still be considerable argument as to whether it is more useful to consider Europe and Asia as separate continents, and whether Arabia should rightly be considered as part of Asia or of Africa.

For better or worse, I shall use such a simplified overview of the structure of human memory as an organizing principle within this book. I shall attempt to fragment memory into subcomponents, fully aware of the fact that while some components would be generally accepted as separable modules, others would be regarded by many as different aspects of a single system. I myself believe that the distinctions discussed are theoretically important, but if you prefer to regard memory as a single monolithic system, then I assume that you have no objection to a book being divided into chapters. The particular chapter topics are not very different from those adopted by virtually every other textbook on memory, a feature that reflects either a great deal of underlying agreement within the field, or an even greater lack of originality—or perhaps both!

Chapter Two

PERCEIVING AND REMEMBERING

Human memory is a system for storing and retrieving information, information that is, of course, acquired through our senses. Whether we see something, hear it or smell it will obviously influence what we recall, since in one sense our memories are records of percepts. One way of obtaining an overview of human memory is to trace the way in which visual and auditory stimuli are processed and remembered. As we shall see, in both cases there are a number of separable processing and memory stages.

The briefest memory stores last for only a fraction of a second. Such sensory memories are perhaps best considered as an integral part of the process of perceiving. Both vision and hearing then appear to have a later but temporary storage stage which might perhaps be termed short-term auditory and visual memory, leaving a memory trace that lasts for a few seconds. In addition to these, we clearly also have long-term memory for sights and sounds. We can remember what a sunset looks like, could probably recognize a photograph of Albert Einstein or Joseph Stalin, or identify the voice of a close friend, or the sound of a creaking door. All these indicate some form of long-term sensory storage.

We shall therefore begin the exploration of human memory by briefly reviewing the evidence for these various types of visual and auditory memory. Similar systems probably exist in the case of other senses such as smell, taste and touch. They have, however, been much less adequately explored, and will not be further discussed.

SENSORY MEMORY

Memory, in the sense of storage of information for subsequent analysis, probably plays an important role in many perceptual systems. Probably the most peripheral effects to which the term memory has been applied with any frequency are the very short-term visual and auditory stores that were labeled by Neisser (1967) *iconic* and *echoic memory.* These systems represent the earlier stages of what could be termed sensory memory, memory that is based on a particular sensory modality. We will discuss these before going on to explore the more characteristic aspects of memory which tend to be much less dependent on the sensory modality of input.

VISUAL MEMORY

Iconic Memory

If you move a brightly glowing cigarette-end around in a darkened room, it will leave a glowing trail, and if it is bright enough and the room dark enough, you can write in the air. This type of visual persistence was studied as long ago as 1740 by the Swedish scientist Segner. He measured the duration of visual persistence in a simple but ingenious experiment in which he attached a glowing coal to a freely-spinning cartwheel. He adjusted the rate at which the wheel revolved to a point at which the visual trace left by the coal formed a circle without a gap. By measuring the time it took for one revolution, he was able to estimate the persistence of vision, and found it to be about 100 milliseconds (cited by Mollon, 1970, p. 182). Segner's estimate is broadly in line with more recent measures using rather more sophisticated equipment (e.g. Haber & Nathanson, 1968).

Early students of visual attention were intrigued by the question of how much could be apprehended in a single glimpse. The philosopher Sir William Hamilton in 1859 carried out a simple experiment in which he cast down a handful of marbles, varying the number of marbles thrown, and attempting to estimate their number visually. He concluded (Hamilton, 1859):

> If you throw a handful of marbles on the floor, you will find it difficult to view at once more than six, or seven at most without confusion; but if you group them into twos, or threes, or fives, you can comprehend as many groups as you can units; because the mind considers these groups as only units.

Exploration of the rate at which the visual system can take up information proved much more feasible with the invention of the tachistoscope, a device for presenting visual material under highly controlled experimental conditions for periods ranging from milliseconds to seconds. In the intervening years there have been many studies exploring the phenomenon described by Hamilton, some of which are described in a notable recent study by Mandler and Shebo (1982). They conducted an extensive series of experiments on the process of "subitizing", as the accurate reporting of small numbers of briefly presented items has come to be known. They conclude that it comprises three separate processes: a response to arrays of one to three items that is fast and accurate and based on familiar "canonical" patterns. The response to arrays of four to seven items is assumed to be based on the mental counting of arrays that are able to be kept in conscious attention for a limited period of time. Arrays containing more than seven items fade from conscious awareness before counting is complete, and hence must be estimated rather than counted, leading to a much lower level of accuracy.

In recent years, however, there has been much less interest in the number of dots that can be perceived, and much more in the perception of more complex stimuli such as strings of letters. This approach was strongly influenced by an elegant study by Sperling (1960) who explored in detail the role of brief sensory stimulation in the tachistoscopic perception of groups of letters.

Sperling presented his subjects with a stimulus comprising three rows of four letters. When shown these for 50 milliseconds, followed by a blank white field, subjects were able to report only about four or five of the twelve letters. Was this because these were the only letters that had been seen, or could the subject have seen them all, but forgotten some of them in the brief period it takes to report five letters? Sperling tested this by instructing the subject that he need only report one line of letters, but that he would not be told which line until just after the letters had been shown. A high tone meant report the top line, a medium tone the middle and a low tone the bottom line. Since subjects did not know in advance which line would be used, they would have to try to remember all the letters. When tested in this way, Sperling's subjects were able to report about three of the four letters comprising the line requested.

How should Sperling's results be interpreted? When asked for a specific line, subjects were able to repeat about three of the four letters. Since the subjects did not know in advance which line was to be probed, we must assume that they also had available about three items from each of the two rows that did not happen to be tested. This suggests that the total number of letters being held was about nine, considerably better than one would expect from the score of about four letters reported in the uncued condition in which the subject was asked to report letters from all three lines.

Sperling interpreted his results as suggesting that the letters were being read out from a rapidly decaying visual memory trace. In support of this view, Sperling describes a study in which the interval between the offset of the letters and the presentation of the cue specifying which line to report is systematically varied. As Figure 2.1 shows, the advantage from cueing a single line declines until at about 500 milliseconds it disappears. This result is consistent with the idea of a visual trace that has a persistence of approximately half a second under these conditions.

In a further experiment, Sperling varied the brightness of the blank field occurring before and after the letters. As Figure 2.1 shows, under these conditions the short-term visual trace, or *icon* as Neisser calls it, persists for a good deal longer, with the line-cueing advantage being present for several seconds after the removal of the target letters.

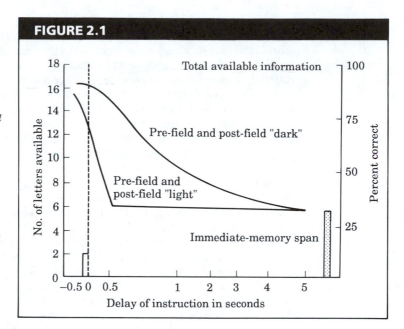

FIGURE 2.1

Information available to one observer from two kinds of stimulus presentation. The right ordinate is the average accuracy of partial reports; the left ordinate is the inferred store of available letters. Average immediate memory span is indicated on the right. From Sperling (1963). Copyright 1963 by The Human Factors Society Inc., and reproduced by permission.

If instead of darkness, or a uniform dim light-field, the letters are followed by a brighter flash of light, then performance is substantially impaired, as if the flash of light were wiping out the icon. This phenomenon had been studied previously by Baxt in 1871. Baxt's results showed two things. First he showed that the brighter the light, the poorer the performance, an effect known as *brightness masking*. Secondly, when he systematically varied the interval between the presentation of the items and the presentation of the flash, Baxt obtained a linear increase in number of letters reported with increased time. His results were consistent with a mechanism whereby the letters were read off sequentially, but very rapidly at a rate of approximately 100 letters per second.

As Sperling points out, these results suggest that the letters are being transferred from some fragile peripheral store into some more durable form. What is the nature of this second stage? Clearly, since the subject is not capable of speaking at the rate of 100 letters per second he was not simply reporting them verbally. In an earlier version of his model of iconic memory, Sperling (1963) suggests that they are read directly into a motor response code. In a later version, Sperling (1967) refers to a buffer containing motor codes for subsequent speech. One reason for drawing this conclusion was the tendency for errors to be similar to the correct item in sound rather than in visual characteristics, hence the letter B might be recalled as V, or the letter F as X.

As we shall see later there is abundant evidence for the role of phonological speech-based coding in the retention of visually presented letters. However, subsequent research has shown that features such as color, shape and indeed direction of movement presented under conditions that make verbalization unlikely can all be stored within the iconic memory system, suggesting that the peripheral iconic information is probably fed into a further visual store, rather than mapped directly on to a speech code.

In an elegant series of experiments, Turvey (1973) showed that iconic memory is better considered as storage occurring at a series of stages in the process of visual perception, rather than being the output of a simple passive peripheral store. Turvey's studies explored the difference between two forms of masking, one, *brightness-masking*, involves the presentation of a flash of light as in the previously described study by Baxt. The other, *pattern-masking*, involves the disruption of performance by the subsequent presentation of a patterned stimulus, typically comprising broken fragments of letters (see Figure 2.2). Turvey showed that these two types of mask behave in very different ways.

One crucial feature of a brightness mask is the amount of energy it contains. As in the case of the perception of brightness, the disruptive effect of the mask is a joint multiplicative function of its brightness and its duration, a phenomenon known in vision as Bloch's Law. Hence a 2-millisecond flash at an intensity of 20 foot lamberts is exactly equivalent to an 8-millisecond flash at 5 foot lamberts.

A second important feature of brightness-masking is that the icon is only disrupted if the mask is presented to the *same* eye as the letters; presenting the letters to the right eye and the flash of light to the left does not lead to masking. This suggests that the masking effect is occurring at the retinal level, before the point at which information from the two eyes is combined.

In the case of pattern-masking, however, intensity is not important, the most crucial feature being the *interval* between the presentation of the letters and the onset of the mask. Furthermore, in contrast to brightness masking, the effect is not dependent on presenting the mask to the same eye as the stimulus. Presenting the letters to the right eye and the pattern to the left will cause just as much masking as presenting both to the same eye. This suggests that pattern-masking occurs at some point in the system after information from the two eyes has been combined.

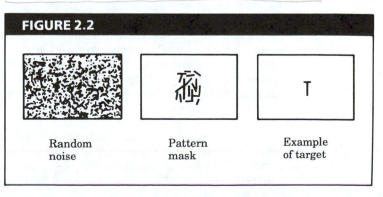

FIGURE 2.2

Examples of noise mask, pattern mask, and target used by Turvey. From Turvey (1973). Copyright (1973) by the American Psychological Association. Reprinted by permission.

Random noise   Pattern mask   Example of target

The concept of iconic memory that emerges from Turvey's investigations is one in which the process of perception involves storage at a number of levels. One of these is relatively peripheral, and as Sakitt (1976) has suggested, this aspect of iconic memory may be based on something resembling a visual after-image. It does, however, seem very unlikely that the later pattern-masked aspect of iconic memory is peripherally based.

What is the ecological function of iconic memory? Does it in fact have any function? Haber (1983) has suggested that it does not, other than the rather esoteric one of allowing one to read by lightning flashes if caught by night in a thunderstorm! Coltheart (1983), however, argues strongly against this view. He points out that the system does not operate by maintaining a stimulus for a standard amount of time after its *offset*, but rather guarantees a given persistence from the *onset* of the stimulus, hence having its maximum effect with briefly presented stimuli. As such, it is likely that it serves the function of ensuring that the perceptual system has some minimum amount of time to process the incoming stimulus.

It is a regrettable feature of studies in iconic memory that so many of them have used letters rather than scenes as targets and that these are typically followed by a mask comprising a completely different stimulus, usually either a blank field or an unrelated visual noise pattern. I assume that the visual system was not designed specifically to cope with this, and that however the system works, it normally is fed with successive glimpses that are broadly similar to each other, as is of course the case in the cinema where each frame is separated from the next by a blank period followed by a frame containing a very similar scene. Presumably this would lead to facilitatory rather than disruptive effects of successive stimuli, since each image will be compatible with what has gone before. Is it perhaps worth exploring these facilitatory effects in more detail if we are interested in the ecological relevance of the iconic store?

Short-term Visual Memory

We have suggested that iconic memory feeds onto some more durable visual storage system. Evidence for such a system was produced in a very neat series of experiments by Posner, Boies, Eichelman and Taylor (1969). They presented subjects with the task of deciding whether two letters did or did not have the same name, hence if shown AA or Aa, the subject should respond "yes", whereas given AB or Ab he should respond "no". Posner observed that subjects were about 80 milliseconds faster when the letters were visually identical as well as having the same name (i.e. AA and aa were faster than Aa or aA).

The second phase of the study involved presenting the letters one at a time, varying the delay between presentation of the first and second letter. As the delay increased, the advantage to having the letters physically identical declined, and was completely lost after a delay of 2 seconds. Posner et al. suggest that this implies a visual trace with a 2-second decay rate.

However, as Phillips and Baddeley (1971) subsequently pointed out, this is not necessarily the case. At the end of the 2-second delay, subjects were presumably relying on some form of name code; at the beginning, they were clearly influenced by a visual code. The fact that the name code was dominant after 2 seconds, however, did not necessarily mean that the visual code had completely vanished.

Phillips and Baddeley investigated this, using patterns that were chosen as being very difficult to name. These comprised matrices of cells with each cell in the checkerboard having a 50% probability of being black or white. A given checkerboard pattern was presented, and after an interval ranging from 0 to 9 seconds was re-presented in either an identical form, or with one cell changed. The subject had to respond "same" or "different". The results are shown in Figure 2.3 in which the subjects' time to respond and accuracy are plotted as a function of delay. The results suggest some form of visual storage that is present for considerably more

Recognition memory for random patterns as a function of complexity. Examples of the three types of pattern are shown. Each pattern was followed by either an identical pattern or one which had a single square changed. From Phillips (1974). Reprinted by permission of the Psychonomics Society Inc.

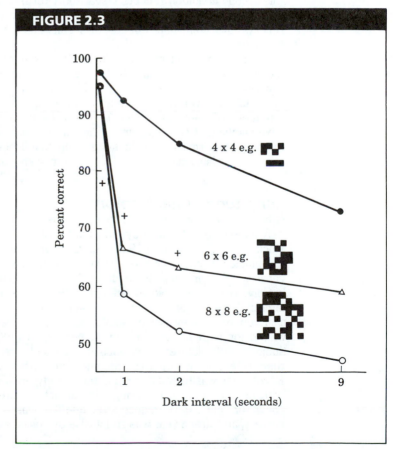

FIGURE 2.3

than the 2-second maximum suggested by the original Posner study.

Could these effects, or those shown by Posner and his colleagues be attributable to iconic memory? This seems extremely unlikely since neither effect is impaired by the presentation of a visual patterned stimulus during the retention interval. Iconic storage effects can however be shown using the checkerboard patterns employed by Phillips. In one study, he presented patterns varying in complexity from 4 to 25 cells, and again tested them after a range of intervals. On half the trials, the second stimulus was presented in an identical place to the first, while on the other half, the stimulus was shifted slightly to the left or the right of the original. When the stimuli were located in exactly the same position, performance was excellent after very brief delays, regardless of the complexity of the pattern. Subjects reported that changes were detectable as a flicker in the stimulus. When the patterns were shifted to one side however, the very high level of initial performance disappeared, and level of recognition was a direct function of pattern complexity. Phillips (1974) suggests that this second condition reflects visual short-term memory, whereas the earlier condition, in which the two patterns were superimposed, reflects the combined effects of iconic and short-term visual storage.

Short-term visual memory does not appear to be masked by intervening visual material which the subject is free to ignore. The capacity to retain an item over a delay *is* impaired however, when subjects are given a demanding intervening task such as mental arithmetic (Phillips & Christie, 1977a,b). Doost and Turvey (1971) have shown that such concurrent activity has little effect on iconic memory performance, again suggesting that iconic memory and short-term visual memory involve different systems.

Long-term Visual Memory

It has long been known, of course, that memory for visual material may extend considerably beyond a matter of seconds. For example Rock and Engelstein (1959) studied memory for a single meaningless shape over periods extending up to a month. While the capacity of their subjects to draw the shape accurately declined rapidly, they were able to recognize the shape from a range of similar shapes almost perfectly four weeks later.

Even more impressive results are found when subjects are tested for recognition of pictures. Nickerson (1965) showed his subjects 600 pictures of various scenes and events, and tested their retention at intervals ranging from a day to a year later. Recognition was tested by mixing the already-presented pictures in with new items, and requiring the subject to categorize each as "new" or "old". Performance after one day was at a level of 92% correct, and after a year was still well above chance at 63%.

An even more dramatic demonstration of memory for pictures was that of Standing, Conezio, and Haber (1970) who presented no fewer than 2,560 color slides, for 10 seconds each. Performance was tested by presenting pairs of items, one new and one old, and requiring the subject to point to the one that had been presented before. Despite the enormous number of items presented, performance was still at 90% when tested several days later.

Does this mean that we are continually storing enormous amounts of visual information? Not necessarily, for the following reason. Note that the technique used by Standing et al. (the two-alternative forced-choice procedure) simply requires the subject to detect which of two items is the more familiar. In order to do this the subject needs only to have stored the minimum amount of information that will allow one of the pictures to appear slightly more familiar than the other. That means that *something* on the picture is stored, not that everything has been remembered.

A study by Goldstein and Chance (1971) explored this issue, changing the material to be remembered and the testing procedure. They used three types of test photographs, women's faces, magnified snowflakes, and ink blots. They presented 14 stimuli from each set at a rate of 3 seconds per stimulus. Recall was tested immediately and after 48 hours by mixing the 14 old stimuli with 70 new ones. The subjects were requested to judge each stimulus and decide whether it was old or new.

Performance was considerably lower than the 90% observed by Standing et al., being 71% for faces, 48% for ink blots and 33% for snowflakes, but note that all of these are substantially above the 14% detection rate to be expected by chance. Furthermore, there was virtually no difference between the immediate test and delayed recognition 48 hours later, suggesting very little forgetting.

This result shows that our visual memory is by no means miraculous, but nevertheless, bearing in mind the nature of the material, the level of recognition performance was still quite impressive. Before moving on from the impressiveness of visual memory however, we should perhaps say something about the phenomenon that has been labeled "flashbulb memory".

Flashbulb Memory

This label was given by Brown and Kulik (1977) who asked their subjects if they could recall how they had heard the news of John Kennedy's death. A similar question had been asked about the assassination of Abraham Lincoln by Colegrove (1899), who observed that of 179 people interviewed, 127 were able to give full particulars as to where they were and what they were doing when the bad news was announced. Brown and Kulik asked similar questions about a total of 10 such dramatic events, and observed that many of them were accompanied by a very vivid recollection of the receipt of the news, the more consequential the event, the greater the probability of a vivid "flashbulb memory". As Neisser (1982) points out, however, a vivid and detailed recollection is not necessarily an accurate one. He cites the case of his own vivid memory of hearing of the bombing of Pearl Harbor. For many years he believed this to be an accurate flashbulb memory. When he later began to explore it in detail, however, he realized that it was so full of inconsistencies it could not possibly be correct. The phenomenon of vivid memories of important events is an interesting one, but as we shall see in exploring the area of eyewitness testimony, a vivid recollection is not necessarily an accurate one.

Eyewitness Testimony

It does not of course greatly matter whether we are correct in our vivid recollections of where we were when we heard of Kennedy's death. There is however one situation in which the accuracy of recollection can be of crucial importance, namely in the case of a witness testifying in a court of law. Almost inevitably, testimony concerns events that are in doubt, and hence it is typically very hard to assess the veracity of a witness's claims. On the other hand there is no doubt that eyewitness testimony can be extremely persuasive.

Consider for example the following case, described by Loftus (1979). On 15 May 1975, the assistant manager of a store in Monroe, North Carolina was forced into a car at gunpoint by two men. They told him to lie down in the back of the car, and he had only a brief glance before they pulled stocking masks over their faces. They drove him to the store and asked him to open the safe. He convinced them that he did not know the combination, whereupon they took the $35 from his wallet and let him go.

All the victim would say about the men was that one of them looked Hispanic, their car was an off-white 1965 Dodge Dart, and that one kidnapper looked like a man who had recently applied for a job at the store. On the basis of this, a composite sketch was made of one of the suspects.

Three days later the police stopped a 1965 white Plymouth Valiant (similar to a Dodge Dart), and arrested the driver and passenger, Sandie and Lonnie Sawyer. Neither looked like the sketch, nor had they applied for a job at the store. Both denied any knowledge of the kidnapping.

At the trial, the manager positively identified the Sawyers as the men who had kidnapped him, and in spite of the presence of four witnesses testifying that Sandie was at home at the time, and four testifying that Lonnie was visiting a girlfriend at a printing plant, the jury nonetheless found them guilty. As they were taken from the court, Lonnie cried "Momma, Daddy, appeal this. We didn't do it".

The family engaged the support of a determined and tenacious detective who continued to investigate the case. About a year later they had a lucky break when a prisoner at a Youth Center admitted to being one of the kidnappers. The detective re-checked some of his leads and found that the man who confessed had indeed applied for a job at the store, and in addition had a friend whose mother owned a 1965 Dodge Dart.

He argued for a re-trial, but the judge refused to accept that sufficient new evidence had occurred to justify this. The Governor of the State was petitioned for a pardon, and while this was under consideration, the prisoner confessed in writing, then on camera, subsequently recanting and finally withdrawing his recantation. On that day, the Governor of North Carolina pardoned the Sawyers. The campaign has cost their impoverished family thousands of dollars, and they had narrowly escaped sentences of 32 and 28 years in prison.

This miscarriage of justice all stemmed from the jury's acceptance of the testimony of the victim who admitted that he had only caught a brief glimpse of his assailants. Despite evidence that the Sawyers were elsewhere at the time, the jury was prepared to accept the testimony of the victim and convict. This is a shocking, but alas by no means exceptional example of the reliance placed by juries on the testimony of eyewitnesses. It has in fact been known since at least the nineteenth century that eyewitness testimony is potentially extremely unreliable. Indeed, the German developmental psychologist William Stern founded a journal entitled *Contribution to the Psychology of Testimony* that was devoted entirely to studies on this topic.

Such imperfect memory is not of course limited to briefly glimpsed faces; even objects and events that are seen very frequently are often poorly recalled. For example, in 1895 J. McKeen Cattell reported a study in which his students were asked a number of questions from which the following are examples:

1. Do chestnut trees or oak trees lose their leaves earlier in the autumn?
2. Do horses in fields stand with head or tail to the wind?
3. In what direction do the seeds of an apple point?

He found that his students' recall was not much better than chance. Chestnut trees lost their leaves first (59% correct); horses stand with their tails to the wind (64% correct); and apple pips point upwards towards the stem (39% correct).

Cattell also asked his students about more specific events, including what the weather had been a week previously, when it had in fact snowed early but subsequently cleared. Of 56 people who responded, only seven mentioned snow, prompting Cattell to suggest that people "can not state much better what the weather was a week ago than what it will be a week hence".

A more recent investigation into the accuracy with which we can recall commonly experienced objects comes from a study by Nickerson and Adams (1979) in which they asked their American subjects to draw from memory what they would expect to find on each side of a U.S. penny piece. On average their subjects recalled correctly only three of the eight critical features of the coin, and even these were often mislocated.

In a subsequent study, Rubin and Kontis (1983) asked 125 U.S. undergraduates to draw both sides of a penny, a nickel, a dime and a quarter. Figure 2.4 (a and b) shows the actual headside of the four coins, together with the modal or most common representation in terms of the features contained. As they point out, their subjects appear to have a very strong general schema or concept of a U.S. coin. What the subjects represent is an approximation to this schema, not what they had actually seen. Rubin and Kontis went on to invite their subjects to suggest a design for a new coin, either a two, seven or twenty cent piece. The drawing produced by these new subjects was virtually identical to the modal recall observed in their previous study. It appears then that what we typically recall in such situations is not what we experience, but what we abstract from that experience.

FIGURE 2.4

(a) Actual coins now in use. (b) Modal coins constructed from recall data. From Rubin and Kontis (1983). Reprinted by permission of the Psychonomics Society Inc.

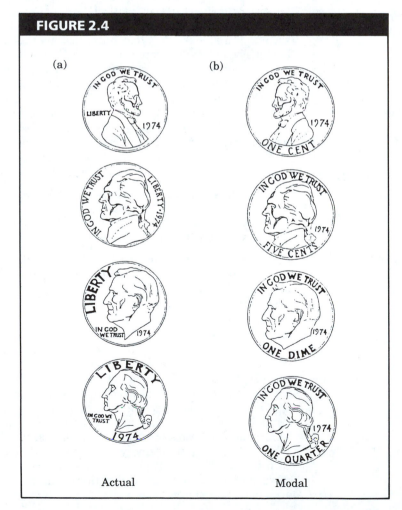

(a)   (b)

Actual   Modal

Recognition of Faces

As we saw from the Goldstein and Chance study, recognition memory for faces, though better than that of snowflakes or inkblots, was not nearly as accurate as earlier studies of pictures and scenes might suggest. In the case of the eyewitness, however, recognition of faces is often of vital importance, as we saw in the case of the department store robbery mentioned earlier. In view of the importance of this issue, a committee under Lord Devlin in 1976 issued a report concerned with identification parades and eyewitness testimony. They analyzed all the identification parades held in England and Wales during 1973, a total of over 2,000. Of these, 45% led to a suspect being picked out, and no fewer than 82% of these suspects were subsequently convicted. In over 300 cases, eyewitness identification was the *only* evidence of guilt, and even here the conviction rate was 74%, suggesting that enormous weight is given to the testimony of the eyewitness.

If a victim has seen the criminal, then his evidence is potentially of enormous value and significance. Such evidence is, however, difficult to evoke accurately, and open to many distortions. Let us suppose that the victim saw the criminal clearly, the first question is how his memory of the person can be turned into some form that could be used to apprehend the criminal. Verbal descriptions are likely to be of very limited value. Try, for example, to describe yourself in such a way that a stranger would recognize you. An alternative is to use artists' sketches, but this again is ultimately dependent on the subject's capacity to describe to the artist what the criminal looked like.

Another apparent solution is the system known as Photofit. This consists of a box comprising large numbers of individual facial features, for example noses, ears, hair and chins. The Photofit operator together with the subject tries to make up a picture that resembles the criminal, and this can then be used in wanted notices or circulated in newspapers (Figure 2.5). This process has been extensively studied by Graham Davies, Hadyn Ellis and John Shepherd at the University of Aberdeen, with results that are far from encouraging (Davies, Ellis, & Shepherd, 1981). Most people have great difficulty in reproducing a likeness, even of a face with which they are very familiar, producing results that are often very poor representations of the original. If one bears in mind the further complication that criminals will often disguise themselves or wear masks, then the limitations of this approach will be obvious. Even when this is not the case, the brevity of the encounter together with possible distraction by incidental features, such as the clothes the criminal was wearing, can make accurate reproduction or indeed recognition very difficult.

A particularly striking incident occurred to the Australian psychologist Donald Thomson who had been carrying out research on exactly this topic. He had previously worked on the role of context in memory for words, and felt that it would be interesting to extend his research to a more realistic problem, that of

FIGURE 2.5

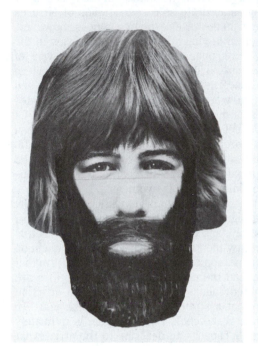
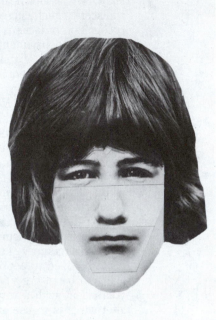
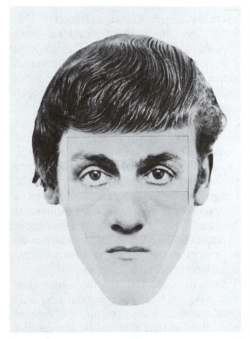

Problems in using Photofit. On the left are four attempts by victims to reconstruct the face of the Cambridge rapist whose actual photograph is shown on the right.

eyewitness testimony. He carried out a number of studies demonstrating that witnesses were likely to be strongly influenced by the clothes the criminal was wearing. A totally innocent person is likely to be picked out of a line-up if he is wearing clothes resembling those worn by the criminal. He became involved in extensive public discussion of this including appearing on a television program. A few weeks later he was picked up by the police, placed in a line-up and picked out by a woman who claimed that she had been raped by him.

It subsequently transpired that the time of the rape exactly coincided with his appearance on the live television discussion. With some relief he pointed out that he had a very good alibi, supported by large numbers of witnesses, including an Assistant Commissioner of the Police and an official of the Australian Civil Rights committee. At this point the policeman taking his statement stopped writing, looked at him sceptically and said "Yes, and I suppose you've also got Jesus Christ and the Queen of England too!". It transpired that the unfortunate woman had actually been raped while watching the television program; she was indeed correct in recognizing Thompson's face, but not in assigning it to the rapist.

It is clear that eyewitness recognition evidence is too important to be ignored, but it is equally essential to remember the unreliability of our capacity for recognizing unfamiliar faces. The Devlin Committee recognized this and recommended that unsupported eyewitness testimony should not be sufficient to convict a criminal. Nevertheless, the power of a victim pointing to the accused and claiming "That's him!" is likely to sway all but the most cautious member of the jury. This is one area in which it is essential to be aware of the limitations of human memory.

AUDITORY MEMORY

Even the simplest of sounds such as a pure tone involves the fluctuation in sound pressure over a period of time. Perception necessarily involves some way of storing the stimulus over time, since even one cycle of a tone at 1,000 cycles per second will take a millisecond. In the case of human speech perception, storage effects clearly operate over much longer intervals. For example Liberman, Delattre, Cooper and Gerstman (1954) showed that the same initial speech sound was perceived as *p* when it preceded an "i", and as a *g* when it preceded "a". This clearly requires that the initial consonant is stored and integrated with the vowel before conscious perception occurs.

Echoic Memory

There is in fact considerable evidence to suggest that sensory storage systems occur in audition, just as in vision, and again the evidence suggests that auditory sensory memory can be split into at least three types, *echoic memory* extending over a matter of milliseconds, *auditory short-term memory* extending up to perhaps 5 or 10 seconds, and *auditory long-term memory*.

Experiments by Efron (1970a,b) involved presenting a series of brief tones to his subjects, and asking them to adjust the onset time of a light to exactly coincide with the end of the tone. He found that regardless of whether the tone actually lasted for 30 milliseconds or 100 milliseconds, its subjective apparent duration was approximately 130 milliseconds. Note that this resembles the case for iconic memory in suggesting a system that prolongs brief stimuli, presumably thereby increasing the chance that they will be present for long enough to be analyzed. A study by Gol'dburt (1961) showed that the apparent duration of a tone was reduced when it was followed by a second tone. Von Békésy (1971) has suggested that this phenomenon may be rather important for the design of concert halls, since there is a very real danger that the echo in a concert hall may reduce the apparent duration and loudness of musical notes. Deatherage and Evans (1969) showed that when a brief target was followed by a masking sound, as in the case of iconic memory, perception was impaired, provided the mask was presented to the same ear as the stimulus, an effect analogous to brightness-masking in vision, where it will be recalled that disruption only occurs when the brightness mask and target are presented to the same eye.

All these results suggest some form of sensory storage which could perhaps be termed "the persistence of audition" by analogy with the persistence of vision effects described previously. A number of attempts have been made to measure the rate at which this effect decays over time. For example, Plomp (1964) presented a 200 millisecond noise burst, followed after varying intervals by a second burst of noise. The subject's task was to detect the appearance of the second noise burst, presumably against a background of a fading trace of the initial burst. By varying the loudness of the second stimulus, it was possible to plot the fading intensity of the first sound. Plomp found evidence of very rapid decay; when the second stimulus occurred only 2.5 milliseconds after the first, it was necessary to present it to an intensity of 65 decibels, whereas after 80 milliseconds, a 15-decibel noise burst was detectable.

A rather different approach to the measurement of the duration of auditory processing was taken by Guttman and Julesz (1963). They took sections of random noise varying in length from 50 milliseconds up to 1 second, and played them repeatedly and continuously to their subjects, asking them to listen and attempt to detect rhythmic periodicities. For a rhythm to be detected, the subject must be able to store the sound from one repetition to the next. Subjects reported clear effects for periodicities separated by up to a quarter of a second; they describe this condition as sounding rather like the throbbing of a motor boat engine. Some subjects reported being able to detect repetition of sequences of up to 1 second, although the effects were more complex and much less clear. This result suggests that the auditory system is capable of storing sequences of at least 250 milliseconds and possibly more.

The effects we have discussed so far are probably broadly analogous with the peripheral iconic memory effects that were described earlier. Like them, they appear to be susceptible to masking, with the intensity of the mask being a crucial factor, as is the need to present target and mask to the same ear. Are there equivalent systems in audition to that disrupted by visual pattern-masking? There almost certainly are, although to the best of my knowledge we do not have as clear a differentiation between the two systems as that suggested by Turvey's research for vision.

Short-term Auditory Memory

A number of workers have attempted to modify the Sperling partial report technique and apply it to auditory memory. Moray, Bates, and Barnett (1965) in what they term the "four-eared man" experiment simultaneously presented sequences of consonants to their subjects from four different locations. They showed that when, following presentation, the subject was cued to recall only one of the locations the estimated total amount of material stored was greater than when total recall was requested. As in the previously described study by Sperling, they argued that this could be treated as a random sample of the total amount of information stored. This was estimated by multiplying the score on the cued sample by four, since only a quarter of the total was sampled.

Darwin, Turvey, and Crowder (1972) used this technique in order to plot the rate of decay of information from this brief auditory store. They used three locations, and cued recall after 0, 1, 2, or 4 seconds, using the partial report or whole report procedure. They found a clear advantage for partial report at short delays, an effect that had almost disappeared after 4 seconds, suggesting a decay function reaching asymptote within about 5 seconds.

Most people have experienced the "double-take" effect whereby something is said to you which you do not understand, but find that you can go back and "re-play" the auditory input, often allowing you to understand it on this second run through. A number of studies have attempted to use this technique to measure the decay rate of the unattended message. One of the best controlled of these is a study by Glucksberg and Cowan (1970). They required their subjects to shadow, that is to repeat back continuously, a stream of prose presented to one ear. At the same time, they presented prose to the other ear which the subject was instructed to ignore. Subjects are quite good at doing this. Embedded in this unattended prose however were occasional digits. From time-to-time, a green light would appear, and this signalled the subject to say whether a digit had just appeared on his unattended ear. Performance of subjects on this task is shown in Figure 2.6 from which it is clear that the unattended items appear to be lost within about 5 seconds,

Probability of reporting a digit presented on the nonattended ear as a function of the delay between digit and cue. From Glucksberg and Cowan (1970).

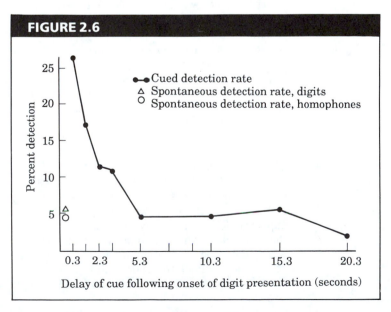

FIGURE 2.6

Delay of cue following onset of digit presentation (seconds)

a time course that is broadly consistent with the other information we have just described.

Subsequent research suggests that when the unattended material is followed by silence rather than speech, the trace may survive for rather longer than 5 seconds (e.g. Cowan, Lichti, & Grove, 1988), although it is not always easy to ascertain in these conditions that the material was completely unattended. In general, however, as the review by Cowan (1984) suggests, there does seem to be clear evidence for two short-term auditory stores, one operating over a timescale of 150–350 milliseconds, and the other lasting somewhere between 2 and 20 seconds.

Modality and Suffix Effects

If you were presented with a string of numbers, say a telephone number for immediate recall, then you are more likely to get it right if the numbers are spoken, than if they are shown visually. Figure 2.7 shows the probability of making an error in recalling a sequence of seven numbers that were either read silently or pronounced out loud. As will be clear, the advantage to the spoken items, termed the *modality effect*, consists mainly in the better recall of the last one or two. Conrad (1960) showed that when a sequence of items is followed by an irrelevant spoken item such as the instruction "recall", then performance is impaired. Hence, if you ring up telephone Directory Enquiries, and the respondent gives you the number and follows this by a cheery "Have a nice day", then you are substantially more likely to forget the sequence. The effect is most marked over the last few items presented, where it tends to reduce the *recency effect*, the term used to describe the enhanced recall of the most recently presented items.

This so-called auditory suffix effect was explored extensively by Crowder and Morton (1969), who showed that a non-speech sound such as a buzzer or tone did not disrupt performance. They also

Effects of an auditory suffix on the retention of spoken digits. The left panel shows the effect of a spoken suffix "zero", and the right panel that of a buzzer. From Crowder (1971). Copyright (1971) The Experimental Psychology Society.

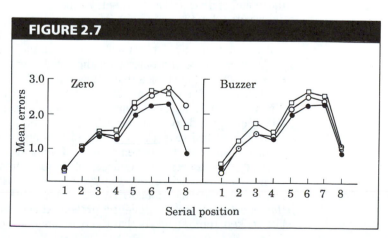

FIGURE 2.7

showed that the meaning of the suffix was unimportant, any speech sound will impair performance. They interpreted their results in terms of a brief *precategorical acoustic store*, which they suggested was disrupted by subsequent acoustic information.

Initially the evidence seemed to support this interpretation; there is for example a close association between the suffix effect and the modality effect whereby acoustically presented items are better recalled than visual. Engle (1974) showed that suffix and modality effects in both free and serial recall extended across the same serial positions. Crowder (1971) and Darwin and Baddeley (1974) studied immediate serial recall of consonant-vowel nonsense syllables. When the material consisted of sequences with differing vowels (e.g. bah, boo, bee, bih), auditory presentation led to better recall than visual, and there was a clear suffix effect, whereas when the vowels were held constant but the consonant varied (e.g. bah, dah, gah) neither a modality nor a suffix effect was found. Such results suggest that the modality effect is based on a temporary peripheral acoustic memory trace which is then disrupted by subsequent acoustic information.

There is, however, evidence against the interpretation of suffix effects as the disruption of a peripheral auditory memory trace. As mentioned earlier, the suffix effect is very much greater for speech material than for non-speech. A study by Ayres, Jonides, Reitman, Egan, and Howard (1979) explored this further. They presented their subjects with sequences of seven single-syllable words, followed by a suffix. In one condition, the suffixes all comprised speech sounds, namely the syllables *da*, *pin*, *wing* and *wa*. In another condition, the suffixes comprised a series of musical sounds, one of which was identical with the spoken syllable *wa*. Results suggested that overall the speech suffixes disrupted performance more than the musical suffixes. The crucial question, however, concerned the *wa* suffix. This was found to disrupt performance much more substantially when it was perceived by the subject as a speech sound, than it did when it was interpreted as the sound of a musical instrument. In short, the disruptive effect is determined by the subject's interpretation, not purely by the acoustic characteristics of the suffix. This suggests that the term *precategorical* may be potentially somewhat misleading.

Another source of problems for the initial interpretation of suffix effects comes from studies that have employed lip-reading. Spoehr and Corin (1978) studied the effect of following an auditory list with a suffix that was spoken silently by the experimenter, and which consequently had to be lip-read by the subject. They found that such suffixes had virtually as great a disrupting effect on the recall of auditory lists as did spoken suffixes. Campbell and Dodd (1980) showed that lip-read sequences of items showed the same pronounced recency effect as did items that were auditorily presented. They also found that an auditory suffix would remove this effect. The fact that silently presented lip-read items behave like spoken items suggests that the phenomenon we are describing is not a purely acoustic one, but occurs at some later stage concerned with the processing of language.

Further evidence that recency and suffix effects do not necessarily imply a peripheral auditory store comes from the demonstration that deaf subjects show similar recency and suffix effects for lists of sequences presented in American Sign Language (Shand & Klima, 1981). Indeed, at this point it is tempting to reconsider the original finding that recency and suffix effects occur with auditory but not visual presentation. Recency is found in a wide range of presentation modalities, including tactile (Manning, 1980; Watkins & Watkins, 1974) and on occasion visual (e.g. Hitch, 1975; Manning & Gmuer, 1985), and the absence of recency with written language-based material such as numbers and letters is perhaps the anomaly. Indeed, lack of recency is not even characteristic of other non-linguistic visual memory studies. Phillips and Christie (1977a,b) have shown, for example, that when a series of random checkerboard patterns are visually presented, there is a clear recency effect, with the last item leading to much better recognition performance than earlier items. It would perhaps be interesting to attempt to explore a wider range of types of material and presentation before drawing too many conclusions from the modality effect.

The experiments we have just discussed emphasize the link between the modality effect and recency in immediate serial recall. However, an auditory advantage has been found in a much wider range of situations, some clearly involving long-term memory. For example, Gardiner and Gregg (1979) found an auditory advantage in a task involving free recall in which a distraction task occurred before and after each list item. Such distraction should presumably have obliterated any short-term traces. However, although there have now been a number of long-term modality effects observed, the pattern appears to be relatively complex. In a recent review of research on modality effects, Penney (in press) suggests that visual and auditory material are processed in separate streams, but within each of these, codes of different duration operate, with acoustic information being stored at both an auditory and a deeper phonological level.

Long-term Auditory Memory

Much long-term memory for material presented auditorily involves language, and is probably stored more in terms of its meaning than its sound. However, it is clear that long-term memory for auditory information does exist, and indeed plays a crucial role in certain occupations such as that of the sonar operator attempting to listen for the engines of approaching ships, having learned to recognize different types of ship by the different sounds given off by their engines. This has led to a certain amount of work on training subjects to detect auditory signals (e.g. Corcoran, Carpenter, Webster, & Woodhead, 1968). The need to learn to recognize auditory patterns is not of course limited to sonar operators. Medical students as part of their training must learn to listen to a chest in the attempt to become expert at interpreting difficulties in breathing, or in detecting irregularities in the patient's heartbeat.

Memory for music is another area of obvious long-term auditory memory. Almost everyone can recognize some tunes, and as we shall see later, some people an enormous number. White (1960) explored some of the features that allow tunes to be recognized. He presented familiar tunes such as "Auld Lang Syne", and studied the extent to which his subjects could recognize them when various features of the pitch and contour of the melody were changed. When both pitch and melody were correct, the recognition rate was 90%; it dropped to 80% when the key was changed, but the contour remained the same, with the magnitude of the rises and falls in the pitch remaining the same. When the key was appropriate, and the contour the same except that all rises and falls comprised one semitone, performance dropped to 60%. Finally, when the contour was maintained in the sense of direction of change, but the degree of change was varied nonlinearly, then performance dropped to around 50%. White's results suggest that both contour and pitch interval information is retained in long-term memory.

In the case of expert musicians, the capacity of long-term memory can be very impressive indeed. A number of instances of this are cited by Marek (1975), reprinted in Neisser (1982). One example concerns Mozart's memory for Allegri's *Miserere* which the Vatican Choir in Rome regarded as its personal property. No-one was to copy it (on pain of excommunication). The young Mozart was taken to hear it by his father, and after one hearing went home and wrote down the whole piece from memory, returning later to check it and noting a few minor modifications on his hat. When it was subsequently performed in the presence of a papal singer who knew the piece well, he confirmed that it was absolutely correct.

Marek cites a number of instances of the phenomenal memory of the conductor Toscanini. For example on one occasion, just before the beginning of a concert, the second bassoonist reported with considerable concern that the lowest note on his instrument was broken. Toscanini thought for a moment and then replied "It is alright, that note does not occur in tonight's concert".

On another occasion, Toscanini decided that he would like the strings of the N.B.C. Orchestra to play the slow movement of *Quartet No. 5* by Joachim Raff. This somewhat obscure piece could not be found in New York, so Toscanini who had probably not seen it for years promptly wrote the whole movement down. Some time later, a collector of musical scores found a copy, checked it against the Toscanini manuscript and detected exactly one error.

While great musicians often have phenomenal memories for music, such memory is not limited to the exceptionally talented performer. For example, according to the *Oxford Companion to*

Music "Mr Napoleon Bird, barber of Stockport Cheshire, in 1894 won the world's record for what has been called 'pianofortitude' by publicly playing for 44 hours without repeating a composition; from 11 p.m. to 3 a.m. he played dance music for hundreds of couples, and, during the subsequent 40 hours, whenever any vocalist or instrumentalist appeared and asked to be accompanied, the mere statement of the title of the piece and the key required were sufficient".

Memory for Voices

It is often the case that when someone telephones you, you know who is speaking immediately from recognizing their voice. I myself have been surprised on a number of occasions to meet someone after many years, and to fail to recognize them until they speak, when it immediately becomes obvious who they are, often despite the growth of a beard or the greying of their hair. How good is our long-term memory for voices?

Such a question can be of considerable importance in the law courts. Consider, for example, the case of Stovall vs. Denno, a case that was considered by the United States Supreme Court on 12 June 1867. The accused, Stovall was said to have entered the home of a doctor, stabbed him to death and afterwards attacked his wife, inflicting multiple stab wounds. Stovall was apprehended and taken to the hospital two days later, being required to utter a few words for voice identification purposes. The doctor's wife gave a positive identification, and subsequently Stovall was convicted and sentenced to death. In a very useful review on voice identification, Clifford (1983) reports that voice identification is far from rare in court cases. For example, in a report for the British Home Office, Clifford and his colleagues identified over 188 cases in which voice identification or testimony was involved (Bull & Clifford, 1984). It is clearly important to know how reliable such evidence is likely to be.

In considering this matter, it is important to distinguish between the recognition of an already familiar voice, and the recognition of the voice of an unknown person heard only once. In the case of familiar people, recognition performance can be very high. For example, Pollack, Pickett, and Sumby (1954) exposed listeners to the speech of 16 talkers, all of whom were familiar to the subjects. Recognition was extremely high at 95%, but declined drastically to 30% when the speakers were whispering rather than talking.

As mentioned earlier, we often retain information about familiar voices over long periods of time. This was studied by Meudell, Northen, Snowden, and Neary (1980) who presented their middle-aged normal subjects and amnesic patients with recordings of the voices of famous people extending back over 50 years. Subjects were able to name speakers who had not been heard since the 1930s about 30% of the time, rising to 60% for more recent speakers, although performance may have been helped by the content of the speech as well as by voice recognition. As Figure 2.8

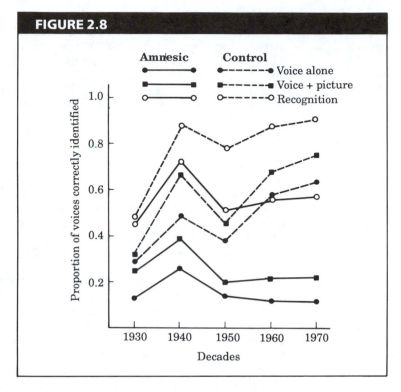

FIGURE 2.8

Proportion of famous voices from different periods identified under each of the three retrieval conditions for amnesic and control subjects. From Meudell, Mayes, and Neary (1980).

shows, identification was increased somewhat when a photograph of the speaker was shown together with three distractor photographs, and was further enhanced by presenting the names of each set of four. Amnesic patients showed a similar pattern of performance, at a much lower level.

In the case of legal testimony, however, it is much more frequently the case that the witness is asked to recognize the voice of a stranger, typically heard only once and often under conditions that are very far from optimal. Performance here is generally rather poorer than one might expect for face recognition. For example, in a series of experiments resulting directly from the Lindberg kidnapping case in 1935, a lengthy passage of prose was read on two occasions, and subjects were required to recognize the speaker (McGehee, 1937; 1944). Identification accuracy for recall within a day or so ranged from 83% to 50% when more than three target voices were being remembered at the same time, after a delay of five months however, it had dropped to 13%.

The overall level of recognition difficulty depends, of course, on the similarity between the target voice and the distractor voices in the recognition set, making it hard to come up with absolute estimates of performance level. However, the following conclusions seem to be broadly justified; first of all, subjects are typically accurate in identifying the sex of an unfamiliar speaker. Secondly, it appears that there is no need for more than a single sentence to be heard for subsequent recognition; typically two, four, or eight sentences are not substantially better than one (Clifford, 1983). Furthermore, although long delays do cause impairment in performance, there does not appear to be a dramatic drop-off within the first day or two of hearing a voice, at least under conditions of intentional learning, where the subject expects to have to recognize the voice later.

Unfortunately, however, absence of forgetting does not appear to be the case under the more realistic condition of incidental memory. For example, an unpublished study by Clifford and Flemming attempted to simulate the sort of low-key interaction that might be associated with a confidence trickster attempting petty fraud. In this study, a male stooge went into a series of banks and shops, introduced himself by name, explaining that he had lost his check validation card and was seeking clarification on the correct procedure in such circumstances. Either immediately afterwards, or after a delay of 1, 4, or 24 hours, a female experimenter approached the bank clerk or shopkeeper and asked him or her to select the stooge from a set of photographs, and identify his voice from a series of tape recordings. On immediate test, voice recognition was at 41%, after 1 hour it had declined to 24%, and to 4% after 4 hours, while at 24 hours no correct recognitions were made. While unalerted recognition is not always as disastrously bad as this, there appears to be general agreement that when a subject is not expecting to remember a voice, performance is substantially poorer (e.g. Saslove & Yarmy, 1980).

The overall implications of this research are clear, that, while recognition of the voice of a familiar person may be reasonably good, that of a stranger is likely to be poor, even under optimal conditions. It seems likely that performance will be even worse when the level of emotion of the speaker differs from one occasion to another, or when some deliberate attempt to disguise the voice is made either by whispering or adopting a voice disguise. Finally, subjects who do not pay particular attention to the voice are unlikely to prove good witnesses, particularly after a delay. As Clifford concludes: "Voice identification by a witness concerning a stranger should be treated with the utmost caution".

OVERVIEW

The storage of sensory information provides a microcosm of the memory system as a whole. It begins with the systems of iconic and echoic memory that store visual and auditory information over a matter of milliseconds, as part of the processes involved in perception. Both of these appear to have characteristics that allow the initial stimulus to be prolonged, probably so as to ensure that adequate later processing is possible.

Further processing and manipulation occurs in short-term visual and auditory memory systems that hold information for a matter of seconds rather than milliseconds. This allows the sensory based information to be integrated with information from other sources through the operation of the limited capacity working memory system that will be discussed later. Such information is also fed into long-term memory, which although relying heavily on coding in terms of meaning, is also able to store more specifically sensory characteristics such as those involved in memory for faces and scenes, voices and tunes. However, although such memories clearly do contain information of a sensory kind, this is probably stored as part of a multi-dimensional memory trace, and for that reason, we shall move now from considering memory as categorized on the basis of the modality of input, to one that categorizes memory in terms of the memory processes involved, and the functions that they serve.

Chapter Three

HOW MANY KINDS OF MEMORY? THE EVIDENCE FOR STM

How long is a moment in time? Long enough to hear one word, or a sentence, or perhaps less than one word? The fact that our consciousness appears to extend in time suggests that it is of some extent, but that extent is clearly limited. In the case of the unfortunate amnesic patient discussed earlier, it is certainly at the very most a few minutes, since he perpetually thinks he has just that very moment woken up. William James used the term *primary memory* to refer to this moment of time, which he also referred to as "the specious present". Writing rather earlier in the nineteenth century, Galton (1883) gives the following description:

> There seems to be a presence-chamber in my mind where full consciousness holds court, and where two or three ideas are at the same time in audience, and an ante-chamber full of more or less allied ideas, which is situated just beyond the full ken of consciousness. Out of this ante-chamber the ideas most nearly allied to those in the presence chamber appear to be summoned in a mechanically logical way, and to have their turn of audience.

The central feature of the account given by both James and Galton is concerned with conscious attention. The later concept of short-term memory that we shall be discussing in the present chapter is clearly related to the question of consciousness, but is not identical with it; ideas in Galton's "ante-chamber" of consciousness would probably still be regarded as being stored in short-term or working memory, even though they are not conscious at that time. The relationship between theories of attention and theories of short-term memory has always been a close one, and remains so as the chapters on working memory will suggest, with the controlling Central Executive component of working memory assumed to function as a supervisory attention system.

THE CAPACITY OF SHORT-TERM MEMORY

Probably the first person to attempt to measure short-term memory directly was a London schoolmaster, Joseph Jacobs who was interested in measuring the mental capacity of his pupils. He devised the technique that has become known as the memory span procedure in which the subject is presented with a sequence of items, often numbers, and required to repeat them back verbatim. The sequences typically begin with one item and are gradually increased in length to a point at which the subject consistently fails to repeat the sequence correctly. The point at which the subject is right 50% of the time is designated as his or her memory span (Jacobs, 1887).

As we saw from Chapter 2, auditory presentation is likely to lead to somewhat better recall than visual. So, if you have just heard a telephone number, you are rather more likely to remember it than if you have just read it. What else might help you retain the number? Recall is usually improved if the numbers are grouped, by inserting a brief pause between successive groupings (Ryan, 1969). Typically, the first and last items of each group are remembered somewhat better than the middle items, with grouping into threes giving the best performance (Wickelgren, 1964). Hence 791 862 534 would be better remembered than 79 18 62 53 4. Even a very brief pause is sufficient to produce the grouping effect, which probably arises as a result of the underlying auditory memory system being specifically evolved to detect and use the rhythmic and prosodic aspects of speech. So if you are giving someone your telephone number, it is best to phrase the digits in groups of three.

A particularly dramatic effect of such rhythmic chunking is given by Hunter (1962) in his account of the remarkable memory capabilities of the mathematician, Professor Aitken of Edinburgh. Aitken had developed a fascination with numbers as a child, and evolved remarkable capabilities as a lightning calculator. On one occasion he had committed to memory the first thousand decimal places of pi, the ratio of the circumference of a circle to its diameter, an achievement which he described as "a reprehensibly useless feat, had it not been so easy". He found that if he laid them out in rows of 50 comprising ten groups of five, and read them rhythmically at a rate of about five per second, he had no difficulty in retaining them.

When Hunter attempted to test Aitken's memory span using the normal presentation rate of one digit per second, Aitken's performance was unremarkable; he complained, however, that it was far too slow, "like learning to ride a bicycle slowly". When the rate was increased to five per second he had no difficult in repeating back sequences of 15 digits either in the appropriate or reversed order. A normal span would be six or seven digits.

While on the subject of digit span, it is perhaps worth mentioning the case of a subject whose digit span exceeded 80 items. He was a subject who agreed to take part in an experiment carried out by Ericsson and Chase (1982) who were interested in what would happen to the digit span, given massive amounts of practice. The subject began with a comparatively normal span. It first showed a modest increase over successive days, reaching something of a plateau, and then increased steadily day after day to a point at which it exceeded 80 items.

How was this achieved? It turns out that the subject was an enthusiastic amateur runner who took the digit sequences as they came in, and encoded them in terms of running times, for example "a good club time for 1500 meters", "just below world record for 400 meters", etc. He was apparently able then to string together these recoded numbers and subsequently repeat them back.

Did this mean then that the underlying memory store had in some sense been increased through exercise? It did not, since when other types of material such as letters were presented, his performance was quite normal. Furthermore, he was able to repeat back a lengthy sequence after a delay, unlike the normal digit span situation in which a brief delay is enough to cause the subject to forget the sequence. In short, Ericsson and Chase's subject was almost certainly using a long-term memory strategy in order to help him perform on a short-term memory task. We will return to this point later in the chapter.

A subsequent study showed that this technique could also be learnt by other subjects, given that they had, of course, the necessary interest in running times. What of non-runners, is there any way in which they can improve memory span? There are in fact mnemonics that have been devised specifically to help subjects remember long sequences of numbers. One type of system involves translating the numbers into letters, using a particular mapping that always allows one to generate consonant-vowel-consonant alternations, and hence sequences that are pronounce-able. Such a system was investigated by Slak (1970). He found that subjects could learn a mnemonic of this type, and could use it to increase digit span and to enhance long-term learning of numbers. Hence, subjects who would find a number sequence like 265070193 quite difficult to learn, found that they could learn the letter-code equivalent BAFDILTUN much more rapidly. Unfortunately, however, Slak found that it took his subjects 20 hours to learn the digit-letter mapping system. Like many mnemonics, for most purposes, its potential advantages are outweighed by the effort needed to acquire and use it.

Why should BAFDILTUN be easier to remember than 265070193? The reason is that it reduces the nine numbers to three chunks, BAF, DIL and TUN. In his classic paper "The magic number seven; plus or minus one", George Miller (1956) showed that immediate memory span was determined by number of "chunks" rather than number of items, averaging about seven chunks. A chunk is an integrated piece of information, where remembering part of it will help you remember the next. Hence a familiar and meaningful date such as 1492 is likely to act as a chunk, while a less significant one such as 1386 would probably not. Memory span as measured in terms of items can be increased by increasing the number of items in each chunk. Thus memory span for letters is about six when they are selected at random, about nine when they comprise consonant-vowel-consonant syllables, rising to perhaps 50 or more when the letters make up the words in a meaningful sentence. In each case, however, the number of chunks remains constant at about six. Chunking also plays an important role in long-term learning and will be discussed in more detail in Chapter 9.

I myself use a rather simpler mnemonic than the system investigated by Slak when I want to remember a new bank card or telephone number. This involves generating a simple phrase or sentence in which the number of letters in each successive word is made equivalent to the number in the sequence. Hence, if my number for obtaining money from my bank cashpoint were 1465, I need a phrase comprising words of one letter, four letters, six letters and five, for example "I want filthy lucre"; if I wanted to remember the Applied Psychology Unit telephone number, which is 355294, then I might remember it as "The Unit's phone is certainly busy". After a while, one tends to recall the number directly and apparently automatically, but even so it is reassuring to be able to check it out using the phrase. Once again, however, it is important to note that although the task of remembering a sequence of numbers might seem like a short-term memory task, I am actually using a strategy of storing the material in long-term memory.

SHORT-TERM FORGETTING

The Brown–Peterson Paradigm

Consider the following incident: I and my wife are invited to a neighbor's party. I meet someone and they tell me their name, asking me how I know the host. I explain briefly and then turn to introduce my wife, only to discover that I have already forgotten the name of my new acquaintance. What do we know about such rapid forgetting?

In the late 1950s, John Brown in England, and the Petersons in the U.S. both devised experimental procedures that showed extremely rapid forgetting of small amounts of information, provided the subject is briefly distracted (Brown, 1958; Peterson & Peterson, 1959). The technique devised by the Petersons involved presenting the subject with a consonant trigram such as HLM, followed by a number such as 492. The subject was required to repeat the number and then proceed to count backwards from it in threes until given a recall signal, whereupon he attempted to repeat back the consonants. Under these circumstances, subjects forgot very rapidly.

Figure 3.1 shows the results obtained by the Petersons, together with the results of a later study by Murdock (1961) in which subjects were presented with either a single three-letter word such as DOG or three unrelated words such as HAT, LID, PEN. As will be clear from the figure, the crucial factor is not the number of letters, but the number of chunks; remembering three words (a total of nine letters) is about as hard as remembering three consonants.

Trace Decay or Interference

The Peterson result caused enormous interest for at least two reasons. First, because it appeared to offer a very neat and economical technique for studying short-term forgetting, and secondly, because the Petersons interpreted their results in terms of trace decay. Since they accepted that long-term forgetting was

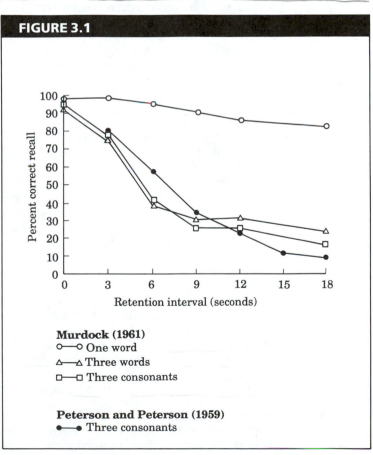

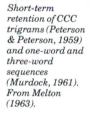

Short-term retention of CCC trigrams (Peterson & Peterson, 1959) and one-word and three-word sequences (Murdock, 1961). From Melton (1963).

FIGURE 3.1

Percent correct recall

Retention interval (seconds)

Murdock (1961)
o—o One word
△—△ Three words
□—□ Three consonants

Peterson and Peterson (1959)
●—● Three consonants

dicotomy

based on the principles of interference rather than decay, their results seemed to suggest the need to assume two separate memory systems, a temporary short-term system where forgetting results from trace decay, and a long-term system where forgetting is the result of interference. Both the assumption of trace decay and the advocacy of two memory systems were controversial viewpoints to hold in North America at that time, although they were much more consistent with views that were current in Britain; Brown (1958) had also shown rapid forgetting of small amounts of material when active rehearsal was prevented. A decay theory of STM was also favored by Broadbent (1958) in his influential book *Perception and Communication* which was one of the first systematic attempts to apply the information processing computer analogy to the study of perception, attention and short-term memory.

A trace decay theory assumes that forgetting occurs as a result of the automatic fading of the memory trace. It can be contrasted with an interference theory; this assumes that forgetting reflects the disruption of the memory trace by other traces, with the degree of interference depending on the similarity of the two mutually interfering memory traces. To give a concrete example; I myself regularly succumb to an interference effect; although I know that in Italian bathrooms "C" stands for "caldo" and means "hot", the English association between "C" and the cold tap is almost always strong enough to guarantee a few scaldings on each trip. I am sure I would have far fewer problems if the initial letters were totally different.

A more detailed account of interference theory will be given in Chapter 10, but for present purposes it is necessary to make one further distinction, namely that between *proactive* and *retroactive* interference or inhibition. Proactive interference (PI) occurs when new learning is disrupted by old habits. Being taught that "C" means "caldo" which means hot, but none the less "forgetting" and turning the wrong tap would be an instance of PI. Retroactive interference (RI) occurs when new learning disrupts old habits. If you change your telephone number, then learning the new number is likely to make it harder for you to recall the old number.

To return to the Petersons' demonstration of short-term forgetting; evidence from long-term learning studies indicated that the numbers involved in backward counting were sufficiently different from the letters to be remembered to produce minimal interference (McGeoch & McDonald, 1931). The Petersons therefore concluded that forgetting could not be due to RI, and must therefore reflect the spontaneous decay of the short-term memory traces.

This interpretation was, however, challenged by an ingenious study by Keppel and Underwood (1962), who argued that short-term forgetting was the result of proactive interference from consonants that had been remembered on earlier trials. They showed that the very first consonant trigram presented showed virtually no forgetting, a fact they attributed to the absence of any similar prior items that might cause PI.

Release from PI

It was possible to test this proposal further; since interference is dependent on similarity, then it should be possible to get rid of the proactive interference by changing the nature of the target items after the first few trials. This was investigated in a study by Wickens, Born, and Allen (1963) in which the subjects remembered consonants for the first few trials and then were switched to remembering numbers. As predicted, immediately after the switch, performance reverted to being almost perfect, a phenomenon that Wickens et al. referred to as release from proactive interference.

The release from PI effect is very robust. In one study, for example, Loess (1968) presented triplets of words from a given semantic category such as animals, in each case requiring recall after 15 seconds of backward counting. After presenting six sequences of animal names without warning his subjects, he switched to another category, say vegetables, and after six further trials switched again to yet another category. The pattern of results was very clear; the first word triplet in each new category was very well recalled, the second somewhat less well, with performance leveling off by about the third or fourth, recovering each time the category was changed.

Before going on to discuss further theoretical developments, it is perhaps worth digressing to mention two subsequent applications of the technique. Wickens (1970) argued that the release from PI effect implied that the subject *must* have processed the particular dimension of the stimulus that had been changed. Hence the fact that changing a dimension such as meaning, sound or print size led to release from PI could be used as a indirect measure of the processing of that dimension. He went on to explore the effects of changing a very wide range of characteristics of the material, from its visual characteristics such as size or background through to semantic characteristics such as category membership or pleasantness. Most changes caused some release, with semantic changes probably being the most effective (Wickens, 1970). However, although in principle the technique offers a useful indirect measure of coding, it does not appear to have been used very widely outside the verbal learning laboratory.

There is, however, some evidence that the phenomenon of build-up and release from PI may have interesting practical implications. Gunter, Berry, and Clifford (1981) had the ingenious idea that PI build-up effects might occur in television news bulletins, where the viewer is presented with a succession of items of news that may or may not be thematically similar. They suggested by analogy with the build-up and release from PI literature, that retention should be best if similar items were separated, rather than being blocked. Subjects watched a series of four TV news items and then attempted to recall either immediately or after a delay. In the control condition, the items were all from the same category, either all home news or all foreign news. There was a clear build-up of PI, with each successive item being less well recalled. In the experimental condition, the fourth item came from the opposite category to the previous three. As Figure 3.2 shows, release from PI occurred, with the item from the new category being better recalled in both the immediate and delayed conditions.

To return to the theoretical fray; by this point, things were looking very promising for the interference theory interpretation of short-term forgetting. But alas, life is never simple. Loess and Waugh (1967) showed that if the interval between trials was increased to two minutes, then no short-term forgetting at all occurred; it was as if each trial became equivalent to the first trial of the experiment. These results did not fit in with interference theory since the delay should have allowed even more interference from the prior items, causing even greater forgetting.

Loess and Waugh's results were, however, consistent with a compromise position, namely that some spontaneous forgetting does occur, but that interference or competition between earlier items and target items is also an important factor. Such a combination of decay and competition is also consistent with a rather striking result obtained by Turvey, Brick, and Osborne (1970). The usual procedure in the Peterson task is to mix up long

Release from PI effects in the immediate and delayed recall of news items. When successive items are from a similar topic, performance declines, and when a new topic is introduced it recovers. From Gunter, Berry, and Clifford (1981). Copyright (1981) by the American Psychological Association. Reprinted by permission.

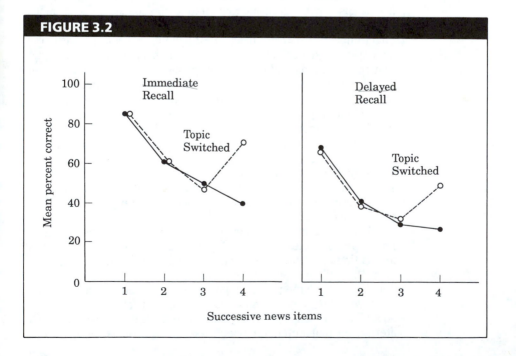

FIGURE 3.2

Temporal discrimination hypothesis of short-term forgetting. P_1 represents the presentation of the first item, P_2 the presentation of the second, and R_2 the recall of the second item. It is assumed that if the two items come from the same general class of material, then the only cue which the subject has in recalling the appropriate item is its time of occurrence. It is further assumed that the discriminability of this temporal cue will determine recall probability. When the critical item is tested after a short delay and the prior item is separated by a long delay, this discrimination will be easy and recall probability will be high. As the delay increases, the relative discriminability of the two items will decrease and recall probability will drop. From Baddeley (1976). Copyright 1976 by Basic Books Inc., Publishers. Reprinted by permission.

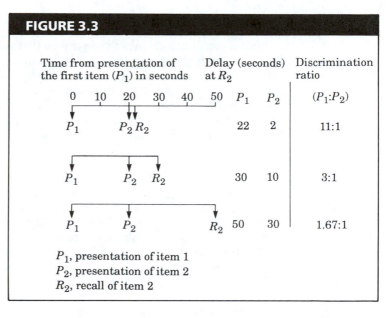

FIGURE 3.3

Time from presentation of the first item (P_1) in seconds	Delay (seconds) at R_2		Discrimination ratio
	P_1	P_2	$(P_1:P_2)$
P_1 ——→ $P_2\,R_2$	22	2	11:1
P_1 ——→ P_2 —→ R_2	30	10	3:1
P_1 ——→ P_2 ————→ R_2	50	30	1.67:1

P_1, presentation of item 1
P_2, presentation of item 2
R_2, recall of item 2

and short delays, but Turvey et al. used a procedure whereby delays were blocked. Hence one group might always have to recall after 5 seconds, another always after 10 seconds, another always after 20 seconds and so forth. Under these circumstances, Turvey et al. found no difference between the amount forgotten, the 5-second group seemed to forget just as much as the 20-second group. In all cases, however, subjects finished the experiment by being tested at the same delay, 15 seconds. On this final trial, those subjects who had previously recalled after short delays forgot considerably more than those who had previously remembered over longer delays.

A Trace Discrimination Hypothesis

How could one explain this result? Consider the task that confronts the subjects; they are asked to recall the *last* item presented. The difficulty of discriminating the last item from the last-but-one is likely to depend on the ratio of the two delays (see Figure 3.3). Under blocked conditions, this ratio will always be the same; 5 seconds versus 10 seconds, 10 seconds versus 20 seconds or 20 seconds versus 40 seconds all give the same target to prior item ratio of 1:2. Hence recall will be equally difficult regardless of delay. On the final trial, however, when all subjects were switched to a 15-second delay, then the ratios will be different. Subjects who were previously recalling after 5 seconds will have to discriminate a 15 from a 20 second record trace (1:1.33), whereas subjects who were previously recalling after 20 seconds will have the rather easier discrimination of 20 against 35 (1:1.75). In the standard Peterson procedure, since delays are scrambled, on average, short delays will have a better ratio than long delays, leading to the standard forgetting function.

Such a discrimination hypothesis makes two assumptions, first that some form of decay occurs spontaneously, and secondly that retrieval involves some form of discrimination. The first of these was explored in a paper by Baddeley and Scott (1971) which argued that the apparent absence of forgetting on Trial 1 shown by Keppel and Underwood (1962) may have been the result of performance being at virtually 100%, meaning that any weakening of the memory trace would not be discernible. It is important to bear in mind the fact that when two subjects are both performing at 100% level, it does not necessarily mean that degree of learning is the same. For example, if you were to tell me your telephone number, I would probably be able to repeat it back correctly, so that we would both be recalling at the 100% level. That would not of course mean that I knew your telephone number as well as you do.

The tendency for differences in learning to be masked when performance approaches 100% is known as a *ceiling effect*. The converse distortion may also occur when performance approaches 0%, the so-called *floor effect*. I suspect that neither you nor I could successfully recall the telephone number of my previous house, so we would both score 0%, but that I would re-learn it more rapidly than you would learn it, indicating some hidden retention on my part.

Denise Scott and I decided to look carefully at the retention by subjects of a single item in a Peterson task, using sequences long enough to avoid ceiling effects. Since each subject contributes only one piece of data, this requires large numbers of subjects, a problem we solved by towing a mobile test cubicle in to the center of the University of Sussex campus and offering a small sum to charity for each subject who would volunteer. This strategy was quite effective since people who would regard the amount that we could afford to pay for a single response as derisory, would nevertheless participate for a good cause, and of course given sufficiently large numbers the good cause did very well out of the arrangement.

Our results were fortunately very clear; forgetting of the first, and only sequence presented certainly occurred, but it was far from massive and levelled off within about 5 seconds. It seems then that something like trace decay occurs in the Peterson task, but is complete within five seconds, and is certainly not sufficiently large as to readily explain the substantial forgetting that occurs in the standard paradigm; this appears to depend crucially on competition from earlier items, and is perhaps better regarded as a phenomenon of long-term rather than short-term memory.

As we saw earlier, the effect of delay between trials is consistent with a discrimination hypothesis, but not with the classical interference view that PI stems from the spontaneous recovery from extinction of earlier items, that is, from their capacity to regain strength to a point at which they are able to compete with the items that followed them. The release from PI effect could be explained by a discrimination hypothesis, if we assume that subjects are able to use the nature of the target item to rule out dissimilar prior items. If the category has just switched from animals to vegetables, then there is no problem in rejecting earlier items (animals) in favor of the target items (vegetables).

A very neat demonstration of the effectiveness of this strategy was provided by Gardiner, Craik, and Birtwisle (1972). They presented their subjects with sequences of flower names in a standard Peterson procedure. The names were in fact separated into clusters of wild flowers such as *dandelion, buttercup* and *bluebell*, and cultivated flowers such as *carnation, wallflower*, and *gladiolus*. After a number of clusters of cultivated flowers, the category was switched to wild flowers. Virtually none of the subjects noticed this, and left to their own devices showed no release from PI. One group, however, was warned of the change from wild to cultivated, and for this group release occurred.

A third group received this information *after* the presentation of the critical sequence, but *before* recall. The crucial question is whether subjects can use this new information to help them discriminate between the target items and earlier potentially interfering items. Subjects were in fact successful in using this cue; they showed substantial release from PI, even though they had presumably not noticed whether the flowers were wild or not during learning. This result supports the discrimination interpretation of the role of PI in short-term forgetting, suggesting that subjects can use the "release" cues to decide whether or not a recalled item is from the crucial last set.

I have gone into some detail in discussing this sequence of experiments because it gives a good idea of the way in which theoretical controversies often operate within a field. At one level, one might conclude that since neither decay theory nor interference theory offered a complete explanation of the phenomenon, both failed, and the answer was a rather boring draw. Another way of looking at the outcome, however, is that we began with two rather crude and broad interpretations, and ended with a much better understanding of the phenomenon that we were trying to explain. The discrimination model has not been worked out in any detail, although some quantitative development is suggested in Baddeley (1976, pp. 126–131). Interestingly, a similar discrimination hypothesis has been suggested for the recency effect in free recall, the tendency for the last few words in a list to be particularly well recalled, a phenomenon which was also one of the major battlefields between interference and trace decay interpretations of short-term forgetting, and which will be discussed in Chapter 4 (see Glenberg & Swanson, 1986; Hitch, Rejman, & Turner, 1980; and further discussion by Baddeley, 1986, Chapter 7).

Although one could probably develop a reasonably good quantitative model of the Peterson task, this has not happened, and theoretical interest in the technique has declined over recent years. Why should this be? I suspect the major reason is that it is no longer clear whether or not the technique reflects anything of basic importance. Initially, when it was thought to reflect directly the fading of a short-term memory trace, this could be regarded as something of fundamental importance to the process of learning and forgetting. Once it has been acknowledged that the major factor is discrimination between closely packed items, then it is less obvious that it reflects anything of fundamental significance, rather than a neat laboratory effect, perhaps playing a role similar to that played by certain illusions in understanding vision. They are intriguing, dramatic and are sometimes claimed to reflect important features of normal perception, but have not in fact proved enormously fruitful as a topic of study so far.

This may, however, be a very unfair assessment of the importance of the Peterson effect; the problem is that there has been little or no concern to explore its real-world significance. It may be the case that it reflects a capacity for keeping track of ongoing events that is essential for adequate orientation in time and place. We simply do not know.

There is in fact one area where the technique has continued to be used extensively. That area is neuropsychology, where it was particularly favored by Cermak, Butters and their colleagues in Boston who used it to study amnesic patients suffering from the alcoholic Korsakoff syndrome. This initially led to a good deal of controversy, since their patients typically performed rather poorly on the Peterson task (Cermak, Butters, & Moreines, 1974), whereas Korsakoff patients studied by Warrington and myself in London appeared to show excellent Peterson performance (Baddeley & Warrington, 1970).

It subsequently transpired that the Boston patients were suffering from subtle but general information processing deficits, whereas the London patients were carefully screened to ensure that this was not the case (Cermak, 1982). The Boston group however continue to use the technique as a sensitive measure of general information processing capacity. The Peterson task might perhaps have theoretical significance as a measure of a subject's capacity to control working memory possibly reflecting the functioning of the attentional Central Executive component of working memory that is described in Chapter 6.

ONE OR TWO MEMORY STORES?

The development of the Peterson task triggered, though did not resolve one of the major controversies of the 1960s, that of whether it was necessary or useful to assume that long- and short-term memory involve separate underlying systems. The trace theorists on the whole argued for a dichotomous or duplex approach, while the interference theorists tended to claim that LTM and STM reflected the operation of a single unitary system. The case for a single system was presented in a cogent paper by one of the most respected interference theorists, Arthur Melton (1963). He argued first, that it was unnecessary to assume trace decay, since interference theory offered a better account of short-term forgetting. Secondly, he pointed out that long-term learning effects could be demonstrated in a number of STM tasks, suggesting a continuity rather than a dichotomy.

The question of trace decay or interference was discussed above, so we will move directly to his evidence for long-term learning in STM. He chose the Peterson task and memory span as the two characteristic STM tasks, and showed first of all that presenting an item several times, enhanced its overall level of retention in the Peterson task. Secondly, he explored an ingenious demonstration that had previously been devised by Donald Hebb (1961). This involves what appears to the subject to be a simple task involving the immediate recall of sequences of random numbers. The sequences are always of fixed length, the length being just beyond the subject span. Unbeknown to the subject, rather than having a different random sequence on each trial, a given number sequence is repeated every three presentations. Under these circumstances, the probability of recalling the repeated sequence gradually increases over successive present-ations, thus showing evidence of long-term learning. Melton argued on the basis of these results that LTM and STM should be regarded as dependent on the same unitary system.

Although there is no doubt that the phenomena described by Melton occur, they do not necessarily present any problem for a dichotomous view of memory. They do so only if one identifies the underlying theoretical *system* with performance on specific *tasks*. If, on the other hand, you assume that particular tasks may reflect more than one underlying system, then these results are no longer worrying; they simply show the contribution of the LTM component of the tasks. To take a concrete example, suppose I were testing your memory span for letters, and happened to present the sequence *abcdefghijkl*. You would almost certainly repeat it back correctly. It would not however mean that you had short-term storage capacity of 10 letters, since your recall would be largely based on prior long-term memory for the alphabet.

The need to distinguish between tasks and underlying memory systems was first argued by Waugh and Norman (1965) who used the old William James term *primary memory* (PM) to refer to the theoretical system they assumed to be responsible for short-term storage, while using the term *short-term memory* (STM) to refer to an experimental situation in which typically, a small amount of information is retained over a short period of time. They used the term *secondary memory* (SM) to refer to a hypothetical *long-term memory* (LTM) system. Performance on short-term memory tasks are likely to reflect both the PM and the SM systems while delayed recall is likely to reflect only SM, since the PM component will have decayed or been over-written by later material.

This distinction between memory system and memory task subsequently became generally accepted, although the particular terminology used by Waugh and Norman was not by any means universal. For example, Atkinson and Shiffrin (1968) used the term *short-term store* (STS) and *long-term store* (LTS) to refer to the theoretical underlying memory systems, and *short-term memory* (STM) and *long-term memory* (LTM) to refer to the experimental situations, situations in which performance might reflect a combination of the effects of STS and LTS.

Although Melton's paper by no means settled the issue, it did make very clear the fact that evidence for a dichotomy was far from convincing, and in the next few years, a flood of experimental evidence appeared. It can be summarized under four broad headings, each relating to an argument against the unitary theory of memory. These will be discussed in turn.

Evidence against a Unitary View of Memory

Two-component Tasks

One of the strongest arguments against a unitary view of memory came from the demonstration that certain tasks appear to have two separable and quite different components. The most extensively studied task of this kind is free recall, in which subjects are presented with a list of unrelated words and asked to recall as many as possible in any order they wish. As Postman and Phillips (1965) and Glanzer and Cunitz (1966) showed, when recall is immediate, there is a tendency for the last few items to be very well recalled, the so-called *recency effect*. After a brief filled delay, however, the recency effect disappears, while performance on earlier items in the curve are relatively unaffected by the delay (see Figure 3.4). One simple interpretation of this result is to suggest that the recency items are held in some temporary and rather fragile short-term store, while earlier items are recalled from LTM. This technique was particularly thoroughly explored by Glanzer (1972) who showed that the recency part of the curve is unaffected by a wide range of variables such as the familiarity of the words, their rate of presentation, the age of the subject or the requirement to perform some other concurrent task. In contrast, all these variables tend to influence long-term learning and to determine level of performance on the earlier part of the serial position curve.

Storage Capacity

A second argument against a unitary memory interpretation comes from evidence suggesting that primary memory (PM) or the short-term store (STS) has a limited storage capacity, but relatively rapid input and retrieval. Secondary memory (SM) or the long-term store (LTS) on the other hand, has an enormous capacity, but tends to be slower to register information and retrieve it. Arguments for the limited capacity of STS come principally from tasks such as the digit span, in which as we saw earlier, the subject

FIGURE 3.4

Serial position curve for lists of 10, 20, or 30 words recalled immediately or after a 15-or 30-second delay. Note that for each list length the last few items presented are very well recalled on immediate test (the recency effect) but not after a delay. From Postman and Phillips (1965). Copyright (1965) The Experimental Psychology Society.

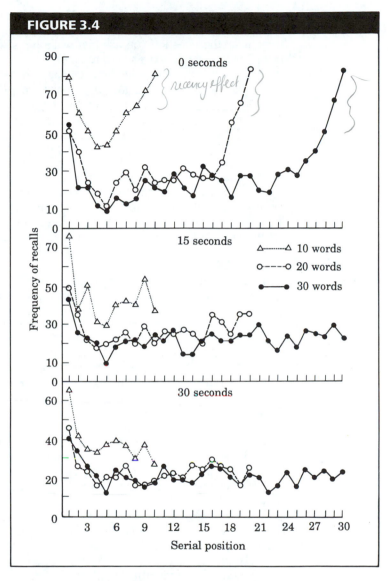

appears to be able to hold about seven chunks of information (Miller, 1956).

Murdock (1965) studied the effect of combining a distracting card-sorting task with free recall. Subjects were required to sort cards into one pile, two colors, four suits or eight categories based on number, at the same time as hearing a sequence of words for immediate free recall. The attentional demand made by the sorting task increased with number of alternatives causing a systematic decrement in performance on the earlier part of the free recall curve. In contrast, however, the recency effect was not influenced by concurrent load, suggesting that input into the PM or STS system may be less attention-demanding than long-term learning. It is probably this effect that allows the airport booking clerk to remember the question you ask him while he is writing out your ticket, and answer it when he has finished.

In a study examining the time taken to retrieve items from memory, Waugh (1970) found that responses from the recency part of the curve were consistently faster than responses from earlier serial positions, prompting her to suggest that retrieval from PM may be easier than from secondary or long-term memory.

It did not of course escape the notice of two-process theorists that the architecture of computers typically involves two kinds of memory, a large capacity long-term storage system, often using disk storage, and a separate working memory system that has more rapid input and storage capabilities, but which is much more limited in storage capacity, and this was used as further support for the plausibility of the two-component model of memory.

Acoustic and Semantic Coding

As part of a series of experiments concerned with the retention of telephone codes, Conrad noted that when such codes comprised consonants, the recall errors made by subjects were typically similar in sound to the correct item even when the letters had been presented visually. Hence *P* was more likely to be misrecalled as *V*, a letter similar in sound, than as a visually similar letter such as *R*. You may recall that Sperling (1960) made a similar observation in his experiments on iconic memory, concluding that the visually presented letters were being stored verbally before being produced as a response. Conrad (1964) showed that the pattern of errors made in remembering visually presented sequences of consonants was very similar to the pattern of listening errors made when the subject was discriminating individual auditorily presented letters presented against a background of noise. On the basis of this, he suggested that the items were stored in some form of acoustic code.

A study by Conrad and Hull (1964) presented further evidence for this view, showing that sequences of items that were similar in sound (e.g. *P*, *D*, *V*, *C*, *T*) were harder to recall than sequences of dissimilar letters (e.g. *K*, *Y*, *Z*, *W*, *R*). Wickelgren (1965) showed that the effect stemmed principally from the difficulty in recalling the *order* of the items; if anything, similarity tended to help recall of the letters themselves.

Conrad's results showed that immediate memory for consonants tends to rely on some type of speech-based code. It was not, however, clear from his results whether this was simply one of many broadly equivalent codes, or whether immediate memory is particularly dependent on such phonological information. I decided to explore this, using words and contrasting phonological similarity with similarity of meaning (Baddeley, 1966a). Subjects were presented with sequences of five words for immediate serial recall.

The effect of similarity of sound and of meaning on immediate serial recall of word sequences: Similarity of sound leads to poor immediate recall, while meaning has little effect. From Baddeley (1966a). Copyright (1966) The Experimental Psychology Society.

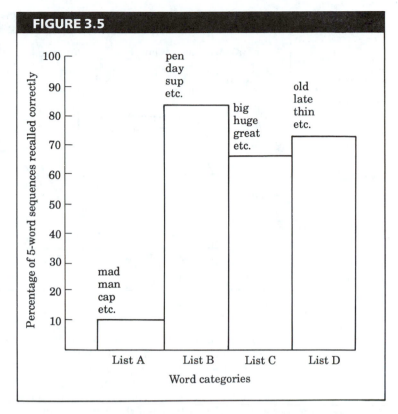

FIGURE 3.5

The words were selected from either a phonologically similar set, which produced sequences such as *man, mad, cap, can, map*, or dissimilar sequences such as *pen, rig, day, bar, sup*. Similarity of meaning was manipulated by using sequences of adjectives having either the same meaning such as *big, huge, broad, long, tall*, or different meanings as in *old, late, thin, wet, hot*. As Figure 3.5 shows, the phonologically similar set were much harder than the dissimilar, while similarity of meaning had a very small effect, suggesting that my subjects were remembering the items in terms of their sound or articulatory characteristics, not in terms of meaning.

I contrasted performance on the immediate memory task with one involving long-term learning (Baddeley, 1966b). Here, subjects were presented with sequences of 10 words to recall, and in order to minimize any use of STS, a filled delay occurred between presentation and test. As Figure 3.6 shows, under these circumstances phonological similarity ceased to be important, and similarity of meaning became the determining feature of learning. These results suggested the simple generalization that the short-term store relies on a phonological code, while the long-term store is primarily concerned with meaning.

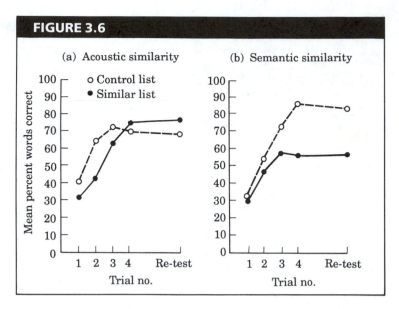

Effect of acoustic and semantic similarity on the long-term learning and retention of word sequences, with STS controlled. Only semantic similarity has a reliable effect. From Baddeley (1966b). Copyright (1966) The Experimental Psychology Society.

Evidence in favor of this view came from a number of other paradigms, including a study by Kintsch and Buschke (1969). They used the probe technique popularized by Waugh and Norman (1965) in which a sequence of items is presented, and recall tested by presenting one of the items again and requiring the subject to say what followed. Hence if the sequence were *1 5 3 9 2* and the probe was *5* then the correct response would be the following item, namely *3*. Waugh and Norman had shown that this task also has a recency component, which they suggested is dependent on PM or STS, whereas the performance on earlier items is assumed to reflect SM or LTS.

Kintsch and Buschke presented sequences containing pairs of similar items. The similarity could be in terms of sound, or in terms of meaning. They observed that both kinds of similarity tended to impair performance compared to lists containing only dissimilar words. However, the pattern of impairment was different for the two types of similarity, with the recency part of the curve suffering most from phonological similarity, while similarity of meaning tended to influence the earlier, LTS-based part of the curve.

Finally, evidence was produced by Sachs (1967) suggesting that the retention of prose passages might show comparable effects of dual coding. She carried out an experiment that was initially designed to test various models of syntax by looking at the role of grammar in memory. She presented her subjects with passages of prose. Occasionally a sentence would be repeated, and the subject's task was to decide whether the sentence was exactly as it had been previously, or whether some change had been made. When a change occurred, it could either involve a syntactic modification, or it could involve a change in meaning. The delay between presenting a target sentence and testing it ranged from an immediate test to several sentences later.

Sachs found that provided the sentence was tested immediately, subjects were relatively good at detecting all changes, whether in meaning or syntax. After one or more intervening sentences, however, the subject's capacity to remember the syntactic and surface features of the prose dropped dramatically, while retention of the meaning remained excellent. It appeared then that subjects listening to prose passages have a very brief retention of the surface characteristics of the sentence, possibly based on a phonological code, while having a much more durable retention of the underlying semantics. Such characteristics would of course be rather useful since one *does* need to remember the meaning of the early part of a passage in order to comprehend it, whereas retention of the specific words in which the meaning was conveyed is of much less significance.

At this point then, it looked as though one could come up with a generalization that short-term storage relies on phonological coding while long-term memory is more influenced by meaning. As we shall see later, although the basic effects described have proved robust, the interpretation proves to be somewhat more complex than at first seemed necessary.

Neuropsychological Evidence

Perhaps the strongest evidence for separate short- and long-term memory systems came from studies of brain-damaged patients. Milner (1966) described the case of H.M. who had undergone an operation in an effort to treat his intractable epilepsy. This involved removing substantial tissue from the temporal lobes and the hippocampus, a subcortical structure of the brain. The lesions were made on both sides of the brain, and had a dramatic effect on the unfortunate patient's capacity to remember. Although H.M. could recall incidents from his earlier life, his capacity for acquiring new information was drastically reduced. He was unable to learn to recognize new people, had no recollection of ongoing events, and could repeatedly read the same magazine without it seeming familiar. He could remember old skills such as mowing the lawn, but not where the lawnmower had been left. A psychologist could test him all morning, and in the afternoon H.M. would not recognize him, and have no recollection of the test session. And yet despite this dramatic impairment in the capacity to learn new material, his immediate memory span was quite normal, suggesting the combination of a defective long-term store coupled with normal primary memory or STS.

The matter was explored further in a study by Elizabeth Warrington and myself in which we carefully selected a group of patients who were severely amnesic, but otherwise intellectually unimpaired (Baddeley & Warrington, 1970). We tested our patients on a series of tasks that were selected so as to allow the separate assessment of STS and LTS. One obvious task to try was immediate and delayed free recall. The results of our study are shown in Figure 3.7, from which it is clear that our subjects showed an excellent recency effect coupled with grossly impaired performance on earlier items; delayed recall was of course also very poor. Like Milner, we found that our subjects had quite normal digit spans. In addition, however, we showed that they were able to perform normally on the Peterson short-term forgetting task. As mentioned earlier, this is not always the case with amnesic patients, since it appears to demand well-preserved general intellectual skills.

In addition to the predicted sparing of performance on STM tasks, we noted two unexpected findings. The first of these was that the point at which performance on the Peterson task levelled out was well above chance, and was identical for our amnesic and control subjects. Since this point of asymptote was assumed to reflect information in LTS, we naturally expected our two groups

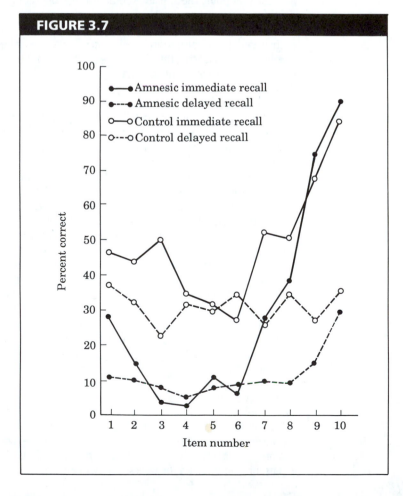

FIGURE 3.7

Immediate and delayed free recall in amnesic and control patients. Amnesic patients show impaired recall of early items, together with a normal recency effect. From Baddeley and Warrington (1970).

Amnesic immediate recall
Amnesic delayed recall
Control immediate recall
Control delayed recall

Percent correct

Item number

to differ. The second anomaly occurred in the results of the Hebb repeated digit sequence task. As you may recall, this involves presenting subjects with a sequence of digits just beyond their span, and surreptitiously repeating the same sequence on every third trial. We found that both amnesic and control subjects showed unspectacular but steady learning on the repeated sequence, again indicating some form of intact long-term learning. We shall return to the issue of preserved LTM performance in the chapter on amnesia.

However, the main conclusion from our study, and from those of others (e.g. Milner, 1966), was that patients suffering from the amnesic syndrome may show normal STS coupled with grossly defective LTS. Shallice and Warrington (1970) showed that the converse could also occur, when they described a patient, K.F., whose immediate memory span was limited to two or three digits, but whose long-term learning appeared to be quite normal. K.F. suffered from a lesion in the left hemisphere of the brain, in the area close to the Sylvian fissure where control of speech is typically located. Although slightly hesitant in his speech, he was by no means aphasic, and subsequent patients have been identified who show perfectly normal speech, coupled with a very specific deficit in immediate verbal memory (e.g. Basso, Spinnler, Vallar, & Zanobio, 1982). Performance on the Peterson task was very poor, particularly with auditory presentation, while K.F.'s free recall performance was exactly the opposite to that found in amnesic patients; the early part of his curve showed excellent retention, while the recency effect was severely reduced.

The demonstration of preserved STM performance in amnesic patients provided strong evidence in favor of a dissociation between two types of memory. Evidence from only one type of patient such as amnesics with impaired LTS and normal STS is, however, open to the objection that perhaps STS-based tests are for some reason "easier" than those testing LTS, and are hence less susceptible to disruption by *any* form of brain damage. The presence of a second type of patient showing the opposite pattern, allows such interpretations to be ruled out; if STS tasks are easier, why were they harder for K.F.? The presence of two such contrasting deficits provides what is usually termed a *double-dissociation* between performance on STS- and LTS-based tasks. As such, it offers a particularly powerful source of evidence for the existence of two separate systems. (For a more detailed discussion of this issue, see Ellis & Young, 1988, Chapter 1 and Shallice, 1988.)

THE MODAL MODEL

Atkinson and Shiffrin's Model

By the late 1960s, the evidence seemed to be accumulating strongly in favor of a separation between short- and long-term memory storage systems. A number of models were formulated, typically having much in common. The most characteristic and influential of these, which is sometimes termed the *modal model* was that proposed by Atkinson and Shiffrin (1968). It is summarized in Figure 3.8.

The Atkinson and Shiffrin model has some similarities to an earlier model by Broadbent (1958), as its authors acknowledge, but it is considerably more detailed. It assumes that information is first processed in parallel by a range of sensory buffer stores. These feed information into a limited capacity short-term store (STS) which in turn communicates with a long-term store (LTS). Note

The flow of information through the memory system as conceived by Atkinson and Shiffrin. Based on Atkinson and Shiffrin (1968). Copyright 1968 by Scientific American Inc. All rights reserved.

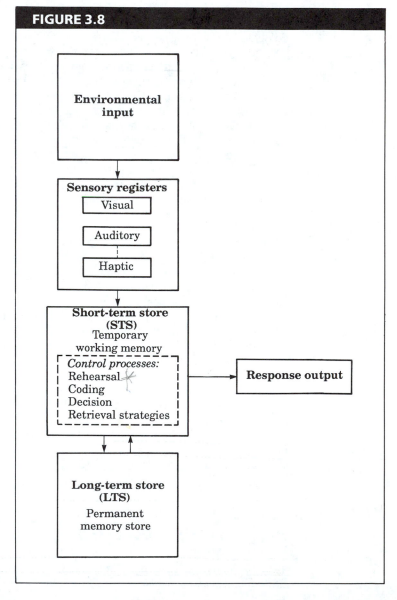

FIGURE 3.8

that the STS plays a crucial role in this model, since without it information can not get into or out of LTS. In addition to storing information, the STS was also assumed to perform certain functions referred to by Atkinson and Shiffrin as *control processes*.

Rehearsal, a process whereby information was maintained in STS, was one such control process that was studied in some detail by Atkinson and Shiffrin. They postulate that the longer an item is held in STS, the greater the probability that it will be transferred or copied into LTS. Although Atkinson and Shiffrin acknowledged the existence and importance of semantic coding, their actual studies were primarily concerned with verbal rote rehearsal. A neat study by one of their students, Rundus (1971) for example, used a free recall task coupled with the instruction that subjects should rehearse out loud. Rundus counted the frequency with which each individual item was rehearsed, and found that the more frequently an item had been rehearsed, the more likely was it to be recalled. An exception to this relationship occurred in the case of items from the last few serial positions, those items that contribute to the recency component, for which recall was excellent despite relatively few rehearsals. Atkinson and Shiffrin interpret this as indicating that the recency effect represents the recall of those items that are already in the STS, whereas recall of earlier items depends on LTS. The longer an item is held in STS however, the greater the probability that it will be transferred to LTS, hence the correlation between number of rehearsals and probability of subsequent recall.

The Atkinson and Shiffrin model probably represents the high-water mark of two-component or dichotomous models of memory. It appeared to be based on a firm foundation of empirical evidence from a wide range of sources. Like many other models of the time, it was expressed in a sophisticated mathematical form that appeared to give an impressive quantitative account of experimental data. As we shall see, however, life once again turned out to be more complicated, and perhaps more interesting than the initial models suggested.

Problems with the Modal Model

Neuropsychological Evidence

It may be recalled that one important source of evidence for the existence of a separate STS came from a study of patients who appeared to have normal long-term learning ability coupled with grossly impaired auditory memory span (Shallice & Warrington, 1970). According to the modal model, the reduced span would indicate that such patients have a greatly reduced STS capacity. Since the limited capacity STS system forms the crucial bottleneck in learning, reasoning and general intellectual performance, such patients should be severely handicapped. They showed no such general impairment, having normal long-term learning capacity and often living an independent and normal life (Shallice & Warrington, 1970; Basso et al., 1982).

STS and Long-term Learning

A second problem for the modal model concerned the learning assumption whereby the probability that an item will be transferred to long-term memory is a direct function of its time of maintenance in STS (Atkinson & Shiffrin, 1968). A number of studies suggested that this was not the case. For example, Tulving (1966) required his subjects to repeatedly read through a list of words which were then included in a larger subsequent list which subjects had to learn. There was no evidence that the previous repetitions had enhanced subsequent learning; simply repeating the words did not increase their accessibility, whereas active subsequent learning did, presumably by strengthening links between the words being learned.

Problems for the modal model also come from a number of rather dramatic instances in which people are shown to learn nothing from the incidental presentation of information many times. For example, Morton (1967) asked his subjects to reproduce the pattern of numbers and letters on the British telephone dial; in those days telephone letter codes were common, and this information was something which his subjects must have used repeatedly. Of 50 subjects tested, none of them was completely correct in reproducing the information. A similar lack of learning following repeated exposure was observed by Nickerson and Adams (1979) in requesting their subjects to recall the characteristics of an American penny, while Debra Bekerian and I (Bekerian & Baddeley, 1980) observed that a saturation advertising campaign in which the BBC presented information about new radio wavelengths on over 1,000 occasions appeared to have virtually no effect in registering that information (see p.159 for further details). In conclusion, the assumption that processing by STS is the straightforward royal road to LTS did not appear to be justified.

Recency and STS

The modal model offers a simple and straightforward account of the recency effect in free recall by assuming that it represents the immediate output of those items currently held in STS. Such a view accounts for the abolition of recency by a few seconds of backward counting since this is assumed to displace the last few words from the STS. The fact that patients with impaired STS show little or no recency is also consistent with this interpretation; reduced STS implies reduced recency. Finally, the experiment by Rundus in which subjects were required to rehearse out loud appeared to give direct confirmation of this interpretation, since the most recent items were typically those that had just been rehearsed, and hence might be assumed still to be within the STS system.

The modal model does however have great difficulty in

accounting for the results of a study by Baddeley and Hitch (1977) in which subjects simultaneously attempted to perform a digit span task while being tested for free recall of lists of unrelated words. Concurrent digit span impaired the long-term component of performance, but had no effect on recency. According to the modal model, both span and recency should have competed for the same limited capacity STS, as a result of which there should have been massive interference. We will return to this point later.

Further potential problems for the modal model were raised by a demonstration of recency effects in LTM for pairs of words by Bjork and Whitten (1972; 1974). This was replicated by Tzeng (1973) in a study using a more standard free recall procedure in which two groups of subjects were presented with lists of unrelated words, and required to recall them after a 20 second delay filled by backward counting. Under standard presentation conditions, this was sufficient to eliminate the recency effect. In a second condition, however, subjects were required to count backwards for 20 seconds after the presentation of each word, and under these conditions, a clear recency effect survived the 20 second filled delay. On the assumption of a simple modal model however, one might have expected all the backward counting in this condition to have wiped out the labile STS trace and hence obliterated the recency effect.

Subsequent studies have extended Tzeng's results (e.g. Bjork & Whitten, 1974), while others have demonstrated recency effects extending over much longer periods. For example, Baddeley and Hitch (1977) showed that when rugby players attempted to recall the teams they had played against earlier that season, they showed clear evidence of recency, as in free recall, with the crucial factor being number of interpolated games rather than simple elapsed time.

It is perhaps worth pointing out that the existence of long-term recency effects is not in itself inconsistent with the modal model; it is entirely possible that there could be different types of recency effect in LTS and STS. However, if the two forms of recency can be shown to behave in a broadly similar way, and can be explained by a single hypothesis, then other things being equal, that hypothesis is to be preferred. We shall discuss later to what extent this is the case. The presence of normal recency despite concurrent digit span (Baddeley & Hitch, 1977) is however a more crucial result, and one that is not easily explained by the modal model.

Coding

It became increasingly clear that a simple association between STS and phonological coding and LTS and semantic coding must be an over-simplification. Indeed, the coding issue was never a very central feature of the modal model which was quite happy to talk about coding in terms of circulating semantic as well as acoustic cues within the STS. Furthermore, it is clearly the case that if we are to learn to speak, then long-term phonological learning must be necessary. Within laboratory tasks, it was becoming increasingly clear that the nature of the task would determine whether or not a subject would use semantic coding. With briefly presented sets of unrelated words, adequate semantic coding tended to be difficult, but provided they were made semantically compatible so that they could be integrated into a meaningful whole, then semantic rather than phonological coding would be used (Baddeley & Levy, 1971). Hence subjects required to repeat back immediately pairs of items such as *priest-delicious* or *vicar-tasty* showed no effect of semantic similarity, whereas when the pairs were made compatible they found *priest-pious* and *apple-delicious* to be consistently easier than semantically similar pairs like *priest-pious* and *vicar-holy*. In short, subjects will encode verbal material meaningfully if they can do in the time available, and will reflect this by showing semantic similarity effects. If not, they rely on phonological coding and show phonological similarity effects.

THE RISE OF LEVELS OF PROCESSING

As problems with the modal model began to accumulate, interest in STM declined, and many of the previously active participants moved into other fields. Atkinson became a senior administrator, Shiffrin became more interested in attention and mathematical models of LTM, while the developing field of semantic memory and of prose comprehension attracted others such as Norman and Kintsch. The field seemed to be becoming increasingly fragmented, with a plethora of STM techniques and of individual models, but a lack of any overall generally agreed framework.

Then, in 1972 Craik and Lockhart published their influential paper on *levels of processing* offering just such a general framework. They suggested that it was more fruitful to concentrate on mode of processing than on hypothetical memory structures such as the long- and short-term stores. Craik and Lockhart suggest that the more deeply an item is processed, the better it will be remembered, with information processed in superficial sensory terms giving rise to relatively short-lived traces, phonological processing producing a somewhat more durable trace, while deep semantic processing produces the most durable learning. They still assumed a separate primary memory system, but within their framework, its main role was to process the incoming information. Longer storage resulted from deeper processing within the LTS, not from transfer from one store to another. A direct result of this viewpoint was a distinction between two modes of rehearsal, *maintenance rehearsal* in which material was recycled without processing it more deeply, and elaborative rehearsal whereby depth of processing was increased.

Levels of processing was welcomed by many as evidence that memory comprised a simple unitary system after all (e.g. Postman,

1975). The approach, however, could be better categorized as being primarily concerned with the role of coding in long-term memory; Craik and Lockhart explicitly favor a dichotomous view, but say relatively little about primary memory. For that reason, we will postpone discussion of levels of processing until Chapter 8 which is concerned with long-term learning, moving instead to a second response to the problems of the modal model, the Baddeley and Hitch model of working memory.

OVERVIEW

Research that began with the attempt to measure a span of conscious awareness gradually extended to investigate the temporary storage of information, as measured by tasks such as the digit span. This in turn led to the question of whether the forgetting shown by the Petersons over brief time intervals when rehearsal is prevented reflects the fading of a memory trace, or the disruption of the trace by other later memories. It eventually became clear that explanation of short-term forgetting involves both of these factors, the weakening of the trace, and the problem of retrieving it or discriminating it from among other competing traces.

In the 1960s, there was considerable controversy as to whether short- and long-term memory should be regarded as involving separate systems, or whether as Melton suggested, all the available results could be explained in terms of a single long-term memory system in which forgetting resulted from interference. Though influential, Melton's views suffered from a failure to distinguish between STM as a hypothetical memory system and STM as an experimental paradigm, typically reflecting the influence of more than one underlying memory system. To avoid this confounding, subsequent theorists have used different terms, with the theoretical system referred to as primary memory (PM) or the short-term store (STS), and the term STM used for the experimental paradigm.

Evidence in favor of at least two systems came from a range of sources including:

1. Tasks such as free recall appeared to have separate long- and short-term components.
2. STS appeared to have a very limited storage capacity, but to have rapid input and retrieval from storage, where LTS appeared to couple massive storage capacity with substantial limitations in the rate of input and retrieval.
3. STS appeared to rely on acoustic or phonological coding while LTS seemed to be more dependent on semantic codes.
4. Neuropsychological evidence suggested that long- and short-term stores could be separately and differentially impaired in different types of patient.

A number of models, including the so-called modal model of

Atkinson and Shiffrin appeared to be able to account for these results. The modal model did however subsequently run into a number of problems including:

1. The model indicated that patients with STM deficits should also have problems in long-term learning; such deficits were not apparent.
2. The assumption that maintaining an item in STS would ensure its transfer to LTS proved to be poorly supported.
3. The existence of long-term recency effects, and the absence of a disruption of recency in free recall by a concurrent memory span task were both inconsistent with the modal model's interpretation of recency.
4. The assumption that STS relies on acoustic coding, and LTS on semantic was clearly over-simplified.

These problems resulted in a loss of interest in the general area of STM, coupled with the development of two new approaches, *Levels of processing* which will be discussed in Chapter 8, and the proposal of a multi-component working memory system in place of the unitary STS. This will be discussed in the following chapter.

Chapter Four

THE ROLE OF MEMORY IN COGNITION: WORKING MEMORY

*T*he study of STM sprang from concern for a number of practical problems, such as the attempt by Jacobs to measure the mental capacity of his pupils, Broadbent's interest in the division of attention and its implications for jobs such as that of the air traffic controller, and Conrad's concern for the memorability of telephone numbers and postcodes. By the late 1960s however, the study of STM had become very much laboratory-bound; it had produced a plethora of novel laboratory techniques and detailed models and theories, often expressed mathematically. Although based almost entirely on laboratory results, none the less the Atkinson and Shiffrin (1968) model did make claims for the general importance of the short-term store. It assumed that the STS acted as a *working memory*, a system for temporarily holding and manipulating information as part of a wide range of essential cognitive tasks such as learning, reasoning and comprehending. Such a view would probably have been quite widely held during the 1960s, although there was little effort to test it directly. The present chapter describes one attempt to investigate the role of short-term storage in a range of tasks and situations, and to ask whether STS really does serve as a general working memory. In attempting to answer that question, the earlier concept of a unitary STS is challenged and replaced by a related but more complex concept, that of a multi-component working memory model. This attempts to account for both the evidence that fitted the earlier STS model and also those features that were problematic. In addition, the concept of working memory attempts to highlight the role of temporary storage in other cognitive tasks such as reasoning, comprehension and learning.

In their levels of processing framework, Craik and Lockhart (1972) continued to assume that primary memory played an important role in cognition, but did they necessarily need to? Given that their framework would deal with coding effects quite effectively, could handle the absence of long-term learning following maintenance rehearsal, and given the uncertainties surrounding the explanation of recency effects, is there any need to assume a short-term store? Even more pressingly, if patients with a severe deficit in short-term storage are apparently otherwise unimpaired and capable of living a full and rich life, is the study of STM anything other than a cul-de-sac in the short but tortuous history of human experimental psychology?

Graham Hitch and I decided to try and tackle this problem by asking the basic question of "What is STS for?" We decided that if the answer was that it merely served to keep experimental psychologists occupied, we would choose to occupy ourselves in other ways.

TESTING THE WORKING MEMORY HYPOTHESIS

A widely held assumption was that STS acts as a temporary working memory that helps us perform a range of other cognitive tasks (Atkinson & Shiffrin, 1968; Hunter, 1957; Newell & Simon, 1972); the concrete evidence for such a view was remarkably sparse. We decided to test it by using a dual-task technique whereby the subject is required to perform one task that absorbs most of the capacity of his working memory, while at the same time performing each of a range of tasks such as learning, reasoning and comprehending that are assumed to be crucially dependent upon working memory. If the assumption is correct, then performing a concurrent STM task should lead to a dramatic impairment in performance.

We selected digit span as our concurrent memory task; although many different models of STS exist, virtually all of them assume that it has a limited storage capacity, and that this capacity is used in performing the standard immediate serial recall task. We began rather tentatively by requiring our subjects to remember only one or two digits while reasoning or learning, but much to our surprise and that of our subjects, they proved to be only minimally encumbered by a few additional items, and we therefore moved to rather heavier concurrent digit loads of three or six items.

We also began by presenting the digits, requiring the reasoning or memory task, and then asking for digit recall. Under these circumstances, however, we found that subjects tended to adopt a strategy of rapidly rehearsing the digits, then switching attention to the reasoning or learning task, before returning to pick up whatever they could of the trace of the digits. As such, we were not obtaining a measure of *concurrent* processing so much as observing the effect of alternating the two tasks. We therefore opted for a policy of requiring the subject always to continue to rehearse the digits out loud, hence ensuring that they were performing both tasks simultaneously. We assumed that if STS serves as a limited-capacity working memory that is used in reasoning or learning, then loading STS with a concurrent task of remembering digits should impair performance. The larger the number of digits being held, the greater the amount of working memory capacity that should be absorbed, and the greater the interference with reasoning or learning performance.

In one study, subjects were required to remember number sequences ranging from zero to eight digits in length, while at the same time performing a reasoning test. This involved verifying a series of sentences each of which purports to describe the order in which two successive letters, *A* and *B*, were presented. The subject's task is to decide whether the sentence correctly describes the order or not. Examples ranged from simple active declarative sentences such as *A follows B – BA* (true) to more complex sentences involving passives and/or negatives such as *B is not preceded by A – AB* (false).

This particular reasoning test is one based on some of the early developments in psycholinguistics which showed that the more complex the sentence, the longer the decision time. I initially devised it to provide a simple robust reasoning test that could be performed underwater as part of a study on the effects on the mental efficiency on deep-sea divers of nitrogen narcosis, the drunkenness that one experiences on breathing air at depth. It proved to be a valid and reliable correlate of verbal intelligence (Baddeley, 1968) and to be sensitive to nitrogen narcosis (Baddeley & Flemming, 1967).

Figure 4.1 shows the effect of concurrent memory load on the speed and accuracy with which subjects performed the syntactic reasoning test. Two points should be noted; first of all, the reasoning time increases clearly and systematically with concurrent memory load, just as a working memory hypothesis would predict. Secondly, however, note that the effect is far from catastrophic; requiring a subject to concurrently rehearse eight items, which in many cases was more than could accurately be maintained, leads to an increase in latency of only about 35%. Even more strikingly, note that error rate remains constant at around 5%. It is not easy to account for this pattern of results if one assumes that working memory involves a single unitary store whose limited capacity is likely to be totally absorbed when the limit of memory span is reached. On this assumption, a concurrent load of eight digits should cause reasoning performance to break down completely. It clearly does not.

A broadly similar pattern of results was obtained across a range of other cognitive tasks. In one study, the free recall of lists of unrelated words was studied when they were accompanied by a concurrent digit span of zero, three or six items. Performance on the earlier part of the serial position curve, normally associated with long-term learning was impaired, but by no means obliterated by the concurrent load of six digits, while a three-digit load had no significant effect on performance. As mentioned earlier, not even

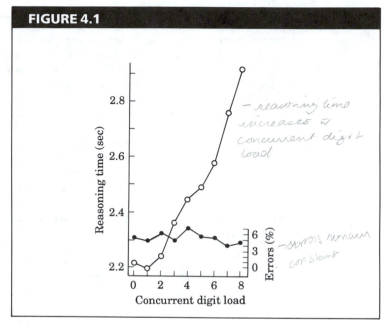

Speed and
accuracy of
grammatical
reasoning as a
function of
concurrent digit
load. From
Baddeley (1986).

FIGURE 4.1

[handwritten: — reasoning time increases w concurrent digit load]

[handwritten: — errors remain constant]

the six-digit load had any effect on the magnitude of recency, suggesting that recency and digit span may well reflect the operation of different memory systems.

In another study, comprehension of prose passages was studied in subjects who were concurrently remembering sequences of zero, three or six unrelated digits. Level of comprehension was significantly impaired by the six-digit, but not the three-digit load (Baddeley & Hitch, 1974).

Finally and most unexpectedly, despite a clear effect on learning, concurrent digit span during *retrieval* from long-term memory was found to have no effect on accuracy of performance, although it did produce an increase in retrieval latency (Baddeley, Lewis, Eldridge, & Thomson, 1984). The requirement to remember and recite a six-digit number had no effect on the accuracy of recalling or recognizing lists of words, whether tested by free recall or paired-associate learning (see Table 4.1). This somewhat surprising result suggests that whatever system is responsible for holding digits in immediate memory might be, it does not play the crucial role in retrieval assumed by many earlier models of memory including that of Atkinson and Shiffrin (1968) and that of Rumelhart, Lindsay, and Norman (1972).

[handwritten margin note: another reason for developing the working memory model]

A WORKING MEMORY MODEL

How well then, did the concept of a working memory survive this initial exploration using the dual-task paradigm? With the exception of retrieval, all the other tasks showed evidence for impaired

A simplified representation of the working memory model.

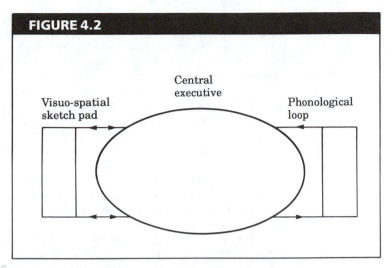

FIGURE 4.2

Visuo-spatial sketch pad

Central executive

Phonological loop

(handwritten margin note: Reasons for model of working memory)

performance, with the degree of impairment increasing with concurrent digit load, a pattern of results that is quite consistent with the working memory hypothesis. On the other hand, the degree of impairment is far from dramatic, particularly bearing in mind that a concurrent load of six digits would approach the span of most of our subjects, and on assumptions such as those of the modal model ought to leave very little processing capacity left for reasoning, learning, comprehending or retrieving. The simplest way out of this paradox seemed to be to abandon the assumption of a unitary STS, and accept that the limits of digit span may be set by one of a number of subsystems, leaving other components of working memory relatively unimpaired.

On the basis of the evidence from these and other tasks, we proposed a model of working memory in which a controlling attentional system supervises and coordinates a number of subsidiary slave systems. We termed the attentional controller the central executive and chose to study two slave systems in more detail, the articulatory or phonological loop which was assumed to be responsible for the manipulation of speech-based information, and the visuo-spatial scratchpad or sketchpad, which was assumed to be responsible for setting up and manipulating visual images. A simple representation of the model is shown in Figure 4.2. I shall begin by discussing the slave systems before going on to talk about the more difficult task of exploring the central executive.

THE PHONOLOGICAL LOOP

We postulated this particular subsystem in order to give an account of the very substantial evidence for the importance of speech coding in STM. It is probably the most extensively worked out component of the model, partly because I suspect it is one of the simpler components, and partly because it is concerned with an area where considerable data already existed. Because of this, it offers a good example of a particular approach to theorizing, namely that of attempting to constrain possible models by using a rich and robust pattern of results, any one of which is capable of being explained in several different ways, but which together place major constraints on possible explanations. The theoretical aim in the short term is to provide a simple account of all the data; such an account need not, and rarely is quantitative and precise, but it represents the basic structure that any more detailed model will need to encompass.

Since the pattern of data is relatively complex, I will begin by giving a brief overview of the assumed structure of the phonological loop system, followed by a description of the individual phenomena, after which an overall mapping of the phenomena onto the model will be suggested.

The phonological loop is assumed to comprise two components, a phonological store that is capable of holding speech-based information and an articulatory control process based on inner speech. Memory traces within the phonological store are assumed to fade and become unretrievable after about one-and-a-half to two seconds. The memory trace can however be refreshed by a process of reading off the trace into the articulatory control process which then feeds it back into the store, the process underlying subvocal rehearsal. The articulatory control process is also capable of taking written material, converting it into a phonological code and registering it in the phonological store. This simple model of a phonological store served by an articulatory control process can give a coherent account of the following phenomena:

presumes read words are converted to phonology

Evidence for the Loop

The Phonological Similarity Effect
As we saw earlier immediate serial recall is impaired when items are similar in sound or articulatory characteristics, hence PGTVCD will be harder to remember than RHXKWY (Conrad & Hull, 1964; Baddeley, 1966a). The question of whether the crucial aspect of similarity is at the level of sounds, phonemes or articulatory commands is one that has created a good deal of discussion over the years, without reaching any very satisfactory conclusion, since the various measures are all extremely highly correlated (e.g. Hintzman, 1967; Wickelgren, 1969). Virtually all the terms used in this respect, including "acoustic", "phonemic" and "phonological" can be taken to imply a particular position on this issue. The present use of the term "phonological" is, however, meant to be relatively neutral on the issue of exactly what level of speech coding is involved. The phonological similarity effect is assumed to occur because the store is based on a phonological code, hence similar items will have similar codes. Recall will require discriminating among the memory traces. Similar traces will be harder to discriminate, leading to a lower level of recall.

The Unattended Speech Effect

Colle and Welsh (1976) carried out a study in which subjects attempted to repeat back sequences of visually presented numbers. In one condition, immediate serial recall was accompanied by the sound of someone reading a passage in German, a language the subjects did not understand. Nevertheless, performance on the immediate memory task showed a clear decrement.

A colleague, Pierre Salamé, and I independently stumbled across the same effect a few years later. Pierre had been working on the effects of noise on memory, in France, and on a collaborative working visit to Cambridge decided that it would be interesting to extend the range of possible distractors to include spoken words. He predicted that being meaningful, the words would be particularly distracting, while I suspected that the subject would be quite capable of ignoring them, producing a negative result.

We therefore set up an experiment in which subjects attempted the immediate recall of nine visually presented digits which were presented either in silence, or accompanied by spoken words or spoken nonsense syllables, both of which the subject was instructed to ignore. Pierre predicted that performance would be more severely disrupted by the words than by nonsense; I predicted no disruption from either. We were both wrong. Performance was disrupted to an equal extent by both words and nonsense syllables. We concluded that the unattended material was gaining access to the phonological store, a store that holds phonological but not semantic information.

This conclusion was reinforced by a subsequent experiment in which subjects again attempted to remember visually presented digit sequences, this time against a background either of other digits, or of other words made up from the same phonemes as digits (e.g. *tun, woo* instead of *one, two*). A third condition involved ignoring words that were phonologically dissimilar disyllables (e.g. *happy, tipple*), while a fourth comprised a silent control condition. The disyllables caused some disruption but not so much as the monosyllables having the same phonological characteristics as digits. These did not, however, differ in their degree of disruptiveness from actual digits, again suggesting that the store contains phonemic information but does not represent items at a word level, otherwise the digits would have been expected to be more disruptive than the non-digits made up from the same phonemes.

Can any sound gain access to the phonological store? The evidence suggests not. In one study, for example, we compared the effects of unattended speech with that of unattended noise on immediate serial recall of digits. We found a clear effect of unattended speech, but no effect of noise, even when the noise was pulsed so as to give the same intensity envelope as continuous speech (Salamé & Baddeley, 1987; 1989). In some ways the effect resembles auditory masking, but in others it does not. The effect is for example unaffected by the intensity of the unattended speech, provided that it is clearly audible (Colle, 1980; Salamé & Baddeley, 1987).

What about unattended music? We studied this in an experiment in which the subject again tried to recall sequences of visually presented digits, this time against a background of either vocal or instrumental music. Whether the vocal music came from nineteenth-century opera in an unfamiliar language, or from a current pop star singing in the subject's native language, the disruption was the same and approximately equivalent to that produced by unattended speech. In the case of instrumental music, the effect was present but rather less marked, and again was uninfluenced by whether it was represented by modern or classical pieces (Salamé & Baddeley, 1989).

What are the practical implications of our results? Should one definitely avoid studying with the radio on? At present we have not explored a sufficiently wide range of tasks to come up with firm recommendations, but it seems that the effect rather specifically impairs tasks that heavily involve the phonological store. We have not so far obtained any indication to suggest that reading comprehension (Baddeley, Eldridge, & Lewis, 1981) or free recall learning (Salamé & Baddeley, unpublished) are impaired by meaningless unattended speech. On the other hand, evidence is beginning to appear suggesting that if the material is meaningful, and evokes at least some of the listener's attention, then impairment in comprehension and/or retention of prose will be observed (Martin, Wogalter, & Forlano, 1988).

In the past, experimental investigations into "noise pollution" have all too frequently opted to study meaningless white noise, regarding sound intensity as the main variable of study. Our results suggest that the qualitative nature of the noise may be a rather more important factor when it comes to disrupting working memory. However, the area clearly needs a good deal more investigation using a wider range of tasks and a wider range of potentially disrupting sounds before valid conclusions can be drawn.

The Word-Length Effect
Another powerful determinant of immediate memory span is the spoken duration of the words presented. Hence most subjects would relatively easily remember a sequence of five monosyllabic words such as *wit, sum, harm, bag, top*, but would have considerable difficulty in repeating back a sequence of polysyllables such as *university, opportunity, aluminium, constitutional, auditorium*. Figure 4.3 shows the relationship between word length, reading rate and memory for words ranging in length from one to five syllables. Figure 4.4 shows the relationship between total spoken duration and probability of recall. The results fall on a straight line which can be reinterpreted as indicating that memory span represents the number of items of whatever length that can be uttered in about two seconds. As one might expect from this, there is a correlation between the rate at which a subject speaks

and his or her memory span (Baddeley, Thomson, & Buchanan, 1975).

Is the crucial feature spoken duration or number of syllables? Duration appears to be the critical variable since sequences of words that tend to have long vowels and be spoken slowly such as *Friday* and *harpoon* lead to somewhat shorter spans than words

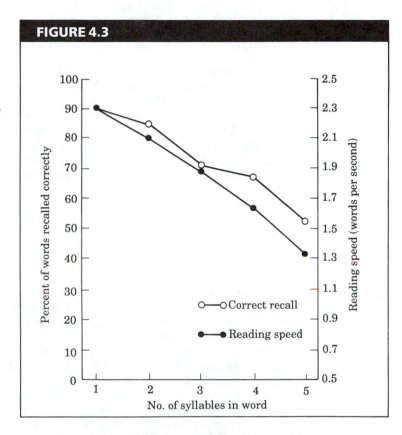

FIGURE 4.3

Relationship between word length, reading rate and recall. Long words take longer to rehearse and produce lower memory spans. From Baddeley, Thomson, and Buchanan (1975b).

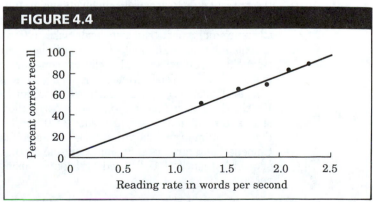

FIGURE 4.4

The relationship between reading rate and recall observed by Baddeley et al (1975b).

Straight line!

TABLE 4.1

Set of Words Used by Baddeley, Thomson, and Buchanan (1975)

Mumps	Measles	Leprosy	Diphtheria	Tuberculosis
Stoat	Puma	Gorilla	Rhinocerous	Hippopotamus
Greece	Peru	Mexico	Australia	Yugoslavia
Maine	Utah	Wyoming	Alabama	Louisiana
Zinc	Carbon	Calcium	Uranium	Aluminium

with the same number of syllables and phonemes that can be spoken more rapidly (e.g. *wicket, bishop*).

Ellis and Hennelly (1980) used this effect to interpret an anomaly in the detailed intelligence test results for Welsh-speaking children. Such children appear to have a consistently lower performance on the digit span subtest of the Wechsler Intelligence Scale than their English-speaking contemporaries. Could this indicate some strange genetic quirk of the Welsh to offset perhaps their prowess at choral singing and rugby playing? Ellis and Hennelly proposed a more prosaic interpretation, observing that the digit names in Welsh, although having the same number of syllables as in English, tend to have longer vowel sounds and take longer to say. They tested this using bilingual Welsh- and English-speaking subjects. Their subjects proved to have a poorer span in their native language of Welsh than in English, but as predicted, their spans were equal when measured in terms of spoken time.

When the subjects were prevented from rehearsing by the requirement to utter an irrelevant sound, the difference between span in the two languages disappeared. Was the effect purely limited to the memory span? Apparently not since their subjects also showed some signs of slower performance and higher error rate in mental arithmetic using Welsh digits. Later research by Naveh-Benjamin and Ayres (1986) has extended the work of Ellis and Hennelly across a range of different languages, and as Figure 4.5 shows obtaining a clear relationship between memory span, and the time it takes to articulate the digits one to ten in that language.

However, the record so far for speed of articulation goes to Chinese for which Hoosain and Salili (1988) report a mean articulation rate of 265 milliseconds per digit compared to Ellis and Hennelly's report of 321 milliseconds for English and 385 milliseconds for Welsh. Mean digit span was no fewer than 9.9 for Chinese subjects compared to a mean of 6.6 for English, and 5.8 for Welsh. Hoosain and Salili also report a correlation between memory span and mathematics exam grades of 0.38. They further report that recitation of multiplication tables is much faster in the case of Chinese undergraduates using Cantonese (mean time = 64.3 seconds) than for U.S. undergraduates using English (134.2 seconds).

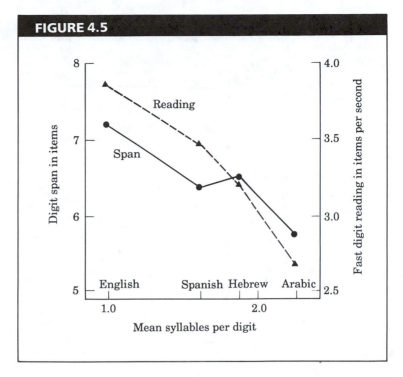

FIGURE 4.5

Memory span and reading rate for digits in four different languages. From Naveh-Benjamin and Ayres (1986). Copyright (1986) The Experimental Psychology Society.

Finally, Hoosain and Salili report a study by Chan (1981) who compared two groups of students in Hong Kong, both from the same Chinese-speaking primary school. One group elected for education in English, the other in Chinese. The groups were equivalent in performance when they transferred schools at age 12. Five years later, those who went to Chinese-speaking schools tended to have poorer grades in everything other than Chinese and mathematics. Such a result is open to a range of possible interpretations, but does support the possibility of a link between language, the phonological loop and mathematics, reinforcing other evidence indicating an involvement of the phonological loop in counting (Logie & Baddeley, 1987) and mental arithmetic (Hitch, 1978).

One of the clearest and most reliable features of the development of memory in children is the tendency for digit span to increase systematically with age. Nicolson (1981) made the interesting suggestion that this might be due to a tendency for older children to rehearse faster. He studied the speed at which children of different ages could articulate and plotted their memory span as a function of this, finding a very clear relationship.

This finding has subsequently been replicated and further extended by Hulme, Thomson, Muir, and Lawrence (1984) and by Hitch, Halliday, and Littler (1984) in a series of studies in which children of various ages were tested for immediate serial recall of

The relationship between word length, speech rate, and memory span as a function of age. From Hulme, Thomson, Muir, and Lawrence (1984).

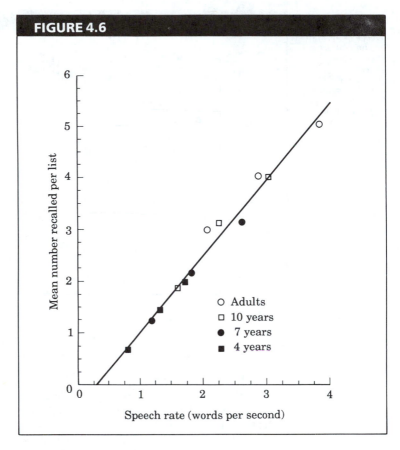

FIGURE 4.6

items that had names varying in length. When presentation was auditory, length had an effect down to children as young as four. As Figure 4.6 shows, when memory span is plotted against articulation rate, the data from all the item lengths and ages fall on the same straight line, suggesting that in this task at least, increased age enhances performance simply because subjects articulate more rapidly.

The presence of a word-length effect implies some form of subvocal rehearsal, and as such appears to conflict with other data from a study for example of free recall in children which seems to suggest that cumulative rote rehearsal is not developed until a somewhat later age (Ornstein, Naus, & Stone, 1977). A subsequent experiment suggests that rehearsal may be very dependent upon a particular experimental situation. For example, if items are presented visually as drawings, rather than spoken, then a word-length effect does not appear in children of the age of 6 and 8, although it is present by the age of 10 (Hitch et al., 1984). It seems likely that the tendency to repeat back either overtly or covertly, items that are heard, is a rather early development, possibly playing an important role in acquiring spoken language. It appears that converting a visual item into a phonological code, and rehearsing that code is something that is acquired considerably later.

How should the word-length effect be interpreted? The simplest account might be to suggest that the process of overt or covert articulation involves setting up and running speech motor programs which operate in real time, with the result that the longer the word the longer it takes to run off. If we assume that this process of subvocal rehearsal has the function of maintaining items in the phonological store by refreshing their fading traces, then the faster it can run, the more items will be maintained and the longer the memory span. If we assume that the memory fades, then the memory span will be determined by the number of items that can be refreshed before they fade away. That number, of course, will depend both on how rapidly the trace fades and on how long it takes to articulate each item and hence refresh each memory trace. Data from studies using English, Welsh, Hebrew, Spanish, Arabic and Chinese all give results suggesting that trace decay time is approximately two seconds, although as mentioned earlier, rehearsal time, and consequently span vary widely from one language to another (Hoosain & Salili, 1988).

Articulatory Suppression

Although overt articulation is not necessary for the operation of inner speech, the operation of the phonological loop is disturbed if overt or covert articulation of an irrelevant item is required. Hence, if a subject in a standard digit span task is required to utter a stream of irrelevant sound, such as repeatedly saying the word *the*, span is likely to be substantially lower, whether presentation is auditory or visual. This is assumed to occur because the articulation of an irrelevant item dominates the articulatory control process, hence preventing it from being used either to maintain material already in the phonological store, or convert visual material into a phonological code. It might furthermore have the additional drawback of creating an unattended speech effect by feeding the irrelevant spoken material into the phonological store.

It is important in interpreting the effects of articulatory suppression to consider another possible interpretation, that suppression impairs performance simply because it demands attention (e.g. Parkin, 1988). There are three arguments against this view:

1. Non-articulatory secondary tasks which might reasonably be regarded as similar in level of demand, such as tapping at the same rate as suppression, typically have little or no effect on STM performance (e.g. Baddeley, Lewis, & Vallar, 1984b).
2. Patient P.V., who does not appear to use the articulatory loop in STM tasks, is not impaired in memory performance by suppression (Vallar & Baddeley, 1984a).
3. The complex pattern of results to be described indicates that

suppression does not have a major general effect, but rather specifically affects phonological and articulatory coding (Baddeley et al., 1984b). It is, none the less, always wise in studies of articulatory suppression to include a tapping condition to control for any general attentional effects on performance.

The effect of articulatory suppression is fortunately very robust, and does not appear to be crucially dependent on the items uttered, with different laboratories tending to favor suppression based on different utterances, ranging from *bla bla bla* through *double double double* to over-learned sequences such as counting or reciting fragments of the alphabet. Developmental psychologists tend to use words they think will appeal to children such as *teddy bear teddy bear*, while one U.S. investigator uses *cola cola cola* which suggests some interesting advertising possibilities within this paradigm.

If we assume that articulatory suppression cuts out the process of subvocal rehearsal, then it ought to interact in predictable ways with some of the other variables we have described, as indeed it does. In the case of phonological similarity, articulatory suppression removes the effect when material is presented visually, presumably since it prevents the visual code from being converted by subvocalization into a phonological code that can be registered in the store. With auditory presentation, however, the phonological similarity effect remains, presumably because the spoken material has direct access to the phonological store without need of the articulatory control process (Baddeley et al. 1984b).

As with phonological similarity, the unattended speech effect should be disrupted by articulatory suppression, given that the material to be recalled is presented visually. If suppression prevents the subject from subvocally registering the material to be remembered in the phonological store, then memory will be based on some non-phonological store. Corruption of the phonological store by unattended speech should hence not affect performance. This is indeed what was found (Salamé & Baddeley, 1982). With auditory presentation however, recall of the items to be remembered will depend on the phonological store, and unattended speech should therefore impair performance, which it does (Hanley & Broadbent, 1987).

What effect should articulatory suppression have on the word-length effect? Since the effect depends directly on subvocal articulation, then articulatory suppression should abolish it, regardless of whether presentation is visual or auditory. If subjects are prevented from rehearsal, it should not matter whether the material is fast or slow to rehearse.

Initial results on this point seemed rather worrying, since Baddeley, Thomson, and Buchanan (1975b) found that articulatory suppression disrupted the word-length effect with visual, but not with auditory presentation. This result went against the predictions of the model which assumes word length to influence rehearsal rate but not storage. Further experimentation however, revealed a critical flaw in the initial experiment using auditory presentation. Articulatory suppression had occurred during presentation but not during recall. It appears that subjects were rapidly rehearsing the auditorily presented items before and during subsequent recall. When suppression is required during both presentation and recall, no significant word-length effect is found (Baddeley et al., 1984b).

A Summary of the Evidence

As explained earlier, the mode of theorizing in working memory has involved taking a relatively complex pattern of data and attempting to fit it into as simple a conceptual structure as possible. In the case of the articulatory loop it has involved a phonological store which will hold information for about two seconds, together with an articulatory control process. This process refreshes items in the store by means of subvocal rehearsal; it is also capable of subvocally recoding printed material, hence registering it in the phonological store.

The phonological similarity effect occurs because the store is based on phonological coding. Similar items have easily confusable codes, leading to impaired performance. Articulatory suppression prevents visual material being recoded, but has no effect on the coding of auditory material, which hence continues to show a similarity effect.

The unattended speech effect is assumed to occur because spoken material gains obligatory access to the phonological store, which is corrupted by the presence of irrelevant material. Suppression prevents the unattended speech effect occurring with visually presented material, since it stops such material being fed into the phonological store. Whether the store is or is not corrupted therefore becomes irrelevant.

Finally, the word-length effect is removed by articulatory suppression, whether material is presented auditorily or visually. Since the word-length effect is dependent on the operation of the articulatory control process, when this system is pre-empted by suppression, word length ceases to be an important variable.

Chunking and the Phonological Loop

The essence of the phonological loop hypothesis is that memory span will depend on rate of rehearsal, being approximately equivalent to the number of items that can be spoken in two seconds. Hence number of items recalled will be a function of how long they take to articulate. Where then does this leave Miller's magic number seven, which suggests that memory span will reflect a constant number of chunks, regardless of the characteristics of those chunks? This question was addressed directly by Herbert Simon who in addition to a distinguished range of other activities in cognitive science had adopted and developed the chunking hypothesis as an important feature of human cognition (Simon, 1974). He and a group of Chinese colleagues took advantage of some of the features of the Chinese language to explore the articulatory loop and chunking hypotheses in more detail (Zhang & Simon, 1985; Yu, Zhang, Jing, Peng, Zhang, & Simon 1985).

In one study, Zhang and Simon directly pitted the two hypotheses against each other, using three types of material which were equivalent in each comprising familiar chunks, but differed in ease and speed of pronunciation. One set of material comprised radicals, the complex components which go to make Chinese characters and words. There are about 200 radicals in the Chinese language, and they are likely to be highly familiar to their Chinese subjects since they are, for example, used for indexing dictionaries. They do not, however, have commonly used oral names. The second set of material used comprised Chinese characters, each of which was made up from two radicals, with each having definite single-syllable pronunciation. The third set of material comprised Chinese words, each comprising two characters and having two syllables in their pronunciation. The different types of material are shown in Figure 4.7.

A simple chunking hypothesis would predict no difference between the three sets of material, since in each case the constituent items comprised familiar chunks. The phonological loop hypothesis on the other hand would predict very poor performance for the radicals which have no familiar name, with somewhat better performance for the disyllabic words, and best performance for the monosyllabic characters. As Table 4.2 shows, it is exactly what was observed. Further evidence for the phonological loop interpretation came from intrusion errors, of which almost half were homophones, items that have the correct pronunciation but are written differently.

FIGURE 4.7

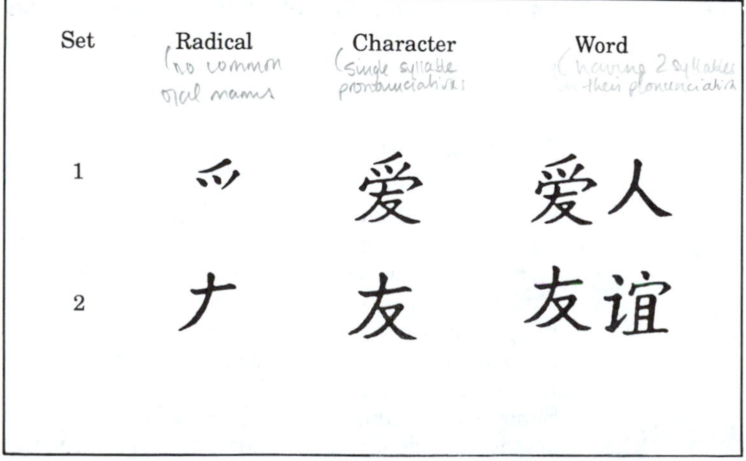

Chinese radicals, characters and words used by Zhang and Simon (1985). Reprinted by permission of the Psychonomics Society Inc.

Set	Radical	Character	Word
1	爫	爱	爱人
2	广	友	友谊

TABLE 4.2

Mean STM Span for Three Types of Chinese Symbol Sequences (Data from Zhang & Simon, 1985)

Type of Item	Mean	s.d
Radicals	2.71	0.52
Characters	6.38	1.08
Words	3.83	0.75

Chinese has a very large number of homophones, and since the pictographic script is not based on the sound of the items depicted, such homophones are typically written quite differently. Zhang and Simon took advantage of this in order to explore further the role of phonological coding in a second study. This used the material shown in Figure 4.8 which comprises nine characters, all of which are pronounced *gong* with high tone in Chinese. Memory span for

FIGURE 4.8

Set of homophonic characters, all pronounced "gong", with high tone, but all with different appearance and meaning, used by Zhang and Simon (1985) to study the role of phonological similarity in immediate memory. Reprinted by permission of the Psychonomics Society Inc.

Chinese character	English translation
工	work, labour
弓	bow
公	public, common
功	meritorious service
攻	attack, accuse
供	supply
宫	palace, temple
恭	respectful
龔	a surname

these items was tested together with memory span for the nonpronounceable radicals described previously. Span for the radicals was 3.00 and for the homophones 2.83, in contrast to the span for characters in the previous study of 6.38. This is of course a very low level of performance, and indeed one subject complained "It seems that my memory doesn't work today". Presumably the items recalled were being remembered on the basis of either a visual or semantic code.

In a third experiment, Zhang and Simon explored memory span for items varying in number of syllables, testing memory for characters, comprising one syllable, words of two syllables and idioms comprising four syllables. Table 4.3 shows the results they obtained measured in terms both of mean number of chunks recalled and mean number of syllables. It is clear that while span does not represent a constant number of chunks, it does not either represent a constant number of syllables. Syllables within chunks tend to lead to faster articulation than do syllables that comprise separate chunks.

Zhang and Simon therefore propose that span is determined by rehearsal rate, but that this in turn depends on three factors, the interval of time (a milliseconds) required to bring each chunk into the articulatory mechanism, an interval of time (b milliseconds) required to articulate each syllable in the chunk beyond the first, and S the average size of a chunk in syllables. This yields an equation that can be used to express either T, the duration of the underlying storage parameter, or C, the STM capacity measured in chunks. They are

$$T = C[a+b(S-1)], \quad \text{or} \tag{1}$$
$$C = T/[a+b(S-1)]. \tag{2}$$

Zhang and Simon show that these equations fit a wide range of experimental results collected in Chinese, and also the data on word length and memory in English reported by Baddeley, Thomson, and Buchanan (1975).

In general, these experiments, taking advantage of some of the

TABLE 4.3			
Mean STM Span for Three Kinds of Chinese Symbol Sequences. (Data from Zhang & Simon, 1985)			
Type of Item or Chunk	No. of Syllables per Chunk	Mean Recall	
		Chunks	Syllables
Characters	1	6.58	6.58
Words	2	4.58	9.16
Idioms	4	3.00	12.00

intriguing characteristics of the Chinese language, produce results that support the phonological loop hypothesis. At the same time they suggest ways in which the more general concept of chunking in STM might be incorporated into the model.

Patients with Impaired STM

A bonus from the phonological loop model is that it offers a straightforward explanation of the memory deficit shown by STM patients. If one assumes a deficit in the phonological store, then this is able to explain both their impaired memory span and their comparatively normal cognitive performance on other tasks such as long-term verbal learning, where one might expect semantic coding to be more important than phonological. One Italian patient, P.V., with a very pure and specific deficit in auditory STM performance was tested with a view to exploring the extent to which her deficit could be explained within the working memory framework (Vallar & Baddeley, 1984a). With the exception of her STM deficit, P.V. appeared to be intellectually entirely normal, with a high level of verbal and performance I.Q., excellent long-term memory, and no apparent problems of speech or language (Basso et al. 1982). P.V.'s immediate memory was influenced by phonological similarity with auditory, but not with visual presentation. She showed no evidence of a word-length effect, and no effect of articulatory suppression. Her speech output appeared to be quite normal as measured both by studying the distribution of pauses in normal speech, and as measured by her capacity to recite the alphabet or count as rapidly as normal control patients of equivalent age and background.

We interpreted her deficit as an impairment though not complete disruption of the phonological storage component of the articulatory loop. We assumed that disruption was not complete since her performance with auditory presentation, though impaired was not completely disrupted, and did show clear evidence of a phonological similarity effect. We assume, however, that she does not attempt to feed visually presented material into the phonological store by the process of articulation. The evidence for this assumption comes from the absence of a phonological similarity effect with visual presentation, the lack of a word-length effect and the absence of any effect of articulatory suppression on performance. We assume that her STM deficit does not stem from an articulatory deficit since her capacity for overt articulation appears to be normal, and since she appeared to be able to make phonological judgments about printed words, deciding for example whether the names of two pictured objects rhymed or not, or where the stress on a particular printed word occurred. We assume that she does not use the articulatory rehearsal process simply because it would feed information into a grossly defective store which would do little to enhance performance.

Dysarthria and the Nature of Inner Speech

To what extent does this process of rehearsal need to involve the overt activity of the speech musculature, and to what extent can it be maintained at some higher more programmatic level? We certainly do not need to rehearse out loud, although it is possible that silent rehearsal still involves some subvocal activity that can perhaps be detected by electromyography, a process whereby electrical activity in the underlying speech musculature can be monitored. A number of studies have attempted to explore the role of subvocal speech in reading using this approach (e.g. Hardyk & Petrinovich, 1970), although the interpretation of the results of such studies remains open to question. Failure to detect any activity could for instance simply reflect insufficient sensitivity in the equipment. Furthermore, if effects are detected, they could reflect a general overflow of activation, rather than an essential feature of subvocal rehearsal. Consequently, electromyography has not featured prominently in recent discussions on the role of inner speech in memory.

An alternative is to examine the memory performance of subjects who are *dysarthric*, that is patients who have lost the capacity to control their articulatory muscles as a result of brain damage. Dysarthria typically results from damage to the brain stem or peripheral aspects of speech control, and as such should be distinguished from *dyspraxia*, problems at the level of setting up and running the motor programs necessary for speech, and *dysphasia*, which would typically involve more central disruption of the capacity to produce and/or comprehend language.

A colleague, Barbara Wilson, and I were able to study the memory performance of a group of dysarthric patients, with relatively severe but peripheral disruption to their capacity to generate speech, and one anarthric patient who was totally unable to make any sound other than an inspiratory groan. This latter patient completely lacked the capacity to articulate, and yet his language capabilities were unimpaired, as indicated both by his comprehension performance, and by his language production using a simple keyboard device.

We tested this patient's memory and found first of all that he had a comparatively normal digit span of six items. Furthermore, he showed a very clear phonological similarity effect, for both visual and auditory material, suggesting that he was using the phonological store in a normal way. We tested for the presence of subvocal rehearsal by means of the word-length effect, and found this to be quite normal. Finally, we assessed his capacity for making phonological judgments on printed material, requiring him to decide whether two items would sound the same if spoken. We tested both words (e.g. *key-quay*) and non-words (e.g. *frelame-phrelaim*), and also asked the patient to judge whether non-words were homophonous with real words (e.g. *oshun*). He was able to perform all of these tasks accurately and with no apparent difficulty. In short then, our dysarthric patient appears to have normal inner speech. Broadly similar results have subsequently been obtained by a range of other studies and are reviewed by Logie, Cubelli, Della Sala, Alberoni, and Nichelli (in press).

We interpreted our results as suggesting that the articulatory control process does not depend upon peripheral speech musculature for its operation. Presumably some form of motor program can be run at a central level, despite the absence of peripheral feedback. Our subjects had all previously had normal language and speech, raising the further question of whether the feedback from overt speech is necessary for a child to learn to use subvocal rehearsal and the articulatory loop. Some recent research by Biship and Robson (1989) suggests that it is not. They studied the memory performance of children who had been anarthric since birth, and who had never in their lives been able to articulate speech. Somewhat surprisingly, these children appeared to have normal functioning of the articulatory loop, with relatively normal memory spans and clear evidence of the effects of phonological similarity and of word-length.

It appears then that inner speech is not dependent on outer speech for either its development or its operation. This suggests that the term "phonological loop" is perhaps preferable to "articulatory loop", since the latter seems to imply a direct involvement of articulation.

The fact that inner speech develops under the apparently inhospitable conditions of congential anarthria is intriguing, and suggests that it might perhaps play a rather important role in the development of cognition. The question of what this might be will be discussed next.

WHAT USE IS THE PHONOLOGICAL LOOP?

We have just described in some detail one hypothetical component of one aspect of memory. The simple model presented may be able to give a reasonably economical account of a relatively wide range of laboratory data, but it leaves open the rather crucial question of what function if any is served by this system. Is the articulatory loop anything more than a way of linking together a number of laboratory phenomena? Is it, to use my colleague Jim Reason's blunt but colorful phrase, anything more than "a pimple on the face of cognition"?

Learning to Read

I believe it is, for a number of reasons. First of all, the evidence seems to suggest that the articulatory loop, or some similar system plays an important role in learning to read (Jorm, 1983). If you select a group of children who have a specific problem in learning to read, despite normal intelligence and supportive background, one of the most striking features they have in common is an impaired memory span (Miles & Ellis, 1981). They also, however, tend to perform rather poorly on tasks that do not directly test memory. Such tasks, typically involve phonological manipulation, or require phonological awareness; examples include judging whether words rhyme, or taking a word and deleting the first phoneme before repeating it (e.g. when the subjects hear *spin* they must respond *pin*). Consequently there is some controversy as to whether the deficit underlying the normal development of reading is one of memory, phonological awareness or some third common underlying factor (Bradley & Bryant, 1983; Morais, Allegria, & Content, 1987).

There is, furthermore, clear evidence for a reciprocal relationship between these factors and learning to read, such that learning to read enhances performance on memory span and phonological awareness, which in turn are associated with improvements in reading (Ellis, 1988). Adults who are illiterate as a result of lack of opportunity tend to show impaired phonological awareness, and to improve as they learn to read (Morais et al., 1987). Which comes first then, phonological memory, phonological awareness, or reading?

In the normal development of reading, there is little doubt that these factors interact, but it seems likely that in the case of a minority of children at least, initial reading is handicapped by some form of phonological deficit, a deficit that can be detected before the child has begun to learn to read (Mann & Liberman, 1984). It seems likely that this deficit is related to the development of the phonological loop system, although at present we know too little about it to draw any firm conclusions.

Language Comprehension

Suppose, however, that we do concede that the articulatory loop is useful in learning to read, from an evolutionary viewpoint, reading surely developed too recently for this to offer a plausible explanation as to why an articulatory loop system should have evolved. A more plausible explanation might be to suggest that the phonological loop developed in the process of the evolution of speech production and comprehension. What is the evidence that the phonological store plays a role in speech comprehension? Surely, if this were the case then our STM patients should be unable to understand normal conversation, and hence should be much more handicapped than they in fact are. This depends crucially on exactly what the role of the phonological loop system is in speech comprehension.

One hypothesis proposed by Clark and Clark (1977) suggests that sentence comprehension demands that the whole of each sentence should be held in some temporary store while it is processed grammatically. This hypothesis implies that a whole sentence must be stored before it can be understood. Since our

Italian patient P.V. can understand sentences that are far longer than she can remember, we can reject this view (Vallar & Baddeley, 1984b).

In stark contrast to the extreme dependence of comprehension on STM suggested by Clark and Clark (1977) is the claim by Butterworth, Campbell, and Howard (1986) that language comprehension is quite independent of STM capacity. They studied the performance of a student who had apparently always had a reduced memory span (four digits). They noted that the reading performance of this particular student was highly atypical, resembling the pattern normally categorized as phonological dyslexia. She could read words relatively normally, but had great difficulty in reading even simple non-words such as *JEX* or *FRIMBLE*. It appeared that this subject had indeed had difficulty in learning to read, and appeared to have learnt almost exclusively by a look-say method, allowing her to identify words that had been encountered and learned before, but giving her no phonological skills for pronouncing new and unfamiliar letter sequences (Campbell & Butterworth, 1985). As such, this case gives further support for the idea that normal STS is necessary for learning to read in the usual way, but gives little comfort for the view that auditory *comprehension* is dependent on normal span, since she appeared to have no difficulty in coping with life as a student on a relatively demanding course.

Interpreting these findings is, however, far from simple. The observed span of four digits was low but not as low as most STM patients. Moreover, there is some evidence to suggest that such cases of developmental phonological processing impairment may show unusual neuro-anatomical features that suggest that generalization to the general population may be unwise. Thirdly, there was evidence to suggest that this student was using somewhat different language comprehension strategies from other subjects. For example, comprehension was not impaired by articulatory suppression, making her performance under these conditions better than that of normal students. These issues are discussed further by Howard and Butterworth (in press) and by Vallar and Baddeley (in press).

Giuseppe Vallar and I studied the comprehension of spoken and written discourse by our STM patient, P.V. Although her digit span is only two, she has a sentence span of about six words, and is able to understand simple sentences such as *"Slippers are sold in pairs"* or *"Archbishops are made in factories"*, and answer them rapidly and accurately. Even when the sentences are made longer by adding verbiage, such as *"It is commonly believed and with justification that slippers belong to the category of objects that are bought in pairs"*, she has no difficulty. She does, however, have problems with long sentences where retention and appropriate processing of word order is essential for their correct comprehension. For example, *"The world divides the equator into two halves, the northern and the southern"* or *"It is fortunate that most rivers are able to be crossed by bridges that are strong enough for cars"*. On these, she performs at chance, whether she is reading them or hearing them. However, when they are reduced in length (*"The world divides the equator"*; *"Rivers are crossed by bridges"*), performance returns to normal (Vallar & Baddeley, 1984b).

Subsequent more extensive investigation of P.V.'s comprehension reinforces the conclusion that she is able to comprehend normally, provided the material does not require the verbatim retention of information over many intervening words; when it does, her performance deteriorates (Vallar & Baddeley, 1987).

These results suggest that the phonological input store does play a role in comprehension, but possibly only for particularly complex or demanding material. One interpretation therefore, is that it merely acts as a supplementary back-up that plays a secondary role in comprehension, but is not of primary importance. A second possibility, however, is that P.V. is able to comprehend most incoming material reasonably adequately because her phonological store, though impaired, is by no means completely defunct. It may well be that an incoming sentence span of six words is enough to cope with most normal language, whereas a subject with no phonological store whatsoever might conceivably be totally incapable of comprehending speech. One way of exploring these possibilities is to look for a patient with an even lower sentence span than P.V. We were fortunate in locating such a patient, and obtaining his cooperation (Baddeley & Wilson, 1988a).

The patient in question, T.B., was a professional mathematician who reported memory problems following an attack of epilepsy. He was intellectually still functioning at a very high level, but had some long-term memory problems coupled with severe impairment in immediate memory performance, with a digit span of one to two items and a sentence span of three words. T.B. reported that he certainly did have problems in comprehension, saying that typically he could understand the beginning of a conversation, but after the first phrase or so, everything became jumbled. His performance on comprehension tests confirmed this. When given the simple sentences such as *"Bishops are made in factories"*, he could confirm or reject them rapidly and accurately. Once the sentences were made verbose by adding additional phrases, however, he had so much difficulty that he became distressed and we had to stop the test.

Using a series of shorter sentences we found the relationship between sentence length and probability of comprehension shown in Figure 4.9. However, as sentences become longer they also tend to become syntactically more complex; could grammatical complexity be the crucial variable?

We first tried to test this by using visual presentation, on the assumption that the printed word might help substitute for his failing memory. This appeared to be the case since his performance substantially improved, although in the case of long and complex

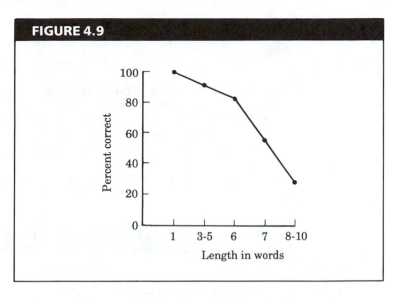

FIGURE 4.9

Probability of sentence comprehension by T.B., a patient with imparied STM, as a function of sentence length. The data are based on Bishops's TROG (test for reception of grammar). From Baddeley and Wilson (1988a).

sentences, this was at the expense of extremely slow performance. He would hunt to and fro through the sentence as if trying to perform some kind of verbal jigsaw puzzle, before eventually coming up with a response which was more likely to be correct than in the auditory condition, but was still far from perfect.

In a second test of grammatical complexity hypothesis, we began by selecting 24 six-word sentences which he was capable of verifying with almost perfect accuracy. We then added redundant verbiage in the form of adverbs and adjectives. For example the sentence *The boys pick the apples* would be changed to *The two boys pick the green apples from the tree*. Under these conditions, performance dropped to chance. Since the additional verbiage all involved syntactic and semantic constructs that we knew he could comprehend, it seems likely that the crucial factor that led to the drop in performance was the increased memory load.

We have spoken as though the sole factor of importance may have been sentence length. This is almost certainly not the case, since some sentences of a given length were more difficult than others. In general, these appeared to be sentences where memory load was greatest, a good example being self-embedded sentences of the kind *The boy the dog chases is big*. In general, the relationship between syntactic factors, semantic factors and imposed memory load is complex, and it has long proved difficult to separate the influence of these factors empirically (see Baddeley, 1976; Chapter 12). Our data from T.B., however, together with data from other STM patients (Vallar and Shallice, in press) does support the view that the phonological store plays a clear role in comprehension, although a comprehension deficit may only become obvious in some patients when tested with materials placing a particularly heavy load on phonological storage. A patient such as

T.B. whose sentence span is limited to three words however is likely to suffer from substantial problems in comprehending language.

Long-term Phonological Learning

What other role might the articulatory loop play in normal comprehension? One hint was given by the observation that children with developmental dyslexia also tend to have impaired vocabulary and to show difficulty in rote learning such as is involved in acquiring the multiplication tables, or the order of months in the year (Miles & Ellis, 1981). We decided therefore that it might be

(a) Paired associate learning of auditorily presented word- word pairs by P.V. and by matched control subjects. (b) Performance on word-nonword paired associate learning with auditory presentation; data from P.V. and matched control subjects. From Baddeley, Papagno, and Vallar (1988).

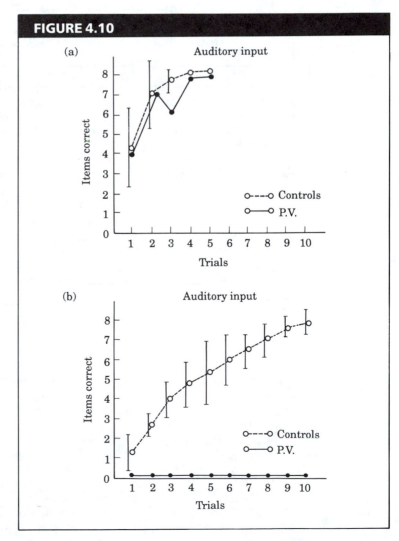

FIGURE 4.10

interesting to explore the capacity for learning novel phonological material in our patient P.V.

We knew that P.V. was good at learning lists of meaningful words, but knew nothing of her ability to learn unfamiliar words such as the vocabulary of a foreign language, for example. We therefore decided to try to teach her both pairs of familiar Italian words (her native language), and items of Italian-Russian vocabulary (Baddeley, Papagno, & Vallar, 1988). We found that with auditory presentation, her capacity to learn pairs of Italian words was well within the range of performance shown by controls of equivalent age and intelligence. Her performance on the auditory learning of Italian-Russian pairs on the other hand is shown in Figure 4.10a,b, from which it is clear that she completely fails to learn. When presentation was visual, performance improved somewhat, but was still well below that of control subjects. It appears then that a second function of the phonological loop system is in new phonological learning. If so, then perhaps it plays a crucial role, not only in second language learning, but also in a child's acquisition of his or her native tongue. We were fortunate in being able to explore this possibility in a study of language and memory development in young children that had already begun (Gathercole & Baddeley, 1989).

Acquiring a Vocabulary

A couple of years earlier, Susan Gathercole and I had begun to study a group of children who were classified as "language disordered". They had normal nonverbal intelligence, but delayed development of language skills, and we were interested in particular in their working memory performance. We found that although they were about two years behind their expected performance on reading, vocabulary and spelling, they were four years behind on one task, the simple repetition of nonwords varying in length and complexity. We interpreted this task as one making particularly heavy demands on the phonological loop, suggesting that a phonological loop deficit might be at the root of their other language problems (Gathercole and Baddeley, 1989).

We decided to investigate this task further, and in particular to see if it would allow us to predict which of a sample of 4–5 year-old normal children entering school and about to learn to read, would subsequently prove to have reading difficulties.

We therefore tested over 100 children before they had acquired any reading skills, planning to re-test them at yearly intervals. In addition to our nonword repetition task and measures of reading, we also tested nonverbal intelligence and vocabulary, using a test in which a word is spoken, and the child points to the appropriate picture. At the time of writing, the children have been tested twice. Not enough children have yet learned to read to allow the original question to be answered, but we were able to follow up our hypothesis about the role of the articulatory loop in vocabulary

TABLE 4.4

Correlations between Vocabulary Scores at Age 4 and other Variables

Measures	Correlation Coefficient	Simple Regression (% Variance)	Stepwise Regression (% Variance)
Chronological age	0.218	5[a]	5[a]
Nonverbal intelligence	0.388	15[b]	13[b]
Nonword repetition	0.525	27[b]	15[b]
Sound Mimicry	0.295	9[b]	0
Total	0.578	33[b]	–

[a]$P < 0.05$; [b]$P < 0.01$.
Source: Gathercole and Baddeley (1989)

development, by looking at the relationship between our nonword repetition test and vocabulary size.

Our results are shown in Table 4.4, which shows that on starting school there is a clear correlation ($r = 0.492$) between nonword repetition and vocabulary. The correlation remains when the effect of nonverbal intelligence is removed statistically. One year later the correlation remains high ($r = 0.572$), and remains statistically significant when the effect of vocabulary level on the previous test is removed, suggesting that the process underlying nonword repetition is continuing to be important for vocabulary learned during the first year at school.

These findings are clearly consistent with the view that the articulatory loop is central both to nonword repetition and to the acquisition of one's native language. However, it is important to remember that correlation does not necessarily mean causation. It is possible, for example, that both phonological STM and vocabulary learning are dependent on some third factor; phonological awareness, or the amount and richness of language that has already been learned, might be two possibilities. Indeed, such results make it clear that our understanding of the processes underlying the operation of the phonological loop is still at a very primitive stage. They do, however, suggest that they are of great potential importance.

Conclusion

We have discussed the phonological loop in some detail since it is the most extensively explored component of working memory. If this aspect of the enterprise fails, then it seems unlikely that it will succeed in the more complex problems of tackling the visuo-spatial sketchpad and the central executive.

How successful has the enterprise been then? It does seem to have provided a simple explanation of the abundant evidence suggesting that STM is in some sense a speech-based system. At the same time it clearly indicates that this is only one component of working memory. However, when looked at from a broader perspective, it appears that this component of working memory is potentially an important one for learning to speak and to read and for comprehending spoken discourse. As such, it is a system worth understanding.

How well do we understand it? At a qualitative level reasonably well, but in detail hardly at all. We know nothing about the nature of the store, its time characteristics, how information is read into it and retrieved from it, and how it relates to the processes involved in speech perception and production. We know relatively little about how it relates to phenomena and concepts based on techniques relying on reaction time measures, an area that is well reviewed by Monsell (1984). At the moment, I am not at all convinced that we even have an adequate language for developing a detailed model, although I have some hopes that the parallel distributed processing models described in Chapter 14 may offer one way of tackling the problem of modeling the phonological loop.

OVERVIEW

The chapter began by discussing a series of experiments concerned with the question of whether STS acts as a working memory, playing an important part in cognitive activities such as learning, comprehending and reasoning. The experiments used a dual-task approach in which working memory capacity was systematically absorbed by requiring subjects to hold sequences of digits in STS at the same time as they performed tasks involving reasoning, learning or comprehending. While clear impairment was found on these tasks, the extent and nature of the disruption was not as great as would be expected on the assumption that the same unitary system both holds digits and acts as a working memory. On the basis of these results, a multi-component working memory was proposed, with a controlling central executive system and a number of subsidiary slave systems.

One of these, the articulatory or phonological loop is described in more detail. It is assumed to comprise a short-term phonological store assisted by a control process based on articulatory rehearsal. It is shown that this simple model can account for a range of factors that influence memory span, including acoustic similarity, word length, unattended speech and articulatory suppression.

We finally considered the question of the role played by the phonological loop in everyday cognition. Evidence is presented to suggest that it plays an important role in learning to read, in the comprehension of language and in the acquisition of vocabulary; in all these areas, the evidence comes both from the development of language in normal children, and from the performance of patients suffering from impaired STM following brain damage.

Chapter Five

VISUAL IMAGERY AND THE VISUO-SPATIAL SKETCHPAD

The second major slave system assumed by the working memory model is the visuo-spatial scratchpad or sketchpad, a system assumed to be responsible for setting up and manipulating visuo-spatial images. In the last decade there has been a great deal of research on the general topic of imagery, much of it concerned with the question of how similar the processes of imagery are to those of visual perception. While I am far from convinced that this is a fruitful or indeed answerable question, the search has certainly produced some interesting phenomena, and these will be described briefly before considering the question of whether the dual-task methodology used in other areas of working memory can fruitfully be applied to the analysis of visual imagery.

VISUAL MEMORY

Visual imagery was one of the first topics to capture the interest of experimental psychologists in the last century. For example, Galton (1883) carried out his well-known survey of the vividness of visual imagery in which he asked a number of eminent people to attempt to recollect their breakfast table, and describe what they saw in their mind's eye. He observed very substantial differences in reported vividness, from some who imaged the scene almost as clearly as if they were seeing it, to others who stoutly denied having any imagery whatsoever. Imagery continued to play an important part during the period when introspection was regarded as the main method of psychological research, but suffered severely during the subsequent period of behaviorism, when inner mental processes were not regarded as a fit topic for scientific study.

Language and Learning

During the 1960s, imagery and imageability gradually began to make its way back into the psychological laboratory. Much of its increase in popularity was attributable to the work of Allen Paivio (1969). He used standard techniques of the verbal learning laboratory, and demonstrated that one of the best predictors of how easy a word would be to remember was given by the extent to which subjects reported that it gave rise to an image. At the same time, people began to explore the use of the visual imagery mnemonics that for centuries had been known to enhance learning and memory. They found that a very good way of learning to associate a pair of words was to form an image of each and imagine the two interacting (e.g. Bugelski, Kidd, & Segmen, 1968). Whether images "existed" or not, instructions to use them appeared to have a marked effect on learning.

In due course, this led to more analytic interest in the nature of imagery. Shepard and Chipman (1970) used newly developed scaling techniques to examine the similarity between judgments made about the relative shapes of U.S. states by subjects on the basis of their imagery, with judgments based on maps of the states when presented visually. They found a close relationship indicating what they term a "second order isomorphism" between imagery and perception.

Analogue or Propositional

One issue that has concerned imagery theorists is that of whether the underlying process is *analogue* or *propositional*. An analogue system is one in which the mode of representation is continuous; the hands of a traditional clock represent time in an analogue way. On the other hand, a digital clock that represents time in a series of discrete steps would offer a propositional representation. The programs that run on digital computers are basically propositional, whereas a servo-system whereby a missile is guided by a joystick that controls a variable voltage would be an example of an analogue system. In the case of visual imagery, analogue theorists such as Kosslyn (1980) and Shepard (Shepard & Metzler, 1971) argue that the imagery process itself is based on an analogue or continuous process. Propositional theorists such as Pylyshyn (1981) argue that imagery is an epiphenomenon, an irrelevant accompaniment to a set of underlying processes that operate upon spatial information that is stored in LTM in terms of discrete propositions.

Mental Rotation

Shepard and Metzler (1971) carried out an elegant experiment that has featured strongly in the controversy of whether or not imagery is an analogue process. Subjects were presented with two-dimensional representations of a pair of three-dimensional shapes (see Figure 5.1). The two shapes could be either identical, or one could be the mirror-image of the other, and the subject was instructed to decide which. Shepard and Metzler observed that the time it took a subject to come to this decision depended on the

FIGURE 5.1

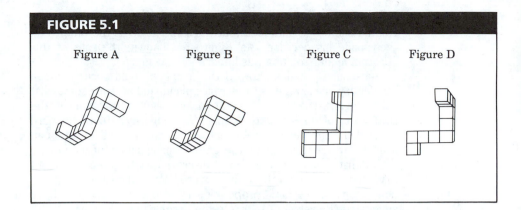

Figure A
Figure B
Figure C
Figure D

Cube clusters used in the study of mental rotation. From Shepard and Metzler (1971).

(analogue process?)

FIGURE 5.2

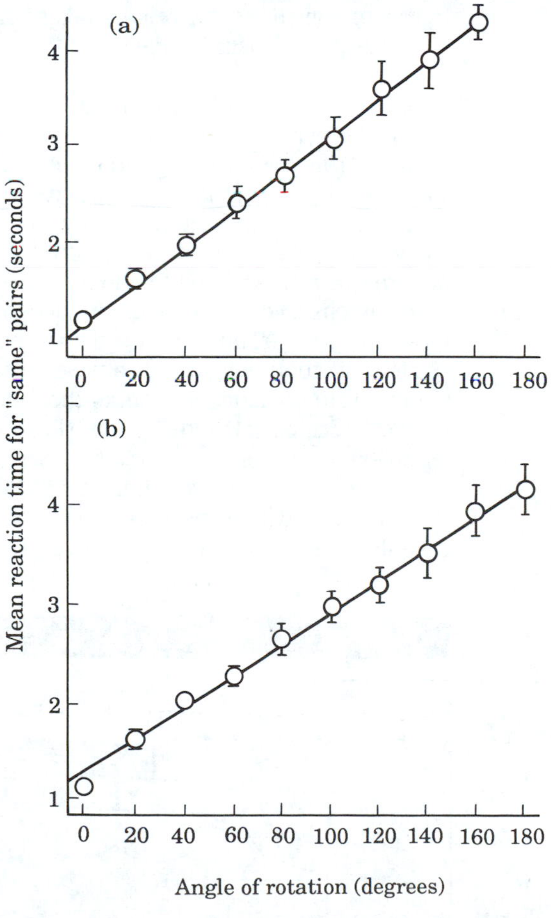

(a)
(b)
Mean reaction time for "same" pairs (seconds)
1
2
3
4
0 20 40 60 80 100 120 140 160 180
Angle of rotation (degrees)

Mean time to decide whether two cube clusters are identical, (a) in the picture plane and (b) in depth. From Shepard and Metzler (1971). Copyright 1971 by the American Association for the Advancement of Science.

angular relationship between the two, just as if the subject mentally rotated one shape until it was at the same angle as the other, and then made his decision. As Figure 5.2 shows, the rate of this apparent mental rotation was linear.

Subsequent studies showed that rotation could occur through the depth plane as well as the surface plane, and perhaps somewhat surprisingly, that rate of rotation was not a function of the complexity of the stimulus (Cooper & Podgorny, 1976). Shepard concluded from these studies that visual imagery was based on an analogue medium, involving the gradual manipulation of the image, rather than reflecting a series of discrete quantal jumps as might have been expected if the system were based on a series of all-or-none steps, as certain "propositional" accounts of imagery have suggested (Pylyshyn, 1973). On the other hand, Pylyshyn (1979) found that complexity *did* influence speed of rotation when the subject's task was to judge whether a rotated figure comprised a part of a complex initial stimulus, rather than make a judgment of whether the comparison item was a mirror-image of the stimulus. Pylyshyn argued that his results favored a propositional rather than analogue view of visual imagery.

Scanning with the Mind's Eye
A broadly analogue interpretation of imagery was proposed by Kosslyn (1980) following a whole range of studies in which subjects were required to read off information from, or make decisions about mental images. In one study, for example, the subject was shown a picture of a boat (see Figure 5.3). Having examined it, the picture was removed and the subject was asked questions about it. Kosslyn observed that when a question about the bows was followed by a question about a distant part of the boat such as the rudder, it took longer to answer than a question about an intermediate component such as the funnel, as if the subject were physically scanning the image, with longer scans taking more time.

An extensive series of studies showed that the time to scan from one part of an image to another was a function of distance, an effect that operated within the depth plane as well as the picture plane (Kosslyn, 1980). Baum and Jonides (1979) showed that a similar

Line drawing of the type used by Kosslyn to study rate of scanning of mental imagery (see text for details).

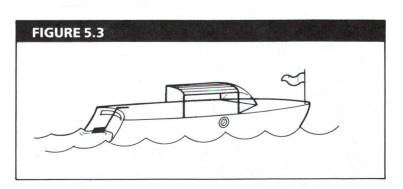

FIGURE 5.3

effect occurs in geographical mental representations; they asked their subjects to judge the distance between locations on a familiar university campus, and found that the further apart the locations, the longer the judgment took. When a barrier occurs between two objects, the judged distance tends to be greater (Kosslyn, Pick, & Fariello, 1974), while distances within town centers, which tend to contain many familiar locations, are judged as further than distances in the suburbs (Byrne, 1979). Thorndyke (1981) showed that a similar effect occurs when subjects are taught fictitious maps, rather than learning from real places, with the estimated distance between two locations increasing with the number of intervening places. He found a similar though smaller effect when the subjects were reading the map rather than remembering it, again suggesting similarities between perception and visual imagery.

Kosslyn and his colleagues demonstrated many other similarities between the scanning of mental images and the processes of perception. For example, when subjects were instructed to imagine walking towards an object, they reported that it expanded and increasingly filled their "visual" field. A scaling effect also occurred; in one study, subjects were asked to imagine a rabbit by the side of either a mouse or an elephant, and then were asked a question about the rabbit's eye. Responses were quicker when the rabbit was imaged beside the mouse, presumably because the eye was a larger and more salient feature of the overall scene than when it was dwarfed by the elephant.

Is Imaging just the Seeing?

Should one conclude then that visual imagery is just like vision? This would almost certainly be a grossly over-simplified view. Indeed, Pylyshyn (1981) argues that there is no reason whatsoever to assume an analogical system on the basis of this evidence, since it can equally well be handled by a model based on separate propositions. He explains the Kosslyn effects as based on tacit knowledge of the world. Subjects take their instruction as one of attempting to produce an internal simulation of vision, and as a result of many years of seeing the world, can reproduce the central characteristics of visual experience. A good example of the effects of tacit knowledge on imagery performance is provided by Intons-Peterson and Roskos-Ewoldsen (1988) who found that their subjects took longer to imagine traversing a familiar route when told they were carrying a cannonball than when told they were carrying a balloon.

Ingenious support for the view that images are not like percepts is provided in a study by Hinton and Parsons (1981). They instructed their subjects to imagine picking up a cube and holding it such that one corner is vertically above the other. They then asked the subjects about the location of the other four corners they are not holding. (Try it yourself, and say where the four corners will be.)

Most subjects report that the four corners lie along a horizontal plane corresponding to the "equator" of the cube. In fact, they form a zig-zag or crown-like structure. Hinton and Parsons suggest that we do not mentally rotate the cube, but rather reconstruct it on the basis of our knowledge of the transformations. In this particular case, the transformations are rather complex and we settle for an incorrect approximation.

In general, the type of cognitive internal psychophysics favored by the studies of Shepard and of Kosslyn, although producing some interesting phenomena, are difficult to interpret. In particular, the question of the extent to which subjects may be responding to experimenter bias raises difficulties. Intons-Peterson (1983) has shown that this can have at least a quantitative effect on subjects' report in this type of task. Other experimenters have also had difficulty replicating some of the more striking effects (e.g. Banks, 1981).

Even if these problems can be avoided, it remains difficult to know just how to interpret the similarities between a subject's report on imagery and normal perception. In so far as imagery is representing in some way an analogical visual representation, then it is likely to attempt to represent these features, and to do so more or less successfully. So far, I would suggest that it tells us relatively little about how the system works, although it does of course give a rich database which can in due course be modeled in more or less detail (see Kosslyn, 1980).

IMAGERY AND WORKING MEMORY

Visual Disruption of Imaging

The approaches of Shepard and of Kosslyn are essentially modeled on the psychophysical technique developed for the study of perception, and they produce results that are analogous to those obtained when the same techniques are applied to visual stimuli. In the next section, I will describe an attempt to tackle a similar problem based on dual-task methods developed for the study of working memory and attention. The aim here is to analyze the processes underlying the use of imagery by seeing what kind of activity will interfere with tasks that are known to rely on imagery.

Some of the pioneering work in this area was done by the Canadian psychologist Lee Brooks. In one study (Brooks, 1967), he devised a task based on STM in which a subject was induced to encode material either verbally or in terms of a visual image. The task involved presenting the subject with a 4 × 4 matrix, and denoting one of the squares as the starting square. Subjects were then required to repeat back sequences of sentences of the following kind:

In the starting square put a 1.
In the next square to the right put a 2.
In the next square beneath put a 3.

Example of stimulus material developed by Brooks and used in experiments on the visuo-spatial sketchpad. From Brooks (1967). Copyright (1967) The Experimental Psychology Society.

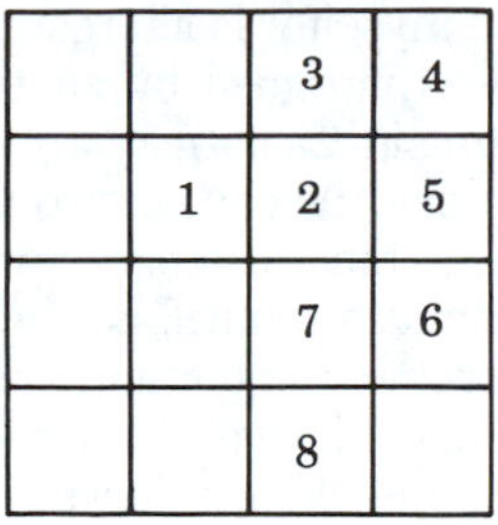

FIGURE 5.4

		3	4
1	2	5	
		7	6
		8	

Spatial material

In the starting square put a 1.
In the next square to the *right* put a 2.
In the next square *up* put a 3.
In the next square to the *right* put a 4.
In the next square *down* put a 5.
In the next square *down* put a 6.
In the next square to the *left* put a 7.
In the next square *down* put an 8.

Nonsense material

In the starting square put a 1.
In the next square to the *quick* put a 2.
In the next square to the *good* put a 3.
In the next square to the *quick* put a 4.
In the next square to the *bad* put a 5.
In the next square to the *bad* put a 6.
In the next square to the *slow* put a 7.
In the next square to the *bad* put an 8.

In the next square beneath put a 4.
In the next square beneath put a 5.
In the next square to the left put a 6.
In the next square to the left put a 7.
In the next square up put an 8.

Subjects almost invariably encode such sequences in terms of an imaged path through the matrix. In order to encourage subjects to abandon the imagery strategy and rely on rote verbal rehearsal, Brooks simply replaced the polar adjectives *up-down* and *left-right* with the non-spatial polar adjectives *good-bad* and *weak-strong*. Under the verbal or non-spatial condition a subject might therefore receive a sequence of sentences such as the following:

In the starting square put a 1.
In the next square to the good put a 2.
In the next square to the strong put a 3.
In the next square to the good put a 4.
In the next square to the good put a 5.
In the next square to the strong put a 6.

Typically, subjects could manage to recall eight of the spatial instructions, but only six of the verbal. Brooks then compared the effect of presenting the instructions auditorily and visually, finding that for the spatial task, auditory presentation was best, while for the verbal task, visual presentation was preferable. He suggested that this reflected the fact that the spatial sentences are remembered by means of visual imagery which uses some of the same processing apparatus as visual perception, while the non-spatial sentences rely on verbal coding, which tends to use systems that are also used in auditory perception.

I myself was interested in the role of visual imagery in memory. I was intrigued by an experience that occurred during a period spent in California, when I became very interested in American football. On one occasion I was driving down the freeway and at the same time listening to a radio broadcast of a football game. American football is of course a game in which spatial location is extremely important, and I found that as I set up my rich and complex image of the football field, my car began to weave from side-to-side. I rapidly switched to music and comparative safety.

Back in Britain I decided to explore this effect more systematically, combining the matrix task devised by Brooks with performance on the pursuit rotor, a traditional laboratory tracking task in which the subject is required to keep a stylus in contact with a spot of light that follows a circular track. Difficulty can be varied by changing speed of rotation, and performance measured by percentage of time on target.

We required our subjects to perform both of the Brooks spatial and verbal matrix tasks alone, and in combination with pursuit tracking (Baddeley, Grant, Wight, & Thomson, 1975a). Our results are shown in Figure 5.5, from which it is clear that tracking seriously disrupted the imagery task, but not its verbal equivalent. Subsequent studies have shown that other concurrent spatial tasks

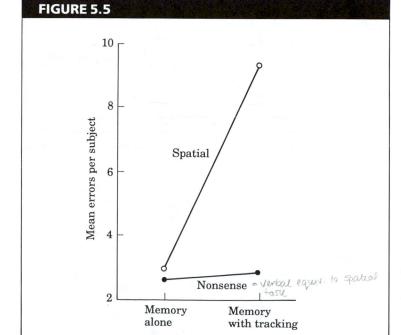

FIGURE 5.5

The influence of concurrent tracking on memory span for visualizable and nonvisualizable sequences. From Baddeley et al. (1975a).

have a similar effect on the suppression of visual imagery. For example, requiring the subject to press the keys of a pocket calculator located out of sight in a systematic spatial sequence is sufficient to disrupt imagery (Moar, 1978).

Is Imagery Visual or Spatial?

We have so far operated on the assumption that the imagery was visual in nature. It could however equally well be a spatial system concerned with location, regardless of whether information on location is based on vision, or some other modality such as hearing or touch. This distinction is perhaps made most simply by describing our next experiment. We again used the Brooks matrix task, this time combining it with a task that was either visual but not spatial, or spatial but not visual. Our visual task involved judging the brightness of a large screen that was illuminated by a slide projector containing slides that were either "bright", covered by one layer of tracing paper, or "dim" (two layers).

Our spatial non-visual condition involved an auditory tracking task that acquired the nickname of "The Pit and the Pendulum Test". The subject was seated in front of a pendulum suspended from the ceiling of a dimly lit room. The bob of the pendulum contained a sound source and a photocell. The subject was given a flashlight and shown that when the light was on the bob, the emitted sound changed. The pendulum was then set swinging, the subject blindfolded and instructed to attempt to keep the flashlight on the pendulum. He could hear where the pendulum was, and tell from the sound whether or not he was on target. It was then, a task that had a heavy spatial component, but no peripheral visual involvement, since the subject was blindfolded.

If the Brooks imagery task is primarily visual, then we might expect it to be most disrupted by the brightness judgment, whereas if it is spatial, then we would expect a greater disruption from the auditory tracking task. The results were clear in showing that the spatial matrix task was most clearly disrupted by tracking, while the opposite pattern held for the verbal matrix. This result suggested therefore that the imagery system responsible for the Brooks task is one based on spatial localization rather than visual characteristics such as brightness (Baddeley & Lieberman, 1980).

Other evidence suggesting that imagery does not necessarily depend on peripheral visual coding comes from a whole series of experiments on visual imagery in the blind. For example, Carpenter and Eisenberg (1978) have shown a tactile equivalent of the Shepard and Metzler mental rotation task in blind subjects, while Kerr (1973) has shown that blind subjects are quite capable of taking advantage of visual imagery mnemonics, and of showing a number of the visual scanning effects of the type explored by Kosslyn and his colleagues.

While our study certainly showed that the Brooks matrix task appears to be more susceptible to spatial disruption than disruption by brightness judgment, it does not of course necessarily follow that this will hold for all visuo-spatial imagery tasks or for that matter all concurrent visuo-spatial disrupting tasks. Indeed, as we shall see later, there is good evidence to suggest that visual imagery is not necessarily purely spatial or purely visual, but may well be both.

Visual Imagery and Verbal Learning

As we mentioned earlier, the revival of interest in visual imagery in the 1960s stemmed largely from evidence that both the judged imageability of words, and instructions to use imagery had powerful effects on the rate of learning lists of words, or for that matter passages of prose. Can our dual-task techniques throw any light on these powerful effects? It seems possible, for example, that rated imageability has its effect through the capacity of highly imageable words to set up both verbal and visual codes, with such dual coding leading to better recall, an interpretation favored by Paivio (1969). If so, then it is conceivable that a spatial disrupting task such as concurrent pursuit tracking might reduce the effect of imageability.

We decided to explore this dual coding interpretation by studying the effect of pursuit tracking on the learning of imageable word pairs such as *bullet-gray* and abstract pairs such as *gratitude-infinite*. Our subjects were presented with lists of pairs of either imageable or abstract words, and were subsequently cued for recall by being given the first word of each pair. We expected a substantial advantage in favor of the imageable pairs, and predicted that if the visuo-spatial sketchpad or temporary imagery storage system was necessary for setting up the image, then tracking would severely disrupt this advantage.

Our results showed a massive advantage in favor of the imageable pairs, a small but significant decrement resulting from tracking, but absolutely no suggestion that tracking disrupted learning of the imageable more than the abstract items (see Figure 5.6). We concluded that the imageability effect is not dependent upon setting up a visuo-spatial representation in the sketchpad system. Our results are more consistent with an interpretation that suggests that concrete and imageable items are easier to remember because they are represented more richly within the long-term semantic memory system, a view that has recently also been advocated by Jones (1988).

Does this result therefore imply that the visuo-spatial sketchpad plays no role in the facilitating effect of imagery in long-term memory? This is certainly one possibility. The sketchpad could simply operate within short-term tasks, having no impact on long-term learning. Another possibility, however, is that the sketchpad system will be used when it is necessary to manipulate images or cause them to interact in novel ways. If so, we might expect concurrent tracking to interfere with the use of a visual imagery mnemonic.

FIGURE 5.6

The influence of concurrent tracking on the retention of concrete and abstract word pairs. From Baddeley et al. (1975a).

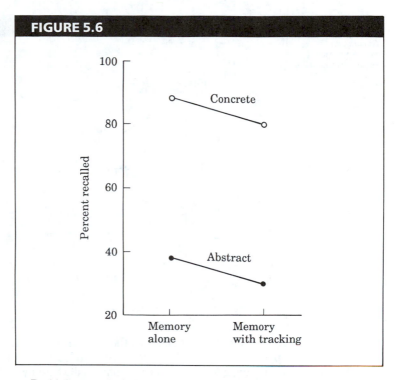

Baddeley et al. (1975a) went on to explore this, using a visual imagery mnemonic in which subjects learnt a 10-word list by associating each item with a location on a specified walk through the university campus. In order to retrieve the items they imagined themselves walking the route through the campus, scanning each location in turn for the item to be remembered. Subjects were encouraged to use either imagery or verbal rote rehearsal, and for each of these were tested with and without concurrent tracking on the pursuit rotor. As Figure 5.7 shows the mnemonic enhanced performance under control conditions, but its advantage was completely wiped out by the spatial tracking task.

This, however, left us with the intriguing question as to whether the sketchpad system is inherently a spatial one, with the result that imageable but relatively non-spatial mnemonics are intrinsically less disruptable, or whether the greater disruption of a spatial mnemonic simply reflects our use of a highly spatial secondary task, that of pursuit tracking. A colleague, Bob Logie, opted for the latter interpretation, and set about trying to explore the use of relatively non-spatial disrupting tasks, patches of color or patterns for which processing of precise spatial location or orientation is not required of the subject.

In a series of experiments (Logie, 1986) he was able to demonstrate a visual imagery disruption effect analogous to that of unattended speech in verbal memory. The subject was simply required to sit facing a screen on which colored patches appeared at

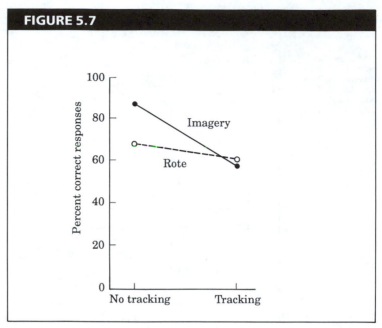

The influence of tracking on the memory for word sequences learnt by rote or by an imagery mnemonic. From Baddeley and Lieberman (1980).

FIGURE 5.7

regular intervals, looking at the screen but ignoring anything that appeared. Meanwhile subjects tried to learn word lists using either visual imagery or a verbal rehearsal strategy. The unattended colored patches caused a significant drop in performance on the imagery condition from 69 to 61% correct, while having no such effect on rote learning, where performance in fact improved non-significantly from 36 to 39% correct.

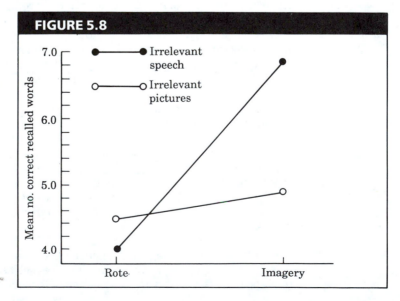

The effect of the presentation of unattended pictures and unattended speech on memory for words using rote rehearsal or a visual imagery pegword mnemonic. Adapted from Logie (1986). Copyright (1986) The Experimental Psychology Society.

FIGURE 5.8

In a final experiment, Logie opted to use line drawings so as to increase the similarity between the imaged material and the irrelevant material, and also included an additional unattended speech condition in which instead of pictures, their names were presented auditorily. Subjects were again told to ignore both the pictures and the words. The results of this study are shown in Figure 5.8 from which it is clear that the imagery mnemonic is disrupted by unattended pictures, while the rote learning condition suffers most from the unattended words.

Characteristics of the Visuo-spatial Sketchpad

The pattern of results is therefore consistent with the assumption of a visuo-spatial system, somewhat analogous to the articulatory loop. Like the loop, it can be fed either directly through perception, in this case visual perception, or indirectly, in this case through the generation of a visual image. The unattended picture effect suggests that access to the store by visual information is obligatory, again a close analogy with the articulatory loop.

The system appears to be used in setting up and using visual imagery mnemonics, but does not appear to be responsible for the imageability effect in long-term verbal memory. While at first, the system appeared to be spatial rather than visual in character, it now seems likely that it either represents a multi-faceted system, with both visual and spatial dimensions, or possibly two separate systems. There is evidence from research on animals and from neuropsychology that the visual system may have two separable components, one concerned with pattern processing and detecting *what*, while the other is concerned with location in space, and conveys information about *where* (Ungerleider & Mishkin, 1982; Weiskrantz, 1986). We shall return to this point after discussing the human neuropsychological evidence in more detail.

THE NEUROPSYCHOLOGY OF VISUAL IMAGERY

Over the years, neuropsychologists have shown a good deal of interest in visual imagery, but it is only recently that a coherent attempt has been made to pull together evidence from psychophysiology, from lesion studies in neuropsychology and from normal experimental psychology to produce a coherent picture. The section that follows has been influenced by a recent paper by Farah (1988) which is recommended for further reading.

Farah begins by pointing to some of the problems in interpreting much of the work on rotating and scanning visual images, problems that have already been discussed. She suggests that combining such tasks with information from psychophysiological measures, and from single case studies of patients with imagery disturbances following lesions, may allow some rather less equivocal conclusions to be drawn.

Psychophysiological Studies

One recently developed technique is that of regional blood flow monitoring (Ingvar, 1979). It has been shown that different tasks lead to a differential rate of blood flow in different parts of the brain, with for example the blood flow in the left hemisphere being associated with language processing, and in the frontal lobes with the performance of complex and demanding tasks. Roland and Friberg (1985) measured regional blood flow in normal subjects performing each of three tasks, one task involved counting backwards in three's from 50, a second verbal task involved imagining a jingle and deleting alternate words, while the third task required the subjects to visualize themselves taking a walk through a familiar location, and alternately taking left and right turns. This latter visual imagery task led to a massive increase in blood flow in the occipital lobes, and the posterior superior parietal and posterior inferior temporal areas. These areas are precisely those that had been shown earlier to produce high rates of blood flow during visual processing (Roland, 1982).

A similar pattern of results is found using techniques based on the electrical activity of the brain. It has, for example, long been known that when the subject's eyes are closed, a pattern of electrical activity known as the alpha rhythm occurs in those parts of the brain concerned with perception, and that this rhythm can be suppressed when subjects open their eyes, or form visual images (Golla, Hutton, & Grey Walter, 1943). In a particularly neat demonstration, Davidson and Schwartz (1977) had their subjects image either a regularly flashing light, a regular tap on the arm, or both. The alpha rhythm was recorded from both the occipital and parietal areas of the brain. Imaging the light suppressed the rhythm in the occipital lobe, imaging the touch inhibited activity in the parietal lobe, while imaging both disrupted both. A separate demonstration of both visual and tactile suppression indicates that suppression could not simply be a general effect of effort.

When a stimulus is presented, its effect can be detected in the electrical activity of the brain, with the location and polarity of such event-related potentials (ERPs) varying with the modality and nature of the stimulus. Farah, Peronnet, and Weisberg (1987) studied the responses evoked by visually presenting words which the subject was instructed either simply to read, or to read and form a visual image of the meaning of the word. The imagery condition led to an increase in the occipital ERP to each word. In order to check that this effect might not have simply been due to the extra effort involved in imagery, a further condition was run in which the subject was required to detect misspellings; this led to an ERP that was different both in polarity and pattern from that evoked by the imagery instruction.

The psychophysiological evidence, whether from blood flow studies, EEG or ERP experiments is consistent in suggesting that instructions to image give rise to increased activity in the occipital lobes and in posterior parietal and temporal areas associated with visual perception. Such studies do, however, leave open the question of whether the observed activity is essential for imagery, or is simply an epiphenomenon, some form of parallel or overflow activity that occurs, but is not actually necessary for the processing of images to occur. Pylyshyn might, for example, argue that such brain activity reflects the subject's attempted simulation of the experience of perceiving, but is not actually necessary for the performance of the imagery task. This point can be checked, however, by using lesion studies, in which neuropsychological patients have accidentally sustained damage to one or more of these areas of the brain. If these areas are important for utilizing imagery, then lesions should disrupt performance on imagery tasks.

Neuropsychological Evidence

It has been known for many years that damage to the occipital lobes may result in color-blindness, and that such patients also appear to lose the capacity to form color images. De Renzi and Spinnler (1967) studied a group of patients all of whom suffered from color-blindness as a result of cortical damage. Such patients also report that they have lost the capacity for color imagery; furthermore, they can not answer questions such as "What color is a banana?" and are not able to select the appropriate color from a set of crayons. A more detailed account of such patients is given by Humphreys and Riddoch (1987), and by Beauvois and Saillant (1985) who describe a patient who is able to draw objects from memory, but cannot say what color they are, unless there is a strong verbal association (e.g. snow-white, sky-blue).

Neuropsychological evidence lends further support to the suggestion that there may be two aspects to visual imagery, one concerned with "what" and the other with "where". Holmes (1919) describes a number of patients who, following head wounds in the First World War, were unable to locate objects, although they were quite capable of recognizing them. One such patient for example correctly identified a pocket knife, but in attempting to grasp it reached in quite the wrong direction. Holmes describes another patient attempting to eat soup. It took many attempts for the patient to locate the soup bowl with the spoon, but once this had been achieved, he was always able to bring the soup to his mouth. The problem was visual not spatial, as indicated by a normal capacity to locate sounds in space.

The converse pattern of visual processing deficit also occurs, with the patient able to localize an object accurately, but not able to recognize it, a deficit known as *agnosia*. One case for example, described in detail by Humphreys and Riddoch (1987) was able to locate and copy drawings of objects, or the objects themselves, but could not recognize them. Shown a drawing of an eagle, he reproduced it very well, but identified it as "a cat sitting up".

Just as perception of "what" and "where" may be disrupted independently, so can their representation in memory. Levine, Warach, and Farah (1985) describe a patient who is unable to draw or describe objects, animals or faces from memory, but shows good retention of the capacity to locate items in space from memory. Hence he can point to the location of cities and states on a map, describe the location of furniture in his house and landmarks in his home city. A second patient described by Levine et al. shows the opposite pattern, being unable to locate cities on a map or local landmarks and being unable to point to the location in his hospital room when his eyes are closed, but nevertheless able to give a detailed description of animals, and of the faces of those familiar to him.

The incapacity to form a visual image of an object may often accompany agnosia, the impairment in the ability to recognize objects from their visual characteristics, despite continuing to understand the meaning of the name. Hence an agnosic patient described by Wilson (1987) completely failed to identify an onion, but given the cue "a vegetable that makes you cry when you cut it", had no difficulty in coming up with the response "onion". When asked what an eagle was, she immediately responded "a bird of prey", but was unable to say how many legs it had. Figure 5.9 shows a series of her attempts at drawing an elephant.

Gradual recovery from agnosia in patient JR who was asked to draw an elephant at various times following her head injury. From Wilson (in preparation).

FIGURE 5.9

(a) Elephant – can't remember what it looks like

(b)

(c)

(d)

Although the neuropsychological literature on imagery is rich, there has been comparatively little work systematically exploring the performance of patients on the tasks that have been developed within the cognitive psychology laboratory. This is now changing, a good example being a study by Farah, Hammond, Levine, and Calvanio (1988), based on a single patient, a 36-year-old minister who had suffered a road traffic accident at the age of 18. This had led to severe damage to the temporal and occipital lobes, but somewhat unusually spared the parietal regions. He was left with no problems of language, memory or motor skill, and a verbal I.Q. of 132, coupled with a performance I.Q. of 93. Visual acuity was, however, very poor, 20/50 for one eye and 20/70 for the other. He had great difficulty in recognizing faces, or other complex stimuli such as plants or animals. He also showed a clear pattern of impairment on a range of tasks that involve the more visual aspects of imagery. These included describing the type of tail different animals would have, giving the color of common objects such as bananas and cactuses, making judgments of the relative size of animals such as a dog and a sheep, and making judgments about the shape of various U.S. states.

In contrast he performed normally on a whole range of tasks that involved primarily spatial processing. These included the Brooks spatial matrix task, Shepard's image rotation test, mental scanning tasks of the type developed by Kosslyn, and locating states on a map of the U.S.

These results are shown in Figure 5.10, from which it is clear that they do fall into two very clearly separate categories, rather than forming a continuous distribution. As such, they tend to argue in favor of two separate locations for visual imagery. One which is primarily concerned with visual aspects of imagery is severely disrupted in this patient, and hence presumably dependent on the occipital lobes. The second system is one that depends principally on spatial coding, and is probably dependent on the functioning of the parietal lobes, which in this patient were intact. The fact that his spatial imagery is normal suggests that spatial imagery is not dependent on an intact visual system. It would be most interesting to locate a patient with the converse damage, and see if intact spatial imagery is necessary for the operation of the more peripheral visual imagery system.

WHAT USE IS THE SKETCHPAD?

What is the sketchpad for? There has been rather less work directly concerned with exploring the role of the visuo-spatial sketchpad in everyday cognition, partly because development of this aspect of working memory has been less intensive, although there has of course been very extensive work on visual imagery from other perspectives. It seems likely that the spatial system is important for geographical orientation, and for planning spatial tasks. Indeed, tasks involving visuo-spatial manipulation have long

FIGURE 5.10

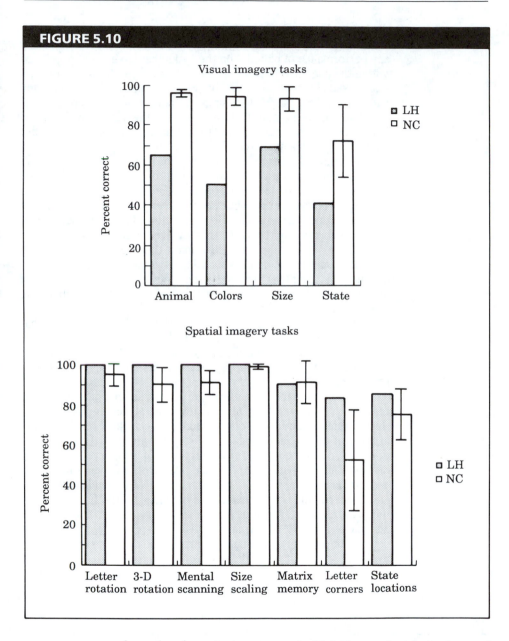

formed an important component of intelligence test batteries, and have tended to be used as selection tools for professions where visuo-spatial planning and manipulation are thought to be important, such as engineering and architecture. There are now, however, starting to appear a number of studies in which dual-task interference techniques developed for the study of the sketchpad are being applied outside the laboratory.

One particularly intriguing study is that by Hatano and Osawa

Data from two patients with impaired imagery, one, L.H., performs poorly on tasks requiring visual imagery judgments, the other, N.C., is impaired on spatial imagery tasks. From Farah et al. (in press).

(1983) of Japanese abacus experts. It appears that people who use the abacus for calculation sometimes become so expert that they can dispense with the abacus itself, using only a mental representation. Competitions are held between such experts in which they perform feats in which they add and subtract up to fifteen numbers, each comprising five to nine digits.

Hatano and Osawa consider three ways in which the users might be holding the numbers while they perform this task. The first possibility they suggest is that they may be using the sketchpad component of working memory. A second possibility is that they use a chunking procedure somewhat similar to that used by the mental calculator Aitken, described in the previous chapter, while a third possibility is that the items are registered in long-term memory, as is the case for the previously described subject of Chase and Ericsson (1982) who developed a digit span of eighty items by using a mnemonic based on running times.

They tested the performance of their subjects using a simple digit span procedure, and initially comparing span for digits with that for letters and for the names of fruits. They found that their abacus experts had extremely long memory spans of approximately sixteen digits forward and fourteen when the order of recall was reversed. They interpret the fact that forward and backward spans were about the same as suggesting the use of a visual image which could be scanned in either direction, since with verbal coding forward span is substantially better than reverse span. Memory span for letters and fruits was no higher in the abacus experts than in control subjects, presumably because letters and fruit names could not be encoded using the abacus system.

Hatano and Osawa tested the imagery hypothesis further by using a dual-task procedure in which subjects were required to remember sequences of digits or letters while performing one of two concurrent tasks. In the visual imagery disruption condition, they were shown the drawing of an object, and then had to recognize that object from a set of six similar pictures. In the verbal disruption condition, they were required to answer questions such as "Who is the Prime Minister of Japan?". While memory for consonants was disrupted most by the verbal processing task, digit span was disrupted by the concurrent visual task, again suggesting that a visuo-spatial system such as the sketchpad was being used to remember the digits.

Finally, the LTM interpretation of the performance of the abacus experts was tested by presenting successively 10 sequences of 10 digits, and in each case requiring the subject to retain them for 30 seconds, a feat they achieved with ease. They were subsequently asked to recall as many of the 10 sequences as possible. Of the two subjects tested on this, one could remember none of the sequences, while the other remembered only the last sequence presented. Unlike the running time mnemonic used by Chase and Ericsson's subject, the enhanced performance of these experts does not depend on LTM. Hatano and Osawa conclude that their abacus experts are using a visuo-spatial representation held in the visuo-spatial sketchpad of working memory.

OVERVIEW

After neglect during the early years of this century, imagery has become a popular research topic. The work on mental rotation carried out by Shepard and his colleagues, and Kosslyn's experiments on the phenomenology of imagery are described.

Two questions that have dominated much of the recent work have been:

1. Is imagery based on a continuous analogue system, or is it better viewed as a representational system based on a combination of discrete propositional components?
2. Are images like percepts?

It is suggested that although these questions have revealed some intriguing empirical data, they are not readily answerable and are unlikely to continue to prove scientifically fruitful.

Work using the working memory dual-task paradigm is then described. Results suggest the separability of a system for setting up and manipulating images, the visuo-spatial sketchpad. The system is shown to be involved in the use of visual imagery mnemonics, but not responsible for the enhanced memorability of highly imageable words.

The question of whether the system should preferably be considered as a visual or a spatial one is then considered using data from the learning and memory performance of normal subjects, and from the pattern of evoked electrical potentials and blood flow observed when subjects are performing verbal or imaginal tasks. The pattern of results suggests separate visual and spatial components of imagery, with different anatomical locations within the brain. Data from neuropsychological studies of patients with damage to these areas of the brain is then reviewed, and is found to support the hypothesis that imagery has related but separable visual and spatial components.

Chapter Six

ATTENTION AND THE CONTROL OF MEMORY

*I*n discussing the structure of working memory, it was suggested that it could usefully be broken down into at least three components, comprising two slave systems, the articulatory loop and the visuo-spatial sketchpad, controlled by a third component, the central executive. What do we know about this all-important third component? The answer unfortunately is that we know considerably less than we know of the two slave systems. Most of the research in the working memory tradition has tended to concentrate on the subsidiary systems, principally on the grounds that they appear to offer more tractable problems than the central executive which from time-to-time has tended to become something of a ragbag for consigning such important but difficult problems as how information from the various slave systems is combined, and how strategies are selected and operated.

It is, of course, entirely legitimate to attempt to tackle a system as complex as working memory bit-by-bit, but sooner or later, it is necessary to grasp the nettle and attempt to understand the component that controls working memory. In some ways, the central executive functions more like an attentional system than a memory store, and a sensible place to start might be to examine theories of attention in the hope that they will provide a suitable model for incorporating into the working memory framework. The study of short-term memory and attention were closely linked during the early days of the information processing approach to cognition, and some of the initial models such as that of Broadbent (1958) were expressly aimed at coping with both attention and STM. Since that time, however, the two areas have drifted apart somewhat, I suspect to their mutual disadvantage. It might therefore be useful to make a small digression at this point to have a brief look at some of the questions that have concerned attention theorists, before returning to the question of the central executive and control of working memory.

THE STUDY OF ATTENTION

Vigilance

Any attempt to survey the literature on attention soon drives the reviewer to the conclusion that the concept of attention is far from unitary. For example one area of research into attention that was discussed in some detail by Broadbent (1958) was that into the sustained attention that is necessary for such tasks as monitoring a radar screen or inspecting items on an industrial production line, an area of research that goes under the general title of "vigilance". This has continued to be studied, since it is of clear practical significance, but my overall impression is that its potential links with, and implications for working memory are rather few.

One possible exception to this absence of a link is the observation by Parasuraman (1979) that while performance on certain vigilance tasks declines systematically over time on task, performance on others holds up reasonably well. Tasks that are vulnerable to decrement in detection over time seem to be those in which some form of short-term storage is required in order to perform the task. Examples include listening to a stream of numbers and attempting to spot three odd digits in succession, or judging whether pairs of adjacent items are of the same hue. On the other hand, tasks in which each item is judged on its own merits, such as detecting faulty bottles on a conveyor belt, show no decrement in performance across time, provided that the subject knows roughly what frequency of faults to expect. This pattern of results suggests that short-term storage may be the vulnerable feature of vigilance, suggesting that it might be worth exploring the role of working memory in vigilance decrement more directly.

Perceptual Selection

There has, of course, been a great deal of theoretical interest in the area of selective attention over the last 30 years. However, as Broadbent (1982) has pointed out, much of the work tends to be focussed on specific laboratory tasks, with different theories tending to be associated with different tasks, and relatively little cross-fertilization.

Much of the work has been concerned with attention as perceptual selection. How, for example, do we manage to converse in a noisy party? How do we manage to tune into the person we are talking to and tune out the many other voices that are surrounding us? There has been a great deal of work on this intriguing problem. Much of the initial work was concerned with working out what features of a voice would allow it to be selected from a babble of competing voices; factors such as the speaker's voice character-istics, loudness and direction all prove to be useful features (Broadbent, 1958).

Later work was concerned with explaining the process of attentional selection, and here results were much more controversial, with some theorists arguing for the process of selecting occurring at a relatively peripheral level in terms of the physical characteristics of the incoming sounds (Treisman, 1964), while others argued that almost all the information was processed by the subject, with selection not occurring until a point at which the system chooses which of the processed items to respond to (Deutsch & Deutsch, 1963).

The sort of evidence that appeared to favor an early selection view is typified by a study by Treisman and Geffen (1967) in which subjects had different streams of words presented to each ear. They were instructed to "shadow" (repeat back) the words presented to one ear, and to press a button whenever they heard an animal mentioned on either ear. Detection of animals was extremely good when they were presented to the ear that was being shadowed, while very few animals were detected on the other ear.

Other studies, however, have suggested that rather more of the information on the unattended ear may be processed than is suggested by the Treisman and Geffen result. An early study by Moray (1959), for example, indicated that subjects were very likely to notice if their own name was presented on the unattended ear. It may, of course, be that there is something rather special about one's own name. Rather subtler effects of material on the unattended ear were, however, shown in a study by Lackner and Garrett (1972) who presented sentences to the attended ear which were subsequently to be remembered. Some of the sentences were ambiguous, containing words with more than one meaning, for example "The boys threw stones at the bank". While this was being presented to one ear, a disambiguating associated word would be presented to the ear that the subject was instructed to ignore. In this case it might be "money" or "river". There was a clear tendency for subjects to recall the sentence later as having the meaning that was appropriate to the unattended word, so if it had been "money", they would recall the boys throwing stones at a building. Despite being influenced by the unattended words, the subjects reported being unaware of them. There is, however, a good deal of evidence to suggest that people may often be influenced by stimuli which they do not report as being within their conscious awareness (Dixon, 1981; Holender, 1986; Marcel, 1983).

It seems clear that any resolution of this theoretical controversy is likely to depend on the development of more detailed and complex models of the way in which language is processed. This is likely to remain an intriguing classic problem, but it is not clear that it will be of direct relevance to the problems of the central executive, which seem to be those of controlling and integrating actions and activities, rather than those of shutting out unwanted information. For that reason we shall move onto a third area of attentional theory, that concerned with doing two things at the same time. Since dual-task performance has formed an important tool in the analysis of working memory, this research area must surely be of relevance.

Dual Task Performance

It is clear that doing two things at the same time can create problems. In some cases the reason for the mutual interference is obvious; try whistling and singing at the same time. Here the problem obviously arises because the lips and vocal apparatus are physically incapable of simultaneously making the appropriate responses.

In other situations, the interference is more subtle. Consider for example a study by Kelso, Southard, and Goodman (1979) in which subjects were required to reach out and touch targets of varying sizes at various distances with right and left hand. As we know from Fitts Law (Fitts & Peterson, 1964), the time it takes to strike a target increases as it becomes smaller or further away. What happens then if we require a subject to touch a small and distant target with his left hand, and a larger near target with his right? In fact the right hand is slowed down so that the two hands hit the targets at the same time. This is not of course logically at all necessary. If one were designing a robot, it would be just as easy to have the hands move independently; human beings, however, do not seem to work that way, presumably because the hands typically work in coordination rather than as independent systems.

One might, however, argue that the hands are a special case in that the two hands operate as a unitary rather than separate system; that does not of course necessarily mean that tasks that use quite separate response systems will show similar interference. In general, however, they do, producing a phenomenon known as *refractoriness*. In general, subjects tend to have difficulty emitting two responses at the same time, and when this is necessary, one of the responses must wait until the other is completed. The delay shown is not constant, however, depending on the relative demands made by the two competing processes. Posner and Boies (1971) used this effect rather elegantly to map the attentional demands made by a cognitive task, that of deciding whether two letters were the same or different.

The procedure involved presenting the first letter (e.g. A) followed after a delay by the second comparison letter (e.g. B) whereupon the subject must decide whether the two were the same or different, and press one of two keys with two of the fingers of his right hand. At the same time as he is performing this task, he must listen for a clearly audible tone. When he hears it, he presses a key with his left hand as rapidly as possible. The tone can be timed to occur at various points during the letter classification task. Posner and Boies assume that the more attentionally demanding that part of the task is, the greater will be its tendency to delay reaction to the tone, allowing this secondary reaction time to plot out the attentional demands of the letter classification task. A

FIGURE 6.1

Reaction time to an auditory probe as a function of its arrival time during the performance of a letter matching task. (○—○) Name identity judgment); (●—●) Physical identity judgment. From Posner and Boies (1971). Copyright (1971) by the American Psychological Association. Reprinted by permission.

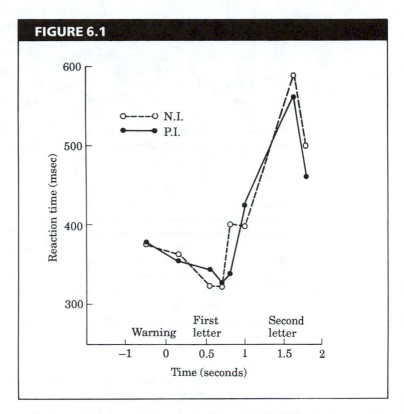

typical result from such a study is shown in Figure 6.1, which suggests that the most demanding point occurs when the second letter arrives, and the decision must be made as to whether it is the same or different.

Elegant though it is, this study can be criticized on the grounds that both tasks involve responding with the hands, and as we saw earlier, the two hands can not be regarded as independent response systems. It is possible therefore that the study is picking up response interference, rather than interference between two decision processes. The possibility that this might be happening was reinforced by an experiment by McLeod (1978) who replicated the Posner and Boies result using a manual response to a tone, but also added a further condition in which the subject responded to the tone verbally by saying "bip". While he obtained the same result as Posner and Boies when the response was manual, McLeod found very little interference when the response was verbal.

Automaticity

Does this then mean that the original result was simply an artefact of using two manual responses? Another possibility was raised by studies that indicate that simple vocal repetition or imitation may be a rather special response that allows a relatively automatic output with little or no attentional capacity required for processing. This is illustrated by a study carried out by Greenwald and Shulman (1973) who combined two reaction time tasks. The first task involved moving a switch in the direction indicated by an arrow presented to the subject. This was combined with each of two other tasks. In one of these the subject heard the number "one" and responded by echoing the word "one", while in the alternative condition, he heard the letter "a" and again responded "one". Responding "one" to the letter "a" substantially slowed down a simultaneous response to the arrow, while simply echoing the word "one" did not.

This suggests the possibility that the original Posner and Boies result might return if the vocal reaction time response was one other than echoing back the spoken stimulus. The relevant study was duly carried out jointly by McLeod and Posner (1984) who showed that interference is indeed minimal when the subject repeats the stimulus (hear "up", say "up"), but that interference does occur between the two tasks when the vocal response required to the stimulus is highly associated (hear "up", say "high"), but not identical. (See Figure 6.2.)

McLeod and Posner refer to the capacity to echo heard speech as operating via a "privileged loop". It may be recalled that a similar mechanism was suggested in the chapter on the articulatory loop, in order to explain the very marked tendency for even young children to show apparent rehearsal of spoken material, a process that it was suggested may form an important component in the process of learning to speak.

Is the auditory-vocal privileged loop the only way in which two tasks can be performed simultaneously without interference? It appears not, as for example was shown by an experiment in which Allport, Antonis, and Reynolds (1972) required a number of skilled pianists to play the piano by sight-reading at the same time as they heard and repeated back a continuous stream of prose, a task

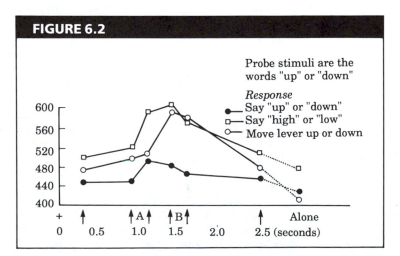

FIGURE 6.2

Probe reaction times to words and tones for mixed word/tone group. From McLeod and Posner (1984).

known as "shadowing". A similar feat was shown by a typist tested by Shaffer (1975) who was able to copy type at the same time as she shadowed prose, though with some decrement in performance, whereas she was not able to combine audio-typing with reading aloud.

The experiments by Allport et al. and by Shaffer involved subjects who were skilled at the relevant tasks of playing the piano, typing and speaking, but who had relatively little practice at combining the skills. Spelke, Hirst, and Neisser (1976) studied the effect of practice on the capacity of two subjects to read stories and write words to dictation simultaneously. After 20 weeks of practice the subjects could not only comprehend the story while copying, but could even write down the semantic category to which the word belonged. In another study, Hirst et al. (1980) had their subjects read aloud while copying short sentences, and were still able to do the task when the reading was switched from stories to much denser and more demanding encyclopaedia passages. Hirst et al. suggest on the basis of this finding that subjects are not performing the task by switching attention rapidly between reading and writing, but it is not clear that this is ruled out; although the encyclopaedia articles may be less redundant than the stories, even difficult prose does involve a good deal of predictability, which could allow an attention-switching strategy to operate.

While these may sound like dramatic demonstrations, most of us can perform complex tasks such as driving and speaking simultaneously with little apparent interference, although one does tend to stop talking when a difficult traffic situation develops. This phenomenon was studied in rather more detail by Brown, Tickner, and Simmonds (1969) in a study that was concerned with the possible adverse effects of telephoning while driving. Subjects were required to hear and verify sentences from the syntactic reasoning test described earlier, giving a vocal "true" or "false" response. The sentences varied from simple such as "A follows B—BA", to relatively complex, "A is not preceded by B—BA". Subjects were required to drive around a course on an airfield that was laid out so as to have a number of "gates" between two sticks. Some of the gates were wide enough, but some were too narrow to negotiate without hitting the sticks. As Table 6.1 shows, the concurrent reasoning task appeared to have no effect on the subjects' capacity to steer between gaps that were large enough, but did impair judgment as to whether to accept the gap or not.

While an experienced driver can talk and drive, the situation is very different when one is first learning to drive, suggesting that one crucial factor in determining the interference between two tasks is the extent to which they have been overlearned. This point has been made very forcefully by Schneider and Shiffrin (1977). They carried out one study in which subjects were required to detect consonants from the first half of the alphabet and reject the rest. During the early stages in performance, both response time and accuracy were affected by both the number of targets and the

TABLE 6.1			
Effect of Telephoning on Driving			
	Driving Alone	*Driving while Telephoning*	*Significance Levels*
Steering Errors	7.2%	9.8%	N.S.
Gap Judgement Errors	42.9%	55.8%	p < 0.01
Reasoning Errors	23.8%	45.0%	p < 0.01
Time to Complete Circuit (Sec)	361.3	385.2	p < 0.01
From Brown et al. (1969)			

number of distractors, with more leading to worse performance. However, unlike most experiments in cognitive psychology which tend to release the subject after about an hour, Schneider and Shiffrin continued to practice their subjects. After 1,500 trials, subjects had become extremely fast and very accurate, with no effect of number of targets or distractors. At this point, subjects were switched and required to respond positively to the items they had previously rejected. Not surprisingly massive proactive interference occurred, with subjects initially being considerably worse than they had been during the early stages of the experiment, and even after 2,100 further trials they were still not up to the level of performance they had reached when they switched.

When a given stimulus is repeatedly paired with the same response, then it progressively appears to take less and less attentional resources, and to interfere less and less with other concurrent tasks, acquiring what it is usually termed "automaticity". The hallmarks of automaticity are said to be an absence of interference between the automatic process and other concurrent activities, together with an apparently unstoppable tendency for the automatic stimulus to evoke its response. An example of the latter is the Stroop effect in which subjects are required to name a color in which words are printed; color naming is slowed down when the letters to be named spell a color that is different from that of the letters, for example the word "red" written in green letters.

There is no doubt that the phenomenon explored by Schneider and Shiffrin is of great importance in the attentional control of skilled behavior. It is perhaps a little unfortunate that the term "automaticity" was selected to describe the phenomenon, however, since it tends to imply an all-or-none phenomenon. This has probably had the effect of deflecting consideration of the processes whereby skills become decreasingly demanding of attention, and emphasizing the possibly less fruitful controversy as to whether any response can ever be truly automatic.

In fact, it seems likely that some interference almost inevitably does occur. For example, McLeod (1977) gave his subjects lengthy practice on a pursuit tracking task in which they were required to keep a spot of light in contact with a target at the same time as they responded by saying "high" or "low" to a high or low pitch tone. Detailed monitoring of the tracking performance indicated no *specific* effect of a concurrent reaction time response. Nonetheless, simply knowing that the trial was one in which it would be necessary to make a reaction time response caused a small amount of *general* impairment in tracking skill, even when no response was being made. Following a later and more detailed study, Shallice, McLeod, and Lewis (1985) conclude that even when the response systems are quite separate and subjects are highly practised, one should expect a decrement of anything up to 10% in performance as a result of the requirement to monitor two tasks simultaneously.

The unstoppability criterion is also somewhat questionable. Even the skilled pianists studied by Allport et al. are presumably not irrevocably bound to hit the appropriate note when they see a piece of music. The essential feature of the work of Schneider and his colleagues, however, is not the issue of whether automaticity is ever complete, but rather that it reflects a crucial factor in the acquisition of skill, namely the repeated association between specific stimuli and responses. Some aspects of a skill such as driving will have this characteristic, the movement required to apply the foot brake for example, while others such as the relationship between the driver's actions and that of other traffic on the road will not.

Thus, while the concept of automaticity focuses on one important feature of the role of skill in the control of action, it does not seem to be flexible enough to offer a plausible model for the operation of something as complex as the central executive component of working memory. This is not of course a criticism of the automaticity model since it does not aim to offer a complete model of attentional control, but it does reduce its relevance to the present discussion.

THE CONTROL OF ACTION

The Norman and Shallice SAS Model

One model that does have the aim of providing a general account of the control of action is that proposed by Norman and Shallice (1986), and as we shall see, although it is not worked out in the degree of detail, or empirically tested as extensively as the Schneider and Shiffrin automaticity model, it nevertheless does appear to provide a very useful basis for conceptualizing the central executive component of working memory. Norman and Shallice were interested in the very broad issue of how activities are controlled, and why this control sometimes breaks down leading to errors which range from the trivial inadvertent eating of a chocolate when one did not intend to, to the disastrous loss of control of a nuclear power plant. Hence, unlike Schneider and Shiffrin's work,

FIGURE 6.3

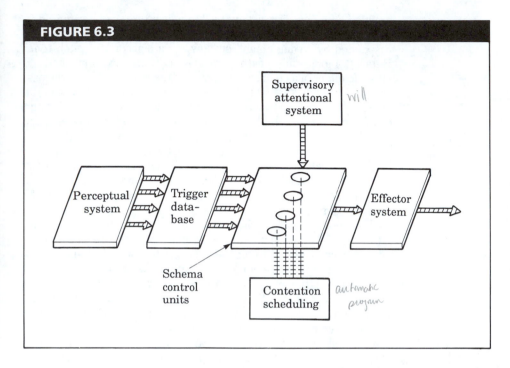

A simplified version of the Norman and Shallice (1980) model representing the flow of control information. The lines with arrows represent activating input, the crossed lines represent the primarily mutually inhibitory function of contention scheduling. The term "effector system" refers to special-purpose processing units involved in schema operation for both action and thought schemas. In the latter case schema operation involves placing information in short-term stores that can activate the trigger data base. From Shallice (1982).

which tends to be based on extensive and rigidly controlled laboratory experimentation, much of the evidence presented in support of the Norman and Shallice model comes from everyday observation of mental lapses, or from the breakdown in control of behavior shown in certain neuropsychological patients.

A representation of their model is shown in Figure 6.3. It assumes that ongoing actions can be controlled in two rather separate ways. The first way occurs in the case of well-learned skills, in which prior learning allows the activity to run off relatively automatically.

Normal driving is a good example of this; most people have occasionally had the experience of driving while thinking about some other issue, and suddenly becoming aware of the fact that they have no recollection of the last few miles, despite the fact that they must have successfully negotiated a winding road, avoided hitting pedestrians and other traffic and found their way. As Schneider and Shiffrin point out, such relatively automated skills can carry on at the same time as other activities, while causing relatively little interference. At the moment, I am walking and talking into a tape recorder, without any obvious signs that I need to stop walking in order to talk.

Occasionally two ongoing activities will come into conflict, and it may be necessary to give one priority over the other. In driving and talking for example, it is usually preferable to stop talking rather than risk hitting the cyclist who has wobbled rather unsteadily out from a side-street. Norman and Shallice suggest that decisions at this level can be carried out by a relatively automatic process known as "contention scheduling", whereby some simple rules as to relative importance are built into the system, and can be operated automatically. Contention scheduling is a standard feature of many computer programs that simulate cognitive activity using the production systems approach to modeling developed by Newell and Simon (1972).

The part of the system we have described so far is entirely consistent with Schneider and Shiffrin's work, but is far from a complete model. It leaves the actor captive to habitual programs, interacting with whatever the environment might present. It leaves no place for the will, a concept that has been conspicuously missing from cognitive psychology for most of this century. Norman and Shallice have a second component to their model which they liken to the operation of the will, something they term the *supervisory activating system* or SAS. In Figure 6.3, the ongoing habits or schema that control routine action are shown going from left to right, while the SAS is represented by a series of vertical arrows that are capable of interrupting and modifying such ongoing behavior. It is assumed to do so by systematically biasing existing probabilities so as to make one line of action more likely and another line less. In my own case, the SAS system has just had to interrupt the walking and talking when I came to a junction and had to decide whether to go straight ahead, left or right.

Slips of Action

One of the interests that generated this model was, as mentioned earlier, an interest in slips of action, such as those collected by Reason (1979). One such example concerns the respondent leaving home to go to work in the morning while somewhat preoccupied, going into his garage to pick up his car, and then suddenly finding that he has put on his gardening clothes and boots as if to work in the garden. The assumption here is that the supervisory system, having set up the going-to-work program was preoccupied with other activities, leaving the program to run on. Presumably, sight of the gardening clothes and boots within the appropriate context was enough to capture the gardening routine, leading to the observed inappropriate activity.

A preoccupation with errors and difficulties of everyday life encouraged Norman (1988) to collect instances where the design of an object or situation guides the user into making the wrong sequence of actions, and contrasting these with good design, whereby the user is steered into making an appropriate response. Norman's book *The Psychology of Everday Things*, shows some characteristic examples of good and bad design. The first draft of the book was written by Don Norman while on a sabbatical visit to my own unit, and he kindly agreed to bequeath us a list of what he termed "ergonomic infelicities" from around the unit, bits of technology which were unnecessarily mystifying and frustrating such as light switches that look as though they are fuse boxes, and slide projection systems that can best be handled by people with three hands. Many of these have now been changed, but no doubt we are inventing more all the time.

Norman points out that an apparently satisfactory engineering solution to a problem often creates problems because it ignores the user and his expectations; as he points out (Norman, 1988, p. viii):

> I can use complicated things. I am quite expert at computers and electronics, and complex laboratory equipment. Why do I have trouble with doors, light switches and water faucets? How come I can work a million-dollar computer installation, but not my home refrigerator? While we blame ourselves, the real culprit — faulty design — goes undetected. And millions of people find themselves to be mechanically inept. It is time for a change.

He begins to try to foster such a change by pointing a rich array of such design blunders, and by coming up with some general design principles. The design of watertaps or faucets is a particularly rich source of misdirected design ingenuity. There are, however, countless other examples which we all encounter, ranging from door handles that trap your fingers, to unfamiliar telephone systems where you need to understand what to do before you can ask for help in understanding what to do. Human–computer interaction, of course, offers this problem to an even greater degree, making attention to the user-friendliness of the system a crucial factor in its success. There is no doubt that much of the popularity of the Apple Macintosh computer, for example, is due to its attention to the needs and limitations of the human user.

Norman suggests a number of general principles for avoiding bad design. One is to optimize the relationship between controls and equipment by mapping the physical lay-out of the one on to the other. Figure 6.4 gives examples of this, based on stove controls. The standard uninformative and frustrating designs are given, together with suggested improvements.

Another approach is to anticipate possible errors and design the system so as to physically guide the user away from them. One of Norman's examples is given in Figure 6.5.

The SAS and the Frontal Lobes

Whereas Norman was interested in having a model that would account for slips of action and lapses of attention in everyday life, Shallice's main interest was in modeling a certain type of neuropsychological patient suffering from what is sometimes termed the *frontal lobe syndrome.* The frontal lobes of the brain, have over the years constituted one of the most fascinating, puzzling and frustrating puzzles in neuropsychology. To some investigators they appear to have given no evidence that they

FIGURE 6.4

Arrangement of stove controls. The top two examples leave ambiguous the relationship between burners and controls. The bottom two examples have a more compatible and less ambiguous mapping of controls onto burners. From Norman (1988). Copyright 1988 by Basic Books Inc., Publishers. Reprinted by permission.

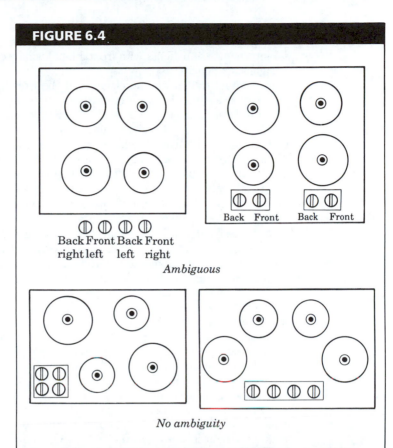

Back Front Back Front
right left left right

Back   Front   Back   Front

Ambiguous

No ambiguity

FIGURE 6.5

Lockout. A form of forcing function that prevents people going into the basement rather than leaving the building. This may be inconvenient for frequent basement users, but could save lives in the case of fire, by discouraging a mad rush into the basement. From Norman (1988). Copyright 1988 by Basic Books Inc., Publishers. Reprinted by permission.

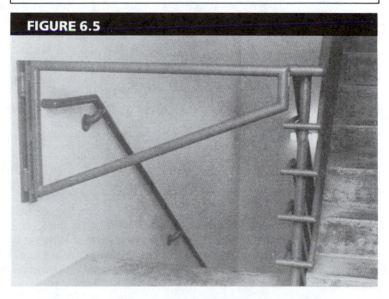

serve any useful function, the so-called "silent areas" of the brain. For example, Hebb (1949, pp. 286–9) and Teuber (1959) studied the intelligence of patients with frontal lobe damage, and observed no significant deficits.

In contrast to this we find claims that the frontal lobes are the source of all abstract behavior (Goldstein, 1936), claims based on a number of very graphic accounts of individual patients with damage to the frontal lobes who show quite marked intellectual deficits. The nature of the frontal deficits is well described by Rylander (1939, p.20) who characterizes them as: "disturbed attention, increased distractability, a difficulty in grasping the whole of a complicated state of affairs … well able to work along old routine lines … (but) … cannot learn to master new types of task, in new situations … (the patient is) … at a loss."

Why these differences of opinion? One reason is almost certainly that the frontal lobes are a very large and complex part of the brain, with the result that damage to different parts of the frontal lobe can probably have quite different effects on behavior. Secondly, those aspects of behavior that are disturbed tend to be relatively subtle and complex with the result that they are much less easy to specify and to measure than are deficits in perception, reading or memory for example. Shallice (1982) argues that the frontal lobes play a crucial role in planning, organizing and controlling action, and using the model of attentional control devised by Norman and himself, suggests that patients suffering from the frontal lobe syndrome have a deficit to the supervisory attentional system (SAS).

Of the many tasks that have been claimed to be dependent on frontal lobes, two that are most consistently shown to be impaired are the Wisconsin Card Sorting Test (WCST) and verbal fluency. The WCST involves presenting the subject with a pack of cards, on each of which is a pattern made up from various numbers of shapes which vary in color, size and surround. The patient is instructed to sort the cards into piles on the basis of some rule. It might for example be color, and the patient is corrected when he attempts to sort a card on a basis that does not fit the rule. Once a rule has been acquired it is changed, and when that rule has been acquired it is changed again, until the cards have been sorted on the basis of all six possible rules. Normal subjects can learn to do this task reasonably easily, acquiring all six rules and making relatively few errors. Patients with frontal lobe damage tend to learn the first rule but appear to be unable to escape that rule, with a very high proportion of their errors being perseverations, based on the old rule.

Perseveration is an important feature of the behavior of frontal lobe patients, who very often tend to become fixed in a routine and find it very difficult to break out. For example, one patient who was cutting up pieces of tape in occupational therapy was about to cut the tape at the wrong end. When this was pointed out he said "Of course I'm not going to cut the tape", meanwhile continuing to cut the tape.

Patients with frontal lobe damage may find it so difficult to initiate activity that they sit motionless and speechless, as if dumb, although their speech and language are perfectly normal once they can be induced to talk. Paradoxically, on other occasions frontal lobe patients can appear to show exactly the opposite behavior, being extremely distractable and unable to concentrate on any single activity for more than a few moments.

Shallice explains this pattern of results as follows. He assumes that patients with frontal lobe damage have an impairment in the functioning of the SAS, with the result that once a strategy has been adopted, it continues to run, since they have lost the capacity to interrupt and change ongoing activity. This accounts for their difficulty in learning more than one category in the card sorting test, and to their tendency to perseverate in ongoing activity. If however there is no well-established current activity, then in the absence of the SAS, the system will remain inert, or else tend to be captured by whatever stimulus the environment happens to present, giving rise to behavior that is distractable and often facetious.

A patient with such a deficit will tend to show what Lhermitte (1983) has termed "utilization behavior", grasping and utilizing any object that is presented, regardless of whether it is appropriate to do so. For example, if a glass is placed on the table, the patient will grasp it. If a bottle of water is then introduced, the patient will tend to seize it, fill his glass and drink. Such behavior was shown by five patients with frontal lesions but was never observed in normal subjects or patients with lesions elsewhere; similar behavior has since been noted in frontal patients by Shallice (personal communication).

A second task that is typically impaired in patients with extensive frontal lobe damage is the task known as verbal fluency, whereby the subject attempts to produce as many words as possible from a given category such as animals, or words beginning with *F*. Frontal patients typically find this task extremely hard, producing only three or four words in a minute, whereas one might expect a normal subject to produce at least a dozen. The problem is not that the material has been lost from memory; in one case, for example, a subject who was unable to generate animal names was able to respond to more specific cues such as an animal beginning with *C*, or an Australian animal that hops (Baddeley & Wilson, 1988b). Patients often tend to break the rules also, for example giving "sausage" as an animal, or repeating the same animal name several times.

The fluency task is presumably difficult for the patient since there is no standard overlearned program for generating sequences of items from a category, with the result that the subject must set up and run his own retrieval strategies, at the same time monitoring that the items do come from the correct category, and are not repetitions. Such a view is supported by the observation that category generation is more susceptible than most retrieval tasks to disruption by an attention-demanding secondary task (Baddeley, Lewis, Eldridge, & Thomson, 1984). Category generation is, however, a task that is quite within the capability of even densely amnesic patients, suggesting that the principal problem is not one of memory in general, but of controlling the retrieval strategy.

THE SAS AS A CENTRAL EXECUTIVE

To what extent might one use the Shallice and Norman model as a model of the central executive of working memory? In considering this possibility I was attracted not only by the way in which the model accounted for the data described by Norman and by Shallice, but also with the way in which it fitted in with our own observations on patients with frontal lobe deficits (Baddeley, 1986; Baddeley & Wilson, 1988b). Indeed we have argued that part of the lack of progress in this area has come from too great a preoccupation with localization, as is suggested by the term "frontal lobe syndrome", and too little concern with specifying the nature of the deficit itself. As a possible way of separating the issues of function and localization, we have suggested the more functional term *dysexecutive syndrome*. I shall return to this issue in the chapter on autobiographical memory when the confabulation shown by dysexecutive patients is discussed.

Why it is Hard to be Random

Another bonus from the Norman and Shallice model was an explanation for some very lawful but somewhat puzzling data I had collected over 20 years before (Baddeley, 1966c). The task in question was that of random generation, whereby subjects are asked to imagine that they have in front of them a hat containing all 26 letters of the alphabet. They are told to imagine dipping into the hat and pulling out a letter at random, and saying it, attempting to make their stream of spoken letters as random as possible. Try doing this yourself at a rate of about one every second.

After about the first 15 or 20 letters, most people find the task becoming increasingly difficult, with the same few letters tending to crop up, and with a tendency for sequences to follow stereotyped patterns such as the alphabet, or familiar acronyms such as CIA, VD and BBC. One can measure the departure from randomness both in terms of the frequency with which individual letters and letter pairs occur, and also in terms of the number of alphabetic stereotypes that are produced. If one systematically varies the rate at which the subject is required to generate letters, then a very lawful pattern emerges, with the randomness increasing with the logarithm of the time available, as is shown in Figure 6.6.

Another way of manipulating the task is to vary the number of

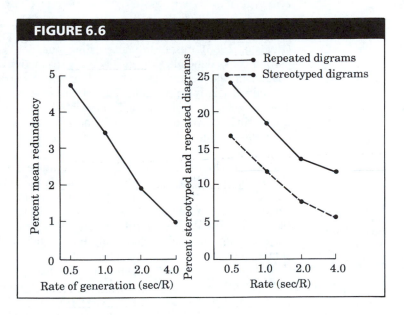

FIGURE 6.6

The influence of the rate at which subjects are required to generate random letter sequences on performance as measured by the redundancy of individual items, the number of different letter digrams and the number of stereotyped digrams per hundred letters. From Baddeley (1966c). Copyright (1966) The Experimental Psychology Society.

alternatives, requiring the subject to generate on the basis of two, four, sixteen or twenty-six letters. This leads to a systematic decrease in the rate at which letters are produced that levels off after about eight alternatives. This suggests that subjects can cope with up to about eight alternatives simultaneously, with smaller numbers of items allowing more attention and faster selection; once the system's capacity has been reached, adding further alternatives will not affect performance since the system will still be operating on its maximum of seven or eight options. This is perhaps another example of Miller's magic number seven, which it will be recalled applies to immediate memory span and to chunking in long-term learning.

While this pattern of results was very lawful, it did not fit easily into any existing information processing model. It does, however, fit neatly into the Norman–Shallice model as follows. The subject is given the task of producing streams of letters, a task for which there are already strong pre-existing but stereotyped patterns in the recitation of the alphabet, and in common abbreviations such as USA and DDT. To rely on these however will produce an extremely stereotyped output, hence breaking the rule that the sequence should be as random as possible. Within the Norman and Shallice model, the stereotyped letter sequences represent good examples of ongoing programs, while the need to break up and avoid such stereotyped responses places a constant demand on the SAS. If we assume that the capacity of the SAS is limited, then the faster the rate of generation required, the less capable will it be of avoiding the domination of existing stereotypes.

An opportunity of exploring further the possible usefulness of random generation as a task dependent on the central executive cropped up as a result of discussing the possible role of working memory in chess. A recent book on the psychology of chess (Holding, 1985) raised the interesting question as to whether playing chess depended principally on verbal activity, visuo-spatial coding, or the central executive. This was explored in a study carried out jointly with a colleague who is an expert chess player, Trevor Robbins, and two undergraduates, Andrew Bradley and Stuart Hudson. We decided to look at memory for complex chess positions so as to avoid the complexity of evaluating the quality of chess moves.

There is already a very substantial literature using memory for chess positions that shows for example that a single glimpse is enough to allow an expert chess player to remember far more of a game than is acquired by a novice player after many such glimpses (de Groot, 1965). We therefore adopted a design in which our subjects were allowed a brief glimpse of a position taken from an actual game between master chess players. The subjects were then required to reproduce as much of the position as possible on a chess board. Testing occurred under either a control condition, where no secondary task was required, or during the performance of tasks that were expected to interfere with various components of working memory. One task, for example, involved articulatory suppression which was assumed to interfere with verbal coding, a second had subjects systematically tapping a particular pattern on a

The effects of articulatory suppression, visuo-spatial suppression and random generation on memory for chess positions of weak and strong players. Data from Bradley, Hudson, Robbins, and Baddeley (unpublished).

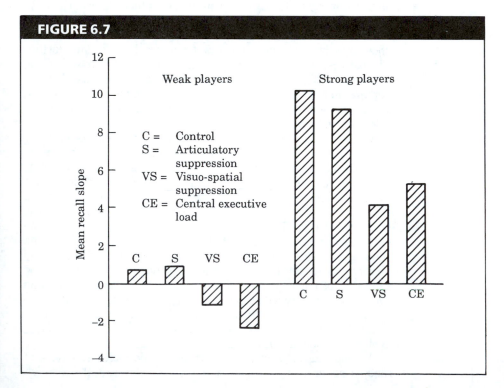

FIGURE 6.7

Weak players   Strong players

C = Control
S = Articulatory suppression
VS = Visuo-spatial suppression
CE = Central executive load

Mean recall slope

series of keys on a calculator hidden from view. This was known to interfere with the operation of the sketchpad, while a third condition involved attempting to generate random letters.

We tested subjects ranging in skill from relatively inexperienced club players to an international grand master. As expected, we found that their memory performance was highly correlated with level of skill, as measured by chess rating. The effect of the secondary tasks is shown in Figure 6.7, where the recall score reflects the number of correctly-placed pieces minus the number that are placed in the wrong location (hence the minus scores). The overall level of performance is clearly different between the novices and the experts, but the pattern is the same, with articulatory suppression having no influence on performance which is, however, markedly depressed by both the visuo-spatial task and random generation. It appears then that chess makes demands both on the sketchpad and the central executive.

So far we have talked about models of attention, settled on one such model and argued that it may well provide a suitable account of the broad functioning of the central executive system. The model is still at a relatively early stage of theoretical development, and one way of attempting to advance it is to explore a number of situations in which the central executive would be expected to play an important part. The remainder of this chapter will be concerned with one such area, the study of fluent reading.

THE CENTRAL EXECUTIVE AND FLUENT READING

Beyond the Phonological Loop

In discussing the phonological, we suggested that it may well play an important part in the development of reading in children, and furthermore suggested that a severe phonological loop deficit could create problems in language comprehension. It is, however, clear that much of the activity that goes on during comprehension of a written text by a fluent reader depends only minimally on the sound characteristics of the material being read, and is much more dependent on its meaning.

As the work by Sachs (1967) and Jarvella (1971) indicates, subjects tend to maintain something approaching a verbatim representation of much of a given sentence, but appear in some sense to "dump" that representation as they move from one sentence to the next. Since comprehension of an integrated passage necessarily involves carrying information over from one sentence to the next, there must presumably be some form of representation that is other than a verbatim record. Evidence of this comes from a series of studies by Glanzer, Dorfman, and Kaplan (1981), who had subjects read passages of prose under either normal conditions, or under conditions whereby they were required to count backwards in between successive sentences. Backward counting markedly impaired their comprehension of a passage.

The disruption observed by Glanzer et al. could of course be either because of the disruption of the phonological loop by counting, or because of the load placed on the central executive by a relatively complex task such as counting backwards in threes. Some evidence as to the relative importance of the phonological loop versus central executive components of working memory are suggested by a number of studies carried out in recent years that have explored individual differences in reading comprehension. An experiment by Perfetti and Goldman (1976) looked at various characteristics of children who were good or poor at reading comprehension, and observed that immediate memory span was not a good predictor, suggesting that differences at this level of reading probably did not stem from differences in the phonological loop capacity, although as we have suggested in Chapter 4, it is likely that the loop is important during the initial stages of learning to read.

Comprehension and Working Memory Span

Daneman and Carpenter (1980) carried out a highly influential study in which they attempted to measure the total capacity of working memory rather than rely on simple memory span. They did so by devising a task in which the subject must simultaneously store and manipulate information. The task which has come to be known as *working memory span* involves presenting the subject with a number of simple sentences with the instruction that each sentence must be processed, and the final word of each retained. After the last sentence, each of the final words must then be reported in order. The nature of the processing of the constituent sentences varies from one experiment to another; in one it involved reading the sentences out loud, in others it has involved hearing them and judging whether a sentence is meaningful or not, but fortunately provided the subject is forced to process the sentence, the exact nature of the processing does not appear to be crucial. Working memory span is measured by starting with one or two sentences and gradually increasing the number of sentences that must be processed and retained up to a point at which performance breaks down. Daneman and Carpenter tested the working memory spans of a range of university students and their reading comprehension and found a correlation between the two of +0.72. Broadly similar correlations have been obtained from other samples coming from a wider range of age and ability (Baddeley, Logie, Nimmo-Smith, & Brereton, 1985; Masson & Miller, 1983).

In a later study, Daneman and Carpenter (1983) explored the relationship between working memory and comprehension further, this time using three groups comprising students who were high, medium or low in working memory span. Subjects were required to read passages which contained apparent inconsistencies, based on the occurrence of words having more than one meaning. For example:

There was a strange noise emanating from the dark house. Bob had to venture in to find out what was there. He was terrified: rumour had it that the house was haunted. He would feel more secure with a stick to defend himself and so he went and looked among his baseball equipment. He found a bat that was very large and brown and was flying back and forth in the gloomy room. Now he didn't need to be afraid any longer.

Most people when reading this passage tend to make the initial assumption that the bat is a baseball bat, a conclusion that is of course inconsistent with the later information that it was flying back and forth. Daneman and Carpenter varied two things, one being the presence of ambiguity, the unambiguous sentence would have for example "bird" instead of "bat". The other factor concerned whether the initial word and the disambiguating phrase were within the same sentence, or were split among two separate sentences. Figure 6.8 shows the percentage of correct interpretations made by subjects of high, medium or low working memory span. All three groups tend to be somewhat misled by the ambiguous sentences, but whereas subjects with a large working memory span are able to come to the right conclusion despite the ambiguity on about 75% of the time, those with a small span are right on only about 25% of trials. The effect of separating the two sources of information is also different for the various groups. Subjects with low working memory spans have more difficulty if the ambiguous word (bat) is in a separate sentence from the disambiguating information (that it is flying about). Subjects with high spans are not

Effects of ambiguity on comprehension by subjects differing in working memory span. Subjects with low spans are more disrupted by misleading context and are less able to use disambiguating information from an earlier sentence. From Daneman and Carpenter (1983). Copyright (1983) by the American Psychological Association. Reprinted by permission.

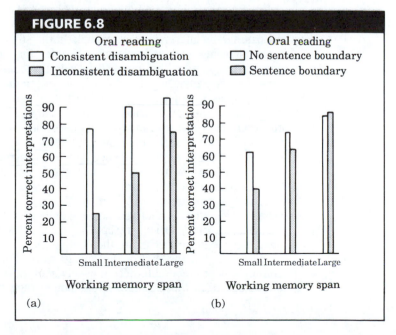

FIGURE 6.8

affected by this, suggesting that they are much more capable of carrying information over from one sentence to the next.

Working memory span is clearly a very powerful predictor of reading comprehension, and has stimulated a good deal of research in recent years. However, both its strength and its weakness stems from the fact that it is itself a relatively complex task, probably involving strategy selection, the articulatory loop, and knowledge of vocabulary as well as the capacity to coordinate these various aspects of memory. Attempts are now being made to decide whether it is, for example, a measure that is specific to language skills, or whether it represents a more general working memory capacity, although as yet the conclusions are far from clear (Daneman & Tardif, 1987). There is, of course, a danger in relying too heavily on a single task, and on this basis there are some advantages to the more varied approach to reading comprehension taken by Jane Oakhill and her colleagues, and reviewed in Oakhill, Yuill, and Parkin (1988).

Comprehension and the Central Executive

Oakhill was intrigued by certain children she had encountered as a teacher of reading. Such children had normal vocabulary for their age, together with a normal capacity to read single words, and yet scored very poorly when they read passages of prose and were tested on comprehension. She chose to study a group of such children, aged between 7 and 8 and compared them with normal children of equivalent age and vocabulary.

Oakhill (1984) began by testing their memory for passages, assessing comprehension both by literal recall of information in the passage, and by recall of information that had to be derived from the passage by inference. For example, if the story mentioned that it was snowing, then it is plausible to infer that the action takes place in the winter. She found that when the questions about the passage were answered from memory, the poor comprehenders were worse at answering both verbatim and inference-based questions. When the children were allowed to answer the questions with the text in front of them, however, both groups were equal on the verbatim answers, but the poor comprehenders still answered few of the inference questions correctly. This latter result suggests that the deficit is not purely due to differences in long-term memory.

A similar conclusion came from another study (Oakhill, 1982) in which subjects heard short stories and subsequently attempted to recognize sentences as having appeared in those stories or not. If a sentence had in fact occurred, then both groups were equally likely to detect it, but the errors they made were different. The high comprehenders tended to accept falsely sentences that were valid inferences from the passage, even though they had not actually occurred, whereas the low comprehenders were more likely than the high to falsely accept sentences that described invalid inferences from the passage. In short, the high comprehenders appeared to have a much better memory for the gist, although they were not found to be any better at verbatim memory.

The fact that verbatim memory does not seem to be critical suggests that it is unlikely that the difference between the two groups lies in differences in the articulatory loop component of working memory. This was tested in a further study by Oakhill, Yuill, and Parkin (1986) which showed that the two groups were equally likely to show a word-length effect in both remembering words and remembering sequences of pictures having names varying in length. In short, both groups appeared to be using the articulatory loop in the normal way.

Oakhill et al. went on to test the two groups on a task based on Daneman and Carpenter's working memory span. However, since they wished to test a more general working memory hypothesis rather than the one that might simply be reflecting specific language difficulties, they modified the task, replacing the sentences used by Daneman and Carpenter with groups of three numbers. The subject's task was to read out the groups of three,and then recall the last number from each group. Subjects were presented with two, three or four groups of numbers, and their results are shown in Figure 6.9. There is clearly a tendency for the working memory span of the high comprehension group to be better than that of the low, and for the difference to increase as the number of digit groups became greater.

A final study resembles that of Daneman and Carpenter (1983) in studying the resolution of ambiguity in the two groups. The children were read stories which had what appeared to be an inconsistent response by an adult to a child, a response that was subsequently explained, either immediately, or after a number of intervening sentences. For example, in one story a mother is pleased with her son for refusing to share his sweets with his sister; it later transpires that his sister is on a diet. After each passage, the child was asked whether the adult should have acted in that particular way, and if so why. When the disambiguating information comes immediately, there is no difference between the two groups, whereas if several sentences are interposed, then the poor comprehenders are much less likely to give the appropriate explanation. The authors conclude that the crucial difference between the two groups is in working memory capacity, and since it is clearly not in the capacity of the articulatory loop, and presumably not in sketchpad capacity, the assumption is that the two groups differ in the attentional capacity of the central executive. It would be interesting to test such groups on other tasks such as random generation and verbal fluency which are also assumed to depend on the central executive.

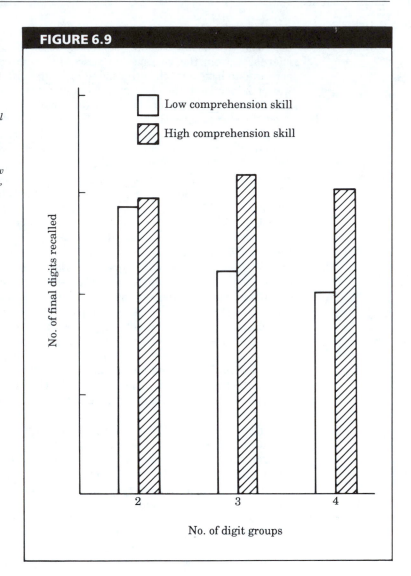

Working memory
span and
comprehension in
children. When
span is measured
by requiring the
reading and recall
of digit groups
rather than
sentences, high
comprehension
children still show
a clear advantage,
suggesting that
working memory
span is not
specifically
linguistic. From
Oakhill, Yuill,
and Parkin
(1968).

FIGURE 6.9

Low comprehension skill

High comprehension skill

No. of final digits recalled

2   3   4

No. of digit groups

OVERVIEW

The concept of attention is briefly discussed, and shown to be somewhat diverse. The concept of sustained attention as studied in vigilance tasks, and of attention as perceptual selection are considered, before going on to discuss the attentional control of action. This is covered in more detail as being directly relevant to the central executive component of working memory, and to the dual-task procedures used extensively in working memory research.

Evidence for the capacity to do two things at the same time is discussed in the light of the concept of refractoriness, and of Schneider and Shiffrin's concept of automaticity. A less precise, but broader and more general model of attentional control is offered by Norman and Shallice. This is described and illustrated by means of its application to slips of action and to the behavior of patients with frontal lobe damage. It is suggested that the Norman and Shallice model gives a good account of the functioning of the central executive in working memory, and experimental evidence is presented in support of this claim, from studies involving random generation, chess playing, and driving.

The chapter concludes with a discussion of the role of working memory in fluent reading, describing the application of Daneman and Carpenter's measure of working memory span to the analysis of reading comprehension. This suggests that subjects with high working memory spans show better comprehension and a better capacity to draw inferences and to integrate information across successive sentences. Subsequent work by Oakhill shows analogous effects in the reading and comprehension skills of children. Her work indicates that the crucial feature that distinguishes good from poor comprehenders is not the articulatory loop but is more likely to be the functioning of the central executive component of working memory.

Chapter Seven

WHEN PRACTICE MAKES PERFECT

The previous chapters have been primarily concerned with the temporary storage and manipulation of information. If this were all we could do, however, we would be doomed to live forever in the "specious present", with our horizons limited to a few moments of time, as indeed is the case with Clive Wearing, the patient described in Chapter 1. To escape from this we need some form of long-term memory. We need to be able to retrieve information from such a memory and to enter new material into it. In short we need to be able to learn.

WHAT IS LEARNING?

As everyone knows, learning is the modification, by experience of ....., of what? Of behavior certainly, although surely behavior is not essential for learning to occur. For example, if you learn someone's name, surely the learning can have occurred before someone actually asks you for it? Perhaps a concrete instance might illustrate the range of processes and activities to which we apply the concept of learning.

One of the most frequent causes of absence from work in our local hospital is back pain. This often happens because hospital staff have to lift heavy patients, and sometimes do so in ways that put unnecessary strain on the back, and for this reason all new employees are expected to attend classes on lifting. Let us consider the case of a new trainee porter who attends a lecture on lifting at the same time as a group of student nurses. He is told about the biomechanics of the spine, the dangers of bad lifting techniques, and taught among other things the Australian lift which is a way of sitting a patient up in bed that minimizes the strain put on the lifter's spine. Let us assume that he is also encouraged always to use this technique when lifting patients. He incidentally makes the acquaintance of an attractive young student nurse and arranges to meet her for a drink later in the week. What might we expect our young man to have learnt and what might he remember one day, or one year later?

At one level he will presumably have added something to his episodic and autobiographical memory. It is reasonable to suppose that he will remember meeting the student nurse, he may remember something about the teacher, and if it is one day later, one hopes that he will remember his arrangement to meet. This is all learning in the sense that it is adding information that was not present before, albeit information about a specific episode in his life.

One hopes that he will also have learnt something about the mechanics of the spine, the need for care in lifting and the various possible ways of coping with heavy patients. If he goes to subsequent classes on the same topic, this information will be presumably reinforced. A year later he may well not be able to remember exactly when he learnt what, nor is he likely to care. The retention of factual information or knowledge independently of remembering the experience of learning is normally classified as semantic memory, the type of information that forms the bulk of what most students are encouraged to acquire, although how much of what emerges in examinations is genuinely semantic, and how much is the regurgitation from episodic memory of information "swotted up" the night before is another matter.

However, being able to give a perfect description of the Australian lift will not guarantee that he is able to perform it. If we want to be sure that he does not hurt his back on the first patient, then it would be wise to ensure that he has acquired the skill of lifting. The way in which this would be assessed would of course be by asking him to lift a patient, that is by performance. This type of skill acquisition is sometimes termed *procedural learning*; as we see in Chapter 14 it appears to represent a mode of learning that is separable from the capacity to learn and remember incidents and events, since the acquisition of new procedural skills may be intact in patients who are densely amnesic.

Finally, although the young hospital porter may be an excellent exponent of the Australian lift when asked to do so, if left to his own devices, he may habitually demonstrate very risky lifting techniques. Knowledge and skill do not guarantee *habitual* performance. Convincing people that smoking is bad for their health, for example, is not enough to change their behavior; entrenched habits die hard.

The term *learning* can be legitimately used for any of the four areas just discussed, remembering a personal incident, acquiring new information, mastering a new skill, or developing a new habit. Curiously enough, psychologists rarely talk about all four. Standard books on human memory tend to concentrate on the first two, both of which could be regarded as examples of "learning that". Books on occupational psychology or perhaps sports psychology would be likely to concentrate on the third, "learning how", while books concentrating primarily on either animal learning, or its extrapolation through behavior modification to clinical psychology would be primarily concerned with the fourth issue of acquiring and changing habits. I shall try in the following chapters to say something about all of these, concentrating, however, primarily on memory as the acquisition of knowledge, if only because this is an area that has been much more extensively explored by those interested in memory than have the issues of mastering skills and developing habits.

LEARNING AS THE ACQUISITION OF NEW INFORMATION

Suppose we go back to Clive, the densely amnesic patient described in Chapter 1, and the imaginary new memory system that it would be nice to be able to give him. Suppose feeding it new information operated on the same principles as feeding information to everyone else's memory, what sort of instructions should we provide with it? What would be the best way of getting new information into the system, or for that matter what would be the best way for someone to acquire the necessary new information to pass their next set of exams?

A considerable amount of work has been done on this question, and although there is no grand generally accepted overall theory, most people would agree on a number of broad general principles. If material is to be learnt, then first of all you must obviously attend to it; secondly, a certain amount of practice will be necessary; thirdly, the material must be organized, and this will involve relating the new information to what you already know. Finally, some form of consolidation must occur, although unlike the previous three aspects of learning, this is unlikely to be under the control of the subject. We will describe these four aspects of learning, before going on to say something about the acquisition of skills and habits. In a later chapter we will go on to discuss the application of these principles to the understanding of memory breakdown in amnesic patients, and to the practical problem of helping such patients cope with their memory problems.

Attention and Learning

On the one hand, it appears obvious that unless you attend to something you are unlikely to learn it; on the other hand, students frequently claim that they learn better when listening to the radio while studying. Similarly, from time-to-time we are urged to take advantage of "sleep-teaching", a painless way of acquiring information while we sleep. Finally, rumors of subliminal advertising seem to suggest that we may be constantly fed information of which we are unaware, and hence uncritical. What is the evidence?

Research on sleep-teaching suggests that if you play information to a subject while he is asleep in bed, and question him next morning, he is likely to be able recall a small amount of the information presented. However, we do not of course sleep soundly all night, and studies that monitor the level of sleep suggest that the learning occurs principally during brief periods of relative wakefulness (e.g. Simon and Emmons, 1956). Studies that ensure that material is presented only when subjects are clearly sleeping, as indicated by electroencephalography do often find some evidence of learning, but this is typically very small (Aarons, 1976), and may not be found at all stages of sleep (Tilley, 1979).

It may be recalled that a similar result occurs when attention is distracted from the learning material by giving subjects two simultaneous auditory messages, and ordering them to repeat one and ignore the other. As Glucksberg and Cowan (1970) showed, although information is stored for the first five seconds or so, virtually nothing remains after this point, even, as Moray (1959) showed, when the unattended material is repeated many many times.

Of course, attention is not something that is simply present or absent. What happens when attention is divided among two or more sources of information? This was explored in a study by Murdock (1965) who required his subjects to listen to lists of unrelated words for subsequent recall, and at the same time perform an attention-demanding card-sorting task. The amount of attention demanded by this task was systematically varied, with the subject either simply turning the cards over or sorting into two, four or eight separate categories. As we know from Hick's Law, the demand of a sorting task increases linearly with the log number of alternatives (Hick, 1952). Murdock found that amount recalled systematically decreased as number of sorting alternatives increased; the more attention taken by card sorting, the less learning occurred. One exception to this generalisation, however, was the last few words presented in each list, the recency portion; it may be recalled from the chapter on working memory that this aspect of performance is typically based on the processes of short-term or working memory rather than LTM. The tendency for recall to be systematically impaired by an attention-demanding secondary task is a very robust one that applies to memory for prose (Baddeley & Hitch, 1974) and paired-associate learning as well as free recall (Baddeley et al., 1984).

Before continuing, however, we should perhaps consider two apparent exceptions to the generalisation that attention is necessary for memory, namely the evidence for subliminal perception, and evidence from studies that appear to suggest that patients sometimes remember events that occurred while they were under anesthetic. In the case of subliminal perception, there is by now relatively substantial evidence to suggest that a subject's behavior may be influenced by information that he is not able to report consciously. For example, Marcel (1983) showed that a subject's responses can be influenced by a word presented so briefly that there is no awareness that anything has been shown.

A typical experiment might involve first presenting a word such as BREAD or PAPER, then following it with a masking pattern made up from letter fragments. As we saw in Chapter 2, if this occurs sufficiently soon after the word, the subject will report seeing only the fragmented letters. Suppose, however, that instead of asking the subject what he saw, we present him briefly with a second word varying the amount of time the word is present, and measuring the time taken to identify this second word. Marcel found under these circumstances that despite denying having seen an earlier word, subjects are influenced by its meaning, being more accurate if the first and second words are meaningfully associated. Thus a subject is more likely to detect the word "butter" if "bread" was the first word presented than if it were "paper", despite having no inkling that the word "bread" had been shown.

Such effects are not always easy to replicate, but have been shown by other investigators (e.g. Fowler, Wolford, Slade & Tassinary, 1981). However, it is notable that what is typically achieved is the easier identification of an already existing word. There is much less evidence for the creation of new learning as opposed to the stimulation of old. Furthermore, the magnitude of such learning is typically very slight, while interpretation is always complicated by the question of specifying a threshold of awareness, so as to be absolutely sure that the first word was not seen (Holender, 1986).

In recent years there has been a number of cases in which patients who have undergone a surgical operation under general anesthetic subsequently claim to remember some incident that occurred while they were presumably unconscious. This has led to a number of attempts to investigate memory for material presented to patients who are anesthetized and undergoing surgery. In an ethically extremely dubious study, Levinson (1965) simulated the conversation surrounding an anesthetic crisis within earshot of the patient undergoing surgery, and reports subsequent behavior implying that this had had a disturbing effect on the patient. Other studies have used the rather less alarming approach of playing a tape of given words to the patient and subsequently testing for memory. In general, asking for recall produces very little, although a carefully designed recognition test did give some evidence of memory (Millar & Watkinson, 1983).

On the whole, indirect measures of memory seem to have been somewhat more successful in detecting learning during anesthesia. In one study, Bennett, Davis, and Giannini (1985) inserted into the conversation during the operation that during a post-operative interview they should indicate that they had heard the message by pulling their ear. There was a greater ear pulling tendency for the instructed group than in uninstructed controls, although Millar (1988) suggests that the difference was primarily contributed by two subjects.

There seems, however, to be evidence that some subjects at least show some form of remembering events that occurred under anesthesia; this does not however necessarily mean that the patient was unaware of the message presented. Indeed, there is evidence to suggest that auditory information will be processed during light anesthesia, and although it may not be readily recalled, it may subsequently influence the patient positively (if encouraging) or negatively. However, while it is important that this is borne in mind by the operating theatre team, the efficiency of such learning is probably very low.

On balance then it appears to be the case that despite some intriguing cases of recalling apparently unattended learning, good learning typically requires focussed attention. What else does it require of the patient? Motivation? Intention to learn? The evidence for both these is curiously enough rather weak, except in so far as they influence what the patient attends to, and how he deals with the information presented.

The Role of Motivation and Memory

It is almost certainly the case that motivation will influence the subject's willingness to attend to the material to be learnt. Suppose, for example, I gave you a list of 10 animals and 10 flower names to remember, and promised you 1 penny for every animal and 50 pence for every flower you recalled. I have little doubt that you would remember more flowers than animals. I suspect, however, that the overall number of items you recalled would not be any greater than would be the case for someone else to whom I offered simply a penny for each word recalled; what you gained in flowers you would lose in animals.

A Swedish psychologist, Lars Göran-Nilsson explored this issue as a result of being confronted every year by sceptical students who assured him that they could of course learn far more in their memory practicals if they were only motivated to do so (Nilsson, 1987). He decided to test this by setting an experiment in which subjects were either given the standard instructions for free recall learning, or were given the offer of a substantial financial reward for good performance. This information was provided either before the start of the experiment, so that it could influence both learning and retrieval, or between learning and recall. The two groups of subjects offered a reward learned no better than the group given no financial incentive.

Why did level of motivation not appear to influence the learning of Nilsson's students? Not because motivation is totally irrelevant; if the students were entirely unmotivated they would probably have refused to participate in the experiment at all. Typically, however, subjects in memory experiments are relatively highly motivated, if only because they feel that memory is related to intelligence, and do not wish to appear stupid. I suspect that this is sufficient to cause them to devote most of their attention to the business of learning, and that any further incentive has little effect. Had the task, however, been a more daunting one such as learning Milton's *Paradise Lost* by heart, I suspect that motivation would have become a factor of crucial importance, because of the need to devote a great deal of time to learning rather than to other less onerous activities.

Another situation in which motivation is probably of considerable importance is in prospective memory, remembering to do things. A bridegroom who failed to turn up at his wedding would have some difficulty convincing his bride that it was simply because he forgot!

Intention to Learn and Automaticity

It is tempting to think of learning as equivalent to storing something in a cupboard or a library, or feeding something into the memory of a computer, all activities in which the intention to store is of crucial importance. This does not appear to be the case with human memory, where the critical feature appears to be exactly *how* you process the material to be remembered, not *why* you process it. Consider, for example, a study by Mandler (1967) in which he presented his subjects with a pack of cards each bearing a word. One group was told to attempt to sort the words into categories, putting together those that had something in common. Nothing was said about subsequent recall. A second group was told to try to commit the words to memory, while a third group was given both sorting instructions and instructions to remember the words. All three groups were given the same number of practice trials, and then asked to recall. There was no difference in amount recalled. On the other hand, a fourth group that had been told not to organize the words but simply to arrange them in columns, showed significantly poorer recall performance. The crucial feature then, appeared to be the semantic organization carried out by the subjects, regardless of whether they were doing this simply in response to the experimenter's sorting instructions, or whether they were trying to learn the words.

Intention to learn, therefore, will help in so far as it encourages the subject to attend to the material and process it in the most appropriate way. Intention to learn *per se*, however, is not crucial. Indeed, Hasher and Zacks (1979, 1984) have suggested that certain features of the environment, including the location of objects and the frequency with which events occur, are stored automatically. By this they mean that such information is encoded without deliberate effort, and is no better retained when subjects are trying to remember than when they are picking up the information incidentally. In addition, they claim that training does not help, and that individual differences between subjects on such tasks are minimal. Finally, they suggest that such encoding is done just as well by young children and the elderly as by normal adults, and is not disrupted by the requirement to perform simultaneous attention-demanding tasks.

There is no doubt that some striking observations of apparent automaticity in encoding frequency and temporal location have been reported both by Hasher and Zacks (1979; 1984), and by others such as Ellis, Katz, and Williams (1987). However, there have also been a number of reported failures to observe automaticity effects in encoding location (Moore, Richards, & Hood, 1984; Naveh-Benjamin, 1987) and in encoding frequency (Ellis, Palmer, & Reeves, 1988; Fisk, 1986; Naveh-Benjamin & Jonides, 1985; Sanders, Gonzalez, Murphy, & Liddle, 1987). This is clearly an intriguing issue, but one that is not yet clearly resolved.

LEARNING AND PRACTICE

It is sometimes claimed of the psychology of memory that we know very little that has not been known for centuries (Tulving & Madigan, 1970; Neisser, 1978). According to our forbears, practice, repetition and frequency lie at the heart of all learning. There is no doubt that practice is an important component of learning, but it has become increasingly obvious over the years that sheer rote repetition is not the best way to acquire new information. Although it is true that learning takes time and effort, some ways of expending effort are more profitable that others.

The first person to explore scientifically the relationship between practice and learning was Hermann Ebbinghaus (1885). He knew, of course, that more practice leads to more learning, but asked the rather deeper question of whether the relationship was a simple linear one, with double the amount of practice leading to twice as much learning, just as doubling the temperature doubles the height of the mercury in a thermometer. There might, of course, be a relationship showing diminishing returns, as is the case with the deflection of a compass needle by a magnetic field. Or, indeed, one might find the opposite relationship with the influence of learning increasing with successive trials, just as a snowball rolled by a child will pick up more and more snow on each revolution.

Ebbinghaus was interested in exploring the development of new memories, new associations between items that had not been encountered before. In an attempt to achieve this he invented nonsense syllables, pronounceable but novel consonant-vowel-consonant triplets such as JEV, ZUD and VAM. He set himself the task of learning sequences of such syllables, reciting them at a rate of 2.5 syllables per second. He was scrupulous in his attempt to control conditions, rigidly avoiding any attempt to seek meaningful associations among the syllables, always testing himself at the same time of day, and if he had to miss a few days due to conflicting appointments or illness, he always ensured that he practised for a few days so as to return to his previous level of performance before beginning to collect new data.

In his study on the relationship between practice and learning, he used a procedure whereby on the first of any pair of days, he would read through the list of 16 syllables for 0, 8, 16, 24, 32, 42, 53 or 64 repetitions, and then 24 hours later measure what had been learnt by seeing how many additional trials were necessary for him to completely master the list to a point at which he could recite it through without error. The results of this study are shown in Figure 7.1 from which two features should be noted. First, note the linear relationship between number of learning trials on day 1, and number necessary on day 2. The fact that the relationship is linear suggests that the amount learnt is a simple function of amount of practice, the appropriate analogy being the thermometer rather than the magnetic needle or the snowball.

A second feature is rather less obvious, but if you work out the relationship between amount of time spent learning on day 1, and the additional learning time needed on day 2 you will note that each learning trial on day 1, which takes about 7 seconds, saves about 12 seconds on day 2.

This is an example of the phenomenon known as *distribution of practice*; in general it is better to spread out learning trials over time, rather than mass them together into one session. This simple experiment thus yielded two important principles of learning. The first of these is sometimes known as the *total time hypothesis*; it simply states that the amount learnt is a direct function of the time devoted to learning. The second principle is in fact a modification of the first, and states that distributed practice is more effective than massed practice.

Influence of number of learning trials on retention after a 24-hour delay. From Ebbinghaus (1885 and 1913).

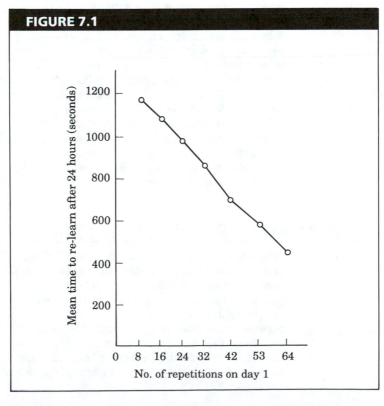

FIGURE 7.1

The Total Time Hypothesis

Although over-simplified, the total time hypothesis represents an important basic feature of human learning that holds across a surprisingly large range of conditions (Cooper & Pantle, 1967). For example, if you take a large list and split it into four subcomponents, each subcomponent will take less than a quarter of the total time. However, by the time you have added the time needed to combine the four together, the additional learning comes to almost exactly the same total time as would have occurred anyhow (Postman & Goggin, 1964).

Before applying the total time hypothesis, however, it is necessary to note a number of caveats. First of all, the hypothesis refers to time actively spent in learning. Hence, doubling the amount of time available for learning does not necessarily increase amount learnt if subjects do not use the available time actively. In a study of patients suffering from senile dementia, Miller (1971) found increasing presentation time did not lead to more learning, presumably because the patients did not use the additional available time for learning. Merely sitting and waiting for something to happen is not an effective means of learning.

A second feature that needs to be borne in mind is the type of processing that occurs. Some learning strategies are better than others, and one would not expect the total time hypothesis to hold when different amounts of time lead to different strategies. For example, Bugelski, Kidd, and Segmen (1968) carried out a study in which subjects were encouraged to associate pairs of words by means of visual imagery. They found that their subjects were able to adopt this strategy very effectively at rates of presentation of 4 or 8 seconds per pair, but not when presentation was at a rapid 2 second rate. One would not therefore expect a linear relationship between time and learning in Bugelski et al.'s study since those subjects given rapid presentation would probably be relying on rote rehearsal, whereas the slower presentation subjects would be basing their learning on visual imagery.

Finally, as we saw earlier, the distributed practice effect represents an exception to the total time hypothesis of some importance.

MASSED AND DISTRIBUTED PRACTICE

How should practice be distributed over time? The previously described results by Ebbinghaus indicate that it is better to distribute it over two days relatively evenly rather than cram it into the first day, but how general is this finding? Is distribution of practice within a day important? If so, the longer the interval between successive practice trials, the better learning should be; and does the distributed practice effect apply to all kinds of learning? The topic has proved to be a relatively complex one with different facets of the question occupying memory theorists at different historical periods, with the result that we have no broad theoretical overview of this important aspect of human learning.

The problem of distribution of practice can, in fact, be broken down into three subquestions, each of which has been tackled using its own methodology, and has come up with its own conclusions. They comprise first of all studies in which the amount of practice per day has been manipulated; this was a popular topic for research during the early years of the century, and produced evidence for the efficacy of distribution of practice across a wide range of tasks from archery to maze-learning in the dancing mouse (Woodworth, 1938).

A second aspect of distribution of practice that became popular during the 1940s and 1950s concerned the question of the length of rest interval between successive blocks of learning. The results here prove to be far less striking, with considerable variability of the occurrence and nature of the effects of distribution of practice.

A third aspect of the question concerns the effect of interval between repetitions of individual items. This became a popular topic of study during the 1970s and 1980s, and proved to have a powerful effect on learning. We will consider these three aspects of distribution of practice in turn.

Amount of Practice per Day
There does appear to be a good deal of evidence suggesting that learning is better if it is spread over many days, rather than crammed into a few. The effects of distribution of practice across days was shown by Perkins (1914) to be more powerful than the effect of rest intervals within a day, a result that is typical of a range of studies reviewed by Woodworth (1938). Although this would appear to be a topic of some practical significance, it seems to have been curiously neglected since the early years of the century, although Woodworth and Schlosberg (1954, p.812) cite an unpublished study by Keller on learning morse-code during the Second World War, where distributed learning proved to be much more effective than massed. A similar effect was observed in a study on learning to type carried out by Longman and myself (Baddeley & Longman, 1978).

Some years ago, the British Post Office decided to introduce postcodes, and to mechanize its letter-sorting procedures. Since the automatic machine recognition of handwritten script was clearly still many years away, they opted instead to have the postmen enter the postcode into a sorting machine by means of a standard typewriter keyboard. This presented the Post Office management with the problem of teaching typing to large numbers of postal workers (mainly postmen since there were relatively few post-women at the time). This prompted them to ask the advice of the Applied Psychology Unit in Cambridge.

The particular question they asked concerned whether they should attempt to teach the postmen as rapidly as possible by giving them several hours of practice per day, or whether learning would be better if practice were distributed. We carried out a study that investigated this, comparing the rate of learning in four different groups, one having a single session of one hour a day, a second having two one-hour sessions, a third having one two-hour session, while the fourth had two sessions of two hours. The rate of learning in the four groups and rate of forgetting are shown in Figure 7.2. Performance is measured in mean keystrokes per minute, and begins only when the locations of keys on the keyboard have been mastered. It will be clear from this that the distributed one-hour per day group learns the keyboard faster, and performs consistently better than the groups practising for two hours a day, which in turn do better than the group that masses its practice in a four-hour training day. In terms of retention, the distributed group again appears to do well, and the massed group to be the poorest (Baddeley & Longman, 1978).

It is perhaps worth pointing out that although the distributed group shows a clear advantage, this does not necessarily mean that it is to be preferred. It takes considerably more weeks to learn to type when practising for one hour a day than practising for four hours a day, and this may be an important factor. Furthermore, subjects in the one hour per day group were the least satisfied of the four groups, presumably because they felt they were not making as rapid progress as their colleagues who had more daily practice. However, other things being equal, our results certainly do support the generalization that skills are best learnt when practised a little and often.

I know of no generally accepted explanation of why it is better to distribute practice over days. One speculative hypothesis might be as follows. The process of long-term learning depends on physical changes within the brain. These in turn depend on neurochemical activity, which may temporarily deplete the available supply of

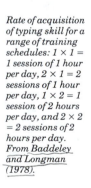

Rate of acquisition of typing skill for a range of training schedules: 1 × 1 = 1 session of 1 hour per day, 2 × 1 = 2 sessions of 1 hour per day, 1 × 2 = 1 session of 2 hours per day, and 2 × 2 = 2 sessions of 2 hours per day. From Baddeley and Longman (1978).

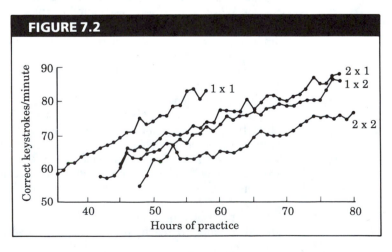

FIGURE 7.2

certain neurochemical substances, which spontaneously regenerate over time (Kopelman, 1985). If one assumes that learning a particular task places particular demands on a specific part of the brain, then it is possible that massed learning is suboptimal because it does not give sufficient time for the underlying neurochemical substances to regenerate. If such processes of regeneration operate over a matter of hours rather than seconds, then the crucial factor is likely to be amount of practice per day, rather than size of rest interval between presentations of the material.

While this hypothesis is not at present easy to test, the rapid development of research into the neurochemical basis of memory suggests that in the not-too-distant future it may be possible to explore this and related hypotheses.

Length of Inter-trial Rest Interval

The effects of inter-trial interval on performance tend to be complex and variable. In the case of learning motor skills, it is relatively easy to demonstrate that performance is impaired when successive trials are separated by too brief an interval. During the 1940s and 1950s, a great deal of research went into studying the effects of massing of practice on tracking performance. Many of these studies used the pursuit rotor in which the subject attempts to keep a stylus in contact with a target revolving in a circular path, with performance scored in terms of time on target. Performance is consistently poorer when the interval between successive trials is short. However, this decrement is in performance not in learning, since when tested the following day, the massed and distributed groups show an equivalent level of performance (Bilodeau & Bilodeau, 1961).

The effect might seem to be one of simple muscular fatigue, but proves to be more complex than this. An ingenious study by Adams (1955) showed that the effect of massing of practice on performance does not dissipate so rapidly over an interval if the subject is required to watch a fellow subject performing the task during that time. Hence, although the effect resembles fatigue, it must be operating at some central rather than peripheral muscular level. Attempts to come up with a good theoretical explanation of this phenomenon were unsuccessful, and the whole phenomenon has tended to disappear from view over the last 20 years.

This may have been partly attributable to the lack of success of extensive attempts to demonstrate equivalent effects in the learning of words and nonsense syllables. An effect of varying the interval between blocks of trials in learning nonsense syllables was reported by Hovland (1938), and this led to a great many further studies, including a marathon series of papers by Underwood and his colleagues. Alas, the effects of varying inter-trial rest periods on verbal learning proved elusive and a paper subtitled *Studies in Distributed Practice No. 23* rather sadly concluded that "The particular situations or conditions which will produce a facilitation by distributed practice in paired associate learning still remain obscure" (Underwood, Ekstrand, & Keppel, 1964, p.212).

Inter-item Repetition Interval

In contrast to the elusive effects of rest interval, a wide range of studies has shown that an individual item will be better learned and recalled if successive presentations of that item are relatively widely separated, even though the interval between presentations is filled with other items (Melton, 1970). Figure 7.3 shows the results of a typical study demonstrating that the greater the separation between successive presentations of individual items, the greater the probability of subsequent recall. This effect is very robust and has been adapted by Landauer and Bjork (1978) to create a new and powerful mnemonic strategy. The strategy is, in fact, derived by combining the distributed practice effect with a second observation regarding human learning, sometimes known as the *retrieval practice effect*. As we shall see in the chapter on retrieval, the act of successfully recalling an item increases the chance that that item will be remembered. This is not simply because it acts as another learning trial, since recalling the item leads to better retention than presenting it again; it appears that the retrieval route to that item is in some way strengthened by being successfully used. This means that in learning, subjects will be helped by being tested at a time when they can still remember an item. Testing them after they have forgotten it and then providing the item is less conducive to learning.

Note then that we appear to have two conflicting principles. The distribution of practice effect suggests that if we regard presenting

Probability of recall of words as a function of number of events occurring between successive presentations. From Melton (1970).

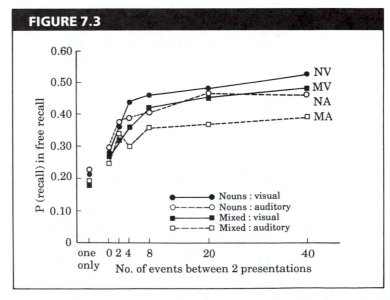

FIGURE 7.3

and testing the item as two successive learning occasions, then they should be separated as far apart as possible. On the other hand, the retrieval practice effect suggests that it is important to test memory while the subject is still capable of recalling. Landauer and Bjork suggested that the optimum is to test a given item at the longest delay compatible with correct recall. As learning proceeds, this delay will increase, suggesting that one should use a strategy of *expanding rehearsal*.

The strategy of expanding rehearsal advocates that a given item should be initially tested after a very brief delay. If the subject correctly recalls it, then the delay should be systematically increased, whereas if he or she is wrong the delay should be shortened. A typical example of such a schedule when employed in the learning of French vocabulary is shown in Table 7.1, and some of the results from its experimental use are shown in Figure 7.4.

TABLE 7.1

Learning Sequence

Teacher	Learner	Teacher	Learner
stable — l'écurie		horse	le cheval
stable?	l'écurie	grass?	l'herbe
horse — le cheval		church — l'église	
horse?	le cheval	church?	l'église
stable?	l'écurie	grass?	l'herbe
horse?	le cheval	church?	l'église
grass — l'herbe		stable?	l'écurie
grass?	l'herbe	grass?	l'herbe
stable?	l'écurie	horse?	le cheval

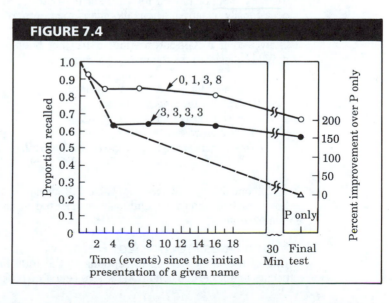

FIGURE 7.4

Results of a study using the expanding rehearsal procedure. Three conditions are tested, a single presentation (P only), four presentations each separated by three other items (3,3,3,3) and an expanding rehearsal schedule in which number of items between successive presentations is increased (0,1,3,8). From Landauer and Bjork (1978).

TABLE 7.2

Effects on Initial Performance and Subsequent Learning of Distribution of Practice

Type of Distribution		Effect on Performance	Effect on Learning
1. Amount of practice per day		Yes	Yes
2. Within-day practice	Motor skills	Yes	No
Length of rest interval	Verbal learning	Results Inconsistent	
3. Within-day practice Inter-item repetition interval		Yes	Yes

This is a very powerful strategy that is easy to use and widely applicable, not only to normal subjects, but also to the learning disabled (Gettinger, Bryant, & Mayne, 1982). Indeed, I would regard it as probably rather more broadly useful than any of the more traditional visual imagery mnemonics, having been shown to be useful in learning a wide range of tasks from multiplication facts to spelling and from lecture material to foreign language vocabulary (Rea & Modigliani, 1988). It goes directly against the assumptions of many teachers and students, who tend to assume that massed practice is best (Landauer & Ross, 1977; Rothkopf, 1963), and as such, offers further refutation of the view that our understanding of memory has not moved forward since Aristotle, as psychologists occasionally claim in their gloomier moments (e.g. Tulving & Madigan, 1970). Indeed, it runs sufficiently counter to Neisser's "Law"—that if X is interesting, it has not been studied—that it moved Neisser to the following epic verse!

> You can get a good deal from rehearsal,
> If it just has the proper dispersal.
> You would just be an ass
> To do it en masse:
> Your remembering would turn out much worsal.
> (Quoted in Bjork, 1988, p.399)

In conclusion, however, as Table 7.2 indicates, the question of how practice should be optimally distributed is an important but complex one.

When Does Practice Not Help?

One of the most striking exceptions to the total time hypothesis occurs under certain conditions where repeated practice appears to lead to little or no learning. Neisser (1982) cites an instance of this from a letter written in 1917 by Professor Sanford to his colleague Professor Titchener. It was, we are told, Professor Sanford's custom to precede meals with family prayers. These were prayers that he had read, or at least skimmed, virtually every day for 25 years, and yet occasionally he would stumble and make a mistake. He therefore decided to test his memory and attempted to write down each prayer, prompting himself from the text whenever he got stuck. He discovered that, apart from two prayers which he had consciously committed to memory, his recall was remarkably poor, on average requiring him to look up the text every five or six words, suggesting that despite his estimate of over 5,000 repetitions, recall was remarkably poor.

A similar phenomenon was studied rather more recently by Debra Bekerian and myself (Bekerian & Baddeley, 1980). A few years ago, the British Broadcasting Corporation was required to change the wavelengths on which it broadcast certain programs in order to comply with an international agreement. Quite rightly, the BBC was anxious to inform its listeners and consequently went in for a saturation advertising campaign in which the date of the change, and the details of the new wavelengths were presented at frequent intervals, sometimes spoken and at other times incorporated into various rhymes and jingles. As listeners, it struck Bekerian and I that not only did this become extremely tedious, but that we had little idea of what the new wavelengths were.

We decided to investigate this, using our panel of subjects, many of whom were housewives who were able to listen to the radio considerably more than we did. We asked our subjects to try to recall the number of the wavelength, but in case this was difficult we also included a drawing of a radio dial with numbers included and invited them to mark the point at which the various radio stations transmitted. We found that accurate recall ranged from 12 to 22% depending on the radio channel, with over 70% of the responses being "don't know". Furthermore, our subjects' attempts to mark the position of the stations on the diagram were little better than chance. And yet, according to the amount of time they claimed to listen to the radio and the frequency with which the information was broadcast, they must have heard the information well over 1,000 times before.

After the changeover had occurred, we carried out another survey, asking different subjects if they had encountered problems, and how they had solved them. We discovered that they had indeed had difficulty in remembering the new wavelengths, but fortunately the BBC had taken the additional precaution of sending everyone adhesive stickers, and most people simply hunted for the various stations, and stuck on the sticker. We discovered at this point that they did not remember the numerical wavelengths of the earlier stations either, and appeared to rely largely on visual cues. It appears that the BBC could probably have achieved virtually the same result without spending half a million pounds on an advertising scheme, and without bombarding their unfortunate listeners with interminable jingles.

What are the more general implications of our results? At a theoretical level they make one simple point, namely that frequent repetition does not guarantee learning. Beyond this, the reason for the failure is less obvious. It might be because our subjects ceased to attend to the message; as the previously described study by Glucksberg and Cowan (1970) suggests, unattended messages are not well retained. The message was clearly not entirely ignored, since most of our subjects were aware that the change was going to occur, and were accurate in reporting the date of the proposed change. It seems likely that repetition may be enough to get across a simple message such as "Boggo washes whiter", but is not good for conveying detailed information.

If number of repetitions or total presentation time is not the crucial determinant of learning, then what is? As we saw earlier, motivation or intention to learn are not essential. What is important is just what the subject does with the material he will subsequently be asked to remember. The relationship between the type of processing and subsequent memory is a topic that has been extensively explored over the last decade, principally stimulated by an influential paper by Craik and Lockhart (1972) on levels of processing and memory.

LEVELS OF PROCESSING

Processing and Structure

Craik and Lockhart present their approach as an alternative to what they describe as structural theories of memory, such as that represented by Atkinson and Shiffrin's model. As explained in Chapter 3, this assumes separate long- and short-term memory stores, with long-term learning being crucially dependent on the short-term store. More specifically, Atkinson and Shiffrin assumed that the longer an item was held in STS, the greater the probability that it would be transferred to LTS and hence stored more durably. As we saw in Chapter 3, this view was already beginning to encounter difficulties by the early 1970s.

Craik and Lockhart suggested that rather than concentrate on a structural view of memory, it might be more profitable to concentrate on the processes that contribute to remembering. They suggest that what is recalled is perhaps not some item that has been lodged in a store, but rather that the after-effects of processing remain, and these can be used as a source of evidence about the item that was processed. They made the further assumption that processing began at a relatively superficial and shallow level and proceeded to deeper and richer levels, with shallow processing giving rise to relatively poorly retrievable traces, while deep and rich encoding will leave traces that are considerably more durable. They referred to already existing evidence to suggest that short-term memory was typically associated with phonological, and long-term with semantic processing, but suggested that rather than regard phonological coding as a characteristic of STS, and semantic coding as a characteristic of LTS, the coding itself should be regarded as primary.

Two Kinds of Rehearsal

While they emphasize the *processing* of information rather than the *structure* of memory, Craik and Lockhart continue to assume a short-term or primary memory (PM) that is separate from LTM. The function of PM, however, is seen principally in terms of the processes it carries out, of which two of the most important are *maintenance rehearsal* and *elaborative rehearsal*. Maintenance rehearsal, as its name suggests, simply maintains or holds information without transforming it into a deeper code; as such, it is assumed to prevent forgetting during the process of maintenance, but not to lead to long-term learning. It is this kind of rehearsal that is assumed to have been used in the study by Craik and Watkins (1973) showing no relationship between the length of time a word was maintained and its subsequent level of learning. Long-term learning was assumed by Craik and Lockhart to depend upon elaborative rehearsal, a process that leads to an increase in the depth at which an item is encoded.

The levels of processing view is perhaps best illustrated by an experimental demonstration from a later paper (Craik & Tulving, 1975). Subjects were presented with a sequence of unrelated words, and instructed to perform one of three possible operations on each word. One condition involved shallow encoding, and for this the subject was required merely to decide whether the word was written in upper- or lower-case letters. In a second condition involving an intermediate level of coding, the subject was asked to make a rhyme judgment, for example "Does the following word rhyme with mat?"—"hat". The third condition involved deep semantic processing, and required the subject to decide whether a word (e.g. meal) fitted in to a sentence, for example "The man ate his .....". Half the items in each condition should evoke a "yes" response and half a "no".

Note that at this stage of the experiment, subjects were not told that their memory would be tested. As such it was an experiment on *incidental learning*, whereas had the subject been told that recall or recognition would be required later, it would be termed *intentional learning*. The reason for using incidental learning is that since the subject is not trying to learn the items, there is no temptation to process or encode a given word in any way other than that specified by the experimenter. If the subject knows he must subsequently recall the item, then he may well try to commit it to memory in other ways, forming images or associations or perhaps just repeating it to himself. Fortunately, as we saw earlier, incidental learning can be excellent, provided the subject processes the material in the right way.

Effects of encoding task on decision latency and subsequent recall. From Craik and Tulving (1975). Copyright (1975) by the American Psychological Association. Reprinted by permission.

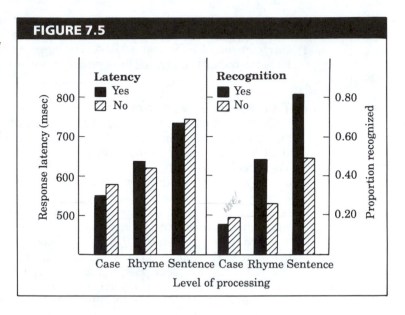

FIGURE 7.5

After answering a large number of such questions, subjects were required to perform a recognition task in which they had to categorize a long list of words as either those that had already been presented, or as "new" words. The results of this recognition test are shown in Figure 7.5.

Two things are clear from this, first that the most superficial coding in terms of the letter case led to the poorest recognition, phonological coding led to somewhat better performance, but the best recognition occurred in the case of the semantic processing task, as levels of processing would predict. Note also, though, that those questions that evoked a "yes" response were better recognized than "no" items, except in the case of the shallowest processing level. We shall return to this point later.

We have described only one study, but could have described many others carried out either earlier than this, testing memory by both recall and recognition (e.g. Hyde & Jenkins, 1969). The result described is extremely robust, and was replicated in one form or another many times in the years immediately following the publication of Craik and Lockhart's paper. As a conceptual framework, levels of processing had many attractions. First of all, it offered to replace the growing complexities of the LTM-STM dichotomy with a simple overriding principle. Secondly, the principle was one that was easy to grasp and easy to apply outside the laboratory. Thirdly, it appeared to suggest a possible answer to a number of questions; for example, "Do the elderly remember less because they code material less deeply?" "Are patients suffering from Korsakoff's syndrome amnesic because they encode their environment too superficially?" Furthermore, levels of processing seem to offer ways of possibly improving memory performance.

Troubles with Levels

Although the levels approach attracted a great deal of interest and much support, it also encountered a good deal of criticism. I myself was one of its critics (Baddeley, 1978), and in the section that follows will try to summarize some of the difficulties raised by the concept, before going on to discuss further developments and possible interpretations of the very robust effects that underlie Craik and Lockhart's approach. I shall begin with objections that are primarily theoretical in nature, and then go on to experimental evidence that appears to argue against the levels of processing approach to memory.

The Problem of Measurement

If the concept of depth of processing is to be testable and useful, then it is important to have some means of measuring it. Without this, the concept can easily become circular; if manipulation A leads to good learning, then it is assumed to involve deep processing, if poor, then the processing must have been shallow. Craik and Tulving (1975) acknowledged this problem and tried to tackle it but without success. Despite some subsequent attempts (e.g. Parkin, 1979), there is no generally accepted way of independently assessing depth of processing. This places major limits on the power of the levels of processing approach.

Serial Stages Assumption

In constructing their framework, Craik and Lockhart very sensibly built upon approaches to perception that were current at the time. These essentially assumed a series of stages. Hence, reading a word was assumed first to require the visual analysis of the letter pattern, followed by the creation of a phonological representation of the word, which in turn led to its semantic processing. Subsequent reading research has suggested that processing is much less clearly dependent on a succession of independent stages, suggesting rather that processing goes on in parallel at several levels, with information feeding both from the visual stimulus to the semantic, and in the opposite direction (e.g. Rumelhart & McClelland, 1982).

Overspill coding

As Craik and Tulving (1975) point out, it is hard to believe that when a subject reads a word such as "dog", that he is not aware of its meaning, even though he is instructed to concentrate on its sound. This still allows the theorist to argue that a phonological processing task leads to *more* phonological coding than semantic coding, but it does mean that the manipulation loses some of its elegance.

Transfer Appropriate Processing

Levels of processing has been criticized by some because of its concentration on encoding, without specifying the relevant retrieval conditions. This argument has been made particularly strongly by John Bransford and his colleagues who emphasize what they term "transfer appropriate processing", by which they mean that the best means of encoding material will depend on the retrieval conditions that are expected. For example, if you were trying to teach students phonetics, then it would be most appropriate to draw their attention to such features of their processing of a word such as the position of their lips and tongue, and the consequent sound that emerges rather than the word's meaning. A form of coding that might be regarded as shallow for one purpose might thus be considered as deep and meaningful for another.

Morris, Bransford, and Franks (1977) illustrated their point with the following experiment. Subjects are given an incidental judgment task typical of that used by Craik and his colleagues, whereby subjects are shown a series of words (e.g. cat) and asked either to make rhyme judgments on them (e.g. Does it rhyme with hat?) or semantic judgments (e.g. Does it have a tail?). The following day, subjects were either required to recognize the items, as in a standard levels of processing experiment, or are shown a sequence of words and asked in each case, whether the word rhymes with a word presented the previous day. When tested in the standard way, the semantic coding condition led to the higher performance, but when judged on the basis of rhyme, the opposite result occurred. Craik himself has made this point (Fisher & Craik, 1977), but argues that other things being equal, semantic coding leads to better learning than phonological coding.

Applications

My own view on the concept of levels of processing was that although it had limited theoretical power, nevertheless it was likely to prove a useful rule of thumb. Unfortunately it has so far proved less generally helpful than at first seemed likely. An initial study suggested that deeper processing might offer a way of improving face recognition; Bower and Karlin (1974) showed that judgments of the honesty of a person in a photograph led to better subsequent recognition than did a judgment of their sex. However, later research indicated that any form of coding that induced perceiving the face as a whole led to slightly better performance than instructions to concentrate on specified physical features, but it did not matter whether the judgment was an apparently deep one such as assessing the intelligence or honesty of the person, or whether the subject was merely trying to assess a person's height from his face (Winograd, 1976).

Somewhat more success appears to have been obtained in relating the memory deficit of the elderly to depth of processing (Craik & Simon, 1979), although even here subsequent work seems to suggest that the picture is much less clear than at first appeared (see Bäckman, in press, for a review of studies on ageing and memory). A third area of application of levels of processing has been in the attempt to explain the memory deficit of amnesic patients. Despite what looked like initially promising results, as we shall see later in Chapter 16, this did not prove to be a particularly good line of attack. Hence, although there is no doubt that levels of processing is a robust phenomenon, it has not so far proved as easy to apply as at first seemed likely (see Baddeley, 1982, for further discussion of this point).

SUBSEQUENT DEVELOPMENTS

The points we have discussed so far have largely been critical, essentially arguing for the limitations of the original concept of levels of processing. However, an important feature of any theory or framework is that it should give rise to questions that actually expand our knowledge of the field and enrich our concept. I shall discuss three such issues, points at which the original framework was clearly not completely adequate, but where useful subsequent developments have occurred, these involve adding the concepts of compatibility, elaboration, and modifying the initial concept of rehearsal.

Compatibility

You may recall that the Craik and Tulving study described earlier had one rather striking feature that I did not discuss at the time, namely the tendency for items evoking a "yes" response to be better recalled than those leading to a negative response. This was not a novel finding, for example having been previously observed by Schulman (1974). Its explanation did, however, appear to require further assumptions, since there is no reason to assume that deeper processing is required for a "yes" than a "no" response.

Craik and Tulving explain this result by suggesting that there is greater *compatibility* between the question and the answer in the case of a "yes" response, and that this will increase the probability of recall or recognition. Why should this be? Let us consider a specific example in which the subject is presented with the word "log" and asked either *"Does it rhyme with 'hog'?"*, or *"Does it rhyme with 'hat'?"* When recognition is tested, he is shown the word "log" and asked if he has seen it before. He may be uncertain, but be reminded of the similar word "hog", which may also seem familiar. The combination of the two is then more likely to convince him that he has indeed encountered the word before. In the case of "hat", this is much less likely to evoke the word "log", and hence is less likely to provide additional confirmatory information.

Note that this is not a dramatic new departure from levels of processing, but it does complicate the picture by adding further assumptions which may make prediction less straightforward.

Elaboration

Craik and Tulving carried out one experiment in which they required their subjects to judge the appropriateness of the target word to complete sentences of varying complexity. A simple sentence might be as follows. "Could the word pen fit the following sentence?: *She dropped her .....*". A slightly more complex sentence might be "Could *hill* fit the sentence: *The young child ran quickly down the .....*", while a more complex sentence might be "Could *watch* fit the sentence: *The little old man hobbled across the room and dropped his ..... in the jug?*". Performance was subsequently assessed either by cued recognition, in which the sentence frame was given, or by recall. In the case of recognition there was a strong tendency for the more elaborated sentences to be better recognized, an effect that was also present although to a much weaker extent in recall. Craik and Tulving suggest on the basis of this and other data that what is critical is not simply the presence or absence of semantic coding, but the richness with which the material is encoded.

This is of course a very plausible assumption, though not a particularly novel one. William James, for example, made a similar point in claiming that of two men with equivalent mental capacity, "the one who THINKS over his experiences most, and weaves them into systematic relations with each other will be the one with the best memory . . . All improvement of the memory lies in the line of ELABORATING THE ASSOCIATES . . ." (James, 1890, p.662). However plausible the assumption is, it makes testing the levels of processing approach even more difficult, since now we have not only the question of depth of processing which we are not able to measure, but we have in addition to concern ourselves with the issue of compatibility and degree of elaboration, neither of which is readily measurable.

Are there Two Kinds of Rehearsal?

Craik and Lockhart can provide a very neat explanation for the failure of subjects to learn when items are presented frequently but processed shallowly, as was presumably the case in Professor Sanford's morning prayers. But is it, in fact, the case that long-term learning only proceeds when information is encoded at a deeper level? Probably not, since there is considerable evidence to suggest that maintenance rehearsal, that simply involves repeating items without changing their level of encoding, may lead to enhanced retention.

Mechanic (1964) used an incidental learning procedure in which his subjects were presented with nonsense syllables and told that the experimenter was interested in how rapidly they could be pronounced. In one condition, subjects merely pronounced each item once, while in a second condition they pronounced each syllable as often as they could in the time available. When subsequently asked to recall the items, it was clear that repetition had indeed enhanced learning (see Figure 7.6). I myself have obtained similar results in a study in which subjects were required to write out nonsense syllables as frequently as possible under the pretext that I was studying code-copying.

Mechanic's result for some reason does not appear to have been much cited, possibly because it was carried out for a different purpose some 10 years before the concept of levels of processing was developed. A rather less dramatic but more influential result was that of Woodward, Bjork, and Jongeward (1973) who found that rote rehearsal had little effect on free recall, but clearly influenced recognition memory. A subsequent study by Glenberg, Smith, and Green (1977) attempted an explicit test of the Craik and Lockhart view. They devised a technique whereby subjects were presented with numbers to remember, and were given words to repeat during the retention interval. By varying the retention interval, the number of repetitions could be manipulated. At the end of the experiment subjects were unexpectedly asked to recall the words they had been repeating. Glenberg et al. found that repetition had a very small effect on recall, a ninefold increase in number of repetitions led to an increase of only 1.5%, but a much more substantial effect on recognition, with the probability increasing from 0.65 to 0.74.

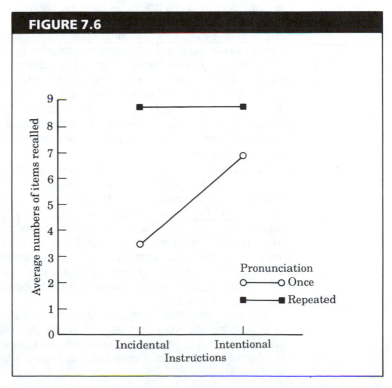

Average number of nonsense syllables recalled as a function of learning instruction and number of repetitions. Rote repetition enhances learning. Data from Mechanic (1964).

FIGURE 7.6

LEVELS OF PROCESSING: CURRENT INTERPRETATIONS

Whatever its adequacy as a complete theory, Craik and Lockhart's paper did capture two important generalisations about human memory, first that, deeper richer semantic processing usually leads to better learning, and secondly that active rehearsal may have two broad characteristics, the maintenance of information over a brief period of time, or the incorporation of new information into old, with the latter enhancing learning much more than the former. The concept of levels of processing does not offer a very detailed explanation of either of these, but over the last decade a number of suggestions have been made in connection with both.

Why Semantic Coding Helps

Curiously enough, there appears to be more agreement as to the explanation of the depth of processing effect than there is to its usefulness as a theoretical concept. Most theorists agree that one component of memory involves the capacity to discriminate the target memory trace from other potential traces. As we saw in the chapter on working memory, phonological similarity creates difficulty in immediate recall, presumably because the phonologically similar items lay down traces that are themselves similar and hence confusable. This tends to result in retrieving the wrong item, or else in having insufficient information left to discriminate between a number of potential items. Consider a situation in which the correct word to recall next is "mad", and all the subject can remember is that it had an *a* sound. The subject would be able to recall the item correctly if he or she knew it came from a set of words all with different vowels such as "pit", "top", and "mad", since only one word will fit the bill, whereas if the potential set of words were *man*, *cad*, *map* and *mad*, knowing the vowel sound is likely to be of very little help.

Suppose we now think about ways in which a given word might be represented. The word "cat" for example, might be represented phonologically or semantically. In terms of the phonological coding we have a rather limited number of dimensions on which it can be represented, possible different types and tones of voice but apart from that very little other than the basic sounds constituting the item. In contrast, the semantics of a cat can include many features including the fact that it is a pet, its habits, the visual appearance of cats, particular cats you have known, the relationship between cats and tigers and so forth.

Let us assume that when a word is presented in a typical levels of processing experiment, the subject will process it in the way specified by the experimenter, and that the operations performed on the word will leave some form of trace. When the word is subsequently presented for recognition, the subject will remember encountering it before if processing it reactivates the old traces sufficiently to allow the conclusion that that word had previously been presented. Note that it is not sufficient for just any feature to have occurred before, since that would cause the subject to say "yes" if he encountered for example any word beginning with a letter *c*; it is necessary to have a pattern of excitation that indicates that that specific word has been encountered. An encoding that leaves multiple rich traces is more likely to allow such a judgment to be made.

This interpretation assumes two things, first, that encoding many distinctive features will help recognition, and second, that deeper semantic and elaborative encoding will tend to lead to the encoding of more features. What is the evidence for these two assumptions? This was explored by Moscovitch and Craik (1976) in a study in which they presented their subjects with a number of words, requiring them to answer either a semantic or a phonological question about each. In each case, the specific question could be applied only to 1 word or to 10 different words. The assumption here is that if 10 words share the same question, then there will be fewer discriminating differences between them than if each word is associated with a different question. In short, they carried out an experiment in which richness of encoding was studied for both phonological and semantic processing. Their results showed that in the case of semantic coding, those items that had each been associated with a separate question were better retained than those that had shared the same encoding with nine other words. In the case of phonological coding no difference occurred. They interpret this as indicating that semantic coding allows potentially a much richer and more finely differentiated code to be created than is the case for phonological coding.

Further evidence that, in the case of semantic coding, greater richness leads to better performance comes from a study by Klein and Saltz (1976) who presented their subjects with words and required them to categorize the words on either one semantic dimension (e.g. pleasant-unpleasant) or on two dimensions (e.g. pleasant-unpleasant and weak-strong). Subjects were then unexpectedly asked to recall the words. As predicted, those words that had been rated on two dimensions were recalled better than those judged on only one dimension, with performance being best when the two dimensions were very different from each other, presumably giving a particularly broad range of encoding cues.

The concept of enhanced memory trace discriminability from multiple coding also offers an explanation of the tendency for motoric enactment to improve learning. For example, Cohen (1981) carried out a study in which subjects were shown a series of objects. Under one condition they were instructed to perform an action on each object. They might, for example, be shown a match and told "break the match". Level of subsequent free recall in this enactment condition was considerably higher than in a condition where the instruction was read but not performed.

Nilsson and Cohen (1988) report a number of other studies indicating excellent learning following enactment, together with an insensitivity of memory following enactment to a range of otherwise powerful factors including the age of the subject, presentation rate and level of processing. They argue that this reflects the fact that enactment produces such a rich and discriminable memory trace that the influence of these factors is swamped. It will be interesting to see if motor coding can be used as a practical memory aid for the elderly.

A parallel series of studies by Saltz and his colleagues produces broadly similar results, but they tend to find that motor enactment reduces effects such as those of ageing but does not remove them (Saltz, 1988). Saltz and Donnenworth-Nolan (1981) tested whether the effect of enactment was indeed due to motor activity and not just to visual imagery by interpolating motoric, visual and verbal tasks between presentation of lists that subjects were induced to learn by motor enactment or visual imagery. Recall of the motor enactment lists were impaired by motor but not visual or verbal interference, while visual imagery lists were impaired by visual but not motor activity, supporting the hypothesis of separate visual and motoric memory codes.

The studies by Moscovitch and Craik, and Klein and Saltz have indicated that better memory follows richer coding when the coding dimension is semantic, while Saltz and Cohen have shown the power of motor enrichment, but what of phonological coding? Is the auditory-verbal dimension so limited that nothing can enrich it? An ingenious study by Eysenck and Eysenck (1980) indicates that this is not the case. The subjects in this experiment were presented with words that normally have a somewhat irregular pronunciation, and on some of the trials were required to pronounce the word as if it had the regular pronunciation; for example they might be given the word "have" and required to pronounce it so that it would rhyme with "rave". On other occasions, the word was pronounced normally, or was processed semantically. When subjects were later unexpectedly tested for recognition, those words that the subject had been instructed to mispronounce were as well recognized as the semantically processed words, with both of these being better recognized than words that had been pronounced normally. It appears then that for phonological coding, the creation of two distinctive codes enhances subsequent recognition. The effect was however considerably less marked in a study where memory was tested by recall rather than recognition (Eysenck, 1979). We shall return to this point later.

To summarize the argument so far, deep, semantic and elaborative encoding appear to enhance memory because they set up memory traces that are more discriminable than items that have been encoded shallowly and with little elaboration. Such effects tend to be most obvious when memory is tested by recognition. Why should this be?

It has long been known that recall requires at least two processes, accessing or generating the item to be recalled, and discrimination of that item from similar but incorrect items. Similarity will uniformly interfere with the discrimination, but it may be actively helpful in accessing an item. To return to the example of phonologically similar words; including a cluster of words such as *man*, *map*, *cad*, *cat*, in a free recall list may actually help performance (Craik & Levy, 1970) because the similarity of the words helps the subject to generate the other three, given that he has one word. The most extreme example of this would of course be a case where the total set was included (e.g. directions *north*, *south*, *east* and *west*). Here the subject would only need to know that such a group had occurred, and remember one item in order to generate the rest. Much more typically, similarity has a rather uncertain effect on recall, depending on the balance between the positive effect of similarity in reducing the number of possible alternatives, and the negative effect of similarity on item discrimination (see Hunt & Seta, 1984, for a fuller discussion of this point).

Perhaps the best way of illustrating the relationship between similarity, recall and recognition is through an experiment carried out by Horowitz (1962). He used paired-associate learning in which the subject had to associate eight pairs of nonsense syllables, and he systematically manipulated the similarity among both the stimulus items and the response items. He predicted that stimulus similarity would have a uniformly negative effect, and this indeed occurred. Similarity among responses however led to much less clear-cut results.

Horowitz then moved to a slightly different paradigm known as associative matching. In this procedure, the subject is given all the eight responses and the eight stimuli, and merely has to assign each response to the appropriate stimulus. In this situation then, learning the responses is not necessary, but discriminating amongst them is. As predicted, under associative matching conditions, both response and stimulus similarity had equivalent deleterious effects on performance.

It appears then that the richness of encoding effect can be explained in terms of earlier concepts of similarity, but what of the further concepts of maintenance rehearsal, compatibility and elaboration? Are these also explicable in terms of more basic concepts?

Maintenance Rehearsal and Elaboration

It may be recalled that while sheer repetition often fails to produce learning, there were some cases when maintenance rehearsal did seem to lead to long-term learning. How should these be explained? Perhaps we should begin by distinguishing two separate effects of learning, namely "priming" and "inter-item association". The concept of priming assumes that there are already existing structures within memory that represent familiar items such as words. When a word is presented, then that representation will be made active or primed. The result of this activity is that subsequently it may be slightly easier to, for example, perceive that word if it is presented very briefly, or perhaps easier to utilize that word. It may also be assumed that the fact that a word has been primed or presented recently may be used in a recognition test.

One can distinguish priming from associative learning, where some new association is built between two previously separate items, or between, for example, a word and a particular experimental context. Recall is assumed to depend on such associations, on items being linked together, possibly through linking to the experimental background.

We have spoken, so far, as though these were quite separate processes, whereas in practice many situations will involve some component of both. Hence, rapidly reciting a sequence of words, such as occurs in maintenance rehearsal, such as Professor Sanford indulged in during his morning prayers, may well build up some links between adjacent words, but inter-word links are likely to be relatively weak since of their very nature, words are used all the time in constantly changing orders. There might well be an initial priming effect, but this would be likely to be relatively short-lived, and enhance recognition but not recall. Such a result was of course exactly what Glenberg et al. (1977) observed, namely an effect of repeated presentation of words on their subsequent recognition but not on their recall.

What of the result obtained by Mechanic (1964), who found that having subjects repeat unfamiliar nonsense syllables enhanced the probability of their later recall? Here, one assumes that the repetition creates new associations among the constituent speech sounds, leading to new learning rather than simply the priming of existing word units. This new learning will be reflected in recall as well as recognition.

In conclusion then, the distinction between maintenance rehearsal and elaboration remains a useful one, although it is neither as absolute, nor as novel as at first seemed likely. Maintenance rehearsal will typically continue to prime an existing representation. This may be useful for certain purposes but is unlikely to lead to substantial long-term learning, since it merely perpetuates the status quo. Elaborative rehearsal on the other hand is an instance of reorganizing the new material to fit in with what is already known. The importance of organization was stressed by Bartlett and by the Gestalt psychologists in the 1930s, and after a period of neglect became prominent in research into memory during the 1960s. It will form the focus of the next chapter.

OVERVIEW

While a single experience may lead to learning, the acquisition of new information typically requires practice. It is important that the learner attends to the material, but is not crucial that he or she is actively intending to commit it to memory, provided the material is processed appropriately.

In general, learning is better when practice is distributed over several days rather than crammed into a single session. Furthermore, individual items show better learning when presentation is distributed rather than massed. This has led to the development of a powerful new mnemonic learning procedure based on a gradually increasing interval between successive presentations of the items to be learnt.

Craik and Lockhart have proposed that probability of learning is a function of level of processing; words that are encoded shallowly by categorizing their visual characteristics are less well retained than words categorized in terms of their sound, which in turn leads to poorer learning than deeper and more elaborate semantic coding. While this is a very robust phenomenon, the adequacy of levels of processing as a theoretical framework has proved a more controversial issue.

It is, however, likely that semantic processing will typically produce richer and more discriminable memory traces than occur with the phonological and visual coding of verbal material, and that this will enhance subsequent recall and recognition.

Chapter Eight

ORGANIZING AND LEARNING

THE ROLE OF ORGANIZATION

Suppose you were given the rather curious task of attempting to learn the following 15 letters and to recall them in any order you wished:

GDOIALAZNRAENENR

You might simply recite them to yourself and try to learn the sequence of letter names off by heart. Or you might try to pronounce them as a word, whereupon you are likely to encounter some difficulties, both in pronouncing the particular combination, and perhaps, remembering how to spell that pronounced unit when you recall it. You might make life easier if you were to rearrange the letters so as to make the whole sequence somewhat easier to pronounce, by alternating consonants and vowels, producing something like:

NARELADENIZAGRON

That would certainly be more pronounceable and almost certainly easier to learn. An even better strategy however would be possible if you happened to notice that these letters can be used to spell out a meaningful phrase:

ORGANIZE AND LEARN

something that has the triple advantage of being readily pronounceable, based on familiar sequences of sounds, and in addition being meaningful.

Artificial though it is, this simple example characterizes the central feature of human learning, namely that it is dependent upon organization. Organization is important at three levels: (1) organization that already exists in one's long-term memory; (2) organization that can be perceived or generated within the material to be learnt; and, (3) organization linking these two, thus allowing the new material to be accessed as and when required. The chapter that follows is concerned with each of these stages; it begins by considering some naturalistic studies carried out on a specific type of memory for which organization is necessary, namely that of a waiter or bartender remembering the orders of his or her customers. The chapter then goes on to discuss a range of laboratory studies of organization, attempting to come up with some generalizations about the nature of mnemonics, before concluding with another practical example, that of attempting to help patients remember the instructions given by doctors.

THE WAITRESS'S DILEMMA

Suppose you are a waitress or waiter and had to look after some dozen or more guests, take down their order for several courses, serve it at the appropriate time and then give them the right bill. How would you do the task? You would probably write the order down, and you could of course rely entirely on the written bill to keep track of everything, continually checking and monitoring as you go. This may be the way in which some waitresses work, but Joy Stevens (1988) observed that this was not the case in the restaurant in which she herself worked for three months. The waitresses here would write the bill, and leave it on the table in front of the customer, relying on memory for everything else. As part of a study of the memory of the waitresses, she encouraged five confederates each wearing a lapel microphone to come into the restaurant and order three dishes from consenting waitresses who also had microphones.

Each customer ordered a hot or cold sandwich, a dessert and a hot or cold drink in that order. Having noted this for all five customers, the waitress left the check behind and went to place and collect the various orders. Stevens notes that in the few seconds between collecting the orders and placing them, the waitresses typically reorganized and clustered the orders so as to fit in with the layout of the restaurant, first placing the hot orders in the hot kitchen, then the cold orders in the cold kitchen, followed by the cold drinks from near the cold kitchen and the hot drinks from a hotplate on the counter. The dessert orders of course came later. In collecting the orders from the kitchens, the waitresses also clustered the items, this time on the basis of the location of the customers within the restaurant, so as to minimize the number of trips that must be made.

At one level, such observations might seem quite commonplace. At another, they clearly tell us a good deal about the flexibility of memory, the way in which the incoming information is categorized and reorganized in order to fit both the geographical constraints of the restaurant, and the order in which the various components of the meal should arrive.

A somewhat more experimental approach was taken by King Beach (1988) who in this case enlisted in a school of bartenders, and studied some of the mnemonic tricks of the trade. Trainees are taught to mix a standard range of drinks, each one being associated with a glass of a particular shape and color. Their training involves standard exercises in which they are required to take an order for four drinks, make them and serve them as quickly as possible. Beach used this task to study the development of expertise, comparing the performance of a group of trainees with a group of bartenders who had graduated from the school, and subsequently had a good deal of practical experience.

The test was run on six successive occasions, with two additional factors being varied. On some of the trials, the tender would have to count backwards in threes from forty while performing the task; this was assumed to interfere with short-term verbal memory (Peterson & Peterson, 1959). On other trials, the task had to be completed using black glasses of identical shapes, rather than the standard glasses that vary in shape and color. This was assumed to interfere with using visual cues to help perform the task.

The experts took only 60% as long to mix the four drinks, showed only 5% as much evidence of overt verbal rehearsal, and only 2% as much tendency to check the recipe in the guidebook. They were also unaffected by the requirement to count backwards, unlike the novices whose performance was impaired by this additional task (see Figure 8.1). On the other hand, the experienced bartenders were much more affected by the change in glasses than the novices, being more likely to forget which drinks they should be preparing, and to make more errors in the ingredients, while the change in glasses does not affect either of these in novices. It appears then that part of the skill of learning to be a bartender is that of relying less on internal rehearsal, a strategy that is subject to distraction, and taking more advantage of the external memory cues provided by the different shapes, sizes and colors associated with different drinks.

Does that mean then that expertise in general involves relying more on external aids and less on internal strategies? Almost certainly not, because many situations occur in which such convenient external cues are simply not available. In these circumstances, internal strategies of organization become crucial, as is demonstrated very clearly in a detailed study of the performance of a single waiter, J.C., who claimed to be able to remember over 20 orders without the necessity of writing anything down (Ericsson, 1988; Ericsson & Polson, in press).

In order to study J.C.'s performance, Ericsson and Polson devised an experimental task which was based on that of remembering restaurant orders. Around a representation of a table they arranged a number of cards. On each card was the photograph of someone taken from a newspaper, representing the customer, and an order which the experimenter would read out. This could involve any of seven different kinds of steak cooked at any of five temperatures and accompanied by any of five salad dressings and

Errors made in recalling drink orders by novice and experienced barmen with and without the presence of mnemonic cues. From Beach (1988).

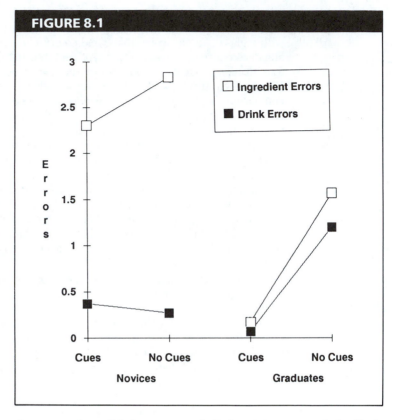

FIGURE 8.1

three starches (fried potatoes, baked potatoes, or rice). Each individual order was produced by randomly selecting from each of these categories.

Ericsson and Polson began by testing their waiter's claim to be particularly good at this task, comparing his performance with that of a group of college students. He did indeed prove to be much more accurate, making only 3% of errors compared to 20% for the students. The next stage was to ask J.C. to "think aloud", describing what was going through his mind as he took the order. Table 8.1 is an example of one of these "think aloud" protocols.

Examining a number of such protocols, Ericsson and Polson isolated the following features:

1. J.C. looks at the picture and those of the other "customers", categorizing them in terms of his experience of customers.
2. This is used to categorize the various orders as expected or unexpected. It is perhaps worth mentioning here that the random nature of the orders in the experiment would make this task harder for J.C. than it would be in actual practice, given that he is correct in his expectations.
3. He categorizes the various orders, and:

4. Notes patterns of repetitions and alternations.
5. He encodes the various features using different systems.

More specifically, they found that he categorized salad dressings in terms of the initial letter, B for blue cheese, T for thousand island and H for house dressing which is creamy Italian. He codes the temperatures visuo-spatially with "well done" represented as the highest point and "rare" as the lowest on a five-point scale,

---

TABLE 8.1

Transcribed Think-aloud Protocol and Retrospective Report from the Study of Dinner Orders from a Table with Five People

E   Why don't you start thinking out loud?

S: Oh, it is five. I thought it was going to be eight. These five people look like they don't fit together. That's unusual. Out of your real estate magazine. This guy, the first guy looks like he's way out of place with this group of people so we'll see how easy his order is. Okay. Go.

E: Steak, Oscar, well done, thousand island, rice.

S: Okay. *Well done and rice seem to fit that guy. Steak Oscar doesn't.* Next.

E: Barbeque, well done, blue cheese, baked potato.

S: *That sounds fairly standard. TB is my salad dressing notation* and next.

E: Filet Mignon, medium well, thousand island, fries.

S: *TBT, rice, baker, fries. Temperatures are making an easy pattern.* Next.

E: Filet Mignon, rare, oil and vinegar, fries.

S: *TB.* What's the salad dressing?

E: Thousand Island

S: *TBTO.* Starch for no. 4?

E: Fries

S: Fries, okay. Rice, baker, fries, fries, TBT. Next.

E: Barbeque, medium well, Creamy Italian, baked potato

S: *TBTOH. Barbeque, that's the second barbeque, medium well,* starch?

E: Baked potato

Okay, *fries, rice, starches are easy.* Done. It seems much easier when I'm not counting, by the way. Thousand, blue, thousand oil, creamy Italian. Temperatures; well, well, medium-well, rare, medium-well. Starches; rice, baked potato, fries, fries, baked potato. Steaks; Oscar, barbeque, filet. I have to think a minute on that guy. And the last one is barbeque. Um, no. 4's steak is rare with fries and he's having oil and vinegar and uh, I have it narrowed down to a filet and a brochette are the two that I'm thinking about. Now, by process of elimination, it seemed to me that there was only one double on this order and that was the barbeques. There were two barbeques, it seemed that everything else was singular, and if there's already a filet that I'm sure of then this guy had a brochette, for no. 4. And I'll go by that. A brochette. No.

Source: Ericsson and Polson (in press).

while the starches, coming from only three categories are remembered principally in terms of the pattern of repetitions.

Finally, the experimenters asked whether this strategy was limited to remembering food, or could be adapted to remember other quite different things. They therefore set up an experiment in which they replaced the various food names with items from other categories, animals, times, flowers and metals. Although performance was somewhat slower, J.C. was able to adapt, and in doing so showed an exactly similar pattern, with the speed of encoding slowing down from the first to the fourth "customer", and then speeding up for the fifth and slowing down for the sixth, seventh and eighth, a pattern that was consistent with J.C.'s claim that he remembered things in clusters of four orders.

Ericsson (1988) relates the findings from this study to those of earlier studies of his own on the subjects who had been taught to remember extremely long sequences of digits (see Chapter 3), and of studies of subjects with phenomenal memory performance from other sources. He concludes that all of these show three characteristics which he argues are central to skill in remembering. They are:

1. That the material is encoded meaningfully, using pre-existing knowledge.
2. That the process involves attaching retrieval cues to some specified structure built on existing knowledge, and:
3. That the process becomes progressively faster with increasing practice.

EXPERIMENTAL STUDIES OF ORGANIZATION

The Gestalt Tradition

While the examples just described are all recent, the study of organization and memory is, of course, far from new. During the 1920s and 1930s, Gestalt psychologists such as Kohler, Wertheimer and Katona tended to view learning in terms of the principles of organization derived from studies of perception, and in terms of the processes of insightful discovery they were investigating in connection with research on problem solving.

An example of a phenomenon derived from the analogy with perception is that of the Von Restorff effect. In a typical experiment, Von Restorff (1933) would present subjects with a single three-digit number embedded in a list of nonsense syllables. Subjects tend to make fewer errors in recalling the isolated atypical item, a phenomenon that Von Restorff likened to the figure-ground effect whereby a figure such as a black square stands out from a white background.

The Von Restorff effect is reliable, and proved useful many years later in designing the British postcode. The Applied Psychology Unit, Cambridge, was asked to advise the British Post Office on code design, but given the constraint that the code had to comprise a mixture of numbers and letters. Effectively, this reduced the question to that of what was the best location in the sequence for the numbers. Bearing in mind the Von Restorff effect, Conrad (1960) suggested that the digits should be used to enhance performance at the point of maximum error, which in the case of auditorily presented items is just beyond the middle of the sequence. He tested this and found that sure enough, errors were minimal when the digits were located at this point. He also found that the worst possible sequence was a regular alternation between letters and digits, a code that has for some reason subsequently been adopted by the Canadian Post Office.

The second feature of the Gestalt approach to memory was the conviction that insightful learning is more durable than that based on rote rehearsal. This was illustrated by Katona (1940) in a study in which subjects were shown a string of numbers and given three minutes to remember them. One group was told nothing else, while the second was encouraged to look for an organizing principle. See if you can find the principle:

2 9 3 3 3 6 4 0 4 3 4 7
5 8 1 2 1 5 1 9 2 2 2 6

The principle involved starting at the bottom row with the digit 5, and successively coding 3 and 4 (i.e. $5 + 3 = 8 + 4 = 12 + 3 = 15$ etc.). On immediate test, both groups showed an equal level of recall, with 33% of the memorizers and 38% of the principle seekers recalling the sequence perfectly. When re-tested three weeks later however, all of the subjects who had been given the learning instruction had forgotten it, whereas 23% of the principle seekers could still recall it perfectly.

Unfortunately, the study of the role of organization in memory was initially largely limited to the continental European Gestalt approach to psychology. This was decimated by the rise of the Nazis in the 1930s, and although individual Gestalt psychologists were offered sanctuary in North America, their influence was never very great, at a time when American psychology was very much dominated by stimulus-response associationism. Furthermore, while Bartlett's approach to long-term memory had been very much concerned with "effort after meaning", his influence on research into long-term memory during the 1950s was much less than it had been, or indeed subsequently became. Consequently, the role of organization in memory had to be re-demonstrated in the 1960s, when it was explored using substantially more rigorous experimental procedures than those that had failed to convince the behaviorists in the 1930s and 1940s.

The demonstration of the importance of organization in human learning was one of the major developments of the 1960s. This work was important in demonstrating the crucial role of the subject as an active processor and organizer of material rather than a passive recipient, an issue that was once sufficiently controversial to merit a complete chapter in many textbooks (e.g. Baddeley, 1976; Crowder, 1976; Zechmeister & Nyberg, 1982). It is, however, now almost universally accepted. For that reason I will simply provide an overview with illustrative studies, devoting more attention to later studies of organization in memory outside the laboratory, studies which grew from the earlier laboratory-based experiments.

The idea that organization might be important for learning was supported by evidence of three kinds: (1) demonstrations that organized material was easier to remember than disorganized; (2) evidence that given random material, subjects spontaneously attempt to organize it; and (3) demonstrations that instructions to organize enhanced learning. These will be considered in turn.

Organized Material is Easy to Learn

Jenkins and Russell (1952) noted that when their subjects were recalling lists of words containing high associates such as *man woman* and *knife fork*, despite the fact that the words were split up during presentation, they tended to be recalled as pairs. This was explored further by Deese (1959) who presented lists of 15 words of three kinds, one list comprised 15 words that were all high associates of a single given starting word, for example: *butterfly*, where the high associate words were: *moth, insect, wing, bird, fly, yellow, net, pretty, flower, bug, cocoon, color, stomach, blue, bees*. A second list comprised low associates, while the third list comprised words that were all unassociated with each other, for example: *book, tulip, government, sofa, early, velvet, winter, payroll, line, zebra, spray, arrow, help, arithmetic, typical*. Subjects recalled a mean of 7.35 words from the high associated lists, 6.08 from the medium and 5.50 from the unassociated sequences.

In a paradigm that was much imitated during the 1960s, Bousfield (1953) presented his subjects with a list of 60 words, comprising 15 animals, 15 boys' names, 15 professions and 15 vegetables in scrambled order. He found that recall was substantially higher than recall of a list of 60 unrelated words; he also noted that recall tended to involve producing clusters of items from the same category.

Some years later, Tulving and Pearlstone (1966) explored this effect further in an experiment in which subjects learnt lists of 12 or 48 words comprising groups of one, two or four words per category. Tulving and Pearlstone found that subjects who were given the category names recalled substantially more than those tested by free recall. This study was important in linking categorization and organization to the process of retrieval, a theme that will be taken up in the Chapter 11.

Although much of the research involved items selected from semantic categories, many other kinds of organization are of course possible. Bower, Clark, Lesgold, and Winzenz (1969) demonstrated the effectiveness of hierarchical semantic organization using

FIGURE 8.2

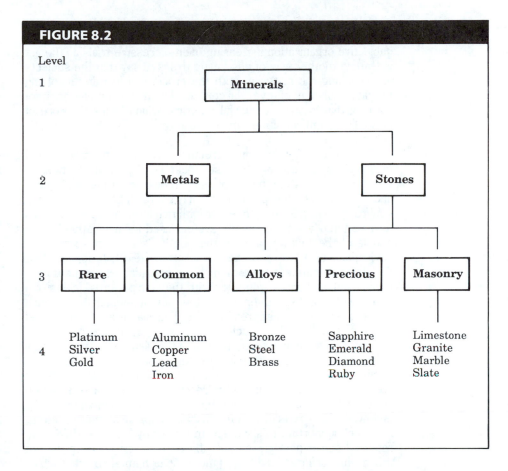

Level

1

*The "minerals"
conceptual
hierarchy used by
Bower et al.
(1969). Recall was
much higher than
when the same
words were
presented in
scrambled order.*

material of the type shown in Figure 8.2. Subjects shown the material laid out in a hierarchical manner recalled a mean of 73 out of 112 words in contrast to a mean of 21 for those in which the hierarchy was obscured. While hierarchical organization is a particularly powerful one, Broadbent, Cooper, and Broadbent (1978) have shown that other organizations such as a matrix comprising rows and columns can be equally effective.

Subjective Organization

A second source of evidence came from observations that given quasi-random material, subjects will attempt to impose their own order, the characteristic "effort after meaning" emphasized by Bartlett (1932). Perhaps the most influential demonstration of this phenomenon was that of Tulving (1962) who repeatedly presented his subjects with a list of words for free recall. On each trial, the words were presented in a different random order; nevertheless the order in which subjects recalled the words tended to become increasingly stereotyped, as if the subject were building up some form of internal organizational structure, with the degree of subjective organization increasing over successive trials as the list is learnt. Another way of describing this is to say that the subjects are chunking the material, with the process of learning involving the accumulation of ever larger chunks, a conceptualization of learning that is still a powerful one, and which forms the core of Newell's recent ambitious model of cognition SOAR (Newell, in press).

The capacity for imposing structure on apparently random and meaningless patterns is of course an old one. The constellations of the stars are a system that helps the perceiver to group, remember and use the major star positions for navigation. The capacity to use minimal cues of this sort, together with rich internal representations forms an important part of the system used for navigation by the people of the Puluwat atoll in the South Pacific, whose amazing navigational skills were studied by Gladwin (1970). It appears that the Puluwat mariners have memorized a spatial representation of islands and landmarks, together with the star patterns linking one island with another. Even given this set of mental maps, such voyages represent an impressive feat. The islands are far apart and hence not visible for much of the voyage; furthermore, the navigator must be able to keep track of the distance covered by his outrigger canoe if he is to utilize his mental map.

Similarly, impressive feats of navigation across trackless wastes are demonstrated by Australian desert Aborigines, and it has on occasion been suggested that they may perhaps be genetically endowed with a particularly effective visuo-spatial memory system. Apparent support for this came from studies by Kearins (1978) who reported better performance of Aborigine desert children than of urban white children on a test of memory for natural objects such as stones and leaves. A certain amount of controversy followed but a study by Klich and Davidson (1983) appears to have clarified the situation.

Klich and Davidson tested desert Aborigine and suburban white children on a task that involved placing 20 objects in a 5 × 4 array. Ten of the objects were manufactured, such as a battery or a clothes peg, and ten were natural, such as a stone or a feather. After this first test, there was indeed an advantage for the Aborigine children, although this was limited to the natural objects. Following this test, the subjects were given training in order to encourage visual coding, presenting them with a set of objects which were visually different, but all had the same name, brown bottles, for instance. Both groups were then re-tested, whereupon the difference in performance disappeared. It seems probable, therefore, that the initial difference was due to a greater tendency of the desert children to rely on visual rather than verbal coding, a characteristic they appeared to share with New York bartenders.

Of course, there are other situations in which verbal coding is advantageous. As Hitch and Halliday (1983) showed, children attempting to learn the order of pictured objects typically tend to rely increasingly on supplementing visual memory with verbal rehearsal as they get older. What strategy will be optimal obviously will depend on the particular task in hand, and it seems entirely plausible that finding one's way across the Australian desert is likely to place a high premium on careful visual observation, and a well-developed spatial long-term memory.

It appears, however, that Aborigine orientation is not purely visuo-spatial, but relies on a very detailed verbal account of routes that may extend over a thousand miles, and that are represented in sacred songs. In his fascinating book *The Songlines*, Bruce Chatwin describes his attempt to learn more about these songs which combine great sacred significance with very practical and detailed information about landmarks, each of which is woven into a narrative about a journey carried out by a totem animal ancestor. The narrative is sung, with certain combinations of notes describing the action of an Ancestor's feet (Chatwin, 1988, p.120): "One phrase would say, 'Salt Pan'; another 'Creek-bed', 'Spinifex', 'Sand-hill', 'Mulga-scrub', 'Rock-face' and so forth. An expert song-man, by listening to their order of succession, would count how many times his hero crossed a river, or scaled a ridge—and be able to calculate where, and how far along a Songline he was. ..... So a musical phrase ..... is a map reference."

As Chatwin points out, it is very difficult to obtain detailed information on songlines because of their sacred nature. However, if he is correct, then they represent a remarkable use of human memory to provide an extremely detailed serial verbal represent-ation of an enormous amount of spatial and geographical information. Such information has probably been the same for many thousands of years, until the coming of European settlers, perhaps giving time for such elaborate mnemonic structures to evolve, being passed on from one generation to the next as something of great religious and practical significance.

Instructions to Organize Enhance Learning

One powerful source of evidence for the importance of organization comes from studies of incidental learning in which subjects are instructed to organize the material in various ways and subsequently tested for recall. The incidental learning study by Mandler (1967) mentioned in a previous chapter is a good example of this; subjects instructed to sort words into categories, with no instruction to learn, retained those words just as well as subjects who were instructed to learn them.

There are of course many ways of organizing material other than semantic categorization. One organization is that of seriation, organizing items in a fixed order. Mandler and Dean (1969) showed that if you repeatedly present lists of words in the same order, then subjects will tend to recall them in a constant order. Sequences like the alphabet are learnt serially, and there is no doubt that serial order does have one crucial advantage, it ensures that every item is produced, whereas free recall tends to be very effective for producing most of the items, but has the drawback that some items will almost always be forgotten. For example, if you try to recall the U.S. states, or the countries of Europe, you are unlikely to be entirely successful. In fact, you will probably find that you tend to move on to using either an alphabetical search or perhaps more likely one based on geographical location, but I suspect you are still likely to leave out a fair proportion.

Another powerful organizing method is that of visual imagery. Suppose you want to associate two words, for example *aeroplane* and *cabbage*, then you simply need to imagine them interacting in some way, for example an aeroplane flying into an enormous cabbage. Subsequently, given one item, the image will pop up, making the other item available.

MNEMONICS

Imagery, Rhyme, and Rhythm

Imagery has formed one of the cornerstones of mnemonic systems through the ages. The Romans, for example, made use of memory theatres, imagined rooms in which different parts of a orator's speech could be stored by representing that part of the speech by an image, and locating the image in a specific location. Hence, if the speech were to begin by discussing the price of corn, and move on to talk about excessive taxation, a cornsheaf would be imagined in the first location, followed perhaps by an image of a man weighted down by a heavy load, to represent the tax burden. At times when literacy was far from universal, and books very expensive, the capacity to remember was an important social skill, and consequently mnemonics played a far more important role than they do today. A detailed and fascinating historical account of mnemonics is given in *The Art of Memory* by Frances Yates (1966).

While visual images provide a very powerful way of associating items, they are not the only one. Indeed, during certain historic periods, images were regarded as sinful and liable to predispose to lewd thoughts, with the result that in puritan times, visual imagery mnemonics were discouraged, and mnemonics based on meaningful associations regarded as more acceptable. For example, Peter Ramus in the sixteenth century proposed an organizational system based on a hierarchical tree with abstract concepts feeding down to ever more concrete instances. Those favoring verbal mnemonics also criticized visual imagery as being inefficient by requiring the memory of a great deal of irrelevant information.

Verbal mnemonics continued to be influential long after the puritans, and in Victorian times they were often used for remembering things like historical dates via a system in which the digits in the date are associated with specific consonants which are then used to produce words by inserting vowels. The words are then incorporated into a piece of doggerel describing the historic event. Hence one example might be:

By *men* near Hastings, William gains the Crown:
A *rap* in forest new brings Rufus down

The first line which refers to William the Conqueror's victory at Hastings represents the date of the battle by the word *men*, where both *m* and *n* are associated with the digit 6. Hence, the word *men* should remind the schoolboy that the Battle of Hastings happened in 1066. The letters *r* and *p* in the *rap* represent the digits 8 and 7, and should remind the pupil that King William Rufus was killed in a hunting accident in the New Forest in 1087.

Mnemonics that rely upon verbal coding often combine it with the more phonological codes of rhyme and rhythm, as for example in the well-known mnemonic for remembering the number of days in a month:

Thirty days hath September
April, June and November

The combination of meaning and rhyme can be a very powerful one, as is demonstrated the work of Wallace and Rubin (1988) on an Apalachian folk singer's memory for ballads.

It used to be thought that singers of ballads and the bards who used to recite epic poetry were literally word perfect. However, studies by Lord (1960) cast doubt on this in an investigation of the traditional bards of Yugoslavia who were the direct descendants of the Homeric tradition. Lord observed that although the bard believed that he always produced the same words, there were subtle differences from one performance to another. Lord concluded that the bards regenerated the epic each time, using their detailed knowledge of the theme together with the highly constrained rhythmic form.

Wallace and Rubin (1988) were able to examine this in the case of their ballad singer, and found that very few errors occurred, but that when they did they almost invariably preserved both the meaning and the prosody, for example:

"Lima it's a three mile grade"
became
"Lima on a three mile grade",
or
"She cried bold captain tell me true"
became
"She cried brave captain tell me true".

Even when changes of meaning do occur, they tend to be minimal, as in

"She had not sailed far over the deep
Till a large ship she chanced to meet"
which became
"She had not sailed far over the main
She spied three ships a sailing from Spain".

This does not, of course, necessarily prove that the singer is able to generate the song each time. Wallace and Rubin therefore tested this directly by giving their singer a newspaper account of a railway disaster and asking him to produce a new ballad about it. After about 5 minutes of study he duly did so, generating a ballad that fitted the overall pattern of disaster ballads that he had previously shown himself to be adept at. If it was possible to generate such a ballad from a completely new story, regenerating a familiar ballad would surely be easy for an experienced singer.

Elaboration Coding Mnemonics

One type of mnemonic operates by elaborating the material to be retained so as to make it more memorable, usually by linking it to something that is already known. A typical example is the pegword mnemonic whereby you first learn to associate the numbers one to ten with a rhyming concrete word as follows:

One is a bun
Two is a shoe
Three is a tree
Four is a door
Five is a hive
Six is sticks
Seven is heaven
Eight is a gate
Nine is wine
Ten is a hen

Having learnt these, they can then be used to learn lists of ten other items by taking each item and imagining it interacting with the item associated with the appropriate number. Let us assume, for example, that the first item is *submarine*, then you might imagine a submarine crashing into a huge floating bun. The second item might be *duck* in which case you might imagine a duck sitting in a shoe and quacking. The third item might be *crocodile*, in which case you might imagine a crocodile with a tree growing out of it, and so forth.

When the time comes to recall you can go through the sequence, thinking first of number one and the bun which in turn will remind you of the submarine running into it and so forth. Alternatively, you can be cued by being given the number, for example three, which should evoke the keyword *tree*, which reminds you that it is growing out of a crocodile. Try it yourself with the following list:

    donkey
    cup
    elephant
    stocking
    fire engine
    ring
    caterpillar
    saucepan
    rabbit
    top hat

Associate each of these in turn with one of the ten pegwords, then close your eyes and try to recall the list.

Most people find that they can get virtually all the items correct after a single trial, considerably more than you would expect if you were not using mnemonics. The words given were all concrete and easy to image, but the system can also be used for abstract material, although in this case one needs to use a little more imagination in order to come up with an imageable representation. For example, in imaging *justice* you might want to imagine the blindfold statue holding the scales, while *strength* might be imaged in terms of a strong man holding aloft a heavy weight. Try it with the following list:

    love
    hope
    disease
    anxiety
    jollity
    success
    eloquence
    kindness
    durability
    lightness

Try forming an image for each and linking it with the appropriate keyword, then see if you can recall the items.

In principle, one can of course learn a much larger range of pegwords, allowing a much more impressive length of list to be recalled. Other more elaborate schemes for remembering specific material such as numbers can also be acquired. On the whole, however, although these may be good for impressing your friends, they tend not to be particularly useful in everyday life since for the most part, if we need the accurate recall of long lists of items, typically we write them down.

There are, however, practical situations where we wish to

commit large amounts of information to long-term memory for subsequent use, rather than to amaze our friends. Acquiring the vocabulary of a foreign language, or indeed of our own language is a case in point. The visuo-spatial imagery mnemonic provides a very useful technique for doing this, as has been demonstrated in a range of studies.

In one such study, Sweeney and Bellezza (1982) studied the process of American students learning the meaning of abstract words, an aspect of knowledge that is tested in the Graduate Record Examination, an important determinant of whether or not one gets into graduate school in the U.S. Subjects were taught either by being given the approximate meaning of a word, together with an example of its use in context, or were taught its meaning, together with a linking word that the subject was instructed to image. For example, in the case of the word *scurrilous* for which they give the short definition as "obscene", the subject was given the linking word of "squirrel" and told to imagine a squirrel making obscene gestures. Subjects were tested after a delay and required to produce an approximate synonym for the word, and use it in context. Mean performance of the subjects who had used the linking imagery mnemonic was 59% compared with 14% for the control group.

Elaborative mnemonics are not of course limited to traditional visual imagery techniques, as the instance illustrated in Figure 8.3 demonstrates. This is a technique invented to help children with reading difficulties learn the correct way to pronounce letters in English by giving them invented characters that link the shape of each letter to its sound, both alone, and in combination with other letters. The elaboration also helps the child to avoid reversing letters.

Reduction Coding Mnemonics

While the systems we have described so far tend to operate by enriching the material to be recalled either by adding more memorable dimensions to the code, or by linking it to existing memory, a class of mnemonics exists which appears to do exactly the opposite, namely to reduce the amount of information stored. A good example of this is one of the two common methods of remembering the order of the colors of the spectrum, namely *Red, Orange, Yellow, Green, Blue, Indigo, Violet*. The reduction code uses the initial letters to create a pronounceable and easily rehearsed acronym of *ROYGBIV*. The equivalent elaboration code that is common in Britain also uses initial letters, but uses them to generate the sentence:

*R*ichard *O*f *Y*ork *G*ains *B*attles *I*n *V*ain.

Opposite page: Illustrations from the Letterland Pictogram System: First Steps in Letterland: Programme One for Teaching Reading and Spelling, by Lyn Wendon. Published (1986) by Letterland Ltd., Barton, Cambridge, CB3, 7AY, UK.

One advantage of reduction coding mnemonics is that they can be rehearsed very rapidly, and hence often verbally maintained while performing some other task. The initial letter system

FIGURE 8.3

Each pictogram is designed to serve several purposes:
- to penetrate the "hieroglyphic barrier" created by the otherwise meaningless abstract symbol;
- to endow the single letters with directional attributes so as to reduce the tendency to reversals in early writing;
- to create a recall route based on story logic which is easier to remember than the arbitrary fact that, for example:

 = "hhh"   = "sss"   = a completely different sound from or in any other letter sequence.

The story logic, given in brief, is as follows:

The Hairy Hat Man hates noise, so

he never speaks above a whisper in words.

Sammy Snake loves to hiss as he

slithers and slides along in words. But

everyone in Letterland knows that the Hat

Man hates noise. So it is not surprising that

whenever he finds himself beside Sammy

Snake in a word he hu es

him up: " "!

(Actual height of cards: 330 mm. Plain letters on reverse sides make the pictogram mnemonics removable by turning over.)

FIGURE 8.4

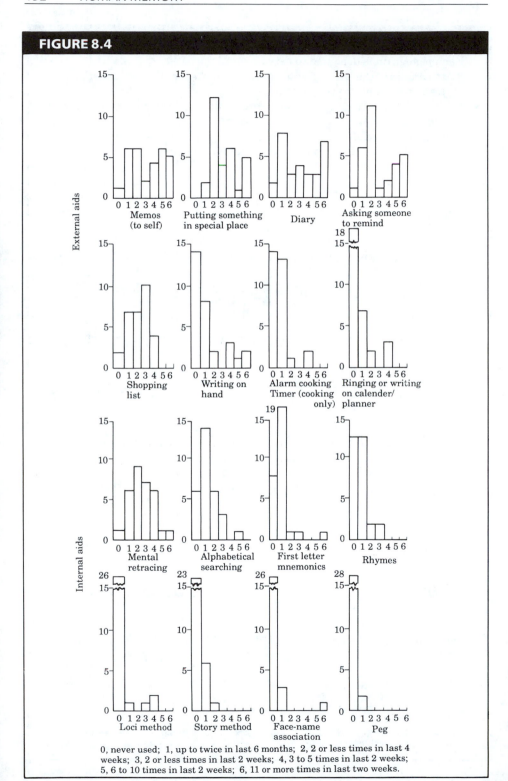

0, never used; 1, up to twice in last 6 months; 2, 2 or less times in last 4 weeks; 3, 2 or less times in last 2 weeks; 4, 3 to 5 times in last 2 weeks; 5, 6 to 10 times in last 2 weeks; 6, 11 or more times in last two weeks.

Figure 8.4 (page 192): Reported frequency of use of memory aids by students (N = 30). The vertical scale is the number of students in each category from 0 (never used) through 3 (about once per week), to 6 (about once per day). From Harris (1980). Reprinted by permission of the Psychonomics Society Inc.

used by the waiter J.C. for remembering salad dressings was a good example of such a code. Other examples include those used for remembering the order of musical notes on the scale such as FACE, and reminders of the order in which particular operations should be performed in simple algebra contained in the acronym BODMAS (Brackets of Division, Multiplication, Addition, Subtraction).

External Aids

We have so far talked as if the only way to improve memory performance is through internal strategies. While these are of particular interest as applications of what we know about the working of human memory, in practical terms they are probably less widely used than external aids such as lists, notes, knots in handkerchiefs and so forth. Harris (1980) conducted a survey of the use of memory aids. His results are shown in Figure 8.4, from which it is clear that people tend to rely more heavily on external aids than on mnemonics, a tendency that seems to be even more marked in the elderly, who according to a recent study by Jackson, Bogers, and Kerstholt (1988), are very sensibly more likely than the young to remember future events and appointments by means of external aids such as notes, calendars and diaries. As we shall see in Chapter 17, external aids probably also are the best and most reliable way of enhancing the memory performance of brain damaged patients, although mnemonic learning strategies can sometimes prove useful.

PROGRAMS TO IMPROVE MEMORY

So how can we apply the information that has been acquired on organization and remembering to the practical aim of improving memory? There are two kinds of answer to this question, the first involves attempting to design materials and arrange situations so as to enhance memorability, the second attempts to teach people strategies whereby they themselves may improve their capacity to learn and remember new material. We will briefly consider both of these in turn.

There is abundant evidence to suggest that material that is presented to the public, is by no means always presented in a way that allows it to be well understood and well remembered. The example of the saturation advertising campaign to inform the British public of the change in radio wavelengths described earlier (Bekerian & Baddeley, 1980) is a case in point. There have in addition been several studies of attempts to convey information to the public, often producing results that should prove very worrying to the media. Wagenaar and Visser (1979) for example studied the extent to which people were able to remember the information presented in the weather forecast, finding depressingly low rates of retention, whether the information is presented purely verbally, or with visual illustrations (Wagenaar, Schreuder, & van der Heijden, 1985).

Making Medical Instructions more Memorable

While accurate memory for weather forecasts may not generally be of great significance, poor recall is of considerable importance in other areas, one striking example being that of communication between doctors and patients. A range of studies reviewed by Ley (1988) showed that patients typically forgot up to half of the information conveyed to them by their doctors (see Table 8.2). He goes on to demonstrate that this is important since there is a high correlation between the extent to which an individual reports understanding the information presented by the doctor, and his general degree of satisfaction. Furthermore, in the case of surgical patients, the provision of adequate information before surgery reduces both the number of analgesics required during recovery, and the time taken to recover sufficiently to be discharged after the operation (Ley, 1979, table 7). Finally, the understanding and remembering of instructions is clearly important in the case of patients who are prescribed drugs or treatment, and again there appear to be significant relationships between reported comprehension and reported compliance (Ley, 1979).

Ley is a clinical rather than cognitive psychologist, but decided that the results of research on the psychology of memory might be applicable to the important practical problem of enhancing the comprehension and retention of medical instructions by patients. He systematically carried out a series of studies exploring the possible ways in which retention could be enhanced. In one study (Ley, 1972), he took advantage of the primacy effect, whereby the first items presented tend to be well recalled, showing that retention of advice and instructions was enhanced when the more important and salient features were presented first.

Another study capitalized on the evidence that semantic categorization enhances memory, and ensured that the statements made by doctors about the patient and his or her illness were explicitly divided into clear categories. For example, the doctor might say "I am going to tell you what is wrong, what tests will be needed, what the treatment will be, what the outcome will be, and what my advice is. First, what is wrong with you; I think you have got bronchitis: Second, what tests will be needed; you will have to have an X-ray and a blood test to make sure: Third, what the treatment will be; I'll give you an antibiotic to take. Take it on an empty stomach, say at least one hour before a meal" and so on. This led to an improvement of recall of 42% in one study, and 24% in another (Ley, Bradshaw, Eaves, & Walker, 1973).

In a further study, Bradshaw, Ley, Kincey, and Bradshaw (1975) showed that recall of advice statements can be substantially improved by using specific rather than general forms of advice. Hence general statements such as "You must weigh yourself

TABLE 8.2

Recall of Information by Hospital Patients

Investigation	Patients	Mean No. of Statements Made	Delay before Recall	Mean % Recalled	Method Assessing Recall
Ley and Spelman (1965)	47 new medical outpatients	5.6	0–80 minutes	63	Free
Ley and Spelman (1967)	(a) 22 new medical outpatients	7.0	0–80 minutes	61	Free
	(b) 22 new medical outpatients	7.9	0–80 minutes	59	Free
Joyce et al. (1969)	(a) 30 new rheumatological outpatients	9.5	Nil	48	Cued
	(b) 24 new rheumatological outpatients	11.9	1–4 weeks	46	Cued
Kupst el al. (1975)	22 repeat visit cardiac patients	?	Nil	76	Cued
Anderson et al. (1979)	151 new rheumatological outpatients	12.1	1 month	80	Written
			Nil	40	Free
Reading (1981)	(a) 20 gynecological inpatients	10.0	Nil	70	Free
				80	Probed
	(b) 16 gynecological inpatients	10.0	3 hours	47	Free
				55	Probed

Source: Ley (1988).

regularly", or "You must lose weight" are much less likely to be recalled by would-be slimmers than more specific statements such as "Weigh yourself every Saturday before breakfast" or "You must lose 15 pounds in weight". Bradshaw et al. found that the specific statements were over twice as well recalled as the general.

Improving Memory Strategies in the Elderly

Can people improve their memories? From the number of courses advertised in the popular press, and the number of "mind and memory" training books available, there is clearly a belief that one can. The memory training courses will tell you about visual imagery mnemonics, about linking things together semantically and organizing in various other ways, and will certainly enable you to develop methods for remembering lists of unrelated material more effectively. However, the evidence seems to suggest that people who take such courses, typically do not put what they learn into practice at all consistently (Higbee, 1981). On the whole, the things that such courses are good at teaching us to do tend not to be particularly useful; if we need to remember lists of unrelated words, we usually write them down.

However, there are occasions where a mnemonic strategy would be useful. For instance I was recently asked if I knew of any work on the best way with which people can learn to memorize the four-digit number that goes with a banking card, where it is inadvisable to write down and carry around one's personal number. We are currently comparing a range of possible strategies. Remembering one's car registration number is another situation where mnemonics can be useful, while any technique that helps the learning and recall of the names of new acquaintances and friends is likely to be very welcome. Having a range of mnemonic strategies to hand can therefore be rather useful, even though one only uses them from time-to-time.

What sort of techniques ought to feature in such a battery of mnemonic skills? One possible collection was devised by McEvoy and Moon (1988) in a program aiming to teach memory skills to the elderly. The areas they chose to tackle were as follows:

Names and faces: Subjects were taught the use of imagery mnemonics, together with techniques of associating the name of the new person with that of someone they already knew. The importance of repeating the name in conversation after gradually increasing intervals was discussed (the expanding rehearsal technique), and they were encouraged to review the names of people they did not meet very frequently, before the meeting (priming). These techniques were then practised.

Appointments: Here, the usefulness of systematically using external aids such as diaries and calendars was emphasized, together with the advantage of reviewing prospective appointments in advance.

Routine tasks: This was concerned with remembering to carry out routine activities such as watering plants or taking medicine. The techniques taught included the use of external memory aids such as checklists, diaries and reminders of various kinds. Internal strategies were also taught, for example always carrying out a task at the same time and linking it with a particular event, e.g. always taking medication after breakfast, or always watering the plants after the weekly TV gardening show.

Spatial orientation: This concerned problems that the elderly reported such as forgetting where their car had been parked, becoming disoriented in an unfamiliar department store or in finding their way through a new town. The sort of skills taught here involved using both verbal and visual coding, making use of landmarks, and looking back at the route as you traverse it for the first time so as to familiarize yourself with how it will look when you are trying to return. The subjects were also taught to analyze new environments before entering them, making use of maps when available, and general knowledge about the layout of buildings. Practice included walking tours through unfamiliar building complexes.

Locating objects: This was concerned with the problem of forgetting where you put things. The skills developed included storing objects in places related to their function, rather than arbitrarily. Objects that are often lost can perhaps be marked with easily visible colors, while the problem of mislaying tools while performing a job can be reduced by remembering to put them down in an obvious and clearly visible place.

Concentration: This involved instructions in the need to maintain concentration on stories or information being presented, the need to review the material as it was encountered and to relate it to what was already known.

The program formed the core of a workshop in memory skills for a group of 34 subjects who averaged 68 years old, and who attended for five one-hour sessions. The course was evaluated by initially requiring the subjects to complete a questionnaire concerned with the frequency with which the subjects experienced memory problems in the six areas taught. For purposes of comparison questions about four other areas that were not taught in the course were also included, namely conversations, new learning, recalling multiple things, and recalling old knowledge.

Approximately two weeks after the final session, the subjects completed the memory questionnaire again, and scores before and after the program were compared. There proved to be significant improvements in rated memory for names and faces, appointments, routine tasks and spatial orientation, while no improvement was reported for locating objects, concentration, or for the four areas not taught in the training program (see Table 8.3).

While self-ratings of the number of memory problems encountered may provide a somewhat unreliable quantitative indication of

TABLE 8.3

Pre- and Post-test Means for Each Problem Area and Direction of Change

	Pre-test	Post-test	Difference
Areas taught in training program			
Names and faces	2.64	2.07	0.57
Appointments	1.32	1.02	0.30
Routine tasks	1.79	1.55	0.24
Spatial orientation	1.43	1.28	0.15
Locating objects	1.86	1.79	0.07
Concentration	2.21	2.37	−0.16
Areas not taught in training program			
Conversations	1.97	1.98	−0.01
New learning	1.56	1.66	−0.10
Recalling multiple things	1.75	1.76	−0.01
Recalling old knowledge	1.81	1.76	0.05

Source: McEvoy and Moon (1988).

everyday memory problems, the results are encouraging. The fact that the improvement does not occur for all items, and in particular does not occur for any of those not trained, suggests that the reported improvements are not simply due to a general reporting bias. As a brief course for elderly people who wish to explore ways of reducing memory lapses, it would seem to hold promise. It would clearly be desirable to have more objective measures of the incidence of memory lapses, although the practical problems of collecting objective evidence of this kind are very great indeed.

However, while the normal elderly may well be able to benefit from such a course, there is little evidence to suggest that patients suffering from major memory problems will be able to develop and apply general mnemonic strategies of this kind, although as we shall see in Chapter 15, therapists and relatives may be able to use such strategies in order to help the patient learn specific and carefully selected pieces of important information.

In conclusion, the question of a relationship between organization and memory is a very simple and straightforward one. Organizing helps learning. Material that is easy to organize will be easy to learn, and subjects who are good organizers of the material are likely to remember it well. At a detailed level, however, the pattern is much more complicated, simply because the number of ways of organizing material is very large, and will depend crucially on the particular material to be learnt. Looked at from this point of view, learning is partly a problem-solving exercise in which one attempts to find the best way of mapping new learning onto old.

OVERVIEW

The chapter begins with a consideration of the practical problem of a waiter or bartender attempting to remember orders, suggesting that memory is enhanced by a range of strategies including categorization, and the use of both internally and externally based mnemonic strategies. Laboratory studies of organization are then described, starting with those providing evidence for the importance of organization in learning. These indicate that the more organized the material, the easier it is to learn, that subjects spontaneously tend to impose organization on random material, and finally that explicit instructions to organize enhance learning.

This is followed by a discussion of techniques designed to enhance learning, with examples both of elaborative mnemonics in which the material to be learnt is elaborated and linked to existing knowledge, and reduction mnemonics. These involve simplifying the material to be learnt in order to enhance speed of rehearsal and learning. A third category of mnemonics involves the use of external aids such as diaries and reminders.

The chapter ends with a discussion of the application of the psychology of memory to two practical problems. The first of these concerns that of improving the communication between doctors and patients, where the work of Ley has been particularly important, while the second concerns more recent attempts to help the normal elderly improve their memory skills.

Chapter Nine

ACQUIRING HABITS

*I*n the 1940s and 1950s, experimental psychology was dominated by theories of learning, and in particular by Clark Hull's monumental attempt to produce a general theory of learning. This was worked out in considerable detail and expressed in equations and postulates that were explicitly aimed at resembling the theories of physics, and in particular Newton's *Principia*. The principal text on human memory, McGeoch and Irion (1952), although much less theoretically oriented, presented a model of learning and memory that was based on the principles of conditioning derived from animal experimentation. However, despite the dominance of this learning theory-based approach up to the late 1950s, it had disappeared almost totally from work on human memory by the 1970s, and a characteristic memory text of the 1980s is likely to have nothing of Hull and precious little of McGeoch.

Has the tradition of research based on animal experimentation therefore vanished without trace? Only from the minds of cognitive psychologists. There continues to be active research on attempting to understand the principles of learning using animals (e.g. Mackintosh, 1974; Rescorla, 1985; Wagner, 1981). Furthermore, at an applied level one could argue that one of the major impacts on society made by psychology has come from work in the area of behavior modification, in which principles originally derived from research on animals continue to be applied to a wide range of practical problems. One could, at the risk of over-simplification, describe behavior modification as the technology concerned with changing habits. Since acquiring and breaking habits clearly forms an important part of human learning, the neglect of research on behavior modification by cognitive psychologists such as myself is clearly regrettable. The chapter that follows is offered as a step in the direction of attempting to redress this omission.

CONDITIONING IN ANIMALS

I should begin by reminding you of two classic experiments, experiments that are included in every basic psychology text, namely the study of classical conditioning in dogs carried out originally by Pavlov, and Thorndike's work on cats in a puzzle box.

Classical Conditioning

You will recall that the Russian physiologist Pavlov working on the reflex of salivation showed that a previously neutral stimulus such as a bell can cause salivation if it is regularly paired with presentation of dry meat powder, a stimulus that automatically evokes the salivary reflex. A similar conclusion was in fact drawn independently by the American psychologist Twitmyer (1902) who, as part of his doctoral dissertation, had been carrying out experiments on the knee jerk reflex using the falling of lead hammers on the subject's knee as the stimulus, and preceding this by sounding a bell. On one occasion the bell sounded but the lead hammers were not released. Nonetheless, the subject's leg responded. The subject said he was conscious of the movement but that it was not under his volitional control.

Twitmyer went on to explore the effect systematically and subsequently reported it, noting its theoretical significance (Twitmyer, 1904). His enthusiasm does not seem to have been shared by the chairman of the session at which he presented it to the American Psychological Association, a certain William James, who cut short the discussion so as not to delay lunch. In classical conditioning then, the previously neutral conditioned stimulus (the bell) becomes in some sense equivalent to the unconditioned stimulus (the hammer), and in doing so evokes the relevant reflex. On the other hand, if the situation changes so that the bell is no longer followed by the hammer tap, then the tendency for the knee jerk will gradually reduce, and eventually vanish, a process referred to as the *extinction* of the conditioned reflex.

Instrumental Learning

At about the same time as Pavlov was working with his dogs, Edward L. Thorndike (1898) was exploring learning in cats. He adopted a procedure whereby the cat was placed inside a box, with food placed outside. The cat could escape from the box by hitting a particular lever, a response that was not likely to be made rapidly by chance (see Figure 9.1). Thorndike observed that the cats initially responded apparently at random, happening eventually, after much varied activity to hit the appropriate lever and get out of the box to claim the food. Over successive trials, the animal became likely to make the appropriate response in less and less time until eventually, the correct response was made almost immediately (see Figure 9.2). Thorndike described the learning as resulting from *trial and error*, with the response that finally led to reward being gradually strengthened, the so-called *Law of Effect*. The basic principle of learning whereby associations between a stimulus and a response that were followed by a reward were strengthened was known as *connectionism*, a term that, as we shall see in a later chapter has once again become popular.

The initial conceptualization of both classical conditioning and instrumental conditioning of the type first studied by Thorndike

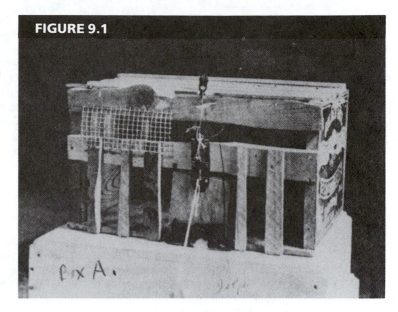

One of the four puzzle boxes used by Thorndike in the research for his doctoral thesis. From Boakes (1984).

FIGURE 9.1

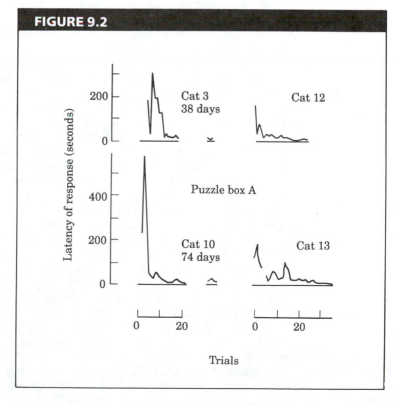

The first learning curves: the results from four cats who learned to escape from Thorndike's Box, showing the general decrease in the latency of the correct response as training was continued and, in the case of cats 3 and 10, good retention of the response after intervals of 38 and 74 days respectively. From Thorndike (1898).

FIGURE 9.2

was in terms of the automatic strengthening of associations. In the case of Pavlov's dogs, the bell became automatically linked with the meat powder, whereas in the puzzle box, the cat's apparently random activity was assumed to become gradually more precise by the automatic strengthening of the association between the apparatus and the target response. Of the many trials that eventually led to escape and food, all of them had in common the one final crucial response, and by principles analogous to natural selection, this response would gradually become ever stronger. It would always eventually be rewarded and hence reinforced, whereas the other irrelevant activities were reinforced only occasionally.

Cognition and Conditioning

An alternative way of conceptualizing both results, however, is in terms of the animals' detection of correlations or perhaps even causal relationships. In classical conditioning, the bell becomes a signal for the presentation of food, while in the puzzle box the pressing of an unobvious and obscure lever becomes eventually associated with escape. Indeed, current developments of animal learning theory often regard traditional conditioning paradigms as ways of studying how animals learn about their environment. Classical conditioning can be regarded as a paradigm for studying the association between events in the world, and instrumental conditioning a way of studying associations between an action and its consequences (Rescorla, 1980).

In the case of human subjects, detecting contingencies, or "understanding what is going on" does seem to be an important component of the process of conditioning. Consider, for example, the study carried out by Hilgard, Campbell, and Sears (1938). Their subjects were required to look at two small windows. The left one became brighter, and 600 milliseconds later an airpuff was delivered to the subject's eye causing a reflex blink. After a few trials, the lightening of the window was enough to cause the subject to blink. On the following day, the subject returned and was tested again. On this occasion however, sometimes the left-hand window brightened and was followed by an airpuff, while on other occasions the right-hand window increased in brightness, and no puff of air followed. As Figure 9.3a shows, subjects gradually learnt this discrimination, blinking to the left-hand window but not to the right. A second group was tested in exactly the same way with one exception. They were told that when the right-hand window brightened, no airpuff would result. As Figure 9.3b shows, learning the "discrimination" was immediate, with no blinks to the right-hand window. However, as we shall see later, the situation is more complex, since subjects can learn associations which they are unable to report (e.g. Berry & Broadbent, 1984).

Just as stimulus generalization can occur through instruction, so can response generalization. Gibson, Jack, and Raffel (1932)

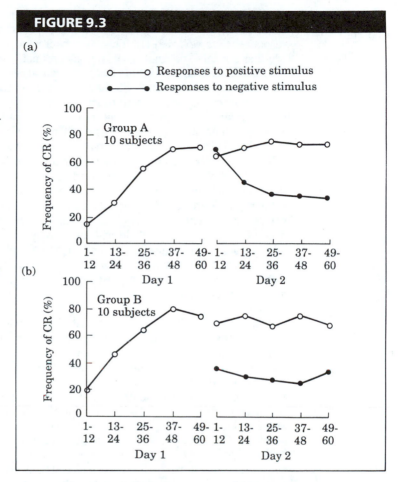

Effect of advance knowledge of stimulus-relationships on the course of discrimination. Subjects were conditioned to blink by an airpuff following a visual stimulus. Extinction of the response occurred when the airpuff no longer followed the stimulus (panel a), but was immediate when subjects were informed that no airpuff would occur (panel b). Data from Hilgard et al. (1938).

FIGURE 9.3

showed that when subjects were conditioned to withdraw their right hand to avoid shock, the response generalized readily to the left hand. An ingenious experiment by Wickens (1938) required the subject to place his finger on an electrode. Following a neutral stimulus, a mild electric shock was given causing the subject reflexly to lift his finger. When the response had been learnt, Wickens instructed the subject to turn his hand over, hence placing the back of his finger on the electrode. If a specific pattern of muscle activity had been conditioned, then the end result should be that the conditioned stimulus should now cause him to press the electrode even harder. In fact, the subject again raised his finger, involving a totally different pattern of muscles, but achieving the same end.

There has been considerable research on the question of whether classical or instrumental conditioning can occur without the awareness of the subject. While the evidence is still not completely clear, on the whole it appears to suggest that subjects do need to be aware of the stimulus-response relationships and contingencies if they are to learn the appropriate conditioned response (Brewer, 1974). This in turn raises the question of whether animal experiments are not also primarily concerned with teaching animals about contingencies and causal links in the world.

Dickinson and Shanks (1985) have approached this issue from a novel viewpoint by attempting to show that judgments of causality in human subjects obey the same rules as govern the behavior of animals in conditioning experiments. They devised a computer game in which an image of a tank moved across a video screen. The subject was given a button and told that when he pressed it a missile would be fired at the tank. If the missile was a "good" one, then the tank would be blown up. The subject's task was to estimate the percentage of "good" missiles. In order to make the situation more complex however, it was explained that the tank was going through a minefield and hence might be blown up by a mine rather than a missile. Dickinson and Shanks showed that when contingencies were systematically manipulated, they were able to predict the subject's estimate of the probability that a missile would explode on the basis of the principles worked out to explain conditioning in animals.

Dickinson and Shanks suggest that the knowledge underlying Pavlovian and instrumental conditioning is different. In Pavlovian conditioning, the animal learns to associate a conditioned stimulus with an unconditioned stimulus, whereby the one comes to be in some sense equivalent to the other, for example, in the case of Pavlov's dogs, the bell comes to automatically have the equivalent properties to the food. This can be contrasted with instrumental learning in which the animal acquires a "belief", for example "pressing the lever causes food". In this case, action results from an inference about what is appropriate and is not in any sense automatic. This type of learning, since it concerns an inference rather than a direct association, can be changed by instruction.

An example of the automatic association that accompanies Pavlovian conditioning is the phenomenon of *autoshaping*. A pigeon is placed in a Skinner box, and from time to time food delivered. If a light is associated with the food, then the pigeon will learn to peck the light, just as if the light were substituting for food. It is of course entirely possible that Pavlovian conditioning may involve both the automatic association of unconditioned and conditioned stimuli, *and* some form of "belief" that the conditioned stimulus causes the unconditioned stimulus, though in the case of animals it is difficult to establish what they "believe" independent of how they respond.

It seems likely that there are at least two kinds of human long-term learning, one of which is open to conscious reflection (perhaps based on instrumental conditioning), and influenced by the capacity to verbalize a strategy, while the other is implicit and independent of verbalization (perhaps based on Pavlovian conditioning?).

Evidence for separate aspects of long-term learning have also been reported by Woltz (1988) in a study using an individual difference approach to demonstrate separate components to learning a complex skill, one concerned with the attentional demands of the early stage of learning, while the other represents the more automatic components of the skill.

In recent years, many studies have suggested the need to fractionate long-term memory into a number of separate systems or processes. The proposed distinctions have included such dichotomies as *procedural-declarative, implicit-explicit, direct-indirect* and *autobiographic-generic* (for a review of this area see Richardson-Klavehn & Bjork, 1988, and Schacter, 1987). As we shall see below, none of these labels is ideal. For present purposes, we will use the procedural-declarative terminology.

Procedural Learning in Amnesia

As long ago as 1911, the Swiss neuropsychiatrist Claparáde observed that amnesic patients with little apparent capacity for new learning were none-the-less capable of learning certain things. It was his custom on morning rounds to shake hands with his patients; on one occasion, when shaking hands with a lady suffering from Korsakoff's Syndrome, a form of amnesia typically associated with alcoholism, he secreted a pin in his hand. The following morning the lady refused to shake hands with him, but was unable to say exactly why. She appeared to have learnt to avoid shaking hands, but had no recollection of the incident that had provoked it.

Schneider (1912), quoted in Parkin (1982), appears to have been the first person to study such preserved learning systematically. He tested three amnesic patients using a number of procedures. In one of these he presented the patient with a picture of an object, subsequently testing retention by presenting a fragment of the original picture and asking the patient to identify the object. He found that although his patients denied ever having seen the picture before, their capacity to identify it from the fragment was enhanced, suggesting that learning had occurred. Schneider also found learning over successive trials on a task analogous to assembling a jigsaw puzzle, and in picture naming and prose completion tasks (Parkin, 1982).

Preserved learning of motor tasks was re-discovered many years later by Talland (1965) who showed that Korsakoff patients could learn to use novel tools, while Corkin (1968) reported that H.M., a patient who was densely amnesic following bilateral lesions to the hippocampus, was able to learn a simple motor skill. Williams (1953) rediscovered the fact that amnesic patients show relatively good learning when the task involves recognizing pictures when cued by a fragment of the original.

The theoretical importance of this preserved learning, was however, first demonstrated by Warrington and Weiskrantz (1968) who found excellent learning in amnesic patients when recall of pictures or words was cued using either fragments of pictures or by presenting the first few letters of target words, for example presenting the word *cyclone* and testing by presenting *cyc*——.

In a study aimed at exploring the extent of preserved learning in amnesia, Brooks and Baddeley (1976) showed normal rates of learning on the pursuit rotor, a task involving keeping a stylus in contact with a moving target. They also noted that their patients were able to learn to assemble simple jigsaw puzzles increasingly rapidly over successive trials, to learn to solve visual mazes and in subsequent unpublished studies showed evidence that they could learn a simple typing task and a verbal equivalent to the jigsaw puzzle task in which patients had to reassemble scrambled sentences.

Since that time there have been many and varied demonstrations of intact learning in amnesic patients. These have included conditioning (e.g. Weiskrantz & Warrington, 1979), enhanced reading of transformed script (Cohen & Squire, 1980), word completion (Graf & Schacter, 1985), the priming of spelling effects (Jacoby & Witherspoon, 1982), the biasing of judgments of pleasantness (Johnson, Kim, & Risse, 1985), and the enhanced learning of complex puzzles such as the Tower of Hanoi (Cohen, 1984). A striking feature about these tasks is that it is frequently the case that the patient will deny having encountered the task before, at the same time as showing clear, and on occasion totally unimpaired learning.

What characterizes these preserved learning tasks? One feature appears to be that in every case, the patient can demonstrate learning without needing to be aware of having encountered the task before. In the case of the pursuit rotor for example, the subject merely performs the task, and happens to do so more efficiently as a result of prior practice. Remembering having practised is not necessary for the practice to be helpful. Making conditioned responses, solving jigsaw puzzles more rapidly, reading transformed script more easily or solving the Tower of Hanoi puzzle more effectively are all activities in which learning is determined by performance, rather than conscious awareness of any previous encounter. In contrast, such patients are very bad at recalling the past, or indeed recognizing that such activities have been practised before.

Normal Procedural Learning

The demonstration of such dramatic effects in amnesic patients led to a wide range of equivalent studies in normal subjects. For example, Jacoby and Dallas (1981) had their subjects process words at different levels, involving either superficial judgments about appearance or sound, or deeper semantic judgments. Learning was then tested in either of two ways, either directly by recognition, or indirectly via the influence of learning on the speed with which the word was identified when presented tachistoscopically. Deeper processing led to consistently better recognition as expected, but the three levels of processing were equally effective in influencing perceptual identification. Similar results demonstrating an absence of an effect of level of processing have been shown using other indirect learning measures, including word completion (Graf & Mandler, 1984; Graf & Schacter, 1985) and time to name pictures (Carroll, Byrne, & Kirsner, 1985). It appears to be the case that those measures of learning that are normal in amnesic patients are also insensitive to level of processing in normal subjects.

Further evidence for separate systems comes from the demonstration of *stochastic independence*, whereby two measures of memory prove to be statistically unrelated. Jacoby and Witherspoon carried out a study in which subjects are given a sentence biasing the subject in the direction of one interpretation of a homophone. For example, given the homophones *read* and *reed*, the latter could be primed by asking the subject "What is the name of the part of a clarinet that vibrates?". On subsequently being asked to spell the word, subjects tend to opt for "reed" rather than "read", a biasing effect also shown by amnesic patients (Jacoby & Witherspoon, 1982). This biasing effect was however, independent of the subject's capacity to recognize having been presented with that word (Jacoby & Witherspoon, 1982). Similarly, Tulving, Schacter, and Stark (1982) showed that the probability of recognizing a word as having been presented earlier in the experiment was independent of the probability of successfully completing that word when given a fragment of the original.

Two kinds of Learning or Many?

Although the evidence for more than one kind of long-term learning is now overwhelming, our theoretical understanding of the under-lying processes is rather less impressive (see Richardson-Klavehn & Bjork, 1988). My own suspicion is that this may reflect a tendency to ask inappropriate questions. For example, we have tended to assume two kinds of learning, and attempt to come up with a dichotomous terminology, which may, I believe have tended to bias our thinking in inappropriate ways. Some of the dichotomous terms are based on a description of some kinds of tasks that are preserved. The term *procedural learning* is a case in point, where it captures the fact that skills are often preserved, whereas the acquisition of knowledge is not. However, some skills do not seem to be learned at all easily by amnesic patients, a case in point being the recent study by Wilson, Baddeley, and Cockburn (1989) of the capacity of patients to learn to enter information into a memory aid, a task that does not logically require conscious recollection, but which is learnt very slowly in amnesic patients. Similarly, the use of the term *procedural* to refer to tasks as diverse as conditioning and the solving of the Tower of Hanoi puzzle suggests a concept of perhaps excessive generality.

Another term that is sometimes used for the preserved

capacities in amnesics is that of *priming*, which suggests the re-activation of some existing mental representation. It is certainly the case that many tasks based on priming do appear to be unimpaired, but one would probably not wish to use the term to refer to other preserved learning involving a totally new skill such as the pursuit rotor, or learning to solve the Tower of Hanoi.

Other approaches have suggested that the crucial distinction is that between *implicit* and *explicit* learning (e.g. Schacter, 1985). This term has the unfortunate implication that provided an amnesic patient is not directly attempting to learn something, then learning will be fine, which it clearly is not. Amnesic patients do not acquire incidental information about the names of their colleagues or the way around the ward, regardless of whether this is learnt intentionally or incidentally, and regardless of whether the patients are assessed directly or indirectly. Of course, it is useful to have a common terminology, and the lack of a consistent terminology in this area probably simply reflects the lack of agreement as to the underlying processes.

My own view is that a dichotomy is probably an over-simplification. I suspect that there is one part of the long-term memory system that is indeed responsible for our capacity to acquire new information and to relate it to ourselves and our environment, a process which one might call *episodic memory*, and which is impaired in the amnesic syndrome. I suspect that there is a wide range of other aspects of learning and memory which have in common the fact that they do not need this autobiographical or episodic component for their acquisition. I see no reason to assume that these will necessarily form a unitary system, and suspect that the processes underlying short-term priming in word identification for example, will prove to be quite different from those involved in classical conditioning, which in turn will be quite different from those involved in acquiring a new motor skill. In short, I believe we need an analysis and taxonomy of procedural learning rather than broad explanations based on an assumed dichotomy.

BEHAVIOR MODIFICATION

In recent years, the flow of theoretical ideas from the animal literature into cognitive psychology has not been particularly notable, with animal work on memory being largely preoccupied with methodological problems rather than conceptual development (Bolles, 1985). However, with the current reawakening of interest in general theories of learning and the development of parallel distributed models of learning and memory described in Chapter 13, there are signs that this may well be changing.

Paradoxically, during the last 25 years, while the theoretical impact of the animal-based associationist theories has been waning, their applied importance has increased enormously. The technology of modifying and changing habits that tends to go under the general title of *behavior modification* is now part of accepted practice in a very wide range of areas from attempts to encourage learning in schoolchildren to marital therapy, and from treatments of obesity to relief of phobias. I myself would regard the advances as more impressive at the practical, rather than theoretical level, but they are nonetheless very important. Furthermore, it seems unlikely that the particular pragmatic advances would have been made other than through the willingness of theorists to attempt to test out their theories in the real world. I believe that cognitive psychologists have something to learn from this.

I shall describe some of the applications of developments from each of the classic paradigms, classical and instrumental conditioning, with the former being applied to the question of how people acquire the irrational but powerful fears known as phobias, and how they can be cured. I shall then go on to describe some of the applications of operant conditioning and of concepts that are descended from Thorndike's Law of Effect.

Learning to Fear

The previous section was concerned with conditioning as a process whereby the organism learns about the world. Although principally concerned with animal research, it focused on cognition and understanding rather than on feeling and emotion. In this respect it contrasts with another approach derived from a classic conditioning paradigm, an approach that had as one of its major aims the understanding and treatment of the irrational but powerful fears known as phobias.

Let me begin with the example of Mrs X, a family friend and neighbor of a few years ago. She and her husband were happily married and had three children. Their lives were contented and unremarkable with one exception, Mrs X suffered from *agoraphobia*. Whenever she went out into crowded public places, she was likely to be overwhelmed by a desperate feeling of panic. This substantially interfered with her everyday life creating major problems for shopping, visits to relatives and of course working. She had undergone a number of treatments ranging from drugs to psychoanalysis, all without success. It put great strain on her husband and the family, and appeared to be a mysterious and quite insoluble problem. In fact her condition could now be treated relatively simply and with a relatively high probability of success using an approach based on learning theory.

The approach in question assumes that fear can be associated with previously neutral stimuli by a process of classical Pavlovian conditioning. Two of the originators of this approach to phobias, Wolpe and Rachman suggested that "any neutral stimulus simple or complex, that happens to make an impact on an individual at about the time a fear reaction is evoked, acquires the ability to evoke fear subsequently ... there will be generalisation of fear reactions to stimuli resembling the conditioned stimulus" (Wolpe & Rachman,

1960). The assumption then is that the phobias or irrational fears shown by various people to objects as diverse as spiders and aeroplanes, and situations as divergent as thunderstorms and public speaking all have in common that the situations were initially by chance associated with some fear-invoking stimulus.

This was not of course an entirely novel view. The originator of behaviorism, J. B. Watson claimed to have conditioned a young baby, Albert, to be afraid of rats by associating the sight of a tame white rat with an unpleasant loud noise. Such conditioned fear has subsequently been extensively demonstrated in animals, which can readily be made to show fear reaction to otherwise neutral stimuli (Wolpe, 1958).

The conditioning interpretation of phobias was also supported by a study in which Lautch (1971) questioned a number of patients showing an extreme and phobic response to dental treatment. They typically reported having had very traumatic earlier experiences in dentistry. However, personality testing suggested that they were also significantly more neurotic than controls, raising the question of which came first, excessive fear or excessive pain. Similar reports of an association between fear and phobia were reported by Grinker and Spiegl (1945) in a study of combat fatigue. They reported that soldiers and airmen who had developed phobias following combat typically reported long periods of prior stress, and often mentioned precipitating stressful incidents. However, it is hard to know how much reliance to place on *post hoc* reports of phobic patients, who may have looked for specific potential causes in order to make sense of what is a very distressing experience.

The experimental induction of phobias in volunteer subjects is of course ethically a very dubious area. However, Sanderson, Campbell, and Laverty (1963) report a study in which patients were given Scoline, a drug that leads to the temporary suspension of breathing, a highly alarming situation that apparently led to fear of the stimulus situation associated with the drug. One might, however, argue that such a fear was a rational response to such a situation, rather than an irrational phobia.

However, whether or not one regards the evidence for the conditioning explanation of phobias as entirely convincing, nevertheless it did offer a coherent interpretation, and suggested new methods of treatment. If phobias could be learnt through conditioning, then presumably they could be unlearnt through extinction, the weakening of an association that occurs when the stimulus and response cease to be presented together. A number of treatments were developed using the principles of classical conditioning and proved gratifyingly successful.

Treating Phobic Fears

Underlying all the methods of treatment was the basic theme of attempting to extinguish the fear response by repeatedly presenting the fear-evoking stimulus, with the intention of adapting it out or extinguishing it. It subsequently proved possible to achieve adaptation not only by presenting the fear-inducing stimulus situation itself, but also by instructing the patient to imagine the situation, a modification that has obvious logistic advantages. Some of the methods that have proved successful include:

Desensitization
The patient is encouraged to indulge in repeated brief approaches to the phobic stimulus, either in reality or in fantasy, without actually contacting it. Periods of systematic relaxation intervene between successive trials; the assumption is that extinction occurs because the physical relaxation is inconsistent with the physical responses associated with fear (Wolpe, 1958).

Modeling
Here the therapist approaches the phobic object first, and the subject is required to imitate (Bandura, 1971).

Flooding
Rapid prolonged approach to the phobic stimulus is required in fantasy or in fact, a procedure that is assumed to lead to massive over-stimulation and rapid adaptation of the fear response (Marks, 1972).

Operant Shaping
In this procedure, the subject is given some positive reward for a steady approach to the phobic situation (Crowe, Marks, Agras, & Leitenberg, 1972).

What all these approaches have in common is that they lead to substantial exposure of the subject to the stimulus, the assumption being that "given enough contact with the provoking situation, the phobic or obsessive person ceases to respond with avoidance or distress" (Marks, 1978, p.499).

All these methods proved successful, to a more or less equal extent. Figure 9.4 shows the results of one study by Mathews, Gelder, and Johnston (1981) comparing flooding with desensitization. Both appeared to work. Rather more worrying for the original hypothesis was evidence suggesting that the inclusion of relaxation was unnecessary (see Marks, 1978, p.500 for a review of the evidence). The original interpretation assumed that conditioning an alternative and incompatible response to the original stimulus was a crucial part of the treatment, and that relaxation involved the necessary incompatible response.

Testing the Conditioning Hypothesis
During the 1970s evidence against the simple conditioning account of phobias began to accumulate, and was summarized by Rachman (1977) one of the original proponents of the interpretation.

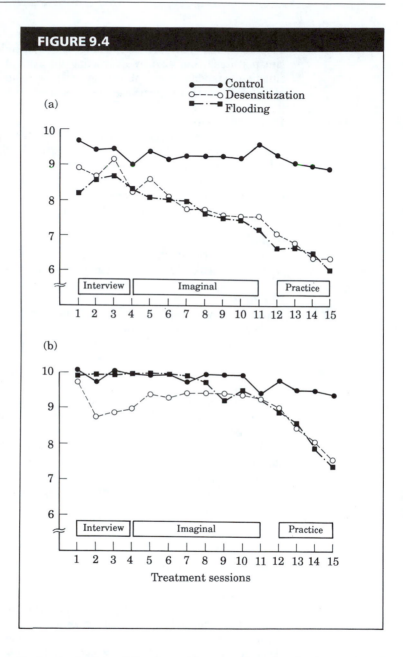

Mean rated anxiety in phobic patients during treatment. Panel (a) gives mean scores when "thinking about" phobic situations and panel (b) gives scores estimated for phobic situations "in real life". The two methods of treatment are equally effective. From Mathews et al. (1970). Reprinted by permission of Tavistock Press, publishers.

FIGURE 9.4

(a)

Control
Desensitization
Flooding

Interview   Imaginal   Practice

1 2 3 4 5 6 7 8 9 10 11 12 13 14 15

(b)

Interview   Imaginal   Practice

1 2 3 4 5 6 7 8 9 10 11 12 13 14 15

Treatment sessions

Rachman cited the following evidence against the simple conditioning view.

Fear-inducing Situations do not Necessarily Induce Phobias

Air-raids during the Second World War were expected to give rise to a great increase in phobic patients, and in Liverpool, for example, additional psychiatric staff were recruited in anticipation of this. There was in fact no rise in neurotic illness; if anything, people adapted and became more courageous, even though the actual bombing was becoming more serious, a pattern of results that was found both in Britain (Lewis, 1951) and in Germany and Japan (Janis, 1951).

Experimental Phobias in Children
Watson's original claims based on little Albert and the white rat proved difficult to replicate (Bregman, 1934). Furthermore, when electric shocks were used as part of an aversion therapy treatment to discourage patients from undesirable habits, they showed no evidence of developing a phobic reaction to the stimuli associated with electric shock; their response was rather one of indifference (Marks & Gelder, 1967).

The Equipotentiality Assumption
The original formulation of the conditioning model assumed that any stimulus was equally likely to become associated with a phobic response. Considerable evidence has now accumulated to indicate that this is not so. One feature that the initial conditioning model finds hard to explain is the uneven distribution of phobias. A survey of phobias in a small town in Vermont indicated that snake phobia was twice as frequent as dental phobia, and five times as frequent as fear of injections. It seems very unlikely that this represents the frequency with which snakes, dentists and needles had happened to be associated with pain or fear. A similar point is made by the observation of Hallowell (1938) who reports that certain American Indian peoples showed little or no fear of bears and wolves, but were very afraid of frogs and toads.

Evidence from the animal learning laboratory was also beginning to indicate that some responses were more easily attached to certain stimuli than to others. Garcia, Kimmeldorf, and Koelling (1955) showed that rats very easily learned an association between a previously attractive taste, and nausea induced by irradiation, despite a relatively long interval between stimulus and reinforcement, whereas associating a taste with shock was much less potent. Seligman (1972) argued that such prepared learning is selective, highly resistant to extinction and can be acquired in one trial.

A series of experiments by Öhman (1979) demonstrate this point for human subjects very neatly. In one study, an electric shock was paired with pictures of snakes and spiders, objects that are frequently associated with phobias, or with flowers and mushrooms. Skin conductance response was used as a measure of emotional conditioning, and occurred readily for all stimuli. However, when the response was extinguished by omitting the shock, extinction was rapid in the case of the neutral stimuli but slower in the case of the snakes and spiders. A similar pattern occurred in a subsequent experiment when extinction was accompanied by the removal of the electrodes that delivered shock, and instructions that there would be no more shock. This immediately extinguished the emotional response to the neutral stimuli, while the snake and spider pictures were still associated with an enhanced emotional responsiveness. Finally, a study by Hugdahl (1978) showed that it was not even necessary to deliver an actual electric shock. Simply telling the subject that he might be shocked in association with a particular type of picture led to an emotional response when that picture appeared. When the electrodes were removed, neutral pictures no longer gave rise to an emotional response, while the snake and spider pictures continued to do so.

This latter study supports other claims that phobias may be induced from watching others. For example, John (1941) reports that fear of air-raids in children tends to be highly correlated with fear in their mothers ($r = 0.59$), suggesting that the child may well have become fearful as a result of observing its mother in air-raids. Presumably this is also the mechanism whereby the American Indians, cited by Hallowell, developed fear of frogs and toads.

It appears then that phobias are not acquired by the chance association of a stimulus with a fearful situation, but can be learned by imitation, and tend to be associated with certain objects rather than others. They can be extinguished very successfully, but counter-conditioning does not seem to be a necessary part of this process. The theory is inadequate but the practice works. How can we come up with a better theory? At this point it might be interesting to digress and talk about a related problem, that of panic attacks.

Treating Panic Attacks

Certain otherwise healthy patients suffer from periodic attacks of intense panic, usually associated with a rapidly beating heart and racing pulse and all the symptoms of extreme fear. The attacks are very distressing, are unpredictable, and resemble the symptoms often shown by agoraphobic patients.

In a recent study of such attacks, Beck (1988) has suggested the following interpretation. Most people will occasionally notice bodily sensations that are slightly unusual: palpitations of the heart; chest pain; tingling; dizziness; or breathlessness, for example. While such symptoms may in fact be entirely normal, they can be interpreted as signifying something much more serious, for example, a heart attack. This will attract the patient's attention to the physical symptoms, making him even more aware of them and thus further increasing his level of anxiety. This in turn will increase the heart-rate, producing a vicious circle whereby the whole process is likely to get out of hand leading to panic.

The crucial problem here is the positive feedback loop between the initial chance symptom and the patient's fearful interpretation of it. Beck's suggested solution is to try to give the subject experience of, insight into, and control over his responses. One of the crucial intervening stages in panic attacks appears to be that of over-breathing. Fear tends to lead the subject to change his breathing pattern to one of rapid shallow breathing. This tends to reduce the level of carbon dioxide in the blood supply to the brain, and can in turn lead to further symptoms and increased panic.

The stages of treatment involve first of all explaining that the symptoms are not a sign of physical pathology, and that they should therefore not be interpreted as directly threatening. This in itself is typically not enough to produce an improvement. It is necessary to go further and teach the patient relaxation and breathing exercises which will alleviate the physical symptoms. The next stage is to induce the symptoms artificially, typically by encouraging the patient to over-breathe, leading to a reduction in the level of carbon dioxide in the blood, which will produce shortness of breath, dizziness, palpitations, etc. The patient is then encouraged to control these symptoms using the methods he or she has just learned (see Beck, 1988, for a more detailed description). Figure 9.5 shows the results of a study by Sokol-Kessler and Beck (1987) who compared treatment of panic disorders based on either the cognitive therapy regime just described, or on non-specific supportive therapy. A group of 13 patients were treated using cognitive therapy, and a control group of 16 patients given brief supportive therapy. As will be clear from Figure 9.5, the treatment was very successful.

Let us return now to the general question of phobias. What do we need to explain? First, we must explain why the phobia develops initially. Secondly, we need to know why it is maintained.

Effects of treatment by Cognitive or Supportive Therapy on the frequency of panic attacks over time. From Sokol-Kessler and Beck (1987) Cognitive Treatment of Panic Disorders. 140th Meeting of the APA, 1987.

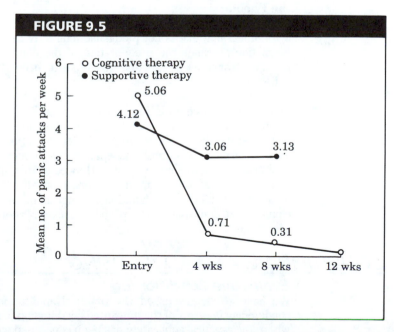

FIGURE 9.5

Thirdly, we must explain why it is not sufficient to tell the patient that his fear is irrational for it to disappear and fourthly, why particular treatment methods appear to be effective. Let us consider these questions in turn.

How do Phobias Develop?

It seems likely that some form of the conditioning hypothesis is appropriate here, with certain modifications. First of all, some stimuli appear to be more readily associated with fear than others. There is probably a large social component here. Monkeys reared in laboratories do not appear to have an inherent fear of snakes, but those reared in the wild do, and appear to be able to communicate this fear to their offspring. It appears then that we can learn fears either directly, or from others.

Why is the Fear Maintained?

One interpretation that used to be popular was that escape from fear was rewarding, and that in turn reinforced the earlier response. Why in that case is the relief more powerful than the original pain? An alternative possibility is that the phobic patient becomes afraid of the fear itself. Hence, a spider phobic is not only afraid of spiders but also of his own response to them. This leads to avoiding situations in which spiders may occur, and hence avoiding a possibility of refuting the conviction of the fearful nature of spiders. This view has the advantage of answering the next question, namely:

Why does Demonstrating Irrationality not Cure the Phobia?

Fear is presumably a Pavlovian conditioned response involving a level of learning that is not modifiable indirectly through language. Extinction demands the presentation of the conditioned stimulus for the elimination of the fear response to occur through direct experience.

Why is Exposure an Effective Treatment?

Exposure allows the subject to indulge in reality testing, encountering the phobic stimulus under conditions in which an anxiety response is entirely acceptable, and indeed possibly even desirable for therapeutic reasons. Hence, in this situation rather than being afraid of his fear, the patient is utilizing the fear. Under these circumstances, the additional complication of being afraid of being afraid does not crop up and the fear response eventually adapts out.

CONDITIONING AND ADVERTISING

Evaluative Conditioning

We have so far discussed the practical applications of classical conditioning in terms of the unwanted conditioning of irrational fear, where the practical application has been concerned with methods of extinguishing the inappropriate fear response. However, it is of course also possible to condition positive responses. Indeed, it has been suggested that much advertising can be regarded as based on the phenomenon of evaluative conditioning, whereby the product is made more desirable by being associated with a positive emotional stimulus such as an attractive scene or person. However, most advertising is probably based on rule of thumb and experience, rather than scientific principles, although there has in recent years been a move in the direction of attempting to understand the possible role of conditioning in advertising.

One of the initial studies was that of Gorn (1982) who suggested that consumer attitudes and choices were modifiable by conditioning, although other studies have been less successful (e.g. Allen & Madden, 1985; Gresham & Shimp, 1985). However, Stuart, Shimp, and Engle (1987) argue that earlier studies in general, and the advertising industry in particular, do not always optimize the chance of conditioning occurring. They point out the need to ensure that the product to be conditioned is relatively novel, that there should be sufficient trials to allow conditioning to occur, that the product should be followed by the pleasant stimulus, (forward conditioning), rather than the reverse, (backward conditioning). Finally, they point out the obvious necessity for a control condition in which the conditioned stimulus and unconditioned stimulus are presented an equivalent number of times, but not paired.

Stuart et al. (1987) carried out a series of studies in which subjects were presented with a slide picture of a "new" brand of toothpaste in a green and yellow tube labeled "Brand L Toothpaste". The unconditioned stimulus was one of four slides that had been selected as being particularly pleasant. They comprised either a mountain waterfall scene, a sunset over an island, sky and clouds seen through the mast of a boat or a sunset over the ocean.

In the first experiment, the toothpaste was presented with slides of three other fictitious commodities, "Brand R Cola", "Brand M Laundry Detergent" and "Brand J Soap", which were paired with twelve neutral pictures. All the stimuli were presented on slides for 5 seconds, with the conditioning procedure involving following the toothpaste with a pleasant slide on one, three, ten or twenty occasions. A control condition involved presenting the toothpaste and the pleasant slides for an equivalent number of trials, but ensuring that the colored slides were not associated with the toothpaste in any way. Performance was measured by requiring the subjects to rate the toothpaste on a number of semantic dimensions such as "good-bad", "attractive-unattractive", "interesting-boring", to rate their "overall feeling about Brand L Toothpaste", and to rate purchasing intentions and general positivity of feeling towards the toothpaste. Figure 9.6 shows the results on these four measures for both the conditioning and the random control conditions. It seems that the experiment was successful in influencing the subjects' responses to the imaginary toothpaste.

FIGURE 9.6

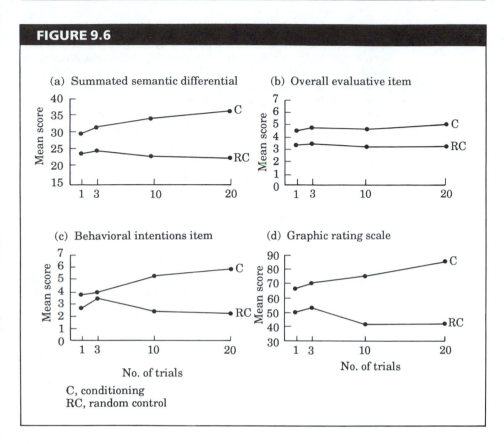

(a) Summated semantic differential

(b) Overall evaluative item

(c) Behavioral intentions item

(d) Graphic rating scale

No. of trials

C, conditioning
RC, random control

Conditioning of attitude to a novel brand of toothpaste as a function of number of trials. From Stuart et al. (1987).

A second study explored the phenomenon of *latent inhibition*, whereby an item that has already been presented under neutral conditions is harder to condition than a novel item. The results suggested that latent inhibition could be found in this context. A third study examined the effectiveness of backward conditioning, in which the pleasant slide precedes the product. As one would expect from the conditioning literature, this led to a much lower degree of attitude change. Stuart et al. conclude that their results offer strong basic support for the application of conditioning theory in advertising.

Work in this area raises some interesting ethical issues. Is one prostituting psychology by attempting to use it to induce people to buy things they would not otherwise buy? Or is one simply helping the wheels of commerce to turn, thereby keeping the economy buoyant for everyone's benefit? Even if one has suspicions about advertising, as I suspect one should, given the role that it is often allowed to play in politics, then one might still argue that it is important to understand advertising in order to control it. For better or worse, I suspect we shall see a good deal more work in this area in the next few years.

CHANGING HABITS

Skinner and Operant Conditioning

During the 1940s and 1950s Thorndike's simple conceptualization of the Law of Effect gave way to a very well-developed technology worked out principally by B.F. Skinner and his followers. Skinner showed that it was possible by carefully selecting responses and then rewarding them, to build up remarkably complex chains of novel behavior.

Skinner's early work was influenced by the methods used by animal trainers, and his methods perhaps reached their most unlikely and complex outcomes in sequences of responses taught to animals, often for the purpose of taking part in films or advertising features (Breland & Breland, 1951). Hence, pigs were trained to push around shopping trolleys and select a particular type of food, pigeons were trained to play ping-pong, and in other studies learned to make apparently subtle discriminations such as choosing between those pictures which had people on them and those which did not. It was shown that such discriminations could be used to control the path of a missile, steering it on to a target such as a ship by pecking at the image of the ship on a screen (Skinner, 1958). At a theoretical level, the operant research remained intentionally very simple, but as a technology of learning concerned with the optimal use of reward and punishment to control behavior, it developed very extensively.

The behavioral programs and treatments developed on the basis of Skinner's work have a number of important characteristics that differentiate them from many other approaches to learning, and from the classical conditioning approach to behavior disorders. The programs depend upon the careful monitoring and observation of behavior, followed by the selective rewarding or punishing of one component of that behavior. Measurement of outcome is built into the process, and one of the major contributions of operant research has been the development of a series of experimental designs that allow clear conclusions to be drawn on the basis of the observation of a single individual. Such designs are particularly appropriate and powerful for the therapeutic situation where it may be necessary to try a whole range of treatments on an individual, and where it is essential to have good evidence as to the efficacy of each. Further description of such designs will be given in connection with the description of methods of helping patients with memory deficits outlined in Chapter 17.

While some of the methods are complex and subtle, the underlying conceptual structure is very simple, that of strengthening and weakening responses by reward and punishment. This assumption proved to be applicable to a wide range of problems, and provided the user was ingenious and patient, the technology often worked. Most importantly, when an attempt to modify a piece of behavior did not work, then it was plainly obvious that the attempt had failed. I would consider this relatively immediate feedback regarding success or failure as one of the most important features of the application of operant principles to applied problems.

This underlying pragmatism has allowed the comparatively limited theoretical structure associated with the behavioral approach to be applied fruitfully to complex and important real-world problems. Given the option of clinging to those variables that could theoretically be readily justified, and opting for messier variables that worked, behavior modifiers have on the whole very sensibly opted for what worked. For example, in discussing social skills training, Hersen and Eisler (1976) mentioned the value of feedback, that is telling the patient what he is doing right and what he is doing wrong. Although the concept of feedback is very well developed in other areas such as the learning of motor skills, Hersen and Eisler seem somewhat puzzled as to how to fit it into an operant theoretical framework, but very sensibly suggest (Hersen & Eisler, 1976, p. 372) that one uses it anyhow: "Although the exact mechanisms accounting for the efficacy of feedback are not fully understood, the administration of feedback to patients regarding specific aspects of their behavior has proven to effect positive changes in relative target behaviors."

Most behavioral programs or treatments can be said to follow a broadly similar pattern involving the following stages:

Designing a Behavioral Program

Stage 1: Specify the behavior to be changed. It is important here to select small, measurable and achievable goals. For example, if a head-injured patient were causing disruption by shouting and behaving abusively on the ward, one would select shouting on the ward as a initial response to modify, rather than opt for a general improvement in social behavior, although the latter might be the longer-term consequence of treatment.

Stage 2: The goal should be stated as specifically as possible, in this case to stop the patient yelling on the ward.

Stage 3: There should be a measure of the baseline rate, extended over a period of several days. This obviously requires a good deal of thought about the methods of measurement and so forth, and in some cases merely observing and measuring the behavior can be enough to change it. During this period it is also often helpful to observe the behavior in more detail, possibly forming some hypotheses as to what maintains it. It might, for example, be the case that yelling attracts attention and that the patient appears to find this rewarding.

Stage 4: Decide on a strategy. In this case it might be simply one of using attention to the patient to reward non-yelling behavior, and ensuring that the yelling behavior is ignored.

Stage 5: Plan treatment. This obviously is a crucial stage since treatment is likely to be carried out in a situation involving people other than the therapist and the patient. It is essential to take this into account and ensure that other staff on the ward, for example, do not provide reinforcement for yelling since this could of course completely disrupt the treatment. It is essential at this stage also to decide on the particular design used. It should be carefully planned and strictly adhered to, otherwise interpreting the outcome may be impossible.

Let us assume that a simple *AB–AB* design is used in which *A* represents the baseline condition in which a patient yelling is likely to attract attention, *B* represents the experimental treatment where attention is withdrawn during the yelling but given during more socially acceptable behavior. If the treatment is working, then the level of yelling during the initial baseline *A* phase should be reduced during the *B* phase. This could however simply indicate improvement for other reasons, such as continued recovery of the patient's health. For that reason, the design requires a return to the original *A* condition. If the treatment is the crucial factor, the yelling behavior will return, and will once again reduce when treatment *B* is re-introduced. There are, of course, many more subtle designs than this, some of which will be described in Chapter 17.

Stage 6: Begin treatment. This should go on hand-in-hand with

Stage 7: Monitor progress, leading to

Stage 8: Change program if necessary.

Hence, if the withdrawal of attention were not sufficient, possibly perhaps because other patients provided the necessary attention then it might be necessary to introduce other rewards or possibly punishments.

If the program is successful, the next question concerns the generalization of the new behavior. Has it led to a decrease of yelling in general, or only on the ward? If the latter, then the program should gradually be extended to other environments until inappropriate yelling disappears completely. One might also ask whether other forms of social disruption are occurring and if so treat them. Finally, it might be necessary to reward and encourage more positive forms of social behavior such as smiling, interacting with other patients and staff, and so forth. Clearly, attempting to control the behavior of another human being in this way raises some important ethical issues. These will be discussed later in the chapter. First of all, however, it might be useful to discuss a number of instances where behavior modification has been applied to specific problems.

Modifying Self-injurious Behavior

One area in which behavioral principles have been applied with considerable success is in that of educating and treating children suffering from severe mental handicap; children who may have very special problems and be very difficult to teach or treat using standard educational procedures. A particularly clear example of this appears in the case of children who attempt to mutilate themselves by biting, scratching, gouging themselves or beating their head against a wall, all forms of behavior that parents and carers find enormously distressing and which can of course be life-threatening (Murphy & Wilson, 1985).

The causes of self-injurious behavior are probably complex. They clearly do offer the child a very powerful weapon for demanding attention, but it is also possible in some cases that the sensory stimulation is in some way rewarding. Head-banging is not entirely dissimilar from the rhythmic rocking behavior that is common in the mentally handicapped, and indeed among certain enthusiasts for "heavy metal" rock music. However, while rhythmic rocking may be harmless, beating the head against a hard object is not, and may indeed endanger the patient's life. Behavior modification offers one way of attempting to tackle this problem, and while treatment is always difficult and success certainly can not be guaranteed, behavioral methods can on occasion be very effective as the following case by Bull and La Vecchio (1978) demonstrates.

The study was concerned with a boy suffering from the Lesch–Nyhan Syndrome, a rare x-linked genetic disorder that typically results in neurological abnormalities, psychomotor retardation and is often associated with self-mutilation. In this case, self-injurious behavior began to appear at about age 3 and from that point seriously interfered with developmental progress. Eventually the child was confined to a wheelchair with his arms constrained by splints, wearing a helmet and shoulder-pads. At night he had to sleep in a jacket and safety straps to restrain his self-injurious activities. These included biting, breath-holding, removing finger and toe nails, spitting, projectile vomiting, head-banging, screaming and foul language. Despite the restraints he was able to inflict wounds on his shoulders, knees, toes, lips and fingers, and while injuring himself would often shout "I hate myself".

The behavior seemed to be associated with periods of anxiety when he would become increasingly agitated, often crying "I hate you, I love you, I hate you, yes, no, yes, no" leading to screaming and self-mutilation. As is often the case, he appeared to have very ambivalent feelings about the restraining devices, attempting to circumvent them, but at the same time becoming very anxious if they were removed. He was extremely dependent, being unable for example, to feed himself, and showed signs of using self-injurious behavior to avoid situations he disliked such as being encouraged to feed himself.

The treatment aimed to do two things, first to allow him to tolerate being without his restraints, and secondly to extinguish the self-injurious behavior. Initially, removing even a peripheral part of his protective equipment generated enormous anxiety, and subsequently such removal was achieved using nitrous oxide as a means of relaxation, initially involving relatively inessential articles of protection such as his socks. Unfortunately, it appeared that

Behaviour modification of self-injurious biting in a child suffering from Lesch-Nyhan syndrome. From Bull and La Vecchio (1978)

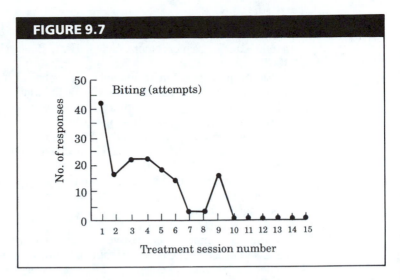

FIGURE 9.7

treatment for his self-inflicted wounds was rewarding, and the therapists went to the lengths of doing this under anaesthetic to try to avoid any association between self-injury and reward.

The child was then placed in a room on his own which contained a one-way viewing screen. A confederate noted that when the therapist left the room, the self-injurious behavior stopped, suggesting that it was motivated by the need for attention, and was not intrinsically rewarding. Attention was therefore used as the reinforcer, being withheld during self-mutilation, and provided at other times.

Figure 9.7 shows the incidence of attempts at self-biting over 15 one-hour sessions. It is very clear that withdrawal of attention during self-injury led to a reduction and ultimate extinction of the biting behavior. A similar pattern was observed in the case of other self-injurious and aggressive behaviors. Initially, however, although self-injury reduced, the child began to show signs of depression; this was treated using standard play therapy techniques, with apparent success. At a follow-up 18 months later, the improvement had clearly been maintained. The child was operating without any restraints, could feed himself and move himself about in his wheelchair. He was learning to walk with crutches. He was attending a special class in a normal school, and was now able to communicate and interact with other children.

TOKEN ECONOMY SYSTEMS

Token Economics in Education

We have so far considered two cases in which a single individual was discouraged from performing some form of antisocial behavior. Needless to say, behavioral methods can be used to strengthen positive behavior rather than weaken negative behavior, as for example when a shy child might be encouraged by attention from the teacher to interact more with other children, leading to an activity which subsequently itself becomes rewarding and no longer needs external reinforcement (Allen, Hart, Buell, Harris, & Wolf, 1964).

Similar principles can be applied to the behavior of a whole class, with attention being paid to behavior of the kind that the teacher wishes to encourage, with other types of behavior being ignored. Clearly such a strategy has its dangers, particularly since a teacher's attention is not the only source of reward for children in a class. Attention from other children can be an equally potent reward, potentially leading to a total breakdown of order and discipline, with the teacher ignoring infringements that may well be reinforced by attention and possibly approval from other children. Once again, it points to the need for behavioral principles to be used sensibly rather than slavishly.

However, another alternative to the selective employment of behavioral techniques is to attempt to control the whole situation by setting up what is known as a *token economy*. This is a system whereby a series of specified behaviors are consistently rewarded by means of tokens which can then be exchanged for rewards in the form of goods or privileges. Hence children might, perhaps, be given tokens which can be exchanged for small toys or for time spent in a desired activity such as painting, or perhaps being taught by an older child.

One example of such a token economy is described by Drabman (1973). It involved a total of 24 11–15-year-old children, the worst behaved in a children's psychiatric hospital. They were presented with a series of clear rules, and the children were told that following the rules would lead to a reward. At regular intervals, the teacher stopped the class and awarded each child a series of tokens for his or her behavior for that period, removing tokens for misbehavior. The tokens were kept in a series of receptacles with children being able to exchange their tokens for small toys at the end of the day or week. Such a system can work reasonably effectively, and on this occasion certainly decreased the number of behavioral problems within the hospital. Such approaches do have problems, however.

First of all, a full token economy is quite demanding to run, requiring as it does constant monitoring and feedback of rewards and punishments. This in turn demands a great deal of control over the social environment, with support from all the relevant staff. A potential drawback of a token economy is that it can lead to a very mercenary approach to learning; it is sometimes claimed for example that "Token economies lead to token learning". Consequently one may find that children will only read or indulge in any educational activity if they are directly rewarded for it. Such an approach to life that may be very effective within the confines of the economy itself, but quite unproductive in the world outside, where it is necessary to learn to operate on a subtler and less immediate reward system.

Thirdly, there is the ethical problem of whether it is appropriate to attempt to manipulate the behavior of another in this way. We will return to this issue after discussing a number of attempts to develop token economies within the prison service.

Token Economies in Prisons

Some of the ethical problems of operating in this area are illustrated by the case of a program of aversion therapy introduced at the prison in Vacaville, California. Recalcitrant prisoners were treated with Anectine, a substance that has the alarming effect of temporarily preventing breathing. This relatively crude form of punishment was both unsuccessful, and subsequently adjudged to be illegal, because although many of the participants had signed consent forms, most admitted that it was only because they felt this would increase their chance of early parole (Kennedy, 1976).

A more elaborate approach to a token economy system was introduced at Patuxent, Maryland in a four-tier system where prisoners could earn promotion and privileges by appropriate behavior. The system did not work; the prison was "besieged by riots", had an atmosphere no better than any other prison and produced no significant drop in probability that its prisoners would subsequently return to crime. It was suggested that the reason for this might lie not in the principle of a token economy, but in the fact that the prison staff were simply not adequately trained to operate such a system. The Federal Bureau of Prisons attempted to avoid this problem in its START (Special Treatment and Rehabilitative Training) program.

The START program carried out at Springfield, Missouri used a points system, rewarding prisoners for personal care, relations with others and good behavior at work. The points could be exchanged for items in the prison store or for renting radios, etc. Discipline was achieved by a "time-out" procedure in which the prisoner would be confined to his room. The prisoners entered into the trial came from the worst behaved group, comprising 21 prisoners who were in general "assaultive, abusive and generally recalcitrant".

The program was not a success. After 15 months, six prisoners were still in the program, eight in a psychiatric hospital, four had been dropped for lack of progress, one returned to his original prison and one had finished his sentence. Seven of the prisoners staged a 65-day hunger strike and then sued the prison service. The judge ruled in their favor describing the program as a punishment inflicted without due hearing. The program was then closed "for economic reasons".

Why did the program fail? Kennedy (1976) suggests the following reasons. First of all, admission to the program was involuntary. This is an interesting reason in the sense that it is not at all clear how volunteering fits into a traditional operant paradigm.

We will return to this point later. Secondly, the system appeared to have the aim of inducing submissiveness in the prisoners. The guards typically would wait until the prisoner submitted, and then reward him. The particular prisoners were not selected on the basis of submissiveness, and the program clearly did not work. The prisoners themselves clearly saw it as aversive, and interpreted the whole system in terms of punishment not reward, which is generally assumed to be the main driving power in a token economy system. Thirdly, there seems to have been a lack of a thorough functional analysis of the original situation and a failure to identify the reinforcement contingencies that were already operating. Finally, no attempt was made to monitor the program and modify it at points of failure. Constant monitoring is an essential component of adequately run behavioral programs.

The START program still leaves open the possibility that a token economy system might work well if it were properly designed and run. A much better example of a token economy was set up at the Draper Correctional Center and is described by Milan et al. (1974). The guards were thoroughly trained, the program was well designed and did lead to an increase in participation in educational programs and in volunteering for jobs such as were necessary for maintaining the fabric of the prison. Even here, however, an 18-month follow-up indicated that there was no significant difference in the likelihood of prisoners returning to crime, suggesting at the very least that the problem of training for generalization to the outside world had not been solved by this program.

What lessons can be learned from the attempt to apply token economies within the prison service? They suggest first of all some of the purely practical difficulties of setting up a token economy, particularly in a system such as the prison service that already has strongly entrenched attitudes, values and ways of attempting to control behavior. Secondly, they suggest that behavioral control is a much more complicated issue than some of the early operant theorists might have suggested. The indication that voluntary participation is an important factor is an interesting one. There is no doubt that token economy systems can work very effectively, but they tend to operate in situations such as the education of the mentally handicapped or treatment of the severely head-injured, where the overall aims of the controllers and the controlled are broadly consistent, and where a smoothly running classroom or ward is itself likely to be reinforcing to the participants. It is also probable that one of the major contributions of such an approach lies in the careful observation during the crucial baseline period. This will often reveal a problem rooted in the current behavior of the staff, for example giving increased attention after disruptive behavior.

I must confess to some relief at discovering that token economies are somewhat less powerful than some of their earlier enthusiasts might have hoped. To quote Kennedy (1976, p. 340)

"Like any technology of control (behavior modification) will be bought, adapted, and monopolized by the powerful for their own not always benevolent purposes". If the techniques were truly as powerful as some of the earlier advocates of behavior modification suggest, then they would be potentially very dangerous indeed.

REFLECTIONS ON BEHAVIOR MODIFICATION

Successes and Failure

The previous chapter has considered some of the applications of behavior modification. It has described them from the viewpoint of a cognitive psychologist, attempting perhaps too hurriedly to obtain an overview of a rich, complex and relatively successful branch of the applied psychology of learning. Only a small sample of the many potential applications have been discussed; I have, for example, said nothing about treatment of depression, of obesity, of alcoholism and drug addiction. I have said virtually nothing about the positive application of behavioral techniques to the development of social skills and to the alleviation of suffering associated with bereavement. The brief conclusions that I draw, therefore, are inevitably somewhat superficial, and should be used as a basis for discussion rather than as reflecting an authoritative view on this important area.

First of all, I am impressed that behavioral approaches are in many cases pragmatically very useful. Successful treatment of phobias is now quite routine, and in the area of mental handicap, I understand that behavioral techniques have revolutionized the methods of teaching and management. In an area such as the treatment of depression, more behavioral approaches have been expanded and developed into cognitive treatments where there is much more concern for the attitudes and beliefs of the patient as well as his or her behavior (Beck, Shaw, Rush, & Emory, 1979; Williams, 1984).

My impression, however, is that there are a number of problem areas that have proved rather less tractable. In addition to the applications to prison management just described, attempts to use operant techniques to cure addictions, whether to alcohol, tobacco or other drugs seem to have had only limited success (Saunders & Allsop, 1985). Behavioral approaches have also been applied in an attempt to help patients control blood pressure, heart rate and other autonomic functions as a means to reducing the incidence of psychosomatic illness and of heart attacks. While such approaches have shown some promise, there is clearly far to go before they play a major role in the treatment of psychosomatic illness. What then are the strengths and what the weaknesses of behavioral treatments?

Some of their strengths are essentially pragmatic. They require a very careful monitoring of the behavior that is to be changed, and encourage a willingness to change behavior in extremely small steps. The combination of careful initial observation with meticulous monitoring of treatment seems to me to be one of the great strengths of the behavior modification approach.

A second strength is the willingness to be eclectic. This I must confess initially came as a surprise to me since the Skinnerian theorists that I myself had come across in the 1960s appeared to be among the more rigid members of my profession. I suspect that the answer here may well stem partly from the fact that behavior modification was largely developed by practising therapists whose concern was to use the theory developed in the animal laboratory to improve the lot of their patients, rather than simply to test existing models.

Those areas in which the behavioral approach seems to have been less successful appear to be those in which motivations are complex, and behavior probably supported by a number of different reinforcers. In the case of giving up smoking, for example, it seems likely that tobacco is rewarding in a number of different ways, in giving an immediately pleasurable sensation, in helping the smoker control level of arousal, as a social activity, on top of which other forces such as advertising tend to maintain the habit.

Why Does it Sometimes Fail?

Behavior modification can be very effective, but often is not. Can we speculate on what allows it to be successful, and what makes it fail? As a non-expert, I would suggest the following. Our behavior is affected by long-term motives, drives and goals, aspects of behavior that cognitive psychology has so far conspicuously failed to address. In general, we opt for courses of action that are consistent with our long-term goals, and for the most part, this is an adaptive way of coping with life. However, conflicts occasionally occur between short-term and long-term goals.

Consider, for example, going to the dentist. Here you have something which in the short-term is almost certainly unpleasant. It disrupts your normal activity, requires arranging a special visit which is likely in turn to lead to someone poking about in your mouth, and quite possibly inflicting pain. You indulge in this activity, I assume, since in the long run you feel that it will preserve your teeth and that on the whole, it is better not to be toothless.

Sometimes, however, the overall drift of behavior in the direction of long-term goals can be disrupted by motivational culs-de-sac, points at which the short-term goal dominates over the long-term aim. I suspect that behavior modification is successful to the extent that it is able to identify these, and provide short-term rewards that allow the person to escape the cul-de-sac.

Let us consider some examples. In the case of phobic patients, the therapist allows the patient to demonstrate to himself that an encounter with a spider or a crowded bus does not have the catastrophic effect that was feared. In the case of the self-mutilating child, the immediate reward of achieving attention from the outside world was enough to compensate him for the wounds he inflicted upon himself. Once this reward was removed, then the short-term gains disappeared and he was able to operate on a more long-term basis.

Token economies tend to be most effective I suspect, among groups that are least capable of taking a longer-term motivational view. Hence, they may well help intellectually handicapped children cope with the problem of learning to dress and feed themselves and establish relationships with their peers. Such a system is much less successful in attempting to impose a general motivational structure on groups of prisoners who probably hold values that are fundamentally at variance with those of their guards. It is perhaps reassuring to learn that those selected for their recalcitrance can not be persuaded to adopt a submissive role simply by means of manipulating rewards. If that were the case, then it would suggest that the technology was sufficiently powerful to dominate ideology. Whether or not one agrees with the ideology, mankind would be the poorer if it could be dominated by any political system that happened to have the appropriate psychological technology.

In conclusion then, what can behavior modification do and what can it not do? I suspect that it is and will continue to be enormously important as a means for helping people to achieve long-term goals which they have selected, but are unable to pursue systematically, because of short-term motivational culs-de-sac. I assume that behavior modification will be successful to the extent that it is able to identify such culs-de-sac, and sensitively provide motivations for behavior that will circumvent them.

I suspect that behavior modification will fail in so far as it attempts to induce habits that go consistently against the long-term motivations and aims of the subject. This does not have to be so, mankind could be infinitely directable and malleable. Behavior modification appears to offer a technology by which we can help people, but we cannot dominate them. Long may that state of affairs continue!

OVERVIEW

The study of the acquisition of habits has been strongly influenced by research on conditioning in animals. The study of classical conditioning, whereby a previously neutral stimulus such as a bell becomes associated with a reflex such as salivation in response to dry food, has led to more recent developments concerned with the acquisition of conditioned emotional responses such as fear. Theories of conditioning based on animal studies have been applied to the problem of understanding and treating phobias in patients. Although there is still disagreement about the underlying theoretical account, these treatments have proved extremely useful.

A parallel development has occurred in the clinical application of instrumental conditioning studies in which responses are strengthened or weakened as a result of reward or punishment. The principles of operant conditioning have been applied to situations ranging from the prevention of self-mutilation in handicapped children to the development of social skills, and from the discouragement of yelling in head-injured patients to the retraining of the skill of drinking from a cup in a dyspraxic patient. The techniques have been rather less successful in attempting to control addictions such as smoking and alcoholism, while their social application within token economy systems has worked under some circumstances but not others. It is suggested that the technology of behavior modification offers a powerful technique for helping patients escape from short-term habits that are incompatible with their long-term aims, but that the techniques are less successful when they are in consistent conflict with the subject's long-term goals.

Chapter Ten

WHEN MEMORY FAILS

The time at which we are most aware of our memory is when it fails. The effect of this is often trivial but irritating; how often have you claimed to have a terrible memory? On the next page is a questionnaire designed to assess the frequency of everyday memory lapses in normal subjects and in patients suffering from memory deficits following head injury. Try completing it yourself and see if you really do have a terrible memory.

Typically, people complain about having a bad memory because they forget appointments or birthdays, lose things around the house or have difficulty remembering someone's name. These are examples of forgetting that are noticeable because they are to some extent unexpected. Most of us do not usually expect to forget important appointments or the names of old and close friends. On the other hand, we would not be surprised to forget the precise date that we last met someone or the detailed content of the first lecture of a new course. What do we know about forgetting, other than that it occurs? The chapter that follows will be concerned with what psychologists have found out about forgetting and what theoretical interpretations have been proposed. These tend to be somewhat dated since interest in forgetting has not featured strongly in the cognitive analysis of memory, possibly because of the dominance of the computer metaphor—computers tend not to forget.

THE FORGETTING CURVE

The Ebbinghaus Function

Once again, we shall begin with Hermann Ebbinghaus who was the first person to plot out systematically what subsequently became known as the *forgetting curve*. Again, he carried out an epic study on himself, learning lists of 13 syllables which he repeated until he was able to recite the list without error on two successive learning trials. Then, after intervals ranging from 20 minutes to 31 days he re-tested himself. He always found that recall was imperfect on the first recall trial, indicating that forgetting had occurred. He was

The *"Everyday Memory Question-naire"* lists 27 common memory lapses. Rate the frequency with which you yourself make each lapse using the scale 1–9.

The number in the right-hand box is the average rating given by a sample of the general public. See Sunderland, Harris, and Baddeley (1983).

EVERYDAY MEMORY QUESTIONNAIRE

1 Not at all in the last six months
2 About once in the last six months
3 More than once in the last six months but less than once a month
4 About once a month
5 More than once a month but less than once a week
6 About once a week
7 More than once a week but less than once a day
8 About once a day
9 More than once a day

1   Forgetting where you have put something. Losing things around the house. ☐ 5

2   Failing to recognise places that you are told you have often been to before. ☐ 1

3   Finding a television story difficult to follow. ☐ 2

4   Not remembering a change in your daily routine, such as a change in the place where something is kept, or a change in the time something happens. Following your old routine by mistake, ☐ 2

5   Having to go back to check whether you have done something that you meant to do. ☐ 4

6   Forgetting when something happened; for example, forgetting whether something happened yesterday or last week. ☐ 3

7   Completely forgetting to take things with you, or leaving things behind and having to go back and fetch them. ☐ 3

8   Forgetting that you were told something yesterday or a few days ago, and maybe having to be reminded about it. ☐ 3

9   Starting to read something (a book or an article in a newspaper, or magazine) without realizing you have already read it before. ☐ 1

10   Letting your self ramble on to speak about unimportant or irrelevant things. ☐ 2

11   Failing to recognize, by sight, close relatives or friends that you meet frequently. ☐ 1

12   Having difficulty picking up a new skill. For example, having difficulty in learning a new game or in working some new gadget after you have practised once or twice. ☐ 1

13   Finding that a word is 'on the tip of your tongue'. You know what it is but cannot quite find it. ☐ 4

14 Completely forgetting to do things you said you would do, and things you planned to do. ☐ 2

15 Forgetting important details of what you did or what happened to you the day before. ☐ 1

16 When talking to someone, forgetting what you have just said. Maybe saying, 'What was I talking about?' ☐ 3

17 When reading a newspaper or magazine being unable to follow the thread of a story; losing track of what it is about. ☐ 1

18 Forgetting to tell somebody something important. Perhaps forgetting to pass on a message or remind someone of something. ☐ 2

19 Forgetting important details about yourself, e.g. your birthdate or where you live. ☐ 1

20 Getting the details of what someone had told you mixed up and confused. ☐ 2

21 Telling someone a story or joke that you have told them once already. ☐ 2

22 Forgetting details of things you do regularly, whether at home or at work. For example, forgetting details of what to do, or forgetting at what time to do it. ☐ 2

23 Finding that the faces of famous people, seen on television or in photographs, look unfamiliar. ☐ 2

24 Forgetting where things are normally kept or looking for them in the wrong place. ☐ 2

25 (a) Getting lost or turning in the wrong direction on a journey, a walk or in a building where you have OFTEN been before. ☐ 2

(b) Getting lost or turning in the wrong direction on a journey, a walk or in a building where you have ONLY BEEN ONCE OR TWICE BEFORE. ☐ 1

26 Doing some routine thing twice by mistake. For example, putting two lots of tea in the teapot, or going to brush/comb your hair when you have just done so. ☐ 2

27 Repeating to someone what you have just told them or asking them the same question twice. ☐ 1

TOTALS ☐ 58

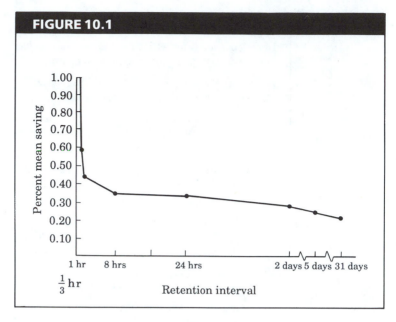

Rate of forgetting nonsense syllables observed by Ebbinghaus. Retention is measured using the saving method, in terms of the number of trials required to relearn a list after varying intervals. From Ebbinghaus (1913).

then able to estimate the amount of forgetting by seeing how long it took him to re-learn the list to the original level; the greater the forgetting, the more trials would be needed to re-learn the list; this is known as the *savings method* of measuring retention. His results are shown in Figure 10.1, from which it is clear that unlike learning which shows a linear relationship between time spent in learning and amount learnt, the rate of forgetting is nonlinear, with amount forgotten being initially rapid, then slowing down in a function that is approximately logarithmic.

Names and Faces
How characteristic is this function of forgetting when tested under rather less artificial circumstances? Plotting accurate forgetting curves over long intervals of time is technically demanding and time-consuming. Consequently the issue has not been extensively explored until a recent series of studies by Bahrick. One of these, (Bahrick, Bahrick, & Wittlinger, 1975) tested the memory of subjects for the names and photographs of high-school classmates. Subjects were tested in a number of ways, some of which showed remarkably little forgetting over periods up to 25 years. Only slight forgetting occurred in the capacity to recognize a name as belonging to a classmate rather than an outsider, to recognize a classmate's picture and to match the classmate's name to his or her high-school graduation photograph. Performance was rather poorer at recalling the name, or putting a name to the picture of a classmate. The results are shown in Figure 10.2 from which it is clear that forgetting is approximately linear when plotted on a log scale with one clear exception, namely that a dip occurs for those

Memory for high-school classmates as a function of retention interval and method of testing. From Bahrick, Bahrick & Wittlinger (1975). Copyright (1975) by the American Psychological Association. Reprinted by permission.

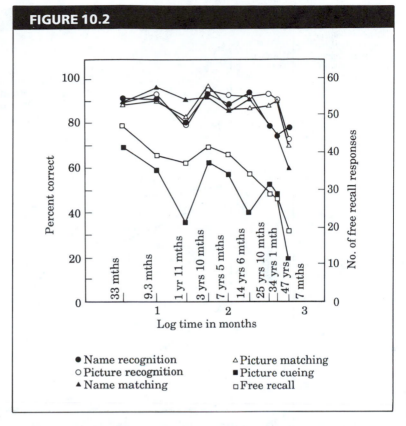

FIGURE 10.2

● Name recognition   △ Picture matching
○ Picture recognition   ■ Picture cueing
▲ Name matching   □ Free recall

subjects who were recalling classmates over the longest delay, from nearly 50 years ago. Whether this sudden dip in the forgetting curve is due to elapsed time, or to the ageing of the subjects who would by this time be well into their sixties, is impossible to tell from the available information.

In a subsequent study, Bahrick explored this issue further by testing the memory of college teachers for the names and faces of former students who had taken a single course with them at a time in the past ranging from 11 days to 8 years before. The results of this study are shown in Figure 10.3. Here, overall level of performance is rather lower, presumably because the amount of contact between the teacher and the student was considerably less than would be the case with fellow high-school students who had grown up together. On the whole, names are retained better than faces, possibly because the teacher has more individual encounters with the student's name in connection with tasks such as grading than with the student's face; typically, classes of 40 were taught.

Three groups of faculty members were tested, a young group with a mean age of 39, a middle-aged group with a mean age of 54, and an older group, mean age 68, some of whom had retired by this time. Bahrick hoped to throw some light on the dip shown in his

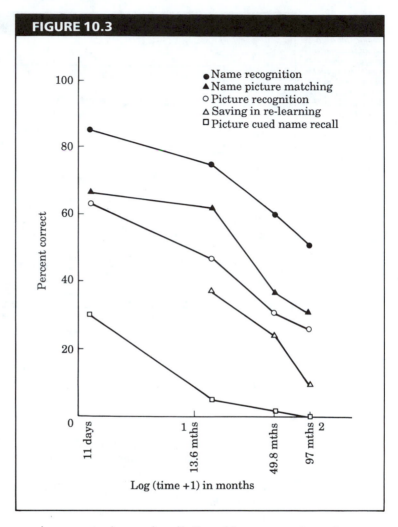

Memory of college teachers for the names and faces of former students. From Bahrick (1984).

FIGURE 10.3

Name recognition
Name picture matching
Picture recognition
Saving in re-learning
Picture cued name recall

Percent correct

Log (time +1) in months

11 days   13.6 mths   49.8 mths   97 mths

previous curve by seeing if the older group showed poorer retention. They did not, suggesting that the previous dip might be a genuine forgetting effect rather than a secondary consequence of the ageing of the subjects.

Foreign Language

In a third study, Bahrick and Phelphs (1987) looked at the retention of a foreign language over intervals ranging up to 50 years. Their results which are shown in Figure 10.4 indicate relatively rapid initial forgetting followed by a very slow forgetting rate, although again there is a tendency for rate of forgetting to increase after 40 or 50 years. Note that level of initial learning continues to be an important factor regardless of delay, with differences in amount learned when young still showing up clearly 40 or 50 years later. A

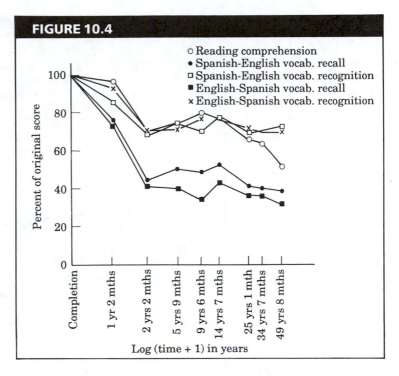

FIGURE 10.4

○ Reading comprehension
● Spanish-English vocab. recall
□ Spanish-English vocab. recognition
■ English-Spanish vocab. recall
× English-Spanish vocab. recognition

Retention of Spanish learnt at college by U.S. students. Note that little further forgetting occurs after two years, suggesting that language is held in some very durable "permastore". From Bahrick and Phelphs (1987). Copyright (1987) by the American Psychological Association. Reprinted by permission.

remarkable, and somewhat comforting feature of this result is the extent to which language is retained despite not being used. Bahrick refers to this stable retention as a *permastore* by analogy with the permafrost, suggesting that its durability is analogous to the unchanging nature of the permanently frozen state of the soil a few feet beneath the ground in Arctic regions.

Complex Skills

An even more dramatic absence of forgetting occurs in the case of *continuous* motor skills. These are skills such as riding a bicycle or steering a car in which performance involves the subject as part of a continuous feedback loop of activity. They can be distinguished from *discrete* skills such as typewriting in which an individual stimulus must be associated with a specific response. For example, Figure 10.5 shows a study by Fleishman and Parker (1962) in which their subjects learnt a task analogous to the skill of flying an aeroplane. They were re-tested after nine months, one year or two years. It is clear that very little forgetting occurs, and even that can be reduced if the subject is given a warm-up trial before the retention test proper is given (Hammerton, 1963).

Unfortunately, discrete motor skills do not show this remarkable retention. In the experiment described in Chapter 7, in which postmen were trained to type using either massed or distributed practice, Baddeley and Longman (1978) found that despite being

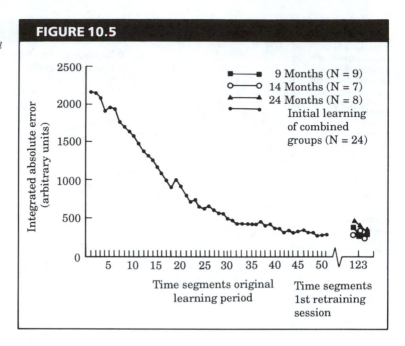

FIGURE 10.5

Retention of a skill analogous to flying an aeroplane after delays ranging from 9 months to two years. After the initial trial, performance is virtually back at the original level of skill. From Fleishman and Parker (1962).

given a warm-up trial before the test, subjects lost a good deal of their typing speed, with the massed practice group that trained for four hours per day showing particularly poor retention.

Many real-life skills are in fact a mixture of several different types of skill and knowledge. A good example is the skill of cardio-pulmonary resuscitation (CPR), the technique for attempting to revive someone who has had a heart attack. It is estimated that this can improve survival chances by up to 40%, and given that there is fair chance that the average person may encounter such an emergency (estimates range from once every 25 years to once every 112 years), if everyone were taught the technique, it could save many lives (Glendon, McKenna, Blaylock, & Hunt, 1987). But are such skills well retained, or are they forgotten, and if forgotten, how often do they need to be revised?

This question prompted McKenna and Glendon (1985) to study forgetting of the skill in 215 shop floor and office worker first aid volunteers, all of whom had mastered the skill. Glendon et al. measured separately:

1. Performance and timing of the crucial component of heart compression;
2. Technique in adequately inflating the lungs and pressing the chest in the right place;
3. Diagnosis, including check for consciousness, breathing and pulse, and
4. Outcome, an expert's judgment of the likelihood that a suitable patient would have been successfully resuscitated.

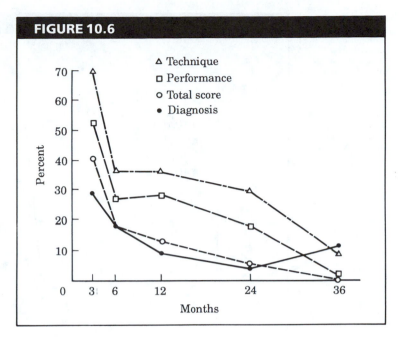

FIGURE 10.6

Effect of delay on the capacity to perform cardio-resuscitation. The figure shows the percentage of trained resuscitations reaching an adequate level of performance on each of four components of the task. Estimated patient survival rate drops dramatically. From McKenna and Glendon (1985).

All of these were measured on Resusci-Anne, a manikin used for training resuscitation that also records the subject's performance, and during training, provides feedback.

Performance on the four measures is shown in Figure 10.6, which indicates clear forgetting, with the result that the expected survival rate of the resuscitable patient drops from 100 to 15% in one year. There is clearly a need for constant revision if the skill is to be maintained.

Autobiographical Incidents

Before leaving the question of long-term forgetting, we should examine one other type of material, namely retention of the events of everyday life. This was studied in a classic experiment by Marigold Linton (1975), who for a five-year period systematically noted everyday two events. At predetermined intervals, she randomly selected a sample of items, read the brief description and attempted to reconstruct each item's date. If she completely failed to remember the incident depicted, then that item was dropped from the sample and the fact noted. She observed, somewhat to her surprise, that the forgetting function appeared to be linear with a slope of about 5% loss per year, rather than logarithmic as the Ebbinghaus result would suggest.

However, the number of samples drawn meant that any given item was likely to be tested on several occasions. When she plotted

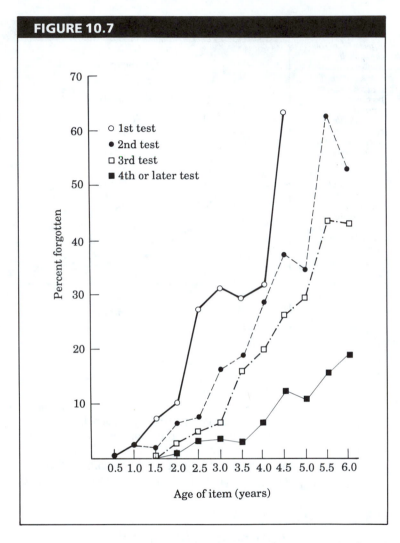

FIGURE 10.7

Probability of forgetting an autobiographical diary item as a function of elapsed time and number of prior tests (rehearsals). From Linton (1975). Copyright 1975 by W.H. Freeman and Company. Reprinted by permission.

○ 1st test
● 2nd test
□ 3rd test
■ 4th or later test

Percent forgotten

Age of item (years)

forgetting rate as a function of number of previous tests, she found this to be a very important factor, as Figure 10.7 shows, with those items which happened not to have been tested before showing much more rapid forgetting than those that had been "rehearsed" by being previously tested. Even so, the forgetting function could not be described as logarithmic.

What can we conclude from this range of forgetting functions? Some types of material appears to show virtually no forgetting as in the case of continuous motor skills, other material such as languages appear to show rapid initial forgetting, followed by excellent further retention, while yet other skills such as those involved in cardiac resuscitation appear to show a relatively steep rate of forgetting, unless they are repeatedly practised. It is hard to escape the suspicion that the "classic" forgetting curve of

Ebbinghaus that is shown in all the introductory psychology texts may be rather less universal than we tend to assume. There are, of course, many differences between the various experiments I have cited, but they reinforce a conclusion that keeps cropping up in discussing the psychology of forgetting, namely that we know surprisingly little about this most fundamental aspect of human memory.

WHY DO WE FORGET?

In the introduction to his book on memory, Ebbinghaus outlines a number of possible explanations of forgetting that had been suggested by philosophers. One which would currently be termed an interference theory assumed that "the earlier images are more and more overlaid so to speak and covered by the later ones".

A second explanation, which would currently be termed a trace decay theory, assumed that memory traces were eroded by the passage of time, much as a range of mountains might be worn down by the elements with time, or to quote Ebbinghaus, "The persisting images suffer changes which more and more affect their nature".

A third possibility is that forgetting involves "crumbling into parts and the loss of separate components instead of general obscuration", a view subsequently proposed by Bower (1967) as a multi-component theory of the memory trace.

Ebbinghaus correctly observed that existing evidence did not allow him to choose between these possibilities. He proposed to carry out experiments which would allow him "a possibility of indirectly approaching the problem just stated in a small and definitely limited sphere and, by means of keeping aloof for a while from any theory, perhaps of constructing one" (Ebbinghaus, 1885/ 1913, p. 65).

Unfortunately, Ebbinghaus never constructed such a theory, and in reviewing his book for the philosophical journal *Mind*, Jacobs (1885) commented that the experiments were "remarkable ... more for their methods than their results" which "... scarcely seemed calculated to set the Spree on fire". This is probably a fair estimation of the theoretical as opposed to methodological contribution of Ebbinghaus' work, but it must be confessed that in terms of coming up with convincing proof of the cause of forgetting, no one else has set the Spree, or the Thames or the Hudson on fire in the intervening century. We certainly do know a good deal more about the determinants of forgetting, but we are still not able to rule out trace decay, interference or fragmentation as mechanisms by which forgetting occurs.

Testing the Trace Decay Hypothesis

It might seem relatively easy to decide whether memory traces fade spontaneously; one simply needs to compare learning after a delay that is unfilled with one that is filled with potentially interfering activity. The problem here, however, is to know what one means by "unfilled" in this context. It is presumably not time itself that causes forgetting, but the neural events that inevitably take place over time in any living organism. Early attempts to explore this possibility involved testing cold-blooded creatures such as insects or fishes under different environmental temperatures. At higher temperatures, metabolism increases and the rate of physiological activity, of ageing and decaying of the memory trace should also increase. However, although some evidence of impaired retention was found in ants by Hoagland (1931), and in goldfish by French (1942), the effects were far from straightforward. Furthermore, higher temperature typically means more activity which could mean more interference, rather than a simple increase in metabolism.

A rather more interesting result was obtained by Minami and Dallenbach (1946) who took advantage of the fact that cockroaches will lie inert, if persuaded to crawl into a narrow cone lined with tissue paper. If placed in a brightly-lit box, cockroaches will spontaneously escape to a dark box. Minami and Dallenbach taught their cockroaches to avoid the dark compartment by shocking them whenever they entered it. When the animals had learnt this, they were either induced to crawl into the tissue paper cone, or allowed to wander about at will in a darkened cage, before being tested at intervals ranging from 10 minutes to 24 hours. The amount remembered was then measured in terms of the number of trials needed to relearn the avoidance.

Forgetting was substantially greater in those subjects that had been active, than in those that had remained inertly in their lined cones. This therefore suggested that activity was an important variable, which might be taken to support an interference interpretation. Two things rule against this, however, first that the inactive cockroaches did show some forgetting. Secondly, it may be that the metabolic processes within the inactive cockroaches were operating much more slowly, and hence the trace was decaying more slowly.

Sleep and Forgetting

There was, however, no doubt that interpolated activity did dramatically increase rate of forgetting. Does the same apply to forgetting in humans, and if so how should it be interpreted? In 1924, Jenkins and Dallenbach conducted an extended study on two students who were required to learn lists of 10 nonsense syllables to a criterion of one perfect recitation. The students were then required to recall them after delays of one, two, four or eight hours during which the subject was either awake or asleep. The interference prediction was that sleep should minimize interpolated interfering activity, and hence should result in less forgetting. This is just what was observed, and the Jenkins and Dallenbach study has figured in introductory texts from that time onwards.

Unfortunately, however, the experiment is open to a number of other interpretations. For instance, since the subjects slept at night, for reasons of experimental convenience, learning for the interpolated sleep condition always took place in the evening, while the waking control learning tended to occur in the morning. When this was controlled, the magnitude of the effect was less (van Ormer, 1932; Ekstrand, 1972), but still remained.

Rather more worrying was a result by Hockey, Davies, and Gray (1972) who used sleep during the day as their intervening activity, and found no evidence that it reduced the rate of forgetting. This suggests that it is not sleep *per se* that is important, but probably some of the diurnal fluctuations in neurochemical activity that occur. Some important neurochemical substances such as growth hormone for example, tend to be secreted during the night rather than during the day. Ekstrand (1972) cites research by Coleman in which she found that sleep leads to the best retention when it immediately follows learning. She interprets this timing effect as consistent with the view that sleep is important because of its role in the initial consolidation of the memory trace, rather than because of its capacity for preventing interference.

It is of course quite wrong to assume that sleep merely represents a cessation of mental activity. The most obvious form of mental activity during sleep is dreaming, and the possibility that the process of dreaming may play an important role in memory is one that seems to appeal to those of a speculative turn of mind. Dreaming is associated with rapid eye movements, which allows the investigator to tell when a sleeping subject is dreaming. In the 1960s, the psychologist Christopher Evans speculated that dreaming might be a form of reprogramming whereby the brain sorts out and catalogues the files of the previous day's memory, making it an essential process in learning. A similar speculation has been made more recently by the Nobel Prize-winning molecular biologist Francis Crick (Crick & Mitchison, 1983), who suggest that dreaming may be a side-effect of a process concerned with consolidating and increasing the discriminability of memory traces.

The idea that dreams and memory processes are linked, is an intriguing one and in the 1970s a number of studies attempted to explore the possible link. Empson and Clarke (1970) taught their subjects verbal material before they went to bed, and then woke their experimental subjects up whenever they began to show the rapid eye movements characteristic of dreaming, waking their control subjects up an equivalent number of times, but ensuring that it did not interfere with their dreams. They found that deprivation of rapid eye movement (REM) sleep did lead to somewhat poorer retention of prose the next day, and interpreted this in terms of the possible role of such sleep in memory trace consolidation. However, Dement (1960) has suggested that the deprivation of REM sleep may have more generally stressful effects, and these could have been responsible for the poorer memory performance the following day.

Ekstrand (1972) used another approach that was based on the finding that REM sleep is comparatively rare during the first half of the night, tending to cluster in the period just before awakening. He had his subjects learn paired associates either in the evening, recalling them in the middle of the night, or learn in the middle of the night, recalling next morning. Those subjects tested in the morning, as expected showed more REM sleep during the retention interval, but tended to remember *less* than those who had learnt in the evening and recalled during the night. This result, therefore, is the exact opposite to that found by Empson and Clarke. Unfortunately, however, while the Ekstrand study avoids the problem of REM deprivation, it introduces two other design problems, the fact that the two groups learn at different times, and that they recall at different times.

It has been known since Ebbinghaus' original work, that the time at which learning takes place affects performance, while subsequent research by Stones (1974) showed that time of awakening is also an important factor. In particular, subjects aroused from REM appear to recall better than those aroused from deep sleep. Indeed, one rather more prosaic interpretation of REM sleep is that it is a progressive warm-up process, preparing the organism to wake up and cope with life at a higher level of physiological arousal. Stones suggests a further complicating factor, namely type of material; he found that REM sleep appeared to favor the retention of meaningful material, but not the rote learning of nonsense material. Perhaps most important of all is the fact that the effects noted by all these studies tend to be very small, suggesting that the intriguing REM sleep reprogramming hypothesis is probably closer to science fiction than to scientific fact.

THE ROLE OF INTERFERENCE

One alternative to attempting to produce a situation in which one tries to get rid of all interfering activity is to explore a weak interference hypothesis. This would argue not that all forgetting is necessarily the result of interference, but that interference is a major determinant of forgetting. This approach has had considerably more success. For example, McGeoch and McDonald (1931) systematically manipulated interference by varying the similarity between the material to be recalled, and the interfering activity.

They had their subjects learn a list of adjectives until they could recall it perfectly. Following this, their subjects spent 10 minutes either resting, or learning new material varying in similarity to the adjective list. Table 10.1 shows the results of this study. As the similarity of the interpolated material to the original adjective list increased, so the amount retained dropped, with the poorest

TABLE 10.1

Effect of Interpolated Learning on Serial Recall and Relearning of a List of Adjectives

Interpolated Activity	Meal Recall (Max = 10) on Trial 1	Mean Trials to a Criterion of One Perfect Repetition
Rest	4.50	4.58
Learn 3-digit number	3.68	4.42
Learn nonsense syllables	2.58	4.50
Learn unrelated adjectives	2.17	5.17
Learn antonyms	1.83	6.67
Learn synonyms	1.25	7.33

Source: McGeoch and MacDonald (1931).

performance occurring when the subjects were required to learn synonyms of the original adjectives. There is no doubt that this is broadly consistent with an interference hypothesis, and suggests that mere disuse is not sufficient to explain forgetting. Notice, however, that even when the subjects rested, a substantial amount of forgetting occurred, from 10 adjectives to 4.5. The amount of forgetting is so large, that I suspect that the subjects may have been boosting their initial learning with information held temporarily in working memory. Nonetheless, the main thrust of the study remains, namely that interfering material will impair retention, with the degree of interference increasing as the interfering material becomes more and more similar to the material learnt.

In the following 30 years, the study of interference came to dominate the North American approach to memory. The approach was based on *associationism*, the assumption that learning could be regarded as the formation of associations between previously unrelated events. This view which had its origins in classical times, was elaborated by the British associationist philosophers Hobbes and Locke in the seventeenth century, and applied to experimental results in the 1890s by the German psychologist G.E. Müller. It was introduced into North America by L.W. Webb in the early years of this century. Associationism formed the basis of the Chicago functionalist school of memory during the middle years of the century, and as the chapters on semantic memory and connectionism indicate, is still a powerful influence in memory theory.

The brand of associationism that became known as *interference theory* was however largely the development of a group working in Chicago during the 1930s, led by Carr, Robinson and McGeoch. The approach was comparatively atheoretical, being more concerned to plot the relationship between well-controlled variables than to speculate about underlying theory, an approach that is sometimes given the unflattering label of "dustbowl empiricism".

With the development of a more cognitive approach to memory in the 1960s, the protagonists of this approach became more speculative and theoretically active (e.g. Melton, 1963; Underwood & Postman, 1960). However, the interference theorists should perhaps best be seen as the heirs to Ebbinghaus, and like Ebbinghaus their main contribution has been the demonstration of empirical effects, rather than the development of sophisticated theory.

In the last decade, the interference approach theory to memory has undergone a very rapid decline. Psychology tends to have a depressingly short memory, and it would be a great pity if the awareness of the very powerful effects of interference were to be lost simply because they tended to be associated with a theoretical approach that became regarded as outmoded and somewhat sterile. I therefore propose to give an overview of the major effects of interference, followed by a rather brief account of the theoretical issues that occupied interference theorists.

Retroactive Interference

The term retroactive interference, often abbreviated as RI, refers to the interfering effect of later learning on recall. In the standard paradigm, the experimental group learns List 1, followed by List 2, and then recalls List 1, whereas the control group learns List 1 then rests during the interpolated learning period before recalling List 1. This is of course the design used in the McGeoch and McDonald study cited above.

Figure 10.8 shows the results of an experiment by Slamecka (1960) who had his subjects learn sentences by heart. The material he chose was hardly deathless prose, an example being: "Communicators can exercise latitude in specifying meaning however they choose provided that such definition corresponds somewhat closely to regular usage". He presented such sequences for two, four or eight trials, and followed this by either a rest period, or a period during which the subjects had four or eight trials learning another equivalent literary gem. As Figure 10.8 shows, the amount learned is a function of the number of initial learning trials, and the amount forgotten a function of the number of interfering trials on the second sentence.

While research on interference has in general been comparatively sparse in recent years, there is one area in which RI effects have been explored in considerable detail. It has been known since the work of Münsterberg (1908) that the testimony of witnesses to a crime is very subject to disruption as a result of interference from subsequent questioning. This phenomenon has been explored in great detail, initially by Elizabeth Loftus, and subsequently by many other investigators. In one study she had her subjects watch a film of a car crash. They were later asked various questions about the incident including how fast the cars were going when they hit each

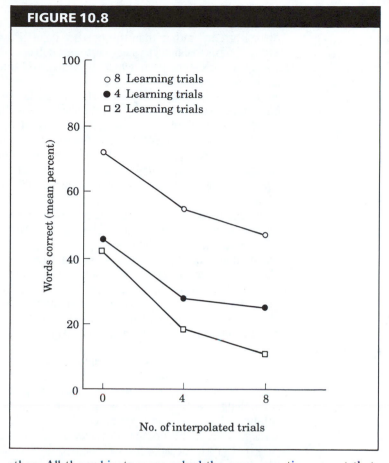

FIGURE 10.8

Effect of retroactive interference on the retention of prose. Recall is affected both by the degree of initial learning and by the number of interpolated trials with other material. From Slamecka (1960).

other. All the subjects were asked the same question except that the word "hit" was replaced by *contacted*, *bumped*, *collided* or *smashed*. The particular word used influenced the speed estimated, with the word *smashed* evoking the highest average speed (40.8 mph) followed by *collided* (39.3 mph), *bumped* (38.1 mph) and *hit* (34.0 mph), with *contacted* being the lowest at 31.8 mph. When further questioned a week later and asked if there was any evidence of broken glass, those who had been tested using the word *smashed* were consistently more likely to incorrectly report the presence of broken glass.

In another study, Loftus (1977) showed her subjects a series of slides representing an accident in which a pedestrian was knocked down at a crossing. A green car was driven past the accident without stopping after which a police car arrived and a passenger from one of the cars involved in the accident went for help. Having seen this, the subjects were asked a total of 12 questions, the tenth of which referred to "the blue car" that drove past the accident. When, 20 minutes later, the subjects were asked the color of the car that had driven by without stopping, subjects given the false information were significantly more likely to choose "blue" or "bluish green" rather than the correct color of green. In another study, Loftus managed to suggest to her subjects the existence of a totally non-existent barn which was inserted into their memory during questioning.

There is no doubt that distortions can be readily induced in subjects by such misleading information. Do they simply represent the response of subjects to social pressure? Or could they imply the destruction and replacement of earlier information by the new? A third possibility is that the new information overlays and interferes with the retrieval of the old but does not destroy it. Loftus explored these possible explanations in a number of experiments.

In one study, she offered rewards of varying sizes for correct response, arguing that if the subject was merely going along with the experimenter's suggestion out of politeness, offering a substantial reward for a correct answer would be likely to reverse this. There was no tendency for a high reward to lead to increased accuracy. In a further study, she showed that her subjects responded just as rapidly and confidently when they were influenced by the misleading information, as they would have been without biasing questions. On the basis of these results, Loftus concluded that the memory trace was actually distorted or destroyed by the subsequent information, rather than merely obscured by it (Loftus & Loftus, 1980).

As Loftus was, of course, well aware, the failure to find something does not prove that it is not there, and a subsequent study by Bekerian and Bowers (1983) showed that under certain circumstances, the original information had not been destroyed, and that given the appropriate conditions, it could be recovered. Bekerian and Bowers pointed out that the standard method of questioning subjects in the Loftus paradigm was to probe for information in a comparatively unstructured way. They argued that if one were to systematically take the subject through the incident, starting with questions about the prior circumstances and systematically moving forward, then there might be a much better chance of reinstating the framework in which the material had first been experienced.

Bekerian and Bowers carried out a study in which they used Loftus' material, followed by misleading material inserted into the subsequent questions. The study then went on to test for memory distortion. One group was questioned in random order while the other was questioned in the order in which the incidents occurred. Subjects tested using the random order Loftus procedure showed the standard distortion effects, while those tested in the order of occurrence of the incidents did not show distortion. It appears then that the initial experience had been overlain by the misleading information, not destroyed by it, as Loftus had previously concluded.

Proactive Interference

This refers to the case in which earlier learning interferes with later. One of the first people to note the proactive interference (PI) effect was the nineteenth century German psychologist Hugo Münsterberg, who happened to change the pocket in which he kept his watch from one side to the other. He kept finding that when he wanted to know the time he would automatically reach into the old pocket rather than the new. A somewhat less antiquated example of the perils of PI is given by Loftus (1980, p.63) who refers to a young lady, who in moments of passion was inclined to cry out the name of her *previous* boyfriend.

The classic experimental demonstration of proactive interference comes from a study by Underwood (1957), one of the most active and influential interference theorists. Underwood was concerned that his subjects showed substantial forgetting of a list of nonsense syllables over a 24-hour delay. Since it seemed unlikely that his student subjects went home and mugged up other interfering nonsense syllables in the interval, it was not clear where the interference might originate.

The phenomenon of PI was known to exist, but was not at that time regarded as a particularly potent source of interference. However, Underwood was a very prolific experimenter, and tended to use the same undergraduate subjects repeatedly, suggesting that PI from earlier experiments might be a source of forgetting. He therefore plotted amount of forgetting as a function of number of previous nonsense syllable experiments the subjects had taken part in. He found a very clear function; the greater the number of prior experiments, the greater the forgetting. He then wrote around to various colleagues asking if they had similar data. For each of the experiments he received, he plotted the amount remembered after 24 hours as a function of number of prior lists. His results are shown in Figure 10.9, which suggests a very clear effect of PI, with amount forgotten over 24 hours increasing substantially with number of prior lists learnt.

In fact, there is a further factor that probably contributed to the size of the effects observed by Underwood. Typically, as subjects take part in more and more experiments they tend to take less and less time to learn a given list. The first list therefore might take say 12 trials, while the tenth list might be learnt in half that time. However, even in the case of the first list, there will be some items that are learnt right from the start, and these will have had 12 trials of practice. In the case of the later list, the maximum amount of practice that any item can have will be six trials, since this is the number of trials it took the subject to master the whole list.

How can one get around this problem? One possibility is to present lists for the same number of trials on each successive occasion. Peter Warr who first pointed out this potential confounding effect in PI used this approach, and found that the amount of PI as a function of successive lists was very much reduced (Warr, 1964). However, it could be argued that if subjects

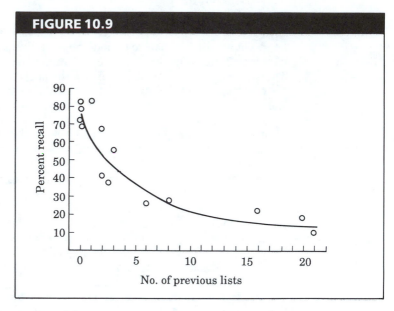

The role of PI in the recall of single lists. Each point represents the recall of a list learned 24 hours previously; the more previous lists the subject has learned, the poorer his retention. From Underwood (1957).

are getting better at learning, then the later lists will be better learnt than the earlier, so Warr's technique is not a fair test of the hypothesis either. A more satisfactory strategy is to select individual items on the basis of the number of times they were correctly recalled during learning. When items are matched for degree of learning in this way, then some effect of PI remains, although it tends not to be as powerful as the initial effect demonstrated by Underwood (Keppel, Postman, & Zavortink, 1968; Warr, 1964).

The Extra-experimental Interference Hypothesis

Although Underwood's initial estimate of the magnitude of PI effects may have been somewhat exaggerated, there is no doubt that PI does lead to greater forgetting. Furthermore, there is abundant evidence in support of the general interference tenet that degree of forgetting is a function of the similarity between the material to be remembered and the interfering material. However, neither of these effects offer a good explanation of the fact that naïve subjects who have not encountered nonsense syllables before, will show forgetting over a 24-hour period during which they presumably do not encounter any further material of the same kind.

In order to explain the fact that forgetting occurred under these circumstances, Underwood and Postman (1960) suggested that forgetting might be due to interference from the subject's language habits. They proposed interference at both the level of individual letter sequences, and at the word level, and made a number of strong predictions. One of these for example, was that words that are common within the language will tend to have strong associations with other words. These will form a powerful source of PI causing such high frequency words to be forgotten more rapidly than less common low frequency words which are assumed to have weaker associations.

Underwood and Postman (1960) tested this prediction in a series of experiments with strikingly uniform results. Rate of forgetting appeared to be quite unrelated to either the frequency of the words, or when nonsense syllables were used, of the frequency with which the constituent letter pairs occurred in English. The attempt to extend interference theory from the strict confines of the verbal learning laboratory by relating it to prior language habits was a resounding flop.

Subsequent work by Underwood and Ekstrand (1966) suggested that the lack of an effect of language habits may be attributable to a tendency for PI to be much less prominent when the interfering material is learnt under distributed practice, as would certainly be the case in a subject acquiring his language. They showed that distributed practice did indeed lead to less PI. Unfortunately, this still leaves the puzzle of why a single individual list should be forgotten, given no prior massed learning of similar material that might interfere. It also suggests that lists of words or nonsense syllables learned under laboratory conditions of massed practice may have even less relevance to normal learning than was suspected.

The response of Postman, the second advocate of the extra-experimental interference hypothesis, to the difficulties raised by the unexpected results was to suggest various ways in which interference theory might be able to explain "deviations from its predictions" (Postman, 1963), an approach that was further elaborated by Postman and Underwood (1973). However, while interference theory was having its crisis, cognitive approaches to memory were rapidly gathering in strength. While some inter-ference theorists became more cognitive in outlook, the theory itself seemed to simply run out of steam. It was as if the two approaches to memory were too dissimilar to talk the same language, so that rather than engage in a controversy, the two merely ignored each other. One unfortunate effect of this has been the subsequent comparative neglect of forgetting as a topic, and an even stronger neglect of the phenomenon of interference. However, as we shall see in chapter 13, the development of connectionist models of learning seems likely to revive the crucial question of when and how memory traces interact with each other.

What Determines Rate of Forgetting?

One of the most striking features of the various experiments carried out by Underwood and Postman (1960) in their attempt to test the extra-experimental interference hypothesis was the lack of any difference in forgetting rate as a function of type of material.

Whether the subject was learning high or low frequency words, or syllables that approximated closely to English like *bal* or differed widely from English, like *zij*, were all factors that had a major effect on learning, but which had no apparent effect on rate of forgetting. Indeed, in another paper Underwood (1964) surveyed the literature and drew attention to this striking feature; provided ceiling and floor effects are avoided, performance measured in terms of number of items correct appears not to depend at all on the nature of the material or the degree of learning.

Following an informal discussion with Norman Slamecka, he and I both agreed that this was an intriguing aspect of the literature, and decided to look at it further. Slamecka's work has resulted in a very carefully conducted set of experiments in which he varied degree of learning within the laboratory and studied the effect of this on forgetting, finding evidence to suggest that the mean number of items lost per unit time does not depend on overall level of learning (Slamecka & McElree, 1983).

I myself used a rather more naturalistic situation. Physiotherapy students in Britain are required to take a national exam at the end of their first year in anatomy. One component of this used to be a multiple-choice paper. We were able to re-test students on the original paper after varying intervals of time, thus allowing us to plot separately the performance of students who did well on anatomy, as indicated by other parts of the examination, and students who did rather poorly. An item analysis of the examination had been carried out on a national basis, so we were able to plot separately the retention of easy and difficult items. We, like Slamecka and McElree, find that the number of items lost per unit time does not depend on level of initial learning (Baddeley, Baddeley, & Nimmo-Smith, submitted).

As we shall see in the section on amnesia, rate of forgetting appears to be surprisingly invariant across many patient groups. Some claims have been made for faster forgetting for certain types of amnesic patient, but the evidence is far from convincing (see Chapter 14).

It is only fair to indicate at this point that the interpretation of such results is not entirely uncontroversial. Loftus (1985a,b) has argued for measuring degree of forgetting in terms of the half-life of a memory trace, an approach that leads to a description of forgetting in terms of the horizontal difference between two functions rather than the vertical, or in other words the amount of time it takes for items from the two curves to reach an equivalent level of retention, a position that Slamecka (1985) does not accept.

My own view on this issue is that the assumption that items are lost at a constant rate regardless of initial level provides a very economical description of a great deal of data. It is far from clear that an equivalently straightforward account can be given by the measure proposed by Loftus. The Loftus measure may have the advantage of being based on a specific model of forgetting, one that is analogous to the decay of a radioactive body such a piece of radium, but the evidence in favor of this model from other sources is not particularly strong. The study of forgetting is an area of considerable theoretical importance, that has in recent years been sadly neglected. It almost certainly needs theoretical modeling skills of greater sophistication than were applied by interference theorists, but such skills will need to be combined with careful empirical research if they are to throw light on this crucial aspect of memory.

Cue-dependent Forgetting

Classical interference theory tended to have a relatively straight-forward view of the way in which interference worked. Forgetting was regarded by Jenkins and Dallenbach as "a matter of the interference, inhibition or obliteration of the old by the new" (Jenkins & Dallenbach, 1924, p.612). Later interference theorists devoted a good deal of attention to the question of whether interference reflected simple competition between responses, or involved the active weakening of the first response by the second. In general, later theorists favored this latter unlearning hypothesis, as a result of a number of experiments in which it was shown that learning a second set of material appeared to block the subject's capacity to recall earlier material, when he was explicitly asked for both (Barnes & Underwood, 1959).

An alternative hypothesis was suggested by Tulving who argued that forgetting might be due to the lack of appropriate retrieval cues, rather than the destructions or over-writing of the initial learning. If this were the case, then one might expect items that appeared to be forgotten as a result of interference, to become accessible once more, given the right retrieval cues.

Tulving and Psotka (1971) attempted to demonstrate the importance of cue dependency in retroactive interference. Subjects were given a list of 24 words to learn. The words comprised six different categories each of four words, hence there might be four types of building, four military titles, four metals, four tools and four flowers. After three presentation trials, subjects tried to recall as many words as possible and then moved on to the second part of the study. This involved learning either zero, one, two, three or five further lists, again for three trials and again with immediate free recall. The third part of the study involved asking the subjects to recall as many items as possible from any of the lists.

Performance showed clear evidence of RI, the more interpolated lists, the poorer the retention. However, as Figure 10.10 shows, this is mainly because subjects tend to forget whole categories; given that one item from a category is recalled, the total recalled from that category shows little effect of RI. In a final condition, after a 10-minute break, subjects were given the names of the categories of the various lists and attempted cued recall. Under these circumstances, performance was as good as the original free recall, and showed no evidence of the effect of interpolated lists.

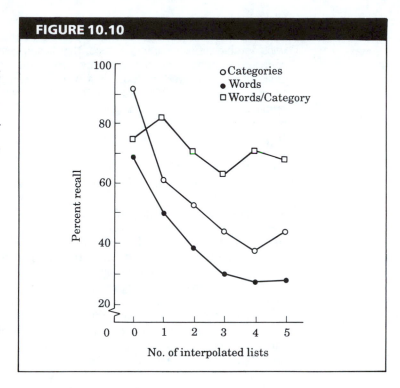

FIGURE 10.10

The effect of RI on the recall of categorized word lists. Overall recall declines with number of interpolated lists, but this is mainly due to forgetting of whole categories. If category cues are given, little or no RI occurs. From Tulving and Psotka (1971).

○ Categories
● Words
□ Words/Category

Percent recall

No. of interpolated lists

Tulving interpreted these results as indicating that the inter-polated trials impaired performance by removing retrieval cues, rather than by loss of information from the memory trace. When such cues were provided by the experimenter, the RI effect disappeared. This issue did of course crop up in the area of eyewitness testimony and the effect of subsequent misleading information. You may recall that the initial work of Loftus and her colleagues (Loftus & Loftus, 1980) seemed to suggest that the misleading information destroyed the earlier memory trace, while subsequent studies (e.g. Bekerian & Bowers, 1983) indicated that the misleading information interfered with retrieval of the original trace, but did not obliterate it, a result that mirrors that of Tulving and Psotka (1971) using word-lists. The role of retrieval failure in forgetting is discussed in the next chapter. Before leaving the investigation of forgetting however, we should say something about the common but vexatious problem of forgetting to do things.

FORGETTING TO DO THINGS

When people complain about having a bad memory, they typically do not mean that they have trouble remembering the Spanish they learnt at school, or how to carry out mouth-to-mouth resuscitation. They are much more likely to mean that they are inclined to forget appointments, or to fail to carry out errands such as collecting the bread on the way home from the office. Until comparatively recently, most theories of forgetting said little or nothing about this all-too-common demonstration of the fallibility of memory, but there has in recent years been a development of interest in remembering to do things, a topic that was christened by Meacham *prospective memory* (Meacham & Singer, 1977).

Prospective and Retrospective Memory

Some of the characteristics of this type of forgetting are illustrated by the following incident that happened to me. I was invited to take part in a live 'phone-in as part of a Scottish radio program called "The Jimmy Mack Show". This required me to arrive at the local studio slightly earlier than I would normally have arrived at work, and join one of two other psychologists in answering questions 'phoned in by radio listeners about memory and its mysteries. On the appointed day, I was looking at the morning paper and wondering what was on television that evening, when suddenly the thought of television reminded me of radio, which produced the horrifying realisation that I should at that time be broadcasting. I rushed off, to arrive at the studio, mumbling about terrible traffic jams and arrived just in time for the final summing up, at which point I was asked what tips I would give the listeners to help them remember!

A number of features of that incident are characteristic of prospective memory and forgetting. One reason that I forgot the appointment was because the timing of going to the studio on my way to work placed it outside the normal structure of my working day. As we shall see later, prospective remembering appears to be tied in closely with the social fabric of one's life. A second feature was the cueing effect whereby reading about television reminded me of radio which in turn reminded me of my appointment. It seems likely that such cues are important, but they are very difficult to study under the naturalistic conditions in which most prospective memory studies have been carried out. A third characteristic feature of such lapses is the degree of embarrassment created by the incident. The implication is that we forget things we do not regard as very important, or perhaps things that we dislike, so that I felt that I could not confess to the radio listeners that I had forgotten to turn up, especially as I was presented as a memory expert.

What then are the crucial differences between *prospective* and *retrospective* memory? First of all, prospective memory tends to be crucially concerned with *when* something should be remembered, whereas retrospective memory is primarily concerned with what. Prospective memory typically has a very low information content, you need to remember to meet someone, or to take a cake out of the oven, but need not remember in great detail what you plan to say, or how to bake a cake. In contrast, retrospective memory tends to be concerned with the amount of information recalled. Thirdly, prospective forgetting appears to have a strong moral component, often producing embarrassment, something that indicates its social importance, whereas retrospective forgetting tend to be very much more neutral in this regard.

So far we have simply speculated about individual instances of forgetting. What is the evidence for a distinction between prospective and retrospective memory? One source comes from a study by Wilkins and Baddeley (1978) who were interested in simulating the task of taking pills four times a day; compliance in taking medicine is, of course, an important everyday prospective memory task that has received a fair amount of attention over the years (Ley, 1988).

The pill-taking task was simulated by requiring the subjects to take with them a small box with a button. When this was pressed the time was automatically recorded, allowing the accuracy of performance to be monitored. Two groups of subjects took part in the experiment, one selected because they had proved to be very good at a task involving the immediate free recall of lists of unrelated words, while the other was particularly poor at this long-term verbal learning task. We were interested in whether they would differ in their prospective memory performance. Indeed they did, with the subjects having good verbal memory actually being *less* accurate in their simulated pill-taking than those with poor memory, a phenomenon we have subsequently labeled the "absentminded professor effect".

However, while it is clear that remembering to do things is a very different task from long-term verbal memory, it would be wrong to assume that having an intact long-term memory is not necessary for good prospective remembering. A test of everyday memory devised to monitor the problems of patients, the Rivermead Behavioural Memory Test, includes a number of prospective memory tasks, for example, having an object such as a comb taken away and secreted with the instruction to ask for it at the end of the test, or being told that when a buzzer rings the patient should ask when the next appointment will be. Patients who show evidence of general memory deficits perform poorly on these tests, just as they perform poorly on more verbal tasks such as remembering people's names, or for that matter learning lists of unrelated words (Wilson, Cockburn, Baddeley, & Hiorns, in press). Indeed, Cockburn and Smith (1988) suggest that prospective memory is one of the most sensitive components of the behavioral memory test to effects of ageing. Does this then mean that the elderly are more likely to forget appointments than the young? On the whole it appears not to be so, although this is probably because the elderly tend to live a rather more structured life, and may make more use of external reminders such as diaries and calendars.

Much of the work carried out so far on prospective memory has been of an observational nature, often using diaries in which the respondents note instances and details of lapses of memory. In one such study Meacham and Kushner (1980) noted that intentions involving other people, such as appointments and meetings are less likely to be forgotten than intentions involving inanimate objects, such for example as remembering to collect a document.

Ellis (1988), as a result of a diary study distinguishes between two types of prospective memory demands, *pulses* and *steps*. A pulse involves the requirement to remember to do something at a specific time, for example to attend for a dental appointment at 4 p.m. next Tuesday. Steps involve remembering to do something over a rather broader period of time, for example, remembering to ring up the travel agent to check that a flight has been confirmed, whereby the telephone call might perhaps be made at any time from now until the end of the day. Ellis notes that pulses tend to be better recalled than steps, to be judged as more important, to be more likely to be remembered by means of a memory aid or diary, and according to her subjects, to be remembered only once at the specific necessary time, or to be something that the subject was aware of for the whole day. Steps on the other hand tend to be less important, are less likely to involve memory aids, and more likely to be recalled from time to time throughout the day.

Motivational Factors

The issue of importance is one that crops up relatively frequently, and was one that particularly interested Freud who was one of the first people to discuss prospective memory. He links memory lapses with motivation and attitude, suggesting "that in these cases the motive is an unusually large amount of unavowed contempt for other people" (Freud, 1960, p. 157), and noting that he himself is more likely to forget his non-paying than his paying patients. While "unavowed contempt" is perhaps putting things a little strongly, the evidence does seem to suggest that the more strongly motivated we are, the less likely we are to forget to do things (Meacham & Singer, 1977). It seems likely that anticipated pleasantness may also be another factor, which is perhaps why U.S. dentists tend to ring up and remind patients the day before an appointment, whereas hairdressers on the whole do not (Winograd, 1988).

We have so far discussed some of the factors that influence the likelihood of prospective forgetting, but have said nothing about the mechanism whereby we do apparently sometimes succeed in remembering to do things at the right time. Freud proposes that "the suggested intention slumbers on in the person concerned until the time for its execution approaches. Then it awakes and impels him to perform the action" (Freud, 1960, p.152), but this provides a colorful description rather than an explanation. How does the intention know when to wake up?

Experimental Studies

Harris and Wilkins (1982) tried to tackle this question by attempting to produce an experimental analogue of one particular prospective memory task, that of monitoring an activity, such as baking a cake, and taking it out from the oven at the appropriate time, while at the same time engaging in other activities. Their subjects were tested in groups, with each subject given a series of specified times at which they should remember to perform an action, namely holding up a particular card. Otherwise, they were free to watch a film. Watches were removed, but subjects were able to see a clock by turning round. Harris and Wilkins used these turning actions as an external indicator that the subject was monitoring the time.

Harris and Wilkins found that the number of clock observations followed a J-shaped pattern, being initially moderately frequent, followed by a period when very few observations were made, with number of observations then increasing steadily up to a point at which the time to hold up their card arrived. They also noted that on a number of occasions, a subject looked at the clock a few seconds early, and between then and the crucial time appeared to forget, suggesting a short-term component to the activity.

They suggest a process model to account for this observation or behavior in which the subject tests the time, waits, tests again until a point at which the time has elapsed whereupon he or she exits with a response, a model they refer to as the Test-Wait-Test-Exit Model. They suggest the J-shape distribution occurs because during the initial tests, it is clear that there is a considerable amount of time to run, allowing a longer wait. Why then should the initial part of the J-shape lead to more observations than the middle? This problem was tackled by Ceci and Bronfenbrenner (1985) who argue that this initial phase is used by the subject to calibrate his time estimation, or in other words to check how quickly subjective time is passing.

Ceci and Bronfenbrenner tested this in an ingenious series of studies in which children perform the task of baking cup cakes, an activity that requires them to wait for 30 minutes while the cup cakes are in the oven. When children are tested at home with a familiar sibling, they show a U-shaped pattern of clock observation responses, suggesting that they initially check the clock rather frequently, gradually becoming better at estimating the rate at which time is passing, and then checking slowly until the latter part of the cooking period.

Ceci, Baker, and Bronfenbrenner (1988) tested the temporal monitoring hypothesis more specifically in a study in which they systematically speeded up or slowed down the clock by 10, 33 or 50%. With the two smaller distortions, the U-shaped pattern remained, but once the distortion reached 50% the pattern changed to one of a steadily increasing frequency of clock monitoring throughout the 30-minute period. This pattern tended to be less efficient, involving about 30% more checks than the U-shaped pattern, but led to the same degree of accuracy. It is a pattern that Ceci and Bronfenbrenner found when the children were placed in a slightly less familiar context than with their family at home, either by requiring them to perform the task in the laboratory, or in having them monitored by an older child from outside the family.

The sensitivity of the pattern of observing responses to social factors again points up the extent to which prospective memory is tied in with factors that extend beyond that of the individual rememberer. It seems likely that we typically remember to do things by embedding the requirement within the planning structure of our day. When we are shopping, for example, we might decide on a route that will optimize the chance of buying everything we need with minimum effort. Once that is done, then position on the route itself can serve as a cue to what must be done next. There is of course always a danger that the ongoing activity will capture our attention, causing us to forget to do something at the right time, or producing one of the slips of action discussed in the chapter on the attentional control of memory. The study of prospective memory should in due course tell us not only about those infuriating occasions on which we forget to do things, but also has implications for the understanding of the important but complex processes whereby we plan and order our lives.

OVERVIEW

The classic study of forgetting carried out by Ebbinghaus using himself as a subject suggested that forgetting follows a logarithmic function, beginning rapidly and then tailing off. Subsequent studies have shown that this is by no means always the case, with some material appearing to be lost at a steady linear rate, while other cases occur such as those of continuous motor skills in which virtually no forgetting is found.

The explanation of forgetting also remains an open question. Interference between memory traces is certainly an important factor, but whether this ever involves the destruction of one trace by another, or simply reflects competition between traces at retrieval remains an unresolved question. There is, however, no doubt that powerful interference effects do occur, with the recall of an event being impaired by interference from both prior learning (proactive interference) and later learning (retroactive interference). Furthermore, it is clear that at least some of these effects occur as a result of problems occurring at retrieval.

Perhaps the most obvious evidence for forgetting in everyday life occurs in the area known as prospective memory, or remembering to do things. Systematic study of prospective forgetting is relatively recent, and it seems clear that it is particularly dependent on motivational factors, and on the way in which the event to-be-remembered is embedded within the social text.

Chapter Eleven

RETRIEVAL

As we saw in Chapter 8, mnemonic systems can be very powerful. The simple *one is a bun* pegword mnemonic for example can, with very little practice, guarantee the average person that they will be able to remember 10 unrelated items in order of presentation, or the reverse order if required, with very little error. Part of the explanation of this effect is that the mnemonic uses an interactive image that appears to lay down a rich, easily evoked and discriminable memory trace. But that is only half the story. The other half is of course the tying in of the mnemonic with the overlearned sequence of numbers 1–10. This has the important additional feature of allowing the subject to be very sure that each item is recalled, and in the appropriate order. It offers, in other words, a highly efficient retrieval structure. Why should such structures be important?

THE CONCEPT OF RETRIEVAL

It is often claimed that memory resembles a vast library, an analogy that has its limitations, but which can be very useful. One way in which memory and a library are closely similar is in the extent to which both will only work efficiently if information is stored in a structured systematic way, with retrieval of information depending on this initial "cataloguing" or encoding. While storing library books on the basis of their size or the color of their covers may be useful for some purposes, it is not very helpful if one wishes to retrieve books on the basis of their contents. For example, a book describing a journey through the jungles of Borneo might be of interest to an expert on butterflies, someone interested in tropical diseases, an anthropologist and possibly a general reader who likes travel. An efficient cataloguing and retrieval system should allow all of these readers to access the book. In exactly the same way, human memory needs to store information in a way that will allow it to be accessed for many different purposes.

I am, for example, at present dictating while retracing a route across a common. My memory is useful in that it will (I hope) allow me to find my way back, and on my outward journey I am consciously encoding the necessary topographical information. However, it is not necessary to encode information intentionally for later recall to occur. In the unlikely event of someone unexpectedly asking me where they could find some heather in North Norfolk, or where on common land there are jumps set up for horses, I would probably be able to recall the information that both of these can be found on Syderstone common, and pass it on, despite the fact that I did not explicitly register this information as something to be remembered. The flexibility with which we retrieve information from memory for novel and unanticipated reasons, is one of the most important and intriguing features of human memory.

Voluntary and Involuntary Remembering

Consider the following description of something which occurred to me some years ago, the sort of experience that most people seem to have from time to time.

Thursday 16 November 1978 On Tuesday I traveled to London. On the platform I notice a vaguely familiar face. I am preoccupied and since the person in question shows no obvious signs of recognizing me I assume that it is someone I have perhaps seen on other occasions on the train or around Cambridge, and I forget about it. As I get off the train I notice him again, since he has been sitting in the same carriage. Again he seems familiar. As I have been thinking about processes of memory and retrieval I decide to see if I can remember who he is.

Two associations occur, the name Sebastian and something to do with children. Sebastian seems to me to be a specific and useful cue, but unfortunately all it calls up is the name of a friend in another city, the schoolboy son of a friend in Cambridge and an association with teddy bears through Evelyn Waugh's *Brideshead Revisited*. I also sense there are some vague associations with a darkish room with books, but nothing clear enough to suggest any useful further search.

A little later, for no apparent reason, the association "babysitting" pops up and I immediately recall that we were both members of a mutual babysitting group; that his name is indeed Sebastian, although I cannot remember his second name, that he lives in a road whose location I am quite clear about and in a house which I could visualize relatively easily. A very clear image of his sitting-room appears together with the fact that it contains a large number of very finely printed books, and that he himself is by profession a printer. I remember noticing in fact that he has a printing press in one room of his house. I have no doubt that I have successfully identified him.

Two days later, thinking about this as an illustration of a certain type of remembering, it occurs to me that I still have not remembered his name or that of the street in which he lives. I have no clues about his name, but know that he lives in either Oxford Road or Windsor Road. The two are linked, one running at right angles to the other, and I have a colleague who lives in the one that Sebastian X does not live in. If I have to guess, I would say that he lives in Oxford Road, and if I have to guess as independently as I can, I would say that my colleague lives in Windsor Road. I therefore opt for Oxford Road, though without any of the certainty which I feel about identifying him. I am, however, certain that he does not live in Richmond Road (since I don't *think* I know anyone who lives in Richmond Road). I also try again to remember his surname. Sebastian ——, nothing, and then for no obvious reason the name "Carter" appears. It feels right, although not overwhelmingly so. Then the association "Penny Carter" appears as his wife's name. I am fairly sure that this is correct and it reinforces my belief that his name is Sebastian Carter. By now, about an hour later, I am quite convinced.

I go and check the babysitting list. There is no Carter. Undeterred, I go to the telephone directory. After all this effort I had better be right! "Carter" is indeed in Oxford Road. That does not of course mean that it actually was Sebastian Carter. I resolve to ring and ask him.

Thursday, 16 November, evening: I ring Sebastian Carter —— was he on the 2:36 train to Liverpool Street on Tuesday, 14 November? He was.

Broadly speaking, the activities that went on in trying to recollect the name of the man in the train fall into two categories, an active search process, with much in common with problem solving, and a more automatic process whereby information popped up as if from nowhere. This distinction is not, of course, a novel one, and indeed Ebbinghaus in his classic book distinguished between *voluntary remembering* and *involuntary remembering*.

Ebbinghaus himself chose to study the process of involuntary remembering, the automatic tendency for one syllable to evoke the next as a result of frequent repetition. In this, as in much else, the researchers of the next 100 years tended to follow his example. In a recent book, the most distinguished modern investigator into the problems of retrieval remarks that so little is known of the processes of voluntary recall that he feels justified in completely leaving it out of his otherwise very broad and ambitious model of retrieval (Tulving, 1983). I shall therefore begin by discussing what we know of the involuntary component of retrieval, leaving until the next chapter the investigation of the process of active recollection.

FORGETTING AS RETRIEVAL FAILURE

Although a concept of retrieval is logically necessary to give a full description of the processes involved in learning and remembering, the idea that it might be an important component is surprisingly new. I still have a very clear memory of sitting on a U.S. Thesis Committee in the early 1970s, and finding myself devoting my attention to attempting to persuade a very able neurobiologist who had done excellent work on learning and forgetting, that the concept of retrieval was an important one, while the candidate patiently waited for us to get on with the oral examination. Indeed, within experimental psychology, the concept of retrieval was not widely utilized until the mid-1960s when a number of studies, notably those carried out by Endel Tulving and his colleagues, began to emphasize its importance.

Availability and Accessibility

So how would I attempt to convince my sceptical neurobiologist of the importance of retrieval? Essentially I would try to convince him that at any given time, more information was stored than the subject could actually report. Perhaps the most obvious example relies on the difference between recall and recognition. For example, Mandler, Pearlstone, and Koopmans (1969) presented their subjects with a list of 100 words for five successive trials. They then tested retention by either recall or recognition, presenting the words mixed in with an equal number of new words that had not been presented. Subjects recalled a mean of 38% of the list, but recognized a mean of 96%, making a false alarm rate of 7%; that is, on 7% of the occasions when a new word was presented, the subjects falsely said that they were "old" words. We shall return to the issue of how to deal with false alarms later in the chapter. The fact that of the 62 words the average subject could not recall, all but about four could be recognized, indicates that they had not been forgotten; to use Tulving's terminology they were *available*, but not *accessible*.

Should my neurobiologist be convinced by this? Probably not, since he might well argue that all he needed to explain my results was the assumption that not all memory traces were equally strong, and that some measures, such as recognition happened to be more sensitive and able to reflect a weak memory trace than others, such as recall. A rather more impressive result however was produced by Tulving (1967) in a study involving the free recall learning of a list of words. In one condition, subjects were tested using the normal procedure of first presenting the list (P), then testing (T), then presenting again, then testing again and so forth (i.e. PT, PT, PT, etc.). In the other condition, the list was presented once, and then tested three times in succession, before the second presentation occurred, followed by a further three recall trials (PTTT, PTTT, etc.).

Two striking features emerged from this study. First of all, the two groups learnt at the same rate. Such a result is consistent with our previous claim that practice at the process of retrieval of an item will itself increase the subsequent probability of retrieving that item. You may recall that this, together with the micro-distribution of practice effect allowed Landauer and Bjork (1978) to devise their very effective mnemonic known as the expanding rehearsal procedure.

The second feature is more directly related to the question of retrieval. Tulving noticed that on each successive retrieval trial, the subject recalled approximately the same number of words, but not the same words. Indeed only about 50% of the words occurred on all three trials, the others appeared and disappeared unpredictably. In Tulving's terminology, they were available, but not reliably accessible. Tulving had thus observed that words that are stored may not always be able to be recalled. He did not so far, however, have any control over the phenomenon.

Retrieval Cues

A number of later experiments attempted to manipulate the accessibility of items experimentally. They involve the utilization of *retrieval cues*, hints or clues that can be used to evoke an item that has been learnt, but can not spontaneously be recalled. The first of these studies, Tulving and Pearlstone (1966) was described in Chapter 8. You may recall that subjects were presented with lists of words comprising items from a number of different semantic categories, for example, animals, birds, boys' names and vegetables. Half the subjects then attempted to recall the items in the absence of any cues, while the other subjects were cued by being given the category names. Tulving and Pearlstone observed that subjects given the category names recalled more items than those given no cues. The latter, when subsequently given the category name cues were then able to recall many words they had previously found inaccessible.

In a later study, Tulving and Osler (1968) further developed the retrieval cue technique. They presented their subjects with a number of words to be remembered, each one typed in capital letters. By the side of each word they printed another word in lower case. Subjects were told to read this since it might help them remember. Subsequently, subjects either attempted free recall, or were cued with the lower-case words. Hence, a subject might be presented with "CITY-dirty", and subsequently given the word "dirty" and asked to recall what went with it. Cued recall was consistently higher than free recall.

Did the cueing advantage occur just because any reminder would help? This was not the explanation, since when subjects were cued with another associate of city such as "village", that had not be presented with the target word, it did not enhance recall. Tulving and Osler (Tulving & Osler, 1968, p.593) state that "Specific retrieval cues facilitate recall if and only if the information about them and about their relationship to the to-be-remembered word is stored at the same time as the information about the membership of the word in a given list". This concept of a retrieval cue is very much like that of a mnemonic handle that must be attached during learning if it is to be usable later.

This rather rigid concept of a retrieval cue seems to exclude the possibility that some cue or hint that was not present during learning, might enhance recall, provided that it does evoke the target item. A number of investigators subsequently showed such cues can be helpful. For example, if one gives a list comprising a single frequent item from each of many different categories, then it is likely that prompting with the categories will enhance recall, despite the fact that the various category labels were not presented during learning (Fox, Blick, & Bilodeau, 1964). Tulving (1983) now makes it clear that he does not wish to argue that only cues that are actually stored at presentation can be useful, although he does continue to emphasize the crucial interaction between the word to be remembered and its cue as central to its effectiveness in helping the subject remember the item.

To recapitulate, Tulving's early work demonstrated that not only was the subject able to recognize more than he could recall, suggesting that he knew more than his recall indicates, but much more powerfully that the experimenter was able to use retrieval cues to manipulate the probability that an item would or would not be accessible to the subject. It seems hard to escape the need for some concept such as retrieval in order to account for these results. We shall continue by describing some of the basic phenomena of retrieval, before exploring attempts to produce models that might explain these and related effects.

Context-dependent Memory

The British associationist philosopher John Locke (Locke, 1690, pp. 339–340) refers to the case of a young man who was taught to dance. His lessons always took place in the same room which contained a large trunk. Alas, it subsequently proved to be the case that:

> The idea of this remarkable piece of household stuff had so mixed itself with the turns and steps of all his dances, that though in that chamber he could dance excellently well, yet it was only while the trunk was there.

While this is a somewhat extreme case, there is no doubt that under some circumstances, material learned in one environment may be difficult to recall in a dramatically different context.

For example, a study carried out by a colleague, Duncan Godden and I was concerned with the memory capacity of deep-sea divers. In one of our experiments, we had our subjects learn lists of words either on the beach, or beneath 15 feet of water, and then recall in either the same or the opposite environment (Godden & Baddeley, 1975). Our results are shown in Figure 11.1; there was no major general effect of environmental context since it did not greatly matter whether our subjects were learning on land or underwater. There was, however, a very clear *context-dependency effect*: if they learnt in one environment and recalled in the other, our subjects remembered about 40% less than if learning and recall occurred in the same environment.

The effect of context on recall of word lists. Words learned underwater are best recalled underwater, and vice versa. From Godden and Baddeley (1975).

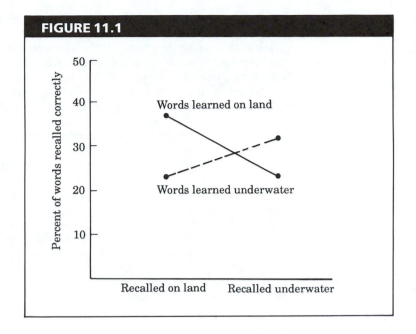

FIGURE 11.1

Context-dependency can of course be quite a problem for the diver since training typically occurs on land, as does instruction for the day's work ahead. If these can not be remembered underwater, the results could be rather unfortunate. Similarly, if a diver is being used to observe or inspect underwater one must expect a relatively poor performance on subsequent debriefing. About the time I was carrying out this research, I had a diving colleague who was running a fisheries project that involved having the divers ride on trawl-nets of various types, and observe the behavior of fish being caught, or evading capture. He found that the amount of detail recalled was so poor he had to opt for a system of underwater tape-recorders into which the divers gave a running commentary describing the behavior of each fish. They were subsequently able to transcribe their account and provide any necessary further details, suggesting that cued recall at least was less disrupted than free recall.

A subsequent study (Godden & Baddeley, 1980) lent further weight to this. We again tested our divers on land and underwater, but this time used a recognition rather than recall measure and found no context-dependency effect; divers could recognize the words they had encountered equally well regardless of whether they were presented in the same or different surroundings.

Our result is just one of many studies that have shown that recall may be impaired when the surroundings are changed (e.g. Smith, Glenberg, & Bjork, 1978; Greenspoon & Ranyard, 1957). However, the magnitude of our underwater effect was substantially greater than we were able to obtain in studies where the degree of environmental change was rather less, such as learning in one room and recalling in another. A number of studies have asked the question of whether students will perform better if their final examinations are in the same room as that in which they received the lectures, typically with results that suggest that any differences are sufficiently small not to be too worrying (Saufley, Otaka, & Bavaresco, 1985), while Fernandez and Glenberg (1985) warn of the unreliability of context-dependency even under controlled laboratory conditions, when the manipulation involves learning and being tested in different rooms.

However, where environmental differences are substantial, then one does need to worry about the transferability of learning. It is commonly asserted that therapists who are treating patients within the hospital, often find that their patients can carry out everyday skills in that environment, but not in their homes. In any situation where training occurs, it is essential to be aware of the danger that it may not transfer to the real-life environment, a problem that is of course central to the whole area of education.

Is it actually necessary for the subject to return physically to the same environment for context-dependent effects to work, or is it sufficient to imagine the original environment? This was explored in a study by Smith (1979) who had his subjects study 80 common words in a distinctive basement room on the first day, and then attempt to recall them on a second day in either the same room, or in a fifth-floor room with very different contents and furnishings. Subjects who recalled in the original basement room tended to remember about 18 words, significantly more than those who remembered in the different upstairs room, who recalled only about 12. Of particular interest however was a third group who were tested in the different upstairs room, but instructed to try to recollect as much as possible of the original learning environment before starting to recall. They remembered an average of 17.2 words, not significantly different from those who had physically returned to the learning environment.

This suggests a useful tip if you are trying to remember something, namely that it is worth taking time to try to recall the surroundings first, a procedure that not only provides a potentially useful mnemonic strategy, but also offers a useful technique for helping an eyewitness recall an incident. Indeed, it seems likely that some at least of the claims made for the usefulness of hypnosis in helping recall stems from the hypnotist's capacity to induce the subject to imagine the context in which the incident occurred before attempting detailed recall.

A danger of using hypnosis in this way however is that it may increase the subject's willingness to provide information, and enhance his confidence in the truth of such information, without actually increasing the amount of information available. In short, while hypnosis may be useful in helping reinstate the context of the crime, its negative effects in encouraging false information may outweigh these advantages (Gregg, 1986; Orne, 1979).

State Dependency

We have so far talked about the role of the external environment in learning, what of the internal environment, the physiological state of the subject and his internal mood states? Here again there is evidence of context-dependency. In one study Goodwin et al. (1969) looked at the effect of alcohol on a number of memory tasks. They used the same design as described in the diving study above, and found broadly the same results; what their subjects learnt when drunk, they recalled better drunk than sober, while what they learnt sober was best recalled sober. They describe cases in which their alcoholic subjects secreted money and alcohol while drunk, but were unable to find it when sober, duly recalling its hiding place when on their next binge.

As in the case of the divers, the alcohol subjects appear to show no state-dependent effects on those tasks where measurement was based on recognition rather than recall. Broadly similar results have subsequently been obtained in an extensive series of experiments reviewed by Eich (1980). Finally, comparable state-dependent effects have been shown to occur when mood is manipulated, with subjects who are sad finding it easier to recollect sad than happy prior experiences (e.g. Teasdale & Fogarty, 1979). The role of mood, however, will be discussed in more detail in Chapter 13.

RECALL AND RECOGNITION

The question of how recall and recognition are related is one of the oldest in the study of memory. It also is one that remains complex and controversial. Even a simple generalization such as "recognition is easier than recall" is questionable. First of all, how do you compare the two? Perhaps in terms of percentage correct? In the Mandler et al. (1969) study mentioned earlier, recall and recognition gave scores of 38% and 96% correct respectively. Surely recognition is better than recall? Not necessarily: suppose for example that a subject in the recognition condition categorized every item he saw as "old", then he would obtain a score of 100%, but show no evidence of memory whatsoever.

Clearly, if a subject behaved like this, then one would feel justified in excluding him from the experiment, but what if you had two subjects, one of whom correctly recognized a large number of old items but also incorrectly said that a large number of new items were old, while the second was more cautious, detecting fewer old items but making very few false alarms. Who has the better memory? This is an important problem for any situation in which you are trying to compare recognition scores. For example, if you wanted to know whether some drug had side-effects that led to impaired memory, then you would need some way of dealing with the problem that subjects given the drug might make both more correct recognitions and more false alarms.

Correcting for Guessing

Perhaps the simplest way of dealing with false alarms is to use what is termed a *guessing correction*. This is based on the simple assumption that if a subject remembers that he has been shown an item, he will correctly categorize it as "old" and that for the rest he will simply guess. If, as in most recognition studies, there is the same number of old items and new distractors, then his chance of guessing an unknown item will be 50%. That being so, for every "new" item he has incorrectly reported as "old", there should by chance be one genuinely "old" item to which he has responded correctly by guessing. One can therefore calculate his "true" detection rate by subtracting the number of false alarms from the number of correct detections.

In the case of the Mandler et al. study just described, the average subject made 94 correct detections and seven false alarms per 100 choices. If we assume that those seven false alarms were seven guesses when he was unlucky, there should on average be another seven occasions on which he was lucky in his guess. If we subtract the seven from his score of 94 correct detections, that gives us a "true" detection rate of 87%.

Signal Detection Theory

Suppose, however, instead of assuming that the subject either knows an item or doesn't, we assume that he bases his judgment on something like level of familiarity, something which in strength rather than being all-or-none. Let us suppose that even before the experiment, words differ in their overall level of familiarity, and that presenting them in a learning experiment adds a little familiarity to each item presented. It may prove to be the case that some items start with such a low level of familiarity that even after they have been presented, their new level of familiarity is still lower than the initial level shown by some other items which may well not have been presented. If the only way the subject can detect whether an item was presented before, is in terms of its level of familiarity, then there will be no way in which these two items can successfully be assigned to the right "new" and "old" category.

That being the case, for this material, the subject will be unable to respond correctly, and consequently he must choose to either accept a relatively low hit rate with few false alarms, or must accept that in detecting most of the old items he will also falsely recognize some of the new. The greater the degree of learning of the material of course, the less this overlap in familiarity between new and old items is likely to be, but until learning is well advanced, the question of criterion is likely to be one that the subject must face.

It is fortunately possible to use a technique initially devised in connection with measuring the efficiency of sonar operators in the Second World War, called *signal detection theory*. It makes certain assumptions about the underlying distribution of familiarity or trace strength, and requires a reasonably stable estimate of false alarm rate. Given these, it produces two separate measures, one of which, d' is a measure of discriminability; in the sonar case it tells you how easy it is to distinguish between the target and background noise. In the case of memory, d' can be regarded as indicating the extent to which the subject is able to discriminate between the old target items and the new distractors, a measure that is sometimes regarded as analogous to a measure of memory trace strength.

The second measure produced by signal detection theory is β, which is assumed to reflect the criterion adopted by the subject, his degree of caution in deciding whether an item is new or old. Note that these two measures are likely to behave in very different ways. If the subjects are encouraged to change their degree of caution, perhaps by paying twice as much for a correct detection as it costs to be wrong, then this would increase both hits and false alarms, producing a change in the β measure. It should, however, leave the d' measure unchanged since the payment will not change the strength of the memory trace. If, on the other hand, items were presented for say five trials rather than one, then this would be likely to increase the d' measure, since the difference in average familiarity between the targets and distractors would be greater. There is, however, no reason to assume that subjects would adopt a different criterion, and hence β would be likely to be unchanged.

Signal detection theory was developed for studying sensory judgments, typically in situations where there is a very high rate of responses, and where hit and false alarm rates can be calculated very reliably. In memory studies, however, the number of responses is typically much smaller, and false alarm rates in particular are often low and unreliable. This has led to a number of suggested modifications in signal detection theory. For these, and further discussion of the strengths and weaknesses of signal detection theory see McNichol (1972) or Wickens (1984).

In citing recognition scores, it is tempting to think of them as absolute, something that directly reflects the degree of learning of the material being recognized. However, as should be clear from our discussion of signal detection theory, what the subject is doing is deciding between target items and distractor items, and the number of targets he detects is likely to be strongly influenced by both the number and nature of the distractors. For example, Davis, Sutherland, and Judd (1961) systematically varied the ratio of targets to distractors, observing that as the proportion of distractor items increased, the probability of making a correct detection of old items systematically dropped.

They attempted to use the statistical concepts of *information theory* to derive a direct measure of the amount of information transmitted, hoping in this way to compare recall and recognition directly. However, as Dale and Baddeley (1962) showed, the crucial feature was not simply number of alternatives, as the information measure assumed, but the similarity between target items and distractors; the greater the number of distractors, the greater the chance of including items that were very similar to the correct items. Indeed, as Bahrick and Bahrick (1964) showed, it is possible to take a set of items, present them under standard conditions, and then show that level of performance can be changed from one in which percentage recognition is substantially higher than recall, to one in which the percentage recognition is lower than percentage recalled, simply by increasing the similarity between the distractors and the target items.

While the issue of the nature of the distractor items in recognition testing may seem to be a somewhat abstruse methodological point, it is of course of considerable importance to anyone involved in setting up identity parades. Here the temptation may be either to ignore the question of distractor similarity, or even worse, to ensure that the distractors do not have the characteristics described by the witness. For example, in one particularly blatant case (Loftus, 1979), where the witness described the criminal as oriental-looking, only one oriental, the suspect was included in the line-up. Rules of thumb for drawing up line-ups and ensuring that they are fair are outlined by Loftus (1979).

The Frequency Paradox

Before going on to discuss retrieval models, it is perhaps worth mentioning one more result, since it places strong constraints on some of the more obvious models. This concerns the relationship between frequency, recall and recognition and can be summarized very briefly; highly frequent words are better recalled than less frequent words, but are less well recognized.

This finding is important since it presents a problem for simple strength theories that argue that learning just involves adding to the strength of the existing memory trace of items presented. Such a simple strength view could account for the easier recall of high frequency words but predicts that high frequency words should also be easier to recognize, which they are not (Gregg, 1976).

One way of thinking about this paradox is perhaps to regard word frequency as being something that helps you retrieve or produce the word. In a recognition test, the word is produced for you by someone else, with the result that word frequency is less important. This provides an explanation of the lack of a frequency advantage in recognition, but does not explain why frequent words should actually be harder to recognize rather than equally difficult. This can be explained by the second aspect of recognition, namely the need to decide whether the word was presented in the list just shown to you. A familiar word is likely to have been encountered recently in other contexts, making it seem familiar, whether or not it has just been presented in the learning list. A rare word however, is much less likely to have been encountered recently, so the fact that it was shown to you may well be a more discriminable event. It is worth pointing out that this effect reverses when the items presented are so unfamiliar as to be regarded by the subjects as nonwords (Schulman, 1976), which typically show poorer recognition than either high or low frequency words. This may be because such items do not have pre-existing representations in long-term memory, making their recognition a different and more difficult task than word recognition.

It should be clear by this point that we do know a good deal more about the characteristics and conditions of involuntary retrieval than can be gleaned by observing our own recollections. If these are to be any more than collections of unrelated facts however, we need to try to incorporate them into some model or theory of the processes involved in involuntary retrieval. By their very nature, these processes are unlikely to be open to introspective investigation, so the problem of the way we derive our models is an important one.

One influential source of ideas on the way in which the human mind works has been the electronic computer. Since this particular information-processing device has been built by man, it is easier to understand than the more complex and ambitious information-processing device that sits inside our skulls. I shall begin by describing one elegant but limited model of retrieval that created great interest in the 1970s, namely Saul Sternberg's *serial exhaustive search model*. I shall move on from that to discuss other models, more directly concerned with explaining the broad phenomena of retrieval, before going on to the most actively explored current approach to retrieval, namely Tulving's *encoding specificity* approach.

MODELS OF RETRIEVAL

Serial Exhaustive Scanning

There are occasional experiments that capture the imagination of the field, either because they appear to offer an elegant new methodology such as occurred with the Peterson and Peterson (1959) short-term forgetting study, or because they appear to make a telling theoretical point, as in the case of Keppel and Underwood's demonstration of proactive interference effects in the Peterson technique. A study published by Saul Sternberg in 1966 caught the imagination of cognitive psychologists for both these reasons. He argued cogently that whereas most memory was concerned with the successful retrieval of information, most memory *experiments* measure errors, that is they study memory failure, not how memory works when it is operating successfully. He argued that in order to do this, one needed to move away from using error measures and towards using time as an indication of the underlying processes. He backed this up with the demonstration of an elegant new technique that appeared to suggest a novel theory of the retrieval processes involved in this task, and by implication in many others.

The task occurs in two forms, one which is typically classified as an STM task, the other as an LTM task. In fact the same broad principles apply to both. I will therefore begin with the STM task, since this is the one that has been cited and used most frequently. The procedure is very simple, the subject is presented with a sequence of between one and six random digits, which he or she is instructed to remember. After a brief delay, a single probe digit is presented. The subject's task is to decide whether or not this digit was part of the set he or she has just seen, and press either a "yes" or a "no" button accordingly.

Since a sequence of six digits was within the memory span of all the subjects tested, errors were very low, so what was being measured was the speed with which the subject could decide whether the probe digit was old or new. On each trial, a separate sequence of digits is presented, so each time the subject has to remember what has just been presented. Sternberg's results are shown in Figure 11.2. Two points should be noted in particular, first that the time to respond increases linearly with the number of digits the subject is remembering. Secondly, note that the slope of this line is the same for "yes" responses, indicating that the probed digit was in the previously presented set, and for "no" responses in which it was not.

In the LTM version of this task, instead of changing the target digits on every trial, the target digits selected remain constant

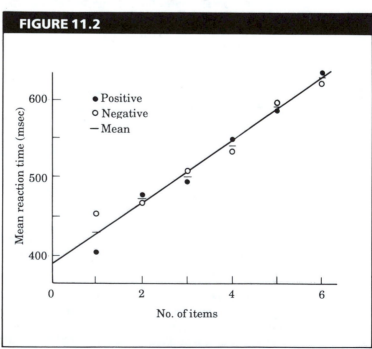

Reaction time as a function of number of items in a series. From Sternberg (1966). Copyright (1966) by the AAAS.

FIGURE 11.2

across a session comprising a substantial block of trials. Hence, Session 1 might consist of a two-choice condition in which the digits 1 and 5 were the targets, whereas Session 2 might have four targets, for example digits 2, 5, 6 and 8. In this paradigm too, there is a linear increase in reaction time as number of items in the target set increases, with positive and negative slopes again being the same.

How did Sternberg explain these findings? He drew an analogy between the way in which the human might perform this task, and ways in which current computers stored and accessed information. He suggested that the digits 1–9 could be regarded as locations, and that the presentation of a sequence of digits would place a marker at the location associated with each of the digits in the sequence. When the probe item followed, then it was successively checked against each of the presented locations. If a "match" occurred, with the probe information identical to one of the previously presented locations, then this was detected by a comparator and a "yes" response was triggered. The linear increase in reaction time with number of alternatives was explained on the assumption that the rate of checking locations was constant, so that two locations would take twice as long to check as one, and so forth.

The model makes one further assumption, that the search is exhaustive. In other words, Sternberg assumes that the search does not end when a match is detected, but goes on until all the locations presented have been checked, and only then is a response made. The reason he suggests this is because a self-terminating search, that is, a search whereby the response is made as soon as a match is detected, would predict different slopes for positive and negative responses. In the case of negative responses, the comparator would have to check every item presented before concluding that there was no match, so reaction time should increase directly with number of items presented. On a quarter of the occasions one would expect the comparator to test the matched item first, on a quarter of the time second, on a quarter of the time third, and only on a quarter of the time would there be any need to check all four locations. On average then, reaction time should increase with number of alternatives more slowly for positive than for negative responses. Sternberg found that the functions relating number of alternatives to speed were parallel, and hence concluded that in the case of both positive and negative responses, all locations were checked before responding. Why should the system check exhaustively rather than responding as soon as the comparator detects a match? Sternberg suggests that it takes a relatively long time to check whether the comparator has or has not made a match, in which case it might be more efficient to wait until all locations have been checked, and then interrogate the comparator, rather than check the comparator after each location.

Sternberg's paper generated a great deal of interest and research activity. Broadly speaking his results have proved to be replicable, although not everyone manages to get such elegant straight lines as Sternberg, who as an experimenter, and a theorist is something of a perfectionist.

Once it became clear that these results were broadly replicable, then the challenge of the day became to find ways of testing Sternberg's model, and to provide alternative models. In fact, simple though they appear, modeling the Sternberg findings proves to be surprisingly difficult, and while a large number of competing interpretations have been presented over the years, few if any of them have the simplicity of Sternberg's original proposals. They include models based on computer stack memories (Theios, 1973), and in addition a range of models based on parallel search and trace strength discrimination, some worked out only crudely, such as my own (Baddeley & Ecob, 1973), while others have been worked out in considerable detail (Anderson, 1973).

A third area of activity concerned the attempt to demonstrate phenomena that were inconsistent with Sternberg's model. For example Corballis, Kirby, and Miller (1972) showed that recency effects occurred in this paradigm, with particularly rapid responses occurring when the last item of the presented sequence was probed. It is not clear why this should occur if search is serial, exhaustive and automatic. Similarly, Baddeley and Ecob (1970) showed that if an item is presented twice within any given set, then if probed, it will give rise to a particularly fast response. Effects such as this suggest that the process of responding may be dependent on trace strength, rather than the simple presence or absence of some form of marker, an approach that has subsequently been developed by Monsell (1978).

Sternberg (1975) presents a very thorough overview of this field, and a response to his critics. Essentially he copes with the effects that do not fit into the model by pointing out that serial exhaustive search is only part of the process whereby the subject responds. This allows him to argue that the effects of the type just mentioned operate elsewhere within the chain of events. While this is plausible, it makes it much harder to test the model, and in losing its simplicity, the model loses a good deal of its scientific attraction. Sternberg himself does not appear to have worked on the model for many years now, and it appears to be losing its popularity as an experimental and theoretical challenge, but continues to be used extensively in studies of the effects of drugs and environmental stressors (e.g. Bhatti, Alford, & Hindmarch, 1988).

The Sternberg paradigm and model has been with us now for over 20 years. It has stimulated an enormous number of papers within experimental psychology journals, and as mentioned above is still very popular in certain applied areas. It combined a neat quantitative technique with a simple but elegant model, and one would like to feel that it provides a way of probing some fundamental characteristic of human memory. But does it?

As a general model of retrieval, a serial exhaustive searching of all possible memory locations must surely be an absurdity, and I am certain that Sternberg would not at any time wish to suggest that it provides a general model of long-term memory retrieval. What then is the current status of the serial exhaustive model? Are there aspects of human behavior that do involve such a process, or is it merely an elegant laboratory reaction time measure in which difficulty can be manipulated in terms of storage load? Even if this were the case, with Sternberg's task simply offering a very artificial procedure that happens to tax the subject in particular ways, then it might still be a useful technique. In the area of physical fitness, for example, the Harvard Step Test in which the subject steps onto and off a box of standard height for a standard period of time, is a useful measure, although I am sure its creators would not argue that it was characteristic of the everyday activity of most people.

In the case of the Sternberg technique however there is a hidden implication that something important is being measured, and certainly its users in applied research typically tend to interpret differences in reaction time slope as differences in rate of memory scanning, lending their results an aura of scientific depth that is attractive but possibly spurious.

There is no doubt that the Sternberg technique is an elegant one that has the advantage of allowing two separate measures, the slope of the function and its intercept. It is, however, far from clear what these measures mean, although they do seem to be sensitive to the effects of drugs and brain damage. Is that sufficient reason for continuing to use them in such applied settings? They seem such neat and elegant tools that it would be a pity to abandon them, but I would feel much happier if I felt I knew what they were measuring. Finding out what the measures mean is, however, a far from easy task, and in the meantime I would settle for a moratorium on interpreting their results as direct measures of mental processes such as "memory scanning".

Generate – Recognize Models

Although Sternberg did not proclaim that his model was character-istic of the processes of retrieval from long-term memory, others have attempted to develop general tagging models, strongly influenced by the way in which memory storage was dealt with in most computer programs. Probably the most influential examples of this approach were the two-process models such as those of Anderson and Bower (1972) and Kintsch (1970). These assume that words are represented as intersections or nodes within a semantic network (see Chapter 13). When a word is presented to a subject, some form of change will occur at the node representing that word, a process analogous to leaving a marker or tag there. Subsequent recall involves two processes, the first comprises the generation or production of possible candidate words, while the second comprises recognizing which of the words has been presented previously, a process that involves detecting the tags or markers. In recognition memory, access to the relevant node is made easy, with performance depending mainly on the second of these processes, namely that of detecting the markers.

Such a model is capable of explaining a number of the phenomena just described. For example, it would predict that on the whole, recall would be harder than recognition, since it involves an extra stage, namely that of generating the candidate items. It can also explain the effect of frequency on recall and recognition; high frequency words are easier to generate, making recall better than for low frequency items. However, high frequency items are likely to have occurred more frequently and more recently, they are thus more likely to have other tags from outside the experiment that may confuse the rememberer, leading to poorer recognition of high frequency words.

Kintsch (1968) showed that, in general, presenting organized material appears to enhance recall much more than it enhances recognition. He explained this on the grounds that organization is important for helping the subject to generate the words, but is much less important for the recognition phase. Such an assumption also explains why maintenance rehearsal, whereby individual words are repeated without the intention to learn them, may enhance recognition, but have little or no effect on recall (Glenberg, Smith, & Green, 1977). The assumption here is that rote rehearsal of an already-existing item will result in incrementing the target tags, hence facilitating recognition, but will not provide the sort of inter-word associative links that would help the subject to generate the relevant words (see Mandler, 1979).

A number of studies have attempted to collect direct evidence for a generation-recognition process. For instance, Bahrick (1970) attempted to predict the probability of recalling words on the basis of their independently assessed probability of being generated, and probability of being recognized. He used words from a given category and used one group of subjects to whom he presented no words but merely the category name, requiring them to generate as many items as possible. This gave a generation probability for each of a series of words. He then presented a list of these to a second group of subjects whose task was subsequently to recognize them from a larger set of items from that category. Finally, he tested a third group in which the items were presented and subjects attempted free recall. Bahrick demonstrated that it was possible to combine the generation probability of the first group with the recognition probability derived from the second group in order to predict free recall probability, as the two-process model would suggest. However, despite the ability of generate-recognize models to account for a great deal of data, they have been strongly attacked by Tulving and Thomson (1973).

The essence of Tulving and Thomson's argument is this: two-process models of recall involve a stage of generating candidate items, followed by a recognition test performed on each candidate. Since recall itself involves this recognition phase, then it follows that any item that can be recalled should also be correctly recognized, since otherwise it would not have passed the second of the two processes involved in recall. They then go on to demonstrate the occurrence of items that can be recalled, even though they failed to be recognized, concluding that this rules out generate-recognize models.

The ingenious paradigm devised to demonstrate this is based on the use of semantic retrieval cues as originally developed by Tulving and Osler (1968). The experimenter begins by selecting pairs of strongly associated items such as *HOT-COLD* and *KNIFE-FORK*. One of each pair of items is then taken and used to make up the learning list. During learning, each of the words is presented, this time accompanied by a low-frequency associate, for example *COLD* might be accompanied by the cue word *ground*, while *KNIFE* might be accompanied by *pen*. Having assembled this material, the experiment then runs as follows.

The subjects are first of all presented with the list of items, each accompanied by its low frequency associate retrieval cue. After a number of learning trials, the subject is presented with a list comprising the strong associates of each of the target words, for example *HOT* and *FORK*, and in each case is told to try to give an associated word. This frequently proves to be the original target word, with *HOT* evoking *COLD* and *FORK* producing *KNIFE*. Having done this, the subject is encouraged to look down the list and tick any item that had been on the previous learning list. Hence if he had produced *COLD* in response to *HOT*, and *KNIFE* in response to *FORK*, he should tick them as *old* items. In fact, although subjects typically did generate a very high proportion of the original list, they were very poor at recognizing them as items that had been presented.

The final stage of the experiment was one in which the retrieval cue words were presented, and the subjects invited to recall the words presented. Under these conditions, many items which the subject failed to recognize were successfully recalled. For example, having failed to recognize *COLD* as a word from the initial list, when they were given the cue word *ground*, the subjects would often correctly recall the word *COLD*.

Tulving and Thomson had clearly demonstrated something which appeared to be inconsistent with the generate-recognize models, namely that an item that could not be recognized, nevertheless could be recalled, a process that was assumed to require both a generation *and* a recognition stage. How does Tulving explain these results? In terms of a concept he refers to as *synergistic ecphory*.

TULVING'S SYNERGISTIC ECPHORY THEORY

The term "ecphory" is based on a Greek word meaning "to be made known", and was first introduced by Semon (see Schacter, Eich, & Tulving, 1978) and subsequently revived by Tulving

(1983). It is assumed to be a process whereby the memory trace or engram is combined with the retrieval cue to give a "conscious memory of certain aspects of the original event" (Tulving, 1976, p.40). Tulving argues that the same processes are involved in recognition as in recall, although the particular retrieval cues are different, in recognition being what Tulving terms "copy cues", that is copies of the original stimuli.

Tulving also differs from those generate-recognition models so far described in rejecting the assumption that the process of learning merely involves marking some semantic node. Learning is assumed to involve laying down a memory trace or engram, while remembering involves a symbiotic process whereby the engram and the retrieval cue interact to produce the conscious recollection of the previous event. This may then be either produced directly as a response, or used as a basis for other processes such as searching for further evidence or further retrieval cues. Tulving represents this process in terms of a General Abstract Processing System (GAPS), an acronym chosen at least in part because it reflects our current state of knowledge about memory (Tulving, 1983, p.130). A simplified version of the model is shown in Fig. 11.3.

The diagram represents the process of learning and subsequent recall at three separate conceptual levels. What is observable is shown on the left, the relevant theoretical processes are shown in the center, and on the right are shown the assumed underlying

Tulving's conceptualization of the elements of episodic memory. Adapted from Tulving (1983).

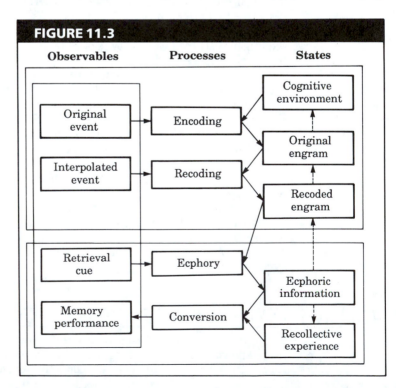

FIGURE 11.3

mental states. Starting at the top left-hand corner: an event occurs and this is encoded by the subject, a process that involves an interaction between the event and the cognitive environment within the subject. Hence, suppose I saw a horse, at a time when I was about to cross a field, the cognitive environment would first of all tell me that it was a horse and not a cow, possibly activate the word "horse", and also be linked to associated information such as whether I was nervous of horses. Combination of event and the internal state would lead to a memory trace or engram, hence completing the learning phase of the process.

Suppose I continue on my walk and meet someone who asks if I have seen a stray horse, this will act as a retrieval cue, which will interact with the memory trace of my encountering the horse, this process of interaction being known as "ecphory" within Tulving's framework. This will produce ecphoric information, which can then lead either directly to a process of conversion from that into a response, in this case presumably the response "Yes, I did just see a horse", or to further state "of recollective experience", conscious awareness of the memory of previously seeing the horse.

How does Tulving's GAPS model explain the Tulving and Thomson results? Let us begin with the original learning trial, where an item such as *COLD* is presented, together with a cue word *ground*; this cue word will presumably form or at least influence the cognitive environment during the encoding of *COLD*. This might plausibly lead to an engram that represents some interpretation or encoding of *COLD* within the context of ground, perhaps images of death, or a field under frost.

Let us now move to the recognition stage. Here, the word *cold* has been generated as a response to the associated word *hot*. Presumably here, the cognitive environment is provided by the associate *hot*, tending to lead to an encoding of *cold* that may be very different from the encoding produced during initial learning, the hot and cold water taps of a bath, for example. Given the difference between this and the initial encoding that led to the engram produced during learning, the process of ecphory is unlikely to yield the original trace, hence recognition is relatively unlikely to occur.

One can contrast this with the cued recall situation in which the original cue word *ground* is presented. Since the word *ground* formed part of the original encoding environment of the word, there is a much better chance that the process of ecphory will occur, with the retrieval cue and the memory trace interacting to produce the necessary ecphoric information for the subject to come up with the response *cold*, together possibly with the recollection of having thought of it in terms of a frosty field.

While Tulving's approach differs in a number of ways from earlier two-process models, two differences are particularly crucial. The first concerns the question of what is learned, while the second concerns the difference if any between recall and recognition. We will discuss these two issues in turn.

Is Verbal Learning Verbal?

It is tempting to think, since the experimenter presented the subject with a word, and subsequently the subject recalls a word, that therefore the underlying process must have been one of storing that word. Over the last decade or so however, it has become increasingly obvious that such a view is a gross over-simplification; words are convenient ways of setting a task for the subject, and a convenient way for him to indicate that he has successfully accomplished the task, but this does not tell us how the word was encoded, stored and retrieved.

One simple interpretation of the power of retrieval cues as used by Tulving and Osler (1968) and Tulving and Thomson (1973) is that they encouraged the subject to form a distinctive semantic representation of that word, hence laying down a distinctive memory trace, and subsequently providing ready access to it. The assumption that learning is not simply the tagging of words is however, not by any means limited to Tulving.

Perhaps the most obvious case in which it is clear that what is remembered is not simply the word itself comes from studies using polysemous words, that is words that have more than one meaning. In one such study, Light and Carter-Sobell (1970) presented a number of such words to their subjects. Half their subjects were initially biased by accompanying the word with one of its two associates, hence "JAM" might be associated for one subject with "traffic" and for another with "strawberry". In a subsequent recognition test, the word would be presented together with the same or a different associate. There was a strong tendency for the changed associate to dramatically impair recognition, presumably because what was encoded in the two cases was the meaning of the two items, not just their visual and phonological characteristics. If the subjects had encoded a traffic jam, they were unlikely to recognize strawberry jam.

The Light and Carter-Sobell study is interesting, but perhaps not very surprising; it merely indicates that words are typically learned in terms of their semantic features rather than their phonological or visual characteristics, and that at this level a single letter sequence may have two meanings and in fact effectively be two separate words. All of this is entirely consistent with evidence cited earlier concerning the importance of deep semantic coding in long-term learning.

A rather more compelling demonstration however comes from a study by Barclay, Bransford, Franks, McCarrell, & Nitsch (1974) in which they showed that what was learned was not simply the meaning of a particular word, but a particular aspect or interpretation of the word's meaning. They presented their subjects with a number of words embedded in sentences. For example, the word *PIANO* might be presented in either *The man tuned the PIANO* or *The man lifted the PIANO*. Recall was subsequently cued with a phrase such as *something melodious* or *something heavy*. Subjects given the first sentence recalled the word substantially more frequently to the melodious cue than to the heavy cue, while the second group that had been told that the man lifted the piano showed exactly the reverse. Clearly what was encoded was not simply the general meaning of piano, but a specific aspect of its meaning.

In conclusion, the evidence does support Tulving on the issue of what is learnt, although the assumption that what is remembered is not a word but an experience is now quite widely held, and should not be regarded as a particular distinguishing feature of Tulving's approach. What does distinguish his approach is the concept of *encoding specificity*.

The Encoding Specificity Principle

This was introduced as an explanatory concept in connection with the powerful retrieval cueing effects demonstrated by Tulving and Osler (1968), who argued that a cue will only be effective if it is specifically encoded at the time of learning. As time went on, it became clear that there are some circumstances in which cues that are not directly present during learning can nevertheless be effective. The study by Fox et al. (1964) mentioned earlier indicated that category names were effective cues for retrieving items from that category, even though the category name had not been explicitly presented. The study by Barclay et al. specifically uses cueing words like *something heavy* that were not directly presented during learning, and yet such cues are very powerful. Although such results might seem to be inconsistent with the strong view implied by the original Tulving and Osler study, over the years, the *encoding specificity hypothesis* has gradually evolved into the more complex but less testable *encoding specificity principle*. This assumes the relationship between encoding and retrieval, and then attempts to use this to interpret the results that are obtained. If the stimulus leads to the retrieval of the item, then it is assumed to have been encoded, whereas if not, then it is assumed not to have been encoded (Tulving, 1983). Tulving is of course aware that it is not, in principle, possible to come up with evidence that will refute such an assumption.

Such a principle is not, therefore, empirically testable, but does that mean that it is not useful? Tulving points out that some of the hallowed principles of physics are also not directly testable. They are supported, however, by a rich network of data that can be held together by a coherent set of principles. Tulving argues that the encoding specificity principle is similarly supported by its capacity to explain a rich and complex pattern of experimental results. While not everyone would agree on this point, there is no doubt that Tulving's many demonstrations of the power of retrieval cueing form an important and impressive body of work.

RECALL: ONE PROCESS OR TWO?

Let us begin with a puzzle that we discussed earlier, namely that context dependency appears to affect recall but not recognition; when the divers tested by Godden and I learnt something underwater, they were better at recalling it underwater than on land, but if we tested them by recognition it did not matter where the test occurred. If, as Tulving claims, recall and recognition are essentially the same processes, then why should providing the appropriate environment be important in one case and not in the other?

It is first of all important to note that, although a range of studies have failed to obtain environmental context-dependent effects when memory is tested by recognition, a series of studies by Thomson and his colleagues does appear to show powerful context effects in the task of eyewitness identification, which appears to be sensitive to influence by both the surroundings in which the initial observation occurred, and to the clothes worn by the person observed and by the suspect (Thomson, Robertson, & Vogt, 1982).

Context and Person Recognition

After working with Tulving, Thomson returned to Australia where he became interested in the question of eyewitness identification. He was particularly struck by a number of incidents in which the witness appeared to be excessively influenced by the clothing worn by the criminal, leading to occasions in which it seemed very probable that misidentification had occurred on this basis. This was used rather neatly by the defense lawyer on one occasion, when he arranged for someone other than the defendant to be wearing the clothes described by the victim. When asked to identify the criminal, the victim confidently picked out the person wearing the clothes of the accused. This seemed to be an interesting example of the influence of environmental cues on recognition memory, and Thomson decided to investigate it further.

In one study, Thomson et al. (1982) took photographs of a number of people in a range of environments, such as running out of a bank or walking into a shop, and wearing a range of different clothing. Subjects were shown one example of pictures of a number of such targets, and then attempted to recognize the targets from among a range of distractor pictures. The study systematically manipulated the question of whether the test item was in the original or a different environment, whether the target was wearing the same or different clothes, and whether distractor photographs involved people in the same or a different environment and were wearing the same or different clothes. Thomson et al. obtained very powerful effects of the context on recognition, in contrast to a rather weaker context effect obtained in a face recognition study by Watkins, Ho, and Tulving (1976) and a complete absence of a context effect in a series of studies by Woodhead and Baddeley (1981).

We appear then to have a situation in which a given feature such as environmental context has an effect on recognition in some cases, in particular the Thomson studies, while having a smaller effect in others, and no effect at all in yet other situations. These negative results include not only the face recognition experiments carried out by Woodhead and myself, but also the data from word recognition in divers (Godden & Baddeley, 1975), and the parallel absence of state-dependency effects of alcohol on recognition shown by Eich and others (e.g. Eich, 1980).

Independent and Interactive Context

My own interpretation of these results is as follows (see Baddeley, 1982 for a more detailed discussion): I suggest that there are two broadly different ways in which the context may be encoded, interactively and independently. An interactive encoding occurs when the context actually changes the way in which the stimulus is perceived. The most obvious example of this is the case of polysemous words where preceding the word *jam* by *strawberry* makes it a different word from preceding it by *traffic*. When this occurs, the memory trace *itself* is changed, so that whether testing occurs by recall or recognition, context will prove to have influenced performance. This is essentially a learning or storage effect rather than an effect on retrieval.

In the case of independent or noninteractive encoding of context, the information is stored together with the trace of the stimulus, but does not fundamentally change the trace. Any effects obtained are based on retrieval effects rather than reflecting a change in the nature of the memory trace itself.

A few examples might help make the distinction clearer. Suppose we begin with the Tulving and Osler semantic cueing effect. Here, as we have mentioned earlier, the semantic cue is likely to influence the interpretation of the presented word. One example was the word *CITY* which was accompanied by either *dirty* or *village*. The former would presumably conjure up a representation of the drabber aspects of city life, such as refuse and squalor, while the latter might conjure up the concept of a small cosy district within a city. The two cues lead to different experiences being stored. In the case of environmental context however, there is no reason to assume that the meaning of words read underwater will differ very much from their meaning when seen on land. Nor is there any reason to believe that a word that is encountered when drunk will be encoded into a different meaning from when it is read sober. In these cases, context may influence the accessibility of the memory trace but will not change its basic characteristics.

What of the case of face recognition and context? The contexts that did not appear to influence recognition were verbal descriptions of the characters of a group of visually rather similar young men. The relationship between the context and the face was entirely arbitrary, and while it is conceivable that subjects might have looked at a face and read into it the generosity, intelligence or lack of imagination described in the cameo, this certainly would not necessarily have been very easy to do, or particularly helpful. In the case of Thomson's study, the people were engaged in activities such as running out of banks, wearing colorful and often rather distinctive clothing, and in general giving a much richer set of cues on which to base assumptions about what the person was doing and why he might be doing it, assumptions that might plausibly be assumed to influence the subject's encoding of the person.

Suppose, for the sake of argument, that we accept this distinction; it still does not provide a complete explanation of the anomalous results. It explains why one does not get an effect on recognition, but not why context does affect recall. I would explain this using a version of the two-component hypothesis, suggesting that reinstating independent context may enhance the probability of accessing a memory trace, but will not influence the issue of deciding whether the trace evoked was or was not part of the material presented for learning. To use William James' previously described analogy of searching for an object in a house, context will influence the area of the house being searched, but will not influence the discriminability of the object that has been lost (for a related viewpoint see Hanley, 1984).

How does this differ from Tulving's view? First of all, it suggests constraints on the way in which stimuli will be encoded, and instead of one general type of interaction that Tulving terms synergistic ecphory, suggests two, one of which, interactive context, is synergistic whereas the other, independent context, is not. Unlike the encoding specificity principle, this is certainly a broadly testable hypothesis. There are ways in which one could certainly encourage the subject to cause the stimulus and the environment to interact, and this should have clear implications, with independent context not influencing recognition, while interactive context should, regardless of whether the contextual effect is based on environment or on semantic features.

The second difference is that this view argues for a rather basic difference between recall and recognition that is closer in spirit to the generate-recognize models, than is Tulving's approach. Tulving and Thomson's "refutation" of generate-recognize models applies only to models that assume that learning occurs by tagging representations of words. Provided one avoids this assumption, then there is no difficulty in explaining the Tulving and Thomson results within a model that separates access to a memory trace from judgments as to its familiarity. What the subject is remembering is not words but experiences, and the experience generated by the word *COLD* in the context of *ground* is simply not the same experience as that generated when *cold* is produced as a response to *HOT*. Given that the same memory is not generated, it is not surprising that it is not recognized.

Although Tulving's own research, and the considerable research that it has stimulated has been predominantly laboratory-based, anything as fundamental as understanding the processes of retrieval is likely to have important applications. The work on context and face recognition carried out by Thomson et al. (1982) is one example, while another is offered by the work in which Geiselman (1988) uses what is known about the processes of retrieval to produce better techniques for interviewing witnesses.

ENHANCING EYEWITNESS MEMORY

Much of the work on eyewitness testimony has been concerned with its unreliability, and with ways in which distortions may be produced. Are there ways in which the psychology of memory could be used to produce improved recall? As we saw in the earlier chapter on organization, psychologists have explored many ways in which learning can be improved, but in the eyewitness testimony situation, learning has typically already occurred, and what is required is some method of improving retrieval. As we have seen, although the process of retrieval is far from well understood, there are certain features that could be used to optimize memory, and these have been put together to produce the "cognitive interview", a recommended interviewing schedule devised by Fisher and Geiselman.

The cognitive interview is based on four general retrieval mnemonics:

1. Mentally reinstating the environmental and personal contact that occurred at the time the crime was witnessed.
2. Encouraging the reporting of every detail, regardless of how peripheral it is to the incident reported.
3. Attempting to recount the incident in several different orders, e.g. both forwards and backwards.
4. Attempting to report the incident from a range of different perspectives, including that of other prominent characters within the incident as well as that of the witness.

The first two of these principles are based on the assumption that the greater the amount of overlap between the reinstated and the initial situation, the better the recall. Principles 3 and 4 are based on the assumption that the observed information can be retrieved through more than one route, suggesting that one should maximize the number of potential retrieval routes that are attempted.

In their initial validation study, Geiselman, Fisher, MacKinnon, and Holland (1985) compared the cognitive interview with a standard interview procedure based on that used by the Los Angeles police force, and a hypnosis interview in which the subject is first hypnotized and then asked to attempt to recall the incident using the standard procedure. It is perhaps worth mentioning again the fact that the use of hypnosis is highly controversial since the scientific evidence for its effectiveness is weak (Smith, 1983). Furthermore, it tends to increase the susceptibility of the subject to suggestion and hence, even when it does increase the amount of accurate information retrieved, it may also lead to a higher level of false information (Orne, Soskis, Dinges, & Orne, 1984).

Geiselman et al. had their subjects view a short police training film of a violent crime. Some 48 hours later they were interviewed by a policeman using one of the three interview schedules. Performance was measured in terms of the number of facts accurately recalled, and number of erroneous items produced. In the standard condition, subjects recalled a mean of 29.40 items, significantly less than either the hypnosis interview (38.0), or the cognitive interview (41.2), while the three conditions did not differ reliably in number of false events reported.

One of the most extensively studied features of eyewitness testimony is the susceptibility of the subject to being misled by leading questions during the process of the interview (Loftus, 1979). However, as Bekerian and Bowers (1983) showed, this process is not inevitable, and can be minimized if the questioning follows the order in which the events occurred (see Chapter 10). Geiselman and his colleagues tested the new interview schedule for its susceptibility to misleading information by carrying out a further study involving a classroom incident. This involved an intruder carrying a blue rucksack. At a later point in the questioning, the subjects were asked "Was the guy with the green backpack nervous?". The effect of this on subsequent recall of the color of the rucksack was then studied for subjects questioned using both the cognitive and standard interview procedures. Those tested using the cognitive interview were less likely to falsely recall the color as green.

In a third study described by Fisher and Geiselman (1988) an attempt was made to improve the cognitive interview as a result of further observations on "good" and "poor" interviewers. As a result of this a number of modifications were made including for example the encouragement to use open-ended questions rather than direct short answer questions, attempting to fit the order of the questioning in with the interviewer's perception of the mental activities of the respondent. Student interviewers were trained on this occasion to use either the original or the modified cognitive interview, and once again respondents were interviewed 48 hours after viewing a film depicting a violent crime. The overall level of reported correct responses using the previous interview was 40% compared with a mean recall of 57.5% using the modified interview.

This improvement of almost 50% was achieved without any increase in the number of incorrect responses elicited.

OVERVIEW

Forgetting often occurs because material that has been learnt can no longer be accessed or retrieved at the appropriate time. It is suggested that retrieval can be divided into two kinds, those processes of conscious recollection that are open to introspection, and the relatively automatic and involuntary retrieval processes that underlie much of our remembering. The present chapter is primarily concerned with these involuntary processes.

The chapter begins by outlining the evidence for the need to assume that retrieval failure represents a major source of forgetting. This includes evidence from comparisons of recall and recognition, evidence that the ability to remember individual items fluctuates over time, and finally evidence for the importance of retrieval cues that can be used to evoke specific memories. A particular example of the importance of retrieval cuing occurs in the case of context- and state-dependent memory, where material learnt in one environment or under one psychological state is shown to be best recalled in that environment or state.

After discussion as to the respective nature of recall and recognition, a brief account is given of the use of guessing corrections, and of signal detection theory to deal with the problem of criterion and bias in recognition memory.

Models of retrieval are then discussed, starting with Sternberg's serial exhaustive scanning model of retrieval from STM. A more extensive discussion follows of models of retrieval in LTM, beginning with generate-recognize models and moving on to Tulving's encoding specificity principle, and his model of synergistic ecphory. The chapter concludes with a discussion of the application of models of retrieval to context-dependent memory, and in particular to the practical issue of enhancing the reliability of eyewitness testimony.

Chapter Twelve

RECOLLECTION AND AUTOBIOGRAPHICAL MEMORY

While there has been a good deal of experimental work on the automatic component of retrieval, there has been far less on the more active processes of retrieval for which we shall use the term *recollection*. Much of this has been carried out quite recently as part of a growing interest in *autobiographical memory*, the recall of the events of one's earlier life. The chapter that follows will be concerned with recollection, principally using studies of autobiographical memory in normal subjects, together with evidence from patients with impaired capacity to recollect the events of their earlier lives.

PROBING AUTOBIOGRAPHICAL MEMORY

The Galton Cueing Technique

Despite its comparative neglect over the last century, autobiographical memory was one of the first areas of memory to be investigated. Sir Frances Galton (1883) invented a technique that is still widely used. This involves presenting the subject with a cue word such as *river*, and asking for the recollection of some personally experienced event associated with a river. The subject typically then attempts to describe and date the recollected incident; the recollection is then rated for various characteristics such as vividness and detail.

The revival of interest in autobiographical memory was based primarily on studies using this technique (e.g. Crovitz & Schiffman, 1974; Robinson, 1976). While it has proved useful (Rubin, 1986), the Galton procedure does have certain technical limitations; it is very open-ended, with the result that a subject may choose to produce all his recollections from one atypical part of his life. This is probably made somewhat more likely by the tendency for one recollection to cue another from the same time period (Rabbitt & Winthorpe, 1988), possibly producing major differences between subjects simply based on the general strategy they adopt. For that reason, there has recently been a development of more structured techniques.

The Autobiographical Memory Schedule

One example of this development is the *autobiographical memory schedule* developed by Kopelman, Wilson, and Baddeley (in press) which systematically questions subjects about both personal information and events from different periods of their lives. For example, during the childhood period the patient will be asked to try to recall such autobiographical facts as the names of teachers, the address of the house he or she lived in, and also to try to recollect some autobiographical incident that happened to them at that time. Figure 12.1 shows the overall performance on the schedule of normal subjects and patients suffering from various forms of amnesia. Note the overall tendency for performance to be substantially poorer in the amnesic patients, together with a trend in the direction of showing a greater deficit for more recent events, an issue we shall return to later. There was a high correlation between performance on the recall of factual aspects of life and recollection of personal events, suggesting that recall of such factual data may provide a reasonably good overall indication of the subject's capacity for recollection of personally experienced episodes.

An as yet unpublished study by Dritschel, Williams, and Baddeley asked a group of 50 normal subjects to perform a similar task, except that instead of asking for the names of only three primary school teachers, or one event experienced during primary school, subjects were instructed to recall as many items as possible within 90 seconds in each of the various categories. The responses were then subjected to cluster analysis, indicating to what extent the capacity to perform well in response to one question was associated to good performance on others. For purposes of comparison, subjects were also asked to generate items from four more purely semantic categories, namely animals, vegetables, post-1930's British Prime Ministers, and post-1930s U.S. Presidents. The results are shown in Figure 12.2 which suggests a structure that indicates similarity among the four semantic memory tasks, separating them somewhat from performance on the more autobiographical questions, which in turn tend to be split into recollection of people and events in a broadly plausible way. As we shall see in the chapter on semantic memory, neuropsychological data is beginning to provide powerful clues as to the way in which long-term semantic and autobiographical memory is organized.

Recollecting Diary Entries

One of the problems with the Galton cue word technique is that of verifying the recollections, and in an effort to avoid this problem a number of investigators have used themselves as subjects,

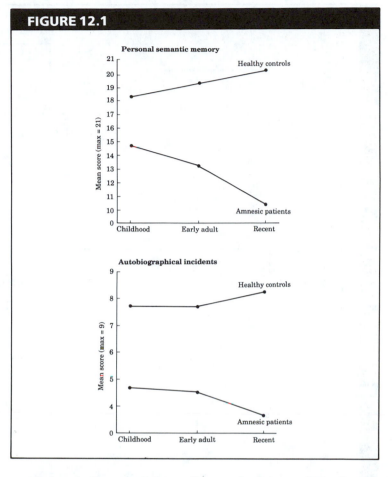

Recall of autobiographical material by amnesic patients and healthy controls. The upper panel shows the recall of autobiographical knowledge of a broadly semantic nature, such as the address one lived at as a child, or the names of friends and teachers. The lower panel shows recall of specific incidents from various periods of life. Both show clear evidence of impairment, and a tendency for this to be more striking for recent than for early material.

regularly entering events into a diary, and subsequently testing for their recollection. In one of the first of these studies, Linton (1975) ensured that every day she noted two events, writing the details on a series of index cards, which she later used to test her capacity to remember. Linton demonstrated that this was a viable if rather demanding method of studying autobiographical memory.

One intriguing feature of her results is the tendency she observed to forget the less pleasant incidents more rapidly than the rest. A second finding was the importance of rehearsal. She sampled cards at random, and noticed that some cards cropped up more often than others; these proved to show less forgetting than those which were being sampled for the first time, indicating that the process of testing was itself acting as a relearning or rehearsal process, something that no doubt happens in natural life when we reminisce and talk about earlier events.

One problem with this diary technique is that it tends to be limited to the recall of events that were sufficiently striking to have merited writing down in the diary, and of course that it is based on the recollection of only one subject. This led to a modification of the

FIGURE 12.2

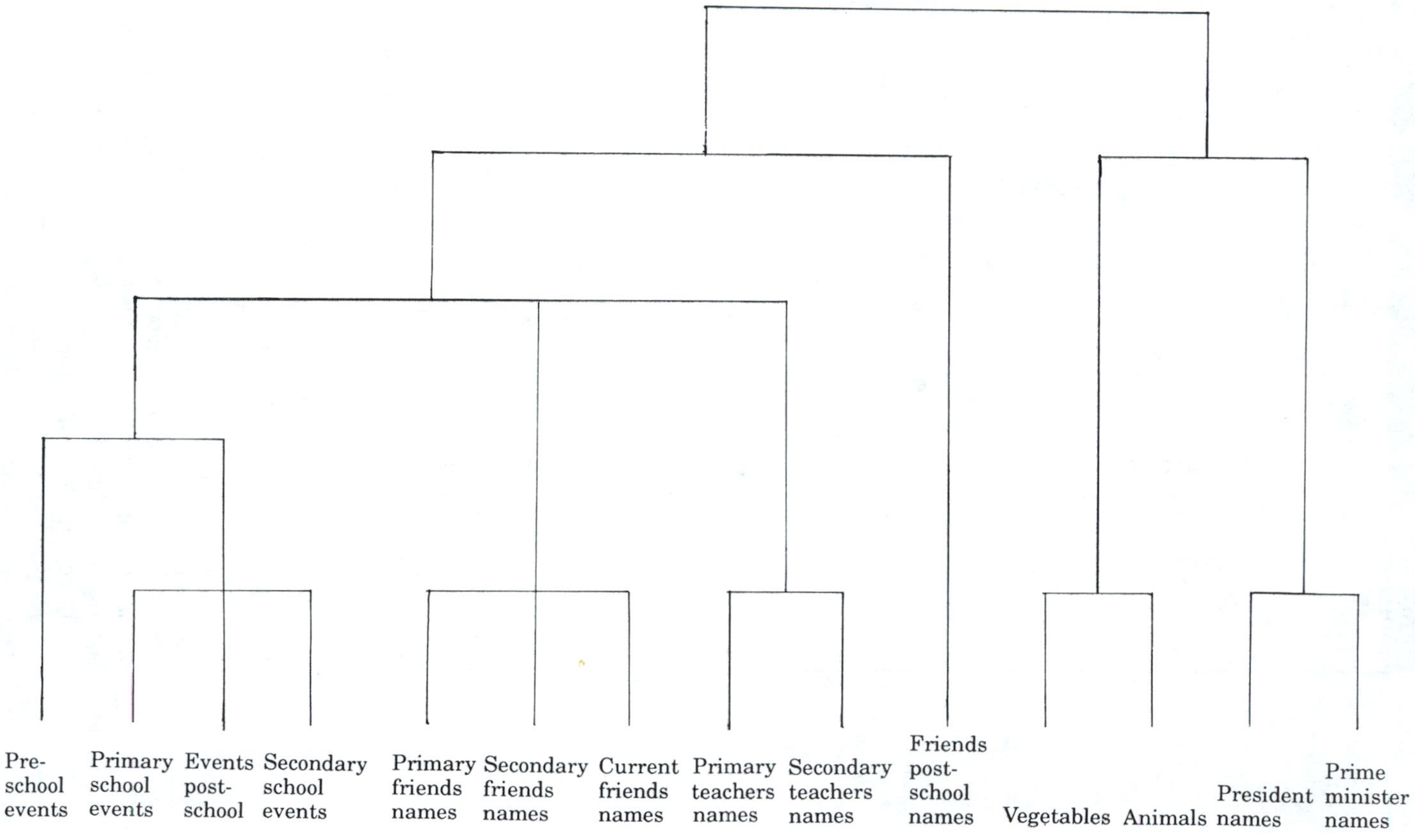

Pre-
school
events

Primary
school
events

Events
post-
school

Secondary
school
events

Primary
friends
names

Secondary
friends
names

Current
friends
names

Primary
teachers
names

Secondary
teachers
names

Friends
post-
school
names

Vegetables Animals
names

President Prime
minister
names

Autobiographical fluency: Subjects attempted to produce as many items as possible in 90 seconds from the various categories. cluster analysis suggests a broad intercorrelation, together with a division in to sub-categories, with events and semantic information being at the two extremes. Data from Dritschel, Williams, and Baddeley (in preparation).

technique by Brewer (1988) who equipped 10 subjects with tape-recorders and beepers. The beepers went off at random intervals, approximately once every two hours, at which time the subject was required to note what he or she was doing at the time, rate the frequency of the activity, its significance, goal-directedness and his or her emotional state at the time. Recall was tested after a delay of 0, 23 or 46 days by being given one of the specified cues of time, location, etc. and asked to recall the incident. Brewer's subjects showed many omissions where nothing could be recollected (190), many occasions on which the wrong event was produced (118), many correct recollections (109), but hardly any overt errors (4) in which the correct event was recalled together with erroneous information.

Dating Autobiographical Incidents

There has been considerable interest in the accuracy with which subjects can date the events they recollect. Theoretical studies that have concentrated on using the Galton technique typically need to rely on dated events in order to plot forgetting functions, since it is often not possible to obtain accurate corroborative information on the material recalled. A second reason for studying event dating is the very practical one of interpreting the data people produce in retrospective surveys. Social surveys concerning people's habits or the events of their lives are often used as a means to assist in optimizing and planning social services. The nature and frequency of use of medical facilities, for example, might be an important factor in the government planning of health resource allocation. A survey concerned for example with frequency of visits to a doctor will typically require the respondent to recall the number of visits within a specified time period. This in turn will require at least approximate memory for *when* the visits occurred.

How do people estimate when events they report occurred, and how can their estimations be improved? Subjects report using a number of cues including such seasonal information as the state of the weather ("it was snowing") or the vegetation ("the trees were just budding") (Baddeley, Lewis, & Nimmo-Smith, 1978), or the ease and clarity with which the memory is evoked (Brown, Ripps, & Shevell, 1985). Loftus and Marburger (1983) showed that it was possible to improve dating by using a striking public event as an anchor point; they used the eruption of Mount St. Helens which was a very prominent event if, like their subjects, you were living in the state of Washington. For many subjects, however, the best cues tend to be associated with events within their own lives, events which themselves can be dated such as "the first Christmas after I began University", or "just after the holiday I had in Paris" (Baddeley, et al., 1978; Thompson, Skownorski, & Lee, 1988).

The application of the psychology of memory to the improvement of survey methods is likely to be an area of increasing importance (Sirken, Mingay, Royston, Bercini, & Jobe, 1988). One problem for example stems from the suggestion that events that occur repeatedly will be under-reported (Neisser, 1986). Means, Mingay, Nigam, and Zarrow (1988) examined this prediction in a study that asked people to remember visits to the doctor within the last year, selecting subjects who had all made at least four visits, and subsequently checking their recall against medical records.

Subjects often clustered visits of the same kind together, saying that they could not recall individual visits. They did indeed recall only 25% of the visits from such repeated sets, compared with 60% of other visits, as Neisser's earlier study would predict. Subjects reporting such clustered "generic" memories were then subjected to the "memory decomposition" procedure. This started with a request for the detailed recollection of the last visit of the cluster, the event that previous research indicated would be easiest to recall (Baddeley et al., 1978; Neisser, 1976).

The subject was asked questions about such potentially discriminating details of the weather at the time, length of wait, and so forth. Subjects then tried to recall the first visit in similar detail, followed by each subsequent visit. Finally, subjects tried to construct a personal "time-line" of the last year, and to mark the various visits on the line. The "memory decomposition" procedure produced a further 51% of the clustered memories, and the time-line added another 12% (Means et al., 1988). There were in addition very few false reports. This was essentially an applied study which does not allow the separate assessment of the importance of cueing, motivation and time spent recollecting. It does, however, support the view that cognitive psychology has a role to play in the development of survey methods.

THE FEELING OF KNOWING

The Tip-of-the-Tongue Effect

One of the most extensively investigated aspects of conscious recollection is that associated with the state of mind whereby a subjects know that they know something, even when they are unable to recall it. Hart (1965) was one of the first to investigate the *feeling of knowing*, and reported that general knowledge questions in which the subject reported a high feeling of knowing, but could not recall the answer, were much more likely to lead to correct recognition than those associated with a low feeling of knowing. A particularly common instance of this feeling occurs in the *tip-of-the-tongue effect*, when we are trying to recall a specific word, and find that it eludes us.

Brown and McNeill (1966) attempted to induce a tip-of-the-tongue (TOT) state in their subjects by reading out definitions of comparatively rare words and asking their student subjects to provide the word. If a subject could not provide it, but felt she knew the word, she was encouraged to stop and try to provide as much information as possible about the missing word. Brown and McNeill found that their subjects very often were quite accurate in recalling a good deal about the word, even though they could not produce the word itself. Typically, when the word was presented, it was recognized immediately.

As Aristotle pointed out (Dennis, 1948), the effect is particularly likely to occur with names. An example in my own case occurred in trying to recall the name of a small Southern California port, Oxnard. I knew it had two syllables, that the first vowel was *o* and the second *a*, but just could not retrieve it. When it was suggested, I recognized it with complete certainty.

Retrieval Blocks

In trying to recall an item while in this TOT state, it is not uncommon to find oneself repeatedly coming up with a related but incorrect response, what Reason and Lucas (1984) have termed the *ugly sister effect*. For example, on one occasion I was attempting to produce the word that an optician would use for "short-sighted"; I continually came up with "astigmatic" which I knew perfectly well was incorrect. When a friend volunteered "myopic", I knew immediately that it was the word I was seeking.

Reason and Lucas (1984) have carried out two diary studies investigating the TOT phenomenon. In their first study, 32 subjects kept a diary for four weeks, recording a mean of 2.5 instances per subject, a rate which Reason and Lucas accept is almost certainly an underestimate. Of these instances, 53% were associated with an "ugly sister". Just as Cinderella's ugly sisters were bigger and older than she was, so the TOT ugly sisters tended to be more frequent and more recent than the target items they were blocking. In those cases where the subject did not feel that recall was blocked by an "ugly sister", about a fifth did involve other types of intermediary words that either helped, or at least did not appear to hinder recall. Typically, these had fewer features in common with the target word than the blocking words did.

In the case of blocked recalls, the subject was more likely to achieve success by means of some external cue such as being reminded by something in the environment, or asking another person (43%) than by using any form of internal strategy (25%). In contrast, the unblocked cases were more likely to yield to internal strategies such as generating further contextual information, going through the alphabet or forming images (54%) than were retrieved through external cueing (14%).

In general, about half of the TOT states were resolved by some form of search procedure, with the remaining cases being split relatively equally between being prompted by some explicit external reminder, and simply popping up apparently spontaneously. Reason and Lucas suggest that some form of search schema is presumably set up and continues to run even though the subject has directed attention elsewhere, or to quote Reason and Lucas, who have an obvious fondness for expressing their concepts in vivid images, "The unrequited schema, like Heathcliff, continues to scan both the inner and outer worlds until the target is found" (Reason & Lucas, 1984, p. 67).

Naturalistic diary studies have the advantage of providing some of the richness of everyday memory, but lack of control makes it difficult to use them to explore the effect in more detail. While research in this area is not yet extensive, some studies have been carried out on broadly related effects within the laboratory. In one study for example, A.S. Brown (1979) read his subjects definitions of relatively infrequent words, followed by a cue word that was either correct, or incorrect but semantically related to the word, orthographically related to the word or totally unrelated. Hence an example might be the definition "to eat greedily" with the words "gobble" (correct), or "cram" (semantic) or "goggle" (orthographic) or "feud" (unrelated). Brown observed that semantically related cues tended to slow down the rate at which the subject produced the correct response.

Another type of inhibitory effect was demonstrated by John Brown (1968) in a study in which subjects were asked to recall as many as possible of the state names of the U.S.A. One group was given no cues, while a second was presented with the names of half the states. This latter group was less successful in recalling the other states than were the group who were given no prompts. Similar effects have been shown in the case of subjects recalling lists of recently presented words. Giving the subject part of the list reduces the probability that he will recall the remaining items (Tulving & Hastie, 1972).

How might one explain these effects? One possibility is that the effect occurs entirely through competition between the ugly sister and the correct item. Let us suppose that for some reason, the competing item is initially rather stronger, in the Reason and Lucas study because it was more frequent and recent, and in the experimental studies because it had just been presented and was hence highly primed. When the process of searching for the appropriate item occurs, then the intruding item will be retrieved instead. The process of retrieval will itself increase the probability that that item will be retrieved later (Landauer & Bjork, 1978), consequently making it even less likely that the correct item will be evoked.

A second possibility is that over and above this strengthening of the competing item, there may be an additional effect that inhibits the correct item. It is possible for example that when the excitation of a particular neural system eventually settles on one item, then other similar and adjacent and hence possibly competing items will be actively inhibited. As Chapter 13 indicates, such inhibitory postulates play an important role in a number of the recently developed models of cognition that assume parallel distributed processing (e.g. Rumelhart & McClelland, 1986). This question was of course a central concern of the interference theory approach to forgetting discussed previously. Interference theorists concluded that the unlearning or weakening of one response by another does occur, although this view is not universally accepted (see Baddeley, 1976 and Chapter 5 for further discussion). In conclusion, while retrieval-inhibition effects certainly exist, they remain, to quote a recent review of this area by Nickerson (1984) "a persisting enigma".

STRATEGIES OF RECOLLECTION

One of the problems of studying memory at point of breakdown is that it tends to tell us more about the relatively few occasions in which the memory is very obviously failing, rather than the enormous number of situations in which it operates successfully. Consider the following questions:

What is your name?
What is the capital city of Australia?
Where were you last Tuesday morning?
How many rooms are there in your present home?
Is *mantiness* an English word?
What was Beethoven's telephone number?

You probably used very different search strategies to answer each of these questions.

I assume that your own name came to you virtually automatically and instantaneously. The capital city of Australia probably took somewhat longer, and may have required you to reject the largest city in Australia, "Sydney", before accepting the correct answer "Canberra". The question of where you were last Tuesday morning is likely to have taken considerably longer. You probably first of all had to find some strategy for identifying the Tuesday, then perhaps reconstructed your timetable, or it may have been that you always do the same thing on Tuesday mornings in which case it would have been semi-automatic. In the case of the number of rooms in your current home, it is probable that you set up some form of spatial image and counted.

The last two are interesting examples discussed among others by Lindsay and Norman (1972). In the case of "mantiness", I suspect you knew immediately that it was not a real word, or at least not a word that you had encountered. How? Not presumably by systematically scanning every word in your vocabulary and eventually concluding that it was not there. We presumably have some more direct access to our knowledge, or lack of knowledge of language. Finally, in the case of Beethoven's telephone number, again you presumably did not need to consult your internal telephone directory. The semantic knowledge that telephones were not invented until long after Beethoven's death was presumably enough to allow you to short-circuit that particular search.

Relatively little research has been done on the rich and complex strategies and tactics we use everyday to interrogate our memory

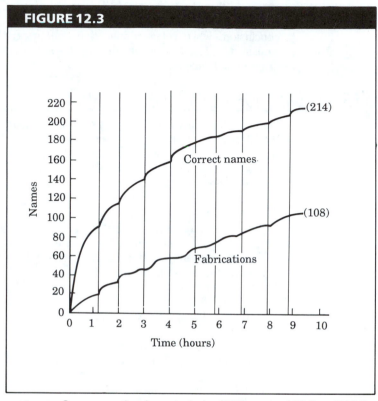

FIGURE 12.3

Cumulative recall over 10 one-hour sessions of the correct names of high-school classmates and number of fabrications produced by a single subject tested many years after leaving high-school. From Williams and Hollan (1981).

systems. One exception is a study by Williams and Hollan (1981), who carried out a naturalistic study in which they asked their subjects to try to recollect as many as possible of the names of children they were at school with. Their subjects were encouraged to attempt this task over a considerable period of time and generated large numbers of names, both correct and incorrect, as Figure 12.3 suggests. They also produced rather rich protocols describing their retrieval attempts. On the basis of these descriptions, Williams and Hollan suggest a process whereby the subject begins by generating the relevant context, then searches that context, subsequently verifying any names that crop up.

How does such verification occur? As St. Augustine observed, this does present something of a paradox:

> When, therefore, memory loses something—and this is what happens whenever we forget something and try to remember it— where are we to look for it except in the memory itself? And if the memory offers us something else instead, as may happen, we reject what it offers until the one thing we want is presented. When it is presented to us we say "This is it", but we could not say this unless we recognized it, and we could not recognize it unless we remembered it.   (St. Augustine, *Confessions* translated by Pine-Coffin, 1961, p. 225.)

As we saw earlier, we do seem to be reasonably good on some occasions at knowing that something has not happened. Brown, Lewis, and Monk (1977) carried out a number of experiments to explore this phenomenon which they called "negative recognition". In one of their experiments, they first established surreptitiously the town of origin of each subject. They then carried out a learning experiment in which town names were presented, carefully ensuring that it did not include the subject's home town. Subjects were later given a recognition test including their home town; they were virtually perfect in correctly saying that this had not been presented, presumably on the grounds that if it had been, they would have noticed and remembered it.

So much for "negative recognition", but what about "positive recognition"? We shall return to this later in the chapter in discussing confabulation in patients who are unable to discriminate between genuine memories and fantasies and inventions. Before doing so, however, research on the autobiographical memory of normal people will be discussed, beginning with a detailed diary study carried out by a single subject who systematically recorded the events of his life, and subsequently tested his capacity to remember them (Wagenaar, 1986).

A Single Case Diary Study

Willem Wagenaar is a Dutch professor who was aged 37 when he began the study, and 43 when he ended it. During this time he was married and had four children and worked first of all as a research scientist in the Institute for Perception in Soesterberg, and subsequently became Professor of Psychology at the University of Leiden. On each day he recorded one or occasionally two incidents, taking care to report *who* was involved, *what* happened, *where* it happened and *when*. He scaled each incident for its saliency, rating whether it was something that happened very frequently or was rather unusual, and assessing the degree of emotional involvement he felt, and the pleasantness of this involvement. He conducted a preliminary experiment over an initial period of 12 months, and a follow-up experiment in the 12 months after the main study. By comparing these two periods he was able to establish that his memory performance had not changed substantially over that time. Had his memory substantially improved or got worse, it would of course have made the interpretation of any apparent forgetting curves rather difficult. Since performance was essentially the same, we can ignore that factor.

During the main part of the experiment, Wagenaar reported a total of 2,400 incidents. He subsequently tested his memory for these, spacing the recall over a period of 12 months, by taking each incident and cueing himself with one piece of information and attempting to recall the rest. The order of the *who, what, where* and *when* questions was randomized so as to allow him to compare the importance of these four aspects of the incident. A combination

Recall of autobiographical incidents as a function of time, given one, two or three retrieval cues. From Wagenaar (1986).

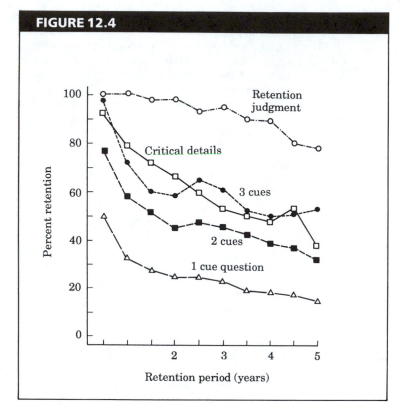

FIGURE 12.4

of single, double and triple cues allows seven different cueing conditions for each of the four basic questions about each incident. Figure 12.4 shows the mean percentage of questions that were answered correctly as a function of number of cues. The function can be described by a power law.

Broadly speaking, this resembles the forgetting pattern reported in earlier studies of autobiographical memory (Rubin, 1982). Wagenaar found the information on *who*, *what* and *where* offered approximately equally powerful cues to memory. On the other hand, telling himself *when* an incident happened proved to be a very poor cue, although combined with other information it could be quite powerful, suggesting that although temporal information is stored, in and of itself it does not provide ready access to remembered events. Can you remember where you were on 14 August last year? Neither can I. Given a particular event however, we do seem quite often to be able to work out the approximate date, as we saw earlier by using target marker dates and various problem-solving strategies, rather than remembering temporal information directly.

Figure 12.5 shows the influence of salience, degree of emotional involvement and pleasantness on level of recall and rate of forgetting. An item that is unusual or salient, and one that evokes

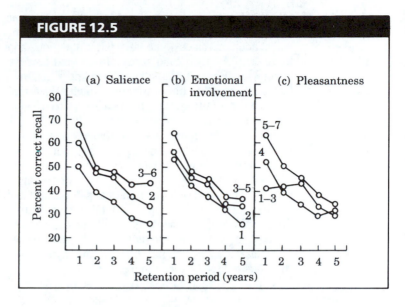

FIGURE 12.5

Forgetting of autobiographical events as a function of rated salience, emotional involvement and pleasantness. In each case "1" represents a low rating. From Wagenaar (1986).

emotional involvement is likely to be better learned, and to retain this advantage over the delay interval. The forgetting curves show essentially parallel functions; this could be taken as indicating equivalent rates of forgetting, although this is a somewhat controversial issue as we discussed in Chapter 10.

The effects of degree of pleasantness on performance shows a rather more complex pattern, with unpleasant items showing considerably poorer recall over the shorter intervals, but being approximately equivalent to more pleasant items after longer periods of delay. Does the unpleasantness simply lose its sting, or is some more complex explanation called for? It is hard to tell from the available data.

On the whole, Wagenaar found that he seemed to forget rather fewer items than did Linton in her earlier study (Linton, 1975), possibly because he used a more detailed cuing procedure than hers. However, some items appeared to have been lost completely, with the result that even when all the information on the card was provided, he still had no recollection of the incident. A proportion of these items concerned incidents in which other people had been strongly involved, and hence were events that they might well themselves remember. In many cases this proved to be so, whereupon the other person was encouraged to provide further information about the event. On almost every occasion it eventually proved possible to recall the incident, and to verify that this was genuine recall since he was able to supply additional information about the event that had not so far been given. This again raises the intriguing central question of forgetting: Is anything ever completely lost, or is everything stored permanently, with forgetting reflecting the fact that it simply becomes harder and harder to retrieve?

Wagenaar's study has been very productive in telling us about rates of forgetting, factors that enhance learning, or possibly subsequent retrieval, the influence of negative emotions on recall, and in addition raises some very basic questions about the nature of forgetting. A single case study of this kind however does have its limitations. First, it is a very demanding and slow way of accumulating information. Interestingly enough, Wagenaar mentions that the process of attempting to recall forgotten events proved to be extremely laborious and stressful.

Secondly, Wagenaar's study tells us only about the memory of one person. While I suspect that his memory does not work in fundamentally different ways from the memories of other people, one is intrinsically limited in such research to studying the memory of certain particularly determined and dedicated individuals. A third problem with studies of this kind is that they are essentially observational. They allow us to study the pattern of events that happen to occur, but do not lend themselves readily to testing particular interpretations. For testing hypotheses, experimental methods tend to be much more powerful.

In short, Wagenaar's study is a first-rate piece of natural history, offering an important initial stage in investigating a hitherto neglected area of human memory, but throwing up questions which are subsequently more likely to be answered by experimental methods. The importance of combining natural history and experimental techniques is, of course, one that crops up with some frequency throughout the present book.

FORGETTING AUTOBIOGRAPHICAL EVENTS

In addition to the dedicated diary studies of Linton and Wagenaar, there have in recent years been a number of group studies of autobiographical memory and forgetting, typically using the Galton verbal cueing method described earlier (Crovitz & Schiffman, 1974; Robinson, 1976; Rubin, 1982).

Rubin, Wetzler, and Nebes (1986) review this recent work, and in particular examine the relationship between elapsed time and probability that an incident will spontaneously be evoked by the provision of a random cue word. Data from a study by Rubin (1982), using 18-year-old student subjects is shown in Figure 12.6. There is a general tendency for older memories to be recalled less frequently. Note, however, that below the age of five, the drop becomes much steeper, a phenomenon known as *infantile amnesia*. When is your own earliest recollection? Few people can remember anything from much below the age of three.

Infantile Amnesia

While infantile amnesia is a well-established phenomenon, its interpretation remains controversial. One explanation claims that crucial aspects of the brain have not yet developed, making infants essentially like amnesic patients (Moscovitch, 1985). Another

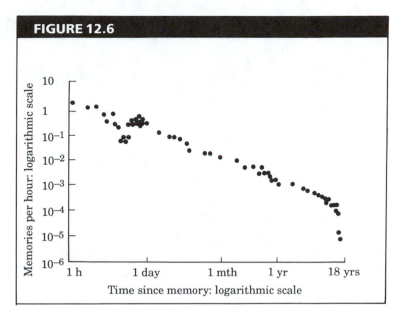

FIGURE 12.6

Probability that a random cue word will evoke a memory, as a function of elapsed time. The data are from student subjects, and the discontinuity around the 18-year delay reflects the inaccessibility of very early memories. From Rubin (1982).

suggestion is that the absence of language in very young children is the crucial variable, while a third suggests that the adult's perception of the world is so different from that of a very young child, that although the memories remain we no longer have adequate access to them, an explanation in terms of context dependency (see Chapter 11). Yet another interpretation is offered by psychoanalysis which suggests that our early experiences are repressed for emotional reasons (Freud, 1901). Unfortunately, our capacity to generate interpretations has so far exceeded our capacity to test them objectively and scientifically, although this continues to be an active research area (Erdelyi, 1985)

Interpretation of the data cited by Rubin et al. (1986) is, of course, complicated by many factors including the age at which the event was experienced, the delay, and the age of the person recollecting. A more tightly designed study was carried out by Sheingold and Tenney (1982) who were interested in the capacity of a child to remember the birth of a younger sibling. In one study they concentrated on children who had had a brother or sister born when they were between 3 and 11 years old, testing the memory for this incident in children aged 4, 6, 8 and 12 years, and in college students. They also tested the recollection of the mothers of the children, allowing them to check the consistency of the reported recollections.

Memory was tested by a number of general questions, supplemented by 37 specific queries asking for details such as who took care of the child while the mother was in hospital, how long she was in hospital, whether the baby received any presents, whether the respondent received presents, and so forth. On average, mothers were able to answer about 18 questions,

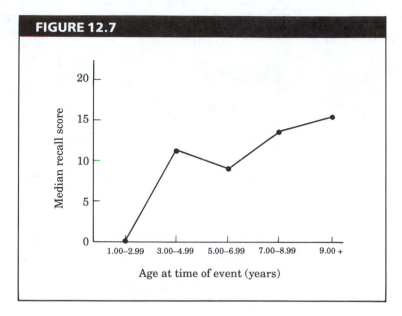

FIGURE 12.7

Median recall scores as a function of age for sibling births reported by college students. From Sheingold and Tenney (1982). Copyright (1982) by W.H. Freeman and Co. Reprinted by permission.

whereas the children recalled an average of 12; there was no substantial reduction in amount recalled as a function of elapsed time for either the mothers or the children, a somewhat surprising finding since in the case of the college students the information had been retained for well over 10 years.

A second study examined recall as a function of how old the respondent was when his or her sibling was born. The results of this are shown in Figure 12.7 from which it is clear that age of learning has a very marked effect on subsequent recollection, with children whose brother or sister was born when they were 3 years old or less, having virtually no recollection of the event, the phenomenon of infantile amnesia discussed previously.

Autobiographical Recollection Cueing

So how well are autobiographical events remembered? We seem to have a very varied picture, ranging from a relatively low recall level shown by Brewer's subjects, coupled with the almost universal finding that dating tends to be unreliable, to quite good recall of details of the birth of a sibling that seem to show no major forgetting after well over a decade. Such apparent inconsistencies are almost certainly partly due to difference in the intrinsic memorability of the events. The birth of a sibling is clearly a very important event for a child, while many of the events recorded by Brewer's subjects were trivial and routine, indeed the uniqueness of the event in his study was quite a good predictor of the likelihood that it would be subsequently recalled.

A second factor of great importance is the number and richness of memory cues provided. You will recall that Wagenaar found that virtually all the events he had recorded in his diary could eventually be recalled, given sufficient prompting. The importance of cueing as a factor in childhood memories is illustrated in a recent study by Hudson and Fivush (1987) in which they studied both free and probed recall of a visit by 5-year-old children to an archaeological museum. The visit seems to have been a relatively memorable one in which the children were encouraged to excavate in a sand pit, where they found various artefacts. They were asked about the event after delays of six weeks, one year and six years. The cues provided were first a very general one, "What happened at the Jewish museum?", followed if necessary by "Do you remember it was a museum of archaeology?", and then "Do you remember you dug in the sand box?", and finally by the presentation of a number of photographs of the visit. While the capacity to recollect details spontaneously fell off quite markedly over the six-year period, given sufficient cueing, subjects were able to recall 87% of the facts initially recollected on the first test six years earlier.

Autobiographical Distortion

The studies by Hudson and Fivush, and by Wagenaar both seem to indicate a very high level of recall of autobiographical events, and a low level of distortion, given adequate cueing. And yet, as we saw, much of the work on eyewitness testimony demonstrates very clearly that distortions do occur. How should we resolve this apparent paradox?

Certainly one factor is the nature of the events being recollected, with both the diary study, and studies of memory in children typically selecting events that stand out as being at least modestly memorable. Furthermore, the amount of detail required is often far less than might be requested of a witness who is attempting to reconstruct the experience of seeing a crime committed. Thirdly, of course, is the question of possible emotional factors; these will be discussed in Chapter 13.

Barclay (1988) describes a study in which he attempts to develop a more demanding test of recollection than that used in the diary studies described so far. He had his subjects keep diaries, and subsequently tested their recollection of the events reported. However, he used a recognition procedure rather than cued recall, selecting as high distractor items events derived from other incidents recorded by the subject, so as to produce items that are inaccurate, but which have many of the characteristics of the sort of event the subject did in fact experience. Under these circumstances, errors were frequent. In discussing his results, Barclay distinguishes between the "truth" of a recollection and its "accuracy". A recollection is true if it represents the person's general experience of the situation and his attitudes to it, in short if it correctly conveys the gist of the experience. It would be accurate however only if the detail were correctly reproduced.

An interesting example of this distinction occurs in the case of the testimony of the Watergate conspirator John Dean (Neisser, 1982). You may recall that during the Watergate investigation, Dean gave very extensive testimony concerning various conversations he had had with President Nixon, accounts that were so detailed that the press dubbed him "the man with the tape recorder mind". Since the conversations had actually been taped, it subsequently became possible to test the accuracy of this claim by comparing his testimony with the actual tapes. As Neisser shows, Dean's testimony proved to be accurate in its broad outlines, but highly inaccurate in its detail. In particular, Dean's own role was presented as more central and important than it proved to have been in practice. In Barclay's sense, his testimony was *true* in correctly reflecting the overall gist of the conversations, but was not *accurate* in its personal detail.

In general, I would agree with Neisser (1988) in concluding that much of our autobiographical recollection of the past is reasonably free of error, provided we stick to remembering the broad outline of events. Errors begin to occur once we try to force ourselves to come up with detailed information from an inadequate base. This gives full rein to various sources of distortion including that of prior expectations, disruption by misleading questions, and by social factors such as the desire to please the questioner, and to present ourselves in a good light.

RETROGRADE AMNESIA (RA)

Memory for Public Events

A problem with many studies of autobiographical memory is that there is rarely a convenient (or inconvenient) tape-recorder that allows the experimenter to check the accuracy of what is recalled. One way of avoiding this problem is to use news events that were sufficiently dramatic for them to have been noted by most of the population at the time they occurred. This approach was first used by Elizabeth Warrington and her colleagues in studies aiming to develop a tool for assessing retrograde amnesia, the tendency for certain types of brain damage to impair a patient's memory for events that happened before the injury. An initial study tested young and elderly normal subjects for both the recall and recognition of news events from the past. In general, the older the event, the lower the probability that it would be remembered. There was a general tendency for the elderly to perform at a lower level than the young for memories from all periods of life (Warrington & Sanders, 1971). When amnesic patients were tested, they showed a lower overall level of performance than normal subjects, with some patients showing a particular marked tendency for poorer performance on more recent items (Sanders & Warrington, in press).

The term *retrograde amnesia* is used to refer to the marked impairment in remote memory found in certain patients. Such patients often fail to recall information that was acquired long before their brain damage. Since the patients were normal at the time of initially encountering such information, it was presumably learnt just as well by the patients as by control subjects. Failure to access it therefore suggests either that the old memory traces have been destroyed, or else that they remain, but have become inaccessible. Such a retrieval failure interpretation is supported by the observation that retrograde amnesia following a blow on the head will sometimes "shrink", with the patient initially able to recall only items from the distant past, but gradually recovering more and more of the past until he may well be able to remember everything up to a few seconds before the accident (see Chapter 16 for further details).

A particularly clear example of retrograde amnesia is shown in a study by Squire and Cohen (1982) of the disturbance of memory by electroconvulsive therapy (ECT), a procedure whereby an electric current is passed through the brain as part of one method of treating depression. Squire and Cohen used as their test material the titles of television shows that had been present for only one season, material that they assumed most of their subjects would have encountered, but not rehearsed since the season in which the show appeared. Figure 12.8 shows the level of performance as a function of delay for a group of patients tested before the ECT and after. There is a very clear tendency for memory for the more recent program to be disrupted by ECT, an effect that does not apply in the case of more distant memories.

Other studies have used the recognition of famous faces, famous voices, and visually and verbally presented news events to test for retrograde memory deficits. The paradigm is full of methodological problems (see e.g. Weiskrantz, 1985), but it is probably true to say that it typically shows that amnesic patients tend to have poorer overall performance, and some of them show a gradient indicating a differential disruption of more recent events.

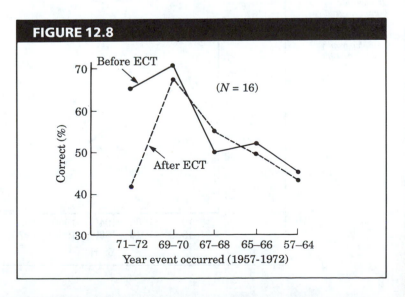

FIGURE 12.8

Temporally limited retrograde amnesia following bilateral electroconvulsive therapy: Recognition of the titles of former one-season television programs before and after ECT. From Squire, Slater, and Chace (1975). Copyright (1975). by the AAAS.

Gradients of RA

Such a gradient is shown particularly clearly in an intriguing single case study by Butters and Cermak (1986) of P.Z., a distinguished but alcoholic scientist who became amnesic in his sixties as a result of Korsakoff's syndrome. This is a condition that may be produced by a combination of alcoholism and inadequate nutrition. The brain develops a thiamine deficiency, leading to damage, typically in the hippocampus and mammillary bodies; this produces an amnesia which may be associated either with substantial other intellectual deficits, or may be relatively pure. The study of such relatively pure cases has played an important part in our investigation of amnesia in recent years, and has interesting implications for the nature of normal memory, as Chapters 15 and 16 will show.

One major advantage enjoyed by Butters and Cermak in studying P.Z. was that he had, a few years before, completed an autobiography. Hence it was possible to be certain that items in his personal life had at one time been recalled by him, and to test his retention of these systematically. Figure 12.9 shows the percentage recall of questions based on his autobiography as a function of date. There is a very clear gradient, with memory for events in his early life being substantially better recalled than memory for events that occurred over the last twenty years.

Butters and Cermak went on to test P.Z.'s professional knowledge, comparing it with that of a colleague of similar age and eminence. In one test, the two subjects were given the names of fellow scientists who had contributed to their subject, either in the period before 1965 or between 1965 and the present. Both subjects were required to say of each scientist, what area he

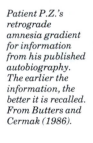

Patient P.Z.'s retrograde amnesia gradient for information from his published autobiography. The earlier the information, the better it is recalled. From Butters and Cermak (1986).

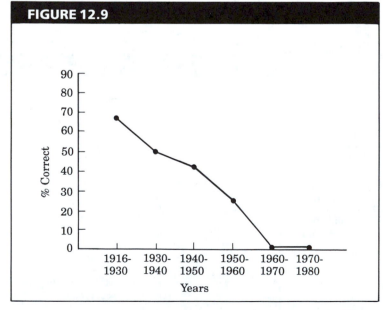

FIGURE 12.9

worked in, and what he was best known for, being given a score of 1 for the first piece of information and 2 for the second. The performance of P.Z. and his control are shown in Figure 12.10 which shows very clearly the overall impairment in the performance of P.Z., together with the gradient; recall of more recent scientists was particularly bad.

Since P.Z. shows a deficit both of autobiographical information and of factual knowledge, one is tempted to assume that this whole area of his memory must have been wiped out. The possibility remains however that the information had not been lost but is merely for some reason inaccessible, a possibility that is emphasized by an even more recent single case study by Warrington and McCarthy (1988).

RA as a Retrieval Deficit

Warrington and McCarthy describe the case of a policeman who developed a devastating amnesia following encephalitis resulting from a brain infection. He remained intellectually well-preserved, but was profoundly amnesic, disoriented in time and place and with no ongoing memory. He did not, for example, remember being told since his illness of the death of his mother. He recognized recent

Performance of patient P.Z. and his matched control subject on the identification of famous scientists. Scores 0, 1, and 2 represent an ordinal scaling of the adequacy of the two subjects' responses. From Butters and Cermak (1986).

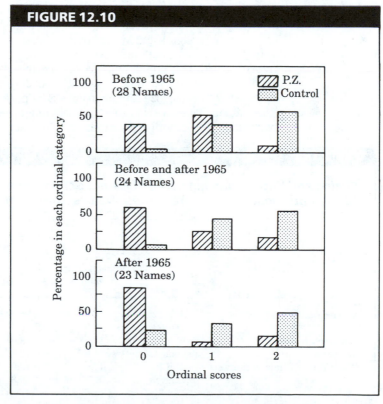

FIGURE 12.10

but not older photographs of his children, was hesitant about recognizing his mother's photograph and sometimes failed to recognize photographs of his wife.

His autobiographical memory was also grossly disrupted. He could remember the broad outlines of his life, knowing for instance that he had been to Egypt in the Services, but not whether he had been to Cairo or not. He knew that he had spent his honeymoon somewhere on the continent of Europe but could not remember where. On the Galton cued autobiographical memory test, he was successful in producing an autobiographical memory for only 3 of 22 cued words, a grossly impaired level of performance. His recall of public events over the last 15 years was similarly impaired, with a score of 1/20 as compared to an average of 15 (range 11–20) for normal control subjects.

When shown pictures of famous personalities from the late 1950s, early 1960s or late 1960s, his capacity to name them was extremely poor, and even when tested by having to select one name from three for each portrait, his performance remained very impaired.

In contrast, however, when he was given a first name and initial, for example David S. for the politician David Steel, his performance improved markedly to within the normal range. When at a later time he was cued by being given the name and initial and asked to generate the famous name in the absence of a photograph, again he performed at a higher level than most control subjects, as Table 12.1 (from Warrington and McCarthy, 1988) shows.

In a subsequent test of recognition, each famous face was presented with two non-famous faces, and the instruction to pick out the one that was famous. A similar procedure was used to test his capacity to recognize famous names. His performance on both these tests was within the normal range, suggesting that information about both the names and the faces was still being

TABLE 12.1

Cueing and Uncued Naming Recall of Names of Photographs of Famous People and Capacity to Generate These Names from an Auditory Cue

		Time Period		
		Contemporary personality	*Mid-1970s*	*Mid-to late-1960s*
Naming photograph	R.F.R.	0	1.0	1.0
	Controls	8.7	6.8	6.3
Naming photograph	R.F.R.	11.0	9.0	7.0
with cue	Controls	14.0	11.3	11.4
Generating name from auditory cue	R.F.R.	12.0	13.0	11.0
	Controls	8.7	6.8	5.5

stored despite his apparently appallingly poor performance on naming faces.

Further evidence of unimpaired performance came when the patient was asked to define a number of words that had come into common currency in recent years, during the time for which his personal autobiographical memory was most blank. For example, he was asked who the Provisionals were (members of a particular group of the Irish Republican Army), what was meant by AIDS and what was Thatcherism. His capacity to define such terms was excellent, in stark contrast to his inability to remember events from his private life over that period.

What can we conclude from this intriguing though tragic case? First of all that remote memory is by no means a simple unitary function. The patient in question appears to have on the one hand a disastrously impaired recollection for personal events and a gross disruption in his capacity to name the portraits of famous people. On the other hand he shows every evidence of preserved learning of the meanings of new words, of recognizing the familiarity of famous faces, and of being able to produce the names if appropriately cued. Warrington and McCarthy suggest that he lacks what they term a "cognitive mediational system" that is necessary for linking the various aspects of his long-term memory.

Clouded Autobiographical Memory

However, although the case described by Warrington and McCarthy is very revealing theoretically, it is not typical of autobiographical memory deficits. A few years ago, a colleague and I became interested in the problems of assessing autobiographical memory in amnesic patients (Baddeley & Wilson, 1986). We used the Galton cueing method, and observed marked differences in the capacity of our patients to recollect a past experience. Some patients, although densely amnesic about recent experiences, appeared to be quite normal in their capacity to recollect events that had happened well before their illness. Others appeared to have very uncertain access to information about their earlier life; recalling events from the past seemed like trying to perceive a scene through a thick mist.

Consider, for example, the following case of a patient who had suffered a bilateral stroke that had left him densely amnesic but otherwise intellectually unimpaired. He could recall the broad outlines of his earlier life, but very little detail. For example in response to the cue word "break" the patient had difficulty coming up with any recollection and was further cued by asking if he had ever broken a limb. He responded as follows:

NW: No, well I have recently had an arm broken....
AB: Can you tell me a bit about that?
NW: Not so easily, no.
AB: How did you break it?

NW: I'm not sure whether it was a break, I think it *was* a break, I thought it was just a strain but I was lifting something heavy to get the lino underneath ... but I have a suspicion that that wasn't how it was caused. I fell, I think, out in the street, I fell and my right arm went back to break the fall.

AB: So where were you when this happened?

NW: In Bodmin.

AB: Do you remember the name of the street?

NW: I don't remember exactly where it was.

His wife subsequently confirmed that he had in fact fallen in the street and broken his arm (Baddeley & Wilson, 1986, p. 233).

Another characteristic of such patients is that very often they would be able to remember something on one occasion but have great difficulty recollecting it on another, although given sufficient detail they could usually show evidence of still having access to the memory, and were able to confirm this by producing further facts. Nevertheless, such patients appear to have what we termed a "clouded" autobiographical memory, suggesting impaired access to stored information about their past.

Autobiographical Confabulation

One of the most intriguing groups, however, occurred in the case of patients suffering from the dysexecutive syndrome described in Chapter 6. They typically are suffering from bilateral damage to the frontal lobes, creating problems in attention and the control of behavior (Shallice, 1982). Some such patients appear to be able to produce fluent recollections of their past, often providing a great deal of detail. Such recollections are often, however, totally unreliable, with the patient subsequently completely denying earlier detailed recollections. Furthermore, when probed, such recollections are often found to contain inconsistencies, and while they are sometimes plausible, they can be completely bizarre.

In the case of one patient, R.J. who suffered from bilateral damage to the temporal lobes following a road traffic accident, confabulation was a very marked feature of his behavior (Baddeley & Wilson, 1986; 1988). He would produce a very detailed but rather varied account of the accident, including verbatim and rambling descriptions of his conversation with the driver of the other vehicle. The account was always different, and since he was unconscious for several weeks following the accident it is very unlikely that he genuinely remembered anything.

In one test, he responded to the cue word *letter* by describing writing a letter to an aunt in which he tells her of the death of his brother. In fact his brother was still alive and well. When this was pointed out, he explained the apparent inconsistency by claiming that after the death of his brother his mother had had another son and given the second son the same name, a claim that not surprisingly was subsequently shown to be quite untrue.

Another patient with frontal lobe damage had initially responded to the cue word *make* with the description of making a record player or phonograph system while at school. On a subsequent test he recalled something different and was prompted to try to remember something else he had made at school. He gave the following account:

AB: Can you think of anything you made at school that is striking?

NW: An Australian wombat.

AB: An Australian wombat?

NW: Ashtray, something different.

AB: That does sound different. How do you make an Australian wombat ashtray?

NW: Get a piece of wood, let your imagination go...

AB: Did you make anything else you can think of? A bit more conventional?

NW: No I don't think so; I made a daffodil, again in wood. That was all to do with the school play.

AB: How was it to do with the school play?

NW: There was a bowl of fruit and flowers which had to be given to the Queen, Queen Diadem. All the various people had to make a flower. We were told to make something out of wood; I happened to be asked to make the daffodil, one of the easier pieces.

Were all our patients lying or perhaps simply teasing an innocent psychologist? We think not. First of all, R.J. was inclined to confabulate quite widely, and independently of being tested. For example, on one occasion while spending the weekend at home from the rehabilitation center, he turned to his wife in bed and asked her:

Why do you keep telling people we are married?

But we are married; we have two children.

That doesn't mean that we are married!

At this point his wife got out of bed and produced their wedding photographs. R.J. looked at them carefully then replied:

That chap certainly looks like me, but it's not me!

R.J. would also act on his confabulations. On one occasion for example he was found pushing a fellow patient in a wheelchair down the road. When questioned he explained that he was taking his friend to see a sewage plant that he (R.J.) was involved in constructing. As a civil engineer, R.J. had in fact been involved in constructing a sewage plant, but that was several years before and over 40 miles away.

Why do such patients confabulate, and perhaps more importantly why do most of us not do so? Impairment of memory is not sufficient, since most amnesic patients show no evidence of genuine confabulation, although they will occasionally attempt to bluff their way out of acknowledging that they don't remember something. The crucial factors seem to be a combination of poor memory and lack of adequate attentional control of working memory, a deficit in the central executive (see Chapter 6). Patients with a deficit in the operation of this system seem to be very poor at sorting out a genuine memory from an invented association, and in the difficult task of filtering out truth from invention, opt for the easy invention rather than the hazy and difficult truth. The fact that the rest of us do not, on the whole, go in for flamboyant confabulation, again emphasizes that the process of recollection is a much more subtle and complex business than merely looking up and reading off an entry in a personal memory encyclopedia.

OVERVIEW

This chapter is concerned with the processes of conscious recollection, and their application to autobiographical memory, recall of the earlier events of one's life. Some of the techniques used in this area are discussed, including the Galton event cueing technique and the more structured interviewing procedures that have developed from it. Diary studies are then discussed as a limited but rich source of evidence which combines an accurate record of the events with the capacity to study their recall systematically. The results of diary studies suggest that rate of forgetting is influenced by such factors as the saliency of the event, its emotional tone, the frequency with which it has been rehearsed, by subsequent recollection, and the richness of the cueing provided. Some of the subjective aspects of recollection are then described, including studies of the feeling of knowing and of the tip-of-the-tongue phenomenon.

As with other aspects of memory, interesting light is thrown on the processes underlying autobiographical memory by clinical studies. One productive line of enquiry has been the investigation of retrograde amnesia, the forgetting of events from one's earlier life following brain damage. Since accurate information on the earlier events of a patient's life are often not available, many of these studies are concerned with the recall of public events. Other studies have used the Galton cueing technique, some patients showing clear evidence of a gradient of retrograde amnesia, with the disruption being greater for more recent events. Finally, the phenomenon of confabulation is discussed. It occurs particularly in patients with frontal lobe damage and it appears to combine the effects of amnesia with the loss of the executive control of memory found in the previously described dysexecutive syndrome.

Chapter Thirteen

KNOWLEDGE

What is the capital of Italy? Do rose bushes have thorns? What is physics? How many inches are there in a foot? Did Plato have ears? What newspaper did he read? What date is Christmas? What does orange juice taste like? What does the word "generous" mean? What is sensory memory? What is meant by the term "levels of processing?"

I trust that you could answer most of these questions relatively rapidly. They reflect just a small amount of the enormous mass of information that we all carry around with us, much of which we are able to access rapidly and almost effortlessly. Consider just a small component of semantic memory, such as our knowledge of the meaning of words. The average man in the street is likely to be familiar with a minimum of 20,000–40,000 words, and many people would have a much larger vocabulary than this. In addition, we all have a great deal of geographical knowledge, knowledge of social customs, knowledge of people and of experiences of the world, the color of things and their smells and textures. This enormous store of information constitutes the core of our semantic memory systems. It clearly is of enormous importance in functioning in everyday life, and adding to this store forms the focus of one of the major world industries, that of education.

Since semantic memory is so important, one might reasonably expect a textbook on memory to have a large and rich section on the topic. In fact, I have found this chapter particularly difficult to write, since despite the obvious importance of semantic memory it was largely ignored during the middle years of this century. While it became a fashionable topic in the 1970s, and continues to be regarded as an area of great importance, it does not seem to have yet acquired any degree of coherence. In one form or another, the study of semantic memory has drawn on philosophy, linguistics, computer science and, in addition, has clear links with fundamental problems of education. My personal view is that we still do not have a sufficiently coherent view of the psychology of semantic memory to integrate these various influences, and that consequently the field remains somewhat fragmented. However, even for psychology this is a very recent area of study, and given the depth and difficulty of the problems it offers, it is perhaps unsurprising that we still lack a generally accepted approach.

SEMANTICS

Much of the research on semantics has been stimulated by an interest in language. As Smith (1978) suggests, much of the early work was aimed at attempting to understand the semantics of individual words, the assumption being that by combining the meanings of individual words and using the rules of syntax, one would be able to derive the meaning of sentences, and from sentences derive the meaning of passages of prose. I will therefore begin by discussing studies concerned with the meaning of individual words and concepts. Related to this enterprise was the attempt by computer scientists to devise computer programs that would in some sense "understand" text. I will describe some of these before going on to discuss some of the evidence that rapidly began to accumulate suggesting that when people understand a sentence, they bring to bear knowledge of the world that extends considerably beyond the simple definition of the constituent words. This leads on to the need for a broader view illustrated by Bartlett's original development of the concept of schema and its subsequent elaborations and refinements into concepts such as "frames" and "scripts". Finally, I will describe the breakdown of semantic memory in patients suffering from brain damage and the implications of this neuropsychological evidence for understanding the organization of semantic memory.

The Linguistic Relativity Hypothesis

It has, in fact, been suggested by the linguist Benjamin Lee Whorfe, that language is one of the major features that determines how we see the world. He argues that a language provides a conceptual framework, and that this framework itself determines what we see. Hence, the very fact that certain Eskimo languages have a very large number of different terms for different types of snow will enable the speaker of that language to perceive and utilize far finer discriminations than would be possible to the non-Eskimo.

A study by Lenneberg and Roberts (1956) showed that members of a North American Indian tribe, the Zuni, who spoke a language that had a single color name for yellow and orange, remembered these colors significantly less well than did English speakers. A subsequent study by Brown and Lenneberg (1954) presented a range of different colors to two groups of subjects. The first group was asked to name the colors, while the second attempted to remember them. They found that certain colors were consistently given the same name, whereas others were given different names by different subjects. When they looked at memory performance, they found that those names over which there was considerable agreement, which they termed "focal" colors were consistently easier to learn than those colors about which there was little agreement. They interpreted their results as support for the Whorfian Hypothesis.

Languages vary substantially in the number of color words they employ. In a study of almost 100 languages, Berlin and Kay (1969) identified 11 basic color names that occurred with some frequency across languages. If only two terms were used, then these were almost invariably black and white, if three, black, white and red. The order of frequency of colors and combinations is given below.

BLACK WHITE
RED
GREEN YELLOW
BLUE
BROWN
PURPLE PINK ORANGE GREY

The salient colors from this set tended to be the focal colors identified by Brown and Lenneberg.

Rosch carried out a very neat series of experiments using this material. She first of all used a separate set of subjects to determine which colors were focal and which non-focal, following which she carried out two experiments comparing American-speaking subjects with members of a New Guinea tribe, the Dani who had a stone-age culture, and a language that had terms only for black and white.

She tested their color memory in two ways: in the first study the subjects were shown a single colored chip, and were then required to recognize it from a set of 160 chips continuously varying in hue. Although performing somewhat more poorly than the U.S. subjects, the Dani nevertheless showed exactly the same pattern of better performance for more focal colors. In a second experiment, the Dani learnt to associate different colors with different clan names. Again performance was better for focal than for non-focal colors (Rosch-Heider, 1972).

What are the implications of these results? Since the same colors were focal for the Dani who had a language without color terms as were focal for American subjects, it seems clear that it is not the language that makes certain colors easier to identify and remember, but the reverse. Dani who have no separate color terms nevertheless find "good" reds and blues and greens easier to remember than intermediate shades like orange, turquoise and magenta. Indeed, those colors that are focal tend to be exactly the colors that studies of color vision indicate are primary. In short, it is perceptual salience that appears to influence language, not the reverse.

Concepts: Features or Prototypes?

Concepts are ways in which we categorize the world in order to understand it and communicate about it. Hence a concept like *DOG* allows us to refer to what poodles and borzois and bull terriers and great danes all have in common. A concept like *DOG* is of course linked with superordinate concepts such as *ANIMAL* and *PET*, and subordinate concepts such as *GREAT DANE*.

The question of how we should think about concepts has interested philosophers since Aristotle who was concerned that words should be properly and logically defined so as to avoid reasoning errors. The system he introduced is shown in Figure 13.1, redrawn by Kintsch (1980) who emphasizes its similarity to virtually all subsequent attempts to give an account of the meaning of words. Aristotle's approach was a logical not a psychological one, and as Kintsch (1980) points out, there is no reason to assume that what is most appropriate for describing a logical system is necessarily a useful way of describing how people deal with meaning. Nonetheless, systems very similar to Aristotle's original have continued to dominate both linguistics (Katz & Fodor, 1963) and psychology (Collins & Quillian, 1969; Smith, Shoben, & Ripps, 1974). Indeed, Kintsch argues that an excessive tendency to base psychological theories on logical models of meaning "has led semantic memory research into avenues of investigation that are barren and lead nowhere" (Kintsch, 1980, p.605). While I would regard the progress in this area as somewhat disappointing, I think we certainly have made some progress, as I hope will become apparent.

Most approaches to semantics have assumed that what specifies a particular concept is some combination of semantic features. Hence a bird would have the features: *has feathers*, *lays eggs*, *has beak*, etc. There are two approaches to the relationship

FIGURE 13.1

A semantic structure (genus-species) after Aristotle. From Kintsch (1980). With permission of the International Association for the Study of Attention and Performance.

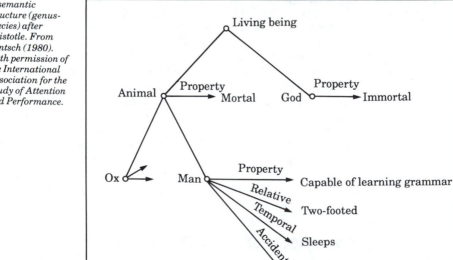

between features and concepts, the *classical theory* and *prototype theory*. The classical theory specified that an item is an example of a concept if, and only if all the necessary defining features apply. Conversely, any item that does not have all the defining features will not be a member of that concept. Take the example of a concept such as *SQUARE*. This requires four features: (1) that it be a closed figure; (2) that it has four sides; (3) that the sides be equal in length; and (4) that the angles be equal. Any shape that fulfils these criteria will be a square, and any square must fulfil these criteria.

However, when we start looking at natural categories, life becomes much more complex. Even with an apparently well-defined concept such as *BIRD*, there are aspects that would certainly be useful in defining most birds, for example ability to fly, that are not true of all birds. Similarly, laying eggs may be characteristic of all birds but it also applies to reptiles and insects. Indeed, some concepts are very useful but appear to be virtually impossible to define clearly and succinctly. The philosopher Wittgenstein discussed this problem in some depth, citing games as an example of such a concept. While games may tend to have certain characteristics such as competition, involving more than one person, etc., exceptions occur; patience or solitaire involves only one person, childrens' games such as ring-a-ring-a-roses are not competitive: and so forth.

Wittgenstein suggested the idea of family resemblance as an alternative to the classical concept of rigidly defined features. Although members of the same family will tend to look somewhat alike, it is not usually possible to specify any one feature that all family members have in common. It might, however, be feasible to specify a typical member of that family. This idea underlies prototype theory, an approach to concept formation that characterizes concepts in terms of typical or central examples that will tend to have a maximum number of features in common with other members of that category.

Prototype theory assumes that natural categories will often have fuzzy boundaries, and this was explored by McCloskey and Glucksberg (1978) in a study in which subjects were given particular category names such as *FRUIT, VEGETABLES, PRECIOUS STONES* and asked to categorize particular instances as to whether or not they belonged to that category. They found that certain items were consistently categorized both by a given subject on different occasions and by different subjects, whereas others were highly inconsistent in their categorization. For example, *tomato* might be categorized as *FRUIT* on one occasion and *VEGETABLE* on another, suggesting that people use these two categories somewhat flexibly.

The concept of a prototype has been explored extensively by Rosch who in one study asked her subjects to rate the degree to which particular instances fitted in with their concept of a particular category. Consistent differences among examples were found, hence given the category *BIRD*, *robin* would consistently be rated as a better or more prototypical example than would *chicken* or *ostrich*. Furthermore, such ratings were highly consistent across subjects. When subjects are asked to verify statements about category membership, then they are consistently faster in processing statements about prototypical items than they are about atypical items. Hence a statement such as *A robin is a bird* would be verified considerably faster than a statement such as *A chicken is a bird* (Rosch, 1973).

Why should some examples be much more prototypical than others? One obvious possibility, suggested by Wittgenstein's family resemblance argument, is that they simply share more common features. Hence a typical bird might be expected to fly, sing, be relatively small, etc. A chicken would deviate from a typical bird in not flying, be rather larger and unbirdlike in shape, not singing, etc. Similarly an ostrich would have many features that are not characteristic of most birds, including lack of flight, extremely long legs and neck, not singing, etc.

Rosch and Mervis (1975) explored this issue by presenting their subjects with 20 objects from each of 6 categories, *FURNITURE*, *VEHICLES*, *WEAPONS*, *CLOTHING*, *VEGETABLES* and *FRUITS*. The subjects were asked to list as many attributes as possible for each of these. Meanwhile, a separate group of subjects rated each of the instances for how typical of the concept it was. The results showed first of all that very few attributes were given to all the items within a given category, suggesting that natural concepts of this sort do not fit in with the classical view that concepts depend on common defining features. Particular instances varied substantially in the number of features they had in common with other members of the category, and as prototype theory predicted, there was a strong correlation between the degree of overlap of features with other members of the category, and the rated typicality of that instance. In short, "good" instances of categories have many features in common with other instances, and few that are different; "poor" instances tend to have fewer similar features and more distinctive features. Hence, *FRUITS* tend to be *round, sweet, colored yellow or red, grow on trees*, whereas *VEGETABLES* are inclined to be *long, non-sweet, green* and *grow in or near the ground*. In this respect a *tomato* is atypical in having a number of the features of a fruit, together with other features that are more vegetable-like.

The Semantic Differential

Although we have talked of concepts and features, we have always referred to the concepts in terms of words, and the features in terms of words or phrases. It is very tempting therefore to regard semantic memory as rather like a dictionary in which words are defined in terms of other words. Such a system would of course be useless, since it would merely link words with other words, which would then link up to other words, without ever conveying what any of the words meant. There is nothing more frustrating than looking up a word in the dictionary only to find it referred to another word, which in turn is defined in terms of the first word. At some point, the words have to be mapped onto concepts which have to link up with our experience of the world. But how should this be expressed?

Osgood, Suci, and Tannenbaum (1957) tried to tackle this problem by means of a device they termed the *semantic differential*. This consisted of a number of bipolar dimensions such as *weak-strong*, *good-bad*, *active-passive* that were derived from a much larger range of dimensions by weeding out those that correlated highly, leaving eventually a much more manageable set that were assumed to cover the whole range of meaning. Osgood et al. then used this as a means of assessing the subject's perception of any given object or situation, requiring the subject to rate the item on each of the various dimensions. They suggest that the particular pattern of responses will capture the underlying meaning of that particular item for the subject.

The technique is one that does have some attractions in that it allows things to be considered where the differences are subtle and perhaps not easily verbalized. For example, it is used by some distillers in connection with the quality control and blending of whiskies. A panel of regular tasters would be required to taste various malt whiskies, and would indicate the characteristics of the particular whisky by marking it on the semantic differential.

However, although the semantic differential does have its uses, one would clearly not wish to claim that it represented the *meaning* of the item rated. I could well imagine rating two individuals in ways that would be analogous to Glenmorangie and Talisker whiskies, and while the analogies might perhaps convey some of the underlying character of the two people, I would obviously not want to say that the whisky and the people had the same "meaning" in anything other than a very metaphorical sense. Indeed, adjectival dimensions seem to capture even less of the essence of a concept than do verbal labels.

MODELS OF SEMANTIC MEMORY

Category Search Models

We have so far been concerned with possible ways in which the meaning of individual words might be represented. However, the comprehension and use of language clearly involves much more than simply interpreting each individual word. In the late 1960s, studies began to appear that were concerned with the verification of simple sentences, typically using reaction time as their principal measure. One of the first of these was a study by Landauer and Freedman (1968) which was a direct attempt to extrapolate Sternberg's work into a broader context.

You may recall that Sternberg showed that the time needed to decide whether an item had or had not just been presented, was a linear function of the size of the set of items the subject was required to hold in memory. Landauer and Freedman (1968) asked their subjects to verify statements such as *A collie is a dog* or negative instances such as *A chair is a dog*. They varied set-size by choosing examples where the smaller set was a subsample of the larger, hence they might compare a statement such as *A collie is a dog* with *A collie is an animal*. The category *ANIMAL* must be larger than the category *DOG* since all dogs are animals, but not all animals are dogs. They found as predicted that it took longer to verify that a collie is an animal than that it is a dog, and argued that this is because is takes longer to scan the larger category.

The model they proposed was similar to Sternberg's except that they assumed the scanning to be self-terminating, that is they assumed that as soon as the necessary information had been achieved, the subject responded, rather than that the subject exhaustively scanned the whole category, as in Sternberg's model. In the case of negative instances, however, the whole set will need to be scanned, a conclusion that predicts that set-size will have a greater effect on reaction time for negative instances than occurs for positive responses. This proved to be the case.

Using this paradigm, Wilkins (1971) showed that subjects were faster at verifying salient items of a given semantic category, that is items that tend to be produced first in a category generation task. Hence, given the category *BIRD*, *robin* would be verified faster than *ostrich*. As we saw from Rosch's work, such salient items tend to be prototypical of the category, having more features in common with other members than is the case for less salient items. The tendency for such items to be processed more rapidly is one of the most important findings in this area, one that runs through a wide range of subsequent studies.

Such a result could in principle be handled by Landauer and Freedman, provided they assume that the scanning process begins with the most typical items. The model does, however, have considerably more problems in the case of a second major empirical finding in this area, namely that it takes consistently longer to reject negative items that come from a similar category than those that come from a dissimilar category. Hence, given the category *TREES*, then it takes longer to reject *potato* as an exemplar than a word from a totally different category such as *rifle*. If verification simply means scanning the category and responding "no" if no match occurs, then the nature of the negative should not be important. Clearly it is.

It is perhaps worth pausing at this point to emphasize the last two findings, since as Kintsch (1980) points out, the tendency for prototypical members of a given category to be verified rapidly, and for similar negative items to be verified slowly can be regarded as the only major experimental findings in this area. A number of other

FIGURE 13.2

Average latencies of true-false judgments as a function of semantic relatedness for true and false sentences. From Kintsch (1980).

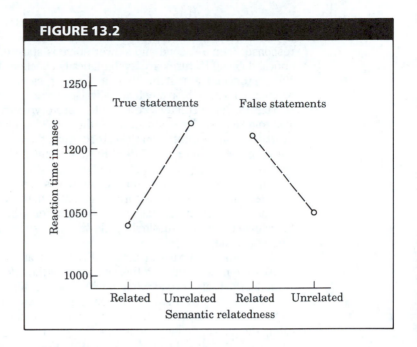

effects that have been noted, can in fact be interpreted in terms of these findings, as we shall see. Figure 13.2 shows data from a study by Kintsch that shows this point particularly clearly (Kintsch, 1974).

Essentially, the fact that the nature of the negative is an important variable suggests that some form of comparison process is involved, rather than a simple category search. One class of models that explicitly attempted to account for the effects of relatedness on true and false judgments are *feature comparison models*, of which the best known is that of Smith, Shoben, and Ripps (1974).

Feature Comparison Models

Such models assume that the meaning of a concept is contained in a bundle of semantic features. The Smith et al. model divides these into two sets, *defining features* which are necessary for membership of a particular category, and *characteristic features* which may apply to most members of the category but are not essential. For example, the category *DOG* would have as defining features characteristics such as *having four legs, having a tail, being covered in fur*, and so forth. Characteristic features might be *being kept as a pet, going for walks on a lead, barking*, etc.

Given the task of verifying a sentence such as *A robin is a bird*, the feature comparison model assumes that the subject begins by comparing the features of *robin* and of *bird*, responding "yes" if there are a sufficiently high proportion of features in common, bearing in mind both defining and characteristic features. If the degree of overlap is not enough to allow a rapid "yes" response, then a second and slower stage is started, in which the critical defining features are systematically checked. If this second stage produces a match, then a "yes" response is provided, whereas a mismatch on any feature will lead to a "no" response.

This model correctly predicts that prototypical examples will lead to a fast "yes" response, since there will be a large degree of overlap of features between the category and the instance, allowing the response to be made after the first stage, whereas atypical examples of a category will require both stages. It can also handle the effect of similarity on "no" responses, since the presence of considerable overlap in features will again demand a two-stage checking process in contrast to the case where the category and the instance are very dissimilar, allowing an instant "no" response after stage one.

The feature comparison model of Smith et al. (1974) certainly handles the major finding in this area, that of the effect of semantic relatedness. It also broadly fits in with work such as that of Rosch on semantic feature models of meaning. It does, however, have some major limitations. First of all, its assumption that natural categories have defining features does not appear to be well supported by the data of Rosch, and as Wittgenstein argued, it seems much more likely that category membership is based on something approaching family resemblance, rather than the possession of a limited set of specific features. A more fundamental problem however is that the model does not appear to be able to distinguish between the statements *A robin is a bird* and *A bird is a robin*, one of which is of course true and one not.

A final problem concerns the extent to which such experiments on the speed with which subjects can make judgments of category membership genuinely advance our overall understanding of semantic memory and comprehension. It is not clear that this rather specific model can be extended beyond the paradigm of category membership judgments and applied to the broader issues of semantic processing.

Semantic Network Theories

My own first contact with semantic memory occurred in the late 1960s, when one of my students with an interest in artificial intelligence lent me a copy of a Ph.D. thesis done by a young computer scientist, Ross Quillian. Quillian was interested in the important but difficult problem of programming a computer to understand text, and for his thesis had produced a model he called the *Teachable Language Comprehender*, or TLC. A prominent feature of the model was its semantic memory system, a sample of which is shown in Figure 13.3.

The model is not entirely dissimilar to that put forward by Aristotle some centuries earlier, but differs in two important

FIGURE 13.3

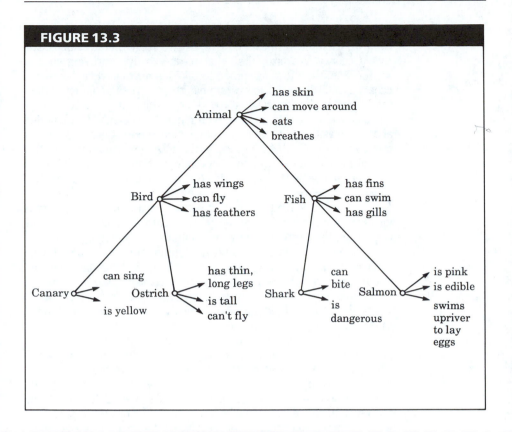

A hypothetical memory structure. From Collins and Quillian (1969).

respects. While both the models assume concepts with associated properties, Quillian's model assumed only one type of association, whereas Aristotle referred to a number of different types of property. Secondly, Aristotle's account was offered as a logical model, Quillian offered his TLC as a psychological model of the way in which people might actually comprehend text. It led to a number of joint experiments with a psychologist, Alan Collins, that were explicitly aimed at using the TLC as a psychological model, and testing it experimentally. Before going on to discuss this, it is necessary to give a brief outline of the way in which the model was assumed to "understand" sentences.

Quillian's model assumes a hierarchically arranged network of links between concepts. The concepts are represented as nodes in the network, with each node being associated with a number of properties. One notable feature of Quillian's model was the assumption of *cognitive economy*. This suggested that the properties that apply to a set of concepts are stored at the highest level to which they are generally applicable. Hence, since most birds can fly, rather than attach this property to every instance of a flying bird, it is more economical to attach it to the general concept BIRD. In the case of birds that do not fly, this is represented at the node relevant to that particular bird.

If the system is asked to verify a statement such as "canaries can fly", then the verification involves two stages, first establishing that a canary is a bird, then that birds can fly. Verifying such a sentence is, therefore, assumed to take longer than verifying that a canary is a bird, since the system has to traverse two nodes rather than one. If the critical feature is something that applies to all animals, then it will be stored even higher at the *ANIMAL* node, and this is assumed to take yet longer, since now it is necessary to move from the *CANARY* node to the *BIRD* node and then to the animal node before the necessary information is made available. This prediction was tested directly in a much quoted study by Collins and Quillian (1969).

The study involved presenting subjects with statements of two kinds, one concerned category membership and the second concerned the properties of given instances. A category membership statement could either involve a statement at the same level, such as *A canary is a canary*, a statement involving one level up, *A canary is a bird*, or two levels up, *A canary is an animal*. It was assumed that these sentences would take increasingly long to verify since the first did not involve moving beyond the initial node, the second involved moving one stage and the third two.

A second class of sentence concerned the property of a particular instance, and again it involved properties that were assumed to be stored at the same level since they were not characteristic of all items at the level above (e.g. *Canaries can sing*), or statements that were assumed tobe verifiable in terms of the level above (e.g. "Canaries have wings"), or statements that were assumed to concern a property that was even more general, and was assumed to involve moving yet one stage further up the hierarchy (e.g. "A canary has skin"). The results of the study are shown in Figure 13.4 from which it is clear that the predictions of the TLC model were well supported.

This intriguing and apparently counter-intuitive result generated a great deal of interest. Unfortunately, it subsequently proved to be considerably less neat than at first appeared, with a study by Carol Conrad (1972) suggesting a more plausible interpretation of the Collins and Quillian result than cognitive economy. Conrad began by presenting instances of particular concepts, such as *DALMATIAN, DOG, SHARK, FISH, ANIMAL*, asking subjects to write down as many properties as they could think of in each case. She found that some properties were mentioned very frequently and others very rarely. She then constructed her material so as to ensure that statements that were assumed to be based on information from different levels were *equal* in the frequency with which they had been listed by her subjects. Having taken this precaution, she re-ran the experiment, and found no evidence for longer responses to categories that were assumed to be stored at higher levels.

Conrad's result does not rule out network theories in general, nor indeed the principle of cognitive economy. What it does

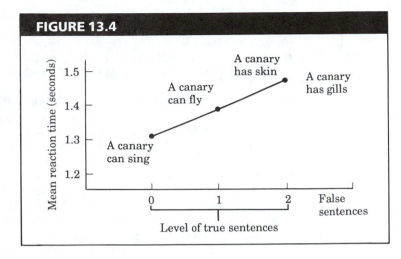

FIGURE 13.4

Average reaction times to saying whether a statement is true or false as a function of the hypothetical distance between the properties in a semantic network hierarchy. From Collins and Quillian (1969).

however, is to show that Collins and Quillian's result could as easily be interpreted in terms of semantic relatedness, which as we saw earlier is one of the few really powerful and robust effects in this field. In order to account for these results, Collins and Quillian would have to explain why semantic relatedness appeared to override the cognitive economy effect, and furthermore to provide additional more robust evidence for cognitive economy. Such evidence is not plentiful, and equivalent studies of my own for example, have typically not shown the differences predicted on the basis of cognitive economy (e.g. Baddeley, Lewis, Eldridge, & Thomson, 1984).

At the same time, other evidence was mounting up that seemed to create problems for Quillian's TLC model. The model assumed that all links were equal in strength; it therefore had difficulty in explaining the very marked tendency for prototypical examples of a category to be verified more rapidly than atypical examples. The link between *BIRD* and *canary* in the TLC model is equivalent to that between *BIRD* and *ostrich*, so why is it quicker to verify that a canary is a bird than that an ostrich is a bird? In the same vein, the TLC model had difficulty in explaining the effects of similarity on negative responses. According to the model, if no link occurs between the two nodes, the subject should give a "no" response. This does not explain why it takes longer to decide that a poodle is not a bird, than to decide that it is not a mineral.

Finally, as Ripps, Shoben, and Smith (1973) point out, the construction of the network in the TLC model is based on logic rather than on empirical evidence. How does one decide where there should be a node? For instance, what about a concept such as *PET*, how could one fit it into the network? And yet it is an entirely appropriate and reasonable concept to hold, and one could very sensibly ask questions about pets in general.

Ripps et al. demonstrate the essential arbitrariness of the

network rather neatly, using the superordinate term *MAMMAL*, which since it is logically a subset of the category *ANIMAL* is presumably lower in the hierarchy. It therefore follows that it should be faster to verify that a *dog* is a *MAMMAL* than that a *dog* is an *ANIMAL*. They tested this and found the reverse to be the case.

Quillian's model is important historically, since it was the first coherent attempt to produce a computer program that would comprehend language. Its assumption of cognitive economy is sensible at one level; if I ask you whether Plato had ears, you would probably answer it on the assumption that Plato was a man and men usually have ears. In short, inference almost certainly does play a role in semantic verification. However, the question of whether it is more economical to infer relatively low-level properties or store them, is one that can not be decided without knowing considerably more about the storage and processing limitations of the brain than we know at present. In general, there appears to be little reason to assume that the type of low-level cognitive economy proposed by Quillian does in fact occur in semantic memory.

Spreading Activation

In response to the many criticisms of the Quillian model, Collins and Loftus introduced a revised network model. This model differed from Quillian's in a number of respects; most notably, it abandoned the assumption of a hierarchical association of semantic nodes, replacing it with a less rigidly structured network. Secondly, in order to account for the many effects of semantic relatedness, it introduced the concept of semantic distance, with highly related concepts being located close together, and distance reflecting the ease with which excitation could flow from one node to the next.

A third major change in the network comprised the introduction of a range of different types of link. These included class membership associations which they label *IS A* links, an example being a *dog is a mammal*. Occasional negative links of this sort were also allowed within the model, to allow for occasions in which the negative information was specifically learnt by the subject; an example might be a *dolphin is not a fish*. Other labeled links include *HAS* links as in an *animal* has skin, *CAN* links as *in a bird can fly* and *CAN NOT* as in the case an *ostrich can not fly* and so forth. The principle of cognitive economy was retained in a much weaker form, so as to allow for the use of inference when no direct information is required, as in our statement *Plato had ears*, but also allowing for such information to be derived directly, should the subject have actually at some point actively encoded the presence of Plato's ears.

In addition to this much richer and more flexible database, Collins and Loftus make some relatively complex assumptions about the processing of information. The basic assumption is that when two concepts are stimulated, activation from each spreads throughout the network until the two concepts are linked. The process of spreading is assumed to take time, hence allowing them to account for the effects of semantic relatedness by assuming that related concepts are closer together. The response, however, is not simply based on the presence or absence of a link; positive and negative evidence is summed, and depending on the criterion set, a "yes" or "no" response is evoked. For example, given the sentence *All animals are dogs*, the presence of an inconsistent instance of one or more animals that are not dogs would be taken into account in coming up with a negative response.

In addition to accounting for the effects of semantic relatedness, which it was of course explicitly designed to do, the Collins and Loftus model is reasonably successful in explaining a number of results involving semantic priming. In one study for example, Meyer and Schvaneveldt (1971) had their subjects deciding whether letter strings were words (e.g. *butter* versus *bunner*). On some occasions, the target item was preceded by another different word; if this word was semantically related to the target however, subjects were significantly faster. Hence subjects were faster at identifying *butter* as a word following *bread*, than following *doctor*. The spreading activation model assumes that because bread and butter are associated, presenting one will lead to excitation flowing to the other, which in turn will lead to its more rapid identification.

Problems and Alternatives

However, although such priming studies appear to give strong support to a spreading activation model, other interpretations are possible. A study by Ratcliff and McKoon (1988) suggests that it is unnecessary to assume a gradual spread of activation. They propose that the priming word and the target combine at retrieval to provide a composite cue that facilitates recall. If the prime and target are associated, as in the case of "bread" and "butter", the match between cue and target is greater, and recall is facilitated. Ratcliff and McKoon argue that this provides a better and more constrained account of the results of their own and other priming experiments than does the concept of spreading activation.

There is no doubt that the Collins and Loftus model is able to account for most of the available data in the area of semantic memory. It does so, however, at the expense of assuming a very complex network and a set of elaborate processing rules. Broadly speaking, there are three criteria that need to be met by a good theory or model; first, it should be able to give an account of the available data, secondly it should do so in a reasonably succinct or parsimonious way, and thirdly it should go beyond the data in suggesting ways in which the phenomena can be further investigated and understood more deeply. The Collins and Loftus model does reasonably well on the first criterion since it does account for available data, but it is not particularly succinct or parsimonious, and in the decade it has been available, it does not seem to have generated much further insight into the problems of semantic memory. Sadly, I am inclined to agree with Kintsch (1980, p.603) in his summing up of the field in 1980:

> So where are we after 10 years of semantic memory? We have an important and well-established experimental phenomenon, the semantic relatedness effect, plus a number of other observations of secondary significance. We have a number of theories that are based on rather different assumptions, but which all explain the experimental phenomena reasonably well (or could be extended in what their authors claim to be minor ways to do so). However, in terms of the issues that really have motivated this research, we have so far not received any clear answers. The impression is unavoidable that questions have been asked in the context of a research paradigm that was simply not rich enough to provide definitive answers.

Kintsch criticizes the poverty of the experimental techniques used in this area, and I am sure he is right in seeing this as a problem. I suspect, however, that there are deeper problems with this area. Two of these are discussed by Johnson-Laird, Herrmann, and Chaffin (1984) who argue that network theories are too powerful, and that they are preoccupied by links between concepts, neglecting the crucial link between such concepts and the world outside the semantic network.

The Symbolic Fallacy

Johnson-Laird et al. argue that, in principle, network theories are so powerful and flexible that they can be made to account for any result. In this respect, network theory is less a theory than a modeling language that will allow a very large number of different models to be constructed. Even so, they argue that a range of phenomena are difficult to model neatly and convincingly in network terms. They cite a number of instances which have in common the feature that the interpretation offered by the network will tend in actual discourse to be overridden by the constraints of real-world knowledge.

Consider the sentence *The ham sandwich was eaten by the soup*. This would appear to be nonsensical since eating requires an animate subject, and soup is inanimate. However, once you are reminded that waiters sometimes label customers on the basis of their order, the sentence immediately becomes understandable.

Another area in which real world knowledge can be crucial concerns the inferences that are drawn in deciding whether a statement is true or not. An inference of the form, *A is on B's right; B is on C's right, therefore A is on C's right*, is valid provided A, B and C are seated down one side of a rectangular table. It may not be true if they are sitting round a circular table.

A network theory can of course always deal with such anomalies by adding further assumptions whenever difficulties arise. Dealing with them in a principled way, however, requires one to break out of the network of interconnections and link into the world. Johnson-Laird et al. refer to this failure to "escape from the maze of symbols into the world" as the *symbolic fallacy*. They illustrate it with the imagined example from science fiction of aliens who are trying to learn the languages of the Earth's inhabitants by listening in to radio transmissions. While they might learn what sounds were most likely to occur they would never learn the semantics of the language, unless they could observe its relationship with the objects and events to which it referred.

SCHEMAS AND FRAMES

Bartlett's Concept of Schema

During the 1970s, it became increasingly obvious that semantic memory must contain structures that were considerably larger than the simple concepts involved in the semantic systems implied by Collins and Loftus and Smith et al. This was not of course a new conclusion. In his classic book *Remembering* published in 1932, Sir Frederic Bartlett proposed an interpretation of memory that assumed that subjects remember new material in terms of existing structures which he termed *schemas* or *schemata*.

The concept of schema was borrowed from a neurologist, Henry Head who used it to represent a person's concept of the location of the limbs and the body. He described it as analogous to having a homunculus inside one's head, keeping track of the position of one's limbs; interpreted more broadly, a person's schema could extend beyond the body to the limits of a car being driven, or as Head points out, to the feather on one's hat. Bartlett generalized this notion far beyond Head's original concept. To Bartlett, a schema referred to an organized structure that captures our knowledge and expectations of some aspect of the world. It is, in other words, a model of some part of our environment and experience.

Bartlett regarded the processes of learning and remembering as essentially active, with the subject showing a constant *effort after meaning*. Applying a schema will typically help the subject to understand since the schema encapsulates what he knows of the world. However, when material is presented that is not readily incorporated into a schema, distortions will occur. Bartlett explored these by presenting his subjects with unfamiliar but structured material, for example a North American Indian folk tale. When subjects recalled the story, they typically distorted it by omitting features that did not fit in with their prior expectations or schemas, and by distorting other features. Hence, an incident where something black came out of the mouth of one of the Indians was often remembered in terms more consistent with the culture of Bartlett's Cambridge subjects, such as the man frothing at the mouth, or his soul leaving his body through his mouth.

Bartlett's work evoked renewed interest, with the return to more naturalistic approaches to memory in the 1960s and 1970s. One of the earlier criticisms of Bartlett's work, however, had been that the concept of a schema was too vague and general to be incorporated into any form of testable theory, although one of Bartlett's ex-students, Carolus Oldfield, suggested as early as 1954 that the development of the computer offered a possible way of developing and elaborating Bartlett's concept of schema. This indeed has proved to be the case, although not until some 20 years after Oldfield's suggestion did schema-based models finally begin to be programmed.

Modern Schema Theories

In 1975, three papers appeared, all of which argued for the importance of knowledge structures that extended beyond the level of an individual concept. Although they did not all use the term schema, all four could be broadly regarded as examples of schema theories. The computer scientist Marvin Minsky (1975, p.211) introduced a schema-like concept which he termed the *frame*, supporting it with the following argument:

> It seems to me that the ingredients of most theories both in artificial intelligence and in psychology have been on the whole too minute, local, and unstructured to account – either practically or phenomen-ologically – for the effectiveness of common sense thought. The "chunks" of reasoning, language, memory, and perception ought to be larger and more structured, and their factual and procedural contents must be more intimately connected in order to explain the apparent power of mental activities.

The second paper was by Rumelhart (1975) and was concerned with an approach to memory for stories using an elaboration of Bartlett's schema notion. The third was a paper by Schank (1975), a computer scientist who introduced the concept of *scripts*, schemas that encapsulate much of our knowledge of social activity.

Although all these approaches were not identical, nevertheless there is a good deal in common between the concept of a frame, a script and a schema. The broad characteristics shared by these are summarized by Rumelhart and Norman (1985) as follows:

Schemas have Variables
Schemas are packets of information that comprise a fixed core and a variable aspect. Hence, a schema for buying something in a shop would have as a relatively fixed feature the exchange of money and goods, but as a variable the amount of money and the actual goods. In particular cases, a variable may be left unspecified, and in this

case it can often be filled by what is termed a default value. This constitutes what might be termed a best guess given the information available. Hence, given a sentence like *The man drank the coffee*, we would probably assume that the coffee was hot unless it were otherwise specified, so for this situation we would be providing a default value for the temperature of the coffee.

Schemas can Embed One Within Another
Schemas are not mutually exclusive packages of information, but can be nested. Rumelhart and Norman give the example of the schema for a head which contains a face, ears, hair, etc. A face itself has a schema that comprises eyes, nose, mouth, and an eye, in turn would have a schema that comprises an iris, an upper and lower eyelid and eyelashes, etc.

Schemas Represent Knowledge at all Levels of Abstraction
The concept of schema is very broadly applicable, from abstract ideologies and concepts such as justice, to very concrete schema such as that for the appearance of a face.

Schemas Represent Knowledge Rather than Definitions
Schemas comprise the knowledge and experience that we have of the world, they do not consist of abstract rules.

Schemas are Active Recognition Devices
This is very reminiscent of Bartlett's original emphasis on effort after meaning.

There have been a number of approaches to comprehension that have used schema concepts. Typically each one is complex and ambitious. They include the already cited work by Minsky, Rumelhart, and Norman and Schank and Abelson, in addition to ambitious enterprises by Kintsch who has carried out an extensive programme of research on comprehension and John Anderson who has elaborated and developed a model originally devised by Anderson and Bower, and attempted to use it across an impressively wide range of situations. For the present purposes, however, I shall limit discussion to a brief overview of two approaches, one concerned with capturing the schematic structure of stories (Rumelhart, 1975), while the other concerns the attempt by Schank and his collaborators to model the social knowledge that underlies efficient communication.

Story Grammars
Bartlett studied the recall of a wide range of different passages, and found marked differences in the amount remembered. On the

whole, descriptions such as an account of part of a cricket match tended to be much less well retained than well-structured narrative stories with a clear plot.

The structures underlying different types of passage are likely to vary, but there was great interest in the late 1970s in the extent to which certain types of passage might have a characteristic structure that could be generated using rules similar to the transformational rules that had been applied to the analysis of syntax, notably by Chomsky (1965).

Rumelhart (1975) attempted to capture the structure of traditional folk tales using what he termed a "story grammar". This essentially involves producing a series of rules that capture the structure of stories, allowing them to be analyzed and compared. A number of related grammars were subsequently developed, one of which was used by Mandler and Johnson (1977) to analyze a range of existing folk tales. Table 13.1 gives a summary of the rules for their simple story grammar. Within the table, each arrow means that the concept on the left can be broken down into the subcomponents on the right. Hence a fable can be regarded as a story with a moral. The story itself can be broken into a setting and an event structure, with each of these being broken down into smaller components. Table 13.2 gives an example of such a story, and Figure 13.6 illustrates the analysis of the story.

Mandler and Johnson discuss the characteristics of a well-formed story, and go on to apply their analysis to a number of conventional stories and to *The War of the Ghosts*, the Indian folk tale that Bartlett had studied. Their analysis indicates a number of anomalous features in the story, including the fact that many of the connections between components which one would normally expect to be causal are simply specified temporally. Table 13.3 and Figure 13.6 show the passage and Mandler and Johnson's analysis of it. A particularly clear instance of a link that one might expect to be causal but which is simply temporal occurs at lines 26 and 27, where the link between concluding that the assailants are ghosts, and the protagonist not feeling sick, is far from clear for most readers. Some evidence for the validity of this interpretation comes from Bartlett's own data, where subjects recalled a mean of 0.61 causally connected episodes compared to 0.48 of the episodes that were connected temporally.

Another curious feature of the story is that despite the title, ghosts do not appear until line 26, where as we saw earlier they are introduced in a somewhat arbitrary way. An earlier study by Paul (1959) introduced the concept of ghosts as the second proposition, and omitted the arbitrary sequences, producing a higher overall level of recall.

Thorndyke (1977) studied the role of the structure of stories within a story grammar resembling those of Rumelhart and of Mandler and Johnson. He began with an original version of a story which started with a general theme and then elaborated it in a subsequent narrative. A second version of the story *(narrative–*

TABLE 13.1

Summary of Rewrite Rules for a Simple Story Grammar

FABLE → STORY AND MORAL

STORY → SETTING AND EVENT STRUCTURE

SETTING → $\begin{bmatrix} \text{STATE (AND EVENT)} \\ \text{EVENT} \end{bmatrix}$

STATE → STATE ((AND STATE))

EVENT → EVENT $\left(\left(\begin{bmatrix} \text{AND} \\ \text{THEN} \\ \text{CAUSE} \end{bmatrix} \text{EVENTS}\right)\right)$ ((AND STATE))

EVENT STRUCTURE → EPISODE ((THEN EPISODE))

EPISODE → BEGINNING CAUSE DEVELOPMENT CAUSE ENDING

BEGINNING → $\begin{bmatrix} \text{EVENT} \\ \text{EPISODE} \end{bmatrix}$

DEVELOPMENT → $\begin{bmatrix} \text{SIMPLE REACTION CAUSE ACTION} \\ \text{COMPLEX REACTION CAUSE GOAL PATH} \end{bmatrix}$

SIMPLE REACTION → INTERNAL EVENT ((CAUSE INTERNAL EVENT))

ACTION → EVENT

COMPLEX REACTION → SIMPLE REACTION CAUSE GOAL

GOAL → INTERNAL STATE

GOAL PATH → $\begin{bmatrix} \text{ATTEMPT CAUSE OUTCOME} \\ \text{GOAL PATH (CAUSE GOAL PATH)} \end{bmatrix}$

ATTEMPT → EVENT

OUTCOME → $\begin{bmatrix} \text{EVENT} \\ \text{EPISODE} \end{bmatrix}$

ENDING → $\begin{bmatrix} \text{EVENT (AND EMPHASIS)} \\ \text{EMPHASIS} \\ \text{EPISODE} \end{bmatrix}$

EMPHASIS → STATE

Source: Mandler and Johnson (1977).

TABLE 13.2

Dog Story. An Example of a Simple Story

1. It happened that a dog had got a piece of meat
2. and was carrying it home in his mouth.
3. Now on his way home he had to cross a plank lying across a stream.
4. As he crossed he looked down
5. and saw his own shadow reflected in the water beneath.
6. Thinking it was another dog with another piece of meat,
7. he made up his mind to have that also.
8. So he made a snap at the shadow,
9. but as he opened his mouth the piece of meat fell out,
10. dropped into the water,
11. and was never seen again.

Source: Mandler and Johnson (1977).

A representation of the underlying structure of the Dog story. The connections AND, THEN, and CAUSE have been abbreviated to A, T, and C, and encircled. The numbers under the terminal nodes refer to the surface statements of the story. From Mandler and Johnson (1977).

FIGURE 13.5

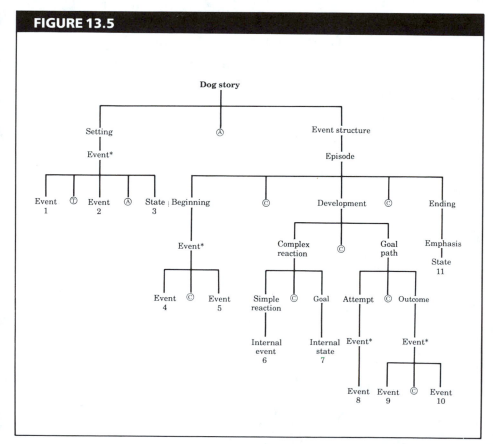

TABLE 13.3

"The War of the Ghosts"   — *Mandler & Johnson*

1. One night two young men from Egulac went down to the river to hunt seals
2. and while they were there it became foggy and calm.
3. They heard war cries,
4. and they thought, "Maybe this is a war party."
5. They escaped to the shore
6. and hid behind a log.
7. Now canoes came up,
8. and they heard the noise of paddles
9. and saw one canoe coming up to them.
10. There were five men in the canoe,
11. and they said, "What do you think? We wish to take you along.
12. We are going up the river to make war on the people."
13. One of the young men said, "I have no arrows."
14. "Arrows are in the canoe," they said
15. "I will not go along.
16. I might be killed.
17. My relatives do not know where I have gone.
18. But you," he said, turning to the other, "may go with them."
19. So one of the young men went,
20. but the other returned home.
21. And the warriors went on up the river to a town on the other side of Kalama.
22. The people came down to the water,
23. and they began to fight,
24. and many were killed.
25. But presently the young man heard one of the warriors say, "Quick, let us go home; that Indian has been hit."
26. Now he thought, "Oh, they are ghosts."
27. He did not feel sick,
28. but they said he had been shot.
29. So the canoes went back to Egulac,
30. and the young man went ashore to his house and made a fire.
31. And he told everybody and said, "Behold, I accompanied the ghosts, and we went to a fight.
32. Many of our fellows were killed,
33. and many of those who attacked us were killed.
34. And they said I was hit
35. and I did not feel sick."
36. He told it all,
37. and then he became quiet.
38. When the sun rose he fell down.
39. Something black came out of his mouth.
40. His face became contorted.
41. The people jumped up and cried.
42. He was dead.

Source: Mandler and Johnson (1977).

FIGURE 13.6

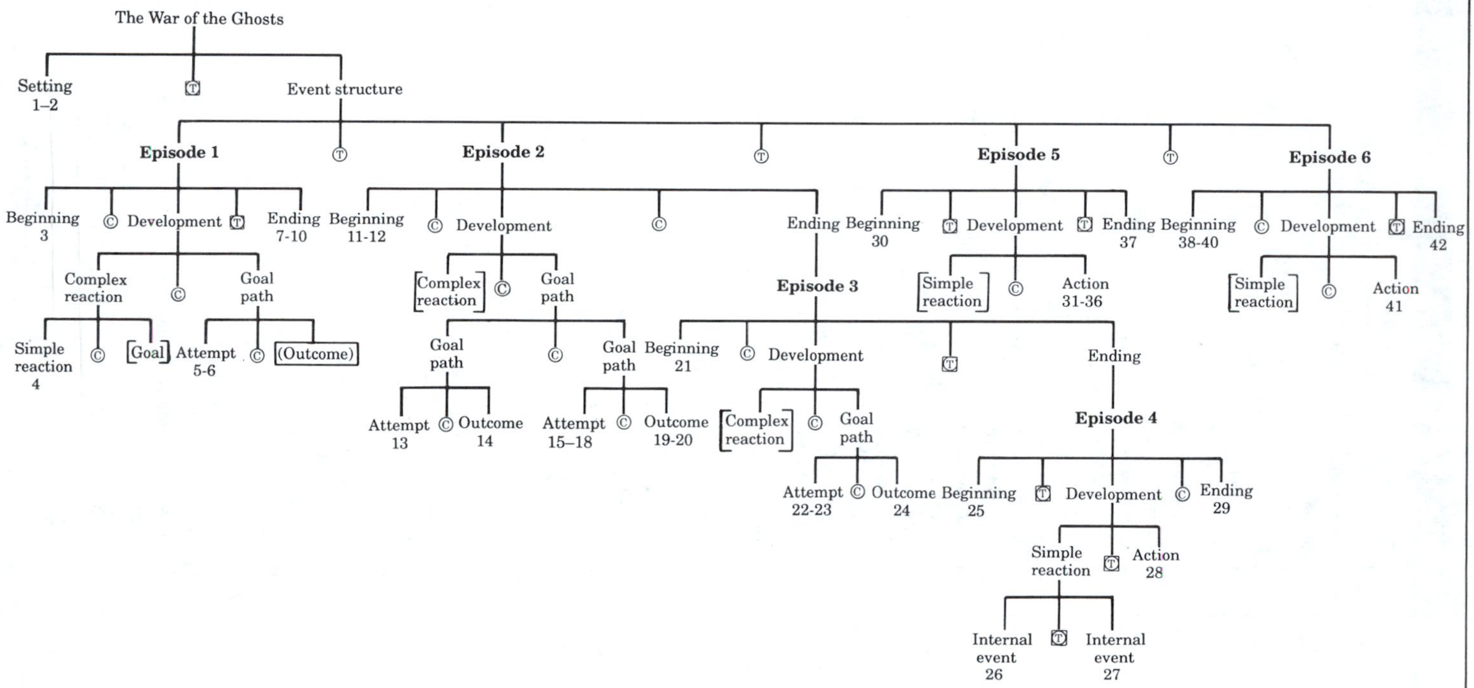

The War of the Ghosts
Setting 1–2
T
Event structure
Episode 1
T
Episode 2
T
Episode 5
T
Episode 6
Beginning 3
C
Development
T
Ending 7-10
Beginning 11-12
C
Development
C
Ending
Beginning 30
T
Development
T
Ending 37
Beginning 38-40
C
Development
T
Ending 42
Complex reaction
C
Goal path
Complex reaction
C
Goal path
Episode 3
Simple reaction
C
Action 31-36
Simple reaction
C
Action 41
Simple reaction 4
C
Goal
Attempt 5-6
C
(Outcome)
Goal path
C
Goal path
Beginning 21
C
Development
T
Ending
Attempt 13
C
Outcome 14
Attempt 15–18
C
Outcome 19-20
Complex reaction
C
Goal path
Episode 4
Attempt 22-23
C
Outcome 24
Beginning 25
T
Development
C
Ending 29
Simple reaction
T
Action 28
Internal event 26
T
Internal event 27

FIGURE 13.7

Recall probabilities for propositions from the "Circle Island" passages as a function of location in the organizational hierarchy. From Thorndyke (1977).

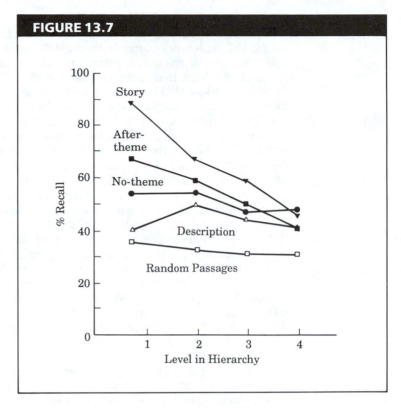

after theme) was identical except that the theme was not introduced until after the narrative, while a third version *(narrative–no theme)* omitted a statement about the theme altogether. A fourth condition *(description)* randomized the order of sentences within the passage, deleting any temporal or causal links. Figure 13.7 shows the overall recall data for one such passage, an account of an imaginary country called Circle Island. Three conclusions can be drawn:

1. There is a tendency for the successive disturbances of the grammatical structure of the passage to lead to successively poorer levels of recall.
2. Propositions that are important to the comprehension of the passage tend to be better recalled.
3. This interacts with structure, with level of proposition being of clear importance in recalling the original story, but completely absent in the less structured description passages.

Opposite page: A simplified representation of the War of the Ghosts *story. Only basic nodes are shown. Violations are enclosed in boxes. From Mandler and Johnson (1977).*

Thorndyke showed that both rated comprehensibility and amount recalled increased as stories became more structured. Finally, when asked to summarize the story from memory, subjects tended to emphasize general structural content rather than specific content, a finding that echoes the earlier observation of Gomulicki (1956) that the processes of recalling and of summarizing prose passages give very similar results.

Schank: Scripts, MOPs and TOPs

Schank and Abelson (1977) suggest that we develop schemas or scripts that represent commonly experienced social events such as catching a bus or going to a restaurant. These allow us to fill in much of the detail that is not specified in text. For example, a statement such as "We had a tandoori chicken at the Taj Mahal last night. The service was slow and we almost missed the start of the play", is interpretable only by bringing in a great deal of additional information. The suggestion that I am eating an Indian meal implies that the Taj Mahal is the name of a restaurant, and not that I had flown over to Agra in order to spend the evening at the world-famous tomb. That in turn implies that I went into the restaurant, probably was shown a seat, and so forth and so on, in short that I used a restaurant script. Table 13.4 shows a theoretical listing of such a script and what might be contained in it. By using implicit default values you can probably conclude a good deal about exactly what went on, since you and I probably share a broadly similar restaurant script. This will not of course be the case if you have lived all your life in the jungles of Borneo and never eaten in a restaurant; scripts are essentially ways of summarizing common cultural assumptions. In this respect they are very useful not only for understanding discourse, but also for predicting what will happen in the future, and enabling one to behave appropriately in given social situations. Part of the fun, and also the frustration of being in another culture, is the way in which well-practised scripts, such as are involved in buying postage stamp or cashing a cheque at a bank, unexpectedly cease to work in quite the way you expect.

Schank and Abelson (1977) built their scripts into a computer program, SAM, and showed that it was capable of answering questions about restaurants, and interpreting restaurant stories. The extent to which the concept of a script helps us understand human memory was explored by Bower, Black, and Turner (1979) who began by asking people to give an account of activities such as going to restaurants. They found that these did broadly agree with the scripts postulated by Schank and Abelson. When such scripts were incorporated in stories, then the sort of distortion that might be expected from the Schank and Abelson model were observed; people tended to falsely recall aspects of the passage that had not explicitly been presented, but which were consistent with the script; when the passage presented details in an order that was inconsistent with the script, subjects tended to change the order to fit what would be expected. Such distortions were of course exactly the sort of error that Bartlett's subjects made, and that initially encouraged him to develop the concept of the schema.

One limitation to the concept of a script however is that it is essentially conservative, storing what one already knows, and as such can only be a partial account of normal memory. Bower et al. noted that their subjects were much better at remembering deviations from the script, for example a waiter bringing fish when you had ordered steak, than at recalling events that were

---

TABLE 13.4

A Simplified Version of Schank and Abelson's (1977) Schematic Representation of Activities involved in Going to a Restaurant

Name:	Restaurant	**Roles:**	Customer
Props:	Tables		Waiter
	Menu		Cook
	Food		Cashier
	Bill		Owner
	Money		
	Tip		

Entry conditions:	Customer is hungry.	**Results:**	Customer has less money.
	Customer has money.		Owner has more money.
			Customer is not hungry.

Scene 1: *Entering*
Customer enters restaurant.
Customer looks for table.
Customer decides where to sit.
Customer goes to table.
Customer sits down.

Scene 2: *Ordering*
Customer picks up menu.
Customer looks at menu.
Customer decides on food.
Customer signals waitress.
Waitress comes to table.
Customer orders food.
Waitress goes to cook.
Waitress gives food order to cook.
Cook prepares food.

Scene 3: *Eating*
Cook gives food to waitress.
Waitress brings food to customer.
Customer eats food.

Scene 4: *Exiting*
Waitress writes bill.
Waitress goes over to customer.
Waitress gives bill to customer.
Customer gives tip to waitress.
Customer goes to cashier.
Customer gives money to cashier.
Customer leaves restaurant.

Source: Bower, Black, and Turner (1979).

---

consistent with the normal script. Indeed, Brewer and Lichtenstein (1981) who had their subjects rate various passages, found that those which conformed to a script without deviation were rated as not at all like stories.

Schank (1982) therefore attempted to extend his earlier work so as to take account of the more dynamic aspects of memory. One piece of evidence that concerned him was the observation by Bower et al. (1979) that subjects would sometimes make confusion errors between two similar scripts, such as going to a doctor and going to a dentist. Clearly, although we do not on the whole make such confusion errors in practice, we are quite capable of noticing analogies between one situation and another, despite the fact that the specifics might be quite different. Freud's observation of analogy between the Oedipus legend in which Oedipus marries his mother and kills his father, and the pattern of loves and jealousies within the family revealed by his patients, is one instance of this.

Similar broad situational analogies also tend to occur at a rather mundane level. Schank gives the example of noticing someone waiting in a long queue at the Post Office to buy a single stamp, saying that it spontaneously reminded him of people who go into petrol stations just to buy a small amount of petrol. What these two have in common presumably is that the actor is deviating from an expected script in an analogous way, undertaking a lengthy procedure for a small item. Schank suggests that memory for incidents may be largely driven by noting such exceptions to existing scripts.

This more dynamic model of remembering incorporates a range of new concepts including *plans, scenes, memory organization packets* (MOPs) and *thematic organization points* (TOPs). *Plans* for example comprise specific motivations and goals. Consider the following instance taken from Rumelhart and Norman (1985): "John knew that his wife's operation would be very expensive. There was always Uncle Harry…. He reached for the suburban 'phone book." Most people reading this assume that John is hoping to borrow money from Uncle Harry in order to pay for his wife's operation. They presumably reach this conclusion because of the combination on the one hand of a problem, paying for the operation, and an implied solution, contacting Uncle Harry. The implication is that reaching for the telephone book is a subgoal concerned with telephoning Uncle Harry, which in turn is a subgoal of the major problem of finding money, which in turn is a subgoal of attempting to allow John's wife to have the necessary operation.

Scenes represent the general structure within which particular actions take place, and will comprise a setting, a goal and the actions attempting to reach a goal, while each scene may form part of one or probably many *memory organization packets* or MOPs. Figure 13.8 shows the three MOPs contributing to the scene representing going to the dentist. Note that each MOP can contribute to more than one scene in somewhat different ways, hence the MOP concerned with health protection might also be

Example of the interconnection of three memory organization packets (MOPs) in the structuring of the scenes (bottom line) for a visit to a dentist. From Schank (1982).

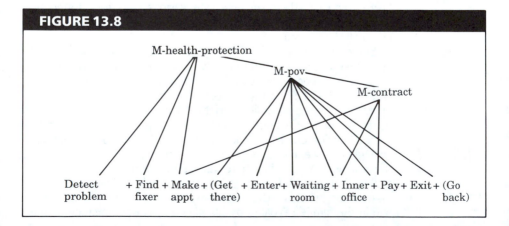

FIGURE 13.8

M-health-protection

M-pov

M-contract

Detect problem   + Find fixer   + Make appt   + (Get there)   + Enter   + Waiting room   + Inner office   + Pay   + Exit   + (Go back)

involved in a scene concerned with immunization against a disease, while the MOP concerned with a contract would be involved in a wide range of activities including, for example, booking a room in a hotel. Schank suggests that MOPs are themselves organized into *metaMOPs* on the basis of higher level structures. The metaMOP representing trips for example might involve the activation of MOPs concerned with aeroplanes, hotels and meetings.

Finally, at a even more abstract level, Schank postulates *thematic organization points* or TOPs. These represent the higher level analogies that exist between situations which are different in detail, but related in structure; the Oedipus and stamp-buying examples described earlier would be instances of the operation of TOPs.

There is no doubt that the social environment within which we operate has a major effect on the way in which we remember. Schank's work is distinguished by a coherent and consistent effort over a period of years to attempt to understand this aspect of memory, and to capture that understanding in the form of well worked out and functioning computer programs. Whatever its ultimate success, it represents a major attack on an important problem.

THE NEUROPSYCHOLOGY OF SEMANTIC MEMORY

Aphasia, Agnosia, and Semantics

In contrast to the analysis of working memory and long-term memory, our discussion of semantic memory has so far made little reference to evidence from neuropsychology. This is because there has so far been relatively little interaction between the theoretical approaches discussed, and neuropsychological evidence, the links being much more strongly connected with linguistics and computer science. I believe that this is likely to change in the next few years, and hence the final section of this chapter will be concerned with some of the fascinating evidence yielded by neuropsychology as to the probable structure and function of semantic memory.

The evidence comes from studies of *aphasia*, which involves a breakdown in the use of language, and *agnosia*, a deficit in object perception, two areas which might not at first sight appear to be closely relevant to semantic memory. However, in both cases, adequate performance involves linking a peripheral stimulus, whether an object or a word, to its meaning, and while some aphasic and agnosic deficits may reflect relatively peripheral perceptual impairment, others are almost certainly the result of problems in semantic processing. I would like to suggest that such problems give important clues as to the way in which semantic memory is organized, and as such are likely to provide valuable constraints on some of the models that have been proposed.

Let us begin with the case of G.L., an 80-year-old salesman who one day was blown by a strong wind against a fence. Following his accident he felt unwell, and complained of difficulties in seeing. Subsequent examination revealed that his visual acuity was normal, and that he could copy objects quite accurately. However, his ability to recognize objects was severely impaired; he mistook his jacket for his trousers, for example, and on another occasion perceived pictures on the wall as boxes and attempted to take things out of them. This case, described in 1888 by Lissauer, was the first detailed report of a patient suffering from agnosia. It is reproduced in translation, together with an introduction by Shallice and Jackson (Lissauer, 1988; Shallice & Jackson, 1988).

The problem appeared to be one of accessing the meaning of objects from their appearance, but did not involve a general semantic deficit; for example, he could not recognize a whistle by sight, but did recognize it from its sound. While perceptual and language deficits may often be rather general, reflecting damage to many aspects of the perceptual or language system, single cases occur in which the deficit is quite limited. These "experiments of nature" in which a small and constrained part of the system is defective, are particularly revealing theoretically.

In addition to patients suffering problems of visual recognition, cases have been identified of specific deficits in other modalities. For example Beauvois, Saillant, Meininger, and Lhermitte (1978) describe a patient who could name objects presented visually but not when presented by touch. This was not a disorder of recognition since the patient could demonstrate the use of the objects, for example using scissors to cut with, but could not access the appropriate name. In other cases, the opposite pattern occurs with subjects being unable to name items presented visually, but able to provide their names when given the opportunity of exploring by touch (Beauvois, 1982).

Such results suggest that semantic memory is not a single unitary system, but rather has a number of subcomponents associated with the modality through which the information reaches semantic memory. Note also that the problem encountered by Lissauer's patient was not simply one of naming, but of recognizing, whereas the patients described by Beauvois et al. appeared to know what the object was that they were perceiving, demonstrating its use appropriately, but could not access the name. This in turn suggests that we should distinguish between the meaning of an object and its name, a distinction that did of course crop up in the discussion on retrieval from long-term memory. The fact that an object can be named when presented in one modality but not in another, suggests that the deficit is not simply one of having lost the name, but rather losing access to it from a given modality.

The evidence we have discussed so far indicates the need to assume different routes into semantics from different modalities, suggesting both that an adequate characterization of semantic memory will need to take account of the contributing perceptual systems, and also that any adequate account of object or word recognition will need to take account of the role of semantic memory.

Suppose we consider a single input modality such as that of the visual presentation of objects, or the auditory presentation of words, does the neuropsychological evidence tells us anything about these processes? In the case of object recognition, it indicates that the process may break down either at the level of perceptually organizing the object, or at the level of accessing its meaning. This distinction is illustrated rather neatly in a study by Warrington and Taylor (1978) in which subjects were given a picture of an object (e.g. a tennis racquet), and asked to choose one of two other pictures on the basis of which was most closely associated in function. For example, the subject might be shown a tennis racquet then given the choice of a tennis ball or a frying pan. Warrington and Taylor found two distinct types of deficit on this task, some subjects simply failed to recognize the object as a tennis racquet, and would select the frying pan as the closest match; these were patients with predominantly right hemisphere damage. Other subjects were quite successful in perceiving the nature of the object but were not able to make the semantic association between racquet and ball. These patients typically had left hemisphere lesions.

A similar distinction between pre-semantic and semantic processing deficits is shown in the case of two studies of aphasia. Both of these concern patients who had difficulty in naming objects. In one of these (Kay & Ellis, 1987), the deficit appeared to be independent of the semantic processing system; pictures of objects that could not be named could nevertheless be categorized quite accurately in semantic terms. One task for example involved showing the patient a picture of a pyramid, and a palm tree and deciduous tree, and asking which tree goes with the pyramid. Despite an inability to name the items however, this patient had no difficulty in performing this semantic matching task. Probability of naming an item was, however, influenced by the frequency of the target word in the language. Kay and Ellis suggest that the problem with this patient is not one of accessing the meaning of the picture, but of moving from meaning to the spoken word, they suggest that the degree of excitation transmitted to the lexicon or set of spoken word forms is not sufficient to trigger off infrequent words, but is sufficient to allow the output of common words which appear to have a lower threshold of excitation.

This pattern of naming problems can be contrasted with that of a patient who also had difficulty in naming objects (Howard & Orchard-Lisle, 1984). For this patient the probability of correctly naming a picture could be substantially increased by providing the initial letter of the name. The authors noted that their patient could be induced to make errors, if the initial letter was appropriate for the name of a semantically related item. Hence, if the subject was shown a picture of a tiger and given the letter L, the response "lion" tended to be made. When the experimenter provided an incorrect but semantically plausible name, for example showing a picture of a tiger and saying "Is this a lion?" on 56% of occasions the subject would say yes, compared to only 2% errors when the name was semantically unrelated to the picture. Howard and Orchard-Lisle conclude that their patient has an impairment in the system responsible for semantic representation of meaning, an impairment that is not total, but which results in an impoverished representation of the meaning of an object. Because of its lack of precision, the subject can be induced to accept an incorrect word as appropriate to that representation, as in the case of accepting lion for a picture of a tiger.

These two aphasic patients thus both appear to have a naming difficulty, but the first seems to be able to make subtle semantic distinctions, suggesting a problem in accessing the name, while the second seems to suffer from an impoverished semantic represent-ation of items rather than a problem at the name level. It is of course a pity that the same tests were not given to both patients. This is probably because this area of cognitive neuropsychology is still at an early stage of theoretical development. While such cases have been recognized for over a century, it is only recently that the link with models of semantic memory has begun tobe explored, with the result that methods of testing and analysis are still developing (see Ellis & Young, 1988 and Humphreys & Riddoch, 1987).

The Organization of Semantic Memory

The evidence presented so far suggests two sets of distinctions, the first based on modality of input, while the second concerns the question of whether the deficit occurs during early processing or within the semantic store itself. Suppose we consider cases in which the deficit is within the store, can the nature of such deficits tell us anything about the way in which semantic storage is organized?

Goodglass, Klein, Carey, and Jones (1966) observed that the naming problems of a range of aphasic patients differed from one to the other, with some subjects finding certain types of words such as colors or body parts particularly hard, while others would find difficult with nouns of a different kind, for example, the names of foods or of kitchen implements. This observation was made before the development of research on semantic memory, and hence tended not to be tied in with the memory literature. It was only in the 1970s that Elizabeth Warrington and her colleagues began to re-explore the phenomenon and realize its implications for the understanding of semantic memory.

In one study, Warrington and Shallice (1984) describe a series of four encephalitic patients who developed brain damage leading to semantic memory problems following the infection of the brain by a herpes virus. These patients were all characterized by a problem in understanding words that referred to living things, while being comparatively normal in processing the names of inanimate objects. For example, given the task of defining words, one such patient, J.B.R. could provide excellent definitions for inanimate objects such as *briefcase*—"small case used by students to carry papers", or *torch*—"hand-held light", but had great difficulty with animate objects, producing either nothing or a very impoverished definition, examples being *daffodil*—"plant", and *ostrich*—"unusual".

It is often the case with patients showing impaired semantic memory that they can produce the superordinate of the item presented, as in the case *daffodil*— "plant". This lends some independent support to the view that semantic memory may be hierarchically organized, as Collins and Quillian suggested. When the system is damaged, then the capacity to access the lower and more detailed nodes of the semantic system is grossly reduced, but the subject still appears to be able to move up to the higher level concepts. This effect is shown in Table 13.5 which shows J.B.R.'s performance on a picture-naming task. Note that he is substantially poorer on living things than on non-living, but that his capacity to come up with a superordinate is still relatively preserved.

While the cases described by Warrington and Shallice all showed this characteristic of finding living objects harder to define than inanimate objects, other patients show other patterns, including the opposite tendency for animate objects to be better named than inanimate (e.g. Nielson, 1946). Such a "double dissociation" with two opposite deficits demonstrated, is important since it allows us to rule out an interpretation that argues that animate objects are simply more difficult to name, and hence more sensitive to any impairment in performance.

The Warrington and Shallice study seems to suggest a broad division of semantic memory into animate and inanimate, but other studies have shown a much finer breakdown. For example, Hart, Berndt, and Caramazza (1985) describe a patient, M.D., who has a particular problem in naming fruit and vegetables. This patient could name such infrequent objects as an abacus and a sphinx, but not an orange or a peach. The problem appeared to be principally

TABLE 13.5

Visual Identification of Foods and Inanimate Objects by Patient J.B.R.

Foods		*Inanimate Objects*	
Identified	Named	Identified	Named
20%	20%	87%	40%

Source: Warrington and Shallice (1984).

one of accessing the name of the object, since M.D. could categorize and sort pictures of the fruits and vegetables that he was unable to name.

The Relation Between Semantic and Autobiographical Memory

Category-specific deficits then are beginning to tell us something about the way in which semantic memory is organized. Before discussing the conclusions that can be drawn from such studies, however, we should consider one more particularly intriguing single case study, that of L.P., a 44-year-old Italian lady who suffered a semantic memory deficit following encephalitis (De Renzi, Liotti, & Nichelli, 1987). L.P. had normal perception and STM performance; her speech and syntax were also normal, but she showed impaired knowledge of word meanings. She also had naming difficulties, being able to correctly name only 5 out of 60 objects, although she could often demonstrate the use of the object. She was also impaired in giving the definitions of words, scoring 36 out of 62; her errors on occasion were quite odd, for example *lemon*— "used by people who study", and *violin*— "used to color glass". On other occasions, she would have some knowledge of the meaning of a word, but be rather hazy on its detailed characteristics; hence she knew that an elephant was an animal, she was able to categorize it as having four legs, but when asked as to its size described it as "rather small", and when asked if it had tusks replied "I can't imagine". Similarly, when given a sensory characteristic and asked to generate items she also tended to be very poor. For example, when asked to produce red objects her response was "apple, orange, mouth, eyes".

So far then, her pattern of performance is not too different from that of a number of other patients already described who have problems in semantic memory. The interesting feature of L.P. however, was the dissociation that occurred in her recollection of incidents from the past, where she seemed to show extremely poor recall of public events, coupled with rather good memory for events that were more autobiographical in nature. She did not know who Garibaldi was, or Mussolini, both of which would have been extremely familiar figures to modern Italians. She remembered little or nothing of the assassination of a recent Italian Prime Minister, and could not recall a very dramatic incident whereby a boy had fallen into a pit and after many days of attempted rescue died.

Her autobiographical memory was investigated by means of a questionnaire constructed with the aid of her relatives, that concerned the events of her life, from childhood to the present. She was able to give precise and accurate responses to virtually all the questions, responses that agreed with the information provided by her family. Those public events that she could remember appeared to be characterized by having had some personal significance. For example, she remembered the Chernobyl nuclear disaster because she had had to refrain from eating the vegetables that she had been growing at that time, while a British royal wedding was remembered because she felt that "The poor boy had been ensnared by a girl whose past history was not immaculate", something she was afraid might happen to her own son.

De Renzi et al. suggest that autobiographical memory and memories related to the self may be stored in a somewhat separate domain of long-term memory, just as fruit and vegetables may reflect a separate domain of semantic memory from animals or kitchen implements, and that this particular aspect of L.P.'s semantic system may have been comparatively spared.

Domains of Semantic Memory

The idea that semantic memory is divided up into domains is one that also fits much of the remaining data in this area. Warrington and Shallice (1984), for example, have suggested that the pattern of semantic deficits may reflect the pattern of sensory dimensions that contribute to the encoding of different classes of items. In the case of items such as fruit and vegetables for instance, then the characteristics of color and taste are likely to be important features, whereas kitchen utensils or furniture are largely defined in terms of their function. If one assumes that different parts of the brain tend to be associated somewhat more strongly with different perceptual input dimensions, and different associative and output characteristics, then one might well end up with a system that was loosely structured (see Shallice, 1988, chapter 12). Items related to the self could be one such domain.

There is some evidence to suggest that, from a computational viewpoint, such clustering will tend to give rise to a relatively efficient system. If features that are likely to occur together are stored closely together, then the links between them will be short and encoding will be rapid, in contrast to the longer and slower links between items that are used together less frequently. Some of the newly developing connectionist models such as that of Kohonen (1984) appear to have this characteristic, as does the proposed overview of memory presented by Minsky (1985) who suggests that: "We keep each thing we learn close to the agents that learn it in the first place. That way, our knowledge becomes easy to reach and easy to use". The theory is based on the idea of a type of agent called a *Knowledge-line* or *K-line* for short. Minsky (1985, p.82) illustrates this using an analogy suggested by a student, Kenneth Haase:

> You want to repair a bicycle. Before you start, smear your hands with red paint. Then every tool you use will end up with red marks on it. When you're done, just remember that red means "good for fixing bicycles". Next time you fix a bicycle you can save time by taking all the red marked tools in advance.

> If you use different colors for different jobs, some tools will end up marked with several colors, that is each agent can be attached to many different K-lines. Later, when there's a job to do, just activate the proper K-line for that kind of job, and all the tools used in the past for similar jobs will automatically become available.

There are welcome signs that with the growth of the interdisciplinary area of cognitive science, there is an increasing concern to develop models that are both computationally adequate from the artificial intelligence viewpoint, and biologically plausible. I would be surprised if the next few years did not see a considerably increased impact of neuropsychological data on psychological and computational models of semantic memory. The development is likely to have the highly desirable effect of reducing the susceptibility of the field to the symbolic fallacy, whereby semantic memory is seen as a rich network of associations between abstract or verbal components, with no connection with the world. The semantic system is part of the processes that have evolved for seeing, hearing and acting; the neuropsychological evidence suggests that we are unlikely to come up with an adequate conceptualization of semantic memory unless we take this into account.

OVERVIEW

Semantic memory is the system whereby we store knowledge of the world. Attempts to study it have been strongly influenced by theories from linguistics and computer science, while some of its conceptual problems, such as the nature of meaning have preoccupied philosophers for centuries.

A good deal of work in recent years has been concerned with the understanding of semantic concepts, with attempts made to use hierarchical structures based on logical analysis as psychological models. In general, it seems clear that the classical theory that attempts to specify precisely each example of a concept in terms of clear features is not suitable for natural language categories, and this approach has been succeeded in popularity by prototype theory. This accepts that natural categories often have fuzzy boundaries, but assumes that exemplars of a given category tend to have many overlapping features.

Attempts to produce models of semantic memory developed during the 1960s and 1970s, often linked with the aim of designing computer programs that will comprehend language. Early models such as that of Quillian had difficulty in explaining the empirical data, and were replaced by more limited models concerned with explaining single tasks, and by more general semantic network theories. While these were more successful in explaining the available evidence in a *post hoc* manner, they have been criticized as being so powerful as to be in principle untestable. They have also been accused of neglecting the link between the semantic system and the outside world, the so-called symbolic fallacy.

Other models have attempted to develop and elaborate the concept of a schema or knowledge structure that captures the subject's knowledge and assumptions about the world. Two examples of schema theory are discussed, one concerned with story grammars, which attempts to encapsulate the characteristic features of stories, the other concerns Schank's attempt to represent our social norms and expectations within a computer model.

The chapter ends by considering the neuropsychological evidence for the nature of semantic memory, citing data from patients with language and perceptual deficits that appear to reflect deficits in the systems responsible for the interface between perception, language and meaning. It is suggested that such evidence may well play an important part in the further development of models of semantic memory.

Chapter Fourteen

WHERE NEXT? CONNECTIONISM RIDES AGAIN!

*T*he last five years has seen some revolutionary new developments in the area of learning and memory that are causing great excitement and already generating controversy. They reflect the development of ideas based on the assumptions of the parallel processing of information distributed across many units, and go under the title of *parallel distributed processing* (PDP) or *connectionism*. Many of the ideas are very new, often quite technical, and hence not always easy to understand. Nevertheless, I think that they are sufficiently important that anyone currently studying learning and memory should at least be aware of the new developments, which will I am sure have a considerable impact on our theorizing about the nature of human learning.

The following chapter attempts to place these developments in their historical context, and to give a simplified overview of some of the underlying concepts. A more extended overview is given by Johnson-Laird (1988, chapter 10); a more detailed introduction to connectionism can be found in McClelland and Rumelhart (1986) and Rumelhart and McClelland (1986) and in a special issue of the journal *Cognitive Science* (1985, vol. 9, part 1). It should, however, be borne in mind that the approach remains controversial (see critical papers by Fodor & Pylyshyn, 1988 and by Pinker & Prince, 1988).

THE ROOTS OF CONNECTIONISM

Theories of Learning

In the early years of this century, Edward Thorndike proposed a series of general principles of learning to which he gave the term "connectionism". Essentially these assumed that learning proceeds by means of a series of trial-and-error steps. Successive steps set up associative connections, and those connections that are followed by reward are strengthened or reinforced, increasing the likelihood that given the first step, the second will occur, the so-called *Law of Effect*. Such a general concept has an attractive similarity to the process of natural selection in evolution, with those habits that lead to reward gradually being selected, and those that do not, falling by the wayside. During the 1930s and 1940s, a series of grand theories of learning developed, and the study of learning was dominated by a few major theorists, notably Guthrie, Skinner, Hull and Tolman (see Hilgard, 1948).

Some of the strongest disagreements occurred between theorists like Clark L. Hull, who attempted to produce a set of detailed learning principles based on the concepts of association and reinforcement, and Edward L. Tolman who emphasized the importance of internal representations, or cognitive maps in learning.

And then, in the mid-1950s, with remarkable suddenness, interest in this area waned. The detailed reasons for this are probably best left to the historians of psychology, but as a graduate student who had just arrived on the scene at this time, the problem seemed to be that people lost their belief in the capacity of experimental research to decide between the competing grand theories. There was no doubt that even the humble white rat, the favored subject of the Hullians, was able to demonstrate relatively intelligent-seeming reorganization of recently acquired habits. For example, when one arm of a complex maze was blocked, the rat was quite able to behave apparently intelligently and select the next best route. Such results were quite consistent with Tolman's views that the rat had formed some kind of internal map, but could they be fitted by the more complex associationist approach? The answer seemed to be yes, provided that the theorists were allowed to postulate so-called "mediating responses". Unfortunately, however, no one knew how to investigate these. Since the major criticism of the Tolmanians had been that the so-called cognitive maps were impossible to investigate, the postulation of internal representations by the associationists seemed to leave both sides with theories that were basically untestable, and hence likely to prove scientifically unfruitful.

Since that time, a concern for general theories of learning has moved away from the center of the psychological stage. There has however continued to be an active movement concerned with studying learning in animals (see Dickinson, 1980 for a review), but this has so far had little impact on research on human learning and memory. As we saw in Chapter 9, some of the technological developments associated with Skinner's work on operant condition-ing, and research on the classical conditioning of fear by clinicians such as Wolpe (Wolpe & Lazarus, 1969) and Rachman (Rachman & Teasdale, 1969) have had a substantial applied impact, but again the work has impinged little on the extensive subsequent research within the cognitive psychology tradition.

Within human experimental psychology, perhaps the last concern with general models of learning came with a controversy that was associated with the development of mathematical models of learning during the 1960s. This was concerned with the question of whether learning was better considered as based on an all-or-none change in the strength of an association, or was based on a gradual increase in associative strength. This particular controversy ran into the sand with the growing conviction that it was apparently impossible to separate the two views, in the absence of a more detailed knowledge of what constituted an association than it appeared to be feasible to achieve empirically (see Kintsch, 1970 for a review of mathematical models of human learning).

The Computer as a Model

From the 1950s then, psychology has been without any general theory of learning. The major model influencing learning during this time was that of the digital computer, and while, as previous chapters have shown, the computer analogy has proved fruitful in analysing many aspects of human memory, it has said little or nothing about the processes underlying learning. One of the reasons for this state of affairs is almost certainly the manner of storage and retrieval of information within digital computers of the type that have dominated the field over the last 30 years. "Learning" in such a computer involves recording information in a specified location, and "retrieval" involves going back to that location and reading out the information stored there. Unlike human memory, provided that there is a storage location available, then storing the information is trivially easy, forgetting is negligible, and retrieval all-or-none. With computers of this kind, recall is either likely to be complete, detailed and accurate, or totally absent. In contrast, retrieval from recall is typically partial and forgetting is substantial. On the other hand, human memory has major virtues in speed and flexibility of access, and in the extent to which it abstracts, yielding ready access to the essentials of complex prior experiences.

While in some respects, the brain is structured like a 1960s digital computer, there are many ways in which it is very substantially different. Most importantly, it appears to comprise a large number of units (neurons), that operate in parallel rather than serially as is the case in most current computers. The speed of operation of the neurons within the brain is very much slower than that achieved by components of current computers, but nevertheless the brain is able to achieve feats in retrieval from memory that are still well beyond that of the average computer. This is presumably because neurons operate in parallel, interacting with each other and probably often operating on approximate solutions rather than completely worked out operations.

Perhaps because of this, the brain has the capacity for so-called *graceful degradation*. At the neuronal level, the brain continues to work in approximately the same way even when it loses large numbers of brain cells as a result of normal ageing, or as a result of brain damage due, for example, to a blow on the head. Compare that with something as simple as the operation of a television set, or indeed the switch on a chainsaw, where I recently had the experience of the whole system stopping simply because one of the connections had worked loose as a result of vibration. Serial machines, including serial computers are very prone to breakdown if any constituent component fails. Fortunately, the human brain is not, nor are the processes involved in human memory search and problem-solving. Then why not develop computers that are based on parallel processing, and study the capacities of such systems to learn, remember and think?

PERCEPTRONS AND PARALLEL PROCESSING

The current generation of computers operates by serial manipulation of symbols which are in turn representations of data. Such an approach to computation has clearly proved enormously powerful, but involves an architecture and a mode of functioning that is very different from at least some aspects of the functioning of the brain. Why then did people develop serial rather than parallel systems? There was in fact considerable interest in developing parallel processing models of cognition during the 1950s and 1960s. Oliver Selfridge's pattern recognition program known as *Pandemonium* was one example (Selfridge & Neisser, 1960), as was the development by Rosenblatt (1962) of a parallel processing machine which he termed the *perceptron*.

A perceptron is a simple device that links a detector unit, analogous to the retina of the eye, to a series of input units, which in turn may activate an output unit causing a response (see Figure 14.1). Both the input and output units may have thresholds, such that they require activity above a certain minimal level before they will fire. The firing will lead to either a positive increment in the probability of the output unit firing (excitation), or will have a negative effect (inhibition). The magnitude of this effect will depend on the weighting of the link. Finally, whether or not the output unit fires will depend on its threshold, and whether the weighted value of the inputs exceeds this.

In the case of Figure 14.1, the input units are assumed to be capable of detecting two distinct features on the retina, represented by a one and a zero. The input units themselves are assumed to have very low thresholds, and for simplicity's sake, both to be excitatory and have a weighting of +1. Let us assume that the output unit has a threshold of 0.5. Given the presentation of a 1, the relevant input unit will detect it, will fire and given its weighting it will produce an excitation from the output unit. Since the excitation will be at level 1, it will exceed the threshold of 0.5, and hence a response will be emitted from the perceptron. Similarly, if the 0 is presented, the process will operate and a response will be made.

Such devices can, of course, be made considerably more complex, and more importantly can be made to learn by giving the

A perceptron that recognizes when one or other (or both) of its inputs is active. From Rosenblatt (1962).

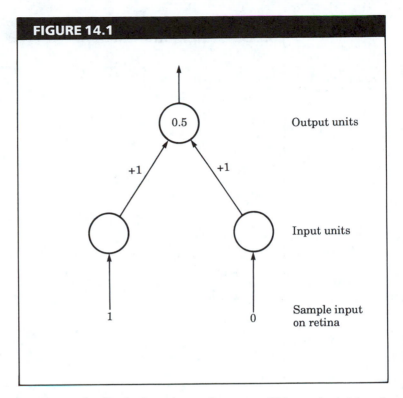

FIGURE 14.1

0.5

+1   +1

Output units

Input units

1   0

Sample input
on retina

perceptron feedback about its performance. This can be achieved by the following simple principle: if the perceptron responds erroneously that the desired pattern is present when it is not, then a reduction is made in the strengths of connections from all units that are currently active. On the other hand, if the perceptron fails to detect a desired pattern when it is there, then all the current levels of excitation are raised. This will gradually produce a state of affairs whereby the perceptron automatically responds when the pattern is present, but not when it is absent.

Since this was already demonstrated by the 1960s, why did such machines not develop? Unfortunately, there are limits to what can be learnt by a simple perceptron. One example is given by the question of teaching a simple machine such as that shown in Figure 14.1 to respond when *either* a 1 *or* a 0 is presented, but not when both are present. Solving such problems demands a major increase in complexity. A highly influential study by Minsky and Papert (1969) performed a detailed mathematical analysis of the capacities and limitations of perceptron-like systems, and concluded that their limitations were sufficiently great as to make them an unprofitable line to follow. Minsky and Papert advocated pursuance of the symbol manipulating approach to artificial intelligence, an approach that has continued to be dominant from that time.

Are there ways around the problems outlined by Minsky and Papert? There certainly are, provided one is prepared to

FIGURE 14.2

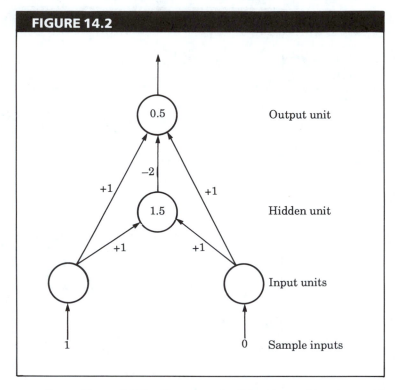

complicate things slightly. One way of solving the problem is to add
a third "hidden unit"; this can be made to fire only when it is
stimulated by both the 1 and the 0 unit, and when it does fire it can
have the capacity to inhibit the response unit, as in Figure 14.2. In
this example, the hidden unit is given a threshold of 1.5 units of
excitation, with the result that it will not be triggered by either of
the input units alone, but will respond when both occur at the same
time. The hidden unit has the effect of inhibiting the output unit,
and hence is able to cancel out the excitatory effects of the two
inputs. Consequently, the system will respond to input unit 1 or
input unit 0, but not to their joint presentation.

Teaching the Hidden Units

The potential value of hidden units was clear to Rosenblatt, but for
many years could not be exploited, simply because of the difficulty
in finding a way in which such hidden units could be "taught". In
recent years, a number of potential learning processes have been
explored, only one of which will be briefly described here, that
known as *backward error propagation*.

This technique, which was developed by Rumelhart, Hinton, and
Williams (1986), can best be understood by considering a system in
which the hidden units within a network are arranged in layers from
the input units at the bottom to the output units at the top, with

activation spreading upwards through the system. The process of learning involves presenting a stimulus to the system and noting the output. This is then compared to a desired output, and the magnitude of the error noted. For example, a printed word might constitute the input and the desired output be the correct pronunciation of that word. This is already known by part of the system that acts as a "tutor", that monitors how far the output deviates from the target pronunciation.

The next stage involves randomly modifying the top-most layer. The strength of connections within this layer are varied until a point is reached at which the error between the actual output and the desired output is minimal. At this point the connections at the top level are stabilized, and a similar operation is performed on the next layer down. When connections on this layer have been optimized, the next layer beneath is then modified, and so forth.

In actual practice such a process can be extremely slow, and there is currently a great deal of activity in exploring alternative ways of learning, some of which do not require a tutor that corrects the network. However, this area is changing so rapidly that anything written now is likely to be out of date by the time this book is published.

Pandemonium

At the same time as people were beginning to work on methods of tutoring hidden units, cognitive psychologists attempting to produce models of reading were becoming increasingly convinced of the need for models that allowed for the interaction of information from a number of different sources, including letter shape, word structure and meaning. Ideas of parallel processing systems had been influential since at least the 1950s with Selfridge's pandemonium model. This assumed a hierarchy of detection units or "demons", each with its own specialized detection task; Selfridge argued that by combining the decisions of the individual demons, it was possible to produce a very effective pattern recognition device (see Figure 14.3). In the case of human pattern recognition, it seemed plausible to assume that the detectors of lines and edges like those recorded in the nervous system of cats by Hubel and Wiesel (1962) might be associated with some of Selfridge's demons.

Consider, for example, the problem of reading a word: the lowest level of demon would be concerned at identifying the strokes that make up the constituent letters. One demon, for example, might be concerned with detecting vertical strokes; when he detects such a stroke, his job is to shout to the demon above him. The demon above might be concerned with a process beyond that of individual strokes, perhaps being a specialist in detecting for example the letter H. As such, he would be encouraged by both vertical and horizontal shouts, but discouraged by shouts from demons representing curved lines or obliques.

Suppose our H demon were to be responding to the letter

FIGURE 14.3

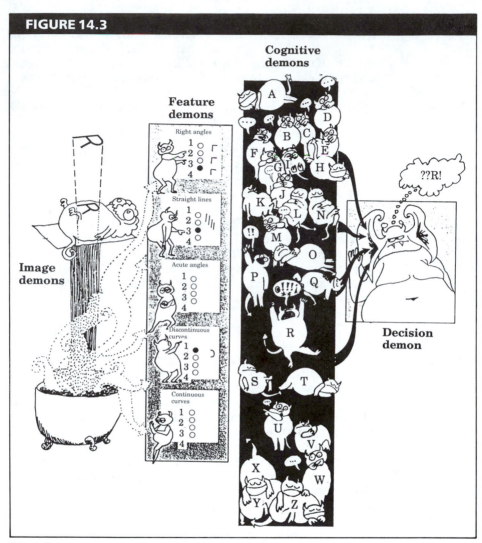

Above: A representation of Selfridge's Pandemonium model of pattern recognition. From Lindsay and Norman (1972).

Right: An ambiguous display in which the context biases the perceiver to see the same letter as "H" in one word and "A" in the next. From Selfridge (1955).

FIGURE 14.4

TAE CAT

The unit for "T" in the first position of a four-letter array and some of its neighbors. Note that the feature and letter units stand only for the first position; in a complete picture of the units needed for processing four-letter displays, there would be four full sets of feature detectors and four full sets of letter detectors. From McClelland and Rumelhart (1981). Copyright (1981) American Psychological Association.

configuration shown in Figure 14.4, how would he react? Presumably he would shout relatively loudly, but so would the demon representing the letter A, and neither presumably shout quite as loudly as they would otherwise. Who would be listening to their shouts? A set of demons higher up who would represent known words. Here the particular demon that won out would depend on the particular word. In the case on the left, the word demons would favor the configuration being perceived as H, whereas if the flanking letters were on the right, then the word demons would favor interpreting the character as an A.

However, although pandemonium models continued to influence the way in which cognitive psychologists talked about perception (e.g. Neisser, 1967), it was only in the 1980s that the development of hardware and modeling skills allowed such models to be constructed and run. One influential example of such a model was that of McClelland and Rumelhart (1981), a small section of which is illustrated in Figure 14.5. The model involves links between units at three levels, features, letters and words. The particular section displayed is concerned only with the first letter of four-letter words. The various links portrayed involve both excitation

FIGURE 14.5

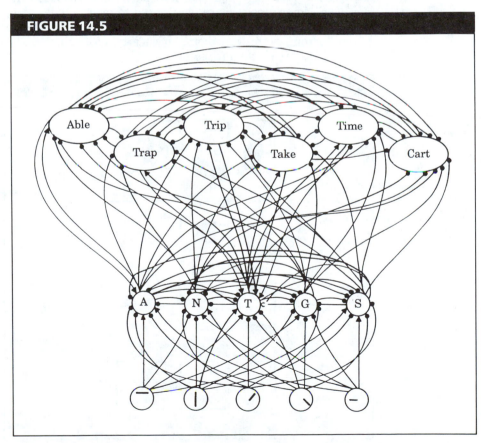

(arrows) and inhibition (blobs). Only some of the features, some letters and some words are depicted here. For example, the letter T receives positive excitation if there is a center vertical, and if there is a horizontal in an upper position. The T unit would receive inhibitory information from the presence of oblique lines, or presumably from curved lines, although these are not reproduced in this illustration of a subsection of the model.

As in the pandemonium model, information from the word level is capable of operating instantly and in parallel to disambiguate letters which on their own might well be totally ambiguous. Figure 14.6 shows a set of examples in which this is illustrated. Note that the effect is immediate and does not require one to systematically work out the options and possibilities. Such a system has then the capacity to take a fragmentary stimulus and allow an unambiguous response. It also is capable of accounting for a good deal of detailed laboratory-based data, indicating that it is a much more ambitious enterprise than earlier and less specific pandemonium-based models.

Selfridge's pandemonium, and the reading model just described, are of course principally models of perception rather than learning. However, similar principles can be applied to models of learning, which as a result yield many of the features that characterize retrieval from normal memory, including most notably the characteristic of *content addressability*.

FIGURE 14.6

Some ambiguous displays. The first line shows that three ambiguous characters can each constrain the identity of the others. The second, third and fourth lines show that these characters are indeed ambiguous in that they assume other identities in other contexts. The ink-blot technique of making letters ambiguous is due to Lindsay and Norman (1972).

Content Addressability

A content addressable memory is one in which access to items can be achieved by giving a partial description of that item, with the memory system providing the rest. For example, if I tell you that I am trying to remember the name of a U.S. President who was involved in a missile crisis, and was subsequently assassinated, you can no doubt provide a great deal of additional information. Similarly if instead of this information, I had provided his name, you would probably be able to tell me that he was involved in the Cuban missile crisis and subsequently assassinated. The flexibility and richness of human memory is, as we have seen, one of its central characteristics; it is moreover a characteristic that makes it very different from standard computer memories.

TABLE 14.1

Characteristics of Individuals Belonging to 2 Gangs, the Jets and the Sharks

Name	Gang	Age	Education	Marital Status	Occupation
Art	Jets	40s	J.H.	Sing.	Pusher
Al	Jets	30s	J.H.	Mar.	Burglar
Sam	Jets	20s	COL.	Sing.	Bookie
Clyde	Jets	40s	J.H.	Sing.	Bookie
Mike	Jets	30s	J.H.	Sing.	Bookie
Jim	Jets	20s	J.H.	Div.	Burglar
Greg	Jets	20s	H.S.	Mar	Pusher
John	Jets	20s	J.H.	Mar.	Burglar
Doug	Jets	30s	H.S.	Sing.	Bookie
Lance	Jets	20s	J.H.	Mar.	Burglar
George	Jets	20s	J.H.	Div.	Burglar
Pete	Jets	20s	H.S.	Sing.	Bookie
Fred	Jets	20s	H.S.	Sing.	Pusher
Gene	Jets	20s	COL.	Sing.	Pusher
Ralph	Jets	30s	J.H.	Sing.	Pusher
Phil	Sharks	30s	COL.	Mar.	Pusher
Ike	Sharks	30s	J.H.	Sing.	Bookie
Nick	Sharks	30s	H.S.	Sing.	Pusher
Don	Sharks	30s	COL.	Mar.	Burglar
Ned	Sharks	30s	COL.	Mar.	Bookie
Karl	Sharks	40s	H.S.	Mar.	Bookie
Ken	Sharks	20s	H.S.	Sing.	Burglar
Earl	Sharks	40s	H.S.	Mar.	Burglar
Rick	Sharks	30s	H.S.	Div.	Burglar
Ol	Sharks	30s	COL.	Mar.	Pusher
Neal	Sharks	30s	H.S.	Sing.	Bookie
Dave	Sharks	30s	H.S.	Div.	Pusher

Source: McClelland (1981).

FIGURE 14.7

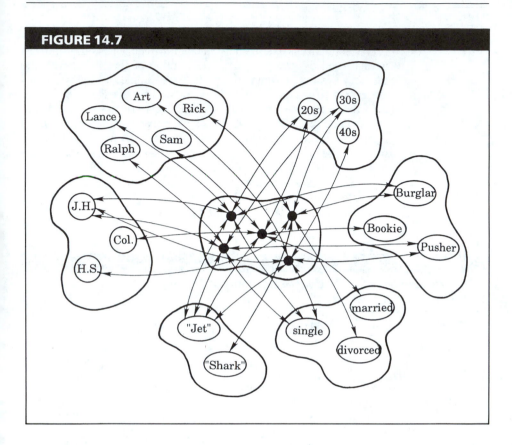

Some of the units and interconnections needed to represent the individuals shown in Table 14.1. The units connected with double-headed arrows are mutually excitatory. All the units within the same cloud are mutually inhibitory. From McClelland (1981).

A study by McClelland (1981) illustrates how a similar parallel distributed architecture can be used to store information about the inhabitants of a rather insalubrious fictitious American suburb. Table 14.1 shows the members of two gangs, together with their educational background, age, marital status and occupation. Figure 14.7 gives a representation of some of the units and interconnections involved in representing the members of the two gangs. A double-headed arrow implies mutual excitation, whereas units within the same cloud mutually inhibit each other. Giving one piece of information will activate others. Hence given the name "Sam", the spread of activation will indicate that he is in his 20s, a bookie, married, a member of the Jets and with a college education. One could instead provide some of the properties and evoke the name— *"Who is in his 40s and a pusher?"*—coming up with the name Art, together with the further facts that he is a member of the Jets and has a junior high-school education.

One characteristic of such a system is that of *graceful degradation*, so that when part of the information is deleted, rather than break down completely, the system gives you the best estimate. Similarly, if a probe contains misleading features, provided the other features give a closer approximation to the correct target than to any other, then the appropriate response will be made.

An analogous virtue of a network of this kind is that of providing a default value, for information that is not directly specified. For example, if we did not know whether Lance was a burglar, a bookie or a pusher, the network would allow us to feed in Lance's characteristics, and come up with a best guess as to his occupation based on the occupations of other gang members who resemble Lance most closely. Such an answer is not of course necessarily correct, it is merely a sensible guess.

Another characteristic of such networks is their ability to perform spontaneous generalization. We could, for example, activate the unit corresponding to membership of the Jets, and this in turn would send activation to the various other properties, producing if you like a stereotype of a Jet. Since nine of the 15 Jets are single, nine in their twenties and nine have only junior high-school education, the stereotype would tend to have these characteristics, even though no individual may in fact fit this stereotype. Where the characteristics are evenly divided, as in the case of occupation, they cancel each other out.

In conclusion, this kind of model offers not only the advantage of a content addressable memory, but it also can fill in missing default values, and form general stereotyped concepts. These are of course all characteristics of human memory. While other models could in principle achieve all these by direct implementation, in the case of parallel distributed processing (PDP) models they are a natural result of the structure of the system and its mode of retrieval.

It is important to note that in a PDP model such as that used for storing information about the Jets and Sharks, the relevant information is contained not in the units representing the individuals or their characteristics, but in the connection strengths between units. In this respect, the models differ substantially from other artificial intelligence (AI) models such as, for example, John Anderson's ACT* (Anderson, 1983), where the process of learning involves the attempt to formulate explicit rules that convey generalizations about the material learnt.

A second crucial difference between PDP models and earlier models of LTM such as, for example, that of Quillian (1969), stems from the assumption that rather than being concentrated in single units or nodes, knowledge is distributed across many different units, each of which contributes to the representation of many different representations, an approach that was first popularized in G.E. Hinton and J.A. Anderson's (1981) *Parallel Models of Associative Memory*.

The idea that memory traces may be distributed across many different brain cells, rather than located in one specific connection was proposed many years ago by Karl Lashley (1929). He carried out an extensive range of studies in which brain lesions were used to attempt to localize within the brains of laboratory rats, the areas responsible for learning and memory. The overall pattern of results seems to suggest that rather than being located in one place, memories were distributed throughout the animal's brain; leading Lashley to propose the principle of *mass action* whereby the cortex was assumed to function as a whole, rather than as a set of separable memory locations. More recently, others have proposed that memory traces are represented as patterns distributed across many brain cells, using mechanisms that are analogous to the storage of information in holograms (e.g. Willshaw, Buneman, & Longuet-Higgins, 1969). In recent years, such distributed models have developed rapidly and seem likely to play an important role in future theories of memory and learning.

DISTRIBUTED REPRESENTATION

There are obvious advantages to distributing a representation over many different units. For example, such systems will still allow the representation to be evoked even though many of the constituent units have been destroyed, a characteristic that Lashley's research showed for the rat brain and which neuropsychological evidence indicates is also true of human learning. But how could it work?

Let us begin with a simple example in which we have two input units, which we wish to associate with two output units such that when a particular pattern of activity stimulates the input, then a given output results. For example the input could be the printed word *dog*, and the output the spoken word. Each unit is assumed to be in one of three states, active (+1), neutral (0), or inhibited (−1).

Association between the visual and auditory patterns requires three steps, the first of which involves establishing connections between the two sets of units. Such connections could be represented by links in a wiring diagram, or the rows and columns of an array such as that shown in Table 14.2. The strengths of the connection between units is assumed to be the same in both directions. Each unit has both a level of activation and a strength of connection to other units, with the magnitude of the resulting activation being determined by the activation of the initial unit multiplied by the strength of its connection. Hence, if a unit has an activity level of +1, and an excitatory connection of +0.5, it will transmit a value of +0.5 to the auditory unit, whereas if a second visual unit has a value of −1.0 and a strength of connection +1.0, it will transmit a value of −1.0, inhibiting the auditory unit.

The next point to note is that a unit's level of activation is determined by the sum of all the values that it receives from all

TABLE 14.2

	Visual units	
		Auditory units

other units, that is $(+1 \times -0.5) + (-1 \times 0.5)$, which equals -1. This principle can be used to adjust connection strengths so as to produce any desired link between the two sets of patterns. Table 14.3 shows a set of weights whereby the visual pattern $+1 -1$ will automatically evoke the auditory pattern $-1 -1$. Since such systems can run in either direction, the auditory pattern $-1 -1$ will also produce the visual pattern $+1 -1$.

In the case of Table 14.4, the unit in the top row will have a level of activity based on the sum of the values it receives from each visual unit, which in this case is $(+1 \times -0.5) + (+1 \times -0.5)$, giving a total of -1. Similarly the bottom row will also give a total auditory weighting of -1. If the pattern is reversed by putting in $-1 -1$, then the visual pattern $+1 -1$ emerges.

Let us consider another array in which the same principles operate, but whereby the visual pattern $+1 +1$ is associated with the auditory pattern $-1 +1$. Such an array is shown in Table 14.4. Note that the combinations of unit values and connection strengths allow the visual pattern to be converted into the auditory and vice versa.

The most intriguing feature of such arrays however, is that if the two sets of connection strengths are added, the resultant array allows both sets of associations to be made. Table 14.5 shows the combined weightings. Given the first set of visual pattern strengths of $+1 -1$, the weightings give the first set of associated auditory giving units of $-1 -1$, while giving the second set of weightings, $+1 +1$ evokes the second set of auditory patterns $-1 +1$.

TABLE 14.3

	Visual units		
	$+1$	-1	
	-0.5	0.5	$+1$ Auditory units
	-0.5	0.5	-1

TABLE 14.4

	Visual units		
	$+1$	$+1$	
	-0.5	-0.5	-1 Auditory units
	0.5	0.5	$+1$

TABLE 14.5

	Visual units	
	-1	0	Auditory units
	0	1	

The example we have given is of course extremely simple, but the same principle can apply to systems having many more units. Such a system will have a number of advantages including, as mentioned earlier, the fact that it is relatively resistant to distortion if some of the units are removed, or for that matter fed with somewhat inappropriate information. Although the output pattern will be weaker, it will be broadly similar to the undistorted output.

How can such pattern associators learn? As mentioned earlier, an increasing number of learning algorithms are being developed, but one of the earliest and best known was that initially proposed by Hebb in 1949. Hebb's rule simply states that: "When unit A and unit B are simultaneously excited, increase the strength of the connection between them." If one allows for the existence of both positive and negative activation values, then the rule can be modified such that the strength of the connection between units A and B is adjusted in proportion to the product of the activation levels of A and B. This will allow the change to increase excitation when the product is positive, or inhibit it if the product is negative. In fact the Hebb rule has now been superseded by other more effective learning algorithms which we need not discuss at this point.

What sort of things can such models accomplish? It is already clear that they have an impressive range of potential applications. For example, Smolensky (1987) reports connectionist models of the following cognitive phenomena:

> Speech perception.
> Visual recognition of figures in the "Origami world".
> Development of specialized feature detectors.
> Amnesia.
> Language parsing and generation.
> Aphasia.
> Discovering binary encodings.
> Dynamic programming of massively parallel networks.
> Acquisition of English past tense morphophonology from examples.
> Tic-tac-toe play: inference about rooms.
> Qualitative problem-solving in simple electric circuits.

PDP AND COGNITIVE PSYCHOLOGY

What is New?

We began this chapter by talking about an earlier version of connectionism, and earlier theories of learning. Is the implication therefore that current developments are merely covering the same old ground and likely to run into the same old problems? Yes and no. There is, first of all, no doubt that these exciting new models are part of an evolutionary development within a long and important tradition. Current approaches have clear links with some of the early general approaches to learning which fell from favor as a result of running into problems which could not be solved. As we have seen, some of these crucial problems have now been solved, with the result that an impressive array of models and examples of learning has already appeared, and given the enormously rapid growth in popularity of this approach, the field seems likely to be deluged in such models over the next few years.

Are connectionist models then simply instantiations of old associationist theories? They are certainly much more than this; for a start, they do actually run, and this requires them to be much more explicit than earlier conceptions of the process of learning.

From an applied viewpoint, such learning models offer the possibility of a very powerful kind of expert system, a system performing complex diagnostic and problem-solving tasks that were until recently able to be performed only by highly trained human experts. Most of the current generation of expert systems are based on the production system methodology (Newell & Simon, 1972), this method of modeling involves providing the computer with a series of rules. These in turn have to be gleaned from human experts, a procedure sometimes known as "knowledge harvesting". A major problem with this is that experts are often not consciously aware of the rules that they use. Indeed, a connectionist might well argue that this is because the rules themselves are fictions, generalizations that attempt to describe processes that are not in fact based on rules. Whether or not this is the case, it is certainly true that experts may have little conscious awareness of the processes underlying their expertise (Berry & Broadbent, 1984).

The advantage of a connectionist machine is that it does not need to be told the rules; given the stimulus input and the desired response, it can work out the relationship for itself. While this applied area of research is still in its infancy, there have already been instances of expert systems that have been taught discriminations using connectionist principles. For example, Gorman and Sejnowski (in press) have devised a system that is capable of discriminating sonar patterns; a complex perceptual task that humans find difficult, and which has so far not proved amenable to automation.

While such developments appear to be promising from an applied viewpoint, they do raise the basic problem of exactly what is happening when the connection machine learns such a discrimination. We know that the relative weightings of connections between the hidden units are being systematically manipulated until the appropriate result is obtained, but is there any meaning to the particular pattern of weights adopted? Is there likely to be only one set of weights, or could one come up with a large or perhaps even infinite range of possible ways of solving the same problem? From an engineering viewpoint, this may not be crucial, but in so far as we are trying to understand the way in which humans perform this task, it is important to know whether the way in which the brain solves the task is the same as the way in which it is solved by a given simulation. Is the brain simply a very large parallel processing machine that can learn anything given long enough?

That this is not the case became obvious to Thorndike (1935) who introduced the concept of "belongingness" to represent the fact that not all associations are equally easy to learn. Similarly, in the area of animal learning, there has in recent years been much evidence to suggest that evolution appears to have prepared certain associations to be learnt more easily than others; hence it is easier to link a taste with subsequent feelings of nausea than with subsequent shock, and easier to associate light or sound with shock than with nausea (see Chapter 9).

Modularity

In the case of human cognition, it seems even more obvious that the brain is not simply a huge and uniform set of units with everything connected to everything else. The concept of *modularity* is important here. Consider the case of a simple piece of domestic equipment such as a television set; it tends to be made up from a number of subsystems or modules, each of which performs an essential but somewhat different task. For example, the aerial and associated components are responsible for picking up the broadcast signals; these are passed in turn to a separate system that controls the firing of a beam of electrons on to the cathode ray tube. Yet another system is involved in picking up the sound signal, and feeding it to the loudspeakers. Each of these components is conceptually separable, and can itself be broken down into smaller modules.

There is currently considerable interest in the question of the extent to which the human brain is modular. Neuropsychological evidence indicates that there is certainly a good degree of modularity. A patient with damage to the perisylvian region of the left hemisphere, for example, is likely to have a language disturbance, but may be otherwise intellectually unimpaired. As we have seen earlier, the memory systems also seem to be modular, at least to the extent of the differentiation of components of sensory, working and long-term memory.

It seems likely that the level of description offered by connectionist models will give a good account of the mode of operation of some of these modules. I am, however, less convinced that they will necessarily provide the best way of understanding the relationship between such modules. In the case of working memory for example, it seems likely that a connectionist architecture would be likely to provide a very good account of the phonological store, since connectionist models are well adapted to storage and retrieval of information within a given domain, although the representation of serial order within a parallel system still presents some problems. Current models might, however, be less appropriate for representing the operation of the central executive, which appears to demand the coordination of information from different modules, rather than the storage and retrieval of information within a single unitary system. It may of course, prove to be the case that if one knows enough about the constituent modules, then the same, or related principles may be sufficient to explain how the submodules intercommunicate. A recent connectionist model of working memory by Schneider and Detweiler (1988) attempts to do just this. To what extent it can give a plausible account of the detailed empirical findings still remains to be seen, but it is, I am sure, the first of many such models.

Levels of Analysis

What then is the relationship between this new type of model, the more traditional Artificial Intelligence models based on approaches such as the production system methodology, and the empirical findings of experimental cognitive psychology? This point is discussed at some length by Smolensky (1987). His views are outlined in Figure 14.8.

Smolensky is concerned with the relationship between neural structures within the brain and mental structures such as goals, knowledge, perceptions and beliefs. He suggests that connectionist systems give an accurate and potentially detailed description of the processes whereby mental structures derive from neural structures. He suggests that more traditional AI models based on sequential symbol processing systems offer a higher level description of these underlying systems. The description is useful, but operates at a level that allows only an approximate description of the underlying

The conceptualization of cognitive science proposal by Smolensky (1987).

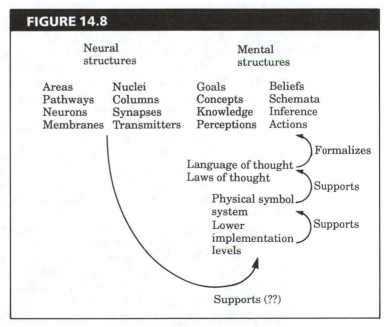

FIGURE 14.8

Neural structures

Mental structures

Areas | Nuclei
Pathways | Columns
Neurons | Synapses
Membranes | Transmitters

Goals | Beliefs
Concepts | Schemata
Knowledge | Inference
Perceptions | Actions

Formalizes

Language of thought
Laws of thought

Supports

Physical symbol system
Lower implementation levels

Supports

Supports (??)

systems, and gives only an approximate mapping on to the subsequent mental structures and cognitive behavior.

A broadly similar point is made by Pylyshyn (1984) who distinguishes between cognitive systems that are "transparent" or "penetrable" and those that are "opaque" or "impenetrable". A transparent system is one that we can access by introspection, and can, by taking thought, modify. Directing attention to the violin rather than the vocal part of a piece of music, or selecting and using a particular learning or retrieval strategy, would be examples of the operation of transparent cognitive systems.

Other parts of our cognitive equipment, however, are simply unavailable to us; we can neither observe nor control their operation. Obvious examples here include such peripheral activities as the reflex mechanism controlling the amount of light entering the eye by adjusting the iris, or the processes increasing the level of adrenalin in the blood following perception of a threat. They would also include more complex mechanisms such as those responsible for stereoscopic depth perception, and probably the procedures involved in automatically retrieving information from long-term memory.

It is possible that models of a connectionist type may be appropriate for opaque processes, processes that operate relatively automatically, while models based on symbol processing will continue to provide a better account of those aspects of cognition that are transparent and open to conscious manipulation and control. As someone whose main interest is in working memory, sitting as it appears to do on the interface between the opaque and the transparent, I hope this is so, since although the new connectionist models appear to offer some exciting prospects, some of the more established symbol processing approaches to cognition still seem to have a great deal to offer.

Finally, what is the relationship between these exciting new models and the more traditional experimental approach to cognition? This is, of course, part of the more general question of the relationship between artificial intelligence, cognitive psychology and *cognitive science*, the term that has come to be applied to the study of cognition in its broadest sense. Cognitive science draws on a range of disciplines including neurobiology, linguistics and philosophy, as well as Artificial Intelligence and cognitive psychology, all of which contribute to the attempt to understand intelligent behavior in both its natural and artificial forms. However, while these participating disciplines have points of overlap, they also have underlying differences.

Artificial Intelligence is concerned to find ways of performing a whole range of tasks that were previously regarded as dependent on human intelligence. To many people in AI, the aim of such research is purely practical: Whether these tasks are performed in the same way as they are performed by humans is irrelevant in so far as this particular aim is concerned. For instance, there are now chess-playing; computer programs that can beat all except the most expert player, it is clear, however, that these do not use the same principles as expert chess players (Holding, 1985). As computer science becomes an increasingly important part of engineering, it seems likely that this aspect of AI will become economically more and more important. This is surely an entirely sensible and appropriate state of affairs.

However, some members of the AI community are interested in cognitive science, and hence in the question of how cognitive tasks are performed by the brain, and while it is possible that attempting to understand how people solve problems may improve our capacity to devise more efficient machines, this need not be the case. The understanding of the human brain and mind is of course intrinsically important and certainly of long-term practical significance. I myself believe that this extremely challenging and difficult enterprise, will be difficult, if not impossible to achieve, without the extensive use of good empirical evidence; cognitive psychology is the discipline that can provide this.

The crucial difference between engineering and science is that whereas for engineering, the acid test is whether the system runs or not, for science one needs further evidence before acceptance. As will have become clear from many of the previous chapters, one of the major difficulties in cognitive psychology is not that of producing alternative plausible theories but in deciding between them.

In conclusion then, cognitive psychology, representing as it does a blend of experimental research and theoretical development, is beginning to enter a very exciting phase of development. We have already reached a stage when models based on the findings of the psychological laboratory are starting to suggest theories that have theoretical implications that extend beyond psychology, to link up with major current developments in neurobiology, biophysics and computer science, as well as suggesting new approaches to some old but important empirical problems.

Meanwhile, at an empirical level we have been moving out of the sheltered confines of the laboratory and exploring some of the richness of memory in the world outside. Some of the newly developing models look as though they may be up to coping with this richness. We still have a long way to go, but the journey looks likely to be an exciting one.

OVERVIEW

The chapter is concerned with a very active and exciting new development in theorizing about learning and memory, namely connectionism, an approach which typically assumes the parallel distributed processing of information. The new developments represent a continuation of a much older tradition of seeking a general theory of learning, extending back at least to Thorndike who himself used the term connectionism, and to the development during the 1940s and 1950s of general theories of learning.

The current approach relies heavily on computer simulation, but differs from most earlier computer models. These typically assumed a sequence of separable stages, whereas connectionism typically opts for models in which a large number of simple units operate in parallel. Such models have intriguing similarities to the way in which the brain appears to operate, and were initially explored during the 1950s and 1960s, producing models such as Rosenblatt's perceptron. However, such models fell from favor in the 1960s because they appeared to have difficulty in learning certain relationships.

In recent years, ways have been found of avoiding these problems by assuming a series of "hidden" units that are interposed between input and output units. Methods of training such systems have been devised, and are continually being developed.

Using such systems, it is possible to distribute the learning across many units. This has the advantage of resulting in memory storage that is much more like the operation of human memory than is the storage of memories in more conventional computers. Conventional computer memories give perfect recall if the correct location is addressed, and zero recall if it is not, unlike human memory which is often partial and fragmentary. Partial recall and generalization occur as a natural feature of some of the parallel distributed representations that have been explored. Such models also have the characteristic of content-addressability, whereby entering part of the material to be recalled will evoke the rest, again a feature of human memory. Finally, as in the case of human memory, such models have the capacity of "graceful degradation", with forgetting, or indeed physical damage to the system, leading to a noisier or weaker recall of the original material, rather than the complete removal of certain fragments and the complete preservation of others.

The chapter concludes with a discussion of the strengths and weaknesses of such systems. They appear to offer a plausible way of theorizing about pattern recognition and retrieval, but may be less effective than more traditional serial or rule-based approaches to describing certain types of problem-solving and reasoning behavior. It is suggested that in the final analysis, it will probably be necessary to blend connectionist approaches with more rule-based models using the empirical methods of experimental psychology to evaluate and shape such developments.

Chapter Fifteen

MEMORY, EMOTION AND COGNITION

I have so far discussed human memory simply as a system for processing, storing and retrieving information, and have interpreted forgetting in purely informational terms. Such an approach implicitly assumes that cognition and memory are insulated from possible distortion by such non-cognitive factors as emotions and moods. But is this the case, or can memory be biased and distorted by emotion? Such a view lies at the heart of one of the most widely known theories of forgetting, namely the suggestion by Sigmund Freud that an important determinant of forgetting is the repression of material that has unpleasant emotional associations. To what extent is human memory likely to distort as a result of emotional pressures?

REPRESSION

Let us begin by discussing the type of evidence that convinced Freud of the power of emotion to block memory. This is well illustrated in the following case of a girl who was treated by the French psychiatrist Pierre Janet, a contemporary of Freud. The quotation is from Morgan and Lovell (1948):

> Irene was a girl of 20 years, who was greatly disturbed by the long illness and death of her mother. Her mother had reached the last stage of tuberculosis, and lived alone in abject poverty with her daughter, in an attic. The girl watched her mother during 60 days and nights, working at her sewing machine to earn a few pennies to sustain their lives. When finally her mother did die, Irene became very much disturbed emotionally. She tried to revive the corpse, to call the breath back again. In her attempts at placing the limbs in an upright position, the mother body fell to the floor, whereupon she went through the strain of lifting her back into bed, alone.
>
> Certainly, such experiences cannot be forgotten in the ordinary course of things. Yet in a little while Irene seemed to have grown forgetful of her mother's death. She would say: "I know very well my mother must be dead, since I have been told so several times,

since I see her no more, and since I am in mourning; but I really feel astonished at it all. When did she die? What did she die from? Was I not by her to take care of her? There is something I do not understand. Why, loving her as I did, do I not feel more sorrow for her death? I can't grieve; I feel as if her absence was nothing to me, as if she were travelling and would soon come back."

There is no doubt that powerful negative emotions can induce amnesia, although the extent to which the patient is totally unable to access the stressful memories, and to what extent he or she "chooses" not to is very hard to ascertain. It certainly seems unlikely that in very many of the cases of psychogenic amnesia, the patient is malingering, and simply pretending not to be able to remember. On the other hand, the line between avoiding searching areas of memory that are associated with anxiety on the one hand, and unconscious repression of unwanted memories on the other is hard to draw. Indeed, it is perhaps neither necessary nor desirable to try to draw such a line.

Repression and Normal Forgetting

While it is clear that strong emotions can produce massive disturbances of memory in hysterical patients, this does not of course necessarily mean that repression forms an important part of normal forgetting. Freud himself, however, certainly claims that it does. His *Psychopathology of Everyday Life* reports a number of instances of symptoms which he suggests are closely analogous to the neurotic symptoms he observed in his patients (Freud, 1901). Perhaps the best known of these are the so-called Freudian slips, slips of the tongue or the pen which are assumed to reveal the unconscious or unexpressed wishes of the speaker or writer. Freud gives the example of the President of the Austrian House of Deputies opening a session from which he expected very little, and mistakenly declaring the session closed. Freud's views have of course evoked considerable controversy, and hence he might have been unsurprised, if unamused by a typographical error that appeared in the *British Psychological Society Bulletin* a few years ago where a list of forthcoming events referred to the "Fraud Memorial Professorship" (*BPS Bulletin*, September 1975).

While slips of the tongue often do seem to be particularly apposite, the evidence he cites for straightforward repression is typically rather less convincing. One of the clearer examples he gives concerns a man attempting to recall a poem, and blocking on a line describing a snowy pine tree as covered "with the white sheet". When Freud asked the man to free-associate this phrase he commented that it reminded him of a sheet that would be used to cover a corpse. This he further associated with the recent death of his brother from a congenital heart condition which he feared would also be the cause of his own death. Other examples he gives tend to be rather less convincing, and depend on rather tortuous interpretations which seem unlikely to convince the sceptic.

How might one therefore test the concept of repression in normal life? Studies have typically been of two types, one based on naturalistic observation, while the second attempts to induce repression experimentally. A rather interesting observation in this connection is made by Linton (1975) who you may recall systematically studied her own ability to remember incidents from her everyday life. She mentions the strange discrepancy between, on the one hand her feeling that her past life has been a reasonably happy one, and on the other the frequency with which the events she has recorded prove to be frustrating, unpleasant or unhappy in some way. It is as if memory selectively preserves what is pleasant.

There have been a number of attempts to explore the tendency of memory to preserve pleasant rather than stressful memories. For example, Waldfogel, cited by Hunter (1957), carried out a study in which people were asked to try to recall as many events from their early life as possible, and subsequently to categorize them as pleasant, unpleasant or neutral. Waldfogel found that about 50% of memories were categorized as pleasant, compared to 30% of unpleasant memories and 20% that were neutral. Could this be because people repressed unpleasant memories? It might, but it might also be that people rehearse pleasant things that happen to them, thinking about them and telling their friends, whereas embarrassing and painful things are not pleasant to recount.

One way of approaching this question might be to study memory for a painful experience. Will recollection of the pain be less as times goes on, or are such experiences very memorable, perhaps even leading to subsequent exaggeration? Robinson et al. (1980) obtained information on this in a study comparing the relative effectiveness of analgesics in childbirth. They had their patients rate the pain associated with birth immediately, and after delays of 24 hours, 5 days and 3 months. Figure 15.1 shows what they found, namely that as time goes on, memory of the pain appears to fade.

However, it is of course entirely possible that the pain associated with childbirth is very atypical of other types of pain. This possibility is supported by the results of a study by Hunter, Philips, and Rachmann (1979) in which the patients were asked to rate the intensity of a pain associated with a medical procedure such as sampling cerebro-spinal fluid, both initially and after a delay. There was no tendency for the rating to decline over a period of a week. Unfortunately, in the case of this study the possibility exists that the patient may have felt that indicating that the procedure was very painful might make it less likely that he or she would have to undergo it again. It would clearly be interesting to have more information on this issue, particularly since studies on pain frequently use retrospective assessments, assessments which

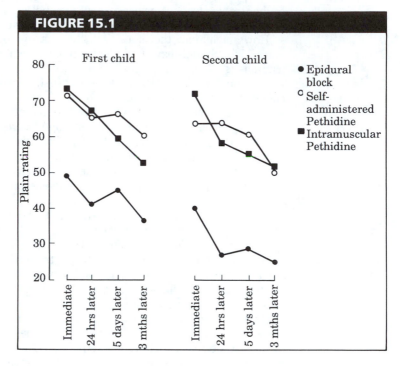

The forgetting of the pain of childbirth by women as a function of method of analgesia employed. From Robinson et al. (1980).

FIGURE 15.1

could well be systematically distorted by any forgetting that might occur.

However, even if we did find that subjects tended to rate their pain as less and less intense as time goes on, this would not necessarily of course imply repression. At the very least, one would need to have comparable data from ratings of non-aversive feelings, such as pleasure; otherwise, our results could be interpreted simply in terms of the normal processes of forgetting. The difficulty in interpreting naturalistic observations of this sort have encouraged some experimenters to try to simulate repression under laboratory conditions.

Laboratory Simulations of Repression

As Erdelyi (1985) points out, there were a number of attempts during the heyday of behaviorism to try to link experimental psychology with psychoanalysis. One feature of this attempted alliance was the occurrence of studies that tried to demonstrate repression within the laboratory.

One attempt to test the repression hypothesis was made by Levinger and Clark (1961). As long ago as 1906, Jung had shown that when subjects are asked to associate to a word, certain items tend to produce very long latencies. Jung suggested that this is because certain words are linked to anxiety-laden complexes which the subject is reluctant to reveal. Levinger and Clark extended this finding, requiring subjects to produce associations to a total of 60 words, some of which were relatively neutral such as *window*, *cow* and *tree* while others were emotionally toned such as *quarrel*, *angry* and *fear*. As Jung would have predicted, they found that emotional words tended to evoke higher galvanic skin response, a measure of emotional arousal. When asked to give free associations to the words, the emotional items also tended to evoke a longer response latency, just as Jung had found.

As soon as the word-association test had been completed, the subjects were given the cue words again, and asked to try to recall the association they had given previously. Subjects were particularly poor at remembering the association they had given to words of high emotionality. Levinger and Clark interpreted their results in terms of Freudian repression; those words that were associated with anxiety-provoking complexes were assumed to be repressed, relative to the neutral control words. However, although this study was frequently cited as supporting the Freudian position, an alternative explanation was proposed by Eysenck and Wilson (1973); this relied on some rather surprising results observed in the early 1960s on the relationship between arousal and memory.

Kleinsmith and Kaplan (1963) carried out an experiment in which their subjects were presented with eight words, each followed by a digit. The words were selected such that some were expected to produce a strongly emotional response (e.g. *vomit*, *rape*), whereas others such as *dance* and *swim* were expected to be more neutral. The arousing effect of each word was measured using the galvanic skin response (GSR) and the words divided into two sets, those above and those below the average in evoked GSR. When tested after a short delay, the high arousal words were poorly recalled, but after a longer delay the function reversed with the high arousal words actually increasing in recall. A subsequent study (Kleinsmith & Kaplan, 1964) replicated this using nonsense syllables rather than words, rather surprisingly finding that differences occurred in the GSR evoked by different nonsense syllables. The results of this second study are shown in Figure 15.2, from which it is clear that the items associated with emotion were poorly recalled initially, but well recalled after a delay, while the low emotion syllables showed the opposite trend. A number of other studies have explored the relationship between arousal and memory with broadly similar results, although typically not so dramatic as those observed by Kleinsmith and Kaplan.

Kleinsmith and Kaplan interpreted their findings in terms of Walker's (1958) action-decrement theory. This assumes that any item presented will set up a memory trace; during the initial period of the trace, an inhibition process will occur that serves to protect the trace during the first stages of consolidation. The inhibitory process however makes it harder to retrieve the trace during this period. Walker assumes that high arousal leads to a higher level of initial state of inhibition, making it less likely that an item will be recalled in the short term, but enhancing consolidation and

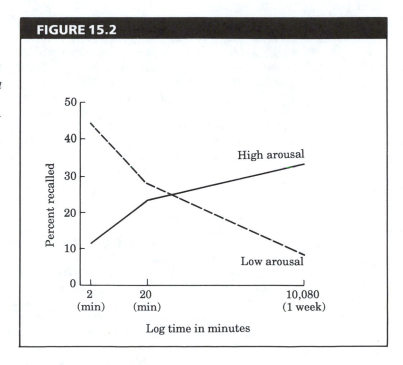

FIGURE 15.2

Differential recall of nonsense syllable paired-associates as a function of arousal level. High-arousal syllables were those evoking a high GSR during the initial learning presentation. From Kleinsmith and Kaplan (1964). Copyright (1964) American Psychological Association.

increasing the likelihood that the item can be recalled after a delay. While evidence for this specific hypothesis is far from convincing, nevertheless there is good empirical evidence to suggest that high arousal does tend to lead to poorer immediate and better delayed recall (see Eysenck, 1977 for a review).

To return to the Levinger and Clark "demonstration" of repression; as Eysenck and Wilson pointed out, this study examined only immediate recall. As Kleinsmith and Kaplan observed, on immediate test, highly arousing items tend to be poorly retained, whereas after a delay the effect reverses, allowing a neat differentiation between the Freudian prediction and that based on arousal theory. If the items are being repressed, then they should continue to be repressed, whereas if arousal is the crucial variable, then the effect should reverse. An unpublished study by two Cambridge undergraduates and I tested this directly (Bradley & Morris, 1976). We repeated the Levinger and Clark study with one exception, instead of testing all subjects immediately, half our subjects were asked to return after 28 days and then given cued recall test. On immediate recall, we obtained the same effect as Levinger and Clark, namely poorer recall of emotional words, whereas after 28 days the effect had reversed strongly, with the subjects remembering more of their associations to emotional than to neutral words.

We had taken the precaution of including words associated with positive as well as negative emotions. This allowed us to separate out the effects of repression which should only occur in the case of negative words, from those of arousal, which would be expected to accompany both. We found that both pleasant and unpleasant arousing words were poorly recalled initially, again supporting the arousal interpretation rather than the repression hypothesis. This study has subsequently been successfully replicated and extended by Parkin, Lewinsohn, and Folkard (1982).

In conclusion, although there does appear to be evidence for powerful effects of emotion on memory in cases of patients suffering from hysteria or fugue, the evidence for repression in everyday life is rather less strong. There does appear to be a biasing towards recalling pleasant memories and forgetting the unpleasant, that crops up sufficiently frequently in observational studies to suggest that it is probably genuine. Attempts to demonstrate repression under experimental conditions however have been surprisingly difficult to produce, prompting Kubie (1952) to comment on "the uselessness of making pallid facsimiles in the laboratory of data which are already manifest in nature, merely to get around the human reluctance to look human nature in the eye" (Kubie, 1952, p. 64). Unfortunately, such exhortations tell us more about the beliefs of the exhorter than the validity of the claim. If Kubie sees evidence of repression all around him, then perhaps like beauty it is in the eye of the beholder?

Nonetheless, one can not help feeling sympathetic to the view that it is difficult to carry out laboratory experiments that manipulate level of emotion, at any rate within the limits of what is ethically acceptable. In general, attempts to test the repression hypothesis have declined over recent years, but in one area, research on effects of emotion on memory has increased, namely that of eyewitness testimony. A person who witnesses a violent crime is likely to experience considerable emotion, and this may well influence the reliability of subsequent testimony.

Memory under Extreme Emotion
In early 1989 I was somewhat surprised one Sunday evening to receive a telephone call from someone who announced himself as a detective with the San Diego Police Force. He explained that he was engaged in the investigation of a multiple throat-slasher whose seventh victim had managed to escape, and claimed to be able to recognize the attacker. What was the effect of extreme emotion likely to be on the accuracy of such recognition? Deffenbacher (1983) reviews the research in this area, pointing out that lawyers tend to have strong, and often conflicting views on the effect of emotion on the reliability of testimony. He cites a survey by Brigham (1981) of 235 lawyers, who among other things were asked whether they felt that a high level of arousal would improve or impair facial recognition. There was an interesting split, with 82% of the defense lawyers feeling arousal would lead to poorer face recognition, while only 32% of the prosecuting attorneys felt this to be the case.

What then is the evidence? Unfortunately, it is rather mixed. A few studies find that higher arousal leads to better recognition. Characteristic of these is a study by Leippe, Wells, and Ostrom (1978) in which they tried to manipulate arousal by simulating either a minor or a more serious crime, the stealing of either a packet of cigarettes or a valuable calculator. The student subjects were subsequently asked to pick out the perpetrator of the crime from a six-person photographic line-up. They were substantially more accurate in identifying the stealer of the calculator (56%) than the stealer of the cigarettes (19%).

Typically, the studies which find a positive effect of arousal are those in which level of arousal is reasonably low, while studies showing impairment tend to be associated with higher arousal levels. For example, Loftus and Burns (1982) had their subjects watch a film of a robbery made as a training feature for bank employees. It involved a hold-up and the subsequent escape of a gunman. In the high-arousal condition, a young boy is brutally shot in the face during the escape, while in the low-arousal condition such violence is avoided. Subsequent memory tests suggested poorer retention of detail in those subjects who had seen the violent version of the film.

A similar picture emerges from a recent study in which the stress was real, although considerably less dramatic than that of shooting a child. Peters (1988) asked subjects to recognize from a line-up a nurse who had given them an inoculation, which physiological and self-rating responses indicated was stressful, or to recognize someone who had interacted with them shortly afterwards. Recognition of the nurse was consistently worse than that of the neutral helper.

However, while studies of film horrors and experienced stresses such as inoculation can tell us something about the influence of emotion on memory, they are likely to cut relatively little ice with a jury attempting to evaluate the testimony of someone who has undergone a horrifying experience, and who states with conviction that they recognize the accused. The task of standing up and arguing that the witness may well be mistaken is often an unenviable one. This was particularly so in the case of John Demjanjuk who was accused of being Ivan the Terrible, the operator of the gas chambers at the Treblinka concentration camp. The defense rested on the claim that this was a case of mistaken identity, whereas the prosecution argued that the horrors of the camps would have left an inextinguishable trace, even after an interval of 35 years.

The Dutch psychologist, Willem Wagenaar agreed to act for the defense, and present the case, not that Demjanjuk was innocent necessarily, but that the strength of the eyewitness evidence was weaker than might appear. Inevitably he encountered the problem of generalizing from laboratory studies which must, of course, be limited to stress levels much below those experienced in Treblinka, and Demjanjuk was duly convicted (an account of the trial and its psychological implications are given in Wagenaar and Groeneweg, personal communication).

Wagenaar subsequently, however, has been able to collect evidence that is directly relevant to this issue from the testimony of 78 witnesses involved in a case against Marinus DeRijke who was accused of atrocities in Camp Erika, a concentration camp in the Netherlands. This study (Wagenaar & Groeneweg, personal communication) was able to take advantage of the fact that some of the witnesses had been questioned shortly after being released from the camp in the period 1943-47, and then subsequently questioned again between 1984 and 1987. The later investigation was complicated by the fact that many of the witnesses had seen a television programme on Camp Erika containing DeRijke's picture before they were re-examined. Of these, 80% recognized DeRijke's photograph, compared to 58% who had not seen the programme. On the other hand, DeRijke's name seemed to be well recalled regardless of whether the witness had or had not seen recent media coverage of the case. Those who had actually been maltreated by DeRijke were slightly more likely to remember him (80%) than those who had not (74%).

In general, survivors remembered a good deal about their experience; the particular punishments given for small or invented misdemeanors, the meals that were deliberately thwarted by not allowing enough time for the food to cool down enough to be eaten, and the particularly wretched treatment of Jewish prisoners. On the other hand, details had often been lost. For example, many respondents forgot that Jewish prisoners were kept in tents rather than barracks, and while those who spontaneously volunteered information on this point were largely correct, 12 out of 13, those who did not mention this but were specifically questioned were much less accurate (14 out of 25). It is perhaps worth noting that this again reinforces Neisser's (1988) point that spontaneous autobiographical memory tends on the whole to be accurate, with errors only introduced when subjects try to go beyond the information that is readily available.

Of particular interest is data from prisoners who were questioned both in the 1940s and in the 1980s. These gave instances of highly dramatic events that appeared to have been completely forgotten. For example one witness reported being beaten up by DeRijke to such an extent that he was unable to walk for days; he also witnessed the murdering of a Jewish fellow prisoner. When re-questioned 40 years later he remembered receiving only an occasional kick, and had forgotten all about witnessing the murder. Another witness reported that two guards who he named had drowned a prisoner in a water trough. By 1984 he had forgotten this and even denied saying it. Yet another witness who recalled being maltreated by DeRijke described how Jews had died after being flogged by the guards; when re-questioned in 1984 he misremembered DeRijke as DeBruin, and had no recollection of the Jews dying after being flogged. Memory for names was also distorted by time, with one witness forgetting the name of the guard who had maltreated him to such an extent that he was unable to work for a year, while another reported in 1943 how prisoner DeVie was violently assaulted by a guard Boxmeer. In 1984, he reported that DeVie was the attacker, not the victim.

The evidence suggests then that after 40 years have elapsed, the victims can still remember the experience, and much of what went on, but however intensely the emotions were felt at the time, and however clearly the images were engraved in the memories of victims, in many cases only the bare bones of the experience remain, with the type of detail that is often so essential in evaluating the testimony of an eyewitness largely being lost. There is no evidence to suggest that intensity of experience is a sufficient safeguard against forgetting. Wagenaar and Groeneweg conclude that the testimony of eyewitnesses should not for that reason be discounted, but that "the extreme horrors of concentration camp experiences do not dismiss the courts of their task to question the evidence critically".

Psychogenic Amnesia

We have argued that extreme emotion does not guarantee good retention, but what of the claims that it can have the exact opposite effect, inducing total amnesia for the horrific event. Bower (1981) cites the case of Sirhan Sirhan who assassinated Senator Robert Kennedy in 1968 in the cause of Arab nationalism, and afterwards claimed to remember nothing of the event. When hypnotized and encouraged to relive the event:

> As Sirhan became more worked up and excited, he recalled progressively more, the memories tumbling out whilst his excite-ment built to crescendo leading to the shooting. At that point Sirhan would scream out the death curses, "fire" the shots, and then choke as he re-experienced the Secret Service bodyguard nearly throttling him after he was caught. (Bower, 1981)

Although he claimed that he would like to have remembered the event in a non-hypnotized state, he appeared to be completely unable to do so.

Such amnesia is not uncommon in the case of violent crime, and in particular homicide, where it can occur in 30–40% of cases (Taylor & Kopelman, 1984). It is particularly likely to occur when the victim is a close relative or lover killed in a crime of passion, or when the crime was committed by a chronic alcohol abuser when severely intoxicated. In addition a small number of cases occur when the crime is committed by a schizophrenic in a floridly psychotic state.

A possibly related phenomenon is the psychogenic amnesia

often associated with "fugue states" in which the patient abruptly loses personal identity, and is often found wandering away from his or her normal home. Such cases typically involve a very dense amnesia, with personal identity frequently lost, together with most of the subject's autobiographical memory. There may be islands of preserved memory, for example, a young man who entered a fugue state following his grandfather's funeral could remember a cluster of details from one period, a period that when he had recovered he identified as being the happiest in his life. Semantic knowledge and procedural skills are often intact, as indeed is often the case in organic amnesia (Schacter, Wang, Tulving, & Freedman, 1982). Attempts to help the patient recover memory by prompting is typically unsuccessful.

The onset of psychogenic amnesia is almost always associated with stress, typically either marital discord, financial problems or possibly the stress of war, and the amnesia can be seen as a flight from this stress. There may also be a past history of organic amnesia. Berrington, Liddell, and Foulds (1956) report that some 16 of their 37 cases had suffered previously from head injury, although Kopelman (Kopelman, 1987, p.438) suggests that "Several authors have remarked that these patients tend to be rather unreliable personalities", one of which, E.F. he cites as an example.

> EF was a 46 year-old man who described 12–15 episodes of going "blank" during the previous 5 years. He said that these episodes lasted 2–36 hours, and that on "coming round", his feet were often sore, he was a long way from home, and he had no idea of the time or what had been happening during the previous hours. For example, he found himself on occasion near the Thames, 10 miles from his home, with his clothes sopping wet. There was a history of epilepsy since he was 19, ECT and bilateral leucotomy at 33, major cardiac surgery, recurrent depression, and two serious suicide attempts. He had recently married for the third time: His wife was many years younger than himself and was pregnant. Marital difficulties were suspected, but were vehemently denied by both partners. Mr EF asked for a psychiatric report after being charged with driving while disqualified, without any insurance, and whilst under the influence of alcohol: His defense was that he had been in a fugue state.

Given such a history, the surprise is not perhaps that E.F. had fugues, but that he ever came out of them.

There is no doubt that powerful negative emotions can induce amnesia, although to what extent the patient is totally unable to access the stressful memories, and to what extent he or she "chooses" not to is very hard to ascertain. Cases of multiple personality represent a particularly intriguing case of hysterical amnesia, where a patient may present as two quite separate individuals, each with his or her own background. Robert Louis

Stevenson's *Dr Jekyll and Mr Hyde* is a fictional account of such a case, but a large number of actual cases have been documented, one of the best known being reported by Thigpen and Cleckley (1957) as described in their book *The Three Faces of Eve*. Their patient had initially two contrasting personalities, Eve Black who was irresponsible, ostentatious and selfish, and Eve White who was gentle, modest and kind. Eve Black was aware of Eve White but the reverse was not true. During the course of treatment a third personality emerged; this was Jane who was aware of both the other personalities and eventually managed to produce a balanced amalgam of the two.

Where does this leave the repression hypothesis? There seems to be little doubt that conditions of extreme emotion can disturb memory, and in neurotic patients can result in very dramatic examples of amnesia. There also appears to be a tendency in everyday life for pleasant events to be favored in memory, although whether this represents active repression of the unpleasant, or favored reminiscence of pleasant events is unclear. Attempts to simulate repression in the laboratory have on the whole had relatively little success, although this may be because it is difficult to set up ethically acceptable experiments in which the levels of anxiety are such as to make it reasonable to assume that repression will occur. However, it seems unlikely that repression is one of the major causes of everyday forgetting, although as we become more adept at collecting reliable information on everyday memory, we may indeed find a more pervasive effect of emotional factors than at present seems likely.

MOOD AND MEMORY

In 1975, Lloyd and Lishman published a study in which patients varying in degree of depression were asked to produce auto-biographical memories in response to a list of neutral words. The more depressed the patient, as measured by the Beck Depression Inventory, the faster the recall of unpleasant experiences. Since depression tends to lead to an overall slowing in mental responsiveness, this seemed to indicate a bias in the direction of negative memories.

Such a possibility was explored by Gordon Bower and his associates, using hypnosis to induce happy or unhappy mood states, and producing effects that they initially attributed to state-dependency (Bower, 1981). Their experiments seem to indicate that mood could act as a powerful associated context, with the result that items that were experienced in a sad mood were much more likely to subsequently retrieved when sad than items experienced in a happy mood. However, while the interpretation placed on many of these early studies was one based on mood dependency, many of them were equally open to an explanation in terms of a related but subtly different phenomenon, mood congruence.

Mood State-Dependency and Mood Congruency

In the case of state-dependency based on mood, anything experienced in a given mood will tend to be recalled more easily when that mood is reinstated, regardless of whether the material experienced in the mood is pleasant, unpleasant or neutral. This can be contrasted with *mood congruency*, whereby a given mood will tend to evoke memories that are consistent with that mood, hence, when sad we will tend to recall sad events, even though we encountered these during a period of happiness. Williams (1984, p.195) gives a good practical example of mood congruency in describing the recollection of a depressed patient of going swimming; when she was in a depressed mood, she remembered the event as being stressful and humiliating, thinking how terrible she looked in her swimsuit and how overweight she was. When in a happier mood, however, she recalled the trip with pleasure, reflecting how much she enjoyed the exercise. The event was the same in both cases, and hence presumably the mood was the same, and yet the aspects remembered vary quite markedly depending on the mood at recall. As we shall see below, the evidence for state-dependency based on mood is somewhat equivocal, whereas that for mood congruence is quite strong.

Suppose we return to the Lloyd and Lishman observation that depressed patients are more rapid at recalling unpleasant incidents; how could we interpret this? One possibility of course is that depressed people experience more unpleasant incidents—perhaps that is why they are depressed. This possibility can be checked by looking for equivalent effects within the same individual during different moods. Such a study was carried out by Teasdale and Fogarty (1979) in which they used normal subjects, and induced high or low mood by using a procedure developed by Velten (1968). This involves encouraging the subject to read out a whole list of statements that are either depressing such as "Every now and then I feel so tired and gloomy that I'd rather sit than do anything", and "I have too many bad things in my life", or in the alternative condition encouraging and positive, such as "If your attitude is good then things are good, and my attitude is good", and "This is great—I really do feel good—I am elated about things". Velten showed that this method was capable of inducing a temporary shift in mood in normal subjects, and the procedure has been used widely in studies of mood and memory. Using this technique, Teasdale and Fogarty (1979) observed that subjects in a sad and anxious mood were slower at evoking positive memories.

There is, of course, always a slight worry with the Velten technique that the results might be based upon the suggestibility of the subjects, with the instruction to think themselves into a depressed mood carrying over to an implied instruction to behave as they imagine a depressed person should. This is not a problem with a subsequent experiment carried out by Clark and Teasdale (1982) in which they took advantage of the fact that certain depressive patients show a diurnal rhythm, being substantially more depressed at one time of day than another. Such patients proved to be significantly less likely to respond to a cue word with a pleasant personal event during their sad phase, than during their comparatively neutral mood stage.

The subject's rating of the happiness of a given event also tended to be dependent on his mood at the time of rating, with depressed mood leading to an average rating that was sadder than a neutral mood, although this was not sufficient to account for the overall effects. It does, however, raise the general problem with autobiographical memory studies of doubt about the nature of the event being recalled.

This problem was tackled in a study by Gilligan and Bower (1984) using a diary method, in which their subjects recorded over a week, the emotionally positive and negative events they experienced. They were then hypnotized and induced to feel either happy or sad. When in a happy mood, they recalled 32% of the happy events, and 28% of the sad, while when in a sad mood, the number of unhappy events that were recalled increased to 38%. The number of happy events remained the same at 32%, an asymmetry that is not uncommon in this literature.

All the results we have discussed so far could be explained either in terms of state-dependency, that reinstating the mood experienced during learning enhances recall, or in terms of mood congruency, whereby happy moods enhance happy memories and vice versa. The crucial issue for state-dependency is whether neutral material shows a similar facilitating effect when the mood during learning is reinstated at recall. The evidence here is much less compelling. Bower, Monteiro, and Gilligan (1978) describe a study in which subjects learnt a single list of neutral words under conditions of either hypnotically induced happiness or sadness, and recalled under the same or a different mood. They found no evidence of state-dependency. In a subsequent study, they did observe a reduction in interference between two lists, when the induced mood differed (Bower et al., 1978), a result that was also obtained by Schare, Lisman, and Spear (1984); however, Bower has subsequently experienced difficulty in replicating this positive result (Bower & Mayer, 1985).

As a recent review by Blaney (1986) indicates, the evidence for the presence or absence of mood state-dependency remains highly equivocal, while the evidence for mood congruency is strong. Why should this be? You may recall that the evidence for context-dependency produces some similar anomalies. While the induction of profound environmental changes, such as that experienced by being tested underwater rather than on land, can produce marked effects, changing the physical environment less drastically from one room to another typically has a much smaller and less reliable influence on recall.

The effects of context-dependency also tend to be detectable using recall but not recognition memory, although some exceptions do appear to occur, as in the studies by Thomson of eyewitness recognition in which reinstating the environment or the clothing in which the target was first seen does appear to have a marked effect on recognition.

Such effects of contextual cues on recognition resemble those obtained using Tulving's retrieval cueing technique, whereby the subject is first induced to encode the target word together with a low frequency associate (*COLD—ground*) and is then shown to be much more likely to recall the target word when the associate, *COLD* is presented. It may be recalled that we suggested that this phenomenon could be explained by assuming that the cue word influenced the way in which the subject *encodes* the target, in this case that he encodes *COLD* in terms of for example, frozen ground or a burial. We suggested that incidental environmental context would typically not change the way in which the stimulus material was encoded, and in the absence of such an encoding effect, its effect at retrieval would be rather less, so that only massive changes in environmental context would give rise to really substantial context-dependency effects.

If we apply this explanation to the evidence on mood dependency, then it suggests that where the material is neutral, as it had to be in order to demonstrate mood dependency rather than mood congruency, then the effect of mood on encoding is not likely to be large, and hence its effect at retrieval is likely to be correspondingly small and unreliable. In contrast, material that can be related much more closely to the patient's ongoing mood is much more likely to be encoded interactively probably by the subject's relating it to himself. Such a situation presents the conditions appropriate for mood congruency, a situation in which the material itself is encoded in a way that is related to the subject's current state of mind, where the context becomes interactive rather than simply additive (Baddeley, 1982).

While the distinction between mood dependency and mood congruency may be important theoretically, the distinction is not of great significance for the depressed patient who finds that he or she can only remember unhappy events. In short, the phenomenon of mood congruency is potentially important and well worth further exploration. To what extent might the effect occur because of bias in initial encoding of the situation experienced? Bower (1981) showed that inducing a happy or sad mood did induce bias in the way in which subjects encoded and recalled a psychiatric interview, although whether or not the mood was reinstated did not prove to be an important variable in recall.

In one study, Bower (1981) hypnotically induced either a happy or sad mood in volunteers who had been selected as being highly hypnotizable. They read a story about two college students playing a friendly game of tennis. One of them, André was happy, with everything in life working out well, while his friend Jack was sad and beset with problems. The two mens' lives, problems and emotional reactions were vividly described by a neutral third person. After the end of the story, the subjects were asked if they had identified with one of the two characters more closely. Those who had been made to feel sad identified with Jack, while the subjects in the happy condition saw themselves through André's eyes.

The mood was then dispersed, and the subjects went away, returning next day and attempting to recall as much of the passage as possible while in a neutral mood. Those who had read the story while sad, recalled 80% of the sad facts compared to 20% of the happy facts, whereas the subjects who had learnt the material while happy recalled about 50% from each condition. Since the subjects were in a neutral mood at recall, the effect is not one of context- or state-dependency, but presumably reflects a bias during initial learning. Sad subjects apparently encode sad facts more richly and deeply than they do happy facts. Note, however, that the happy encoders were equally good at either, and hence did not show the impaired retention of unhappy items that would have been predicted in terms of a repression interpretation.

However, while mood at retrieval did not influence performance on these tasks, a study by Teasdale and Russell (1983) required subjects to remember statements about themselves and found that mood at recall was a crucial factor. The critical feature here was presumably that of self-reference which was explicitly present in the Teasdale and Russell study, whereas the Bower experiments involved an interview and a story about other people.

Before going on to discuss broader interpretations of mood congruency, we should note a number of other features. First, as we have mentioned previously, there is a tendency for the effect of mood to be asymmetric, with happy memories more likely to be dependent on mood than sad. In a study by Isen, Shalker, Clark, and Carp (1978) for example, mood was manipulated by arranging success or failure on a computer game. Subjects attempted to recall adjectives referring to positive or negative personality traits. Success or failure influenced the recall of positive but not negative traits. The previously described study by Teasdale and Fogarty also found an effect on positive but not negative items, while studies by Teasdale and Russell (1983) and Dunbar and Lishman (1983) both observed effects on positive items, but not on negative or neutral. It should perhaps however be noted that the previously described diary study by Gilligan and Bower (1984) showed the opposite effect.

So far, all the studies we have described have been concerned with differences in happiness or elation as contrasted with sadness or depression. The implication has been that these are typical of other emotions. In fact that proves not to be the case. For example, Mogg, Mathews, and Weinman (1987) tested patients with general anxiety state, and observed no tendency for them to recall threat-related words, indeed there was a non-significant tendency in the opposite direction. Watts (1986) in a study of spider phobics did find a somewhat greater tendency for them to subsequently *recognize* words associated with spiders such as *crawly* and *hairy*, but to be significantly less likely to *recall* such phobia-related words. This observation of an effect for recognition and the reverse for free recall, is exactly the opposite to what one might expect from the state-dependent literature in general, where recognition effects are much less likely to be observed than recall. As we shall see below, this is not because anxiety has no effect on performance, but rather that it influences perception and attention rather than memory. Watts suggests that while phobics may be particularly alert to any stimulus that might suggest the presence of the phobic object, they tend not to analyze such stimuli in detail, leading to a relatively impoverished memory trace. Williams and Broadbent (1986) have shown a similar qualitative difference in the memory performance of depressed patients, this time occurring in their retrieval of semantic memories. Williams and Broadbent used the Galton single-word cueing technique in a study in which patients who had recently attempted suicide were encouraged to come up with specific and detailed autobiographical memories. They found that regardless of whether the memory was good or bad, their patients had much greater difficulty than non-depressed controls in coming up with a rich and detailed recollection. Hence, in response to the cue word "happy", the subject might respond "playing squash", but be unable to come up with any particular happy squash game.

A subsequent study indicated that this phenomena was shown by depressed patients generally, not only those who had recently attempted suicide (Moore, Watts, & Williams, 1988); 40% of the recollections of the depressed patients were excessively general, as compared to 19% in the case of controls. Williams suggests that this may be an important variable in treating patients, where cognitive therapy techniques often require the patient to remember incidents and events from a time when he or she was less depressed and hopeless. It seems likely that remembering an event in a relatively abstract way may be much less helpful in treatment than a richer and more detailed recollection.

Learning, Memory and Depression

Patients suffering from depression frequently complain that their memory is bad, and while the elderly depressed certainly do not have the memory deficits shown by those suffering from senile dementia, there is abundant evidence for a milder disturbance of memory (see Watts, 1988 for a review). It is less clear wherein lies the source of such memory problems; depressed patients tend to be lacking in drive and energy, and hence might encode less, or retrieve less actively. Furthermore, it is possible that the depressed state, or possibly drugs taken to attempt to relieve that state, might have a more direct physiological effect on the memory trace.

Johnson and Magaro (1987) suggest that depression has its effect by reducing the effort at encoding, a conclusion that is also supported by an earlier study by Weingartner et al. (1981) who observed less semantically based category clustering in the free recall performance of depressive patients when compared to non-depressed controls. A study by Leight and Ellis (1981) induced depressed or happy mood in normal subjects, and found that induced depression impaired recall. This result suggests that the effect of depressed mood on learning is at least partly an effect of mood, and is not dependent on basic biological differences between depressed patients and controls.

The possibility does remain, however, that such effects could be due to the unwillingness of the depressed patient to invest the necessary effort for performing a recall task. If this were the case, then one might expect that providing retrieval cues would reduce the difference between depressed and control memory performance by minimizing the demands at recall. This was tested by Watts and Sharrock (1987) in a study involving prose recall, followed by cueing so as to produce a task in which the subject would be only required to provide a single word answer to each cue word. They observed a decrement in the depressive group that was if anything slightly greater in the cued than in the free recall condition, suggesting that a retrieval deficit was probably not the primary problem experienced by these subjects.

Two studies have provided evidence that depression may influence performance by inducing a response bias. In one of these, Zuroff, Colussy, and Wielgus (1983) tested subjects who were high or low on the Beck depression scale on a task whereby subjects judged the applicability to themselves of positive or negative adjectives. They were subsequently required to try to recall the adjectives, and then recognize them from a larger set of positive and negative items. The depressed subjects recalled more negative items, but in the recognition task were also more likely to falsely recognize negative items that had not been presented. When separate measures of memory sensitivity and memory bias were calculated, the difference between the high and low depressed groups proved to be attributable to a difference in bias rather than sensitivity.

A similar bias was noted by Dunbar and Lishman (1984), who observed that their depressed subjects were more cautious in recognizing positively toned items. On the other hand, Watts, Morris, and MacLeod (1987) obtained a significant impairment in the d' measure of sensitivity in depressed patients, with the bias effect depending on the particular encoding instructions to the subjects. When the subjects were left free to encode in any way they wished, they tended to be more cautious, but showed the opposite bias in a condition where an overt verbal response was required during learning.

This result suggests that although bias effects may well occur when depressed patients are attempting to remember material with happy or sad associations, there is a further learning decrement over and above this. This may well stem from the tendency for depressed subjects to be comparatively hopeless and unable or unwilling to process the material in the active way that is likely to lead to good learning. Fortunately, as Watts, MacLeod, and Morris (1988) have shown, depressed patients are able to take advantage of memory processing strategies such as visual imagery, and do show the expected enhancement in recall. In many cases, such as that of depressed students with study problems, the demonstration that memory *can* be improved may well be the first stage in the lifting of the depression and the resolving of the study problems.

ANXIETY, MEMORY AND PERCEPTION

Patients who are depressed often tend to be anxious, which is probably one reason why it took some time to separate out the rather different effects on cognition of depression and anxiety. As we have seen, depression tends to impair overall performance by reducing processing and input, and by biasing both learning and recall through the mood congruency effect, whereby the depressed subject is biased in the direction of both perceiving and recalling items that are consistent with the depressed mood. Hence, depression appears to have its main effect on memory via the subject's preoccupation with the negative events of his or her life and character. In contrast, the main effect of anxiety is to distort the subject's perception of future threats. The following quotation from Beck (1976, p.164) gives the flavor of the problem faced by someone with a phobia about flying:

> When the patient (a flying phobic) was not planning a flight in the predictable future, he would feel that the chances of the plane's crashing were 1 in 100,000 or 1 in a million. As soon as he decided to make a trip by air, his estimated probability of a crash would jump. As the time for the flight approached, the likelihood increased progressively. By the time the airplane took off, he would figure the chances as 50-50. If the trip was bumpy, the odds would switch over to 100 to 1 in favour of a crash.

At least the aeroplane phobic has the advantage of knowing exactly where and when he is likely to be subjected to the fearful situation, this is not the case with many other phobics whose symptoms are likely to be more general and incapacitating. The following hypothetical example from Williams, Watts, MacLeod, and Mathews (1988, p.13) gives a general idea of the state of mind that one might expect to find in an anxious and depressed patient:

> I feel so low and depressed that everything is just too much effort. I can't even manage very simple jobs without getting distracted or confused. I just can't concentrate anymore. And I feel afraid all the time too. Society is so dangerous nowadays. Everything I read in the papers is about some terrible accident, or about violence. It's

not even safe on the streets—everywhere I look there are dangers. But I can get anxious even when I'm just sitting quietly, thinking about nothing. Anxiety just seems to come out of the blue and sweeps over me. I am doing less and less nowadays, and seldom see friends anymore. Whenever I'm out socially I get uncomfortable. People find it difficult to accept me now. It's clear that they either find me boring or embarrassing, so I prefer to avoid these situations...

As part of his series of experiments investigating the effect of mood on cognition, Bower (1983) asked subjects to assess the probability of various causes of death while under a positive mood, and under a unhappy mood induced by hypnosis. The negative mood led to a general increase in the assessed likelihood of the various causes of fatality. Butler and Mathews (1983) carried out a similar study in which normal subjects or depressed or anxious patients rated the likelihood of occurrence of a range of pleasant and unpleasant events. The subjects were required to estimate likelihood both that the events would happen to themselves and to others. There was no difference between the three groups in the assessed likelihood of positive events, but both the anxious and the depressed rated the unpleasant events as more likely to happen to them, though not to others.

It is, of course, possible that the anxious and depressed were genuinely more afflicted by the sorrows of this world than the controls; this suggests the need for replication using a within-subject design which allows the same subject to make judgments when he or she is at different levels of anxiety. Butler and Mathews (1987) carried out such a study using students selected as being high or low in trait anxiety as assessed by a questionnaire. Subjects were tested either one month or one day before an important examination, or at a time when no examination was imminent. Both high and low trait anxiety groups showed a similar response to the imminence of the exam, rating disasters as more likely to happen to them, but not changing their estimate of the likelihood of negative events for others. It appears then that anxiety increases your expectation of dangers and disasters happening to yourself, but not to others.

So far we have talked about estimated probabilities. It is conceivable that these simply represent a form of "superstitious" behavior on the part of the subject, announcing for example the imminence of an exam disaster so that if he or she fails, they will at least have the consolation of being able to say "I told you so". If that were the case however, one might expect little actual impact of this on behavior. A number of studies have shown that genuine distortions of attention do indeed occur and do influence performance.

In one study for example, Eysenck, MacLeod, and Mathews (1987) tested subjects who were either high or low in trait anxiety as measured by their response to a questionnaire. Their task was to listen to and then recall items from a list of unrelated words. The words however were carefully selected so as to comprise homophones, with one spelling having a neutral and the other a negative meaning (e.g. *dye*, *die*; *pane*, *pain*). Subjects wrote their recall, which revealed a significantly greater tendency for the anxious group to recall the negative spelling. Since subjects in free recall typically store the incoming words in terms of their semantic characteristics (Light & Carter-Sobell, 1970), it seems likely that the effect stems from a tendency for the anxious subjects to be more alert to threatening words than are control subjects.

Evidence that anxiety may bias perception comes from a study by Parkin and Rachman (1981) comparing mothers who were anxious because their child was about to undergo tonsillectomy the following day, with mothers whose children were not about to undergo any such operation. The experiment involved playing a tape which comprised mainly music, but which had embedded in it a number of words varying in loudness from clearly audible to extremely quiet. The words were either associated with a probable source of worry (e.g. *bleeding*) or were similar in sound to such words (e.g. *breeding*), or were neutral (e.g. *newspaper*). The subjects were asked to report any words they heard. The anxious mothers tended to report a higher proportion of worrying words than the controls for all except the loudest intensity, for which there was no difference. The words that were acoustically similar to worrying words were also more likely to be reported at the quietest level, but did not show any difference at the intermediate or louder levels. It seems likely then that the worry was biasing the anxious mothers in the direction of words that were related to that worry.

One might argue that in this case, the worry was actually helpful, and indeed one assumes that the evolutionary advantage to anxiety is that it alerts the organism to potential threat. There are, however, occasions in which this may be counter-productive, when worrying simply gets in the way of the task in hand.

A neat demonstration of difficulty in avoiding distraction from such unwanted associations is given in a study by Watts, McKenna, Sharrock, and Trezise (1986) in which spider phobic or control subjects were required to perform the Stroop task. This is a test in which words are written in different colors, and the subject required to name the color. In its standard form, the crucial test involves a conflicting situation in which color names are written in different ink colors, hence the name *green* might be written in red and the name *blue* in green. This conflict typically slows down the naming of the color of the ink. In the study by Watts et al. (1986), instead of color names, the critical condition used words that are semantically associated with spiders, such as *hairy* and *creepy*. The spider phobics were significantly more slowed down by this than the controls, an effect that was reduced following treatment of the phobia. Williams and Broadbent (1986) showed a similar phenomenon using patients who had just attempted suicide by taking an overdose of drugs, showing color naming to be slowed down substantially more by words associated with their plight such as *overdose* and *drug*, than by words of a more generally negative nature such as *helpless* and *immature*.

Anxiety and Performance

If the effects of anxiety were limited to impairing performance on the Stroop test, this would be theoretically interesting, but with little practical significance. Unfortunately, however, the effects tend to be very much more widespread. One aspect that has been particularly extensively studied, presumably because it is of direct relevance to academics, is that of examination anxiety. Sarason (1975) suggests that test anxiety can be split into two components, a general increase in emotional responses such as heart rate and sweating together with an increase in "self-centered" interfering responses, such as saying "I am stupid" or "I'll fail!". Spiegler, Morris, and Liebert (1968) showed that as exams approach, there tends to be an increase in the worry or self-centered responding, rather than an increase in overall emotionality, while Morris and Liebert (1970) found that amount of *worry* was significantly correlated with subsequent exam result, when emotionality was allowed for statistically, whereas *emotionality* did not have an effect over and above that of worry.

One possibility is that the worry has its effect by interfering with performance during the exam. While this is certainly likely, recent work by H. Baddeley (1987) suggests that the effect of worry might already be present before the examination. She had samples of physiotherapy and psychology students complete two question-naires, one concerned with study methods and the other with worries. The study method questionnaire was based on one devised by Schmeck (1983) which probed the extent to which the student used rote memorization, elaboration or deep processing strategies during study; the questionnaire had previously been validated, with deep processing shown to be correlated with subsequent academic success. The worries questionnaire asked her students to report the things that worried them, and subsequently explored these in further detail. Although the two student samples were very different in both subject of study, background and nature of worries, the pattern for physiotherapists and psychologists was the same, namely the tendency for students reporting more worrying to be less likely to use deep processing strategies in studying.

Eysenck (1983) discusses the experimental evidence for disruption of performance by anxiety, whether studied through individual differences between anxious and non-anxious subjects, or as a result of the imposition of environmental stressors. While performance does in general tend to be impaired, the pattern is far from straightforward; in many cases, for example, Eysenck is driven to listing the number of studies that show a negative effect that is significant, the number that show an effect that is non-significant and the number that show no effect, or indeed an enhancement. He suggests that this complex pattern arises because anxiety has two main effects. The first is that it tends to increase worry which will serve as a distraction in many cases, but at the same time it increases the overall arousal level of the subjects inducing them to put more effort into the task, which may or may not be sufficient to counteract the negative effects of worry.

This hypothesis gives a plausible account of the available literature. For example Dornic (1977) asked two groups of subjects to rate the effort expended on a task they performed at two levels of difficulty. One group comprised stable extroverts who were low in anxiety while the other were neurotic introverts who tend to have a high anxiety level. The two groups rated the effort involved by the task as equivalent at the low loading, but the anxious subjects rated their effort as significantly higher when performing under conditions of high load. In another study Ganzer (1968) had subjects low and high in test anxiety attempt to learn a serial list of words either alone, or in front of an audience. The audience condition tended to evoke many more apologetic responses from the high test anxiety group, suggesting a higher level of worry and distraction.

Danger, Memory and Performance

We have so far concentrated on the effects on performance of anxiety as a trait that is characteristic of some subjects but not others. However, in certain situations, everyone is anxious. To what extent is such *state anxiety* that depends on the situation equivalent in its effects to *trait anxiety*?

There has been over the years a good deal of work attempting to measure the performance of subjects in dangerous or threatening environments. While such research is difficult to do for obvious ethical and practical reasons, it is sometimes the case that one can capitalize on a situation in which subjects voluntarily place themselves in a threatening situation. Such a situation need not necessarily be physically threatening as the following description by Mosso (1896) of the experience of giving his first public lecture illustrates:

> Never shall I forget that evening. From behind the curtains of the glass door I peered into the large amphitheatre crowded with people. It as my first appearance as a lecturer, and most humbly did I repent having undertaken to try my powers in the same hall in which my most celebrated teachers had so often spoke. All I had to do was communicate the results of some of my investigations into the physiology of sleep and yet, as the hour grew nearer, stronger waxed within me the fear that I should become confused, lose myself, and finally stand gaping, speechless before my audience. My heart beat violently, its very strings seemed to tighten, and my breath came and went as when one looks down into a yawning

abyss.... As I cast the last glance at my notes, I became aware, to my horror, that the chain of ideas was broken and the links lost beyond recall.... Long periods which I thought myself able to repeat word for word — all seemed forgotten.... There was a singing in my ears.... After a few sentences jerked out almost mechanically, I perceived that I had already finished the introduction to my speech.... Trembling of the hands ... my knees shook.... My trembling voice ... I was perspiring, exhausted.

A study by Idzikowski and Baddeley (1983a) took advantage of this "stage fright" effect by asking a number of new members of staff at the Applied Psychology Unit, Cambridge, if they were prepared to undergo testing immediately before they gave their first public talk at the Unit. Figure 15.3 shows the heart rate of one such subject before, during and after the talk. We found clear evidence of anxiety as measured both by physiological measures such as heart rate and by subjective estimates. We found small but significant decrements in two aspects of memory performance, namely digit span which fell from an average of 8 digits to 7.25, and verbal fluency, where the mean number of words beginning with a specified letter that could be produced within one minute fell from 22 to 20. On the other hand, performance on a reasoning task was not impaired.

A subsequent study (Idzikowski & Baddeley, 1987) used a similar range of tasks to look at the effects of anxiety on performance in a group of novice parachutists who were tested immediately before their first jump. Again we found clear evidence of an increase in anxiety, accompanied by a drop in digit span. Fluency was not measured on this occasion, but speed of searching for letters was impaired, as was the accuracy although not the speed of performing a verbal reasoning task.

The main evidence for an effect of danger on memory in fact comes from the digit span task, which has been shown to be impaired by anxiety in a number of studies (e.g. Moldawsky &

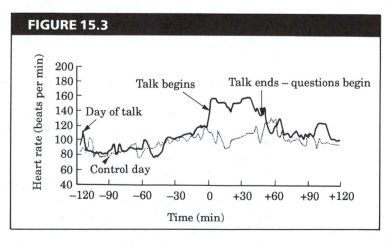

FIGURE 15.3

Heart-rate of subject A.S. when he presented a paper at a lunch-time seminar at the Applied Psychology Unit, Cambridge. From Idzikowski and Baddeley (1983a).

Moldawsky, 1952; Mueller, 1979). There is also some evidence for an effect of anxiety on perception. Simonov, Frolov, Evtushenko, and Sviridov (1977) tested parachutists on the aircraft, just as they were about to jump, requiring them to recognize numbers composed of dots against a distractive background. They observed a decrement in performance, of which perhaps the most plausible interpretation is that the parachutists had their mind on other things than performing adequately on psychological tests.

Indeed, as we saw earlier, one of the major ways in which anxiety affects performance may well be through worry, whereby the subject is distracted from performance on the cognitive task by thoughts about potential threats. This is likely to produce a rather general impairment in performance on a range of tasks, which is the pattern observed in a review of research on performance in dangerous environments by Idzikowski & Baddeley (1983b).

One aspect of performance that may be particularly impaired is that of motor control, where high levels of arousal may cause tremor which may well interfere with accurate performance. Analysis of data from weapon control during the Second World War suggests that an interaction may occur between the complexity of the control system and degree of anxiety. Walker and Burkhardt

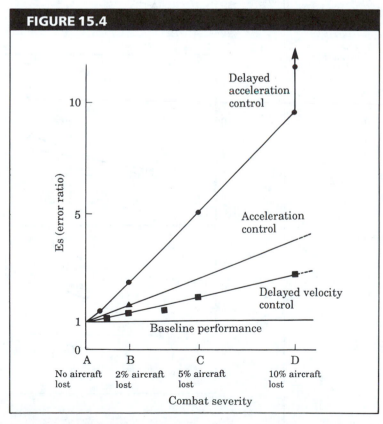

FIGURE 15.4

Performance decrement as a function of combat severity and weapon control. From Walker and Burkhardt (1965).

(1965) looked at the mean error observed using a range of bomb and missile control systems during training and during combat varying in degree of severity. Figure 15.4 shows the mean error they report, which escalates quite dramatically as stress level increases.

The influence of anxiety on performance is of course something familiar to any sportsman. It has recently been studied in a series of experiments by Bäckman and Molander on miniature golf, a popular and very competitive sport in Sweden. It has the advantage of

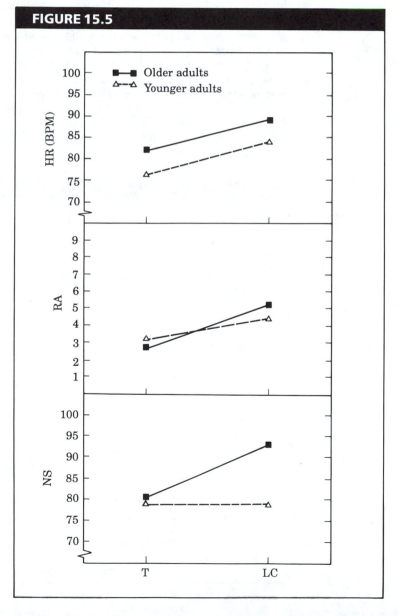

FIGURE 15.5

Mean heart-rate in beats per minute (top panel), mean rated anxiety (middle panel), and mean number of shots per two rounds (bottom panel) for older and younger adults during training (T) and club championship (LC). From Bäckman and Molander (1986b). Copyright (1986) American Psychological Association.

involving a complex skill across a range of different tasks set by the standard obstacles on each hole. Since the obstacles and the course is always the same, it offers much better controlled conditions than are found in most sports. In one experiment, Bäckman and Molander (1986a) studied the performance of young players (mean age 27.7) and older players (mean age 51.0) during practice and during the club championship. As Figure 15.5 shows, both groups showed a similar increase in anxiety during competition. However, the young performed just as well under stress as in training, while the older players showed clear deterioration in their golfing skill.

In another study, Bäckman and Molander (1986b) studied the performance of young and old miniature golf players of two levels of skill on an indoor course. All subjects subsequently returned and took part in a competition for a cash prize. Performance was measured in terms of the total number of shots to complete the 10-track course, together with a test of their capacity to remember the first shot on each track. The results of their study are shown in Figure 15.6 from which it is clear that all groups show an increase in anxiety between training and competition, and that there is an overall increase in number of shots taken under competitive conditions. However, this decrement is largely attributable to the older players who are significantly more likely to show decrement than the young. In the case of recall, while the young recall marginally more shots in competition, the old recall significantly fewer.

Bäckman and Molander suggest that the decrement in the elderly may stem from an impaired capacity to concentrate on the task in hand and shut out intrusive and worrying thoughts. In order

Recall of miniature golf shots in training and more stress-ful competition for young and old players. Competition reduces amount recalled by the old but not the young. From Bäckman and Molander (1986b). Copyright (1986) American Psychological Association.

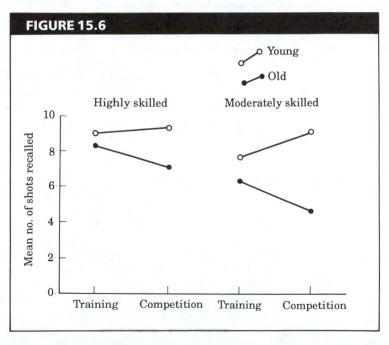

FIGURE 15.6

to test this, they took advantage of the finding that heart-rate tends to decelerate during concentration, hence giving an indirect measure of the mental activity of the two groups. Molander and Bäckman (in press) therefore measured the heart-rate of young and older, miniature golf players during relaxed training and during competition rounds. The results supported the hypothesis, with the overall heart-rate of the elderly remaining high during the shot, whereas the young showed clear evidence of heart-rate deceleration, suggesting successful concentration. It appears to be the case, then, that even the motor skill performance decrements shown may indirectly be due to the influence of anxiety on attentional control, rather than to peripheral motor effects.

OVERVIEW

We began by considering one of the classic explanations of forgetting, namely that unpleasant events are repressed. While psychogenic amnesia does occur, causing on occasion a complete blanking out of whole areas of autobiographical memory, the evidence for repression as an important component of everyday forgetting is much less strong. Studies of autobiographical memory do show a tendency for people to remember more pleasant than unpleasant events, but attempts to reproduce this in the laboratory have met with mixed results. Indeed, there is some evidence to suggest that high arousal may actually lead to enhanced later recall under certain circumstances, probably because of its positive effect on memory trace consolidation.

Under more realistic conditions, however, such as those encountered by an eyewitness to a serious crime, emotional factors may well reduce recall accuracy. This is probably because the stress distorts the normal pattern of attention; thus an eyewitness to a violent crime may tend to focus on the gun held by a robber rather than on his physical appearance.

There is considerable evidence that mood may influence memory retrieval, with subjects in a gloomy mood tending to recall more sad than happy thoughts, and vice versa. There is, however, much less consistent evidence for context dependency, the phenomenon whereby a neutral event learned in one mood will be better recalled under that mood than it will be under a different mood. The chapter goes on to discuss the effects of emotion on cognition more generally, describing evidence that suggests that depression leads to impaired learning. The evidence seems to suggest that this is probably a result of less adequate and rich encoding, rather than from a deficit in retrieval.

In the case of anxiety, its effects tend to be greater on the direction of attention than on memory. Anxious patients tend to be particularly sensitive to potential sources of threat, while normal subjects in threatening or competitive situations may often perform more poorly as a result of distraction from the task in hand by intrusive and worrying thoughts.

Chapter Sixteen

UNDERSTANDING AMNESIA

There is no doubt that the study of memory over the last 100 years has been largely confined to the laboratory. Some psychologists would argue that it should remain in the laboratory since once we move out, we lose the experimental control that is so important in teasing apart the complexities of a system as complex as human memory. As I hope will be clear by now, my own view is that we need to blend the control of the laboratory with the richness of the everyday world if we are to understand the whole of human memory, rather than selected easily investigated subcomponents. I would furthermore, argue that in the process of moving from the laboratory we are likely to point out the limitations of existing theories, and obtain valuable insights into how they should be improved. I would therefore like to conclude with two chapters concerned with a very practical real-world problem, namely that of the memory deficit that is so frequently suffered by patients following brain damage. It is an area that has attracted increasing interest from cognitive psychologists in recent years, and the study of amnesia has amply repaid that interest in the contributions it has made to understanding normal memory. At the same time, the enormously difficult problem of how one can help such patients demonstrates the limitations as well as the strengths of the psychology of memory.

After a brief overview of the study of amnesia, this chapter will concern itself with two questions. First, can we analyze the memory deficit observed in our unfortunate patients? Secondly, can we explain it theoretically? The next chapter will be concerned with what, if anything, psychology can do to help?

AMNESIA

The Patient's Viewpoint

Impaired memory is one of the commonest symptoms following any kind of brain damage. Whether the damage is due to a blow on the head, to a brain infection such as viral encephalitis, to a stroke, to senile dementia, or for that matter to normal ageing, one of the first complaints tends to be of difficulty in remembering, and one of the most sensitive tests tends to be a standard word-learning test of the type that we have discussed at great length in earlier chapters. In most cases, the deficit may be relatively mild, and may present no more than a slight social embarrassment. In more severe cases however, the memory deficit can be a major problem, and in the case of a very dense amnesia, as we saw in the case of Clive Wearing discussed in the first chapter, it can be absolutely crippling.

A very good account of what it is like to have moderate memory deficit is given by a clinical psychologist Malcolm Meltzer who encountered memory problems as a result of anoxia following a heart attack. His was not a pure memory deficit, since he had some perceptual and emotional problems, but his principle difficulty was a result of his poor memory (Meltzer, 1983). When Meltzer came out of a six-week coma, he was not densely amnesic. He knew who he was, knew his job and recognized his family, although not all his friends. He initially thought he had two children not one, and thought that his age was 33, whereas it was 44. He failed to recognize the route home even though it was previously very familiar. His house was familiar but he could not remember where things were kept. He had to relearn how to play the stereo, set the alarm clock, change a razor blade etc. Relearning these was relatively slow. Meltzer also seemed to have lost access to what Schank would term "scripts" (Meltzer, 1983, p. 3):

> the feeling engendered by this inability to do things done in the past was that of incompetency. When should bills be paid? What is used to fix a broken chair? When should oil be changed in the car?... Which are good places to go for a vacation? How do you get there? Where do you stay? What have you enjoyed and not enjoyed in previous vacations?

Other problems occurred in general cognitive processing (Meltzer, 1983, p.4):

> Organization of thinking was hampered... I had trouble keeping the facts in mind, which made it difficult to organize them..... Comparing things along a number of variables is difficult to do when you can not retain the variables or retain the comparison after you have made it.

As a result of his memory problem, even recreation became difficult (Meltzer, 1983, p.4):

> Movies and T.V. watching became work. If it is a story, the trouble is remembering the beginning of the story or who the characters are...... In terms of sports on T.V. there is trouble remembering which team is which, which team is ahead, which players did the scoring, and how it all relates to their past performance.

Meltzer also had considerable trouble in spatial memory (Meltzer, 1983, p.5):

> Even inside a building, getting lost was commonplace, and sometimes it took days for me to figure out and remember how to get out of a building. In taking walks, even in a familiar neighborhood I could get lost.

Finally, interpersonal relationships were hampered by his memory deficit (Meltzer, 1983, p.6):

> Having conversations could become a trial. Often in talking with people I was acquainted with, I had trouble remembering their names or whether they were married or what our relationship had been in the past. I worried about asking where someone's wife is and finding out that I had been at her funeral two years ago.

And participating in a conversation was difficult for other reasons too:

> Often if I didn't have a chance to say immediately what came to mind, it would be forgotten and the conversation would move to another topic. Then there was little for me to talk about. I couldn't remember much about current events or things I read in the paper or saw on T.V. Even juicy titbits of gossip might be forgotten. So in order to have something to say, I tend to talk about myself and my "condition". My conversation became rather boring.

In fact, Meltzer persevered, and with help was able to show sufficient improvement that eventually he was able to return to his job, and as is clear, to write at least one paper. His account is well worth reading for the insight it gives into the problem of having a memory deficit, and also for the hints it provides to carers and those responsible for treating the brain-damaged.

Categorizing and Studying Memory Disorders

However, although Meltzer's account gives us a very vivid picture of what it is like to have a memory problem, it does not, and of course was not intended to give an objective description of amnesia. One of the problems in coming up with such a description is the doubts surrounding the question of whether amnesia is a unitary affliction, or whether it comprises many different deficits. If you read the amnesia literature, you may be puzzled to find that different workers appear to categorize their patients on a different basis. Some papers categorize their patients according to the origin of the amnesia, whether it be from viral encephalitis or from closed head injury or from alcoholism. Others appear to base their categorization on the area of the brain that is presumed to be damaged, the temporal lobes or the limbic system or perhaps the frontal lobes. Yet others categorize their patients functionally, selecting them on the basis of a very pure memory deficit, regardless of how this was acquired. There is no doubt that this mix of ways of categorizing patients has caused difficulties in the past, and probably will do so in the future. Since all three are appropriate for certain questions, but not others, it is perhaps wise at this point to consider the issue.

Studies Based on Disease

If the paper in question is concerned with the outcome of a particular type of illness or brain damage, then clearly it is important to select patients on this basis. Hence, if I wanted to write about the outcome of senile dementia of a particular kind, then it would be important for me to include in my group patients who have that dementia, and exclude all others. However, patients who have the same illness may be very different in their behavior, and indeed may show quite marked differences in the amount and distribution of underlying brain damage. Hence, having a group that is diagnostically pure does not mean that one can assume a pure or indeed homogeneous memory deficit.

Studies Based on Brain Localization

A second way of classifying patients is according to area of brain damage. It may be the case that two patients with quite different diseases happened to have damage to the same part of the brain, and behave quite similarly, whereas two patients with the same disease may have very different memory deficits. If the primary question is one of brain localization, then this is obviously the most appropriate way of assigning patients. On the other hand however, techniques for localizing brain damage are still very far from perfect. Some types of brain damage such as that following carbon monoxide poisoning may not be detectable on a standard brain scan. Furthermore, lesions are very rarely clearly circumscribed and will usually affect more than one part of the brain. Hence, although such studies are essential for work on brain localization, if one's main interest is in the functional characteristics of memory, then categorizing patients on the basis of localization may be inappropriate.

Studies Based on Functional Deficit

The third way of classifying patients is to assign them on the basis of their functional characteristics. Hence, if one is interested in long-term memory for example, one might wish to confine the study to patients who are amnesic but have normal working memory and are otherwise intellectually intact. This will allow one to draw conclusions about memory that are not distorted by the presence of other separate deficits such as problems in perceiving or attending. If one is primarily interested in theoretical questions concerning the functioning of human memory then such patients with pure deficits offer the most powerful source of evidence, and it is patients of this type that have yielded the most revealing data, examples being Milner's study of the amnesic patient H.M., and Shallice and Warrington's study of the short-term memory patient K.F. (Milner, 1966; Shallice & Warrington, 1970). However, such pure cases are rare; consequently they are usually reported as single cases.

There is one particularly pure pattern of amnesia that has been very extensively and profitably studied in recent years. It can occur in a very dense form in the absence of any general cognitive deficit, and in the presence of excellent working memory, and good autobiographical and semantic memory. This classic *amnesic syndrome* has been so extensively studied that it is easy to get the impression that all amnesics are like this. In fact such pure cases are rare, and for that reason I shall begin by talking about the form of memory deficit that is much more common, before going on to discuss the amnesic syndrome and then returning to the question of whether or not there are many different kinds of amnesia.

CLOSED HEAD INJURY AND MEMORY

A few years ago, I was sitting in my car in a line of traffic waiting behind a tractor to cross a busy seaside road. Quite suddenly I saw the body of a man with a blue crash helmet sail high in the air across the front of the tractor to land in the road, where it lay motionless. He was apparently a motorcyclist who had been struck by a car turning into our side road. Helpers swarmed around; a woman began to weep hysterically, someone else called for the ambulance, here was yet another head injury.

In Britain there are approximately 7,500 serious cases of head injury a year, of whom about 97% survive. Until quite recently, there was comparatively little solid information on the probable outcome of head injury. Head injury patients tend to have deficits that are rarely sufficiently pure to interest the research-minded neuropsychologist, while the neurosurgeon is typically more interested in the acute problem of keeping the patient alive than in the question of what happens afterwards. In the 1970s, however, a number of people in different countries began to point out that this was an important practical question. The number of head injuries from causes such as road traffic accidents was large, and unlikely to drop very substantially. Furthermore, many such casualties were young, and if severely disabled might require care of an expensive kind for many years to come.

This concern resulted in a concerted attack on the problem which I became peripherally involved in through an interest in memory and amnesia. The resulting research was not, of course, by any means limited to psychology, being concerned with the medical, surgical, psychiatric and social aspects of head injury as well as its psychological concomitants. It has more recently been overtaken as the popular topic for concern by senile dementia.

However, work continues albeit at a steadier rate, and there is no doubt that we now know considerably more about head injury than we did 10 years ago (see Levin, Grafman, & Eisenberg, 1987 for an overview of current research).

A blow on the head may cause damage, not only through large lesions, but also as a result of the twisting and tearing of the microstructure of the brain. Furthermore, as the brain moves about inside the skull, bony protuberances are likely to cause lacerations, commonly in the area of the temporal lobes which are particularly relevant to the functioning of long-term memory. The resulting memory deficit is of three possible kinds, *post-traumatic amnesic* (PTA), *retrograde amnesia* and *anterograde amnesia*.

Post-traumatic Amnesia

Following a severe head injury, the patient is likely to remain unconscious for some time, gradually recovering consciousness and entering the stage known as post-traumatic amnesia. This is a relatively confused stage during which patients may have difficulty keeping track of ongoing activities, knowing where they are or remembering material presented to them. The degree of confusion may vary considerably, with islands of lucidity being interspersed with periods of relatively dense amnesia, something which makes the assessment of post-traumatic amnesia (PTA) rather difficult. Measuring length of PTA is of some interest as one predictor of the probable eventual degree of disability, although not a very precise one.

Retrograde Amnesia

After a head injury, it is commonly the case that the patient will have difficulty recalling events before the accident. This may extend back for many years, as the following quotation illustrates. It is taken from the work of Ritchie Russell (1959, pp.69–70), an Oxford neurologist who carried out pioneering work on head injury.

> A greenkeeper, aged 22, was thrown from his motorcycle in August 1933. There was a bruise in the left frontal region and slight bleeding from the left ear, but no fracture was seen on X-ray examination. A week after the accident he was able to converse sensibly, and the nursing staff considered that he had fully recovered consciousness. When questioned, however, he said that the date was February 1922, and that he was a schoolboy. He had no recollection of five years spent in Australia and two years in this country working on a golf course. Two weeks after the injury he remembered the five years spent in Australia, and remembered returning to this country; the past two years were a complete blank. Three weeks after the injury he returned to the village where he had been working for two years. Everything looked strange, and he had no recollection of ever

having been there before. He lost his way on more than one occasion. Still feeling a stranger to the district, he returned to work; he was able to do his work satisfactorily, but he had difficulty in remembering what he had actually done during the day. About 10 weeks after the accident the events of the past two years were gradually recollected and finally he was able to remember everything up to within a few minutes of the accident.

Retrograde amnesia typically shrinks in this way, suggesting that some process has interfered with the retrieval of old memories. It is also characteristically the case that recent memories are most severely affected. However, although some shrinkage is likely to occur, subjects typically do not recover their memory for the period immediately before the accident. This was well illustrated in a study by Yarnell and Lynch (1970) of American footballers who had been "dinged" (concussed) during a game. They were able to report the name of the play (e.g. pop 22) as they were led off, but when tested a few minutes later were quite unable to recall the play or its name. Yarnell and Lynch point out that the information had clearly been encoded, and suggest that subsequent failure to recall may have been the result of failure of the memory trace to consolidate. However, although consolidation may appear to be the most obvious interpretation of the effects of concussion or electro-convulsive therapy, it is not the only possible explanation, and a number of people have suggested that the problem may be one of retrieval rather than failure to consolidate (e.g. Miller & Springer, 1974).

Although shrinkage of the amnesia may frequently occur, it is not at all unusual for autobiographical memory to continue to be rather patchy, and if the amount of brain damage is substantial, it may be very dense (e.g. Baddeley & Wilson, 1986; Kopelman, Wilson, & Baddeley, in press).

Anterograde Amnesia

Anterograde amnesia refers to problems in ongoing memory and new learning, as opposed to retrograde amnesia which reflects a problem in recalling things from the distant past. It is the most characteristic and striking feature of almost all memory deficits. There are very occasional cases in which retrograde amnesia is present but no anterograde learning difficulty, suggesting that these are separable functions, but such cases are rare. It is much more common to have the reverse, namely learning deficits, with relatively little difficulty in recalling items that occurred well before the onset of amnesia.

Anterograde amnesia affects a wide variety of new learning, and while occasionally patients occur who have a specific deficit in remembering verbal material, usually associated with damage to the left cerebral hemisphere or with specific visuo-spatial learning deficits, typically associated with damage to the right hemisphere

(Milner, 1968, 1971), such cases are very much the exception rather than the rule, even in the case of stroke patients whose damage may be largely confined to one hemisphere (Faglioni & Spinnler, 1972; Wilson, Cockburn, Baddeley, & Hiorns, in press).

THE AMNESIC SYNDROME

Most head injury patients, and indeed most patients with memory problems have deficits that extend beyond memory. These may influence the patient's capacity to perceive, to attend, or may influence the patient's emotional state, making him irritable, or possibly excessively passive. Any of these might plausibly interfere with efficient learning, and could give rise to a secondary memory deficit, a problem in remembering that stems from difficulties of another kind. To take an extreme example, an aphasic patient who can not comprehend language would obviously have great difficulty in remembering a passage of prose. Nevertheless, one would not wish to say that the poor score was due to amnesia. There are, however, some patients who appear to have an extremely pure amnesia, unaccompanied by any of the many problems that typically beset a seriously head-injured patient. This relatively isolated but dense form of memory deficit is typically referred to as the *amnesic syndrome*.

The amnesic syndrome can result from a variety of causes. One of the most frequent of these is Korsakoff's syndrome, an affliction resulting from drinking too much and eating too little, resulting in a thiamine deficiency and subsequent brain damage. While Korsakoff cases can be very pure, more typically they have deficits that extend beyond memory, often being linked with damage to the frontal lobes and resulting in a general intellectual deficit which may be associated with impairment in the operation of the central executive component of working memory (Baddeley, 1976).

Another source of the amnesic syndrome is damage to the brain following viral infection. Clive Wearing, the desperately amnesic patient discussed in the introductory chapter, became amnesic as a result of viral encephalitis. Yet another source of amnesia is lesion to critical areas of the brain; the classic amnesic patient, H.M., you may recall became amnesic as a result of bilateral removal of large parts of his hippocampus and temporal lobes. Damage may also result from lack of oxygen, as in Meltzer's case, or from poisoning as occurs occasionally in cases of attempted suicide.

What do all these cases have in common? While they do not all show lesions to one single part of the brain, they do typically appear to be associated with lesions somewhere within a circuit linking the temporal lobes, the hippocampus, the mamillary bodies and the frontal lobes. Work on monkeys by Mishkin (Mishkin, 1982; Mishkin, Malamut, & Bachevalier, 1984) suggests a similar area of vulnerability in non-human primates. As such, it suggests that an animal model of amnesia that has been sought with apparently little success for many years may now be in sight (see Weiskrantz, 1982).

Functional Characteristics

As you may recall from the chapters on short-term and working memory, information from amnesic patients has played an important role in shaping current concepts of memory. This in turn has led to a much more detailed understanding of the amnesic deficit. In describing this, it might be helpful to use a specific case, that of K.J., a man of 59 who developed a dense but pure amnesia following meningitis (Wilson & Baddeley, 1988). He was a highly intelligent man with a verbal I.Q. of 133 and a performance I.Q. of 131, suggesting no impairment in general intellectual function. He showed no sign of perceptual problems and no evidence of the attentional executive problems that go with frontal lobe damage; he was in short, a very pure case of the amnesic syndrome.

Working Memory

This can be quite intact in amnesic patients. For example, K.J. had a digit span that was above average and showed excellent recency in free recall. Performance on the Peterson task can also be extremely good; probably the best Peterson performer I have ever encountered was a densely amnesic Korsakoff patient (described in detail in Warrington, 1982), while Cermak (1976) describes similarly high performance in a patient suffering from amnesia following encephalitis.

Long-term Memory

The central and most striking feature of the amnesic syndrome is difficulty in new episodic learning. Hence, K.J. had great difficulty for example in learning to recognize new therapists or to learn their names, to find his way about in new environments, or to remember what he had read in the paper or seen on television. His performance on more formal tasks was also extremely poor when tested after a brief delay. Hence, although his capacity to repeat back a paragraph of prose immediately was quite good, a few minutes later he was able to recall none of it. His visual memory was similarly poor; he was able to make a good copy of a complex figure, but when asked to reproduce it a few moments later was quite unable to do so.

Semantic Memory

This was apparently unimpaired in K.J. His vocabulary score was extremely high, but then this is often preserved in patients who are otherwise severely impaired. An aspect of semantic memory that is much more vulnerable to brain damage, however, is speed of sentence verification, using sentences of the type developed by Collins and Quillian (1969) in which the subject must verify statements about the world. In this version of the test, a sheet of such sentences is presented, and the subject required to tick those that are true and put a cross by those that are false, doing as many as possible in a standard period of time, usually three minutes. K.J.'s performance on this was extremely good both in terms of speed and accuracy, being comparable with an equivalently intelligent control group. He was also normal in his capacity to generate items from a semantic category such as birds or vegetables, and in the speed and accuracy with which he was able to categorize items as belonging to the same category or not (e.g. *table-sweater*—no; *swimming-rugby*—yes).

Autobiographical Memory

We tested this both by the Galton method of presenting cue words and asking for associates, and by means of structured interview. Both suggested that his capacity to remember incidents from well before his illness was excellent, although there was a suggestion of poorer retention of information from the period immediately preceding the onset of amnesia.

It is by no means always the case that pure amnesic patients have intact autobiographical memory. A case studied by Wilson (1982) showed very similar performance to K.J. on tests of working memory, semantic and episodic memory, but nevertheless had very poor autobiographical memory (Baddeley & Wilson, 1986).

Procedural Learning

The most striking developments of research in amnesia over the last few years has been the realisation that there is a remarkably large number of tasks in which amnesic patients show normal rates of learning. The observation that some such preserved learning can occur is not a new one, but what is novel is the discovery of the extent of this learning.

Since this was discussed in Chapter 9 (see p.207), it will not be further elaborated here, other than to mention that in the case of patient K.J., we observed normal procedural learning on the pursuit rotor, normal perceptual learning in reading reversed script, together with rapid acquisition of jigsaw puzzles and excellent performance on the Tower of Hanoi puzzle (Wilson & Baddeley, 1988).

There is now general acceptance that amnesic patients are capable of showing normal learning on a surprisingly wide range of tasks. What do such tasks have in common? They all appear to have the characteristic of testing learning without requiring the subject to be aware of the source of the information. In the case of the incomplete words and pictures, the patient presumably regards the task as one of solving a visual puzzle. Having previously seen the word or picture will prompt him to make the appropriate response, but the patient need not be aware of the source of this information; indeed amnesic patients typically deny ever having encountered the task on which they show clear evidence of earlier learning (see Baddeley, 1982; Parkin, 1982; and Schacter, 1987 for reviews).

In the case of motor skills, for example, it is unnecessary for the patient to remember that he has encountered that task before; it is enough for him simply to perform it to the best of his ability. The same explanation can be applied to classical conditioning, the reading of transformed script, the biasing of spelling patterns and even the solving of puzzles, both simple such as childrens' jigsaws, and complex such as the Tower of Hanoi. As we saw in Chapter 9, there is now extensive further evidence for at least two types of long-term learning based on normal subjects, although the detailed nature and explanation of this distinction remains controversial (see Chapter 9, p.209 and the review by Richardson-Klavehn & Bjork, 1988).

Theoretical Implications

We have then a reasonably clear and uncontroversial picture of the pattern of deficits shown by amnesic patients. Broadly speaking they can have perfectly normal working memory, good semantic and autobiographical memory, and be capable of procedural learning, despite a very dense amnesia that interferes with the acquisition of new episodic memories. From a clinical viewpoint, a clear description of the syndrome is useful, at least as a first step in helping such patients. There is now, for example, no excuse for the type of misdiagnosis I came across a few years ago, where a woman had attempted suicide and been left with a classic amnesic syndrome. The psychiatrist who saw her was puzzled by the fact that her immediate memory was normal, and diagnosed her as suffering from hysterical amnesia. Understanding the pattern of deficits should also give us clues as to how to provide suitable clinical tests, an issue I will return to later in the chapter.

What are the theoretical implications of this line of research? I would claim that these have been very substantial. As we saw earlier, the amnesic syndrome played an important role in establishing the distinction between long-term and short-term or working memory. While the exact characterization of the distinction is still somewhat controversial (Crowder, 1982), I think that most theorists would now accept the value of separating the study of such active temporary memory systems as are involved in working memory from the study of long-term learning and forgetting. However, this development essentially reflected the application to clinical cases of distinctions already suggested on the basis of research carried out on normal subjects.

The observation of intact procedural learning in amnesic patients is an interesting example of the flow of ideas in the opposite direction. Here, data from patients suggested a distinction that had not previously been made in normal subjects. Subsequent work for example by Jacoby and Dallas (1981) has suggested that a similar distinction operates within normal human memory, with procedural learning being insensitive to a number of factors that influence episodic learning, such as depth of processing and degree of elaboration.

Further evidence for procedural learning within normal subjects comes from studies by Mayes and Meudell (1981), who show that when the level of retention of normal subjects is reduced to that of amnesics, they show similar phenomena. In one study they presented their subjects with pictures and asked them to look for a particular item, for example, a cup or a dog. On subsequent tests, amnesics were more rapid in finding the designated item, even in those cases where they failed to recognize ever having seen the picture before. An exactly equivalent effect was observed in normal subjects, provided the delay between the initial presentation and the later test was sufficiently great for recognition memory to drop to a level equivalent to that found in the amnesic patients.

Evidence from the amnesic syndrome, therefore, has caused not only a fractionation of memory into long-term and working memory, but is now leading to a further fractionation of long-term memory itself. The distinction between semantic and episodic memory had of course already suggested a split. However, it has never been clear that the semantic-episodic definition represented separate systems rather than two modes of operation of the same system. In the case of procedural learning, there is probably considerably more general agreement that it does represent a separate system. Indeed, the analysis of procedural learning is probably one of the liveliest areas of research in long-term memory at present. Does procedural learning represent a single type of learning, or are there many types of procedural learning that simply have in common the fact that they do not depend upon recollection of the source of the information?

One conceptualization of the structure of memory that may not be generally accepted, but at least has the merit of coherence and simplicity is that recently proposed by Tulving (1985). It is shown in Figure 16.1, and comprises two continua, one specifying the nature of the memory involved, paralleled by the second system which specifies the involvement of conscious awareness. As ever, Tulving has a fondness for neologisms and uses the term "noetic" to refer to this degree of conscious awareness. Note that at the highest level it has episodic memory which is classified as *autonoetic*, meaning that it is dependent on the subject's self-awareness.

Episodic memory in turn can build up into semantic memory, which is categorized as *noetic*. Here, the subject is aware of the information stored, but not of its point of origin. An even deeper level of learning produces the procedural learning we have just been discussing. This is described as *anoetic*, requiring no conscious awareness. Riding a bicycle, for example, is not typically enhanced by recollecting the occasions on which you learnt to ride; indeed as anyone who has tried to improve a tennis shot knows, becoming aware of your muscle patterns is rarely associated

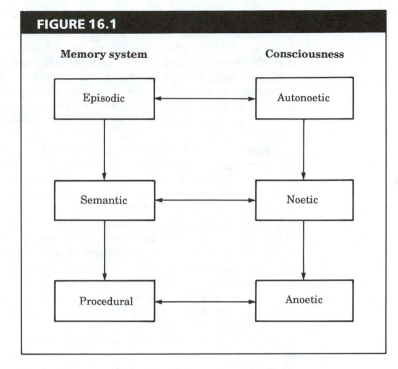

FIGURE 16.1

A schematic diagram of the relations between memory systems and varieties of consciousness. From Tulving (1985). Copyright (1985) American Psychological Association.

Memory system

Consciousness

| Episodic | ←→ | Autonoetic |

| Semantic | ←→ | Noetic |

| Procedural | ←→ | Anoetic |

with playing good shots, although it may be useful in breaking up old habits so as to give new ones a chance to develop.

EXPLAINING THE AMNESIC SYNDROME

So far we have concentrated on describing the pattern of memory deficits associated with amnesia. This has had interesting theoretical implications, but these do not tell us just why the amnesic patient has a memory deficit. It is, of course, not logically necessary that an information-processing account of the amnesic syndrome will be particularly revealing. The deficit is clearly physiological in origin, and it is possible that the breakdown does not influence any single component of the information-processing sequence involved in learning and memory. While this should always be borne in mind, it is clearly worth exploring the possibility of isolating the memory stage at which the deficit occurs, since this may have implications not only for memory theory, but also for helping patients to cope with their memory deficit. A good deal of research over the last decade has attempted to tackle this problem. As a result, we are able to rule out a number of previously plausible theories, although we still do not have a generally accepted answer. On the whole, the theories have tended to be associated with the hypothetical stages of learning, namely input, storage and retrieval.

Input Theories

One influential input theory has been that proposed by Cermak within a levels of processing framework; Cermak suggested that perhaps amnesic patients do not spontaneously encode material at a deep semantic level, resulting in inadequate learning. He and his colleagues ran a number of experiments using alcoholic amnesic patients suffering from Korsakoff's syndrome. In one study Cermak and Moreines (1976) required their patients to listen to sequences of words, responding when a word was immediately repeated, or when it was followed by a rhyme, or by a word from the same semantic category. The amnesic patients were well able to detect repetitions and rhymes, but were severely impaired in their capacity to detect items from the same semantic category.

Although this is an impressive result, its interpretation is not entirely unequivocal. If one assumes a discrimination interpretation of release from proactive interference (PI) (see pp.250–252), then it is conceivable that the amnesic patients do not use the difference in category simply because they have forgotten that the change had occurred, rather than because they had failed to encode the material semantically. For example, an amnesic patient I tested using this technique showed the same lack of release from PI, coupled with clear evidence of semantic coding; her remarks on the items made it clear that she was encoding them semantically, but had simply forgotten that all the previous words were from a different category when it came to recalling the critical items.

Cermak's interpretation of amnesia as an encoding deficit was an attractive one in many ways. It has the advantage of linking the neuropsychological data to a well-established and well-researched area of normal memory, and furthermore held out the promise of a possible way of alleviating the memory deficit by encouraging deeper levels of coding.

A number of groups have explored this possibility of reversing the amnesic deficit. In one study, Cermak and Reale (1978) carried out an experiment in which they used the standard Craik and Lockhart procedure for manipulating depth of encoding, requiring subjects either to make a physical judgment concerning the letters in which a word was written, a slightly deeper phonological judgment, or a semantic judgment which would be expected to lead to the deepest encoding and the best retention. While the control patients showed these effects clearly, the amnesic subjects in this study learnt virtually nothing in any of the conditions.

Such a result could be interpreted in two ways, either as indicating that amnesic patients fail to obtain the usual benefit from deeper coding, which would support a coding interpretation of their deficit, or alternatively that their learning deficit was so great that even given the advantage of deep encoding, their performance was still below the floor level. Just as a *ceiling effect* where two groups are both at 100% recall, may mask differences in degree of over-learning, so *floor effects*, where two groups are at zero recall can mask genuine differences in degree of learning (see p.423 for a further discussion).

In order to settle the question, Cermak and Reale carried out a further experiment in which they ensured that their amnesic subjects were given enough training on the task to avoid floor effects. Under these circumstances, the amnesic patients showed the standard levels of processing effect, with deeper processing leading to better learning.

A similar result was obtained by Meudell, Mayes, and Neary (1980) in a study using drawings and cartoons. They had three instruction conditions, in one the subjects were simply told to remember the cartoons, in a second, a low level of encoding was encouraged by showing the subject two almost identical cartoons and requiring the subject to spot the difference, while a third condition encouraged deep encoding by asking the subjects to describe the cartoons, and also rank them for degree of humor. The results of this study are shown in Figure 16.2 from which two things are clear, first that the amnesic Korsakoff patients tested do show the standard levels of processing effect, and, secondly, that this is not sufficient to explain their memory deficit since even when they are encouraged to encode deeply, their level of learning is substantially below that of controls. In a further study, when level of performance was equated by inserting a delay between presentation and test for the control subjects, the results of the

FIGURE 16.2

Effect of encoding instructions on subsequent recognition of humorous or neutral cartoons by amnesic patients and controls. Both groups are helped by humor and by deeper encoding instructions. Adapted from Meudell, Mayes, and Neary (1980).

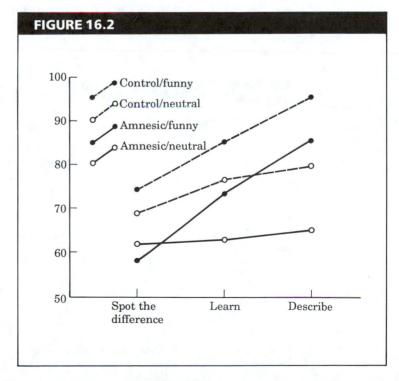

two groups were essentially identical, as was the overall assessment of the humoressness of the cartoons. It is nice to know that unlike memory, sense of humor is not apparently dissolved by alcohol.

Is Amnesia due to Faster Forgetting?

One obvious possibility is that amnesics learn normally, but forget faster, possibly because of inadequate consolidation of a memory trace. In the early days, this looked a promising interpretation since amnesics do appear to "forget" very rapidly in that they can remember long enough to carry on a conversation, but are not able to recall the conversation later. However, as we saw earlier, the initial level of performance is probably largely based on working memory rather than LTM, so there is no reason to assume that degree of long-term learning of the conversation was ever very high. In those situations in which learning can be shown to occur, then there appears to be no evidence of faster forgetting in amnesics, whether tested by completion of words and pictures (Warrington & Weiskrantz, 1970) or by other methods of procedural learning such as motor skills, jigsaw puzzle learning or the acquisition of mazes (Brooks & Baddeley, 1976).

It could be argued however that these results simply reflect equivalent rates of forgetting for procedural learning; what about episodic memory? This was explored in a careful study by Huppert and Piercy (1978a) in which they presented a series of distinctive colored photographs to their subjects for subsequent testing by recognition. As mentioned in the chapter on visual memory,

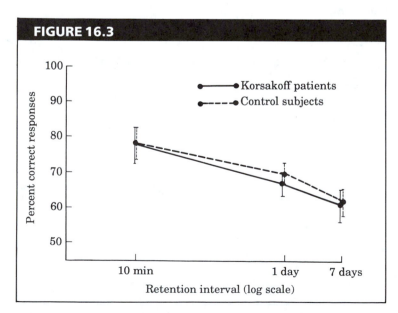

Korsakoff patients forget no faster than controls on picture recognition when performance at 10 min has been equalized. From Huppert and Piercy (1978).

FIGURE 16.3

memory for pictures tends to be rather good. Furthermore, by presenting the pictures much more slowly to the amnesic patients, Huppert and Piercy were able to equate their level of initial learning with that of control subjects. They then tested samples of their list at varying intervals after presentation. The results of their study are shown in Figure 16.3, from which it is clear that amnesic and control patients were forgetting at the same rate.

There have been suggestions that while certain types of amnesic patient may show general forgetting, others show rapid forgetting (e.g. Squire, 1982). The evidence for this will be discussed later, but can at best be considered equivocal.

Amnesia as a Retrieval Deficit
The Interference Hypothesis

Given that amnesics do not appear to encode material any differently, and do not forget any faster, can they therefore be shown to have a retrieval deficit? One possible explanation was suggested by Warrington and Weiskrantz (1970) who suggested that amnesics might be particularly vulnerable to interference effects. They suggest that the capacity for amnesics to benefit from partial cueing might stem from the tendency of this procedure to rule out competing items from earlier learning. It is the case that most of the procedural learning tasks could probably be regarded as having this characteristic of minimizing interference from competing responses.

The interference interpretation continued to be an influential one for many years, but was finally rejected by Warrington and Weiskrantz themselves (1978) as a result of experiments that attempted to explore directly the interference effects between successive lists. They used the previously described procedural learning procedure of letter-cueing in which the words to be learnt were selected so as to have relatively few potential competing responses. They chose two of these, for example *cyclone* and *cycle*. Subjects first had to learn to respond to the cue letters *cyc* with "cyclone", after which they were required to learn to respond instead with the alternative response "cycle". On the very first transfer trial the performance of the two groups was equivalent, whereas the interference hypothesis would predict greater impairment in the amnesic patients.

In a second experiment a similar procedure was used, again requiring subjects to learn two lists in which the target words were based on the same three initial letters. In this case, however, learning of the second list was followed by a test in which subjects were asked to provide responses from both the first and the second list. Both amnesic and control subjects showed the standard interference effect, but the magnitude of the effect was the same in the two groups, suggesting that the amnesic subjects were no more susceptible to interference than the controls.

The Contextual Hypothesis

As we saw from the chapter on retrieval, recent research has highlighted the importance of contextual cues, and a number of people have suggested that amnesics may be deficient in associating the material learned with the cues necessary for subsequent retrieval. Winocur and Mills (1970) suggested a contextual cue interpretation of results showing impaired memory in rats following brain lesions, and Winocur (1978) followed this up in a study concerned with the role of context in human learning. He carried out an experiment in which an amnesic and a control group learnt potentially interfering material in either the same or a different environment from that in which the initial learning took place. The amnesic subjects showed a much more powerful effect of environment than the controls, a result that Winocur interpreted as supporting the contextual cue hypothesis. Unfortunately, however, the control subjects were performing at near ceiling level, which meant that any advantage from the changed environment would have been masked.

A contextual cueing hypothesis was also favored by Huppert and Piercy (1978b) following a study in which subjects were required to make separate judgments of the recency and frequency with which they had seen a particular picture. The design was as follows; on day 1, subjects were shown a long sequence of distinctive photographs of scenes and objects, half of which appeared once and half twice. On day 2 they saw a second list, involving different pictures which again were presented either once or twice. After a brief delay they were then shown a sample of items from the two lists; on half the occasions they were asked to judge whether the items had appeared once or twice, while on the other occasions they had to judge whether they had seen them that day or the day before.

Control subjects perform this task reasonably well, amnesics not so well. The crucial question, however, was the exact nature of the decrement, and focuses in particular on judgments made about items presented the previous day. Control subjects were more likely to be correct in saying that a given item occurred on day 1 if that item had occurred twice, suggesting perhaps that they were associating each presentation of the item with some representation of that particular session, with two such presentations being better than one. The amnesics however showed the opposite pattern, and were more likely to say that a day 1 picture had been presented on day 2 if it had been presented twice on the first day, as if they were relying on overall level of familiarity to tell them how recently an item had been presented; items that had been presented twice would be more familiar, and hence likely to be wrongly categorized as seen on day 2. In short, amnesic patients appear to rely on trace strength whereas controls appear to rely on some form of association between an item and its context in order to remember when it was encountered.

Meudell, Mayes, Ostergaard, and Pickering (1985) point out

that this is virtually the only experimental result which suggests a qualitative difference between the memory performance of amnesics and controls. All the other results can be replicated in normal subjects given sufficiently weak memory traces. They therefore set out to replicate this and include conditions in which the overall level of performance shown by controls is as low as that shown by amnesics. They succeeded in doing this by using extended delays, and found that even under these circumstances, normal subjects were more accurate in assigning items to day 1 when they have occurred twice than when they were only presented once, while amnesics show the opposite pattern.

This is probably the strongest evidence in support of any specific model of amnesia, but is it convincing? What it suggests is that amnesic patients and controls will tackle the same task in a different way, one relying on trace strength and the other relying on contextual association. It is plausible to assume that such associations are difficult for amnesic patients to form, but then so are any other novel associations. Is there any need to assume that contextual associations are more vulnerable than others? I think not.

Another phenomenon that has been used to argue for an interpretation of amnesia in terms of a contextual learning deficit is that of *source amnesia*, the tendency sometimes shown by amnesic patients to be more impaired in their capacity to remember *where* they have acquired new information than *what* that information comprises (Mayes, Meudell, & Pickering, 1985). Schacter, Harbluck, and McLachlan (1984) had amnesic and control patients learn trivia such as "What is Bob Hope's favorite food?" Amnesic patients were more severely impaired in recollecting the source of any such facts they could recall than were controls. Shimamura and Squire (1987) have replicated this finding, but report substantial differences among patients in the extent to which they show source amnesia, with degree of source amnesia being uncorrelated with degree of impairment in fact retention. This would seem to suggest that if source amnesia is indeed an indication of degree of impairment in contextual encoding, then such a deficit is unlikely to provide a general explanation of amnesia, since this would lead one to expect a strong positive correlation between fact and source amnesia. It seems possible that source amnesia is associated with a cognitive deficit that is additional to the amnesic syndrome, possibly related to frontal lobe damage.

Hence, although the contextual coding and retrieval hypothesis remains popular, the evidence for it is still far from conclusive.

A Modal Model of Amnesia

In the last few years, with the general acceptance of the theoretical importance of intact procedural learning in amnesic patients, there has been a tendency for interpretations of amnesia to emphasize similar points and possibly move in the direction of a common interpretation, perhaps a modal model of amnesia. Weiskrantz (1982), in outlining the revised view taken by Warrington and himself acknowledges its similarity to a number of other more recent approaches. Warrington and Weiskrantz now suggest that amnesia may be due to the disconnection between two sources of information involved in learning. On the one hand, certain types of learning can occur as the evidence of procedural learning indicates. On the other, subjects can create cognitive links between previously separate events, the process involved in organizing material. Weiskrantz and Warrington suggest that what amnesics miss is the capacity to relate these two, and in particular to store a record of such organizing or cognitive mediation.

In an earlier review of the literature (Baddeley, 1982) I myself suggested that retrieval might involve two components, an automatic retrieval process, and one based on the more problem-solving processes of recollection. I suggested that there might be a defect in the amnesic patient's capacity to recollect, and that this might be responsible for the anterograde learning deficit that characterizes amnesia. I would now modify my view somewhat, to emphasize that I do not believe that the active search processing involved in recollection is what is lost; K.J. for example, shows excellent recollective powers when asked about his early life. What appears to be lost is the sort of material that the recollective process might utilize, namely the record of new links formed in the process of episodic learning. In this respect then, my views are now very similar to those of Warrington and Weiskrantz. Furthermore, the contextual view could be made very similar if one abandons the hypothesis that there is something different about contextual information, and instead suggest that all conscious links between new experiences are hard to form for amnesics. These will include links to contextual cues but also will extend beyond this to associations between novel target items. This avoids one of the problems of the contextual hypothesis, namely the fact that amnesics are poor at recognition memory, although recognition memory appears to be much less sensitive than recall to change in environmental cues (see Chapter 11).

To summarize then, the evidence seems to be pointing increasingly strongly in the direction of the assumption that one aspect of learning, that involved in episodic memory, involves storing the product of cognitive links or associations made between items that were previously separate. As Weiskrantz (1982) points out, amnesic patients are very good at learning high association pairs where links already exist, but become progressively worse as the link becomes more and more remote, being particularly bad when previously unrelated material must be linked.

Suppose that this characterization of the amnesic syndrome is correct, it still leaves the question of why this particular form of brain damage should have this specific effect. I would suggest that this is the point at which an information-processing interpretation probably needs to map onto some more physiologically based hypothesis. It offers an interesting challenge, but one that goes beyond the remit of the present chapter.

How Many Kinds of Amnesia?

I have so far discussed the amnesic syndrome as if all patients with memory problems are alike. Are they? At a clinical level they are certainly not, since memory deficits are seldom pure, and problems of perception, attention of language will all contribute to any difficulty the patient may have in learning and recalling new material.

A particular source of additional problems occurs in patients who have extensive bilateral damage to the frontal lobes. Such patients are often amnesic, but in addition have further problems such as difficulty in initiating an action, or changing it. Hence, the patients may alternate between periods of inertia and periods of activity, between extreme distractability and stubborn perseveration. For example, one such patient with frontal lobe damage, R.J., discussed in the chapter on autobiographical memory, would frequently be mistaken about his rehabilitation programme, but stubbornly refused to accept any correction.

There is a good deal of current discussion in the case of Korsakoff patients as to whether some of their non-memory performance deficits might be related to the fact that frontal damage is not uncommon in this syndrome (Moscovitch, 1982; Squire, 1982). Although frontal amnesic patients certainly differ in important ways from pure amnesics, it is entirely feasible to explain their behavior in terms of two separate syndromes, one producing their amnesia and the other their dysexecutive frontal behavior (Baddeley & Wilson, 1988).

A second distinction between types of amnesia is proposed by Squire (1982) who claims that amnesic patients with damage in the temporal lobes form a different group from those whose damage is primarily in subcortical structures such as the hippocampus and mammillary bodies. The main critical evidence presented in support of this came from a study by Huppert and Piercy (1979) that suggests that the classic amnesic patient H.M. whose amnesia resulted from bilateral temporal lobectomy shows faster forgetting than do alcoholic Korsakoff patients. However, the magnitude of the difference is very small, and one might expect to find larger differences than this even within a group of normal subjects.

A subsequent study by Kopelman (1985) suggests that rate of forgetting is broadly equivalent in normals, patients suffering from senile dementia of the Alzheimer type, who typically show temporal lobe atrophy, and alcoholic Korsakoff amnesics whose characteristic damage is subcortical. Similarly, a study by Baddeley et al. (1987) showed no evidence for differential rates of forgetting in head-injured patients as compared with the normal elderly, or with young normals. Indeed, the only convincing evidence so far for differential rates of forgetting comes from subjects undergoing electro-convulsive therapy (e.g. Squire, 1982). I would be very dubious about interpreting these transient effects in the same way as the much more permanent effects found in the classic amnesic syndrome, where the memory problems almost certainly result from the loss of brain tissue rather than its temporary disruption.

ALZHEIMER'S DISEASE

Characteristics of the Disease

One memory deficit that certainly does differ from the classic amnesic syndrome is that found in Alzheimer's disease. This is a progressive dementia that has memory deficit as one of its earliest and most pronounced symptoms (Morris & Kopelman, 1986). Typically, the patient becomes steadily worse, showing perceptual, language and emotional problems as the disease moves towards its terminal stage. At a neuropathological level the disease is associated with the development of plaques and neuro-fibrillary tangles within the brain, but in the early stages is often hard to diagnose unequivocally. With improved general medical care, the average age within Western societies is steadily increasing. The frequency of senile dementia is substantial and its cost to society in terms of nursing, medical care and, of course, human suffering, is very great. For that reason there is considerable current interest in the possibility of alleviating dementia.

Neurochemical studies a few years ago showed that the brains of patients suffering from Alzheimer's disease were typically reduced in the level of choline, a substance that has been claimed to play an important role in the neurochemical basis of memory. Attempts were made to alleviate the effects of Alzheimer's disease by feeding the unfortunate patients with choline, an approach that sceptical critics described as equivalent to attempting to help a country with a petrol shortage by flying over in helicopters and pouring the petrol out. Alas, the analogy proved all too apt since the only effect of ingesting choline appears to be to make the patient smell of bad fish.

Other more sophisticated approaches have been taken since that time, and this remains one of the most active areas of neurochemical research, with the cholinergic hypothesis continuing to receive experimental support (Kopelman, 1985). At the time of writing I know of no clear evidence that a neurochemical treatment for Alzheimer's disease is in sight, although in the long term one hopes that either pharmacological treatment or possibly treatment by implanting the diseased brain with regeneration-producing tissue may prove successful (Dunnett, 1989).

Analyzing the Memory Deficit

Should a treatment be discovered, then it will be important to identify patients suffering from the disease as early as possible, since clearly it is important to treat the disease before too much brain damage has occurred. There is hence a good deal of interest in understanding the functional nature of the memory deficit in Alzheimer's disease, from both a theoretical and applied viewpoint.

While memory deficits are certainly not the only cognitive impairments shown by patients suffering from Alzheimer's disease they are among the most prominent and early symptoms. In some respects the Alzheimer patient resembles the classic amnesic, with the deficit in free recall being much more strongly evident in the long-term or secondary memory component, and much less in the recency effect (Wilson, Bacon, Fox, & Kaszniak, 1983; Spinnler, Della Sala, Bandera, & Baddeley, 1988). As with the amnesic syndrome, the functioning of the articulatory loop component of working memory is qualitatively normal, with patients showing phonological similarity and word length effects (Morris, 1984). However, Alzheimer patients differ from amnesic patients in showing a clear deficit in working memory, with both verbal and spatial memory span being impaired (Spinnler et al., 1988) and a clear impairment in performance of the Peterson short-term retention task, where even a relatively undemanding interpolated task such as articulatory suppression may be enough to induce rapid forgetting (Morris, 1986).

One way of conceptualizing the memory deficit shown in Alzheimer patients is to argue that they show a combination of the amnesic syndrome together with the disturbance in central executive functioning, similar to that found in dysexecutive frontal lobe cases (Baddeley, 1986; Becker, 1987).

We decided to try to explore the possibility of a specific central executive deficit by setting up a task which made heavy demands on the central executive capacity to coordinate information from different sources (Baddeley et al., 1986). One problem in setting up such a study is to avoid the objection that any task given to Alzheimer patients will simply overload their limited capacity, with dual tasks being even more demanding and hence causing more overloading.

We therefore opted for two tasks in which we could adjust the level of difficulty so that Alzheimer patients, normal elderly and young control subjects were all performing at a similar level. As one of our tasks we used pursuit tracking whereby the subject attempted to keep a stylus in contact with a spot of light moving around the screen of a visual display unit; the level of difficulty was adjusted by varying the speed so as to ensure that all subjects performed the task at the same level as measured by time on target. We combined this tracking task with digit span; here we adjusted the length of digit sequence until our three groups were performing with an equal error rate. We then required our subjects to perform both tasks simultaneously. The results showed that while the normal elderly are no more hampered by the need to combine two tasks than are the young, the Alzheimer patients are very seriously disrupted by this requirement to coordinate the two.

We followed up our Alzheimer and elderly patients, testing them after six months and a year had elapsed. Alzheimer's disease is progressive, and within 12 months, half of the Alzheimer group had either become so cognitively impaired that they were no longer testable, or had died. As in the initial study, the level of difficulty of the individual tasks was adjusted so that Alzheimer and normal subjects were performing equally well. When the two tasks were combined, however, the effects of dementia were clear, with the decrement growing steadily worse as the disease progressed (see Figure 16.4).

Do our results necessarily suggest a specific deficit in co-ordinating tasks, as the central executive interpretation suggests? Could they not equally well be interpreted in terms of a general limitation in overall processing capacity in patients suffering from dementia? We think not for two reasons. First of all, the progressive decline over time occurred just as clearly in a second experiment in which we combined pursuit tracking with articulatory suppression, a much less demanding task than digit span. A second reason for not interpreting our results in terms of general processing comes from other studies we have carried out in which Alzheimer and normal elderly patients are required to keep track of a number of sources of information simultaneously; in one condition they were making semantic categorization judgments on words, while in another they were keeping track of conversations involving varying numbers of people. Both the controls and the dementia patients showed a tendency for performance to decline as number of alternative sources increased. However, the effect was no greater for patients with dementia than for the controls, suggesting that an increase in difficulty is not enough to penalize the Alzheimer patients differentially.

Given the complexity of the cognitive deficit in Alzheimer's disease, and the relatively primitive state of our understanding of the executive control of working memory, the interpretation of these results must remain tentative. However, they do suggest the potential usefulness of attempting to apply laboratory-based models to practical problems. We are at present attempting to develop a simpler and more easily portable form of the dual-task procedure, which we hope, given suitable development, may prove to be a useful weapon in the armory of the clinician given the difficult task of attempting to decide whether an elderly patient is or is not suffering from the early stages of Alzheimer's disease. It would be nice to think that if and when suitable neurochemical treatments are developed, cognitive psychologists will be able to play their part in ensuring that the treatment reaches the patient while the disease is still at an early stage.

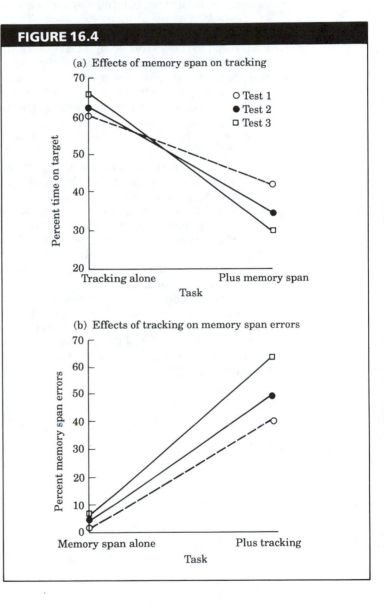

Effects of memory span on tracking, and tracking on memory span in patients suffering from Alzheimer's disease. The three tests were separated by intervals of six months. Progression of the disease has relatively little effect on the tasks when performed alone, but substantially impairs the patients' capacity to perform them at the same time. From Baddeley, Logie, Della Sala, and Spinnler (in preparation).

FIGURE 16.4

(a) Effects of memory span on tracking

○ Test 1
● Test 2
□ Test 3

Percent time on target

Tracking alone   Plus memory span

Task

(b) Effects of tracking on memory span errors

Percent memory span errors

Memory span alone   Plus tracking

Task

OVERVIEW

The chapter began by describing a memory problem from the patient's point of view, before going on to give an account of some of the major causes of memory deficit. The first of these was amnesia following closed head injury. A blow on the head may intially lead to coma followed by a confusional state known as post-traumatic amnesia. The patient typically recovers from this but may have an amnesia for events extending long before the accident, known as retrograde amnesia, and a persistent difficulty with new learning, so-called anterograde amnesia.

The purest and most extensively studied form of memory disorder is the classic amnesic syndrome which is usually associated with damage to the temporal lobes, or to subcortical structures such as the hippocampi or the mammillary bodies. This may result from the alcoholic Korsakoff's syndrome or from damage to these structures as a result of brain infection, stroke or poisoning. The amnesic syndrome is characterized by a marked deficit in episodic memory, typically with preserved working memory, semantic memory and procedural learning. Attempts to give a theoretical explanation of the syndrome are evaluated, and it is concluded that none of the information processing interpretations receives unequivocal support.

The final section considers the memory deficit that accompanies Alzheimer's disease, describing its functional characteristics and suggesting that it may comprise a combination of the classic episodic memory deficit of the amnesic syndrome, coupled with an impairment in the functioning of the central executive component of working memory.

Chapter Seventeen

TREATING MEMORY PROBLEMS

*I*t is sometimes said that "there is nothing so useful as a good theory". But is that true, and if so, why should a theory be useful? I would like to suggest that in this instance, our theoretical knowledge of the way in which memory functions can be helpful in three ways; first, in giving an overview of the problem that will help the clinician provide useful advice to patients and their relatives; we discussed this in the previous chapter. Secondly, the theorist can help provide the clinician with tools for assessing memory. Finally, the theorist can generate ideas for treatment and techniques for monitoring their effectiveness. Each of these will be considered in turn.

ASSESSING MEMORY DEFICITS

As mentioned before, memory problems are often the first and most sensitive indicator of brain damage; on the other hand, some decrement in memory is the normal accompaniment of growing older. Suppose someone complains to their doctor about memory problems; is it possible to tell whether these are likely to be serious, or whether he or she is simply worrying unnecessarily?

There are indeed many tests of memory, some of which have extensive norms, and most of which are sensitive to moderate-to-severe disruption of normal memory functioning. Such tests do a reasonably good job in telling the clinician how a patient's score compares with that of the general population. There are, however, a number of reasons why they are not entirely satisfactory, indicating that further test development would be useful. Many such tests are relatively long, and since they are often also correlated with intelligence, need to be interpreted in the light of current and estimated premorbid I.Q. They are thus likely to require a good deal of time from a qualified clinical psychologist, something that few patients in Britain at least, can expect, since clinical neuropsychologists are few and patients with memory problems numerous. A shorter test that can be given by an occupational or speech therapist would therefore be helpful.

Such a test would ideally map onto the practical problems experienced by the patient, something that is not common among most available clinical tests which are typically based on laboratory tasks, whose relationship to memory problems in everyday life is usually very unclear. Scores on such tests may give the therapist little idea as to what the practical effects of any memory deficit might be, and hence give few clues as to possible treatment strategies. Finally, subjects may resist being tested on material that appears to be of little obvious relevance to their own problems and this may affect their motivation; non-psychologists may also be relatively unimpressed by changes that occur in apparently artificial tests.

An interesting example of this was drawn to my attention a few years ago when I was approached by psychologists from a drug company. They had developed a drug which appeared to alleviate somewhat the symptoms of senile dementia as measured by standard memory tests. The effect was not, however, apparent to the physicians who regularly examined the patients; the doctors rated both experimental and control patients as a little better each time they were examined! As the company pointed out, drugs are bought by doctors, who tend to be unimpressed by a slight improvement on an unrealistic test. Could we suggest something with a higher degree of plausibility?

Perhaps the doctors would have been right to have discounted changes in performance on psychometric tests. Could we really, hand-on-heart, say that the changes were clinically important? Some colleagues and I became intrigued by this question a few years ago, and decided to try to tackle the issue of the relationship between performance on standard memory tasks, and the memory problems encountered by patients in their everyday life (Sunderland, Harris, & Baddeley, 1983).

Measuring Everyday Memory Questionnaires and Standard Tests

The great problem in attempting to validate any memory test is obtaining adequate measures of everyday memory. My colleagues, Alan Sunderland, John Harris and I decided that we would tackle the problem by using a structured interview of the patient and a near relative or spouse, together with diaries in which the subject was encouraged each day to write down any instances of memory lapses. We began by interviewing patients and relatives, and on the basis of this came up with the questionnaire which you may remember having completed on p.234.

We selected as our target group patients who had suffered a moderate-to-severe head injury, with a period of post-traumatic amnesia lasting for at least 24 hours. We knew that such a group would be likely to have memory problems varying in severity. This should give us a good chance of seeing which of a range of existing memory tests might be the best predictor of memory problems in everyday life. We tested two groups of patients, one who had recently returned home, having had their injury within the last few months, and a second who had experienced their head injury several years before. Most of our subjects had acquired their head injuries as a result of a road traffic accident, and we therefore selected a control group of patients who had also been in accidents, but had sustained fractured limbs but no head injury. For all these subjects, everyday memory was assessed using an extensive series of interviews and checklists, while objective memory performance was measured using a large battery of memory tests, most of which had previously been shown to be sensitive to the effects of head injury.

Our results, which are shown in Figure 17.1, suggested first of all that our head-injured patients did indeed have memory problems, whether these were assessed in terms of the number of everyday memory complaints, or performance on the wide range of memory tests used. Furthermore, there was no evidence that the problems were any less in the patients who had had their head injury several years before, although most of this group were now back at work and managing to cope, in some cases extremely well: one of our patients, for example, who was a lecturer in Hebrew had learnt Aramaic since his head injury. However, the subjective reports indicated that our head-injured patients did continue to have problems, and other long-term follow-up studies suggest that memory problems will continue for many years (Thomsen, 1984).

The main purpose of our study however was to look at the relationship between laboratory measures and real-life problems. Here the pattern was far from straightforward. First of all, some measures of memory performance were extremely sensitive to the effects of head injury, but did not correlate with complaints voiced either by the patient or the relative. A test measuring the memory for repeated nonsense figures was one example of this, as was speed of performing the Collins and Quillian (1969) semantic memory task. On the other hand, some tests did correlate with reports of everyday memory problems, most notably a test involving remembering a brief passage of prose.

Finally, we were somewhat disappointed in the low apparent reliability of the questionnaire and checklist measures themselves. In the patients who had had their head injury some years before, the patient's own assessment was consistently more poorly correlated with objective performance than was the relative's assessment. Even more strikingly, for the group of patients who had only just returned home, none of the everyday assessments correlated well with objective performance, although the memory for prose was the best of a bad lot. This is unfortunate since it is exactly at this stage that the therapist is likely to need an accurate assessment of the problems being encountered by the patient.

Why were our subjective measures so disappointing? I suspect that the major reason is summed up in the following quotation. It

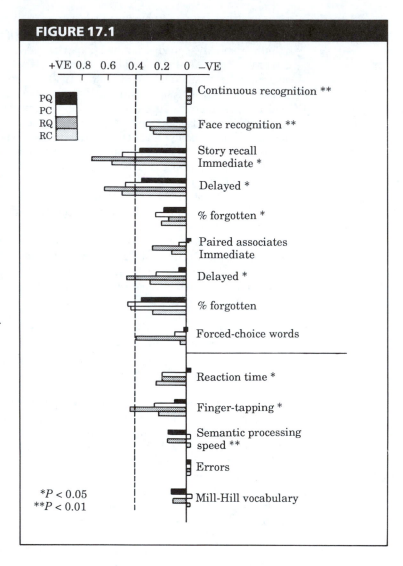

FIGURE 17.1

Relationship between reports of everyday memory problems and performance on a range of laboratory tests. The histograms on the left indicate the degree or correlation between performance on the test in question and four estimates of everyday memory lapses: PQ, patient's interview; PC, patient's checklist; RQ, relative's interview; RC, relative's checklist. The laboratory tests are listed on the right. Those showing significantly poorer performance in patients who suffered a head injury 2-8 years before are marked *(P<0.05) or **(P<0.01). From Sunderland et al. (1986).

does not come from this study but from the diary of a law student who became amnesic following a brain haemorrhage. "Late last night I remembered that I'd forgotten to list those things that I had forgotten. But then how do I know what I'd forgotten?"

This is presumably why the normal relative's report of memory problems tended to correlate more highly with objective test scores than did the head-injured patient's.

In the case of the group of patients who had just returned home, a further source of unreliability probably stems from the fact that some would be living a very sheltered life, being protected by relatives and placing minimal demands on their memory, while others would have returned to work, producing a much greater opportunity for memory lapses to occur. Indeed, the less serious the patient's cognitive impairment, the more likely that he would have returned to a more demanding environment.

We later carried out a similar study, this time concerned with the memory problems of normal elderly subjects rather than head-injured patients, and came up with comparable results, except that subjective estimates of problems appeared to be even less reliable, with the assessment of memory problems provided by the spouse, correlating no better with objective performance than did the subject's own assessment. This is presumably because the spouse, like the subject, was elderly and forgetful (Sunderland, Watts, Baddeley, & Harris, 1986).

What general lessons could we learn from our two studies? First, that a sensitive memory test is not necessarily a good predictor of everyday memory problems. Presumably recognizing nonsense figures does not figure very prominently in everyday life, while the speed of access to semantic memory may be less important than its reliability, which remained high in our patients. We suspect that recalling a prose passage was a good predictor because it involves many different aspects of memory, working memory and semantic memory for comprehension, and episodic memory for retention of the meaning of the passage once it had been understood.

Our second conclusion was that questionnaires may be useful for giving *qualitative* information about those aspects of memory that are most troublesome to the patient, but are likely to be unreliable indicators of how serious the deficit is. Memory for a prose passage appears to be a useful measure, which is somewhat reassuring since it is already extensively used clinically, and does indeed form part of the Wechsler Memory Scale. It does however give only a single score, providing very little detailed information to the therapist who may want help in deciding what aspects of a patient's memory problem to treat.

A Behavioral Memory Test

At about the time we were beginning to publish our work on the validity of memory tests, Barbara Wilson, a clinical psychologist at Rivermead Rehabilitation Center in Oxford became interested in the problem of devising better objective tests of everyday memory performance. She adopted a strategy of first of all attempting to characterize the various memory problems that cropped up frequently both in our study and in her own observations, and then turning each of these into an objectively scorable test. The result of this was the Rivermead Behavioral Memory Test (RBMT), the components of which are shown in Table 17.1.

A patient doing this test would have separate measures of capacity to remember names, to recognize faces, to remember named objects, to learn a route, to indicate orientation in time and

TABLE 17.1

The Rivermead Behavioral Memory Test

1. Remembering a new name — first name.
2. Remembering a new name — second name.
3. Remembering a belonging.
4. Remembering an appointment.
5. Picture recognition.
6. Newspaper story — immediate and delayed recall.
7. Face recognition.
8. Remembering a new route — immediate recall.
9. Remembering a new route — delayed recall.
10. Remembering to deliver a message.
11. Orientation.
12. Date.

space, and to remember to do things. It is, to the best of my knowledge, the only standardized memory test that includes prospective memory items of this kind, despite the fact that forgetting to do things is one of the most frustrating and pervasive features of poor memory.

Having devised the test, the next problem was to validate it, and obtain standard norms. Bearing in mind the problems encountered in using information from patients and relatives in the previous studies, we decided to take advantage of the fact that Rivermead was a rehabilitation center in which a large number of patients with brain damage, and probably memory problems would be treated for a period of several weeks. It also had a team of very keen and co-operative therapists, who agreed to observe each patient during each day's therapy for a period of two weeks. This gave us many hours of observation per subject. At the end of each therapy session, the therapist would mark a checklist indicating any lapses that had been observed. This measure has the advantage that the same therapist will see many different patients, that they will be seen under relatively standard conditions, and that the therapists will be much less emotionally involved in the decision as to whether a lapse has occurred than would be the case with relatives. When a mean number of items passed on the RBMT was correlated with number of lapses per session observed by the therapist, the correlation was a very respectable +0.75 (Wilson, Cockburn, Baddeley, & Hiorns, in press).

Another way of assessing whether the test will pick out patients who have everyday problems was used during the early stages of the project. The occupational therapists were asked to categorize each patient on the basis of whether the patient had sufficient memory problems to create difficulties in treatment. Figure 17.2 shows the performance of these patients on the RBMT. In general, any patient failing more than three or four items on the RBMT is likely to have difficulties. Densely amnesic patients such as the previously described patient K.J., who became amnesic following meningitis, tend to fail virtually all the items. Colleagues elsewhere are using the RBMT to investigate the memory deficit in early Alzheimer's disease, and appear to be finding it sensitive to dementia, but resistant to the effects of depression (Poon, 1987). It is readily acceptable to patients, has high face validity and we think looks quite promising as a sensitive predictor of everyday memory problems.

TREATMENT AND ITS EVALUATION

To what extent can a patient with memory problems be helped? It is important, first of all, to bear in mind that patients are typically amnesic because of damage to the brain. While they may acquire ways of making better use of what remains, they are unlikely to show dramatic recovery after the early months. The brain tissue that has gone will not return.

On the other hand, some recovery almost always occurs, and this can on occasion be quite marked. Nevertheless, the best that can usually be achieved is to encourage the patient to continue to try to cope, while teaching skills for solving the particular memory problems that are most disruptive of the patient's life. Very often external aids such as notebooks, digital watches, calendars and reminders are the most effective. However, there are techniques that can be used to help the patient learn material where necessary. Learning will tend to be slow and laborious, but it may be important that the patient realizes that learning is still possible. Furthermore, a relative or therapist can be given a series of techniques which can be used when an occasion crops up where it is important for the patient to learn something such as the names of new neighbors, or routes from a new house to the shops.

One of the major general problems in teaching mnemonic strategies, whether to normal subjects or brain damaged patients, is that applying them tends to demand ingenuity and persistence. Consequently, although classes in mnemonics may impress the participants with their capacity to remember large amounts of material, very few people who undergo such classes appear to actually put what they learn into practice subsequently (Higbee, 1981).

If this is the case with students who are intelligent and motivated to improve their learning skills in order to pass examinations, how much harder is it likely to be for a brain damaged patient to use mnemonics spontaneously. Therefore, it is important to use such mnemonic techniques as specific tools to be employed only when the patient needs to learn something important, and not as general principles which the patient is expected to apply to his day-to-day problems.

But are such techniques in fact helpful to patients? It is of course important to assess any form of treatment, and given that patients vary enormously in their problems and their capabilities, group studies of mnemonic techniques are unlikely to be very satisfactory. Fortunately, there are techniques that were specially devised to investigate the effects of treatment on a single patient. Most of these originated in the operant conditioning laboratory, they have been adapted for clinical purposes by behaviorally minded clinicians, and are now being used to assess the effectiveness of cognitive rehabilitation. They tend not to be well known to cognitive psychologists who are generally much more familiar with large group designs, or in the case of neuropsychology to single case studies that are concerned with assessing and describing the patient's deficits, rather than evaluating treatment.

TREATMENT DESIGNS

Single-case Designs

Much of what follows is based on the work of Barbara Wilson, a clinical psychologist who has taken particular interest in developing and evaluating ways of helping patients with memory problems. A more detailed description of this work is given in Wilson (1988) and in two books, *The Clinical Management of Memory Problems* (Wilson & Moffat, 1984), and *Rehabilitation of Memory* (Wilson, 1987). The single-case experimental designs are adapted from research on evaluation of behavioral treatments in clinical psychology (see Chapter 9); a more detailed account of such designs is given in Hersen and Barlow (1976).

Stages of Treatment

The procedures typically involve three general stages, first defining the behavior that one wishes to modify or improve, followed by a second stage in which the baseline level of performance is established, followed by the third phase involving a combination of treatment and simultaneous monitoring of treatment effectiveness.

All of these stages are important. It is first of all essential to choose some aspect of behavior that is sufficiently clearly defined to be measurable, and that one has a good chance of changing within a reasonable time scale. A vague goal like "improving memory" would be totally unsatisfactory, whereas attempting to teach the patient a route from home to a local shop and back, or to learn the names of a number of people with whom he or she interacts would be much more sensible.

A crucial second stage is establishing the baseline level of performance. Occasionally, this in itself could be therapeutic, since it may demonstrate that the problem is far less serious than was suspected. More likely is the possibility that improvement is already ongoing. In this case, it may not be necessary to change anything, but simply continue to monitor so as to ensure that progress continues, and of course encourage the subject. The main purpose, however, is to establish the current level of performance in order to allow the later assessment of whether the patient has indeed improved following treatment.

The third phase involves the treatment itself, which should have performance measures built into it, so as to allow evaluation. The critical feature here is that the design should allow one to rule out the possibility that factors other than treatment might be leading to any improvement shown by the patient, who may for instance still be undergoing a gradual natural recovery from his injury. There are several standard procedures for achieving this, and I will describe some of them in the process of giving an account of the ways in which different methods may be applied to helping a patient cope with memory problems.

A Simple AB-AB Design: Remembering Names

This very basic design is one in which the baseline level of performance A is first of all established, after which some therapeutic aid B is provided; if this leads to an enhancement of performance, then the importance of the aid may be assessed by removing it and reverting to A, whereupon performance may drop. If so, treatment B is reinstated, whereupon the patient should then begin to improve once again.

Wilson (1988) describes a case using the AB-AB design involving a young man with a head injury who had great difficulty remembering names for more than a few seconds. She decided to explore the effect of increased rehearsal, using the task of remembering a single name, her own, and an expanded rehearsal procedure whereby the subject is initially tested after a short delay, with each subsequent test delay being longer than the last.

Testing this aspect of behavior went on in parallel with a treatment of other aspects of his memory problems, and involved first of all establishing how long the patient could remember her name, and ascertaining that this length of time did not increase over successive therapy sessions in the absence of treatment. Having established a stable baseline, Wilson then instituted a procedure whereby a timer would buzz, whereupon the young man would be asked to recall the therapist's name. The interval was initially set at a very short period of time, and over successive sessions gradually extended, reaching a point at which the name was retained over a period of nine minutes. Wilson then reverted to the A condition, with no buzzer, and as Figure 17.2 shows, performance began to decline. After a number of sessions during which this decline became very apparent, the buzzer was again introduced, again using an expanded rehearsal procedure, and once again performance improved.

What can one tell from such a study? First of all it is clear that

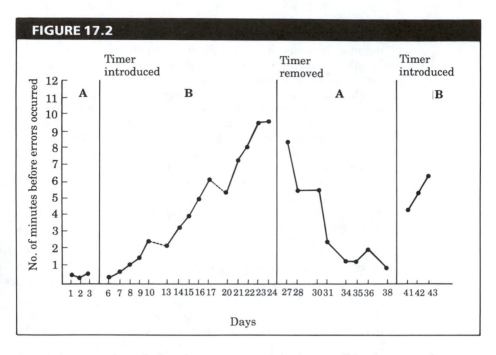

FIGURE 17.2

A simple ABAB design used to test the use of rehearsal to retain a person's name. From Wilson (1988).

introducing the strategy and the buzzer did enhance performance during the session, but the fact that the name was forgotten again suggested that it was simply being maintained without being learnt, an interesting confirmation of the literature discussed in Chapter 3 indicating that maintaining material at a shallow level does not necessarily lead to good learning. The fact that withdrawing the buzzer led to a decline in performance demonstrates the importance of the buzzer to the use of the strategy, a demonstration that is reinforced by the recovery of performance when the buzzer was re-introduced.

While AB-AB designs can be useful, they have severe limitations. In many cases, once something has been learned, then removing the aid to learning does not cause forgetting, or at least one hopes it does not. Hence, if one has taught a patient the route from his ward to the canteen, then one would hope that this information would be retained. On other occasions, when the behavior acquired is of some importance, it would often be unpopular, or even unethical to attempt to revert to baseline. For example, one common use of behavioral programs in head-injured patients is to discourage them from disruptive behavior such as yelling and shouting; re-establishing such behavior does not do much for the popularity of the patient or the psychologist with other patients and staff. In other cases, reverting to baseline would be quite unethical, as for example if a patient had been trained to ensure that a gas cooker is not turned on and then forgotten. Much more widely useful are the multiple baseline designs which will be described next.

Multiple Baseline Designs
Multiple Baseline Across Settings:
Acquiring a Habit

This design is useful if one is attempting to teach a patient a particular form of behavior that is applicable to a range of different settings; very often teaching in one setting will not spontaneously generalize, a major problem for therapy of all kinds, when all too often it is found that what is learnt in the clinic is not necessarily applied when the patient returns home.

A good example of this design is provided in a study by Carr and Wilson (1983) concerned with a paraplegic patient who in addition to being confined to a wheelchair had memory problems following head injury. One unexpected difficulty created by this combination was a tendency to develop pressure sores as a result of failing to lift his buttocks from the wheelchair at sufficiently regular intervals to allow adequate circulation.

Carr and Wilson began by obtaining a pressure sensor that would record every time the patient lifted, and placing this in the wheelchair, initially in only one of the environments in which he operated, namely the occupational therapy workshop. The pressure sensor was set so that it sounded a buzzer if 10 minutes had elapsed since the last lift. As Figure 17.3 shows, the mean number of lifts within the workshop immediately began to increase, while remaining low in the other areas monitored.

When it was clear that lifting within the workshop was satisfactory, the buzzer signal was introduced into a second location, the restaurant during the lunch-break. As Figure 17.3 shows, at this point, lifting during the lunch-break began to increase in frequency, while lifting during the coffee-break and on the ward remained at a low level. In the next phase, lifting was reinforced by the buzzer in a third location, during the coffee-break. As before, lifting in this location began to increase, but note that finally the response was beginning to generalize, so that lifting on the ward also increased.

What can we conclude from this design? It provides strong evidence that the introduction of the pressure-sensing, timing and reminding device enhanced the patient's tendency to lift; we can be reasonably confident that the device itself was important since improvement occurred only when it was introduced, and except at the end, *only* in the location where the buzzer was operating. The possibility that the improvement in lifting might have occurred by chance, or from spontaneous improvement is therefore extremely low, since such general improvement ought to have had equal effects in all environments. Finally, one crucial measure of the effectiveness of the program was that the patient's pressure sores healed.

Multiple Baseline Across Subjects: Testing an
Imagery Mnemonic

This is a procedure for looking at the effectiveness of a particular

A multiple base-line across settings design involving the use of a buzzer to remind a paraplegic patient to lift from his wheelchair. The fact that improvement does not occur until the reminder is introduced into that context indicates that the reminder is crucial. From Carr and Wilson (1983).

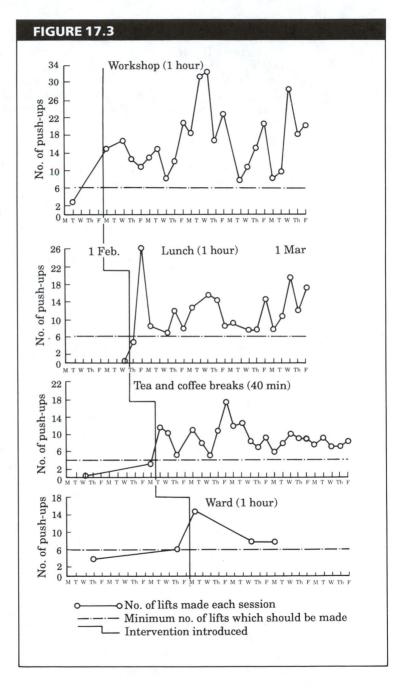

FIGURE 17.3

treatment being given to a group of broadly similar patients, and since several patients are involved it is not, strictly speaking, a single case design. However, conceptually it is very similar to other multiple baseline experimental designs and hence it makes sense to include it at this point. The essence of the procedure is that the crucial intervention is made at different pre-planned times for different patients, the prediction being that if the method is effective, then each patient will only begin to improve when the method has been introduced to that patient.

Wilson (1988) gives an example in which a group of patients with memory problems were taught the names of members of the staff of the rehabilitation unit. Remembering names may appear to be a rather trivial task to a normal healthy person, but it is something that patients often find very difficult, and something that can create considerable social embarrassment. Furthermore, in any social environment discussion about what has happened or what will happen almost inevitably involves referring to people by name; if you cannot remember anyone's name then this further adds to the problems of coping.

The names of members of the rehabilitation unit staff were selected, and each of a group of patients with memory problems were first of all tested for their knowledge of these. As can be seen from Figure 17.4, this was universally low. One of the patients was

FIGURE 17.4

A multiple baseline across subjects design to demonstrate the effectiveness of visual imagery for learning names. None of the four subjects tested begin to improve until the imagery mnemonic is introduced. From Wilson (1988).

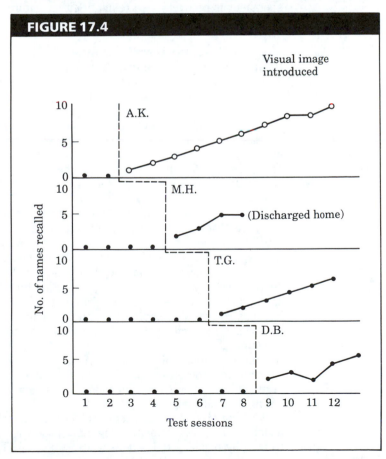

then selected at random, and taught the names systematically, introducing a few each day.

The method of learning was one based on visual imagery. It involved first of all forming an image from the name, and then attempting to link that image with some feature of the named person. Hence, a physiotherapist called "Stephanie" might, for example, be represented by a simple drawing of a step and a knee, and this in turn associated with step-up exercises for knees as carried out by physiotherapists. The patient was encouraged to find his or her link, with help from the psychologists as and when necessary.

Figure 17.4 shows the effect of introducing such a visual imagery mnemonic on retention of the names. Note that performance improves very clearly once the mnemonic is introduced, but that equivalent improvement does not occur in the case of those patients who have not yet been taught to use the imagery system. As each patient is introduced to the system, so performance improves, strongly suggesting that the improvement is due to the introduction of the mnemonic technique, not to spontaneous recovery as a result of either natural recovery of the brain, or longer exposure to the names of the staff.

Multiple Baseline Across Behaviors: Routes, Names and Comprehension

This has much in common with the previous design, in that treatment is introduced at different times. However, rather than having a group of patients all receiving the same treatment, this concerns a single patient who has a number of different memory problems, as is of course frequently the case. In this design, the method of treatment for each problem is introduced at a different time, the prediction being that if the treatment is effective, improvement on that behavior will begin only when the treatment is instituted.

Wilson (1988) describes the case of a patient who had memory problems that affected a number of areas of everyday life, three of which she decided to attempt to treat, namely problems in learning routes, difficulties in understanding and retaining the content of newspaper articles, and problems in learning the names of new people. She began by establishing a baseline for all three of these areas, and during this period it became obvious that one of these, learning a route was improving without treatment, since level of performance steadily increased throughout the baseline period. It appeared then that the simple rehearsal involved in repeatedly testing the route was enough for the patient to improve; unfortunately routes are not always so easily acquired. In the case of the other two problems, no spontaneous improvement occurred during the baseline period.

The first of the two remaining problems to be tackled was that of understanding and remembering newspaper articles. This was treated by teaching the patient to use the PQRST strategy. This approach is named after the four successive steps the subject is encouraged to take, namely, "Preview" wherein the material is given a preliminary reading, "Question" wherein the salient points are identified, "Read" in which the article is carefully read, then "State" involving a statement of the major features of the article followed by a "Test" in which memory for the content is self-assessed. The PQRST technique is, of course, a way of ensuring the reader processes the material deeply, elaborates it and organizes it. It tends to be an effective way of helping patients to ensure that they can read and understand articles, although it is of course unlikely that the method would be used for the casual reading of a newspaper. It proved to be an effective method for this particular patient, and recall duly improved. The third problem to be tackled was that of remembering names; as before, a visual imagery method was used, and again it proved effective.

What then can we conclude from this design? First of all, we note that the mastery of routes in this patient does not need special training, and that for this task, simple repetition is sufficient for learning to occur. Secondly, the fact that improvement in prose comprehension and the learning of names occurs only when the particular treatment strategy was introduced indicates that the strategies themselves were helpful. Had improvement simply occurred as a result of general recovery from brain damage, then the point of improvement should not have exactly coincided in each case with the beginning of treatment.

Multiple Baseline Across Items:
Relearning the Alphabet
A final variant on the multiple baseline approach I would like to discuss comes from a study involving a girl who had become dyslexic after a head injury following a riding accident. She had many problems, including memory difficulties, perceptual problems and agnosia, a difficulty in object-recognition. This probably lay at the base of at least part of her reading problem since she had great difficulty in recognizing many letters of the alphabet, although she could often describe them and trace them (Wilson & Baddeley, 1986).

We began the treatment by assessing her capacity to recognize individual letters, and then selectively began to train her on groups of unknown letters, systematically introducing one group at a time. The method of teaching was eclectic, for example the letter Y gave her particular difficulty, and in order to teach her it we used a whole range of strategies, including tracing it, relating it to phrases such as "Why is Y so difficult?" and so forth. These individual strategies were not themselves being evaluated; rather we were interested in whether whatever we could do to teach her individual letters was in fact being effective.

It was a slow business, since she had both perceptual and memory problems, but given a great deal of determination, and some systematic reinforcement (being taken to see horses was a

FIGURE 17.5

A multiple baseline design to demonstrate a head-injured patient's relearning of letters of the alphabet. O, errors made in test session; *, no errors made in test session; --, next stage of treatment introduced. From Wilson and Baddeley (1988). Reprinted by permission of John Wiley and Sons.

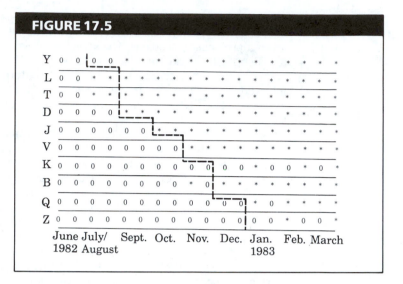

particular favorite), she did slowly begin to learn. As Figure 17.5 shows, the learning was associated with the introduction of training for that particular group of letters, and once learnt, the letters were rarely forgotten. Having learnt the individual letters, the rules of combining letters were then taught. During this period she was moved from the rehabilitation center back home, but I am happy to say has continued to improve, and now reads at the level of an 11-year-old (Wilson, 1986), although still making errors on irregular words such as *yacht* that are characteristic of patients with surface dyslexia (Patterson, Marshall, & Coltheart, 1985).

Group Designs

The previous section has concentrated on single case treatment designs. There is no doubt that these are particularly useful in clinical practice since they can form an integral part of treatment, allowing the therapist to evaluate the treatment while it is in operation, and of course providing valuable feedback for the patient. This latter point should not be underestimated, since improvements tend to be slow and it is very easy for both the patient and the therapist to become discouraged when problems persist.

Both the strength and the weakness of a single case design, however, is that it tells you whether a particular method works with a specific patient; it leaves open the question of how far the results may be generalized. Is this particular patient typical of many others or is he or she very unusual in responding to this particular approach? In order to answer questions of this sort, it is necessary to test groups of patients, and such group studies form a useful further stage in evaluating methods of treatment. Note, however, that even if a treatment did not offer significant help when assessed statistically across the group, it is entirely possible that one or two patients might have been helped very substantially by the method.

Group designs and single case designs are therefore aiming to answer different questions, the single case design is concerned with whether that particular patient was helped, while the group design indicates the extent to which any improvement shown is characteristic of all the patients tested.

A Small Group Design Testing Procedural Learning

The techniques so far described for helping the patient with a memory problem have drawn extensively on behavioral psychology, using reinforcement and chaining paradigms, for example, and from methods of improving normal learning such as the employment of expanded rehearsal, richer encoding or visual imagery. Rather less of a contribution has so far been made to treatment by recent work concerned with understanding the nature of amnesia at a more basic and theoretical level, although such studies have played an important role in improving methods of diagnosis and assessment. There is, however, one theoretical development that appears to hold some considerable promise, namely the observation that procedural learning tends to be spared in amnesic patients. This preservation of an important aspect of long-term learning would seem to have exciting implications for treatment. It has, however, so far proved much more difficult to exploit this insight than at first seemed likely.

One problem is that acquiring a task that may subsequently become a procedural skill often appears to rely on some form of episodic memory, either to remember the instructions, or to avoid errors that are made on early trials. This was demonstrated very clearly in a study in which brain damaged patients or normal controls attempted to learn a simple task involving an electronic memory aid. The task involved putting in the time and date and required six successive steps. The task might appear to comprise only procedural learning, since performance is not logically dependent on recalling having encountered the task before. In actual practice this proved to be a difficult task for amnesic patients to learn, suggesting that episodic memory may play an important role in acquiring such skills, reinforcing the observation that electronic memory aids may be less useful to patients than at first seemed likely (Wilson, Baddeley, & Cockburn, 1989).

However, while taking advantage of intact procedural learning may be more difficult than seemed likely, it is possible, given patience, to teach patients quite complex skills. For example, Glisky, Schacter, and Tulving (1986) were able to teach quite densely amnesic patients to program and interact with a microcomputer.

The first stage of training involved teaching the patients the necessary vocabulary. This was done using the priming method which had originally been shown by Warrington and Weiskrantz

(1968) to be a very effective way of teaching amnesics to learn lists of unrelated words. Glisky et al. presented their subjects with the necessary definition followed by the appropriate word, for example "a repeated portion of a program—LOOP". Recall would then be tested by presenting the definition and giving everything except the last letter. Each time the subject was successful, the number of letters was reduced, until eventually the definition itself was sufficient to allow the subject to produce the correct term. Figure 17.6 shows the performance of four subjects on successive sessions, which were held twice a week. It is clear that all subjects learned successfully using this approach.

When compared with a standard procedure of simply repeating the item and the definition, the stem completion or vanishing cues prove to be somewhat more effective both in learning and retention, and was much preferred by the patients.

Having learned the terminology, subjects then went on to acquire simple programming skills, using training programs that were initially very supportive, and where prompting was provided whenever necessary. Gradually the amount of prompting was reduced as the patients successfully mastered the skills. The procedure was a long and laborious one compared to the rate of learning in normal subjects, but there is no doubt that the patients were able to acquire a complex set of skills that could subsequently prove useful for example in learning to use a word processor, or to

Use of the vanishing cues prompting technique to teach amnesic patients computer-related vocabulary. Data from four patients over successive training sessions. From Glisky, Schacter, and Tulving (1986).

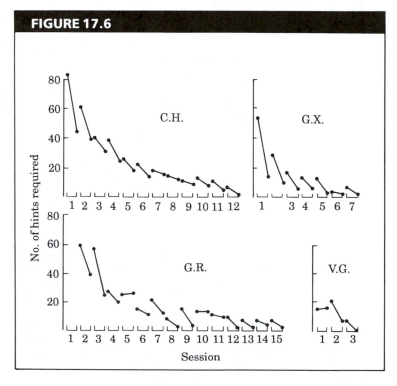

FIGURE 17.6

program a computer so as to help them cope with ongoing memory problems.

For the patient who is unfortunate enough to be really densely amnesic then, the best hope is probably to attempt to capitalize on procedural learning. While the work of Glisky et al. is a promising start, we are still not very skilled in knowing how preserved procedural learning can best be used. It may be, however, the case that this is an area in which the psychologist can learn from the patient. I was particularly impressed in this respect by the case of a woman who became very densely amnesic following encephalitis (Moakes, 1988). Initially, her life was devastated by her problem, but gradually with the aid of her husband and a great deal of perseverance and courage, she has been able to reconstruct her life in a restricted but still very fulfilling way.

The essence of the strategy that she and her husband have adopted is to ensure that her whole life is regular and ordered. The organization includes her daily schedule, the layout of the kitchen, and the routes she follows around her home, with the result that after many many repetitions, she is able within her domestic routine to do the right thing without needing to remember. Using this technique she has even been able to return to her job at a school, and to drive, keeping to a small number of routes, and always having the back-up of knowing that if lost she can ask someone to take her to the nearest police station from which she can ring for help.

As Schacter points out in the case of his patients, the penalty of such learning is that it tends to be extremely rigid, making generalization and flexibility very difficult. It is far from ideal, but compared to the mental chaos that she first encountered, it is a major achievement that might perhaps give us some important clues as to how we can help other patients with similar problems.

OVERVIEW

As I hope the earlier examples have shown, even densely amnesic patients can learn new material given patience and the appropriate mnemonic strategies. Memory deficits can be enormously frustrating and incapacitating, and for that reason there is likely to be a ready market for anyone claiming to rehabilitate the memory of the many patients with problems in learning and remembering. It is, however, important to point out the limits of what we can achieve.

First of all, while memory capacities do sometimes spontaneously recover to a surprising extent, despite the excitement raised by the possibility of brain implants, there is currently no evidence that anything that the therapist or the doctor does can bring back or replace the brain cells whose loss has led to the memory deficit.

Secondly, although mnemonics and strategies can certainly be used to help patients, it is unlikely that these will be spontaneously used in the patient's everyday life. In general, external aids such as notebooks, diaries and alarm watches are likely to be more practically useful on a day-to-day basis. What the mnemonic techniques described *can* do however is to allow the patient, with the help of a relative or therapist, to identify things that it is particularly important for him or her to learn, and having identified them learn them. It is not a great deal to offer a patient who has lost so much, but it is a start. For the future we need to know more about the preserved procedural memory capacities of patients and to develop ways in which these can be used to compensate, at least in part, for the patient's defective episodic memory.

REFERENCES

Aarons, L. (1976). Sleep-assisted instruction. *Psychological Bulletin, 83*, 1–40.

Adams, J.A. (1955). A source of decrement in psychomotor performance. *Journal of Experimental Psychology, 49*, 390–394.

Allen, K.E., Hart, B.M., Buell, J.S., Harris, F.R., & Wolf, M.M. (1964). Effects of social reinforcement on isolate behavior of a nursery school child. *Child Development, 35*, 511–518.

Allen, C.T. & Madden, T.J. (1985). A closer look at classical conditioning. *Journal of Consumer Research, 12*, 301–315.

Allport, D.A., Antonis, B., & Reynolds, P. (1972). On the division of attention: A disproof of the single channel hypothesis. *Quarterly Journal of Experimental Psychology, 24*, 225–235.

Anderson, J.A. (1973). A theory for the recognition of items from short-term memorised lists. *Psychological Review, 80*, 417–438.

Anderson, J.L., Dodderman, S., Coppleman, M., & Fleming, A. (1979). Patient information recall in a rheumatology clinic. *Rheumatology and Rehabilitation, 18*, 18–22.

Anderson, J.R. (1983). *The architecture of cognition.* Cambridge, Mass.: Harvard University Press.

Anderson, J.R. & Bower, G.H. (1972). Configurational properties in sentence memory. *Journal of Verbal Learning and Verbal Behavior, 11*, 594–605.

Atkinson, R.C. & Shiffrin, R.M. (1968). Human memory: A proposed system and its control processes. In K.W. Spence (Ed.), *The psychology of learning and motivation: advances in research and theory Vol. 2* (pp.89–195). New York: Academic Press.

Ayres, T.J., Jonides, J., Reitman, J.S., Egan, J.C., & Howard, D.A. (1979). Differing suffix effects for the same physical suffix. *Journal of Experimental Psychology: Human Learning and Memory, 5*, 315–321.

Bäckman, L. & Molander, B. (1986a). Adult age differences in the ability to cope with situations of high arousal in a precision sport. *Psychology and Aging, 1*, 133–139.

Bäckman, L. & Molander, B. (1986b). Effects of adult age and level of skill on the ability to cope with high-stress conditions in a precision sport. *Psychology and Aging, 1*, 334–336.

Baddeley, A.D. (1966a). Short-term memory for word sequences as a function of acoustic, semantic and formal similarity. *Quarterly Journal of Experimental Psychology, 18*, 362–365.

Baddeley, A.D. (1966b). The influence of acoustic and semantic similarity on long-term memory for word sequences. *Quarterly Journal of Experimental Psychology, 18*, 302–309.

Baddeley, A.D. (1966c). The capacity for generating information by randomization. *Quarterly Journal of Experimental Psychology, 18*, 119–129.

Baddeley, A.D. (1968). A three-minute reasoning test based on grammatical transformations. *Psychonomic Science, 10*, 341–342.

Baddeley, A.D. (1976). *The psychology of memory*. New York: Basic Books.

Baddeley, A.D. (1978). The trouble with levels: A re-examination of Craik and Lockhart's framework for memory research. *Psychological Review, 85,* 139–152.

Baddeley, A.D. (1982). Domains of recollection. *Psychological Review, 89,* 708–729.

Baddeley, A.D. (1986). *Working memory*. Oxford: OUP.

Baddeley, A.D., Baddeley, H.A., & Nimmo-Smith, M.I. (in prep.). What do physiotherapy students remember of their first year anatomy?

Baddeley, A.D. & Ecob, J.R. (1973). Reaction time and short-term memory: a trace strength alternative to the high-speed exhaustive scanning hypothesis. *Quarterly Journal of Experimental Psychology, 25,* 229–240.

Baddeley, A.D., Eldridge, M., & Lewis, V.J. (1981). The role of subvocalization in reading. *Quarterly Journal of Experimental Psychology, 33,* 439–454.

Baddeley, A.D. & Flemming, N.C. (1967). The efficiency of divers breathing oxy-helium. *Ergonomics, 10,* 311–319.

Baddeley, A.D., Grant, S., Wight, E., & Thomson, N. (1975a). Imagery and visual working memory. In P.M.A. Rabbitt & S. Dornic (Eds.), *Attention and performance V* (pp. 205–217). London: Academic Press.

Baddeley, A.D., Harris, J., Sunderland, A., Watts, K., & Wilson, B. (1987a). Closed head injury and memory. In H.S. Levin, J. Grafman, & H.M. Eisenberg (Eds.), *Neurobehavioral recovery from head injury* (pp. 295–317). New York: Oxford University Press.

Baddeley, A.D. & Hitch, G. (1974). Working memory. In G.A. Bower (Ed.), *Recent advances in learning and motivation, Vol. 8*. New York: Academic Press.

Baddeley, A.D. & Hitch, G. (1977). Recency re-examined. In S. Dornic (Ed.), *Attention and performance VI* (pp.647–667). Hillsdale, N.J.: Lawrence Erlbaum Associates.

Baddeley, A.D. & Levy, B.A. (1971). Semantic coding and short-term memory. *Journal of Experimental Psychology, 89,* 132–136.

Baddeley, A.D., Lewis, V., Eldridge, M., & Thomson, N. (1984a). Attention and retrieval from long-term memory. *Journal of Experimental Psychology: General, 113,* 518–540.

Baddeley, A.D., Lewis, V.J., & Nimmo-Smith, I. (1978). When did you last.....? In M.M. Gruneberg, P.E. Morris, & R.N. Sykes (Eds.), *Practical aspects of memory* (pp.77–83). London: Academic Press.

Baddeley, A.D., Lewis, V.J., & Vallar, G. (1984b). Exploring the articulatory loop. *Quarterly Journal of Experimental Psychology, 36,* 233–252.

Baddeley, A.D. & Lieberman, K. (1980). Spatial working memory. In R. Nickerson (Ed.), *Attention and performance VIII* (pp.521–539). Hillsdale, N.J.: Lawrence Erlbaum Associates Inc.

Baddeley, A.D., Logie, R., Bressi, S., Della Sala, S., & Spinnler, H. (1986). Dementia and working memory. *Quarterly Journal of Experimental Psychology, 38A,* 603–618.

Baddeley, A.D., Logie, R., Nimmo-Smith, I., & Brereton, N. (1985). Components of fluent reading. *Journal of Memory and Language, 24*, 119–131.

Baddeley, A.D. & Longman, D.J.A. (1978). The influence of length and frequency on training sessions on the rate of learning to type. *Ergonomics*, 21, 627–635.

Baddeley, A.D., Papagno, C., & Vallar, G. (1988). When long-term learning depends on short-term storage. *Journal of Memory and Language, 27*, 586–595.

Baddeley, A.D. & Scott, D. (1971). Short-term forgetting in the absence of proactive interference. *Quarterly Journal of Experimental Psychology, 23*, 275–283.

Baddeley, A.D., Thomson, N., & Buchanan, M. (1975b). Word length and the structure of short-term memory. *Journal of Verbal Learning and Verbal Behavior, 14*, 575–589.

Baddeley, A.D., Vallar, G., & Wilson, B.A. (1987b). Sentence comprehension and phonological memory: Some neuropsychological evidence. In M. Coltheart (Ed.), *Attention and performance XII: The psychology of reading* (pp. 509–529). London: Lawrence Erlbaum Associates Ltd.

Baddeley, A.D. & Warrington, E.K. (1970). Amnesia and the distinction between long-and short-term memory. *Journal of Verbal Learning and Verbal Behavior, 9*, 176–189.

Baddeley, A.D. & Wilson, B. (1986). Amnesia, autobiographical memory and confabulation. In D. Rubin (Ed.), *Autobiographical memory* (pp. 225–252). New York: Cambridge University Press.

Baddeley, A.D. & Wilson, B. (1988a). Comprehension and working memory: A single case neuropsychological study. *Journal of Memory and Language, 27*, 479–498.

Baddeley, A.D. & Wilson, B. (1988b). Frontal amnesia and the dysexecutive syndrome. *Brain and Cognition, 7*, 212–230.

Baddeley, H.A. (1987). *Acceptance of behavioural science in physiotherapy education.* Paper presented at Psychology and Physiotherapy working group conference on Psychological Principles in Physiotherapy Practice, University of Manchester.

Bahrick, H.P. (1970). Two-phase model for prompted recall. *Psychological Review, 77*, 215–222.

Bahrick, H.P. (1984). Memory for people. In J.E. Harris & P.E. Morris (Eds), *Everyday memory, actions and absent mindedness* (pp.19–34). London: Academic Press.

Bahrick, H.P. & Bahrick, P.O. (1964). A re-examination of the interrelations among measures of retention. *Quarterly Journal of Experimental Psychology, 16*, 318–324.

Bahrick, H.P., Bahrick, P.O., & Wittlinger, R.P. (1975). Fifty years of memory for names and faces: A cross-sectional approach. *Journal of Experimental Psychology: General, 104*, 54–75.

Bahrick, H.P. & Phelphs, E. (1987). Retention of Spanish vocabulary over eight years. *Journal of Experimental Psychology: Learning, Memory and Cognition, 13*, 344–349.

Bandura, A. (1971). Psychotherapy based upon modelling principles. In

A.E. Bergin & S.L. Garfield (Eds.), *Handbook of psychotherapy*. New York: Wiley.

Banks, W.P. (1981). Assessing relations between imagery and perception. *Journal of Experimental Psychology: Human Perception and Performance, 7*, 844–847.

Barclay, C.R. (1988) Truth and accuracy in autobiographical memory. In M.M. Greenberg, P.E. Morris, & R.N. Sykes (Eds), *Practical Aspects of Memory. Current research and Issues; Volume 1 Memory in Everyday Life* (pp. 289–294). Chichester: John Wiley.

Barclay, J.R., Bransford, J.D., Franks, J.J., McCarrell, N.S., & Nitsch, K. (1974). Comprehension and semantic flexibility. *Journal of Verbal Learning and Verbal Behavior, 13*, 471–481.

Barnes, J.M. & Underwood, B.J. (1959). "Fate" of first-list associations in transfer theory. *Journal of Experimental Psychology, 58*, 97–105.

Bartlett, F.C. (1932). *Remembering*. Cambridge: Cambridge University Press.

Basso, A., Spinnler, H., Vallar, G., & Zanobio, E. (1982). Left hemisphere damage and selected impairment of auditory verbal short-term memory: A case study. *Neuropsychologia, 20*, 263–274.

Baum, D.R. & Jonides, J.J. (1979). Cognitive maps: Analysis of comparative judgements of distance. *Memory and Cognition, 7*, 462–468.

Baxt, N. (1871). Über die Zeit welche nötig ist, damit ein Gesichtseindruck zum Bewusstsein kommt. *Pflüger's Arch. ges. Physiol, 4*, 325–336.

Beach, K.D. (1988). The role of external mnemonic symbols in acquiring an occupation. In M.M. Gruneberg, P.E. Morris, & R.N. Sykes (Eds.), *Practical aspects of memory: Current research and issues, Vol. 1: Memory in everyday life* (pp. 342–346). Chichester: John Wiley & Sons.

Beauvois, M.-F. (1982). Optic aphasia: A process of interaction between vision and language. *Philosophical Transactions of the Royal Society of London B, 298*, 35–47.

Beauvois, M.-F. & Saillant, B. (1985). Optic aphasia for colours and colour agnosia: A distinction between visual and visuo-verbal impairments in the processing of colours. *Cognitive Neuropsychology, 2*, 1–48.

Beauvois, M.-F., Saillant, B., Meininger, V., & Lhermitte, F. (1978). Bilateral tactile aphasia: A tacto-verbal dysfunction. *Brain, 101*, 381–401.

Beck, A.T. (1976). *Cognitive therapy and the emotional disorders*. New York: International University Press.

Beck, A.T. (1988). Cognitive approaches to panic disorder: Theory and therapy. In S. Rachman & J.D. Maser (Eds.), *Panic: Psychological perspectives* (pp. 91–109). Hillsdale, N.J.: LEA Inc.

Beck, A.T., Shaw, B.F., Rush, A.J., & Emory, G. (1979). *Cognitive therapy of depression*. Chichester: John Wiley & Sons.

Becker, J.T. (1987). A two-component model of memory deficit in Alzheimer's Disease. In R.J. Wurtman, S.H. Corkin, & J.H. Growdon

(Eds.), *Alzheimer's Disease: Advances in basic research and therapies* (pp. 343–348). Cambridge: Center for Brain Sciences and Metabolism Charitable Trust.

Bekerian, D.A, & Baddeley, A.D. (1980). Saturation advertising and the repetition effect. *Journal of Verbal Learning and Verbal Behavior, 19*, 17–25.

Bekerian, D.A. & Bowers, J.M. (1983). Eyewitness testimony: Were we misled? *Journal of Experimental Psychology: Human Learning and Memory, 9*, 139–145.

Bennett, H.L., Davis, H.S., & Giannini, J.A. (1985). Nonverbal response to intraoperative conversation. *British Journal of Anaesthesia, 7*, 174–179.

Berlin, B. & Kay, P. (1969). *Basic color terms: Their universality and evolution.* Berkeley: University of California Press.

Berrington, W.P., Liddell, D.W., & Foulds, G.A. (1956). A re-evaluation of the fugue. *Journal of Mental Science, 102*, 281–286.

Berry, D.C. & Broadbent, D.E. (1984). On the relationship between task performance and associated verbalisable knowledge. *Quarterly Journal of Experimental Psychology, 36A*, 209–231.

Bhatti, J.Z., Alford, C.A., & Hindmarch, I. (1988). Lormetazepam, memory and information processing: A review. In I. Hindmarch & H. Ott (Eds.), *Benzodiazepine receptor ligands, memory and information processing* (pp. 169–179). Berlin: Springer-Verlag.

Bilodeau, E.A. & Bilodeau, I.McD. (1961). Motor skills learning. *Annual Review of Psychology, 12*, 243–280.

Bishop, D.V.M. & Robson, J. (1989). Unimpaired short-term memory and rhyme judgement in congenitally speechless individuals: Implications for the notion of 'articulatory coding'. *Quarterly Journal of Experimental Psychology, 41a*, 123–141.

Bjork, R.A. (1988). Retrieval practice and the maintenance of knowledge. In M.M.Gruneberg, P.E. Morris, & R.N. Sykes (Eds.), *Practical aspects of memory: Current research and issues Vol. 1: Memory in everyday life* (pp. 396–401). Chichester: John Wiley & Sons.

Bjork, R.A. & Whitten, W.B. (1972). *Recency-sensitive retrieval process in long-term free recall.* Paper presented at the meeting of the Psychonomic Society, St. Louis, Missouri.

Bjork, R.A. & Whitten, W.B. (1974). Recency-sensitive retrieval processes. *Cognitive Psychology, 6*, 173–189.

Blaney, P.H. (1986). Affect and memory: A review. *Psychological Bulletin, 99*, 229–246.

Boakes, R. (1984). From Darwin to behaviorism: Psychology and the minds of animals. Cambridge University Press.

Bolles, R.C. (1985). Short-term memory and attention. In L.G. Nilsson & T. Archer (Eds.), *Perspectives on learning and memory*. Hillsdale, N.J.: Lawrence Erlbaum Associates Inc.

Bousfield, W.A. (1953). The occurrence of clustering in recall of randomly arranged associates. *Journal of General Psychology, 49*, 229–240.

Bower, G.H. (1967). A multicomponent theory of the memory trace. In K.W. Spence & J.W. Spence (Eds.), *The psychology of learning and motivation: Advances in research and theory, Vol. 1* (pp. 299–325). New York: Academic Press.

Bower, G.H. (1981). Mood and memory. *American Psychologist, 36,* 129–148.

Bower, G.H. (1983). Affect and cognition. *Philosophical Transactions of the Royal Society of London B, 302,* 387–402.

Bower, G.H., Black, J.B., & Turner, T.J. (1979). Scripts in memory for text. *Cognitive Psychology, 11,* 177–220.

Bower, G.H., Clark, M.C., Lesgold, A.M., & Winzenz, D. (1969). Hierarchical retrieval schemes in recall of categorized word lists. *Journal of Verbal Learning and Verbal Behavior, 8,* 323–343.

Bower, G.H. & Karlin, M.B. (1974). Depth of processing pictures of faces and recognition memory. *Journal of Experimental Psychology, 103,* 751–757.

Bower, G.H. & Mayer, J.D. (1985). Failure to replicate mood-dependent retrieval. *Bulletin of the Psychonomic Society, 23,* 39–42.

Bower, G.H., Monteiro, K.P., & Gilligan, S.G. (1978). Emotional mood and context for learning and recall. *Journal of Verbal Learning and Verbal Behavior, 17,* 573–587.

Bradley, L. & Bryant, P.E. (1983). Categorising sounds and learning to read: A causal connection. *Nature, 301,* 419–421.

Bradley, B.P. & Morris, B.J. (1976). *Emotional factors in forgetting. Part II Research Project.* Cambridge University Department of Experimental Psychology.

Bradshaw, P.W., Ley, P., Kincey, J.A., & Bradshaw, J. (1975). Recall of medical advice: Comprehensibility and specificity. *British Journal of Social and Clinical Psychology, 14,* p. 55.

Bregman, E. (1934). An attempt to modify the emotional attitudes of infants by the conditioned response technique. *Journal of Genetic Psychology, 45,* 169–196.

Breland, A. & Breland, M. (1951). The field of applied animal psychology. *American Psychologist, 6,* 202–204.

Brewer, W.F. (1974). There is no convincing evidence for operant or classical conditioning in adult humans. In W.B. Weiner & D.S. Palermo (Eds), *Cognition and the symbolic processes* (pp.1–42). Hillsdale, N.J.: Lawrence Erlbaum Associates Inc.

Brewer, W.F. (1988). A qualitative analysis of the recalls of randomly sampled autobiographical events. In M.M. Gruneberg, P.E. Morris, & R.N. Sykes (Eds.), *Practical aspects of memory, Vol. 1: Memory in everyday life* (pp. 263–268). Chichester: John Wiley & Sons.

Brewer, W.F. & Lichtenstein, E.H. (1981). Event schemas, story schemas, and story grammars. In J. Long & A. Baddeley (Eds.), *Attention and performance IX.* Hillsdale, N.J.: Lawrence Erlbaum Associates Inc.

Brigham, J.C. (1981). The accuracy of eyewitness evidence: How do attorneys see it? *The Florida Bar Journal,* November, 714–721.

Broadbent, D.E. (1958). *Perception and communication.* London: Pergamon Press.

Broadbent, D.E. (1982). Task combination and selective intake of information. *Acta Psychologica, 50,* 253–290.

Broadbent, D.E., Cooper, P.J., & Broadbent, M.H. (1978). A comparison of hierarchical matrix retrieval schemes in recall. *Journal of Experimental Psychology: Human Learning and Memory, 4,* 486–497.

Brooks, D.N. & Baddeley, A. D. (1976). What can amnesic patients learn? *Neuropsychologia, 14,* 111–122.

Brooks, L.R. (1967). The suppression of visualization by reading. *Quarterly Journal of Experimental Psychology, 19,* 289–299.

Brown, A.S. (1979). Priming effects in semantic memory retrieval processes. *Journal of Experimental Psychology: Human Learning and Memory, 5,* 65–77.

Brown, I.D., Tickner, A.H., & Simmonds, D.C.V. (1969). Interference between concurrent tasks of driving and telephoning. *Journal of Applied Psychology, 53,* 419–424.

Brown, J. (1958). Some tests of the decay theory of immediate memory. *Quarterly Journal of Experimental Psychology, 10,* 12–21.

Brown, J. (1968). Reciprocal facilitation and impairment of free recall. *Psychonomic Science, 10,* 41–42.

Brown, J., Lewis, V.J., & Monk, A.F. (1977). Memorability, word frequency and negative recognition. *Quarterly Journal of Experimental Psychology, 29,* 461–473.

Brown, N.R., Ripps, L.J., & Shevell, S.K. (1985). The subjective dates of neural events in very-long-term memory. *Cognitive Psychology, 17,* 139–177.

Brown, R. & Kulik, J. (1977). Flashbulb memories. *Cognition, 5,* 73–99.

Brown, R.W. & Lenneberg, E.H. (1954). A study in language and cognition. *Journal of Abnormal and Social Psychology, 49,* 454–462.

Brown, R. & McNeill, D. (1966). The 'tip of the tongue' phenomenon. *Journal of Verbal Learning and Verbal Behavior, 5,* 325–337.

Brunswik, E. (1957). Scope and aspect of the cognitive problem. In R. Jessor & K. Hammond (Eds.), *Cognition: The Colorado symposium* (pp. 1–27). Chicago: University of Chicago Press.

Bugelski, B.R., Kidd, E., & Segmen, J. (1968). Image as a mediator in one-trial paired-associate learning. *Journal of Experimental Psychology, 76,* 69–73.

Bull, M. & La Vecchio, F. (1978). Behavior therapy for a child with Lesch-Nyhan syndrome. *Developmental Medicine and Child Neurology, 20,* 368–375.

Butler, G. & Mathews, A. (1983). Cognitive processes in anxiety. *Advances in Behaviour Therapy, 5,* 51–62.

Butler, G. & Mathews, A. (1987). Anticipatory anxiety and risk perception. *Cognitive Therapy and Research, 91,* 551–565.

Butters, N. & Cermak, L.S. (1986). A study of the forgetting of autobiographical knowledge: Implications for the study of retrograde amnesia. In D. Rubin (Ed.), *Autobiographical memory* (pp. 253–272). Cambridge: Cambridge University Press.

Butterworth, B., Campbell, R., & Howard, D. (1986). The uses of short-term memory: A case study. *Quarterly Journal of Experimental Psychology, 38A,* 705–738.

Byrne, R. (1979). Memory for urban geography. *Quarterly Journal of Experimental Psychology, 31*, 147–154.

Campbell, R. & Butterworth, B. (1985). Phonological dyslexia and dysgraphia in a highly literate subject: A developmental case with associated deficits of phonemic processing and awareness. *Quarterly Journal of Experimental Psychology, 37A*, 435–476.

Campbell, R. & Dodd, B. (1980). Hearing by eye. *Quarterly Journal of Experimental Psychology, 32*, 85–99.

Carpenter, P.A. & Eisenberg, P. (1978). Mental rotation and the frame of reference in blind and sighted individuals. *Perception and Psychophysics, 23*, 117–124.

Carr, S. & Wilson, B. (1983). Promotion of pressure relief exercising in a spinal injury patient: A multiple baseline across settings design. *Behavioural Psychotherapy, 11*, 329–336.

Carroll, M.V., Byrne, B., & Kirsner, K. (1985). Autobiographical memory and perceptual learning: A developmental study using picture recognition, naming latency, and perceptual identification. *Memory and Cognition, 13*, 273–279.

Cattell, J.M. (1895). Measurement of the accuracy of recollection. *Science, 20*, 761–776.

Ceci, S.J., Baker, J.E. & Bronfenbrenner, U. (1988). Prospective remembering, temporal calibration, and context. In M.M. Gruneberg, P.E. Morris, & R.N. Sykes (Eds.), *Practical aspects of memory: Current research and issues, Vol. 1: Memory in everyday life* (pp. 360–365). Chichester: John Wiley & Sons.

Ceci, S.J. & Bronfenbrenner, U. (1985). Don't forget to take the cup cakes out of the oven: Prospective memory, strategic time monitoring, and context. *Child Development, 56*, 152–164.

Cermak, L.S. (1976). The encoding capacity of a patient with amnesia due to encephalitis. *Neuropsychologia, 14*, 311–326.

Cermak, L.S. (1982). The long and short of it in amnesia. In L.S. Cermak (Ed.), *Human memory and amnesia* (pp. 43–60). Hillsdale, N.J.: Lawrence Erlbaum Associates.

Cermak, L.S., Butters, N., & Moreines, J. (1974). Some analyses of the verbal encoding deficit of alcoholic Korsakoff patients. *Brain and Language, 1*, 141–150.

Cermak, L.S. & Moreines, J. (1976). Verbal retention deficits in aphasic and amnesic patients. *Brain and Language, 3*, 16–27.

Cermak, L.S., & Reale, L. (1978). Depth of processing and retention of words by alcoholic Korsakoff patients. *Journal of Experimental Psychology: Human Learning and Memory, 4*, 165–174.

Chan, J. (1981). A crossroads in language instruction. *Journal of Reading, 22*, 411–415.

Chase, W.G. & Ericsson, K.A. (1982). Skill and working memory. In G.H. Bower (Ed.), *The Psychology of learning and motivation, Vol. 16*. New York: Academic Press.

Chatwin, B. (1988). *The songlines*. London: Picador.

Chomsky, N. (1965). *Aspects of the theory of syntax*. Cambridge, Mass: M.I.T. Press.

Clark, H.H. & Clark, E.V. (1977). *Psychology and language*. New York: Harcourt Brace Jovanovich.

Clark, D.M.. & Teasdale, J.D. (1982). Diurnal variations in clinical depression and accessability of memories of positive and negative experiences. *Journal of Abnormal Psychology, 91*, 87–95.

Clifford, B.R. (1983). Memory for voices: The feasibility and quality of earwitness evidence. In S. Lloyd-Bostock and B.R. Clifford (Eds.), *Evaluating witness evidence* (pp. 189-218). Chichester: John Wiley.

Cockburn, J. & Smith, P.T. (1988). Effects of age and intelligence on everyday memory tasks. In Gruneberg, M.M., Morris, P.E., & Sykes, R.N. (Eds.), *Practical aspects of memory: Current research and issues. Vol. 2: Clinical and educational implications* (pp.132–136). Chichester: John Wiley & Sons.

Cohen, N.J. (1984). Preserved learning capacity in amnesia: Evidence for multiple memory systems. In L.R. Squire & N. Butters (Eds.), *The neuropsychology of memory* (pp. 419–432). New York: Guilford.

Cohen, N.J. & Squire, L.R. (1980) Preserved learning and retention of pattern analyzing skill in amnesia: Dissociation of knowing how and knowing that. *Science, 210*, 207–210.

Cohen, R.L. (1981). On the generality of some memory laws. *Scandinavian Journal of Psychology, 22*, 267–281.

Colegrove, F.W. (1899). Individual memories. *American Journal of Psychology, 10*, 228–255.

Colle, H.A. (1980). Auditory encoding in visual short-term recall: Effects of noise intensity and spatial location. *Journal of Verbal Learning and Verbal Behavior, 19*, 722–735.

Colle, H.A. & Welsh, A. (1976). Acoustic masking in primary memory. *Journal of Verbal Learning and Verbal Behavior, 15*, 17–32.

Collins, A.M. & Quillian, M.R. (1969). Retrieval time from semantic memory. *Journal of Verbal Learning and Verbal Behavior, 8*, 240–247.

Coltheart, M. (1983). Iconic memory. *Philosophical Transactions of the Royal Society, London B, 302*, 283–294.

Conrad, C. (1972). Cognitive economy in semantic memory. *Journal of Experimental Psychology, 92*, 149–154.

Conrad, R. (1960). Very brief delay of immediate recall. *Quarterly Journal of Experimental Psychology, 12*, 45–47.

Conrad, R. (1964). Acoustic confusion in immediate memory. *British Journal of Psychology, 55*, 75–84.

Conrad, R. & Hull, A.J. (1964). Information, acoustic confusion and memory span. *British Journal of Psychology, 55*, 429–432.

Cooper, E.C. & Pantle, A.J. (1967). The total time hypothesis in verbal learning. *Psychological Bulletin, 68*, 221–234.

Cooper, L.A. & Podgorny, P. (1976). Mental transformations and visual comparison processes: Effects of complexity and similarity. *Journal of Experimental Psychology: Human Perception and Performance, 2*, 503–514.

Corballis, M.C., Kirby, J., & Miller, A. (1972). Access to elements of a memorized list. *Journal of Experimental Psychology, 94*, 185–190.

Corcoran, D.W.J., Carpenter, A., Webster, J.C., & Woodhead, M.M. (1968). Comparison of training techniques for complex sound identification. *Journal of the Acoustical Society of America, 44*, 157–167.

Corkin, S. (1968). Acquisition of motor skill after bilateral medial temporal lobe–excision. *Neuropsychologia, 6*, 255–265.

Cowan, N. (1984). On short and long auditory stores. *Psychological Bulletin, 96*, 341–370.

Cowan, N., Lichti, W., & Grove, T. (1988). Memory for unattended speech during silent reading. In M.M. Gruneberg, P.E. Morris, & R.N. Sykes (Eds.), *Practical aspects of memory: Current research and issues, Vol. 2: Clinical and educational implications*, pp. 327–332. Chichester: John Wiley & Sons.

Craik, F.I.M. & Levy, B.A. (1970). Semantic and acoustic information in primary memory. *Journal of Experimental Psychology, 86*, 77–82.

Craik, F.I.M. & Lockhart, R.S. (1972). Levels of processing: A framework for memory research. *Journal of Verbal Learning and Verbal Behavior, 11*, 671–684.

Craik, F.I.M. & Simon, E. (1979). Age differences in memory: The role of attention and depth of processing. In L.W. Poon, J.L. Fozard, L.S. Cermak, D. Arenberg, & L. Thompson (Eds.), *New directions in memory and ageing: Proceedings of the George Talland Memorial Conference*. Hillsdale, N.J.: Lawrence Erlbaum Associates Inc.

Craik, F.I.M. & Tulving, E. (1975). Depth of processing and the retention of words in episodic memory. *Journal of Experimental Psychology: General, 104*, 268–294.

Craik, F.I.M. & Watkins, M.J. (1973). The role of rehearsal in short-term memory. *Journal of Verbal Learning and Verbal Behavior, 12*, 599–607.

Crick, F. & Mitchison, G. (1983). The function of dream sleep. *Nature, 308*, 111–114.

Crovitz, H.F. & Schiffman, H. (1974). Frequency of episodic memories as a function of their age. *Bulletin of the Psychonomic Society, 4*, 517–518.

Crowder, R.G. (1971). The sound of vowels and consonants in immediate memory. *Journal of Verbal Learning and Verbal Behavior, 10*, 587–596.

Crowder, R.G. (1976). *Principles of learning and memory*. Hillsdale, N.J.: Lawrence Erlbaum Associates Inc.

Crowder, R.G. (1982). The demise of short-term memory. *Acta Psychologica, 50*, 291–323.

Crowder, R.G. & Morton, J. (1969). Precategorical acoustic storage (PAS). *Perception and Psychophysics, 5*, 365–373.

Crowe, M.J., Marks, I.M., Agras, W.S., & Leitenberg, H. (1972). Time-limited desensitization, implosion and shaping for phobic patients: A cross-over study. *Behaviour Research and Therapy, 10*, 319–328.

Dale, H.C.A. & Baddeley, A.D. (1962). On the nature of alternatives used in testing recognition memory. *Nature, 196*, 93–94.

Daneman, M. & Carpenter, P.A. (1980). Individual differences in working memory and reading. *Journal of Verbal Learning and Verbal Behavior, 19*, 450–466.

Daneman, M. & Carpenter, P.A. (1983). Individual differences in integrating information between and within sentences. *Journal of Experimental Psychology: Learning, Memory and Cognition, 9*, 561–584.

Daneman, M. & Tardif, T. (1987). Working memory and reading skill re-examined. In M. Coltheart (Ed.), *Attention and performance XII*, pp. 491–508. Hove: Lawrence Erlbaum Associates Ltd.

Darwin, C.J. & Baddeley, A.D. (1974). Acoustic memory and the perception of speech. *Cognitive Psychology, 6*, 41–60.

Darwin, C.J., Turvey, M.T., & Crowder, R.G. (1972). An auditory analogue of the Sperling partial report procedure: Evidence for brief auditory storage. *Cognitive Psychology, 3*, 255–267.

Davidson, R.J. & Schwartz, G.E. (1977). Brain mechanisms subserving self-generated imagery: Electrophysiological specificity and patterning. *Psychophysiology, 14*, 598–602.

Davies, G.M., Ellis, H.D., & Shepherd, J.W. (1981). *Perceiving and remembering faces*. London: Academic Press.

Davis, R., Sutherland, N.S., & Judd, B.R. (1961). Information content in recognition and recall. *Journal of Experimental Psychology, 61*, 422–428.

De Groot, A.D. (1965). *Thought and choice in chess*. New York: Basic Books.

De Renzi, E., Liotti, M., & Nichelli, N. (1987). Semantic amnesia with preservation of autobiographic memory. A case report. *Cortex, 23*, 575–597.

De Renzi, E. & Spinnler, H. (1967). Impaired performance on color tasks in patients with hemispheric damage. *Cortex, 3*, 194–216.

Deatherage, B.H. & Evans, T.R. (1969). Binaural masking: Backward, forward and simultaneous effects. *Journal of the Acoustical Society of America, 46*, 362–371.

Deese, J. (1959). Influence of inter-item associative strength upon immediate free recall. *Psychological Reports, 5*, 305–312.

Deffenbacher, K.A. (1983). The influence of arousal on reliability of testimony. In S.M.A. Lloyd-Bostock & B.R. Clifford (Eds.), *Evaluating witness evidence*, pp. 235–254. Chichester: John Wiley.

Dement, W.C. (1960). The effect of dream deprivation. *Science, 131*, 1705–1707.

Dennis, W. (1948). *Readings in the history of psychology*. New York: Appleton-Century-Crofts.

Deutsch, J.A. & Deutsch, D. (1963). Attention: Some theoretical considerations. *Psychological Review, 70*, 80–90.

Dickinson, A. (1980). *Contemporary animal learning theory*. Cambridge: Cambridge University Press.

Dickinson, A. & Shanks, D. (1985). Animal conditioning and human causality judgement. In L.G. Nilsson and T. Archer (Eds.), *Perspectives on learning and memory*. Hillsdale, N.J.: LEA Inc.

Dixon, N.F. (1981). *Preconscious processing*. London: Wiley.

Doost, R. & Turvey, M.T. (1971). Iconic memory and central processing capacity. *Perception and Psychophysics, 9*, 269–274.

Dornic, S. (1977). *Mental load, effort, and individual differences*

(Report No. 509). Report from the Department of Psychology, The University of Stockholm.

Drabman, R.S. (1973). Child versus teacher-administered token programmes in a psychiatric hospital school. *Journal of Abnormal Child Psychology, 1*, 66–87.

Dritschel, B., Williams, J.M.G., & Baddeley, A.D. (in prep.). *On the structure of autobiographical memory.*

Dunbar, D.C. & Lishman, W.A. (1984). Depression, recognition memory and hedonic tone: A signal detection analysis. *British Journal of Psychiatry, 144*, 376–382.

Dunnett, S.P. (1989). Anatomical and behavioral consequences of cholinergic-rich grafts to the neocortex of rats with lesions of the nucleus basalis magnocellularis. *Annals of the New York Academy of Sciences, 495*, 415–429.

Ebbinghaus, H. (1885). Über das Gedächtnis. Leipzig: Dunker. (Translation by H. Ruyer and C.E. Bussenius, (1913), *Memory*. New York: Teachers College, Columbia University.

Efron, R. (1970a). The relationship between the duration of a stimulus and the duration of a perception. *Neuropsychologia, 8*, 37–55.

Efron, R. (1970b). The minimum duration of a perception. *Neuropsychologia, 8*, 57–63.

Eich, J.E. (1980). The cue-dependent nature of state-dependent retrieval. *Memory and Cognition, 8*, 157–173.

Ekstrand, B.R. (1972). To sleep, perchance to dream. In C.P. Duncan, L. Sechrest, & A.W. Melton (Eds.), *Human memory: Festschrift in honor of Benton J. Underwood*, pp. 59–82. New York: Appleton-Century-Crofts.

Ellis, A.W. & Young, A.W. (1988). Human cognitive neuropsychology. Hove: Lawrence Erlbaum Associates Ltd.

Ellis, J.A. (1988). Memory for future intentions: Investigating pulses and steps. In M.M. Gruneberg, P.E. Morris, & R.N. Sykes (Eds.), *Practical aspects of memory: Current research and issues,Vol. 1: Memory in everyday life*, pp. 371–376. Chichester: John Wiley & Sons.

Ellis, N.C. & Hennelly, R.A. (1980). A bilingual word-length effect: Implications for intelligence testing and the relative ease of mental calculation in Welsh and English. *British Journal of Psychology, 71*, 43–52.

Ellis, N.R., Katz, E., & Williams, J.E. (1987). Developmental aspects of memory for spatial location. *Journal of Experimental Child Psychology, 44*, 401–412.

Ellis, N.R., Palmer, R.L., & Reeves, C.L. (1988). Developmental and intellectual differences in frequency processing. *Developmental Psychology, 24*, 38–45.

Empson, J.A.C. & Clarke, P.R.F. (1970). Rapid eye movements and remembering. *Nature, 225*, 287–288.

Engle, W. (1974). The modality effect: Is precategorical acoustic storage responsible? *Journal of Experimental Psychology, 102*, 824–829.

Erdelyi, M.H. (1985). *Psychoanalysis: Freud's cognitive psychology*. New York: W.H. Freeman.

Ericsson, K.A. (1985). Memory skill. *Canadian Journal of Psychology, 39*, 188–231.

Ericsson, K.A. & Chase, W.G. (1982). Exceptional memory. *American Scientist, 70*, 607–615.

Ericsson, K.A. & Polson, P.G. (in press) A cognitive analysis of exceptional memory for restaurant orders. In M. Chi, R. Glaser and M. Farr (Eds.), *The nature of expertise*. Hillsdale, N.J.: Lawrence Erlbaum Associates Inc.

Eysenck, H.J. & Wilson, G.D. (Eds.) (1973). *The experimental study of Freudian theories*. London: Methuen.

Eysenck, M.W. (1977). *Human memory: Theory, research and individual differences*. Oxford: Pergamon Press.

Eysenck, M.W. (1979). Anxiety, learning, and memory: A reconceptualisation. *Journal of Research in Personality, 13*, 363–385.

Eysenck, M.W. (1983). Anxiety and individual differences. In G.R.J. Hockey (Ed.), *Stress and fatigue in human performance*. Chichester: John Wiley & Sons.

Eysenck, M.W. & Eysenck, M.C. (1980). Effects of processing depth, distinctiveness, and word frequency on retention. *British Journal of Psychology, 71*, 263–274.

Eysenck, M.W., Macleod, C., & Mathews, A. (1987). Cognitive functioning in anxiety. *Psychological Research, 49*, 189–195.

Faglioni, P. & Spinnler, H. (1972). Visual perception versus memory of abstract spatial patterns and unilateral brain damage. *International Journal of Mental Health 1*, 65–77.

Farah, M.J. (1988). Is visual imagery really visual? Overlooked evidence from neuropsychology. *Psychological Review, 95*, 307–317.

Farah, M.J., Hammond, K.M., Levine, D.N., & Calvanio, R. (1988). Visual and spatial mental imagery: Dissociable systems of representation. *Cognitive Psychology, 20*, 439–462.

Farah, M.J., Peronnet, F., & Weisberg, L.L. (1987). *Brain activity underlying mental imagery: An ERP study*. Paper presented at the 28th Annual meeting of the Psychonomic Society, Seattle.

Fernandez, A., & Glenberg, A.M. (1985). Changing environmental context does not reliably affect memory. *Memory and Cognition, 13*, 333–345.

Fisher, R.P. & Craik, F.I.M. (1977). Interaction between encoding and retrieval operations in cued recall. *Journal of Experimental Psychology: Human Learning and Memory, 3*, 701–711.

Fisher, R.P., & Geiselman, R.E. (1988). Enhancing eyewitness memory with the cognitive interview. In M.M. Gruneberg, P.E. Morris, & R.N. Sykes (Eds.), *Practical aspects of memory: Current research and issues, Vol. 1: memory in everyday life*, pp. 34–39. Chichester: John Wiley & Sons.

Fisk, A.D. (1986). Frequency encoding is not inevitable and is not automatic: A reply to Hasher and Zacks. *American Psychologist, 41*, 215–216.

Fitts, P.M., & Peterson, J.R. (1964). Information capacity of discrete motor responses. *Journal of Experimental Psychology, 67*, 103–112.

Fleishman, E.A., & Parker, J.F. Jr. (1962). Factors in the retention and relearning of perceptual motor skill. *Journal of Experimental Psychology, 64*, 215–226.

Fodor, J., & Pylyshyn, Z. (1988). Connectionism and cognitive architecture: A critical analysis. *Cognition, 28*, 3–71.

Fowler, C.A., Wolford, G., Slade, R., & Tassinary, L. (1981). Lexical access with and without awareness. *Journal of Experimental Psychology: General, 110*, 341–362.

Fox, P.W., Blick, K.A., & Bilodeau, E.A. (1964). Stimulation and prediction of verbal recall and misrecall. *Journal of Experimental Psychology, 68*, 321–322.

French, J.W. (1942). The effect of temperature on the retention of a maze habit in fish. *Journal of Experimental Psychology, 31*, 79–87.

Freud, S. (1901). *The psychopathology of everyday life*. Translated by Tyson, A. (1971). New York: W.W. Norton.

Galton, F. (1883). *Inquiries into human faculty and its development*. Everyman Edition, London: Dent.

Ganzer, V.J. (1968). Effects of audience presence and test anxiety on learning and retention in a serial learning situation. *Journal of Personality and Social Psychology, 8*, 194–199.

Garcia, J., Kimmeldorf, D.J., & Koelling, R.A., (1955). Conditioned aversion to saccarin resulting from exposure to gamma radiation. *Science, 122*, 157–158.

Gardiner, J.M., Craik, F.I.M., & Birtwisle, J. (1972). Retrieval cues and release from proactive inhibition. *Journal of Verbal Learning and Verbal Behavior, 11*, 778–783.

Gardiner, J.M. & Gregg, V.H. (1979). When auditory memory is not overwritten. *Journal of Verbal Learning and Verbal Behavior, 18*, 705–719.

Gathercole, S.E., & Baddeley, A.D. (1989). Development of vocabulary in children and short-term phonological memory. *Journal of Memory and Language, 28*, 200–213.

Gathercole, S.E. & Baddeley, A.D. (in press). Immediate memory deficits in language disordered children. *Journal of Memory and Language*.

Geiselman, E. (1988). Improving eyewitness memory through mental reinstatement of context. In G.M. Davies & D.M. Thomson (Eds.), *Memory in context: Context in memory*, pp. 245–266. Chichester: Wiley.

Geiselman, R.E., Fisher, R.P., MacKinnon, D.P., & Holland, H.L. (1985). Eyewitness memory enhancement in the police interview: Cognitive retrieval mnemonics versus hypnosis. *Journal of Applied Psychology, 70*, 401–412.

Gettinger, M., Bryant, N.D., & Mayne, H.R. (1982). Designing spelling instruction for learning-disabled children: An emphasis on unit size, distributed practice, and training for transfer. *Journal of Special Education, 16*, 439–448.

Gibson, J.J. (1979). *The ecological approach to visual perception*. Boston, Mass.: Houghton Mifflin.

Gibson, J.J., Jack, E.G., & Raffel, G. (1932). Bilateral transfer of the conditioned response in the human subject. *Journal of Experimental Psychology, 15,* 416–421.

Gilligan, S.G., & Bower, G.H. (1984). Cognitive consequences of emotional arousal. In C. Izard, J. Kagan, & R. Zajonc (Eds.), *Emotions, cognitions and behavior.* New York: Cambridge University Press.

Gladwin, T. (1970). *East is a big bird.* Cambridge, Mass: Harvard University Press.

Glanzer, M. (1972). Storage mechanisms in recall. In G.H. Bower (Ed.), *The psychology of learning and motivation: Advances in research and theory, Vol. V.* New York: Academic Press.

Glanzer, M., & Cunitz, A.R. (1966). Two storage mechanisms in free recall. *Journal of Verbal Learning & Verbal Behavior, 5,* 351–360.

Glanzer, M., Dorfman, D., & Kaplan, B. (1981). Short–term storage in the processing of text. *Journal of Verbal Learning and Verbal Behavior, 20,* 656–670.

Gleitman, H. (1986). *Psychology.* New York: Norton.

Glenberg, A.M., Smith, S.M., & Green, C. (1977). Type I rehearsal: Maintenance and more. *Journal of Verbal Learning and Verbal Behavior, 16,* 339–352.

Glenberg, A.M., & Swanson, N.G. (1986). A temporal distinctiveness theory of recency and modality effects. *Journal of Experimental Psychology: Learning, Memory, and Cognition, 12,* 3–15.

Glendon, A.I., McKenna, S.P., Blaylock, S.S., & Hunt, K. (1987). Evaluating mass training in cardiopulmonary resuscitation. *British Medical Journal, 294,* 1182–1183.

Glisky, E.L., Schacter, D.L., & Tulving, E. (1986). Computer learning by memory-impaired patients: Acquisition and retention of complex knowledge. *Neuropsychologia, 24,* 313–328.

Glucksberg, S., & Cowan, G.N. Jr. (1970). Memory for nonattended auditory material. *Cognitive Psychology, 1,* 149–156.

Godden, D., & Baddeley, A.D. (1975). Context-dependent memory in two natural environments: On land and under water. *British Journal of Psychology, 66,* 325–331.

Godden, D., & Baddeley, A.D. (1980). When does context influence recognition memory? *British Journal of Psychology, 71,* 99–104.

Gol'dburt, S.N. (1961). Investigation of the stability of auditory processes in micro-intervals of time (new findings on back masking). *Biofizika, 6,* 717–724. (English translation: *Biophysics,* 1961, *6,* 809–817.)

Goldstein, A.G., & Chance, J.E. (1971). Recognition of complex visual stimuli. *Perception and Psychophysics, 9,* 237–241.

Goldstein, K. (1936). The significance of the frontal lobes for mental performance. *Journal of Neurology & Psychopathology, 17,* 27–40.

Golla, F.L., Hutton, E.L., & Grey Walter, W.G. (1943). The objective study of mental imagery. I. Physiological concommitents. *Journal of Mental Science, 75,* 216–223.

Gomulicki, B.R. (1956). Recall as an abstractive process. *Acta Psychologica, 12,* 77–94.

Goodglass, H., Klein, P., Carey, P., & Jones, K. (1966). Specific semantic word categories in aphasia. *Cortex, 2,* 74–89.

Goodwin, D.W., Powell, B., Bremer, D., Hoine, H., & Stern, J. (1969). Alcohol and recall: State dependent effects in man. *Science, 163*, 1358.

Gorman, R.P. & Sejnowski, T.J. (in press) Learned classification of sonar targets using a massively-parallel network. *IEEE transactions in acoustics and speech signal processing.*

Gorn, G.J. (1982). The effects of music in advertising on choice behaviour: A classical conditioning approach. *Journal of Marketing, 46*, 94–101.

Graf, P. & Mandler, G. (1984). Activation makes words more accessible, but not necessarily more retrievable. *Journal of Verbal Learning and Verbal Behavior, 23*, 553–568.

Graf, P. & Schacter, D.L. (1985). Implicit and explicit memory for new associations in normal and amnesic subjects. *Journal of Experimental Psychology: Learning, Memory and Cognition, 11*, 501–518.

Greenspoon, J., & Ranyard, R. (1957). Stimulus conditions and retroactive inhibition. *Journal of Experimental Psychology, 53*, 55–59.

Greenwald, A., & Shulman, H. (1973). On doing two things at once: II. Elimination of the psychological refractory period. *Journal of Experimental Psychology, 101*, 70–76.

Gregg, V. (1976). Word frequency, recognition and recall. In J. Brown (Ed.), *Recognition and recall*. Chichester: John Wiley & Sons Ltd.

Gregg, V.H. (1986). *Introduction to human memory*. London: Routledge and Kegan Paul.

Gresham, L.G., & Shimp, T.A. (1985). Attitude toward the advertisement and brand attitude: A classical conditioning perspective. *Journal of Advertising, 14*, 10–17.

Grinker, R., & Spiegl, J. (1945). *Men under stress*. Philadelphia: Blakiston.

Gunter, B., Berry, C., & Clifford, B.R. (1981). Proactive interference effects with television news items: Further evidence. *Journal of Experimental Psychology: Human Learning and Memory, 7*, 480–487.

Guttman, N., & Julesz, B. (1963). Lower limits of auditory periodicity analysis. *Journal of the Acoustical Society of America, 35*, 610.

Haber, R.N. (1983). The impending demise of the icon: A critique of the concept of iconic storage in visual information processing. *Behavioral and Brain Sciences, 6*, 1–11.

Haber, R.N., & Nathanson, L.S. (1968). Post-retinal storage? Park's camel as seen through the eye of a needle. *Perception and Psychophysics, 3*, 349–355.

Hallowell, A.I. (1938). Fear and anxiety as cultural and individual variables in a primitive society. *Journal of Social Psychology, 9*, 25–47.

Hamilton, W. (1859). *Lectures on metaphysics and logic*, Vol. 1. Edinburgh: Blackwood.

Hammerton, M. (1963). Retention of learning in a difficult tracking task. *Journal of Experimental Psychology, 66*, 108–110.

Hanley, J.R. (1984). Dual processes in recognition and in recognition failure. *Memory and Cognition, 12*, 575–580.

Hanley, J.R., & Broadbent, C. (1987). The effect of unattended speech on serial recall following auditory presentation. *British Journal of*

Psychology, 78, 287–298.

Hardyk, C.D., & Petrinovitch, L.R. (1970). Subvocal speech and comprehension level as a function of the difficulty level of reading material. *Journal of Verbal Learning and Verbal Behavior, 9*, 647–652.

Harris, J.E. (1980). Memory aids people use: Two interview studies. *Memory and Cognition, 8*, 31–38.

Harris, J., & Wilkins, A.J. (1982). Remembering to do things: A theoretical framework and illustrative experiment. *Human Learning, 1*, 1–14.

Hart, J.T. (1965). Memory and the feeling of knowing experience. *Journal of Educational Psychology, 56*, 208–216.

Hart, J., Berndt, R.S., & Caramazza, A. (1985). Category-specific naming deficit following cerebral infarction. *Nature, 316*, 439–440.

Hasher, L., & Zacks, R.T. (1979). Automatic and effortful processes in memory. *Journal of Experimental Psychology: General, 108*, 356–388.

Hasher, L., & Zacks, R.T. (1984). Automatic processing of fundamental information: The case of frequency of occurrence. *American Psychologist, 39*, 1372–1388.

Hatano, G., & Osawa, K. (1983). Digit memory of grand experts in abacus-derived mental calculation. *Cognition, 15*, 95–110.

Hebb, D.O. (1949). *Organization of behavior*. New York: Wiley.

Hebb, D.O. (1961). Distinctive features of learning in the higher animal. In J.F. Delafresnaye (Ed.), *Brain mechanisms and learning*, pp. 37–46. London: Oxford University Press.

Hersen, M., & Barlow, D.H. (1976). *Single case experimental designs: Strategies for studying behavior change*. New York: Pergamon Press.

Hersen, M., & Eisler, R. (1976). Social skills training. In W.E. Craighead, A.E. Kazdin, & M.J. Mahoney (Eds.), *Behavior modification, principles, issues and applications*. Boston: Houghton Mifflin Co.

Hick, W.E. (1952). On the rate of gain of information. *Quarterly Journal of Experimental Psychology, 4*, 11–26.

Higbee, K.L. (1981). *What do college students get from a memory improvement course?* Paper presented at the April meeting of the Eastern Psychological Association, New York City.

Hilgard, E.R., (1948). *Theories of Learning*. New York: Appleton–Century–Crofts.

Hilgard, E.R., Campbell, R.C., & Sears, W.N. (1938). The effect of knowledge on stimulus relationships. *American Journal of Psychology, 51*, 498–506.

Hinton, G.E., & Anderson, J.A. (1981). *Parallel models of associative memory*. Hillsdale, N.J.: Lawrence Erlbaum Associates Inc.

Hinton, G.E., & Parsons, L.M. (1981). Frames of reference and mental imagery. In J. Long & A.D. Baddeley (Eds.), *Attention and performance IX*. Hillsdale, N.J.: Lawrence Erlbaum Associates Inc.

Hintzman, D.L. (1967). Articulatory coding in short-term memory. *Journal of Verbal Learning and Verbal Behavior, 6*, 312–316.

Hirst, W., Spelke, E.S., Reaves, C.C., Caharack, G., & Neisser, U.

(1980). Dividing attention without alternation or automaticity. *Journal of Experimental Psychology: General, 109*, 98–117.

Hitch, G.J. (1975). The role of attention in visual and auditory suffix effects. *Memory and Cognition, 3*, 501–505.

Hitch, G.J. (1978). The role of short-term working memory in mental arithmetic. *Cognitive Psychology, 10*, 302–323.

Hitch, G.J., & Halliday, M.S. (1983). Working memory in children. *Philosophical Transactions of the Royal Society London B, 302*, 325–340.

Hitch, G.J., Halliday, M.S., & Littler, J. (1984). *Memory span and the speed of mental operations*. Paper presented at the joint Experimental Psychology Society/Netherlands Psychonomic Foundation Meeting, Amsterdam.

Hitch, G.J., Rejman, M.J., & Turner, N.C. (1980). *A new perspective on the recency effect*. Paper presented at the July Experimental Psychology Society meeting, Cambridge.

Hoagland, H. (1931). A study of the physiology of learning in ants. *Journal of General Psychology, 5*, 21–41.

Hockey, G.R.J., Davies, S., & Gray, M.M. (1972). Forgetting as a function of sleep at different times of day. *Experimental Psychology, 24*, 386–393.

Holding, D.H. (1985). *The psychology of chess skill*. Hillsdale, N.J.: Lawrence Erlbaum Associates Inc.

Holender, D. (1986). Semantic activation without conscious identification in dichotic listening, parafoveal vision, and visual masking: A survey and appraisal. *Behavioral and Brain Sciences, 9*, 1–66.

Holmes, G. (1919). Disturbances of visual space recognition. *British Medical Journal, 2*, 230–233.

Hoosain, R., & Salili, F. (1988). Language differences, working memory, and mathematical ability. In M.M. Gruneberg, P.E. Morris, & R.N. Sykes (Eds.), *Practical aspects of memory: Current research and issues, Vol. 2: Clinical and educational implications*, pp. 512–517. Chichester: John Wiley & Sons.

Horowitz, L.M. (1962). Associative matching and intralist similarity. *Psychological Reports, 10*, 751–757.

Hovland, C.I. (1938). Experimental studies in rote learning theory: III. Distribution of practice with varying speeds of syllable presentation. *Journal of Experimental Psychology, 23*, 172–190.

Howard, D. & Butterworth, B. (in press) Developmental disorders of verbal short-term memory and their relation to sentence comprehension. *Cognitive Neuropsychology*.

Howard, D., & Orchard-Lisle, V. (1984). On the origin of semantic errors in naming: Evidence from the case of a global aphasic. *Cognitive Neuropsychology, 1*, 163–190.

Hubel, D.H., & Wiesel, T.N. (1962). Receptive fields, binocular interaction and a functional architecture in the cat's visual cortex. *Journal of Physiology, 160*, 106–154.

Hudson, J.A., & Fivush, R. (1987). *As time goes by: Sixth graders remember a kindergarten experience (Report No. 13)*. Emory Cognition Project.

Hugdahl, K. (1978). Electrodermal conditioning to potentially phobic stimuli: Effects of instructed extinction. *Behaviour Research and Therapy, 16*, 315–321.

Hulme, C., Thomson, N., Muir, C., & Lawrence, A. (1984). Speech rate and the development of short-term memory span. *Journal of Experimental Child Psychology, 38*, 241–253.

Humphreys, G.W., & Riddoch, J. (1987). *To see but not to see: A case study of visual agnosia*. London: Lawrence Erlbaum Associates Ltd.

Humphreys, G.W., & Riddoch, M.J. (Eds.) (1987). *Visual object processing: A cognitive neuropsychological approach*. London: Lawrence Erlbaum Associates Ltd.

Hunt, R.R. & Seta, C.E. (1984). Category size effects in recall: The roles of relational and individual item information. *Journal of Experimental Psychology: Learning, Memory and Cognition, 10*, 454–464.

Hunter, I.M.L. (1957). *Memory: Facts and fallacies*. Baltimore: Penguin.

Hunter, I.M.L. (1962). An exceptional talent for calculative thinking. *British Journal of Psychology, 53*, 243–258.

Hunter, M., Philips, C., & Rachman, S. (1979). Memory for pain. *Pain, 6*, 35–46.

Huppert, F.A., & Piercy, M. (1978a). Dissociation between learning and remembering in organic amnesia. *Nature, 275*, 317–318.

Huppert, F.A., & Piercy, M. (1978b). The role of trace strength in recency and frequency judgments by amnesic and control subjects. *The Quarterly Journal of Experimental Psychology, 30*, 346–354.

Huppert, F.A., & Piercy, M. (1979). Normal and abnormal forgetting in amnesia: Effect of locus of lesion. *Cortex, 15*, 385–390.

Hyde, T.S., & Jenkins, J.J. (1969). Differential effects of incidental tasks on the organization of recall of a list of highly associated words. *Journal of Experimental Psychology, 83*, 472–481.

Idzikowski, C. & Baddeley, A.D. (1983a). Waiting in the wings: Apprehension, public speaking and performance. *Ergonomics, 26*, 575–583.

Idzikowski, C., & Baddeley, A.D. (1983b). Fear and dangerous environments. In G.R.J. Hockey (Ed.), *Stress and fatigue in human performance*, pp. 123–144. Chichester: John Wiley & Sons.

Idzikowski, C. & Baddeley, A.D. (1987). Fear and performance in novice parachutists. *Ergonomics, 30*, 1463–1474.

Ingvar, D. (1979). Patterns of activity in the cerebral cortex related to memory functions. In L.-G. Nilsson (Ed.), *Perspectives on memory research*, pp. 247–255. Hillsdale, N.J.: Lawrence Erlbaum Associates Inc.

Intons-Peterson, M.J. (1983). Imagery paradigms: How vulnerable are they to experimenters' expectations? *Journal of Experimental Psychology: Human Perception and Performance, 9*, 394–412.

Intons-Peterson, M.J., & Roskos-Ewoldsen, B. (1988). *Sensory/perceptual qualities of images*. Paper presented at the 29th Annual meeting of the Psychonomics Society, Chicago.

Isen, A.M., Shalker, T.E., Clark, M., & Carp, L. (1978). Affect, accessibility of material in memory and behavior: A cognitive loop.

Journal of Personality and Social Psychology, 36, 1–12.

Jackson, J.L., Bogers, H., & Kersholt, J. (1988). Do memory aids aid the elderly in their day-to-day remembering? In M.M. Gruneberg, P.E. Morris, & R.N. Sykes (Eds.), *Practical aspects of memory: Current research and issues, Vol. 2: Clinical and educational implications*, pp. 137–142. Chichester: John Wiley & Sons.

Jacobs, J. (1885). Review of "The Psychology of Memory" by H. Ebbinghaus. *Mind, 10.*

Jacobs, J. (1887). Experiments on 'prehension'. *Mind, 12*, 75–79.

Jacoby, L.L., & Dallas, M. (1981). On the relationship between autobiographical memory and perceptual learning. *Journal of Experimental Psychology: General, 110*, 306–340.

Jacoby, L.L., & Witherspoon, D. (1982). Remembering without awareness. *Canadian Journal of Psychology, 36*, 300–324.

James, W. (1890). *Principles of psychology*, Vol. 1. New York: Holt.

Janis, I.L. (1951). *Airwar and emotional stress*. New York: McGraw Hill.

Jarvella, R.J. (1971). Syntactic processing of connected speech. *Journal of Verbal Learning and Verbal Behavior, 10*, 409–416.

Jenkins, J.G., & Dallenbach, K.M. (1924). Obliviscence during sleep and waking. *American Journal of Psychology, 35*, 605–612.

Jenkins, J.J., & Russell, W.A. (1952). Associative clustering during recall. *Journal of Abnormal and Social Psychology, 47*, 818–821.

John, E. (1941). A study of the effects of evacuation in air-raids on pre-school children. *British Journal of Educational Psychology, 11*, 173–179.

Johnson, M.H., & Magaro, P.A. (1987). Effects of mood and severity on memory processes in depression and mania. *Psychological Bulletin, 101*, 28–40.

Johnson, M.K., Kim, J.K., & Risse, G. (1985). Do alcoholic Korsakoff's syndrome patients acquire affective reactions? *Journal of Experimental Psychology: Learning, Memory, & Cognition, 11*, 22–36.

Johnson-Laird, P.N. (1988). *The computer and the mind*. London: Fontana.

Johnson-Laird, P.N., Herrmann, D.J., & Chaffin, R. (1984). Only connections: A critique of semantic networks. *Psychological Bulletin, 96*, 292–315.

Jones, G.V. (1988). Images, predicates, and retrieval cues. In M. Denis, J. Engelkamp, & J.T.E. Richardson (Eds.), *Cognitive and neuropsychological approaches to mental imagery*, pp. 89–98. Dordrecht: Martinus Nijhoff.

Jorm, A.F. (1983). Specific reading retardation and working memory: A review. *British Journal of Psychology, 74*, 311–342.

Joyce, C.R.B., Caple, G., Mason, M., Reynolds, E., & Matthews, J.A. (1969). Quantitative study of doctor patient communication. *Quarterly Journal of Medicine, 38*, 183–194.

Jung, C.G. (1906). *Experimental researches*. Republished in *Collected works*, 1973. London: Routledge and Kegan Paul.

Katona, G. (1940). *Organizing and memorizing*. New York: Columbia University Press.

Katz, J.J., & Fodor, J.A. (1963). The structure of a semantic theory. *Language, 39,* 170–210.

Kay, J., & Ellis, A.W. (1987). A cognitive neuropsychological case study of anomia: Implications for psychological models of word retrieval. *Brain, 110,* 613–629.

Kearins, J. (1978). Visual memory skills of Western Desert and Queensland children of Australian Aboriginal descent: A reply to Drinkwater. *Australian Journal of Psychology, 30,* 1–5.

Kelso, J.S., Southard, D.L., & Goodman, D. (1979). On the coordination of two-handed movements. *Journal of Experimental Psychology: Human Perception and Performance, 5,* 229–238.

Kennedy, R.A. (1976). Behavior modification in prisons. In W.E. Craighead, A.E. Kazdin, & M.J. Mahoney (Eds.), *Behavior modification, principles, issues and applications.* Boston: Houghton Mifflin Co.

Keppel, G., Postman, L., & Zavortink, B. (1968). Studies of learning to learn: VIII. The influence of massive amounts of training upon the learning and retention of paired–associate lists. *Journal of Verbal Learning and Verbal Behavior, 7,* 790–796.

Keppel, G., & Underwood, B.J. (1962). Proactive inhibition in short–term retention of single items. *Journal of Verbal Learning and Verbal Behavior, 1,* 153–161.

Kerr, B. (1973). Processing demands during mental operations. *Memory and Cognition, 1,* 401–412.

Kintsch, W. (1968). Recognition and free recall of organized lists. *Journal of Experimental Psychology, 78,* 481–487.

Kintsch, W. (1970). *Learning, memory and conceptual processes.* New York: Wiley.

Kintsch, W. (1974). *The representation of meaning in memory.* Hillsdale, N.J.: Lawrence Erlbaum Associates Inc.

Kintsch, W. (1980). Semantic memory: A tutorial. In R.S. Nickerson (Ed.), *Attention and performance VIII,* pp. 595–620. Hillsdale, N.J.: Lawrence Erlbaum Associates Inc.

Kintsch, W., & Buschke, H. (1969). Homophones and synonyms in short-term memory. *Journal of Experimental Psychology, 80,* 403–407.

Klein, K., & Saltz, E. (1976). Specifying the mechanisms in a levels-of-processing approach to memory. *Journal of Experimental Psychology: Human Learning and Memory, 2,* 671–679.

Kleinsmith, L.J., & Kaplan, S. (1963). Paired associated learning as a function of arousal and interpolated interval. *Journal of Experimental Psychology, 65,* 190–193.

Kleinsmith, L.J. & Kaplan, S. (1964). Interaction of arousal and recall interval in nonsense syllable paired associate learning. *Journal of Experimental Psychology, 67,* 124–126.

Klich, L.Z., & Davidson, G.R. (1983). A cultural difference in visual memory: On le voit, on le voit plus. *International Journal of Psychology, 18,* 189–201.

Kohonen, T. (1984). *Self-organization and associative memory.* Berlin: Springer-Verlag.

Kopelman, M.D. (1985). Rates of forgetting in Alzheimer-type dementia and Korsakoff's Syndrome. *Neuropsychologia, 15*, 527–541.

Kopelman, M.D. (1987). Amnesia: Organic and psychogenic. *British Journal of Psychiatry, 150*, 428–442.

Kopelman, M.D., Wilson, B.A, & Baddeley, A.D. (in press) The autobiographical memory interview: A new assessment of autobiographical and personal semantic memory in amnesic patients. *Journal of Clinical and Experimental Neuropsychology*.

Kosslyn, S.M. (1980). *Image and mind*. Cambridge, Mass.: Harvard University Press.

Kosslyn, S.M., Pick, H., & Fariello, G. (1974). Cognitive maps in children and men. *Child Development, 45*, 707–716.

Kubie, L.S. (1952). Problems and techniques of psychoanalytic validation and progress. In E. Punpian-Mindlin (Ed.), *Psychoanalysis as science*. Stanford: Stanford University Press.

Kupst M.J., Dresser, K., Schulman, J.L., & Paul, M.H. (1975). Evaluation of methods to improve communication in the physician-patient relationship. *American Journal of Orthopsychiatry, 45*, 420–429.

Lackner, J.R., & Garrett, M.F. (1972). Resolving ambiguity: Effects of biasing context in the unattended ear. *Cognition, 1*, 359–372.

Landauer, T.K., & Bjork, R.A. (1978). Optimum rehearsal patterns and name learning. In M.M. Gruneberg, P.E. Morris, & R.N. Sykes (Eds.), *Practical aspects of memory*, pp. 625–632. London: Academic Press.

Landauer, T.K., & Freedman, J.L. (1968). Information retrieval from long-term memory: Category size and recognition time. *Journal of Verbal Learning and Verbal Behavior, 7*, 291–295.

Landauer, T.K., & Ross, B.H. (1977). Can simple instructions to use spaced practice improve ability to remember a fact? An experimental test using telephone numbers. *Bulletin of the Psychonomic Society, 10*, 215–218.

Lashley, K.S. (1929). *Brain mechanisms and intelligence: A quantitative study of injuries to the brain*. Chicago: University of Chicago Press.

Lautch, H. (1971). Dental phobia. *British Journal of Psychiatry, 119*, 151–158.

Leight, K.A., & Ellis, H.C. (1981). Emotional and mood states, strategies, and state-dependency in memory. *Journal of Verbal Learning and Verbal Behavior, 20*, 251–266.

Leippe, M.R., Wells, G.L., & Ostrom, T.M. (1978). Crime seriousness as a determinant of accuracy in eyewitness identification. *Journal of Applied Psychology, 63*, 345–351.

Lenneberg, E.H., & Roberts, A.M. (1956). *The language of experience: Memoire 13*. University of Indiana Publications in Anthropology and Linguistics.

Levine, D.N., Warach, J., & Farah, M.J. (1985). Two visual systems in mental imagery: Dissociation of "what" and "where" in imagery disorders due to bilateral posterior cerebral lesions. *Neurology, 35*, 1010–1018.

Levin, H.S., Grafman, J., & Eisenberg, H.M. (Eds.) (1987). *Neuro-

behavioral recovery from head injury. New York: Oxford University Press.

Levinger, G., & Clark, J. (1961). Emotional factors in the forgetting of word associations. *Journal of Abnormal and Social Psychology, 62*, 99–105.

Levinson, B.W. (1965). States of awareness during general anaesthesia. *British Journal of Anaesthesia, 37*, 544–550.

Lewis, A. (1951). Incidence of neurosis in England under war conditions. *Lancet, 2*, 175–183.

Ley, P. (1972). Primacy, rated importance and the recall of medical information. *Journal of Health and Social Behaviour, 13*, 311.

Ley, P. (1979). Improving clinical communication: Effects of altering doctor behaviour. In D. Oborne, M.M. Gruneberg, & J.R. Eiser (Eds.), *Research in psychology and medicine*. London: Academic Press.

Ley, P. (1988). *Communicating with patients*. London: Croom Helm.

Ley, P., Bradshaw, P.W., Eaves, D., & Walker, C.M. (1973). A method for increasing patients' recall of information presented by doctors. *Psychological Medicine, 3*, 217–220.

Ley, P. & Spelman, M.S. (1965). Communications in an out-patient setting. *British Journal of Social and Clinical Psychology, 4*, 114-116.

Ley, P. & Spelman M.S. (1967). *Communicating with the patient*, London: Staples Press.

Lhermitte, F. (1983). "Utilisation behaviour" and its relation to lesions of the frontal lobe. *Brain, 106*, 237–255.

Liberman, A.M., Delattre, P.C., Cooper, F.S., & Gerstman, L.J. (1954). The role of consonant-vowel transitions in perception of the stop and nasal consonants. *Psychological Monographs, 68*, 1–13.

Light, L.L., & Carter-Sobell, L. (1970). The effects of changed semantic context on recognition memory. *Journal of Verbal Learning and Verbal Behavior, 9*, 1–11.

Lindsay, P.H., & Norman, D.A. (1972). *Human information processing*. New York: Academic Press.

Linton, M. (1975). Memory for real-world events. In D.A. Norman & D.E. Rumelhart (Eds.), *Explorations in cognition*, Chapter 14. San Francisco: Freeman.

Lissauer, H. (1988). A case of visual agnosia with a contribution to theory. Original 1888, translation published in *Cognitive Neuropsychology, 5*, 157–192.

Lloyd, G.G., & Lishman, W.A. (1975). Effect of depression on the speed of recall of pleasant and unpleasant experiences. *Psychological Medicine, 5*, 173–180.

Locke, J. (1690). *An essay concerning human understanding*. (Everyman's Library Edition, 1961.) London: Dent.

Loess, H. (1968). Short-term memory and item similarity. *Journal of Verbal Learning and Verbal Behavior, 7*, 87–92.

Loess, H., & Waugh, N.C. (1967). Short-term memory and inter-trial interval. *Journal of Verbal Learning and Verbal Behavior, 6*, 455–460.

Loftus, E.F. (1977). Shifting human color memory. *Memory and Cognition, 5*, 696–699.

Loftus, E.F. (1979). *Eyewitness testimony*. Cambridge, Mass.: Harvard University Press.

Loftus, E.F. (1980). *Memory*. Reading, Mass: Addison-Wesley.

Loftus, E.F. & Burns, T.E. (1982). Mental shock can produce retrograde amnesia. *Memory and Cognition, 10*, 318–323.

Loftus, E.F., & Loftus, G.R. (1980). On the permanence of stored information in the human brain. *American Psychologist, 35*, 409–420.

Loftus, E.F., & Marburger, W. (1983). Since the eruption of Mount St Helens, has anyone beaten you up? Improving the accuracy of retrospective reports with landmark events. *Memory and Cognition, 11*, 114–120.

Loftus, G.R. (1985a). Evaluating forgetting curves. *Journal of Experimental Psychology: Learning, Memory, and Cognition, 11*, 397–406.

Loftus, G.R. (1985b). Consistency and confoundings: Reply to Slamecka. *Journal of Experimental Psychology: Learning, Memory, and Cognition, 11*, 817–820.

Logie, R.H. (1986). Visuo-spatial processes in working memory. *Quarterly Journal of Experimental Psychology, 38A*, 229–247.

Logie, R.H., Cubelli, R., Della Sala, S., Alberoni, M., & Nichelli, P. (in press). Anarthria and verbal short-term memory. In J. Crawford & D. Parker (Eds.), *Developments in clinical and experimental neuropsychology*. New York: Plenum Press.

Logie, R.H., & Baddeley, A.D. (1987). Cognitive processes in counting. *Journal of Experimental Psychology: Learning, Memory, and Cognition, 13*, 310–326.

Lord, A.B. (1960). *The singer of tales*. Cambridge, Mass.: Harvard University Press.

McClelland, J.L. (1981). Retrieving general and specific knowledge from stored knowledge of specifics. *Proceedings of the Third Annual Conference of the Cognitive Science Society*. Berkeley, California.

McClelland, J.L., & Rumelhart, D.E. (1981). An interactive activation model of context effects in letter perception: Part I. An account of basic findings. *Psychological Review, 88*, 375–407.

McClelland, J.L. & Rumelhart, D.E. (Eds) (1986). *Parallel distributed processing. Explorations in the microstructure of cognition. Vol 2: Psychological and biological models*. Cambridge Mass.: M.I.T. Press.

McClelland, J.L., Rumelhart, D.E., & Hinton, G.E. (1986). The appeal of parallel distributed processing. In D.E. Rumelhart & J.L. McClelland (Eds.), *Parallel Distributed Processing*. Cambridge, Mass.: M.I.T. Press.

McCloskey, M.E., & Glucksberg, S. (1978). Natural categories: Well defined or fuzzy sets? *Memory and Cognition, 6*, 462–472.

McEvoy, C.L., & Moon, J.R. (1988). Assessment and treatment of everyday memory problems in the elderly. In M.M. Gruneberg, P.E. Morris, & R.N. Sykes (Eds.), *Practical aspects of memory: Current research and issues, Vol. 2: Clinical and educational implications*, pp. 155–160. Chichester: John Wiley & Sons.

McGehee, F. (1937). The reliability of the identification of the human voice. *Journal of General Psychology, 17*, 249–271.

McGehee, F. (1944). An experimental investigation of voice recognition. *Journal of General Psychology, 31*, 53–65.

McGeogh, J.A., & Irion, A.L. (1952). *The psychology of human learning.* New York: Longmans.

McGeoch, J.A., & McDonald, W.T. (1931). Meaningful relation and retroactive inhibition. *American Journal of Psychology, 43*, 579–588.

McKenna, S.P., & Glendon, A.I. (1985). Occupational first aid training: Decay in cardiopulmonary resuscitation (CPR) skills. *Journal of Occupational Psychology, 58*, 109–117.

McLeod, P. (1977). A dual-task response modality effect: Support for multiprocessor models of attention. *The Quarterly Journal of Experimental Psychology, 29*, 651–667.

McLeod, P. (1978). Does probe RT measure control processing demand? *The Quarterly Journal of Experimental Psychology, 30*, 83–89.

McLeod, P., & Posner, M.I. (1984). Privileged loops from percept to act. In H. Bouma & D.G. Bouwhuis (Eds.), *Attention and performance X*, pp. 55–66. London: Lawrence Erlbaum Associates Ltd.

McNicol, D. (1972). *A primer of signal detection theory.* London: Allen and Unwin.

Mackintosh, N.J. (1974). *The psychology of animal learning.* New York: Academic Press.

Mandler, G. (1967). Organization in memory. In K.W. Spence & J.T. Spence (Eds.), *The psychology of learning and motivation*, Vol. 1, pp. 327–372. New York: Academic Press.

Mandler, G. (1979). Organization and repetition: Organizational principles with special reference to rote learning. In L.-G. Nilsson (Ed.), *Perspectives on memory research*, pp. 293–327. Hillsdale, N.J.: Lawrence Erlbaum Associates Inc.

Mandler, G., & Dean, P.J. (1969). Seriation: Development of serial order in free recall. *Journal of Experimental Psychology, 81*, 207–215.

Mandler, G., Pearlstone, Z., & Koopmans, H.S. (1969). Effects of organization and semantic similarity on recall and recognition. *Journal of Verbal Learning and Verbal Behavior, 8*, 410–423.

Mandler, G., & Shebo, B.J. (1982). Subitizing: An analysis of its component processes. *Journal of Experimental Psychology: General, 111*, 1–22.

Mandler, J.M. & Johnson, N.S. (1977). Remembrance of things parsed: Story structure and recall. *Cognitive Psychology, 9*, 111–151.

Mann, V.A., & Liberman, I.Y. (1984). Phonological awareness and verbal short-term memory. *Journal of Learning Disabilities, 17*, 592–598.

Manning, S.K. (1980). Tactual and visual alphanumeric suffix effects. *Quarterly Journal of Experimental Psychology, 32*, 257–267.

Manning, S.K., & Gmuer, B.A. (1985). Visual suffix effects on the optacon: A test of changing state, primary linguistic and attentional theories. *Bulletin of the Psychonomic Society, 23*, 1–4.

Marcel, A.J. (1983). Conscious and unconscious perception: Experiments on visual masking and word recognition. *Cognitive Psychology, 15*, 197–237.

Marek, G.R. (1975). *Toscanini*. London: Vision Press.

Marks, I. (1978). Behavioral psychotherapy of adult neurosis. In A.E. Bergin & S.L. Garfield (Eds.), *Handbook of psychotherapy and behavioral change*, pp. 493–547. New York: John Wiley & Sons.

Marks, I.M. (1972). Flooding (implosion) and the related treatments. In W.S. Agras (Ed.), *Behavior modification: Principles and clinical applications*. Boston: Little Brown.

Marks, I., & Gelder, M. (1967). Transvestism and fetishism: Clinical and psychological changes during voradic aversion. *British Journal of Psychiatry, 117*, 173–185.

Marshall, J.C., & Fryer, D.M. (1978). Speak, memory! An introduction to some historic studies of remembering and forgetting. In M.M. Gruneberg & P.E. Morris (Eds.), *Aspects of memory*, pp. 1–25. London: Methuen.

Martin, R.C., Wogalter, M.S., & Forlano, J.G. (1988). Reading comprehension in the presence of unattended speech and music. *Journal of Memory and Language, 27*, 382–398.

Masson, M.E.J., & Miller, G.A. (1983). Working memory and individual differences in comprehension and memory of text. *Journal of Educational Psychology, 75*, 314–318.

Mathews, A.M., Gelder, M.G., & Johnston, D.W. (1981). *Agoraphobia: Nature and treatment*. London: Tavistock Publications.

Mayes, A., & Meudell, P. (1981). The Claparède phenomenon: A further example in amnesics, a demonstration of a similar effect in normal people with attenuated memory, and a reinterpretation. *Current Psychological Research, 1*, 75–88.

Mayes, A.R., Meudell, P.R., & Pickering, A. (1985). Is organic amnesia caused by a selective deficit in remembering contextual information? *Cortex, 21*, 167–202.

Meacham, J.A., & Kushner, S. (1980). Anxiety, prospective remembering and performance of planned actions. *Journal of General Psychology, 103*, 203–209.

Meacham, J.A., & Singer, J. (1977). Incentive effects in prospective memory. *Journal of Psychology, 97*, 191–197.

Means, B., Mingay, D.J., Nigam, A., & Zarrow, M. (1988). A cognitive approach to enhancing health survey reports of medical visits. In M.M. Gruneberg, P.E. Morris, & R.N. Sykes (Eds.), *Practical aspects of memory: Current research and issues, Vol. 1: memory in everyday life*, pp. 536–542. Chichester: John Wiley & Sons.

Mechanic, A. (1964). The responses involved in the rote learning of verbal materials. *Journal of Verbal Learning and Verbal Behavior, 3*, 30–36.

Melton, A.W. (1963). Implications of short-term memory for a general theory of memory. *Journal of Verbal Learning and Verbal Behavior, 2*, 1–21.

Melton, A.W. (1970). The situation with respect to the spacing of repetitions and memory. *Journal of Verbal Learning and Verbal Behavior, 9*, 596–606.

Meltzer, M.L. (1983). Poor memory: A case report. *Journal of Clinical Psychology, 39*, 3–10.

Meudell, P.R., Mayes, A., & Neary, D. (1980). Orienting task effects on the recognition of humorous material in amnesia and normal subjects. *Journal of Clinical Neuropsychology, 2*, 1–14.

Meudell, P.R., Mayes, A.R., Ostergaard, A., & Pickering, A. (1985). Recency and frequency judgements in alcoholic amnesics and normal people with poor memory. *Cortex, 21*, 487–511.

Meudell, P.R., Northen, B., Snowden, J.S., & Neary, D. (1980). Long-term memory for famous voices in amnesic and normal subjects. *Neuropsychologia, 18*, 133–139.

Meyer, D.E., & Schvaneveldt, R.W. (1971). Facilitation in recognizing pairs of words: evidence of a dependence between retrieval operations. *Journal of Experimental Psychology, 90*, 227–234.

Milan, M.A., Wood, L.F., Williams, R.L., Rogers, J.G., Hampton, L.R., & McKie, J.M. (1974). *Applied behavior analysis and the important adult felon project I: The cellblock token economy.* Elmore, Alabama: Rehabilitation Research Foundation.

Miles, T.R., & Ellis, N.C. (1981). A lexical encoding difficulty II: Clinical observations. In G.Th. Pavlidis & T.R. Miles (Eds.), *Dyslexia research and its applications to education*, pp. 217–244. Chichester: John Wiley & Sons.

Millar, K. (1988). Memory during anaesthesia. In M.M.Gruneberg, P.E. Morris & R.N. Sykes (Eds.), *Practical Aspects of Memory: Current Research and Issues Vol. 2: Clinical and educational implications*, pp. 230–235. Chichester: John Wiley & Sons.

Millar, K., & Watkinson, N. (1983). Recognition of words presented during general anaesthesia. *Ergonomics, 26*, 585–594.

Miller, E. (1971). On the nature of the memory disorder in presenile dementia. *Neuropsychologia, 9*, 75–78.

Miller, G.A. (1956). The magical number seven, plus or minus two: Some limits on our capacity for processing information. *Psychological Review, 63*, 81–97.

Miller, R.R., & Springer, A.D. (1974). Implications of recovery from experimental amnesia. *Psychological Review, 81*, 470–473.

Milner, B. (1966). Amnesia following operation on the temporal lobes. In C.W.M. Whitty & O.L. Zangwill (Eds.), *Amnesia*, pp. 109–133. London: Butterworths.

Milner, B. (1968). Visual recognition and recall after right temporal-lobe excision in man. *Neuropsychologia, 6*, 191–209.

Milner, B. (1971). Interhemispheric differences in the localization of psychological processes in man. *British Medical Bulletin, 27*, 272–277.

Minami, H., & Dallenbach, K.M. (1946). The effect of activity upon learning and retention in the cockroach. *American Journal of Psychology, 59*, 1–58.

Minsky, M.L. (1975). A framework for representing knowledge. In P.H. Winston (Ed.), *The psychology of computer vision*, pp. 211–277. New York: McGraw Hill.

Minsky, M.L. (1985). *The society of mind.* London: Heineman.

Minsky, M., & Papert, S. (1969). *Perceptrons.* Cambridge, Mass.: M.I.T. Press.

Mishkin, M. (1982). A memory system in the monkey. *Philosophical Transactions of the Royal Society London B, 298*, 85–96.

Mishkin, M., Malamut, B., & Bachevalier, J. (1984). Memories and habits: Two neural systems. In G. Lynch, J. McGaugh, & N.M. Weinberger (Eds.), *Neurobiology of learning in memory*, pp. 65–77. New York: Guilford Press.

Moakes, D. (1988). *The viewpoint of the carer*. Paper presented at the Amnesia Association Course on Memory and Amnesia. Isle of Thorns Conference Centre, Sussex.

Moar, I. (1978). *Mental triangulation and the nature of internal representations of space*. Unpublished PhD thesis, University of Cambridge.

Mogg, K., Mathews, A., & Weinman, J. (1987). Memory bias in clinical anxiety. *Journal of Abnormal Psychology, 96*, 94–98.

Molander, B., & Bächman, L. (In press). Adult age differences in heart rate patterns during concentration in a precision sport: Implications for attentional functioning. *Journal of Gerontology*.

Moldawsky, S. & Moldawsky, P.C. (1952). Digit span as on anxiety indicator. *Journal of Consulting Psychology, 16*, 115–118.

Mollon, J.D. (1970). *Temporal factors in perception*. Unpublished DPhil. Thesis, Oxford University.

Monsell, S. (1978). Recency, immediate recognition memory and reaction time. *Cognitive Psychology, 10*, 465–501.

Monsell, S. (1984). Components of working memory underlying verbal skills: A "distributed capacities" view—A tutorial review. In H. Bouma & D.G. Bouwhuis (Eds.), *Attention and performance X*, pp. 327–350. London: Lawrence Erlbaum Associates Ltd.

Moore, R.G., Watts, F.N., & Williams, J.M.G. (1988). The specificity of personal memories in depression. *British Journal of Clinical Psychology, 27*, 275–276.

Moore, T.E., Richards, B., & Hood, J. (1984). Aging and the coding of spatial information. *Journal of Gerontology, 39*, 210–212.

Morais, J., Allegria, J., & Content, A. (1987). The relationships between segmental analysis and alphabetic literacy: An interactive view. *Cahiers de Psychologie Cognitive, 7*, 415–438.

Moray, N. (1959). Attention in dichotic listening: Affective cues and the influence of instructions. *Quarterly Journal of Experimental Psychology, 11*, 56–60.

Moray, N., Bates, A., & Barnett, T. (1965). Experiments on the four-eared man. *Journal of Acoustical Society of America, 38*, 196–201.

Morgan, J.J.B., & Lovell, G.D. (1948). *The psychology of abnormal people*. London: Longmans.

Morris, C.D., Bransford, J.D., & Franks, J.J. (1977). Levels of processing versus transfer appropriate processing. *Journal of Verbal Learning and Verbal Behavior, 16*, 519–533.

Morris, L.W., & Liebert, R.M. (1970). Relationships of cognitive and emotional components of text anxiety to physiological arousal and academic performance. *Journal of Consulting and Clinical Psychology, 35*, 332–337.

Morris, R.G. (1984). Dementia and the functioning of the articulatory loop system. *Cognitive Neuropsychology, 1*, 143–157.

Morris, R.G. (1986). Short-term forgetting in senile dementia of the Alzheimer's type. *Cognitive Neuropsychology, 3*, 77–97.

Morris, R.G. & Kopelman, M.D. (1986). The memory deficits in Alzheimer-type dementia: A review. *Quarterly Journal of Experimental Psychology. Special Issue: Human Memory, 38A*, 575–602.

Morton, J. (1967). A singular lack of incidental learning. *Nature, 215*, 203–204.

Moscovitch, M. (1982). Multiple dissociations of function in amnesia. In L.S. Cermak (Ed.), *Human memory and amnesia*. Hillsdale, N.J.: Lawrence Erlbaum Associates Inc.

Moscovitch, M. (1985). Memory from infancy to old age: Implications for theories of normal and pathological memory. *Annals of the New York Academy of Sciences, 444*, 78–96.

Moscovitch, M., & Craik, F.I.M. (1976). Depth of processing, retrieval cues, and uniqueness of encoding as factors in recall. *Journal of Verbal Learning and Verbal Behavior, 15*, 447–458.

Mosso, A. (1896). *Fear*. London: Longman, Green & Co.

Mueller, J.H. (1979). Test anxiety and the encoding and retrieval of information. In I.G. Sarason (Ed.), *Test anxiety: Theory, research and applications*. Hillsdale, N.J.: Lawrence Erlbaum Associates Inc.

Münsterberg, H. (1908). *On the witness stand: Essays on psychology and crime*. New York: Clark, Boardman.

Murdock, B.B.Jr. (1961). The retention of individual items. *Journal of Experimental Psychology, 62*, 618–625.

Murdock, B.B.Jr. (1965). Effects of a subsidiary task on short-term memory. *British Journal of Psychology, 56*, 413–419.

Murphy, G., & Wilson, B. (1985). *Self-injurious behaviour*. Kidderminster: British Institute of Mental Handicap.

Naveh-Benjamin, M. (1987). Coding of spatial location information: An automatic process? *Journal of Experimental Psychology: Learning, Memory, and Cognition, 13*, 595–605.

Naveh-Benjamin, M., & Ayres, T.J. (1986). Digit span, reading rate, and linguistic relativity. *Quarterly Journal of Experimental Psychology, 38*, 739–751.

Naveh-Benjamin, M., & Jonides, J. (1985). The effects of rehearsal on frequency coding. *Bulletin of the Psychonomic Society, 23*, 387–390.

Neisser, U. (1967). *Cognitive psychology*. New York: Appleton-Century-Crofts.

Neisser, U. (1976). *Cognition and reality*. San Francisco: W.H. Freeman.

Neisser, U. (1978). Memory: What are the important questions? In M.M. Gruneberg, P.E. Morris, & R.N. Sykes (Eds.), *Practical aspects of memory*. London: Academic Press.

Neisser, U. (1982). *Memory observed*. San Francisco: Freeman.

Neisser, U. (1986). Nested structure in autobiographical memory. In D.C. Rubin (Ed.), *Autobiographical memory*, pp. 71–81. Cambridge: Cambridge University Press.

Neisser, U. (1988). Time present and time past. In M.M. Gruneberg, P.E. Morris, & R.N. Sykes (Eds.), *Practical aspects of memory: Current research and issues, Vol. 2: Clinical and educational implications*, pp. 545–560. Chichester: John Wiley & Sons.

Newell, A. (in press). *Unified theories of cognition; the 1987 William James Lectures*. Cambridge Mass.: Harvard University Press.

Newell, A., & Simon, H.A. (1972). *Human problem solving*. Englewood Cliffs, N.J.: Prentice-Hall.

Nickerson, R.S. (1965). Short-term memory for complex meaningful visual configurations: A demonstration of capacity. *Canadian Journal of Psychology, 19*, 155–160.

Nickerson, R.S. (1984). Retrieval inhibition from part-set cueing: A persisting enigma in memory research. *Memory and Cognition, 12*, 531–552.

Nickerson, R.S., & Adams, M.J. (1979). Long-term memory for a common object. *Cognitive Psychology, 11*, 287–307.

Nicolson, R. (1981). The relationship between memory span and processing speed. In M. Friedman, J.P. Das, & N. O'Connor (Eds.), *Intelligence and learning*, pp. 179–184. Plenum Press.

Nielsen, J.M. (1946). *Agnosia, apraxia, aphasia. Their value in cerebral localisation*. New York: Hoeber.

Nilsson, L-G. (1987). Motivated memory: Dissociation between performance data and subjective reports. *Psychological Research, 49*, 183–188.

Nilsson, L-G., & Cohen, R.L. (1988). Enrichment and generation in the recall of enacted and non-enacted instructions. In M.M. Gruneberg, P.E. Morris, & R.N. Sykes (Eds.), *Practical aspects of memory: Current research and issues, Vol. 1: Memory in everyday life*, pp.427–432. Chichester: John Wiley & Sons.

Norman, D.A. (1988). *The psychology of everyday things*. New York: Basic Books.

Norman, D.A., & Shallice, T. (1986). Attention to action: Willed and automatic control of behavior. In R.J. Davidson, G.E. Schwarts, & D. Shapiro (Eds.), *Consciousness and self-regulation. Advances in research and theory*, Vol. 4, pp. 1–18. New York: Plenum Press.

Oakhill, J.V. (1982). Constructive processes in skilled and less skilled comprehenders' memory for sentences. *British Journal of Psychology, 73*, 13–20.

Oakhill, J.V. (1984). Inferential and memory skills in children's comprehension of stories. *British Journal of Educational Psychology, 54*, 31–39.

Oakhill, J.V., Yuill, N., & Parkin, A.J. (1986). On the nature of the difference between skilled and less-skilled comprehenders. *Journal of Research in Reading, 9*, 80–91.

Oakhill, J.V., Yuill, N., & Parkin, A.J. (1988). Memory and inference in skilled and less-skilled comprehenders. In M.M. Gruneberg, P.E. Morris, & R.N. Sykes (Eds.), *Practical aspects of memory: Current research and issues, Vol. 2: Clinical and educational implications*, pp. 315–320. Chichester: John Wiley & Sons.

Öhman, A. (1979). Fear-relevance, autonomic conditioning, and phobias:

A laboratory model. In P.-O. Sjöden, S. Bates, & W.S. Dockens III (Eds.), *Trends in behaviour therapy*. New York: Academic Press.

Orne, M.T. (1979). The use and misuse of hypnosis in court. *International Journal of Clinical and Experimental Hypnosis, 27*, 311–341.

Orne, M.T., Soskis, D.A., Dinges, D.F., & Orne, E.C. (1984). Hypnotically-induced testimony. In G.L. Wells & E.F. Loftus (Eds.), *Eyewitness testimony: Psychological perspectives*. New York: Cambridge University Press.

Ornstein, P.A., Naus, M.J., & Stone, B.P. (1977). Rehearsal training and developmental differences in memory. *Developmental Psychology, 13*, 15–24.

Osgood, C.E., Suci, G.J., & Tannenbaum, P.J. (1957). *Measurement of meaning*. Urbana, Ill.: University of Illinois Press.

Paivio, A. (1969). Mental imagery in associative learning and memory. *Psychological Review, 76*, 241–263.

Parasuraman, R. (1979). Memory load and event rate control sensitivity decrements in sustained attention. *Science, 205*, 924–927.

Parkin, A.J. (1979). Specifying levels of processing. *Quarterly Journal of Experimental Psychology, 31*, 175–195.

Parkin, A.J. (1982). Residual learning capability in organic amnesia. *Cortex, 18*, 417–440.

Parkin, A.J. (1988). Review of "Working Memory". *Quarterly Journal of Experimental Psychology, 40A*, 187–189.

Parkin, A.J., Lewinsohn, J., & Folkard, S. (1982). The influence of emotion on immediate and delayed retention: Levinger and Clark reconsidered. *British Journal of Psychology, 73*, 389–393.

Parkinson, L., & Rachman, S. (1981). Intrusive thoughts: The effects of an uncontrived stress. *Advances in Behaviour Research and Therapy, 3*, 111–118.

Patterson, K., Marshall, J., & Coltheart, M. (1985). *Surface dyslexia: Neuropsychological and cognitive studies of phonological reading*. London: Lawrence Erlbaum Associates Ltd.

Paul, I.H. (1959). Studies in remembering: The reproduction of connected and extended verbal material. *Psychological Issues, 1*, 1, 2.

Penney, C.G. (in press). Modality effects and the structure of short-term verbal memory. *Memory and Cognition*.

Perfetti, C.A., & Goldman, S.R. (1976). Discourse memory and reading comprehension skill. *Journal of Verbal Learning and Verbal Behavior, 14*, 33–42.

Perkins, N.L. (1914). The value of distributed repetitions in rote learning. *British Journal of Psychology, 7*, 253–261.

Peters, D.P. (1988). Eyewitness memory and arousal in a natural setting. In M.M. Gruneberg, P.E. Morris, & R.N. Sykes (Eds.), *Practical aspects of memory: Current research and issues, Vol. 1: Memory in everyday life*, pp. 89–94. Chichester: John Wiley & Sons.

Peterson, L.R., & Peterson, M.J. (1959). Short-term retention of individual verbal items. *Journal of Experimental Psychology, 58*, 193–198.

Phillips, W.A. (1974). On the distinction between sensory storage and short-term visual memory. *Perception and Psychophysics, 16*, 283–290.

Phillips, W.A., & Baddeley, A.D. (1971). Reaction time and short-term visual memory. *Psychonomic Science, 22*, 73–74.

Phillips, W.A., & Christie, D.F.M. (1977a). Components of visual memory. *Quarterly Journal of Experimental Psychology, 29*, 117–133.

Phillips, W.A., & Christie, D.F.M. (1977b). Interference with visualization. *Quarterly Journal of Experimental Psychology, 29*, 637–650.

Pinker, F., & Prince, A. (1988). On language and connectionism: Analysis of a parallel distributed processing model of language acquisition. *Cognition 28*, 73–193.

Plomp, R. (1964). Decay of auditory sensation. *Journal of the Acoustical Society of America, 36*, 277–282.

Pollack, I., Pickett, J., & Sumby, W. (1954). On the identification of speakers by voice. *Journal of the Acoustical Society of America, 26*, 403–406.

Poon, L.W. (1987). *Sleep and ageing progress report (cognitive evaluation).* Gerontology Center, Athens, Georgia.

Popper, K. (1959). *The logic of scientific discovery.* London: Hutchinson.

Posner, M.I., & Boies, S.J. (1971). Components of attention. *Psychological Review, 78*, 391–408.

Posner, M.I., Boies, S.J., Eichelman, W.H., & Taylor, R.L. (1969). Retention of visual and name codes of single letters. *Journal of Experimental Psychology, 79*, 1–16.

Postman, L. (1963). Does interference theory predict too much forgetting? *Journal of Verbal Learning and Verbal Behavior, 2*, 40–48.

Postman, L. (1975). Verbal learning and memory. *Annual Review of Psychology, 26*, 291–335.

Postman, L., & Goggin, J. (1964). Whole versus part learning of serial lists as a function of meaningfulness and intralist similarity. *Journal of Experimental Psychology, 68*, 140–150.

Postman, L. & Phillips, L.W. (1965). Short-term temporal changes in free recall. *Quarterly Journal of Experimental Psychology, 17*, 132–138.

Postman, L., & Underwood, B.J. (1973). Critical issues in interference theory. *Memory and Cognition, 1*, 19–40.

Pylyshyn, Z.W. (1973). What the mind's eye tells the mind's brain: A critique of mental imagery. *Psychological Bulletin, 80*, 1–24.

Pylyshyn, Z.W. (1979). The rate of "mental rotation" of images: A test of a holistic analogue hypothesis. *Memory and Cognition, 7*, 19–28.

Pylyshyn, Z.W. (1981). The imagery debate: Analogue media versus tacit knowledge. *Psychological Review, 86*, 16–45.

Pylyshyn, Z.W. (1984). *Computation and cognition: Toward a foundation for cognitive science.* Cambridge, Mass.: Bradford Books, MIT Press.

Quillian, M.R. (1969). The teachable language comprehender: A simulation program and theory of language. *Communication of the ACM, 12*, 459–476.

Rabbitt, P.M.A., & Winthorpe, C. (1988). What do old people remember? The Galton paradigm reconsidered. In M.M. Gruneberg, P.E. Morris, & R.N. Sykes (Eds.), *Practical aspects of memory: Current research and issues, Vol. 1: Memory in everyday life*, pp. 301–308. Chichester: John Wiley & Sons.

Rachman, S. (1977). The conditioning theory of fear acquisition: A critical examination. *Behaviour Research and Therapy, 15*, 375–387.

Rachman, S.J., & Teasdale, J. (1969). Aversion therapy: An appraisal. In C.M. Franks (Ed.), *Behaviour therapy: Appraisal and status*, pp. 279–320. New York: McGraw Hill.

Ratcliff, R., & McKoon, G. (1988). A retrieval theory of priming in memory. *Psychological Review, 95*, 385–408.

Rea, C.P., & Modigliani, V. (1988). Educational implications of the spacing effect. In M.M.Gruneberg, P.E. Morris, & R.N. Sykes (Eds.), *Practical aspects of memory: Current research and issues Vol. 1: Memory in everyday life*, pp. 402–406. Chichester: John Wiley & Sons.

Reading, A.E. (1981). Psychological preparation for surgery: Patient recall of information. *Journal of Psychosomatic Research, 25*, 57–62.

Reason, J.T. (1979). Actions not as planned: The price of automatisation. In G. Underwood & R. Stevens (Eds.), *Aspects of consciousness Volume 1: Psychological issues*. London: Academic Press.

Reason, J.T., & Lucas, D. (1984). Using cognitive diaries to investigate naturally occurring memory blocks. In J.E. Harris & P.E. Morris (Eds.), *Everyday memory, actions and absent-mindedness*, pp. 53–70. London: Academic Press.

Rescorla, R.A. (1980). *Pavlovian second-order conditioning*. Hillsdale, N.J.: Lawrence Erlbaum Associates Inc.

Rescorla, R.A. (1985). Associationism in animal learning. In L.G. Nilsson & T. Archer (Eds.), *Perspectives on learning and memory*. Hillsdale, N.J.: Lawrence Erlbaum Associates Inc.

Richardson-Klavehn, A., & Bjork, R.A. (1988). Measures of memory. *Annual Review of Psychology, 39*, 475–543.

Ripps, L.J., Shoben, E.J., & Smith, E.E. (1973) Semantic distance and the verification of semantic relations. *Journal of Verbal Learning and Verbal Behavior, 12*, 1–20.

Robinson, J.A. (1976). Sampling autobiographical memory. *Cognitive Psychology, 8*, 578–595.

Robinson, J.O., Rosen, M., Revill, S.I., David, H., & Rus, G.A.D. (1980). Self-administered intravenous and intramuscular pethidine. *Anaesthesia, 35*, 763–770.

Rock, I., & Engelstein, P. (1959). A study of memory for visual form. *American Journal of Psychology, 72*, 221–229.

Roland, P.E. (1982). Cortical regulation of selective attention in man: A regional cerebral blood flow study. *Journal of Neurophysiology, 48*, 1059–1078.

Roland, P.E., & Friberg, L. (1985). Localization of cortical areas activated by thinking. *Journal of Neurophysiology, 53*, 1219–1243.

Rosch, E. (1973). Natural categories. *Cognitive Psychology, 4*, 328–349.

Rosch, E., & Mervis, C.B. (1975). Family resemblances: Studies in the internal structure of categories. *Cognitive Psychology, 7*, 573–605.

Rosch-Heider, E. (1972). Universals in color naming and memory. *Journal of Experimental Psychology, 93*, 10–20.

Rosenblatt, F. (1962). *Principles of neurodynamics*. New York: Spartan.

Rothkopf, E.Z. (1963). Some observations on predicting instructional effectiveness by simple inspection. *Journal of Programmed Instruction, 2*, 19–20.

Rubin, D.C. (1982). On the retention function for autobiographical memory. *Journal of Verbal Learning and Verbal Behavior, 21*, 21–38.

Rubin, D.C. (1986). *Autobiographical memory*. Cambridge: Cambridge University Press.

Rubin, D.C., & Kontis, T.C. (1983). A schema for common cents. *Memory and Cognition, 11*, 335–341.

Rubin, D.C., Wetzler, S.E., & Nebes, R.D. (1986). Autobiographical memory across the lifespan. In D.C. Rubin (Ed.), *Autobiographical memory*, pp. 202–224. Cambridge: Cambridge University Press.

Rumelhart, D.E. (1975). Notes on a schema for stories. In D.G. Bobrow & A. Collins (Eds.), *Representation and understanding*, pp. 211–236. New York: Academic Press.

Rumelhart, D.E., Hinton, G.E., & Williams, R.J. (1986). Learning representations by back-propagating errors. *Nature, 323*, 533–536.

Rumelhart, D.E., Lindsay, P.H., & Norman, D.A. (1972). A process model for long-term memory. In E. Tulving & W. Donaldson (Eds.), *Organization and memory*. New York: Academic Press.

Rumelhart, D.E., & McClelland, J.L. (1982). An interactive activation model of context effects in letter perception. Part 2: The contextual enhancement effect and some tests and extensions of the model. *Psychological Review, 89*, 60–94.

Rumelhart, D.E., & McClelland, J.L. (Eds.) (1986). *Parallel distributed processing: Explorations in the microstructures of cognition Vol. 1: Foundations*. Cambridge, Mass.: M.I.T. Press.

Rumelhart, D.E., & Norman, D.A. (1985). Representation of knowledge. In A.M. Aitkenhead & J.M. Slack (Eds.), *Issues in cognitive modelling*, pp. 15–62. London: Lawrence Erlbaum Associates Ltd.

Rundus, D. (1971). Analysis of rehearsal processes in free recall. *Journal of Experimental Psychology, 89*, 63–77.

Russell, W.R. (1959). *Brain, memory, learning: A neurologist's view*. London: Oxford University Press.

Ryan, J. (1969). Temporal grouping, rehearsal and short-term memory. *Quarterly Journal of Experimental Psychology, 21*, 148–155.

Rylander, G. (1939). Personality changes after operation on the frontal lobes. *Acta Psychiatrica Neurologica* (Supplement No. 30).

Sachs, J.S. (1967). Recognition memory for syntactic and semantic aspects of connected discourse. *Perception and Psychophysics, 2*, 437–442.

Sakitt, B. (1976). Iconic memory. *Psychological Review, 83*, 257–276.

Salamé, P., & Baddeley, A.D. (1982). Disruption of short-term memory by unattended speech: Implications for the structure of working memory. *Journal of Verbal Learning and Verbal Behavior, 21*, 150–164.

Salamé, P., & Baddeley, A.D. (1987). Noise, unattended speech and short-term memory. *Ergonomics, 30*, 1185–1193.

Salamé, P., & Baddeley, A.D. (1989). Effects of background music on phonological short-term memory. *Quarterly Journal of Experimental Psychology, 41A*, 107–122.

Saltz, E. (1988). The role of motoric enactment (m–processing) in memory for words and sentences. In M.M. Gruneberg, P.E. Morris, & R.N. Sykes (Eds.), *Practical aspects of memory: Current research and issues, Vol. 1: Memory in everyday life*, pp. 408–414. Chichester: John Wiley & Sons.

Saltz, E., & Donnerwerth-Nolan, S. (1981). Does motoric imagery facilitate memory for sentences? A selective interference test. *Journal of Verbal Learning and Verbal Behavior, 20*, 322–332.

Sanders, H.I., & Warrington, E.K. (in press). Memory for remote events in amnesic patients. *Brain*.

Sanders, R.E., Gonzalez, E.G., Murphy, M.D., & Liddle, C.L. (1987). Frequency of occurrence and the criteria for automatic processing. *Journal of Experimental Psychology: Learning, Memory, and Cognition, 13*, 241–250.

Sanderson, R.E., Campbell, D., & Laverty, S.G. (1963). Traumatically conditioned responses aquired during respiratory paralysis. *Nature, 196*, 1235–1236.

Sarason, I.G. (1975). Anxiety and self-preoccupation. In I.G. Sarason & C.D. Spielberger (Eds.), *Stress and anxiety, Vol. 2*. London: Hemisphere/Wiley.

Saslove, H., & Yarmy, A. (1980). Long-term or auditory memory: Speaker identification. *Journal of Applied Psychology, 65*, 111–116.

Saufley, W.H., Otaka, S.R., & Bavaresco, J.L. (1985). Context effects: Classroom tests and context independence. *Memory and Cognition, 13*, 522–528.

Saunders, W., & Allsop, S. (1985). Giving up addictions. In F.N. Watts (Ed.), *New developments in clinical psychology*. Chichester: John Wiley & Sons.

Schacter, D.L. (1985). Priming of old and new knowledge in amnesic patients and normal subjects. *Annals of the New York Academy of Sciences, 444*, 41–53.

Schacter, D.L. (1987). Memory, amnesia, and frontal lobe dysfunction. *Psychobiology, 15*, 21–36.

Schacter, D.L., Eich, J.E., & Tulving, E. (1978). Richard Semon's theory of memory. *Journal of Verbal Learning and Verbal Behavior, 17*, 721–743.

Schacter, D.L., Harbluk, J.L., & McLachlan, D.R. (1984). Retrieval without recollection: An experimental analysis of source amnesia. *Journal of Verbal Learning and Verbal Behavior, 23*, 593–611.

Schacter, D.L., Wang, P.L., Tulving, E., & Freedman, M. (1982). Functional retrograde amnesia: A quantitative case study. *Neuropsychologia, 20*, 523–532.

Schank, R.C. (1975). *Conceptual information processing*. Amsterdam: North-Holland.

Schank, R.C. (1982). *Dynamic memory*. New York: Cambridge University Press.

Schank, R.C., & Abelson, R. (1977). *Scripts, plans, goals and understanding*. Hillsdale, N.J.: Lawrence Erlbaum Associates Inc.

Schare, M.L., Lisman, S.A., & Spear, N.E. (1984). The effects of mood variation on state dependent retention. *Cognitive Therapy and Research, 8*, 387–408.

Schmeck, R.R. (1983). Learning styles of college students. *Individual Differences in Cognition, 1*, 233–279.

Schneider, K. (1912). Über einige klinisch-pathologische Untersuchungsmethoden und ihre Ergebnisse. Zugleich ein Beitrag zur Psychopathelogie der Korsakowschen Psychose, *Zeitscrift für Neurologische Psychiatrie, 8*, 553–616.

Schneider, W. & Detweiler, M. (1988). A connectionist control architecture for working memory. In G.H.Bower (Ed.) *The psychology of learning and motivation, 21*, 54–119. New York: Academic Press.

Schneider, W., & Shiffrin, R.M. (1977). Controlled and automatic information processing I: Detection, search and attention. *Psychological Review, 84*, 1–66.

Schulman, A.I. (1974). Memory for words recently classified. *Memory and Cognition, 2*, 47–52.

Schulman, A.I. (1976). Memory for rare words previously rated for familiarity. *Journal of Experimental Psychology: Human Learning and Memory, 2*, 301–307.

Selfridge, O.G. (1955). Pattern recognition and modern computers. *Proceedings of the Western Joint Computer Conference*. New York: Institute of Electrical and Electronics Engineers.

Selfridge, O.G., & Neisser, U. (1960). Pattern recognition by machine. *Scientific American, 203*, 60–68.

Seligman, M.E.P. (1975). *Helplessness: On depression, development, and death*. San Francisco: Freeman.

Shaffer, L.H. (1975). Multiple attention in continuous verbal tasks. In P.M.A. Rabbitt & S. Dornic (Eds.), *Attention and performance V*, pp. 157–167. New York: Academic Press.

Shallice, T. (1982). Specific impairments of planning. *Philosophical Transactions of the Royal Society London B, 298*, 199–209.

Shallice, T. (1988). *From neuropsychology to mental structure*. Cambridge: Cambridge University Press.

Shallice, T. & Jackson, M. (1988). Lissauer on agnosia. *Cognitive Neuropsychology, 5*, 153–156.

Shallice, T., McLeod, P., & Lewis, K. (1985). Isolating cognitive modules with the dual-task paradigm: Are speech perception and production separate processes? *Quarterly Journal of Experimental Psychology, 37A*, 507–532.

Shallice, T., & Warrington, E.K. (1970). Independent functioning of verbal memory stores: A neuropsychological study. *Quarterly Journal of Experimental Psychology, 22*, 261–273.

Shand, M.A., & Klima, E.S. (1981). Nonauditory suffix effects in congenitaly deaf signers of American sign language. *Journal of Experimental Psychology: Human Learning and Memory, 7,* 464–474.

Sheingold, K., & Tenney, Y.J. (1982). Memory for a salient childhood event. In U. Neisser (Ed.), *Memory observed*, pp.201–212. San Francisco: Freeman.

Shepard, R.N., & Chipman, S. (1970). Second-order isomorphism of internal representations: Shapes of states. *Cognitive Psychology, 1,* 1–17.

Shepard, R.N., & Metzler, J. (1971). Mental rotation of three-dimensional objects. *Science, 171,* 701–703.

Shimamura, A.P., & Squire, L.R. (1987). A neuropsychological study of fact memory and source amnesia. *Journal of Experimental Psychology: Learning, Memory, and Cognition, 13,* 464–473.

Simon, C.W. & Emmons, W.H. (1956). Responses to material presented during various levels of sleep. *Journal of Experimental Psychology, 51,* 80–97.

Simon, H.A. (1974). How big is a chunk? *Science, 183,* 482–488.

Simonov, P.V., Frolov, M.V., Evtushenko, V.F., & Sviridov, E. (1977). Effect of emotional stress on recognition of visual patterns. *Aviation, Space and Environmental Medicine,* 856–858.

Sirken, M.G., Mingay, D.J., Royston, P.N., Bercini, D.H., & Jobe, J.B. (1988). Interdisciplinary research in cognition and survey measurement. In M.M. Gruneberg, P.E. Morris, & R.N. Sykes (Eds.), *Practical aspects of memory: Current research and issues, Vol. 1: Memory in everyday life*, pp. 531–536. Chichester: John Wiley & Sons.

Skinner, B.F. (1958). Teaching machines. *Science, 128,* 969–977.

Slak, S. (1970). Phonemic recoding of digital information. *Journal of Experimental Psychology, 86,* 398–406.

Slamecka, N.J. (1960). Retroactive inhibition of connected discourse as a function of practice level. *Journal of Experimental Psychology, 59,* 104–108.

Slamecka, N.J. (1985). On comparing rates of forgetting: Comment on Loftus (1985). *Journal of Experimental Psychology: Learning, Memory, and Cognition, 11,* 812–816.

Slamecka, N.J., & McElree, B. (1983). Normal forgetting of verbal lists as a function of their degree of learning. *Journal of Experimental Psychology: Learning, Memory, and Cognition, 9,* 384–397.

Smith, E.E. (1978). Theories of semantic memory. In W.K. Estes (Ed.), *Handbook of learning and cognitive processes*, Vol. 6. Hillsdale, N.J.: Lawrence Erlbaum Associates Inc.

Smith, E.E., Shoben, E.J., & Rips, L.J. (1974). Structure and process in semantic memory: A featural model for semantic decisions. *Psychological Review, 81,* 214–241.

Smith, M.C. (1983). Hypnotic memory enhancement of witnesses: Does it work? *Psychological Review, 94,* 387–407.

Smith, S.M. (1979). Remembering in and out of context. *Journal of Experimental Psychology: Human Learning and Memory, 5,* 460–471.

Smith, S.M., Glenberg, A., & Bjork, R.A. (1978). Environmental context and human memory. *Memory and Cognition, 6,* 342–353.

Smolensky, P. (1987). Connectionist AI, symbolic AI, and the brain. *Artificial Intelligence Review, 1,* 95–109.

Sokol-Kessler, L., & Beck, A.T. (1987). *Cognitive treatment of panic disorders.* Paper presented at the 140th meeting of the American Psychiatric Association, Chicago.

Spelke, E.S., Hirst, W., & Neisser, U. (1976). Skills of divided attention. *Cognition, 4,* 215–230.

Sperling, G. (1960). The information available in brief visual presentations. *Psychological Monographs: General and Applied, 74,* 1–29.

Sperling, G. (1963). A model for visual memory tasks. *Human Factors, 5,* 19–31.

Sperling, G. (1967). Successive approximations to a model for short term memory. *Acta Psychologica, 27,* 285–292.

Spiegler, M.D., Morris L.W., & Liebert R.M. (1968) Cognitive and emotional components of test anxiety: temporal factors. *Psychological Reports, 22,* 451–456.

Spinnler, H., Della Sala, S., Bandera., R, & Baddeley, A.D. (1988). Dementia, ageing and the structure of human memory. *Cognitive Neuropsychology, 5,* 193–211.

Spoehr, K.T., & Corin, W.J. (1978). The stimulus suffix effect as a memory coding phenomenon. *Memory and Cognition, 6,* 583–589.

Squire, L.R. (1982). Comparisons between forms of amnesia: Some deficits are unique to Korsakoff's Syndrome. *Journal of Experimental Psychology: Learning, Memory, and Cognition, 8,* 560–571.

Squire, L.R., & Cohen, N.J. (1982). Remote memory, retrograde amnesia, and the neuropsychology of human memory. In L.S. Cermak (Ed.), *Human memory and amnesia.* Hillsdale, N.J.: Lawrence Erlbaum Associates Inc.

Squire, L.R., Slater, P.C., & Chace, P.M. (1975). Retrograde amnesia: Temporal gradient in very long-term memory following electro-convulsive therapy. *Science, 187,* 77–79.

St. Augustine (Trans., 1961). *Confessions,* p.225. Translated by Pine-Coffin.

Standing, L.G., Conezio, J., & Haber, N. (1970). Perception and memory for pictures: Single-trial learning of 2500 visual stimuli. *Psychonomic Science, 19,* 73–74.

Sternberg, S. (1966). High speed scanning in human memory. *Science, 153,* 652–654.

Sternberg, S. (1975). Memory scanning: New findings and current controversies. *Quarterly Journal of Experimental Psychology, 27,* 1–32.

Stevens, J. (1988). An activity theory approach to practical memory. In M.M. Gruneberg, P.E. Morris, & R.N. Sykes (Eds.), *Practical aspects of memory: Current research and issues, Vol. 1: Memory in everyday life,* pp. 335–341. Chichester: John Wiley & Sons.

Stones, M.J. (1974). *Sleep and the storage and retrieval processes in humans.* Unpublished PhD thesis, University of Sheffield.

Stuart, E.W., Shimp, T.A., & Engle, R.W. (1987). Classical conditioning of consumer attitudes: Four experiments in an advertising context. *Journal of Consumer Research, 14,* (December) 334–349.

Sunderland, A., Harris, J.E., & Baddeley, A.D. (1983). Do laboratory tests predict everyday memory. *Journal of Verbal Learning and Verbal Behavior, 22,* 341–357.

Sunderland, A., Watts, K., Baddeley, A.D., & Harris, J.E. (1986). Subjective memory assessment and test performance in the elderly. *Journal of Gerontology, 41,* 376–384.

Sweeney, C.A., & Bellezza, F.S. (1982). Use of keyword mnemonics in learning English vocabulary. *Human Learning, 1,* 155–163.

Talland, G.A. (1965). *Deranged memory: A psychonomic study of the amnesic syndrome.* New York: Academic Press.

Taylor, P.J., & Kopelman, M.D. (1984). Amnesia for criminal offences. *Psychological Medicine, 14,* 581–588.

Teasdale, J.D., & Fogarty, S.J. (1979). Differential effects of induced mood on retrieval of pleasant and unpleasant events from episodic memory. *Journal of Abnormal Psychology, 88,* 248–257.

Teasdale, J.D., & Russell, M.L. (1983). Differential effects of induced mood on the recall of positive, negative and neutral words. *British Journal of Clinical Psychology, 22,* 163–172.

Teuber, H–L. (1959). Some alterations in behaviour after cerebral lesions in man. In A.D. Bass (Ed.), *Evolution of nervous control from primitive organisms to man.* Washington: American Association for the Advancement of Science.

Theios, J. (1973). Reaction time measurements in the study of memory processes: Theory and data. In G.H.Bower (Ed.), *The psychology of learning and motivation,* Vol. 7, pp. 43–85. New York: Academic Press.

Thigpen, C.H., & Cleckley, H. (1957). *The three faces of Eve.* London: Secker and Warburg.

Thomsen, I.V. (1984). Late outcome of very severe blunt head trauma: A 10-15 year second follow-up. *Journal of Neurology, Neurosurgery and Psychiatry, 47,* 260–268.

Thomson, D.M., Robertson, S.L., & Vogt, R. (1982). Person recognition: The effect of context. *Human Learning, 1,* 137–154.

Thompson, C.P., Skowronski, J.J., & Lee, D.J. (1988). Reconstructing the date of a personal event. In M.M. Gruneberg, P.E. Morris, & R.N. Sykes (Eds.), *Practical aspects of memory: Current research and issues, Vol. 1: Memory in everyday life,* pp. 241–246. Chichester: John Wiley & Sons.

Thorndike, E.L. (1898). *Animal intelligence.* New York: Macmillan.

Thorndike, E.L. (1935). *The psychology of wants, interests and attitudes.* New York: Appleton-Century.

Thorndyke, P.W. (1977). Cognitive structures in comprehension and memory of narrative discourse. *Cognitive Psychology, 9,* 77–110.

Thorndyke, P.W. (1981). Distance estimation from cognitive maps. *Cognitive Psychology, 13,* 526–550.

Tilley, A.J. (1979). Sleep learning during stage 2 and REM sleep. *Biological Psychology, 9*, 155–161.

Treisman, A.M. (1964). Monitoring and storage of irrelevant messages in selective attention. *Journal of Verbal Learning and Verbal Behavior, 3*, 449–459.

Treisman, A.M. & Geffen, G. (1967). Selective attention: Perception or response? *Quarterly Journal of Experimental Psychology, 19*, 1–18.

Tulving, E. (1962). Subjective organization in free recall of "unrelated" words. *Psychological Review, 69*, 344–354.

Tulving, E. (1966). Subjective organization and effects of repetition in multi-trial free-recall learning. *Journal of Verbal Learning and Verbal Behavior, 5*, 193–197.

Tulving, E. (1967). The effects of presentation and recall of material in free-recall learning. *Journal of Verbal Learning and Verbal Behavior, 6*, 175–184.

Tulving E. (1976). In J. Brown (Ed.), *Recall and recognition*. London: John Wiley & Sons.

Tulving, E. (1983). *Elements of episodic memory*. Oxford: OUP.

Tulving, E. (1985). How many memory systems are there? *American Psychologist, 40*, 385–398.

Tulving, E., & Hastie, R. (1972). Inhibition effects of intralist repetition in free recall. *Journal of Experimental Psychology, 92*, 297–304.

Tulving, E., & Madigan, S.A. (1970). Memory and verbal learning. *Annual Review of Psychology, 21*, 437–484.

Tulving, E., & Osler, S. (1968). Effectiveness of retrieval cues in memory for words. *Journal of Experimental Psychology, 77*, 593–601.

Tulving, E., & Pearlstone, Z. (1966). Availability versus accessibility of information in memory for words. *Journal of Verbal Learning and Verbal Behavior, 5*, 381–391.

Tulving, E., & Psotka, J. (1971). Retroactive inhibition in free-recall: Inaccessibility of information available in the memory store. *Journal of Experimental Psychology, 87*, 1–8.

Tulving, E., Schacter, D.L., & Stark, H.A. (1982). Priming effects in word-fragment completion are independent of recognition memory. *Journal of Experimental Psychology: Learning, Memory and Cognition, 8*, 336–342.

Tulving, E., & Thomson, D.M. (1973). Encoding specificity and retrieval processes in episodic memory. *Psychological Review, 80*, 352–373.

Turvey, M.T. (1973). On peripheral and central processes in vision: Inferences from an information-processing analysis of masking with patterned stimuli. *Psychological Review, 80*, 1–52.

Turvey, M.T., Brick, P., & Osborn, J. (1970). Proactive interference in short-term memory as a function of prior-item retention interval. *Quarterly Journal of Experimental Psychology, 22*, 142–147.

Twitmyer, E.B. (1902). A study of the knee jerk. Reprinted in *Journal of Experimental Psychology, (1974), 103*, 1047–1066.

Twitmyer, E.B. (1904). *Knee-jerks without stimulation of the patella tendon*. Report to the American Psychological Association.

Tzeng, O.J.L. (1973). Positive recency effects in delayed free recall. *Journal of Verbal Learning and Verbal Behavior, 12*, 436–439.

Underwood, B.J. (1957). Interference and forgetting. *Psychological Review, 64*, 49–60.

Underwood, B.J. (1964). Degree of learning and the measurement of forgetting. *Journal of Verbal Learning and Verbal Behavior, 3*, 112–129.

Underwood, B.J., & Ekstrand, B.R. (1966). An analysis of some shortcomings in the interference theory of forgetting. *Psychological Review, 73*, 540–549.

Underwood, B.J., Ekstrand, B.R., & Keppel, G. (1964). Studies in distributed practice: XXIII. Variations in response-term interference. *Journal of Experimental Psychology, 68*, 201–212.

Underwood, B.J., & Postman, L. (1960). Extra-experimental sources of interference in forgetting. *Psychological Review, 67*, 73–95.

Ungerleider, L.G. & Mishkin, M. (1982). Two cortical visual systems. In D.J. Ingle, M.A. Goodale, & R.J.W. Mansfield (Eds.), *Analysis of visual behavior.* Cambridge, Mass.: M.I.T. Press.

Vallar, G., & Baddeley, A.D. (1984a). Fractionation of working memory. Neuropsychological evidence for a phonological short-term store. *Journal of Verbal Learning and Verbal Behavior, 23*, 151–161.

Vallar, G., & Baddeley, A.D. (1984b). Phonological short-term store, phonological processing and sentence comprehension: A neuropsychological case study. *Cognitive Neuropsychology, 1*, 121–141.

Vallar, G., & Baddeley, A.D. (1987). Phonological short-term store and sentence processing. *Cognitive Neuropsychology, 4*, 417–438.

Vallar, G. & Baddeley, A.D. (in press) Developmental disorders of verbal short-term memory and their relation to sentence comprehension. A reply to Howard and Butterworth. *Cognitive Neuropsychology.*

Vallar, G. & Shallice, T. (Eds.) (in press) *Neuropsychological impairments of short-term memory.* New York: Cambridge University Press.

Van Ormer, E.B. (1932). Sleep and retention. *Psychological Bulletin, 30*, 415–439.

Velten, E. (1968). A laboratory task for induction of mood states. *Behavioral Research and Therapy, 6*, 473–482.

Von Bekesy, G. (1971). Auditory inhibition in concert halls. *Science, 171*, 529–536.

Von Restorff, H. (1933). Über die Wirkung von Bereichsbildungen im Spurenfeld. *Psychologische Forschung, 18*, 299–342.

Wagenaar, W.A. (1986). My memory: A study of autobiographical memory over six years. *Cognitive Psychology, 18*, 225–252.

Wagenaar, W.A., & Groeneweg, J. (Pers. Comm.). *The memory of concentration camp survivors.*

Wagenaar, W.A., Schreuder, R., & van der Heijden, A.H.C. (1985). Do TV pictures help people to remember the weather forecast? *Ergonomics, 28*, 765–772.

Wagenaar, W.A., & Visser, J.G. (1979). The weather forecast under the weather. *Ergonomics, 22*, 909–917.

Wagner, A.R. (1981). SOP: A model of automatic memory processing in animal behavior. In N.E. Spear, & R.R. Miller (Eds.), *Information processing in animals: Memory mechanisms*, pp. 5–47. Hillsdale, N.J.: Lawrence Erlbaum Associates Inc.

Walker, E.L. (1958). Action decrement and its relation to learning. *Psychological Review, 65*, 129–142.

Walker, N.K., & Burkhardt, J.F. (1965). *The combat effectiveness of various human operator controlled systems*. In Proceedings of the 17th U.S. Military Operation Research Symposium.

Wallace, W.T., & Rubin, D.C. (1988). Memory of a ballad singer. In M.M. Gruneberg, P.E. Morris, & R.N. Sykes (Eds.), *Practical aspects of memory: Current research and issues, Vol. 1: Memory in everyday life*, pp. 257–262. Chichester: John Wiley & Sons.

Warr, P.B. (1964). The relative importance of proactive inhibition and degree of learning in retention of paired associate items. *British Journal of Psychology, 55*, 19–30.

Warrington, E.K. (1982) The double dissociation of short- and long-term memory deficits. In L.S. Cermak (Ed.), *Human memory and amnesia*, pp. 61–76. Hillsdale, N.J.: LEA Inc.

Warrington, E.K., & McCarthy, R.A. (in press) Categories of knowledge: Further fractionations and an attempted integration. *Brain*.

Warrington, E.K. & Sanders, H.I. (1971). The fate of old memories. *Quarterly Journal of Experimental Psychology, 23*, 432–442.

Warrington, E.K., & Shallice, T. (1984). Category specific semantic impairments. *Brain, 107*, 829–854.

Warrington, E.K., & Taylor, A.M. (1978). Two categorical stages of object recognition. *Perception, 7*, 695–705.

Warrington, E.K., & Weiskrantz, L. (1968). New method of testing long-term retention with special reference to amnesic patients. *Nature, 217*, 972–974.

Warrington, E.K., & Weiskrantz, L. (1970). Amnesic syndrome: Consolidation or retrieval. *Nature, 228*, 628–630.

Watkins, M.J., Ho, E., & Tulving, E. (1976). Context effects in recognition memory for faces. *Journal of Verbal Learning and Verbal Behavior, 15*, 505–517.

Watkins, M.J., & Watkins, O.C. (1974). A tactile suffix effect. *Memory and Cognition, 2*, 176–180.

Watts, F.N. (1986). Cognitive processing in phobias. *Behavioural Psychotherapy, 14*, 295–301.

Watts, F.N. (1988). Memory deficit in depression: The role of response style. In M.M. Gruneberg, P.E. Morris, & R.N. Sykes (Eds.), *Practical aspects of memory: Current research and issues, Vol. 2: Clinical and educational implications*. pp. 255–260. Chichester: John Wiley & Sons.

Watts, F.N., MacLeod, A.K., & Morris, L. (1988). A remedial strategy for memory and concentration problems in depressed patients. *Cognitive Therapy and Research, 12*, 185–193.

Watts, F.N., McKenna, F.P., Sharrock, R., & Trezise, L. (1986). Colour naming of phobia related words. *British Journal of Psychology, 77*, 97–108.

Watts, F.N., Morris, L., & MacLeod, A. (1987) Recognition memory in depression. *Journal of Abnormal Psychology, 96,* 273–275.

Watts, F.N., & Sharrock, R. (1987). Cued recall in depression. *British Journal of Clinical Psychology, 26,* 149–150.

Waugh, N.C. (1970). Retrieval time in short-term memory. *British Journal of Psychology, 61,* 1–12.

Waugh, N.C., & Norman, D.A. (1965). Primary memory. *Psychological Review, 72,* 89–104.

Weingartner, H., Cohen, R.M., Murphy, D.L., Martello, J., & Gerdt, C. (1981). Cognitive processes in depression. *Archives of General Psychiatry, 38,* 42–47.

Weiskrantz, L. (1982). Comparative aspects of studies of amnesia. *Philosophical Transactions of the Royal Society London B, 298,* 97–109.

Weiskrantz, L. (1985). Issues and theories in the study of the amnesic syndrome. In N.M. Weinberger, J.L. McGaugh, & G. Lynch (Eds.), *Memory systems of the brain.* New York: Guilford Press.

Weiskrantz, L. (1986). *Blindsight: A case study and implications.* Oxford: Oxford University Press.

Weiskrantz, L. & Warrington, E.K. (1979). Conditioning in amnesic patients. *Neuropsychologia, 8,* 281–288.

Wendon, L. (1986). *First steps in Letterland Programme One for teaching reading and spelling.* Cambridge: Letterland Ltd.

White, B. (1960). Recognition of distorted melodies. *American Journal of Psychology, 73,* 100–107.

Wickelgren, W.A. (1964). Size of rehearsal group and short-term memory. *Journal of Experimental Psychology, 68,* 413–419.

Wickelgren, W.A. (1965). Short-term memory for phonemically similar lists. *American Journal of Psychology, 78,* 567–574.

Wickelgren, W.A. (1969). Auditory or articulatory coding in verbal short-term memory. *Psychological Review, 76,* 232–235.

Wickens, C.D. (1984). *Engineering psychology and human performance.* Columbus, Ohio: Charles Merrill.

Wickens, D.D. (1938). The transference of conditioned excitation and conditioned inhibition from one muscle group to the antagonistic muscle group. *Journal of Experimental Psychology, 22,* 101–123.

Wickens, D.D. (1970). Encoding categories of words: An empirical approach to meaning. *Psychological Review, 77,* 1–15.

Wickens, D.D., Born, D.G., & Allen, C.K. (1963). Proactive inhibition and item similarity in short-term memory. *Journal of Verbal Learning and Verbal Behavior, 2,* 440–445.

Wilkins, A.J. (1971). Conjoint frequency, category size, and categorization time. *Journal of Verbal Learning and Verbal Behavior, 10,* 382–385.

Wilkins, A.J., & Baddeley, A.D. (1978). Remembering to recall in everyday life: an approach to absentmindedness. In M.M. Gruneberg, P.E. Morris, & R.N. Sykes (Eds.), *Practical aspects of memory,* pp. 27–34. London: Academic Press.

Williams, M. (1953) The effect of progressive prompting on memory after head injuries. *Journal of Neurosurgery and Psychiatry, 16,* 14–18.

Williams, J.M.G. (1984). *The psychological treatment of depression: A guide to the theory and practice of cognitive-behaviour therapy.* London: Croom Helm.

Williams, J.M.G., & Broadbent, K. (1986). Distraction by emotional stimuli: Use of a Stroop task with suicide attempters. In J.M.G. Williams (Ed.), *The psychological treatment of depression: Guide to the theory and practice of cognitive behaviour therapy.* London: Croom Helm/New York: Free Press.

Williams, J.M.G., Watts, F.N., MacLeod, C., & Mathews, A. (1988). *Cognitive psychology and emotional disorders.* Chichester: John Wiley & Sons.

Williams, M.D., & Hollan, J.D. (1981). The process of retrieval from very long-term memory. *Cognitive Science, 5,* 87–119.

Willshaw, D.J., Buneman, O.P., & Longuet-Higgins, H.C. (1969). Non-holographic associative memory. *Nature, 222,* 960–962.

Wilson, B.A. (1982). Success and failure in memory training following a cerebral vascular accident. *Cortex, 18,* 581–594.

Wilson, B.A. (1986). *Jane: Lif arfta hed inharee.* May Davidson Award Presentation, April 1986.

Wilson, B. A. (1987a). *Rehabilitation of memory.* New York: Guilford Press.

Wilson, B.A. (1987b). Single case experimental design in neuropsychological rehabilitation. *Journal of Clinical and Experimental Neuropsychology, 9,* 527–544.

Wilson, B., & Baddeley, A.D. (1986). Single case methodology and the remediation of dyslexia. In G.Th. Pavlidis & D.F. Fisher (Eds.), *Dyslexia: Its neuropsychology and treatment,* pp. 263–277. London: John Wiley & Sons.

Wilson, B., & Baddeley, A. (1988). Frontal amnesia and the dysexecutive syndrome. *Brain and Cognition, 7,* 212–230.

Wilson, B.A., Baddeley, A.D., & Cockburn, J.M. (1989). How do old dogs learn new tricks: Teaching a technological skill to brain injured people. *Cortex, 25,* 115-119.

Wilson, B., Cockburn, J., Baddeley, A., & Hiorns, R. (in press). The development and validation of a test battery for detecting and monitoring everyday memory problems. *Journal of Clinical and Experimental Neuropsychology.*

Wilson, B.A., & Moffat, N. (1984). *Clinical management of memory problems.* London: Croom Helm.

Wilson, R.S., Bacon, L.D., Fox, J.H., & Kaszniak, A. (1983). Primary memory and secondary memory in senile dementia of the Alzheimer type. *Journal of Clinical Neuropsychology, 5,* 337–344.

Winocur, G. (1978). Discussion of paper by Weiskrantz. In *Functions of the septo-hippocampal system,* pp. 388–394. (CIBA's Foundation Symposium, 58). North-Holland: Elsevier.

Winocur, G., & Mills, J. (1970). Transfer between related and unrelated problems following hippocampal lesions in rats. *Journal of Comparative and Physiological Psychology, 73,* 162–169.

Winograd, E. (1976). Recognition memory for faces following nine different judgments. *Bulletin of the Psychonomic Society, 8,* 419–421.

Winograd, E. (1988). Some observations on prospective remembering. In M.M. Gruneberg, P.E. Morris, & R.N. Sykes (Eds.), *Practical aspects of memory: Current research and issues, Vol. 1: Memory in everyday life*, pp. 348–353. Chichester: John Wiley & Sons.

Wolpe, J. (1958). *Psychotherapy by reciprocal inhibition*. Stanford: Stanford University Press.

Wolpe, J., & Lazarus, A.A. (1969). *The practice of behavior therapy*. New York: Pergamon.

Wolpe, J., & Rachman, S. (1960). Psychoanalytic evidence: A critique based on Freud case of little Hans. *Journal of Nervous and Mental Diseases, 131*, 135–145.

Woltz, D.J. (1988). An investigation of the role of working memory in procedural skill acquisition. *Journal of Experimental Psychology: General, 117*, 319–331.

Woodhead, M.M., & Baddeley, A.D. (1981). Individual differences and memory for faces, pictures and words. *Memory and Cognition, 9*, 368–370.

Woodward, A.E., Bjork, R.A., & Jongeward, R.H. (1973). Recall and recognition as a function of primary rehearsal. *Journal of Verbal Learning and Verbal Behavior, 12*, 608–617.

Woodworth, R.S. (1938). *Experimental psychology*. London: Methuen.

Woodworth, R.S., & Schlosberg, H. (1954). *Experimental psychology*. New York: Holt.

Yarnell, P.R., & Lynch, S. (1970). Retrograde memory immediately after concussion. *Lancet, 1*, 863–865.

Yates, F.A. (1966). *The art of memory*. London: Routledge & Kegan Paul.

Yu, B., Zhang, W., Jing, Q., Peng, R., Zhang, G., & Simon, H.A. (1985). STM capacity for Chinese and English language materials. *Memory and Cognition, 13*, 202–207.

Zechmeister, E.B. & Nyberg, S.E. (1982). *Human memory*. Monterey, California: Brooks/Cole.

Zhang, G., & Simon, H.A. (1985). STM capacity for Chinese words and idioms: Chunking and acoustical loop hypotheses. *Memory and Cognition, 13*, 193–201.

Zuroff, D.C., Colussy, S.A., & Wielgus, M.S. (1983). Selective memory and depression: A cautionary note concerning response bias. *Cognitive Therapy and Research, 7*, 223–232.

AUTHOR INDEX

SUBJECT INDEX